KISSINGER AND BRZEZINSKI

Also by Gerry Argyris Andrianopoulos

WESTERN EUROPE IN KISSINGER'S GLOBAL STRATEGY

Kissinger and Brzezinski

The NSC and the Struggle for Control of US National Security Policy

Gerry Argyris Andrianopoulos

St. Martin's Press   New York

© Gerry Argyris Andrianopoulos 1991

All rights reserved. For information, write:
Scholarly and Reference Division,
St. Martin's Press, Inc., 175 Fifth Avenue,
New York, N.Y. 10010

First published in the United States of America in 1991

Printed in Hong Kong

ISBN 0–312–05743–1

Library of Congress Cataloging-in-Publication Data
Andrianopoulos, Gerry Argyris, 1954–
Kissinger and Brzezinski : the NSC and the struggle for the control of
US national security policy / Gerry Argyris Andrianopoulos.
p.   cm.
Includes bibliographical references and index.
ISBN 0–312–05743–1
1.   United States—Foreign relations—1969–1974.   2.   United States—
Foreign relations—1974–1977.   3.   United States—Foreign
relations—1977–1981.   4.   Kissinger, Henry, 1923– —Philosophy.
5.   Brzezinski, Zbigniew, 1928– —Philosophy.   6.   National Security
Council (U.S.).   7.   United States—National security.   I.   Title.
E855.A85   1991
327.73—dc20   90–9133
                                                                              CIP

To Marti

Contents

Preface   x

Acknowledgements   xi

Glossary   xiii

1   Introduction   1

   Overview   1
   Why Kissinger and Brzezinski?   4
   Sources for the Study   9
   Limitations of the Study   10
   Organization of Chapters   11

2   The Philosophical Beliefs of Henry Kissinger   13

   Introduction: The Content of Philosophical Beliefs   13
   The Nature of Politics   13
   Image of Adversaries: The USSR and the PRC   17
   Image of Alliances   21
   Image of the New States   25
   Eventual Realization of Fundamental Political Values:
      Optimism/Pessimism   28
   Predictability of the Political Future   30
   Control of Historical Development   32
   Chance (and Tragedy) in Human Affairs   34
   Conclusion   35

3   The Philosophical Beliefs of Zbigniew Brzezinski   38

   Introduction: The Content of Philosophical Beliefs   38
   The Nature of Politics   39
   Image of Adversaries: The USSR and the PRC   43
   Image of Alliances   55
   Image of the New States   61
   Eventual Realization of Fundamental Political
      Values: Optimism/Pessimism   64
   Predictability of the Political Future   66
   Control of Historical Development   69

Chance (and Tragedy) in Human Affairs   71
Conclusion   72

4   The Instrumental Beliefs of Henry Kissinger   76

Introduction: Notions of Correct Strategy and Tactics   76
Best Approach for Selecting Goals for Political Action 76
Most Effective Pursuit of Goals   81
Calculation, Control, and Acceptance of Risks   85
The Best "Timing" of Action   89
Utility of Different Means for Advancing
    One's Interests   90
Conclusion   97

5   The Instrumental Beliefs of Zbigniew Brzezinski   100

Introduction: Notions of Correct Strategy and Tactics   100
Best Approach for Selecting Goals for Political Action 101
Most Effective Pursuit of Goals   106
Calculation, Control, and Acceptance of Risks   112
The Best "Timing" of Action   113
Utility of Different Means for Advancing
    One's Interests   115
Conclusion   119

6   Kissinger Organizing Power for Decision-Making   122

Nixon/Ford and Kissinger: A Shared Perspective   122
The Question of Roles: The Adviser and
    the Secretaries of State and Defense   125
The National Security Council System   127
Informal Structures: The "Backchannel" System   130
Conclusion   131

7   Brzezinski Organizing Power for Decision-Making   133

Carter and Brzezinski: A Shared Perspective   133
The Question of Roles: The Adviser and
    the Secretaries of State and Defense   138
The National Security Council System   139
Informal Structures: "Friday Presidential Breakfast"
    and the "V-B-B"   143
Conclusion   144

8	Kissinger and the Adversaries: The USSR and the PRC	147
	The Need for Strategy	147
	A Triangular Balance: The Opening to the PRC	150
	US-Soviet Relations: From Confrontation to Détente	155
	Force and Diplomacy: Détente Tested	170
	Conclusion	174
9	Brzezinski and the Adversaries: The USSR and the PRC	178
	The Need for Architecture	178
	US-Soviet Relations: From Détente to Contestation	182
	Force and Diplomacy: Détente Tested	194
	A Triangular Balance: Normalization of US-PRC Relations	201
	Conclusion	212
10	Kissinger and the Allies: Seeking a Common Policy	215
	The Nixon Doctrine: Genuine Partnership	215
	The Dilemmas of Common Defense: Maintaining the Power Equilibrium	218
	European Unity: Paying the Economic Price for It	227
	"Selective Détente": Ostpolitik, Berlin, and the CSCE	232
	The Year of Europe: Seeking Atlantic Unity	240
	Conclusion	245
11	Brzezinski and Alliances: Trilateral Cooperation	248
	Introduction: The Challenge of Collective Leadership	248
	The Need for Architecture	248
	The Common Defense: The European Military Balance	250
	The Threat of Selective Détente: Afghanistan and Poland	260
	Conclusion	271
12	Conclusions	274
	Notes	286
	Select Bibliography	360
	Primary Sources	360
	Secondary Sources	366
	Index	376

Preface

This study examines the impact of Kissinger's and Brzezinski's beliefs on US national security policy by comparing their views on world politics and strategy and tactics for achieving national goals, and then analyzing the consistency of those beliefs with their recommendations and/or actions while serving as National Security Advisers. They were selected for this study because: (a) a major purpose of their academic writings was to influence policy; and (b) they were appointed by Nixon and Carter, respectively, on the basis of policy beliefs shared with the two presidents. Despite apparent divergences, this study found that Kissinger and Brzezinski both believed that the greatest threat to peace is Moscow's and Peking's commitment to world-wide communist expansion, that divergent national interests undermine cooperation even among allies, and that the exploitation of Third World conflicts by Moscow and Peking would eventually undermine peace. They also believed that, within limits, man can shape history. For them, national goals should be selected on the basis of power-realist, non-ideological, and strategic approaches, and could be effectively pursued through power, leadership, the linkage of issues, the use of force and diplomacy, and the rapid application of power in the protracted conflict with the East. However, they disagreed about the necessity of injecting morality into policymaking and had different conceptions of leadership. This study found that, while in office, Kissinger's and Brzezinski's recommendations and/or actions were especially consistent with their beliefs about Moscow's and Peking's negative impact on global stability and their conceptions of power, diplomacy, linkage, and leadership. Indeed, those conceptions were clearly evident in their organization of the National Security Council system and more informal policymaking structures and their handling of relations with allies, the USSR, and the PRC. Moreover, since leaving office they have been making proposals consistent with their beliefs. The fact that the consistency is encountered repeatedly in a sequence of interrelated recommendations and/or actions by Kissinger and Brzezinski while in and out of office, permits the conclusion that their policymaking behavior was, indeed, strongly influenced by their conceptions and beliefs.

Acknowledgments

The author and publisher wish to acknowledge with thanks the following text sources and to state that in any case where they may have failed they will be pleased to make the necessary arrangements at the first opportunity.

I am indebted to several individuals and organizations who were particularly helpful in the preparation of this study. For their patience in reading through the entire manuscript I am most grateful to Professors Burton M. Sapin, William H. Lewis, Michael J. Sodaro, Linda P. Brady, Charles F. Elliott, and Carl A. Linden. Their help was of great value in many ways, from reassuring me that what began to appear patently persuasive had not been said before, to offering incisive critiques that led to my rethinking some basic concepts and arguments. I am also indebted to the Department of Political Science, its chairman, Professor Bernard Reich, and its former chairman, Hugh L. LeBlanc, and to The Institute for Sino-Soviet Studies, its acting director, Carl A. Linden, and former director, Gaston J. Sigur.

My wife, Martha L. Melzow, was a source of unwavering encouragement and support. My friend, Thanos Tsimberdonis, facilitated its completion by teaching me the latest computer research skills. Dr Susan K. Mahoney and Philip Valahu assisted with the editing of the manuscript. Ms Wendy Kolker of the Department of Political Science, Ms Suzanne Stephenson of The Institute for Sino-Soviet Studies, and Ms Kay K. Beach of the Computer Information and Resource Center provided their administrative assistance.

Finally, I owe a very special debt to my parents Sotirios and Katina, to my uncle Kimon, to my sister Dimitra, to my brothers Lambros and George, and to the younger members of my family Peter and Tiffany. Their understanding, assistance, and patience made this study possible.

Choice (Copyright © 1961 Henry A. Kissinger); *The Troubled Partnership* (Copyright © 1965 Henry A. Kissinger); *White House Years* (Copyright © 1979 Henry A. Kissinger); *Years of Upheaval* (Copyright © 1982 Henry A. Kissinger); *For the Record* (Copyright © 1981 Henry A. Kissinger); *Observations* (Copyright © 1985 Henry A. Kissinger); *Newsweek*, March 2, 1987, "How to Deal with Gorbachev" (Copyright © 1987 Henry A. Kissinger); *Ibid.*, December 21, 1990, "The Dangers Ahead" (Copyright © 1990 Henry A. Kissinger); *The Washington Post*, January 19, 1988, "Arms Control Fever" (Copyright © 1988 Henry A. Kissinger); *Ibid.*, February 7, 1989 "Dealing with Moscow: A New Balance" (Copyright © 1989 Henry A. Kissinger).

I would also like to express grateful acknowledgment for permission to quote from *Power and Principle* by Zbigniew Brzezinski (Copyright © 1983, 1985 by Zbigniew Brzezinski), reprinted by permission of Farrar, Straus and Giroux, Inc.; Praeger Publishers for *Ideology and Power in Soviet Politics*; Foreign Policy for "America in a Hostile World", "Recognizing the Crisis", and "The Deceptive Structure of Peace"; the Council on Foreign Relations for *Alternative to Partition*; Foreign Affairs for "US Foreign Policy: The Search for Focus"; Viking Penguin Inc. for *Between Two Ages*.

GERRY A. ANDRIANOPOULOS

Glossary

ABM	Anti-ballistic missile
APNW	Agreement on Prevention of Nuclear War
CSCE	Conference on Security and Cooperation in Europe
CEMA	Council of Economic Mutual Assistance
CIA	Central Intelligence Agency
COCOM	Co-ordinating Committee on Export Controls
DEFCON	Defense Condition
DPRC	Defence Program Review Committee
EAG	Energy Action Group
EDIP	European Defence Improvement Program
EEC	European Economic Community
EFTA	European Free Trade Association
ERW	Enhanced Radiation Weapon
FBS	Forward Based Systems
FRG	Federal Republic of Germany
GLCM	Ground Launched Cruise Missile
GDR	German Democratic Republic
IG	Interdepartmental Group
ICBM	Intercontinental Ballistic Missile
INF	Intermediate Nuclear Forces
JCS	Joint Chiefs of Staff
LTDP	Long-term Defense Program
MBFR	Mutual and Balanced Force Reductions
MIRV	Multiple Independently Re-entry Vehicles
NATO	North Atlantic Treaty Organization
NEP	New Economic Policy
NPG	Nuclear Planning Group (NATO)
NSC	National Security Council
NSDM	National Security Decision Memorandum
NSSM	National Security Study Memorandum
PD	Presidential Directive
RDF	Rapid Deployment Force
PRM	Presidential Review Memorandum
PRC	Peoples Republic of China

SALT	Strategic Arms Limitation Talks
SCC	Special Coordination Committee
SDI	Strategic Defense Initiative
SLBM	Submarine Launched Ballistic Missile
SRG	Senior Review Group
START	Strategic Arms Reduction Talks
TNF	Theater Nuclear Force
USC	Under Secretaries Committee
V-B-B	Vance-Brown-Brzezinski luncheon
VSSG	Vietnam Special Studies Group
WSAG	Washington Special Actions Group
WTO	Warsaw Pact Treaty Organization

1 Introduction

OVERVIEW

The persistent interest in US national security policy and the intensity of the debate revolving around it emanate from the following factors: (a) America's predominant role in the international arena, yet its often limited ability to influence desired outcomes; (b) the West European and Japanese dependence on US protection accompanied by a reluctance to support, consistently, US policies; (c) the growing linkage of traditional security issues with domestic concerns; (d) the increasing military power and expanding influence of the USSR; (e) the perception of an increasing risk of nuclear war between the superpowers; (f) the growing global interdependence and the emergence of new security issues such as energy and economic stagnation; and (g) the evident inability of recent US administrations to formulate and execute policies that preclude and/or reduce damage to vital US global interests. The consensus is that national security policy is in a permanent state of challenge, yet few agree on the nature of the challenge and on the means and methods to meet it.

Kissinger and Brzezinski intensified the national security policy debate with their pre-and-post appointment writings and their actions while serving as National Security Advisers.[1] As scholars they strongly criticized both the style and the substance of that policy. As National Security Advisers they tried to implement views of world politics and strategy and tactics they advanced in their academic writings. Their prominence, deriving from the determination of Presidents Nixon and Carter to play an active international role by controlling the formulation and execution of policy through the National Security Council (NSC) system, exacerbated the controversy over policy and focused attention on the role of the National Security Adviser as architect, advocate, and orchestrator of policy. Kissinger and Brzezinski were strongly criticized for their style as well as for the substance of their conceptions and policy recommendations. Many observers charged that by dominating policymaking Kissinger and Brzezinski exacerbated the problems of coordination and consistency in national security policy. Kissinger and Brzezinski ultimately leveled this same charge at one another.

During the Nixon-Ford Administrations the critics, Brzezinski being the most severe, attributed national security policy successes and debacles

1

primarily to Kissinger's conceptions and highly personal and secretive diplomatic style. However, while concurring on his personality and his imperious role in the policymaking process, most critics conceded that his views on world politics and strategy and tactics for achieving national goals led to a consistent national security policy. But they felt that his world view and strategy were devoid of morality and humanitarianism, the essential requisites for building a domestic consensus which is necessary for a successful national security policy. They also maintained that an obvious gulf existed between the views and policy proposals he advanced prior to his appointment and his recommendations and/or actions while in office.[2]

In the Carter years, Brzezinski was criticized for contributing to the confusion in national security policy. But unlike the attacks on Kissinger, the critiques were less severe and contained contradictory assessments of Brzezinski's personality, conceptualizations, and his role in the Administration. Critics saw Brzezinski as an unreconstructed anticommunist; an overly ambitious conceptualizer or a tactician lacking a consistent world view; a futurist with insightful and sound practical solutions for emerging global problems or an unimaginative futurist better at stating problems than at formulating solutions; brilliantly imaginative or virtually ignorant of many important issues in international relations; and either politically sophisticated or politically naïve. In short, unlike Kissinger, Brzezinski could not be easily categorized. The critics concurred, however, that a blatant inconsistency existed between the conceptions and policy proposals Brzezinski advanced before his appointment and his policy recommendations and/or actions while in office.[3]

The departures of Kissinger and Brzezinski did not end the debate over their impact in national security policy. Most, if not all, studies focusing exclusively on either Kissinger or Brzezinski examined the discrepancies between specific proposals advanced in their writings and specific policies of the Nixon, Ford, and Carter administrations rather than on the intellectual underpinnings of their recommendations and/or actions, concluded that Kissinger and Brzezinski were primarily responsible for the policy successes and debacles. The studies ignored most of their academic writings, and as a result assessments which do not fit the pattern were given only superficial treatment. Moreover, few systematic efforts were made to distinguish between their policy recommendations and/or actions and those that might more reasonably be attributed to the Presidents they served or to other high-level policymakers. Most studies, while justifiable, have yet to answer the question that should be asked: Was national security policy under Nixon, Ford, and Carter shaped by concepts and operational procedures bearing significant resemblance to those advanced by Kissinger and Brzezinski prior to their appointment? This study examines the impact of Kissinger's and Brzezinski's beliefs on US national security policy by comparing their views on world politics and strategy and tactics for achieving national goals, and then analyzing the consistency of those beliefs with their recommendations and/or actions while serving as National Security Advisers. Moreover, it examines the impact of their beliefs on their policy recommendations since leaving office.

A study on Kissinger and Brzezinski is warranted for a number of reasons. First, the choice for National Security Adviser has a direct impact on national security policymaking. Serving at the President's pleasure, the Adviser is an extension of him. Therefore, since he can be used by the President to make changes in national security policy, changes in the substance and/or style of policy can, to a large extent, be explained in terms of the Adviser's influence on whom the President might assign responsibility for either its formulation, implementation, or both. Second, like the Presidents they served, Kissinger and Brzezinski were determined, to formulate and implement a "new" coherent national security policy. As academics, they did not simply write to set the record straight: their goal was to influence policy.[4] Therefore, unlike their predecessors, they came into office with definite views on world politics and strategy and tactics for achieving national goals. Third, each President declares a "new" approach in the substance and style of national security policy; an approach emerging from the intense and rigorous policy review undertaken at the outset of each new administration under the direction of the Adviser. Once the most salient problems are identified and policy initiatives are determined, the focus of the Adviser shifts to policy implementation, program decisions, and day-to-day issues. The writings of Kissinger and Brzezinski make it possible to examine whether their influence, and in turn the "new" approach of the Nixon, Ford, and Carter administrations, can be understood by reference to some new set of ideas about the goals and means of national security policy or whether there is nothing distinctive about their vision of world affairs. Fourth, it appears that Kissinger and Brzezinski are still trying to influence national security policy. Hence, a more thorough understanding of their beliefs will make the prediction of their future recommendations possible.

However, the consistency between the views advanced by Kissinger and Brzezinski prior to their appointment and their policy recommendations and/or actions while in office have been attributed primarily to the following factors: (a) the compatibility of their world views and operating styles with those of the Presidents they served; (b) the structure of the National Security Council system; (c) the overlap in the designated roles and priorities of the Secretaries of State and Defense and the National Security Adviser; and (d) the use of more informal procedures in the formulation and execution of policy. Therefore, particular attention will be given to them.

WHY KISSINGER AND BRZEZINSKI?

Brzezinski's criticisms of the Nixon-Kissinger national security policy and Carter's reiteration of those criticisms during the campaign led to the misperception that the premises, goals, and means of that policy under Carter were radically different from those under Nixon and Ford. Brzezinski's endeavors to project himself as the "good Kissinger", i.e., as equal in ability to Kissinger but as less imperious and secretive and more sensitive to morality and humanitarianism, enhanced this misperception. The longing of most Americans, and especially Carter, to discard Kissinger's Machiavellianism and recapture American idealism facilitated Brzezinski's task. Few noted that as Kissinger met some of Brzezinski's criticisms by trying to improve relations with allies and by injecting more humanitarianism into policy, Brzezinski drew away from Trilateralism and emphasis on North-South relations and focused more on US-Soviet relations. This comparative study of Kissinger and Brzezinski explores the hypothesis that despite apparent differences in their views on world politics and strategy and tactics for achieving national goals, their recommendations and/or actions while in office can be understood on premises of Realpolitik. Both believed that the greatest threat to peace is Moscow's and Peking's commitment to world-wide communist expansion, that divergent national interests limit the degree of cooperation among allies, and that the exploitation of Third World conflicts by Moscow and Peking would eventually undermine peace. For them, national goals should be selected on the basis of power-realist, non-ideological, and strategic approaches, and could be effectively pursued through power, leadership, the linkage of issues, the use of force and diplomacy, and the rapid application of power in the protracted conflict with the East. Moreover, believing that, within limits, man can shape history, both tried to control national security policymaking in order to move history in the direction they desired.

   Unlike most, if not all, comparisons of Kissinger and Brzezinski which have focused on superficial similarities (both were European refugees with Harvard degrees, both had Council on Foreign Relations connections and a Rockefeller for a patron, etc.), and differences (Kissinger a Jewish schoolteacher's son, Brzezinski an aristocratic Polish diplomat's son, Kissinger a Republican, Brzezinski a Democrat, etc.), this study uses Alexander L. George's "Operational Code" construct to compare their views on world politics and strategy and tactics for achieving national goals prior to their appointment, and then examines the impact of their beliefs on US national security policy by analyzing the consistency of those beliefs with their recommendations and/or actions while in office. The analysis focuses on Kissinger's and Brzezinski's preferred policy options rather than on the options they finally supported since the influence of beliefs is likely to be greater in determining the options they preferred than the options they finally recommended and/or acted upon. The latter could have been influenced by domestic politics, the necessity to compromise, organizational considerations, etc., which could have run counter to the options they preferred. The operational code construct consists of two sets of questions about one's beliefs:

(A) *Philosophical Questions*
1. What is the "essential" nature of political life? Is the political universe essentially one of harmony or conflict? What is the fundamental character of one's political opponents?
2. What are the prospects for the eventual realization of one's fundamental political values and aspirations? Can one be optimistic or pessimistic on this score; and in what respects the one and/or the other?
3. Is the political future predictable? In what sense and to what extent?
4. How much "control" or "mastery" can one have over historical development? What is one's role in "moving" and "shaping" history in the desired direction?
5. What is the role of "chance" in human affairs and in historical development?

(B) *Instrumental Questions*
1. What is the best approach for selecting goals or objectives for political action?
2. How are the goals of action pursued most effectively?
3. How are the risks of political action calculated, controlled, and accepted?
4. What is the best "timing" of action to advance one's interest?
5. What is the utility and role of different means for advancing one's interests?[5]

By asking the same general questions, this study hopes to avoid the all-too-familiar and disappointing experience of previous unsystematic comparisons of Kissinger and Brzezinski. But while the philosophical and instrumental questions reveal a significant part of their entire set of beliefs about politics, they do not include all dimensions of their belief systems, much less all cognitive or psychological aspects of policymaking.

The operational code construct focuses on one's orientation toward domestic and international opponents since a belief system about politics is influenced primarily by one's assumptions about the nature of political conflict and the image of opponents. The characteristics one attributes to political opponents exercise a subtle influence on many of his other beliefs regarding world politics and strategy and tactics for achieving national goals.[6] The image of the opponent, however, may play a less central role in the operational code of individuals who do not attribute an irreconcilable hostility to their political enemies. When opponents are perceived as limited (and perhaps temporary) adversaries it is advantageous to supplement the image of opponents with observations about the images of allies and followers. But since beliefs can change due to the impact of significant historical developments, the centrality of the opponent's image for the operational code requires that particularly close attention be given to possible shifts in that image and to related changes in the fundamental nature of political conflict. However, the changes are more likely to be modifications of one's belief system, rather than its abandonment or radical transformation.[7] Those considerations lead to two hypotheses: (a) Kissinger's and Brzezinski's images of the USSR and the PRC and their images of allies and the Third World greatly influenced their other beliefs; and (b) significant changes in the international system led to modifications in Kissinger's and Brzezinski's image of the USSR and the PRC and to compensating changes in the images of allies and the Third World. Knowledge of Kissinger's and Brzezinski's philosophical and instrumental beliefs does *not* provide a simple key to explanation and prediction, but it helps to narrow the range of alternatives from which their policy recommendations and choices were made.[8]

The assumption that operational code beliefs are linked to one's actions derives from the special nature – centrality – of those beliefs. Unlike attitudes, they are concerned with fundamental issues of history, politics, and political action. They provide the basic framework within which one approaches the task of processing available information and making "rational" calculations in pursuit of his values and interests. Hence, one premise is that operational code beliefs influence policymaking indirectly by influencing the definition of the situation and the formulation of policy options that precede and accompany the choice of action.[9]

The image of the opponent (first philosophical belief) held by an individual is especially important in shaping his definition of a new situation/issue, particularly regarding a threat posed by that opponent's actions. The definition of a new situation can be of great importance in shaping one's response to that situation, so much so that his definition is likely to eliminate from serious consideration certain policy options and favor others.[10] An image of one's opponent as being inherently hostile leads him to define situations of interaction with that opponent as dangerous to his nation's interests. Ambiguous situations are perceived as threatening or as posing latent crises. Equivocal information about an adversary's behavior or intentions is probably to be interpreted as evidence of hostility. Information that challenges the existing image of the opponent as essentially hostile is discounted or ignored.[11] But an image of the opponent as a limited adversary who is interested in moderating conflict and in striving for accomodations encourages one to choose a conciliatory response. The type of conciliatory response he chooses may be influenced by other beliefs, such as the fifth instrumental belief regarding the utility and role of different means for advancing one's interests, that further refine his general propensity for making such a response. In brief, a policymaker's operational code beliefs introduce "diagnostic propensities" into his information processing.[12]

The actor's philosophical and instrumental beliefs also introduce "choice propensities" into his information processing. An actor who is essentially optimistic about his ability to achieve his fundamental political values (the second philosophical belief), is likely to avoid knowingly choosing high-risk options. One that believes that political outcomes are predictable (the third philosophical belief), is more likely to engage in extensive analysis of the possible consequences of different policy options.[13] Choice is also affected by the actor's intrumental beliefs regarding correct strategy and tactics. An actor who is an "optimizer" rather than a "satisficer" in his approach to goal selection (the first instrumental belief), is more likely to seek to formulate and choose options that offer the prospect of greater payoffs. If he believes that risks can generally be calculated and often controlled (the third intrumental belief), he is more likely to pursue risky objectives by means of controlled risk options rather than to settle for conservative strategies that trade off the possibility of major payoffs in preference for options that entail low risks. It is important to note that beliefs do not act separately. A combination of several beliefs may further narrow a decision-maker's choice propensities, thereby increasing the explanatory-predictive power of the belief system as a whole.[14]

In summary, the actor's operational code beliefs by performing certain functional and substantive tasks in information processing, introduce two types of propensities, *not determinants*, into his decision-making: first, "diagnostic propensities" which extend or restrict the scope of search and evaluation and influence his "definition of the situation" in certain directions; and second, "choice propensities" which lead him to support certain types of action alternatives over others.[15] In short, the role of operational code beliefs is conceptualized as a set of general guidelines to decision-making, and "not as a set of rules and recipes to be applied mechanically to the choice of action."[16]

The impact of philosophical and instrumental beliefs in policymaking is likely to emerge in a more striking and plausible way when two or more leaders are compared who, ideally, are matched in every important respect and differ only in their beliefs.[17] Such an ideal matching of two policymakers is rarely possible. Kissinger and Brzezinski, however, do, to a great extent, meet the ideal matching. They are approximately the same age (Kissinger was born in 1923 and Brzezinski in 1928),[18] and they have similar personalities in the sense that their "ambitions agenda was almost identical," that is, both sought high appointive office within the foreign/defense policy arena.[19] Both lived in the same sociohistorical epoch, (in 1938 Kissinger immigrated to the US and Brzezinski to Canada), and underwent similar political socialization experiences. They were European refugees (Kissinger fleeing the Nazis and Brzezinski the Communists), who completed their education in North America, receiving their doctorates from Harvard.[20] They embraced the same anti-communist ideology (as reflected in the Council on Foreign Relations), and occupied similar political roles. Prior to their appointment as National Security Advisers they served as consultants to high level policymakers in the national security field in Washington and as advisers to presidential candidates on foreign/defense policy issues.[21] Finally, they had similar roles as National Security Advisers.

The use of the operational code construct to ascertain Kissinger's and Brzezinski's views on world politics and strategy and tactics is ideal for another reason as well.[22] Their extensive academic writings on international politics and contemporary international issues provide a good data base and satisfy several prerequisites for a useful utilization of the operational code construct. First, Kissinger's and Brzezinski's attention to history and its meaning (especially in Kissinger's case) provide clear answers to the philosophical and instrumental questions of the operational code. Second, their writings are broad, in that they cover a wide range of topics to reveal an operational code. Third, secondary sources reveal that their writings can be considered "honest," in that they manifest the real beliefs of Kissinger and Brzezinski.[23] Finally, their writings reflect significant continuity – an important criterion for using the operational code construct. In their writings Kissinger and Brzezinski generalize and hypothesize lessons and conclusions from the analysis of historical cases, thereby outlining their operational code beliefs, and thus providing a "guide" to their future actions.[24]

In summary, Kissinger's and Brzezinski's philosophical and instrumental beliefs represent their views on world politics and strategy, and their tactics for achieving national goals. This study treats their beliefs as intervening variables since "reality," whatever that might have been for outside observers, for them existed only as it was perceived through their belief lenses. In this sense their beliefs acted as a mediator in a stimulus-response process. How they responded to incoming information about national security issues depended upon how much and which parts of that information they took in and the subsequent interpretation of that information. In short, before they could respond, the information had to go through the "screens" of their philosophical and instrumental beliefs.

SOURCES FOR THE STUDY

This study is based on both primary and secondary sources. The primary sources are: (a) the writings of Kissinger and Brzezinski, as well as those of the other participants in the policymaking process; and (b) the official statements and speeches of these individuals as published in governmental documents and the press. In the case of Kissinger and Brzezinski neither private correspondence nor classified documents need to be consulted to ascertain what they thought about national security policy before coming into office. Kissinger's writings were a running commentary on the policy achievements and failures of the Truman, Eisenhower, and Kennedy administrations while Brzezinski's writings focused on the policy achievements and debacles of the Nixon and Ford administrations. The secondary sources include both studies on Kissinger and Brzezinski and on national security policy for the period between 1969 to 1981. The use of content analysis makes it relatively easy to misconstrue Kissinger's and Brzezinski's philosophical and instrumental beliefs by an unsystematic examination of their writings. To avoid the most common error in linking their beliefs to their behavior, that is, determining their beliefs from their official statements and/or behavior, a number of safeguards have been used. First, Kissinger's and Brzezinski's operational code beliefs are ascertained by examining only their academic writings. The examination is based on their books rather than their articles on the assumption that their books present their most carefully considered views since, with few exceptions, their arcticles were incorporated into their books. The exceptions, more in the case of Brzezinski, are articles published after their last book but prior to their appointments. Second, the analysis of their recommendations and/or actions while in office is based on official documents and press statements published during that time, as well as on their memoirs and the memoirs of the other policymakers. Third, an examination of Kissinger's and Brzezinski's other writings (not memoirs) since leaving office will determine whether the views advanced in them reflect any changes in their operational code beliefs. Finally, the secondary sources provide the "inside" information not available in the primary sources.

LIMITATIONS OF THE STUDY

There are, of course, difficult problems in using the knowledge of a policymaker's operational code beliefs for explaining and predicting his actions in specific instances. Knowledge of a policymaker's beliefs can assist, but not substitute for, analysis of specific situations and assessment of institutional (and other) pressures on his actions. A policymaker's beliefs do not provide a simple key to explanation and prediction, but they can assist in identifying the alternative ways in which he may perceive different types of situations, and approach the task of making a rational assessment of alternative options of action. Kissinger's and Brzezinski's control over crucial documents and the fact that most official documents regarding national security policy are classified make it difficult to determine precisely many of the objectives and apparent intentions underlying their recommendations and/or actions. But it is important to note that my final evaluation of Kissinger and Brzezinski presupposes that ideas play a very important role in their lives. In fact, I have tried to understand them on their own terms, which has not previously been done adequately. This approach runs the risk of taking them at their own word. Hopefully, this critical examination of their views on world politics and strategy and tactics for achieving national goals and their recommendations and/or actions while in and out of office will offset any suggestion that they be allowed to provide the only definite interpretation of their role in shaping national security policy in the 1970s.

To determine the impact of their operational code beliefs on their policymaking behavior, this study employs a historical-descriptive perspective and examines the consistency between their beliefs and their recommendations and/or actions regarding US policy toward major allies, the USSR, and the PRC while in and out of office. Realistically, no analysis of the motivational background of any policy can ignore the essentially multicausative nature of political actions. Hence, influences from other sources are not ignored. However, this is not a study of the policymaking process, nor is it particularly concerned with uncovering the bureaucratic rivalries in the Nixon, Ford, and Carter Administrations. Elements of the policymaking process and the bureaucratic struggles are unavoidable in any treatment of policy, and they will not be ignored. The main thrust of this study, however, is to establish a broader understanding of the linkage between a policymaker's operational code beliefs and his policies. In addition, the hope is that by enhancing our understanding of Kissinger's and Brzezinski's impact on national security policy, this study would facilitate the development of a consensus which both viewed as vital to the achievement of national goals in this area.

ORGANIZATION OF CHAPTERS

This study contains twelve chapters. The introduction deals with the intellectual underpinnings of this study. Chapter 2 examines the philosophical beliefs of Kissinger which are presented, quite frequently, in his own words. The study begins with Kissinger because he preceded Brzezinski as National Security Adviser. But more important, as Kissinger's beliefs were manifested in his critiques of the policies of the administrations preceding Nixon's, Brzezinski's beliefs became evident in his criticisms of Kissinger's conceptions and policies. Chapter 3 analyzes the content of Brzezinski's philosophical beliefs and highlights the points on which his views and those of Kissinger coincide. Chapter 4 deals with Kissinger's views on correct strategy and tactics for achieving national goals. Chapter 5 examines Brzezinski's views regarding correct strategy and tactics that provided the underpinnings of his evaluation of the Nixon-Kissinger approach to policymaking and policies. Chapter 6 examines Nixon's and (Ford's) views on international affairs and their congruence with Kissinger's operational code, the definitions of one's role by the principal policymakers, and the impact of these on the organization of the formal and informal policymaking structures which could have affected the consistency between Kissinger's beliefs and his recommendations and/or actions while in office. It also examines whether the policymaking structures under Nixon and Ford reflect any of Kissinger's beliefs. Chapter 7 examines the congruence between Brzezinski's and Carter's views on world politics and strategy and tactics for achieving national goals, the definitions of one's role by the principal policymakers, and the impact of these on the organization of the formal and informal policymaking structures which could have affected the consistency between Brzezinski's beliefs and his recommendations and/or actions while in office. It also examines whether the policymaking structures reflect any of Brzezinski's beliefs. Chapter 8 examines Kissinger's impact on US policy toward the PRC and the USSR by analyzing the consistency between his beliefs and his recommendations and/or actions while in office. Chapter 9 examines Brzezinski's influence on US policy toward the PRC and the USSR by analyzing the consistency between his beliefs and his recommendations and/or actions while in office, and underlines the similarities and differences with those of Kissinger. Chapter 10 analyzes Kissinger's influence on policy toward allies by examining the consistency between his beliefs and his recommendations and/or actions while in office. Chapter 11 deals with Brzezinski's impact on US policy toward allies by examining the consistency between his beliefs and his suggestions and/or actions while in office and compares them with Kissinger's. The four preceding chapters also examine the consistency between Kissinger's and Brzezinski's beliefs and their recommendations since leaving office. Chapter 12 presents the findings of this study.

2 The Philosophical Beliefs of Henry Kissinger

INTRODUCTION: THE CONTENT OF PHILOSOPHICAL BELIEFS

There is substantial agreement that the intellectual capital political leaders bring to their office has an impact on their actions. Indeed, Kissinger, declared:

> It is an illusion to believe that leaders gain in profundity while they gain experience. As I have said, the convictions that leaders have formed before reaching high office are the intellectual capital they will consume as long as they continue in office. There is little time for leaders to reflect . . .
>
> When I entered office, I brought with me a philosophy formed by two decades of the study of history . . . [1]

This chapter examines Kissinger's academic writings to ascertain the content of his philosophical beliefs, the intellectual capital he consumed while in office. The content of his beliefs, however, is presented quite frequently in his own words.

THE NATURE OF POLITICS

What is the "essential" nature of political life? Is the political universe essentially one of harmony or conflict? What is the fundamental character of one's political opponents?

Kissinger believed that the essential nature of politics is conflictual. He viewed politics as a process by which differences are resolved. But this process is beset with conflict, disagreement, compromise, and above all violence. This characterization of politics stemmed from Kissinger's understanding of "History" which "is the past and the past represents the most inexorable necessity with which we live." At the end of his undergraduate thesis he stated: "Man's existence is as transcendental a fact as the violence in history."[2]

The conviction that the political universe is essentially one of conflict and violence rather than harmony is evident in all of Kissinger's scholarly writings. In *A World Restored*, Kissinger presented his models for stable and revolutionary international systems.[3] These models derived from Kissinger's conception of peace which he defines as stability based on an equilibrium of forces within a legitimate international order. As he explained: "Stability . . . has commonly resulted not from a quest for peace but from a generally accepted legitimacy," which "means no more than an international agreement about the nature of workable arrangements and about the permissible aims and methods of foreign policy." Kissinger maintained that legitimacy "implies the acceptance of the framework of the international order by all major powers, at least to the extent that no state is so dissatisfied that . . . it expresses its dissatisfaction in a revolutionary foreign policy."[4] Hence, an international order whose structure is accepted by all major powers is legitimate and thus stable.

In Kissinger's view conflict was inherent in both models which were distinguished primarily by the degree of conflict present in them. He stressed that "A legitimate order does not make conflicts impossible, but it limits their scope. Wars may occur, but they will be fought *in the name* of the existing structure, and the peace which follows will be justified as a better expression of the 'legitimate', general consensus" (his italics). However, "whenever there exists a power which considers the international order or the manner of legitimizing it oppressive, relations between it and other powers will be revolutionary. In such cases, it is not the adjustment of differences within a given system which will be at issue, but the system itself."[5] In short, for Kissinger conflict is inherent in the nature of relations among sovereign states. But conflict within the system has been more limited than conflict about the system.

For Kissinger a revolutionary power is one that believes that relations among nations should be conducted on ideological premises.[6] In his view it makes no difference whether a revolutionary is red or white.[7] As he explained: "It is the essence of a revolutionary power that it possesses the courage of its convictions, that it is willing, indeed eager, to push its principles to their ultimate conclusion . . . therefore, it tends to erode, if not the legitimacy of the international order, at least the restraint with which such an order operates." Kissinger stressed that in revolutionary situations the injection of ideology into foreign policy leads "the contending systems [to be] less concerned with the adjustment of differences than with the subversion of loyalties," and as a result, "diplomacy is replaced either by war or by an armaments race".[8] In other words, the political contest becomes doctrinal, the revolutionary power pursues unlimited objectives, hence, an international order based on incompatible philosophies leads to conflict.

Kissinger believed that

> the distinguishing feature of a revolutionary power is not that it feels threatened – such feeling is inherent in the nature of relations among sovereign states – *but that nothing can reassure it.* Only absolute security – the neutralization of the opponent – is considered a sufficient guarantee, and thus the desire of one power for absolute security means absolute insecurity for all the others. (his italics)[9]

He maintained that "absolute security . . . is never obtainable as a part of a 'legitimate' settlement, and can be achieved only through conquest."[10] Hence, "the quest for absolute security leads to permanent revolution."[11] Kissinger is convinced that "no major power will give up its minimum claim to security – the possibility of conducting an independent foreign policy – merely for the sake of legitimacy."[12] Therefore, the feeling of absolute insecurity among sovereign states which seek to protect their national interests leads to conflict.

Kissinger's belief that the political universe is basically conflictual was also evident in his rejection of peace conceived as the avoidance of war. He constantly reiterated that the quest for peace based on this conception will be self-defeating, and explained why this will be the case.

> Whenever peace – conceived as the avoidance of war – has been the primary objective of a power or a group of powers, the international system has been at the mercy of the most ruthless member of the international community. Whenever the international order has acknowledged that certain principles could not be compromised even for the sake of peace, stability based on an equilibrium of forces was at least conceivable.[13]

This belief led to Kissinger's emphatic rejection of the conception of "peace . . . as an end in itself, and its manifestation . . . the *absence* of struggle" (his italics),[14] and to his criticism of the prevailing notion in the US and the West in general, "which considers peace as the 'normal' pattern of relations among states and which has few doubts that reasonable men can settle all differences by honest compromise."[15] For Kissinger then, the primary objective of states must be not to preserve peace – avoid war – but to achieve stability. Consequently, conflict is inherent even in a stable international system since limited war is an acceptable means to preserve the principles on which the system is based.

The models presented in *A World Restored* were not altered in Kissinger's subsequent studies because, as he explained in *Nuclear Weapons and Foreign Policy*, "in a revolutionary period like the present . . . we are confronted by two revolutionary powers, the USSR and Communist China, which pride themselves on their supperior understanding of 'objective' forces and to which policies unrelated to a plausible possibility of employing force seem either hypocrisy or stupidity." [16] Kissinger saw no need to modify his models because only the superpowers have the formidable military capability to transform the existing international system or, by seeking to do so unilaterally, ignite an all-out nuclear war that could destroy the world.

Changes in Beliefs Regarding the Nature of Politics

The examination of Kissinger's writings revealed that he modified some of his beliefs in order to account for some significant historical developments. Kissinger did not alter his models, but he incorporated some new factors which in his view reinforced the revolutionary character of the contemporary international system, thus shifting his emphasis from the revolutionary actor to the revolutionary period. This shift was first evident in *Nuclear Weapons and Foreign Policy*, and resulted according to Kissinger from the following developments: "(a) the number of participants in the international order increased and their nature has altered; (b) their technical ability to affect each other has vastly grown; [and] (c) the scope of their purposes had expanded." The first development resulted from decolonization which brought new states into the international system which inject into their foreign policies the revolutionary fervor that got them independence, hence giving priority to change over harmony. The second emanated from the scientific and technological revolutions, particularly in the fields of nuclear weapons and communications, which removed technical limits from the exercise of power in foreign policy, thereby magnifying insecurities since any diplomatic and military move immediately involves global consequences and makes survival apparently dependent on technological breakthroughs. This development is compounded by the democratization of politics which enables states to marshal ever more resources for their competition. Third, the ideological conflict intensifies international tensions since political loyalties no longer coincide with political boundaries, and conflicts among states merge with divisions within them to reduce the distinction between domestic and foreign policy. As a result states feel threatened not only by the foreign policy of their adversaries but also by domestic transformations. In addition, the instabilities produced by ideological conflict are exacerbated by the reduced influence of the traditional great powers.[17] Kissinger believed that these developments not only intensified conflicts among states, but they were "manipulated by the Sino-Soviet bloc, which is determined to prevent the establishment of an equilibrium . . . "[18] that he regarded as an essential requisite for the establishment of a stable international order.

IMAGE OF ADVERSARIES: THE USSR AND THE PRC

In Kissinger's view, political adversaries were those who threatened the stability of the international order by rejecting its legitimacy. The revolutionary actor by injecting ideology into foreign policy undermined the international agreement regarding the nature of workable arrangements and the permissible aims and methods of foreign policy. For Kissinger, America's main adversaries, the USSR and the PRC, were revolutionary in nature because they rejected the legitimacy of the contemporary international system. He stressed that, the Soviet doctrine "explicitly rejected [the existence of] harmony between different social systems [and that the Soviet leadership] has been careful to insist . . . that real peace is attainable only *after* the triumph of Communism" (his italics). He also pointed to Mao Tse-tung's assertion that "political power . . . grows out of the barrel of a gun . . . " and his advocacy of "the omnipotence of the revolutionary war".[19] Criticizing Western leaders "for their penchant on insisting that dictators do not mean what they say,"[20] he argued, "the non-Communist world, for a variety of motives, has been easy prey to each new Soviet change of line because of its eagerness to integrate the Soviet power center into a legitimate system – the contingency above all others which Bolshevik doctrine explicitly rejects".[21] For Kissinger, then, the leadership of the USSR and the PRC meant what they said, that is, they will do everything they could to transform the existing international order.

According to Kissinger, the USSR and the PRC had "the distinguishing feature of a revolutionary power . . . ," that is, "not that it feels threatened . . . *but that nothing can reassure it*" (his italics).[22] This belief was clearly stated in *Nuclear Weapons and Foreign Policy*. In Kissinger's words:

> . . . the Soviet leaders have been most insistent about feeling threatened. And they are probably sincere in these assertions. Their revolutionary quality derives, however, not from the fact that they feel

threatened – a measure of threat is inherent in the relations of sovereign states – but that nothing can reassure them. Because their doctrine *requires* them to fear us they strive for absolute security: the neutralization of the United States and the elimination of all our influence from Europe and Asia. And because absolute security for the USSR means absolute insecurity for us, the only safe United States policy is one which is built on the assumption of a continued revolutionary struggle, even though the methods may vary with the requirements of the changing situation.[23]

In short, as he put it, the USSR and the PRC are "avowedly revolutionary powers."[24]

What made the USSR and, to a lesser extent, the PRC, the primary threat to stability was the fact that their ideology was combined with awesome military capabilities, specifically, the growth of the Soviet nuclear stockpile.[25] As Kissinger explained:

Only two powers – the United States and the Union of Socialist Republics – possess the full panoply of military might. Over the next decade, no other country or group of countries will be capable of challenging their physical preeminence. Indeed, the gap in military strength between the two giant nuclear countries and the rest of the world is likely to increase rather than diminish over that period.[26]

For Kissinger then, the USSR is the main adversary of the US, and thus, it should be the focus of US national security policy.

Changes in Beliefs Regarding Adversaries

In Kissinger's view, nuclear weapons did not change the revolutionary nature of the USSR and the PRC. In 1969, he wrote: "From Lenin, to Stalin, to Mao, and to the current Soviet leadership, the insistence on superior historical understanding, on endless and inevitable conflict with non-Soviet states, on ultimate victory, has been unvarying . . . the attitudes of the current Soviet leadership . . . have not been basically changed even by the enormity of the new technology".[27] For Kissinger, the Cuban missile crisis in 1962 injected a greater degree of realism into Soviet views regarding nuclear war, but it did not reduce their ideological hostility. He noted that Soviet leaders who "[had] been careful to insist that no technological discovery, however powerful, can abolish the laws of history and that real peace is attainable only *after* the triumph of communism" (his italics),[28] now "share[d] our reluctance to engage in any adventures which may involve th[e] risk [of all-out war]."[29] In his view, the mutual fear of nuclear war injected a degree of limited cooperation in the nuclear field of US-Soviet relations as was evident in the Partial Test-Ban Treaty in 1963.[30] Kissinger warned, however, that the mutual fear of nuclear war "does not automatically produce détente."[31] Recognizing that the Soviet fear of nuclear war increased the possibility of a split within the Soviet bloc since Moscow would not risk such a war to support Peking's objectives, Kissinger endorsed a strategy of limited war because it would create situations that would accentuate this possibility.[32] Rejecting the proposition that US policy can promote a split, Kissinger argued, "if it occurs, we should take advantage of it."[33] By 1968 the Brezhnev doctrine, according to Kissinger, "made a Sino-Soviet war at least conceivable." [34]

The limited US-Soviet cooperation in the nuclear field and the possibility of a Sino-Soviet split did not change Kissinger's view regarding the revolutionary nature of the USSR or the PRC. He insisted that while "the nuclear stalemate may prevent all-out war . . . it will not deter other forms of conflict; in fact it may even encourage them."[35] Kissinger constantly stressed that for Soviet leaders "peaceful coexistence would thereby become the most efficient offensive tactic, the best means to subvert the existing order by means other than all-out war".[36] He warned, however, that "should the strategic balance shift so that this condition (Soviet fear of nuclear war) is no longer met, the reason for even the formal defense of peaceful coexistence will fall away,"[37] because "what is permanent in Soviet theory is the insistence upon the continuing struggle, not the form it takes at any given moment."[38] Discussing the Soviet doctrine on nuclear weapons, Kissinger criticized the "tendency in the West to overlook Soviet doctrinal disputes . . . ", and declared, "Yet they are the most profitable indication of Soviet intentions, far more rewarding than Soviet actions which are often deliberately designed to mislead or to lull."[39] Indeed, in his view, the significance and danger of Khrushchev's "peaceful coexistence" was that "after thirty years such shopworn phraseology could still lull the non-Soviet world and be seriously debated as ushering in a new era of Soviet behavior."[40]

Kissinger's conviction that the Soviet willingness to cooperate with the US in reducing the threat of nuclear war was only a change of tactics, was reinforced by "the exasperation with which the Soviet leaders regularly have repudiated the notion that a change of tactics on their part implies an abandonment of their basic doctrines." To falsify "the insistence by the intended victims (the West) that the Bolsheviks do not 'mean' what they have so often proclaimed . . . " Kissinger quotes Khrushchev declaring, at the height of the "peace offensive," "if anyone thinks . . . that we shall forget about Marx, Engels, and Lenin, he is mistaken. This will happen when shrimps learn to whistle."[41] Kissinger stressed, that "as in all past periods of peaceful coexistence, Khrushchev was at pains to point out that this change of tactics did not imply a modification of revolutionary goals."[42] For Kissinger then, "the slogan of 'peaceful coexistence' cannot obscure the fact that we are living in a revolutionary period."[43]

In *American Foreign Policy*, Kissinger warned "we should not again confuse a change of tone with a change of heart."[44] As he explained:

> [S]ome Soviet leaders may have become more pragmatic; but in an elaborated Communist state, the results of pragmatism are complex. Once power is seized and industrialization is largely accomplished, the Communist Party faces a difficult situation . . . In order to justify its continued existence and command, it may develop a vested interest in vigilance against outside danger and thus in perpetuating a fairly high level of tension.[45]

In brief, nuclear weapons have not eradicated the distinguishing features of revolutionary powers, namely, the injection of ideology into foreign policy and the desire for absolute security.[46] For Marxists, Kissinger argued, "a genuine settlement between different social systems can come about . . . only with the end of the class struggle. In any other situation the Communists assign themselves the task of exacerbating all tensions."[47] Therefore, Kissinger never wavered from his belief that the Soviet Union is still committed to transforming the international system and, in the process, to perpetuating international conflict.

Moreover, Kissinger rejected the prevailing theory of convergence and the notion that the liberalization of Soviet society would lead to a settlement of East-West issues.[48] Accepting the view that in time the emerging middle class in the USSR may loosen the rigidity of Soviet doctrine, he argued, that historically "a revolutionary movement has lost its messianic *elan* . . . only when [it was] opposed with equal fervor or when it reached the limit of its military strength" (his italics). Not reassured by the history of middle-class revolutions, Kissinger feared, that "a middle class deprived of Marxist theory might be even more inflexible than the present Soviet leadership."[49] He also insisted, that "a Communist bureaucratic structure [like the Soviet], however pragmatic, will have different priorities from ours; it will give greater weight to doctrinal considerations and conceptual problems. Bureaucratization and pragmatism may lead to a loss of elan; they do not guarantee convergence of Western and Soviet thinking."

Turning to the PRC, however, he pointed out that its less bureaucratic structure "may permit a wider latitude for new [policy] departures."[50] In short, he did not believe that change within the USSR would have a positive impact on East-West relations.

Kissinger believed that the new revolutionary developments (discussed previously) helped sustain the revolutionary momentum of the USSR and the PRC. He stressed that "the greatest need of the contemporary international system is an agreed concept of order. In its absence, the awesome available power is unrestrained by any consensus as to legitimacy; ideology and nationalism, in their different ways, deepen international schisms."[51] The nationalism and domestic weakness of the new states encouraged foreign intervention, while the ideological conflict facilitated the USSR's and the PRC's efforts to subvert the political loyalties of the West and the Third World.

IMAGE OF ALLIANCES

Kissinger's belief in the conflictual nature of politics was also manifest in his views of alliances. His writings focused primarily on US-West European relations and the role of allies in the establishment of a stable international system. Therefore, it would be useful to ascertain his images of alliances, and especially of NATO.

For Kissinger, the unity of the US alliance system is vital for developing a stable international system which depends on an equilibrium of power and legitimacy. In 1969 he wrote, "in a very real sense, the world balance of power depends on our ability to deny the resources and manpower of Western Europe to an aggressor."[52] The legitimacy of the system requires its acceptance by all major powers, and he regarded the major West European allies and Japan as great powers. Yet, believing that only the superpowers could transform the present international system, Kissinger stressed the need to focus on the US-Soviet relationship. He was not greatly concerned with the allied reaction to such a policy given their military dependence on the US. As he explained:

> Third-force dangers . . . have been overdrawn. It is hard to visualize a deal between the Soviet Union and Europe which would jeopardize our interests without jeopardizing European interests first . . . .Whatever their formal autonomy, *it is almost inconceivable* that our allies would prefer to go to war without the support of the United States, given the relatively small nuclear forces in prospect for them. Close coordination

between Europe and the United States in the military sphere is dictated by self-interest, and Europe has more to gain from it than the United States. (my italics)[53]

In short, Kissinger believed that a crisis serious enough to lead NATO to consider a nuclear attack will reveal the underlying community of interest "which is the best guarantee of the cohesion of the Alliance."[54] Moreover, he was convinced that as long as Western security rests on the US nuclear guarantee US allies will acquiesce to US strategic hegemony convinced that their acquiescence is the price for it.[55] However, he feared that acquiescence can mean either a sincere commitment to Atlantic partnership or a neutralist wish to abdicate responsibility.[56] For Kissinger, allied neutralism was a threat to global stability because it would give the USSR an additional veto on US efforts to get an international agreement about the nature of workable arrangements and about the permissible aims and methods of foreign policy.

Kissinger also believed, however, that the impossibility of an isolated military strategy permits allies to pursue their own objectives since in the political field "the temptations for independent action are great and the penalties small."[57] Convinced that these gain momentum with the real or imaginary expansion of détente, he stressed that "a true relaxation of tensions [in East-West relations] presupposes Western unity."[58] Economic developments within the Alliance did not concern Kissinger given his belief that economic competition between Europe and the US "involves, at best, indirect risks."[59] Again, as in the military field, these beliefs were also applicable in the case of Japan and allies in general.

Kissinger also believed, however, that despite the common interest in defense, "American and European interests outside of Europe are not identical".[60] For him, "Phrases like 'indivisible interest' are correct when applied to the defense of Europe or East-West relations; they come close to being platitudes in other parts of the world."[61] This was evident in the bitter intra-alliance disputes regarding burdensharing and European unity which US policymakers advocated as a means to enable Europeans to share US burdens on a world-wide scale. But Kissinger was convinced that due to "decolonization, Europeans are unlikely to conduct a significant global policy whatever their resources or their degree of unity."[62] In his view, "European unity is not a major cure-all for Atlantic disagreements . . . in many respects . . . it may magnify rather than reduce differences" since a united Europe "will be in a better position to insist on differences whose ultimate cause is structural rather than personal."[63]

Kissinger's beliefs regarding the US alliance system issued from his analysis of the reasons for the creation of alliances, the prerequisites for their effectiveness, and the requirements for their cohesiveness. He argued, that historically alliances have been established for three basic reasons: (a) to provide an accretion of power – the wider the alliance, the greater its power to resist aggression – and to leave no doubt about the alignment of forces; (b) to transform a tacit interest in mutual assistance into a formal obligation; and (c) to legitimize the assistance of foreign troops or intervention in a foreign country.[64] From Kissinger's viewpoint, "even before the advent of nuclear weapons, there was some inconsistency among these requirements."[65] The efforts to combine the greatest number of states for joint action occasionally conflicted with the need to remove any doubt about the collective motivation (goal for resisting aggression). The wider the alliance, the more divergent the motives of its members, and more intense and direct had to be a threat to produce a united response.[66] In NATO, however, the inconsistency among these requirements has been largely eclipsed by the perception of a Soviet threat and the fear of Western Europeans that the US might withdraw its forces from Europe.

In Kissinger's view, to be effective, alliances

> must meet four conditions: (1) a common objective – usually defense against a common danger; (2) a degree of joint policy at least sufficient to define the *casus belli*; (3) some technical means of cooperation in case common action is decided upon; and (4) a penalty for non-cooperation – that is, the possibility of being refused assistance must exist – otherwise protection will be taken for granted and the mutuality of obligation will break down.[67]

For Kissinger, NATO meets three of those conditions: (1) NATO's common objective is deterring a Soviet attack on Western Europe; (2) a degree of joint policy sufficient to define the casus belli exists (Article 5 of The North Atlantic Treaty);[68] (3) NATO's military organization enables joint action when the political desicion is made. The fourth condition, however, is not met; in military and in political matters, penalties for non-cooperation do not exist since "in the nuclear field – the closest association between Europe and the United States is in the self-interest of both sides." For Kissinger, the fact that the "[US] can no more withdraw from Europe than from Hawaii,"[69] undermined NATO's effectiveness because very often the Europeans take US protection for granted and the reciprocity of obligation is in danger of breaking down.

Kissinger believed that nuclear technology compounded the problem of maintaining NATO unity. As he explained:

[. . .] the deepest problem before the Alliance is that the pressures of the new technology run counter to traditional notions of national sovereignty. The risks of nuclear warfare may be too great to be combined reliably with . . . a key attribute of sovereignty: the unilateral right of a sovereign state to alter its strategic or political views. The destructiveness and range of modern weapons have a tendency to produce both extreme nationalism and neutralism. A wise alliance policy must take care that in dealing with one of these dangers it does not produce the other.[70]

In his view, the controversy over NATO strategy demonstrated the incompatibility between an alliance of sovereign states and tight command and control of all nuclear weapons which is indispensable for nuclear war. He stressed that the risk of nuclear war weakened the credibility of the traditional pledges of mutual assistance. Historically, the unity of alliances rested on the belief that the "immediate" risk of war was less than the "ultimate" danger of facing a preponderant enemy alone.[71] But the growing Soviet nuclear capability made nuclear war the worst contingency for NATO, and generated uncertainties both in the US and Europe about the course of action allies would take in a time of crisis. Western Europeans seriously question whether Washington will risk a nuclear war to defend them while the US fears European neutralism or extreme nationalism. Kissinger believed that if Western Europe moved in either of these directions it could lead to the transformation of the international system. In his view, this threat was real because Moscow "[has] skillfully fomented neutralism by giving the impression that local resistance must inevitably lead to all-out war."[72] For Kissinger, de Gaulle exploited the structural limits of NATO but did not disrupt it by himself. In his view, "Allied relationships would have to be adapted to new conditions, no matter who governed in Paris – or in Washington . . . "[73] In short, he believed that while allied support was vital to establishing a stable international system it was being undermined by new limits introduced by the fusion of sovereignty with nuclear weapons.

For Kissinger, unlike NATO, the Southeast Asia Treaty Organization (SEATO) and the Central Treaty Organization (CENTO), never met the four conditions of effectiveness. There is no consensus as to the common danger, hence, the members of those alliances never developed joint policies regarding the issues of war and peace. The technical means of cooperation do not exist because most states do not have the resources and/or the will to provide mutual support. In Kissinger's view, "SEATO and CENTO have become, in effect, unilateral American guarantees. At best, they provide a legal basis for bilateral U.S. aid." The fact that Washington was more eager to defend its SEATO and CENTO allies than they were in defending themselves convinced them that "non-cooperation will have no cost. In fact, they have been able to give the impression that it would be worse for [the US] than for them if they fell to Communism."[74] Kissinger believed that military bipolarity encourages political multipolarity; "Weaker allies have good reason to believe that their defense is in the overwhelming interest of their senior partner. Hence, they see no need to purchase [US] support by acquiescence in [US] policies."[75]

In summary, Kissinger believed that in the foreseeable future the fusion of sovereignty with nuclear weapons precludes any changes in the US-West European relationship since "no nation will give up its vital interests simply for the sake of allied unity."[76] Nevertheless, he stressed the need for creating an Atlantic Commonwealth in order to fullfil the aspirations of the peoples in it and maintain the West's relevance to the rest of the world.[77] Although Kissinger focused on NATO, it is implicitly evident that in his view the new limits also affected the whole US alliance system.

IMAGE OF THE NEW STATES

Kissinger believed that the new states "weigh little in the physical balance of power."[78] Yet, he also believed in their importance[79] because "the forces unleashed in the emergence of so many new states may well affect the moral balance of the world – the convictions which form the structure for the world of tomorrow." Kissinger's primary interest in the new states, however, issued from his conviction that "the principal threats to peace came from the emerging areas," as a result of the following reasons. First, the domestic weakness of the new states encourages foreign intervention. Second, their leaders are unfamiliar with the elements of international stability and with the nature of contemporary power relationships. Third, they feel little sense of responsibility to an overall international equilibrium and are much more conscious of local grievances. Fourth, the need to deflect domestic dissatisfaction leads to foreign adventures which lead to conflict. And fifth, the rivalry of the superpowers provides the new states with many opportunities for blackmail.[80]

The beliefs of Kissinger with respect to the new states are closely related to his conceptions of stable and revolutionary international systems. He argued that in the present revolutionary period international relations take on a special urgency because many different revolutions occur simultaneously while isolated diplomatic and military actions are no longer possible given the transformation in the nature of military power and in communications. The special urgency emanates from the emergence of the new states which inject into their foreign policy the revolutionary zeal that gained them independence. On the political plane, this makes it very difficult to integrate them into the international community.[81] On the ideological plane, the revolutionary turmoil is fed by the rapid communication of ideas by the new technology and by "the inherent impossibility of fulfilling the expectations aroused by revolutionary slogans." On the economic and social plane, the masses are rebelling against inadequate standards of living as well as against archaic social and racial barriers. But more important for Kissinger was the belief that global instability is further intensified because these serious problems "are manipulated by the Sino-Soviet bloc which is determined to prevent the establishment of an equilibrium and which is organized to exploit all hopes and dissatisfactions for its own ends."[82] In short, his image of the new states was closely related to his image of America's main adversaries.

The leaders of the new states according to Kissinger "challenge the West . . . [by] demanding that the West live up to its own principles."[83] He maintained that "precisely because they are inwardly so close to the West, many of [these] leaders . . . cannot afford to align themselves with it politically." Therefore, in his view, their "neutralism and anti-colonialism are not so much a policy as a spiritual necessity." Nonalignment is the means by which they reassure themselves. Kissinger recognized that those closest to the West were the most strident advocates of neutrality while those with firm roots in their own traditions were more prepared to act jointly with it when their interests coincided.[84] For him anti-colonialism was a means by which they attempt to achieve personal as well as a national identity. The extent of anti-colonialism reflects the difficulty of creating a national consciousness. Kissinger argued that until the leaders of the new states develop a stronger sense of personal identity and national goals "not drawn from the struggle for independence, they will require anti-colonialism, and it must have an anti-Western connotation. For beyond anti-colonialism lies psychological chaos." He believed that the close identification of nationalism with colonial rule by Western powers had established a "blind spot" in many new states with respect to Soviet colonialism.[85] This blind spot was of particular concern for Kissinger who was convinced that it was exploited by Moscow and Peking to prevent the establishment of an equilibrium of forces – a prerequisite for a stable international order.

The anti-Americanism of the new states did not really concern Kissinger since he believed that as the most powerful nation the US is "the natural target for all frustrations" and, more importantly, that "a great deal of anti-Americanism hides a feeling of insecurity, both material and spiritual." For Kissinger, the US, which is the main defender of the free world, is "unpopular with all who are so preoccupied with their own national development that they are unwilling to pay sufficient attention to foreign threats." The unwillingness of the new states to deal with threats emanating from the Soviet bloc led him to conclude that, while the US "should . . . seek to allay legitimate grievances," it "would be wrong to take every criticism at face value." In his view, "the neutrality of the uncommitted is possible . . . only so long as the United States remains strong, spiritually and physically".[86]

For Kissinger, the unfamiliarity of many of the leaders of the new states with the elements of international stability and with the nature of modern power relationships increased the importance of US leadership in efforts to create a stable international system. Their unfamiliarity resulted from the reliance of independence movements more on ideological agreement, especially the pacifism of Liberalism, than on an evaluation of power factors. Kissinger maintained that "if it is difficult for the leaders to retain a sense of proportion, it is next to impossible for the mass of the population." Hence, in the new states "there is an overestimation of what can be accomplished by words alone," and this "is a dangerous trend."[87] In Kissinger's words:

> In the present revolutionary situation . . . the dogmatism of the newly independent states makes them susceptible to Soviet "peace offensives" and their lack of appreciation of power relationships causes them to overestimate the protection afforded by moral precepts. Indeed, their very insistence on principle contributes to the demoralization of international politics, for it tempts them to accept at face value the protestations of peaceful intentions with which the Soviets inevitably accompany their aggressive moves. It reinforces the quest for a "pure" case of aggression which almost insures that the actual aggressions which may take place will not be dealt with and in many instances not even be recognized as aggression.[88]

Kissinger insisted that the US must educate the new states by word and deed that "the inexorable element of international relations resides in the necessity to combine principle with power" since an exclusive reliance on either one is irresponsible.[89] In the final analysis, Kissinger's image of the new states was very closely linked to his beliefs regarding America's main adversaries, and specifically the USSR.

EVENTUAL REALIZATION OF FUNDAMENTAL POLITICAL VALUES: OPTIMISM/PESSIMISM

What are the prospects for the eventual realization of one's fundamental political values and aspirations? Can one be optimistic or pessimistic on this score; and in what respects the one and/or the other?

Kissinger was essentially pessimistic, but not fatalistic,[90] regarding the eventual achievement of his fundamental political goals, that is, the creation of a stable international system and the prevention of a nuclear holocaust. His pessimism was evident in his preocupation with survival and limits, and his conviction that his fundamental goals could not be achieved in the foreseeable future. Yet, his pessimism was tinged with conditional optimism, namely, an underlying belief that a thermonuclear war could be avoided and a stable international order created although not in the foreseeable future.[91]

Kissinger's declaration that "a state will not easily risk its survival to defeat an aggression not explicitly directed against its national existence,"[92] reflected his survivalist mentality. In the nuclear era, Kissinger believed, survival took on a special importance because "technology . . . has magnified insecurities because it has made survival seem to depend on the accidents of a technological breakthrough."[93] Moreover, given military bipolarity "every issue seems to involve a question of survival."[94] Kissinger placed physical survival above the promotion of Western values, explaining: "we should never give up our principles nor ask other nations to surrender theirs. But we must also realize that neither we nor our allies nor the uncommitted can realize any principles unless we survive."[95]

The frequency and intensity with which Kissinger invoked the notion of limits is another indication of his pessimism.[96] He believed that the acceptance of limits is vital to establishing international stability and he distinguished stable from revolutionary international systems by their acceptance of limits. In a stable system states seek limited objectives while in a revolutionary system states seek unlimited goals, such as, absolute security.[97] Kissinger argued that while Napoleon recognized no limits, his defeat in Russia demonstrated that "Europe could not longer be governed by force . . . the man of will would have to find safety in the recognition of limits."[98] In his view, "Freedom derives not merely from an inward state but from an experience that has come to the recognition of limits. This acceptance is tolerance, the knowledge that one must set boundaries to one's striving."[99] For Kissinger, the belief in limits derived from the cool calculation of power and, intellectually, it was the touchstone of his conservatism.[100]

Although Kissinger did not provide a systematic definition of his concept of limits, it permitted him to predict future developments within NATO. He saw nuclear weapons as a conservative force imposing limits on statesmen; the most obvious being that the enormous increase in power eroded its relationship to policy, therefore, "power no longer translates automatically into influence."[101] This is manifest in the inability of NATO to resolve its strategic dilemmas. Kissinger believed that given "the incompatibility between central control over nuclear weapons and undiluted sovereignty,"[102] for these issues, "no final solution is possible so long as the Alliance remains composed of sovereign states."[103]

Moreover, Kissinger was pessimistic about America's vitality, and its potential to shape the future of the international system. His pessimism derived from his belief that "any society faces a point in its development where it must ask itself if it has exhausted all the possibilities of innovation inherent in its structure. When this point is reached, it has passed its zenith. From then on, it must decline, rapidly or slowly, but nonetheless inevitably." In Kissinger's view, "America is now at such a critical juncture." He argued that "for a while longer we may be able to hold on to what we have and perhaps even extend our achievement by proceeding along familiar routes." But "the question before America is whether it can muster the dedication and creativity *before* the worst has happened" (his italics).[104] His analysis of American traits, i.e., empiricism and the quest for certainty, the reluctance to think in terms of power, and the notion of peace as the avoidance of war, implied that for him the US could not.[105]

Yet, Kissinger's basic pessimism had a trace of optimism. He explained: "it would be a mistake to be pessimistic" about America's potential since "the performance of the United States, for all its failings, compares favorably with that of the other nations of the non-Soviet world." In his view, "our shortcomings are imposing only because of the magnitute of the threat confronting us." His optimism, however, was dependent on the willingness of the US to "face the challenge of demonstrating that democracy is able to find the moral certainty to act without the support of fanaticism and without a guarantee of success."[106] For Kissinger: "in foreign policy courage and success stand in a causal relationship".[107]

Kissinger's faith in man's freedom to act – most apparent in his endeavors to conceive options that would prevent a nuclear war and eventually lead to the creation of a stable international system – fed his optimism.[108] This was evident in his conviction that the divergent US and West European perspectives can be turned into a source of strength that eventually would help create an Atlantic Commonwealth.[109] While recognizing that its creation "will not come quickly," he believed that it was not too early to take the first step beyond the nation state.[110] One might even argue that Kissinger's advocacy for a strategy for limited nuclear war, when most analysts were arguing against it, is another manifestation of his optimism.[111] Although he later rejected it, his proposal for such a strategy demonstrated his belief in man's ability to eventually overcome the limitations of his environment.

Kissinger's basic pessimism, and his conditional optimism, presented him with the fundamental problem of how to transcend the past and the limitations of the present through the perpetual exercise of one's freedom and the exertion of personal will.[112] However, he rejected the kind of optimism which assumed that all problems are soluble with the right formula, and shunned the search for simple technical solutions for realizing man's fundamental political values and aspirations.[113]

PREDICTABILITY OF THE POLITICAL FUTURE

Is the political future predictable? In what sense and to what extent?

Kissinger believed that the political future, and specifically the foreseeable future, is predictable in a negative sense. He stressed what is not likely to happen as opposed to what will happen. His negative predictions reflected his pessimism and emanated from his belief in limits.

Believing that NATO's strategic dilemmas cannot be resolved "so long as [it] remains composed of sovereign states,"[114] and that "an Atlantic Commonwealth . . . will not come quickly",[115] Kissinger predicted that "the pressures within the Alliance against the need for any effective military policy are likely to mount."[116] Convinced that "the interests of Europe and America are not identical everywhere," and particularly outside Europe,[117] he concluded that "a united Europe is likely to insist on a specifically European view of world affairs," and thus "it will challenge American hegemony in Altantic policy,"[118] even though "for the foreseeable future we are likely to be by far the stronger partner."[119] For Kissinger, "over the next decade, no other country or group of countries will be capable of challenging [the superpowers'] physical preeminence."[120] Hence, he predicted that the formal autonomy of Western Europe will not reduce its military dependence on the US.[121] In short, Kissinger believed that, on the basis of historical experience and an analysis of the present, it is possible to forecast political developments, specifically, in the foreseeable future.

Kissinger's belief in the predictability of the political future was balanced by his belief in the unpredictability of specific developments. His notion of unpredictability was evident in his conception of policy. In his words: "the essence of policy is its contingency; its sucess depends on the correctness of an estimate which is in part conjectural."[122] Kissinger stressed, that "the conjectural element of foreign policy – the need to gear actions to an assessment that cannot be proved true when it is made – is never more crucial than in a revolutionary period," when the old order is disintegrating while the shape of the new one is highly uncertain.[123] The acceptance of a degree of unpredictability was also evident in his conception of "diplomacy, which symbolizes the contingency of application."[124] For Kissinger, while the consequences of specific events and policies are not predictable, statesmen should plan long-range national strategy. He argued that "the obsession with safety and predictability must produce an attitude fearful of risk and striving to reduce everything, including man himself, to manipulable quantities."[125] In brief, the statesmen's willingness to take risks and act could lead to the resolution of foreign policy dilemmas.

This balance in Kissinger's beliefs regarding the predictability and unpredictability of the political future had an important impact on his approach to policymaking. His "passive" orientation to policymaking, implicit in his "deterministic" view of history, i.e., that all societies inevitably decline, was offset by the indeterministic conception of policymaking, i.e., that "heroic and deliberate" decisions could influence historical developments. From the operational point of view the indeterminist component of Kissinger's beliefs was dominant, in that it stressed the importance of man's imagination and will in taking well-calculated action for achieving his fundamental political goals, and perhaps, arresting the historical process, even within the constraints forged by sovereignty and nuclear weapons. As he stated:

> The overemphasis on "realism" and the definition of "reality" as being entirely outside the observer may produce a certain passivity and a tendency to adapt to circumstance rather than to master it. It may also produce a gross underestimation of the ability to change, indeed to create, reality. To recapture the ability and the willingness to build our own reality is perhaps our ultimate challenge.[126]

In other words, America's decline does not have to be inevitable, and the dilemmas of NATO could eventually be resolved if its leaders act on their vision of the future.

CONTROL OF HISTORICAL DEVELOPMENT

How much "control" or "mastery" can one have over historical development? What is one's role in "moving" and "shaping" history in the desired direction?

Kissinger's answers to those questions flow from his conception of history and his study of it in terms of the actions of Napoleon, Castlereagh, Metternich, Bismarck, and other statesmen. He viewed history as an unending process devoid of any ultimate value or purpose. Yet, he did not perceive it as being totally chaotic because he believed that there is a certain degree of order in the affairs of men which reveals two basic realities: (a) the cool calculation of power reveals its inherent limit; and (b) in any historical period there is a certain structure to international relations. The notion that there is a limit and structure to power provided an intellectual framework which enabled Kissinger to deal rationally with history – the inherently formless and irrational process.[127] The inherent limit and structure of power is demonstrated, according to Kissinger, by "history . . . the memory of states."[128] He maintained that "history is the past and the past represents the most inexorable necessity with which we live. We know the past only as phenomena . . . The past sets the framework which our spirituality must transcend . . . The experience of freedom enables us to rise beyond the suffering of the past and the frustration of history."[129] In other words, relations among states reveal the limit and structure of power, and statesmen, who recognize and accept limits and are willing to act with self-restraint, can move history in the desired direction.

Kissinger believed that the meaning of history is whatever meaning men choose to give their lives. In *The Troubled Partnership*, Kissinger stated: "Free from the shackles of a doctrine of historical inevitability, the nations of the West can render a great service by demonstrating that whatever meaning history has is derived from the convictions and purpose of the generation which shapes it."[130] Rejecting social determinism, which "has reduced the statesman to a lever on a machine called 'history', to the agent of a fate which he may discern but which he accomplishes regardless of his will,"[131] he constantly declared, "we can still shape our future."[132] In his view, history places limits on man's ability to control it by confronting "the statesman . . . with material he must treat as given." However, the ability to interpret the facts and choose between policy alternatives gives man control over historical development.[133] In short, man can control historical development, but the degree of his control depends on "his ability to recognize the real relationship of forces and make this knowledge serve his ends." For Kissinger, this was "the test of a statesman."[134]

To shape history, according to Kissinger, statesmen must play three vital roles. First, they must provide a conception of alternatives – a vision of the future. Hence, "statesmen must be judged not only by their actions but also by their conceptions of alternatives."[135] Second, "the statesman must . . . be an educator; he must bridge the gap between a people's experience and his vision, between a nation's tradition and its future." Kissinger realized, however, that "in this task [a stateman's] possibilities are limited," because "nations learn only by experience; they 'know' only when it is too late to act." Therefore, in shaping history "statesmen must act as *if* their intuition were already experience, as if their aspiration were truth" (his italics). Third, believing that "statesmanship . . . involves not only a problem of conception but also of implementation, an appreciation of the attainable as much as the desirable,"[136] Kissinger, stressed "it is dangerous to separate planning from the responsibility of execution".[137] In brief, Kissinger believed that in order to move history in the desired direction a statesman must provide a vision, implement it, and educate his nation.

The belief in man's capacity for self-transcendence is crucial to Kissinger's political philosophy which stresses the need to deal always with empirical reality in the context of a vision and the will to create a new reality.[138] This is manifest in his criticism of Metternich.

> Lacking in Metternich is the attribute which has enabled the spirit to transcend an impasse at so many crises of history: the ability to contemplate an abyss, not with the detachment of a scientist, but as a challenge to overcome – or to perish in the process . . . For men become myths, not by what they know, nor even by what they achieve, but by the tasks they set for themselves.[139]

For Kissinger, "those statesmen who have achieved final greatness did not do so through resignation, however well founded. It was given to them not only to maintain the perfection of order, but to have the strength to contemplate chaos, there to find material for fresh creation."[140] In brief, Kissinger believed in the existence of man's freedom in history. As he explained: "an analysis of historical phenomena reveals but the inevitability inherent in completed action. Freedom, on the other hand, testifies to an act of self-transcendence which overcomes the inexorability of events by infusing them with its spirituality. The ultimate meaning of history – as of life – we can find only within ourselves."[141] The balance and/or conflict evident in Kissinger's other general beliefs is also manifested here. His beliefs in man's freedom in history and in the recognition and acceptance of limits created the dilemma with which he struggled: How to shape history in the desired direction through the perpetual exercise of one's freedom and the exertion of personal will.[142]

CHANCE (AND TRAGEDY) IN HUMAN AFFAIRS

What is the role of "chance" in human affairs and in historical development?

The belief that both chance and tragedy play a role in human affairs and in historical development was manifest in Kissinger's reflections on Bismarck – the White Revolutionary – and in his conception of foreign policy. He quoted approvingly the German liberal Bamberger, who in explaining the enigma of Bismarck wrote: "People are born as revolutionaries . . . the accident of life decides whether one becomes a Red or a White revolutionary." In the same discussion, Kissinger stressed, that "a society that must produce a great man in each generation to maintain its domestic or international position will doom itself; for the appearance and, even more, the recognition of a great man are to a large extent fortuitous."[143] Considering the impact of Robespierre in France and Lenin in Russia, he stated: "in the early stages of a revolutionary movement . . . the accident of personalities can be decisive."[144] His belief in the role of chance led Kissinger to warn that "a statesman who leaves no room for the unforeseeable in history may . . . mortgage the future of his country."[145]

Kissinger's belief that history can be shaped by accidental events was also apparent in his conception of foreign policy. In his words: "the tragic element in foreign policy is the impossibility of escaping conjecture; after the 'objective' analysis of fact there remains a residue of uncertainty about the meaning of events and the opportunities they offer."[146] Believing that "only the risks are certain; the opportunities are conjectural,"[147] Kissinger was willing to act in the face of uncertainty because, as he explained:

> The quest for certainty . . . may be paralyzing when pushed to extremes with respect to policy. The search for universality . . . may lead to something close to dogmatism in national affairs. The result can be a tendency to recoil before the act of choosing among alternatives, which is inseparable from policymaking, and to ignore the tragic aspect of policymaking, which lies precisely in its unavoidable component of

conjecture. There can come about a temptation to seek to combine the advantage of every course of action: to delay commitment until "all the facts are in," until, that is, the future has been reduced to an aspect of the past.[148]

For Kissinger then, "certainty is purchased at the cost of creativity."[149] Convinced that "many of the difficulties of the non-Soviet world have been the result of an attempt to use the element of uncertainty as an excuse for inaction," he declared: "but in foreign policy certainty is conferred at least as much by philosophy as by fact. It derives from the imposition of purpose on events."[150] For Kissinger, "to deal with problems of such ambiguity [as Soviet aggression] pressupposes above all a moral act: a willingness to run risks on partial knowledge and for a less than perfect application of one's principles."[151] His belief that chance and tragedy affect human affairs was balanced by his conviction that man can control historical development. Hence, he was not deterred from attempting to move history in the direction he desired.

CONCLUSION

The preceding analysis indicates that for Kissinger the essential nature of politics is conflictual. His conception of peace/stability and his models for stable and revolutionary international systems were characterized by conflict. Indeed, the difference between the two models was the degree of conflict present in them. In a stable system conflict was limited since states went to war to adjust differences within it while in a revolutionary system conflict was total given the determination of a state to change it. For Kissinger, the present international system is revolutionary since the USSR and the PRC reject its framework and are committed to transform it. Their search for absolute security and their pursuit of an ideological foreign policy have intensified the conflict within the present system which has been further exacerbated by the increase in the number of states in the system which inject into their foreign policy the revolutionary fervor that gained them independence, by the technological revolutions in the nature of military power and communications which globalize the consequences of each diplomatic and military move, and by the ideological conflict which reduces the distinction between foreign and domestic policy and facilitates the subversion of political loyalties. In his view, the exploitation of those developments by the USSR and the PRC undermines efforts to create an equilibrium of power – a prerequisite to stability. However, since Moscow could combine an ideological foreign policy with awesome nuclear and conventional capabilities, Kissinger viewed the USSR as the primary threat to international stability.

For Kissinger, nuclear weapons did not change the revolutionary nature of the USSR and the PRC. But he recognized that since the Cuban missile crisis Moscow accepted the risk of nuclear war and has been willing to cooperate in order to reduce it. However, he did not believe that the mutual fear of nuclear war automatically produces détente. Indeed, he believed that peaceful coexistence was the most efficient offensive tactic by which Moscow sought to subvert the present international system through means other than nuclear war. He rejected the view that Soviet pragmatism would reduce international conflict since the CPSU justifies its continued existence by exacerbating all tensions and claiming vigilance against outside danger. Moreover, he rejected the argument that convergence would lead to a settlement of East-West issues.

Kissinger believed that the conflictual nature of politics is also evident in US relations with its allies and the new states. He viewed US allies as vital to establishing a stable international order since they help maintain the equilibrium of power and its legitimacy. Kissinger believed that allied dependence on the US strategic guarantee ensures the cohesion of the US alliance system despite the US focus on relations with the USSR and the PRC. But he also believed that the impossibility of an isolated military strategy by the US and its allies permits allies to pursue their own objectives, especially outside of Europe, thereby generating intra-alliance conflicts. In Kissinger's view, European unity would magnify those conflicts since a united Europe will be in a better position to insist on differences whose causes are structural rather than personal. Moreover, he believed that while allied support is vital to global stability, allied cohesion is being undermined by the incompatibility between sovereignty and the tight control of all nuclear weapons which is indispensable for nuclear war. However, despite his belief that NATO's nuclear issues could not be resolved as long as it remains composed of sovereign states, Kissinger urged the creation of an Atlantic Commonwealth to maintain the West's relevance to the world.

Unlike major allies, the new states, according to Kissinger, weigh little in the physical balance of power but like allies they are important to establishing the legitimacy of the international system. He believed that the conflict in the present system is intensified when new states try to deflect domestic weakness through foreign adventures, by their leaders' unfamiliarity with the elements of international relations and the nature of modern power, by their lack of commitment to the international system, and by their neutralism and anti-Americanism which were exploited by Moscow and Peking to prevent the establishment of a stable international system.

Kissinger's preoccupation with survival and limits indicate his pessimism, not fatalism, regarding the prevention of nuclear war and the eventual creation of a stable international system. He placed physical survival above the promotion of Western values. Believing that no values can be realized unless we survive, he refused to risk the balance of power on which survival depends for the sake of allied unity or the support of new states. His belief that only the acceptance of limits by states will produce a stable international system was balanced by his conviction that the fusion of sovereignty with nuclear weapons impose new limits which preclude the resolution of NATO's dilemmas. While pessimistic because the US was at that critical juncture that only creativity can preclude its decline, he was optimistic given the US potential relative to other states. Kissinger's faith in man's freedom to act fed his optimism that eventually the US will find the moral certainty to act to overcome the limitations imposed by the environment. Yet, he rejected the optimism that assumed that man's political values can be realized by technical solutions. Kissinger's pessimism and his belief in limits led him to stress what is not likely to happen in the foreseeable future. However, his belief that the predictability of future trends permits man to make long-term strategy was not undermined by his belief that specific developments are unpredictable. Indeed, he insisted that unless statesmen leave room for the unforeseeable in history they may mortgage the future, and warned that a society that depends on the appearance of a great man in each generation dooms itself since the recognition of "great men" is accidental. Rejecting the obsession with safety and the avoidance of risks, he stressed the importance of man's will in overcoming the limits of his environment and achieving his goals. For Kissinger, a statesman who recognizes and accepts limits and acts with self-restraint can shape history. But to do so he must provide a vision of the future and implement it, and he must be an educator and bridge the gap between his nation's history and his vision.

3 The Philosophical Beliefs of Zbigniew Brzezinski

INTRODUCTION: THE CONTENT OF PHILOSOPHICAL BELIEFS

Zbigniew Brzezinski, a relentless critic of the Nixon-Kissinger approach to national security decision-making, wrote in July of 1973,

> Richard Nixon . . . has perceived more sharply than many of his contemporaries – certainly more clearly than his rivals – the nature of the changed circumstances in which America finds herself. He sees – in part correctly – his foreign policy as a realistic response to worldwide and domestic changes . . . Nixon – though obviously the beneficiary of able advice from his Special Assistant – is to a greater extent the conceptual architect of his Administration's policy . . . (a point rarely conceded by his critics, who prefer to deny Nixon any credit.)[1]

This statement indicates that for Brzezinski, Kissinger's conceptual impact on US national security policy was not as great as Nixon's. Brzezinski conceded, however, that Nixon and Kissinger were successful in establishing a more stable relationship with America's adversaries, and specifically the USSR. At the same time he stressed that, while East-West relations can be handled on the bases of power-realism, the condition of the Third World, and the planet as a whole, requires greater concentration on the issues raised by planetary humanism, while relations with allies demand the creative blend of both approaches.[2]

This chapter examines the philosophical beliefs of Brzezinski in order to accertain the premises on which his criticisms of the Nixon-Kissinger approach to decision-making and policies were based, but more importantly, to determine the basic conceptions influencing his recommendations and/or actions regarding policy toward US allies, the USSR, and the PRC, while he was National Security Adviser. As in the case of Kissinger, Brzezinski's beliefs will be determined by analyzing his academic writings. In this context, Brzezinski will be allowed to speak for himself. In addition, this chapter highlights the similarities and differences between his beliefs and those of Kissinger.

THE NATURE OF POLITICS

What is the "essential" nature of political life? Is the political universe essentially one of harmony or conflict? What is the fundamental character of one's political opponents?

Brzezinski, like Kissinger, believed that the essential nature of politics is conflictual. In his view, conflict, hostility, and violence emanated from "man's inherent aggressiveness." Convinced that "man's primary self-identification is still on the basis of nationalism,"[3] Brzezinski maintained that "rivalry between nations is inherent in an international system that functions without global consensus – the result of centuries of the conditioning of man's outlook by competitive nations that insisted on their individual superiority and particular values." In his view, this rivalry can be terminated only by a fundamental restructuring of international relations that would limit, if not discard, national sovereignty.[4]

Brzezinski's belief in the conflictual nature of politics was strengthened by his orientation toward America's main adversaries – the USSR and the PRC. Focusing on the USSR, Brzezinski explained:

> The Soviet Communist ideology has made an important contribution toward the transformation of international politics from a "game" with certain commonly accepted rules into a profoundly intense conflict, insoluble without a major social transformation either of some of the participating societies or at least of the outlook of some of their elites . . . . The Soviet Communist ideology, even while consciously grappling with certain social problems, introduces into international affairs an element of profound instability and conflict by rejecting the notion that social-economic change might be *unconsciously* taking place in all societies faced with certain similar difficulties, thereby reducing the degree of their diversity. (his italics)[5]

He constantly pointed to the emphasis of Communist ideology, and particularly Soviet ideology, on the intensified class struggle, to Lenin's concepts of the seizure of power with its stress on violent revolution, and to "the notion that social developments throughout the world operate on the basis of a sharply definable dichotomy – that is proof per se of an unbridgeable hostility between the emerging socialist state (latter a system of socialist states) and the rest of the world."[6] Believing that ideology is "the link between theory and action,"[7] Brzezinski considered Soviet ideology as "an ideology of conflict",[8] and the primary contributor to the conflict in the international system. For Brzezinski, the conflict between Communism and Capitalism was fundamental and irreconcilable because of the Soviet "militant conceptions of relations, in which reality is viewed as being a continuing conflict . . . until such time as socialism becomes a world system."[9] In short, Brzezinski believed that whatever conflict existed in the world due to social-economic change has been intensified primarily by the injection of Soviet ideology backed with nuclear weapons.[10]

The focus on the USSR does not indicate that Brzezinski underestimated the PRC's contribution to the conflict in the international system. The Communist schism convinced him that, despite the PRC's military weakness, Peking, fearing that in the long-run Moscow will abandon the revolutionary struggle, was actively promoting international instability and encouraging insurgency not only to promote revolutionary situations but also to embroil the USSR in a more direct conflict with the West. Moreover, he maintained that "as the revolutionary Communism gains in strength, the Chinese may eventually expect to be able to 'slight' imperialism tactically as well, thereby precipitating a major threat to peace."[11] For Brzezinski, then, as the PRC's power increased its contribution to international conflict was likely to increase.

Changes in Beliefs Regarding the Nature of Politics

In the 1950s and early 1960s, Brzezinski's writings pointed to the USSR and the PRC as the main sources of conflict and violence in the international system. In the late 1960s and early 1970s, however, his analysis of the "technetronic" revolution and the globalization of nuclear weapons technology, economics, and ideology led him to refine his beliefs regarding the conflictual nature of politics. Brzezinski concluded that the linkage of old conflicts, i.e., nationalist, religious, and ideological, with the accelerating pace of change brought about by the technetronic revolution, increased the threat of global fragmentation and the possibility of international chaos.[12]

Brzezinski's conception of the technetronic revolution derived from his definition of the "technetronic" society.[13] He maintained that American society – the model technetronic society – "is the principal global disseminator" of this revolution.[14] But while viewing the US as "the innovative and creative society of today," Brzezinski also believed that "it is also a major disruptive influence on the world scene."[15] He declared that America's global impact is contradictory because:

(. . .) it both promotes and undermines American interests as defined by American policymakers; it helps to advance the cause of cooperation on a larger scale even as it disrupts existing social or economic fabrics; it both lays the groundwork for well-being and stability and enhances the forces working for instability and revolution . . . Implicitly and often explicitly modeled on the American pattern, modernization makes for potentially greater economic well-being, but in the process it disrupts existing institutions, undermines prevailing mores, and stimulates resentment that focuses directly on the source of change – America. The result is an acute tension between the kind of global stability and order that America subjectively seeks and the instability, impatience, and frustration that America unconsciously promotes.[16]

In short, while the US is the primary source of global change, it unconsciously and unintentionally promotes revolutionary forces, thus intensifying international conflict and violence. However, it is important to realize Brzezinski's distinction between the type of change promoted by the USSR and the PRC and that promoted by the US. For him, the conflict and violence supported by Moscow and Peking were intended to transform the international system, therefore they were "bad" since they threatened world stability, while the change resulting from America's impact was "good" since the conflict emanating from it was unintentional. Brzezinski warned, however, that "an America that turns inward – repelled by the ugliness of the world around it and beset by internal ideological conflict – would create a vacuum that would be filled less by any single power, though that might be the result in some regions, and more simply by escalating chaos."[17]

Convinced that "real unity of mankind remains remote," despite the emerging global consciousness, Brzezinski argued, that "concentrated humanity is [characterized by] the routinization of conflict."[18] This belief was evident in his rejection of the concept of "global village." He argued that "the new reality . . . will not be that of a 'global village', since the "analogy overlooks the personal stability, interpersonal intimacy, implicitly shared values, and traditions that were important ingredients of the primitive village." He maintained that "a more appropriate analogy is that of the 'global city' – a nervous, agitated, tense, and fragmented web of interdependent relations."[19] Brzezinski found the concept of a global city more suitable because today city life "is definitely leading to mass mental disease, to growing vandalism, and possible eruptions of mass violence."[20] Rejecting the prevailing assumption that the world, shaped increasingly by the industrial and urban revolutions, will become more homogeneous in its outlook, and thus more stable, he stated that "this may be so, but it could be the homogeneity of insecurity, of uncertainty, and of intellectual anarchy. The result, therefore, would not necessarily be a more stable environment."[21] Convinced that the gap between the pace in the expansion of knowledge and the rate of its assimilation poses the threat of intellectual fragmentation, he maintained that the sharing of new common perspectives becomes more difficult as knowledge expands with man's increased involvement in global affairs while traditional perspectives can no longer be sustained. Brzezinski predicted "the end of ideology," arguing that "terms such as capitalism, democracy, socialism, and communism – even nationalism – are no longer adequate to provide relevant insights."[22] For Brzezinski then, the contemporary change caused by the technetronic revolution is likely to intensify the conflict and violence in the international system.

Brzezinski believed that these problems were compounded by "the triumph of equality." Arguing that "the relationship between the technetronic age and the passion for equality – if not the idea of equality itself – is quite causal," since inequality is no longer insulated by time and distance, he stressed that although "the commitment to the idea of equality currently commands the greatest allegiance, the definion of equality remains elusive." In Brzezinski's view, "with real equality impossible, equality through emotion becomes a substitute, with passionate conflict and hostility creating the illusions of equality."[23]

The changes brought about by the technetronic revolution were, according to Brzezinski, a threat to stability, especially if the intensifying confrontations between the advanced and the developing countries revive the USSR's and the PRC's waning ideological aspirations."[24] In his view, "communism, which many Americans see as the principal cause of unrest, primarily capitalizes on frustrations and aspirations, whose major source is the American impact on the rest of the world. The United States is the focus of global attention, emulation, envy, admiration, and animosity."[25] Therefore, he criticized the Nixon Doctrine as "insufficiently concerned with what might well emerge as the central threat to international stability in this and the next decade: the contagious spread of global anarchy."[26] The belief that the revolutionary powers could prevent the establishment of a stable international system by exploiting the instability and frustration unconsciously promoted by the US was shared by both Kissinger and Brzezinski.

IMAGE OF ADVERSARIES: THE USSR AND THE PRC

Brzezinski, like Kissinger, believed that the USSR and the PRC are revolutionary powers, and referred to them as such in all of his writings,[27] since they conducted an ideological foreign policy, that is, insisting on the universality of their goals,[28] and after the Sino-Soviet split on the universality of their respective models of communism.[29] Focusing on the USSR, Brzezinski explained:

> Soviet insistence (derived from the conceptual elements of ideol- ogy . . . and from their general impact on Soviet foreign policy) that ultimate peace depends on the total victory of a particular social system led by a particular political party injects into international affairs an element of a fundamental struggle for survival not conducive to conflict resolution.[30]

In short, for Brzezinski, as for Kissinger, the essence of a revolutionary power is the belief in its principles and the willingness, if not eagerness, to push them to their ultimate conclusion.[31] Brzezinski's definition of a "modern revolutionary ideology" led him to conclude that both Communism and Fascism or Nazism are revolutionary ideologies since their goal was the transformation of the international system.[32] For him, as for Kissinger, then, revolutionary powers whether red or white were equally threatening to international stability.[33] Indeed, he admitted, that "the views I have of the Soviet Union happen to be somewhat similar to the views of Henry Kissinger . . . "[34]

Brzezinski also attributed to the USSR and the PRC what Kissinger called the distinguishing feature of a revolutionary power, that is, the desire for absolute security.[35] In 1966 Brzezinski wrote, that although Soviet foreign policy in its short-term is concerned with Russia's traditional concerns for security, frontiers, and national power, the Soviet leaders, unlike the Czars,

> view these issues in terms of certain long-term perspectives and not as ends in themselves. Indeed, the Soviet conception of their own security is inherently offensive; as long as alternative political systems exist, there is continued need to be preoccupied with security issues. Because they see themselves as part of a historical process toward a defined end, the Soviet leaders are compelled to view any effort to "stabilize" or to "normalize" the international situation as a hostile design.[36]

For Brzezinski, then, Moscow's and Peking's insistence on ultimate peace, which they equated with "the goal of an ultimate world-wide Communist society . . . ,"[37] led to absolute insecurity for all the other states and, as Kissinger maintained, to permanent revolution.[38] Moreover, Brzezinski believed that Soviet ideology "as an ideology of conflict, [has] given them a more effective basis for a strategy of conflict . . . "[39] in the pursuit of their goal.

Like Kissinger, Brzezinski focused on the USSR since it could back its revolutionary ideology with overwhelming military power. As he stated: "the global ambitions of Communist ideology have now been harnessed to a new sense of national self-assertion, intensified by power and achievement. That combination drives the Soviet Union toward global primacy." In 1967 Brzezinski warned:

> It would be a mistake to consider the Soviet leaders simply as nationalists, cynically manipulating Communist slogans to gain support. In all probability, they believe themselves to be true Communist internationalists, but they interpret that internationalism in terms of Soviet interests and purposes. Thus, they will use foreign revolutions . . . in their struggle against the United States . . . but . . . in moments of crisis they will be ready to sacrifice the foreign revolution for the sake of the U.S.S.R.[40]

He maintained that the distinction between ideological and power considerations in analyzing Soviet behavior is "an artificial abstraction" and a "misleading issue," since they "become so enmeshed in the performance of a particular political act that to isolate one from the other is to deny that which is precisely most characteristic of the [Communist] movement – the blending of ideology with power."[41] Soviet international achievements, according to Brzezinski, demonstrate the correctness of the ideology to the Party membership, "thereby preserving the inner sense of ideological purpose without which the Party could decay." In his view, the USSR's involvement in the international system "on a massive scale – an involvement that in part is also a function of size and power and would continue to generate conflicts between the U.S.S.R. and the United States even without ideology – tends to revitalize the ideology and to translate even simple issues into broader conflicts."[42] Brzezinski argued that there is a kind of a "dialectical" relationship between an ideological party and reality which "permits the ideology to exercise a continuing influence and prevents it from becoming sterile and irrelevant."[43] In short, he believed that the USSR, as well as the PRC, will remain revolutionary powers for the foreseeable future.

Brzezinski's belief that Moscow and Peking were committed to creating a world-wide Communist society did not change as a result of, what he called, the relativization of ideology emanating from changes in the Soviet Bloc, and particularly from the Sino-Soviet schism. In 1961, attacking those in the West claiming that the schism would lead to changes in Communist objectives, he stated:

> The bloc is not splitting and it is not likely to split. Talk of a Sino-Soviet conflict, of even a war between them, merely illustrates a profound misconception of the essence of the historical phenomenon of Communism, which, while affected by traditional national considerations, has from its very beginning reflected a conscious emphasis on supranational perspectives.[44]

For Brzezinski, as for Kissinger, then, the USSR and the PRC were revolutionary powers given their commitment to world-wide communist expansion. By 1967, however, as a result of new developments in the Sino-Soviet conflict Brzezinski modified his views regarding the possibility of war between the USSR and the PRC, but he did not change his belief about their commitment to transforming the existing international system.[45]

Changes in Beliefs Regarding Adversaries

The examination of Brzezinski's scholarly studies reveal that in order to account for some significant historical developments in international Communism he refined his images of the USSR and the PRC, but he did not change them. For Brzezinski, Khrushchev's declaration that war is no longer "a fatalistic inevitability," and the increasing Soviet willingness to concede that war would be mutually destructive, indicated that the increasing number of nuclear weapons was the most important aspect of international affairs that could promote the erosion of Soviet ideology.[46] He also noted Moscow's view that the emergence of the world socialist system is a decisive force of change that accelerated the pace of the socialist revolution while successfully deterring Western countermeasures.[47] Those changes in Soviet perceptions, according to Brzezinski, led to peaceful coexistence as an alternative to mutual destruction. He warned, however, that

> (. . .) there can be little doubt that if the military situation were to become onesidely favorable to the USSR, making it invulnerable, the

Soviet viewpoint might change again . . . It would be naive, of course, to assume that Soviet commitment to such peaceful coexistence is irreversible; but given a general fear of war, the Soviet leaders would have to think twice before restoring "the inevitability of war" principle.[48]

For Brzezinski, as for Kissinger, then, the adjustment in Soviet perceptions regarding the inevitability of war was the product of necessity and interest; it did not indicate the abandonment of the goal of a world-wide communist society.[49] This belief was also evident in his criticism of those in the West who made "the triumphant assertions that the Soviet leaders are abandoning their Marxism or Communism . . . with such monotonous regularity and persistent ignorance . . . "[50] In short, Brzezinski, like Kissinger, concluded that the fear of thermonuclear war (and the increasing domestic social desire to enjoy the "good life") might induce the USSR to cooperate with the US in reducing the risks of such war.[51]

Brzezinski's recognition that the increasing ideological diversity within the Soviet bloc threatens the universal validity of the Soviet ideology itself, thereby undermining one of the factors that shape the Soviet approach to the world,[52] did not change his belief that the USSR is a revolutionary power. Convinced that the sources of ideological vitality, that is, the CPSU's determination to maintain ideological consciousness in its ranks, the personal commitment of Soviet leaders for whom "ideology is the source of their insight into reality . . . ", a broad social commitment, and action commitment crowned by success, minimized the threat to the universal validity of Marxism-Leninism, he explained:

> It is these forces that impede the erosion of the ideology and inhibit the Soviet leadership from accepting international affairs as a game with a series of rules; instead, these forces make them insist on treating international affairs as a conflict with only *one* solution . . . In the near future, an international "conflict resolution" is unlikely. (his italics)[53]

This statement indicates that although Brzezinski did not develop models for stable and revolutionary international systems, he shared Kissinger's belief that the present international system is revolutionary because the USSR and the PRC are seeking to transform it, not to adjust differences within it. Brzezinski maintained that the cumulative effect of the fear of nuclear extinction, of the impact of domestic change, and of the emergence of ideological relativism resulting from the spread of Communism, could be the gradual erosion of the "oversimplified conception of an antagonistic confrontation between two social systems and of historical change in general, the commitment to conflict, the universality of goals, the sense of self-righteousness, and the belief in the imminence of victory . . . " He argued that as a result, "a growing willingness to accept some common and overt rules of behavior could follow, buttressing the existing informal and undefined restraints on violence that both sides have tacitly recognized." He recognized, however, that at the present time this erosion is balanced by the sources of ideological vitality, which reassert and even revitilize the ideology."[54]

Indeed, in 1970, with the USSR approaching strategic parity with the US, Brzezinski wrote in *Between Two Ages*, "it would . . . be rash to expect in the near future a fundamental revision of the Soviet attitude toward the world."[55] He tirelessly reiterated that for top Soviet leaders

> The basic premise continues to be the Manichaean notion of the antago-nistic dichotomy between the socialist and the capitalist worlds . . . Though war between these two worlds is no longer said to be "fatalisti-cally inevitable", and the destructiveness of nuclear weapons dictates the necessity of peaceful coexistence . . . the underlying reality of our age is still said to be the competition between the two systems . . . Event-ually one or the other will have to prevail . . . [56]

In short, for Brzezinski, Moscow's rejection of the inevitability of war led only to new Soviet tactics for transforming the international system.

The Soviet declarations that the underlying reality of our age is the struggle between capitalism and socialism and that socialism will prevail, led Brzezinski to warn that:

> It would be an error to dismiss [ideology] as merely a ritualistic act of obeisance to doctrine, or to view it as a sign of fanatical and implacable militancy. Its importance lies in the influence of the ideological frame-work on more immediate, and otherwise quite well-informed, policy judgements. Though far from committing Soviet leaders to short-term militancy, the ideological framework does inhibit them from thinking of accomodation and stability as ends in themselves, since that would be tantamount to negating the communist view of history as a fluid, dialectical process.[57]

Brzezinski believed that for Soviet leaders peaceful coexistence was "an ideological offensive," most evident in their encouragement of radical nationalist revolutions made possible by the peaceful and paralyzing mutual nuclear blackmail of the USSR and the US,[58] their attacks on the notion of "ideological coexistence" advocated by some Soviet intellectuals,[59] and the April 1968 statement of the Soviet Central Committee that "the contemporary stage in historical development is distinguished by intense sharpening of the ideological struggle between capitalism and socialism."[60] He insisted that "peace with victories will serve to strengthen the Party's claim that history is still unfolding, that it must continue its mission, that there is no fraternization with the enemy – but all without war."[61] For Brzezinski, then, as for Kissinger, since peaceful coexistence was an ideological offensive the USSR remained a revolutionary power. Yet, this offensive was not the real threat to international stability, according to Brzezinski, since the CPSU had transformed the most important revolutionary doctrine of this century (which could have made the USSR the standard-bearer of the most influential system of thought and the model for resolving the key dilemmas facing man) into a dull social and political orthodoxy that is revolutionary in rhetoric but conservative in practice.[62]

For the PRC leadership, according to Brzezinski, Sputnik signaled a decisive shift in the balance of military power between East and West. Mao insisted that now the East would prevail over the West since the USSR had the means to affect more revolutionary changes in the world despite of the militarization of imperialism. Hence, he pressured Moscow to adopt harsher ideological positions and more militant policies toward the West, and in particular the US.[63] But the Cuban missile crisis which reduced Moscow's confidence in its ability to extort concessions from the West by military threats,[64] convinced Peking that while Moscow had the means, it lacked the will to promote revolution globally. Peking viewed détente with the US as dangerous to the interests of world revolution, and the Test Ban Agreement as a Soviet step "toward *an alliance* with the principal 'imperialist' power directed *against* China's interests" (his italics).[65] This perception, Brzezinski argued, led to a qualitative change in the Sino-Soviet conflict, since Peking felt "duty bound to infuse international Communism with the will to prevail." He maintained:

> The Chinese did not desire war per se, but they were convinced that increased pressure on the West, including that of local wars, was justified and that the West would yield step by step. Furthermore, the Chinese were concerned that fear of war would inevitably lead to the fear of revolution and hence to the extinction of revolutionary zeal in the international movement itself . . . They felt that continuous pressure by the militarily superior Soviet bloc would encourage revolutionary upheavals, particularly in the colonial areas. The disintegration of imperialism would soon follow.[66]

Peking's total unwillingness to cooperate in reducing the risks of nuclear war, led Brzezinski, in 1967, to reiterate his belief that the PRC "is our most immediate concern."[67]

The willingness of the USSR and the reluctance of the PRC to assist in reducing the risks of nuclear war, was in Brzezinski's view, only a difference in tactics and timing, not in their commitment to transform the international system. He explained:

> In the short run, then, the revisionist Communism is the more dangerous, because it is based primarily on Soviet power, reflects intense Soviet national ambitions, and is backed by a nuclear rocket force . . . However, the gradual decline in the revolutionary orientation of the Soviet leaders, their growing recognition that a nuclear war would not bring about a Communist victory, and their increasing stress on economic competition leave room for the optimism concerning a future adjustment with the West. The orthodox Communism, because of its military impotence, is less of an immediate danger, but it represents the greater long-range threat to peace. One may presume that its Chinese leaders will strive to promote international instability, not only in order to promote revolutionary situations but also to embroil Moscow's revisionist Communism in more direct conflict with the West.[68]

This statement reiterates Brzezinski's belief that the USSR is a greater immediate threat to world stability and indicates that, like Kissinger, he believed that the USSR should be the focus of US national security policy since its nuclear capability made it more dangerous and at the same time more "willing," given its fear of thermonuclear war (and desire for trade with the West), to cooperate with the US in reducing the risk of such war.

For Brzezinski, then, while Moscow threatened world stability primarily with its military power, Peking threatened it with its ideological puritanism and militancy. However, as in the case of the Soviet conservative bureaucratized doctrine, he was not really concerned with the appeal of the PRC's orthodox communism because: (a) the PRC, unlike the USSR, represents only a potential and not a relevant model of how communism responds to the problems of modern man given its industrial backwardness, its conflicts with its immediate neighbors, and its political uncertainties; and (b) because the cultural, linguistic, and racial distinctiveness of the Chinese automatically made their communism much more difficult to export or emulate.[69] But Brzezinski conceded that the PRC appeals to the more disaffected and emotional Western intellectuals and to some would-be Third World revolutionaries because of its alleged puritanism, its ideological militancy, and its seemingly permanent revolution; for them it is an attractive example of national discipline, of ideological dedication, and of a massive social effort to modernize despite its technological backwardness.[70]

The death of the Sino-Soviet alliance as an active political force[71] did not change Brzezinski's belief regarding the revolutionary nature of the USSR and the PRC. In 1967, criticizing those in the West who argued that the USSR might give up its universal goal, he declared:

> Focusing more specifically on international Communism, it is hence most unlikely that the international scene will soon see a realignment of forces which pits, as some seem to expect, a coalition of the U.S. and the USSR against Communist China. For this to happen, a major domestic transformation of the Soviet system would be necessary, with its Communist elite losing all hope of a Communist victory, in effect moving over into the doctrinal position of its erstwhile enemies and, consequently, giving up its doctrinal claim to domestic power. This transformation could only occur in conditions of prolonged international stability . . . However, such an impasse is very unlikely, since it would have to include not only the so-called Western world but also the underdeveloped areas, which at the moment seem to offer the best revolutionary prospects.[72]

Recognizing that Moscow and Peking will openly pursue different strategies against the West to thwart each others' international objectives,[73] Brzezinski suggested, in 1968, that the US should respond favorably to any PRC interest in broadening contacts in order not to appear as a tacit partner of the USSR in the isolation of the PRC. He admitted that this was a major change of his belief that the PRC must be isolated for the sake of improved relations with the USSR.[74]

Rejecting the widespread argument that the "liberalization" or "democratization" of the Soviet political system was taking place and the inference that Moscow would abandon its goal to change the international system, Brzezinski declared, such terms "are somewhat misleading" since the system "involves one-party dictatorship, with its outstanding characteristic being the active indoctrination of the society in the Party's ideology and the shaping of all social relations according to that ideology."[75] For him, the abandonment of indoctrination "would signal the first real step in the direction of the transformation of the system."[76] He noted, however, that Khrushchev's successors "re-emphasiz(ed) the imperative necessity of ideological orthodoxy and more vigorous ideological indoctrination"[77] because they recognized that "even a limited democratization of the Soviet society – that is, freedom of expression and of travel – would threaten [them]".[78] In Brzezinski's view, democratization in the USSR requires positive political reforms, not mere changes in mood and style, or reductions in terror and fear.[79] For Brzezinski, then, Moscow's continued stress on ideological indoctrination would perpetuate the East-West conflict.

For Brzezinski, the Soviet adjustments to the threat of nuclear war and to the diversity within international communism suggested, that if "gradual erosion is to take place and if, in its wake, the Soviet political system is to change fundamentally, the change will have to come primarily from the outside and not from the inside."[80] He stressed that unlike Stalin's time, "what happens abroad is now much more relevant to domestic Soviet politics."[81] But he also believed, that only changes which originate in Communist states and are formulated within the framework of the common ideology, might gradually penetrate the ruling elite and only afterward affect society as a whole. However, looking at the flow of foreign ideas into far less controlled Czarist Russia and the control of internal power by the Communist regime, Brzezinski concluded, "one may well be justified in cautioning that this erosion should be awaited with a great deal of patience."[82] In his view, a prevailing mood of general social relaxation both at home and abroad would be politically very dangerous for the Party. Hence, it must preserve the sense of dynamism by demonstrating the continuous need for its dictatorship and for its ideology-action.[83] He argued that the Party did this by the policy of peaceful coexistence which called for intensifying the ideological conflict.

Brzezinski also rejected the widespread theory of convergence. Both the Communist version which stated that the world will converge into an essentially communist form of government, as well as the Western version which assumed that the fundamental aspects of democracy will be retained after the US and the USSR "converge" in the indeterminate future. Convinced that theories of convergence "in reality posit not convergence but submergence of the opposite system," he insisted that both versions of convergence "are basically revolutionary: both predict a revolutionary change in the character of one of the present systems."[84] For him, a highly unlikely possibility in the foreseeable future.[85] Brzezinski explained that,

> The theory of convergence thus minimizes or ignores the totality of the Russian and the American historical experience – political, social, and economic – and exaggerates the importance of one factor alone. It minimizes also the uniqueness of the historical process and it

forces it into a common pattern with fundamentally the same outcome
for all. It asserts the repetitiveness of the historically familiar and
ignores the probability that the future will see in both the United
States and in the Soviet Union novel forms of government which
will *evolve* out of the present on the basis of the *uneven* importance
of political and social-economic determinants in the two countries. (his
italics)[86]

In short, he believed that because both "political systems, each in its own
way, have been highly successful . . . they are not likely to change drastically . . . The evolution of the two systems, but not their convergence,
seems to be the undramatic pattern of the future."[87]

For Brzezinski, the steady convergence of the West and the East,
including China, in terms of contemporary styles and values, that is, in
clothing, in social behavior, in some private aspirations, as a result of
industrialization and urbanization, does not reduce the political differences
since "a political system has its own staying power and helps shape the
course of economic and social development."[88] This was evident in
the Soviet attacks on the notion of ideological coexistence, efforts to
revitalize Marxism-Leninism, and the vigorous efforts of Soviet scholars in rejecting the theory of convergence of the Soviet and Western, particularly US, systems.[89] Moscow viewed the theory of convergence and Brzezinski's theory of evolution as attempts to undermine
the ideological foundation of Soviet power.[90] In other words, the Soviet
efforts to assert and to prove the distinctive character of the communist system convinced Brzezinski that the USSR is still a revolutionary
power.

Rejecting the belief that convergence "represents the only hope for
peace," Brzezinski declared, that "history shows that social-political uniformity and peace need not go hand in hand. In fact, the latter may
be a more comforting conclusion than the propostion – shared by both
the Marxists and the 'convergists' – that peace depends on uniformity.
Such a premise is both curiously escapist and utopian." His study of the
Communist bloc led him to conclude that the Communist advocates of
convergence "should realize that a communist America and a communist
Russia would be likely to engage in a competition more intense than the
relatively unequal struggle between Russia and China." He also stressed,
that "noncommunist believers in convergence also have no reason to
assume that a noncommunist Russia, with its nationalist ambitions, would
be less likely to strive to dominate the Eurasian continent than a communist
Russia." Brzezinski acknowledged that "both America and Russia may

learn from each other ('codiscovery') . . . ", but stressed, "this is not tantamount to becoming more alike, nor indeed is there much reassurance that their becoming more alike would necessarily diminish tensions between them." He believed that "the new sense of Soviet nationalism is merged with the ideological interests of the ruling bureaucracy, and the competition with America is the national expression."[91] For Brzezinski, then, short of thermonuclear war and despite the relativization of communist ideology, the US-Soviet conflict will continue given the incompatibility of their national interests.

Focusing on great power nationalism Brzezinski stated:

> Great-power nationalism can be very assertive and tenacious. Therefore, it would be premature to expect a precipitous decline in the intensity of Soviet-American tensions because of the domestic changes. The competition between these two superpowers will continue because both continue to have, however vaguely defined, a global sense of mission and both remain the world's principal military powers. Conflicts of interest between them are inescapable. But both the nature of the conflict and its geographic focus may change with the evolution of Soviet society and national orientation. Europe could become an area where both sides see an advantage in obtaining stability, even while waging political warfare elsewhere.[92]

This statement demonstrates that, despite Brzezinski's focus on Soviet ideology in explaining the revolutionary nature of the USSR, he did not underestimate the impact of Soviet nationalism. In his words, "today the Soviet Union has a foreign policy that is intensely nationalistic."[93] Indeed, his analyses of state relations in the Communist bloc and among the new states convinced him that national interest considerations influence the foreign policy of all states.

US-Soviet détente did not change Brzezinski's beliefs regarding the USSR since the Soviet concept of détente, which in his view had primarily shaped US-Soviet relations, stressed intensified ideological hostility and absolute security – the characteristics of a revolutionary power.[94] In 1975, he wrote, this concept "is that of a limited and expedient arrangement, which in no way terminates the ideological conflict even as it yields tangible economic benefits." His conviction rested on Soviet statements emphasizing that "'peaceful coexistence' is a form of class struggle and that ideological conflict, far from abating, is to intensify during détente."[95] Noting the continued expansion of the Soviet defense effort, Brzezinski concluded, that "the Soviet agreement to SALT has been more tactical than strategic in nature, and at least some Soviet leaders are still attracted by the notion of strategic superiority," that is absolute security. He insisted that the SALT I agreements resulted from the Soviet fear of nuclear war, the emerging US-PRC rapprochement, and the Soviet economic and technological vulnerabilities, and were more beneficial for the USSR than the US because Washington conceded numerical superiority in strategic weapons, thus granting the USSR the symbolic status of co-equality with the US that it did not deserve. Brzezinski saw those agreements as the partial codification of "the rules of the game" under which the superpower rivalry is to be conducted.[96] Moreover, he opposed Soviet access to US credits and technology and the collaborative efforts in space because in his view they helped the Soviet economy and buttressed the Soviet political system, thus, reducing domestic pressures for needed reforms.[97] Brzezinski considered détente as both limited and unstable since "alleged concessions" by the USSR "were on matters peripheral to the U.S.-Soviet relationship and were transient in nature, while the U.S. concessions have been on matters directly *central* to that relationship and have been continuing" (his italics). Hence, while acknowledging that détente itself was "a welcomed development," he attacked the Nixon-Kissinger "passive" approach to détente.[98] For Brzezinski, the Nixon-Kissinger approach lacked the necessary linkage between the political, economic, and cultural aspects of détente.[99] In short, he believed that through détente Moscow is still pursuing its objective of a world-wide communist expansion.

For Brzezinski, US-PRC rapprochement did not indicate a change in the PRC's revolutionary nature. He stressed that given the Maoist principal that the revolutionary process has to be indigenous and truly spontaneous in any country, "China's general support of and assistance to revolutionary activity does not stand in the way of its negotiating transitional and more expedient arrangements with individual states, especially if such arrangements are clearly in China's national and political interest." Acknowledging that Nixon's visit to Peking benefited the US by putting a higher premium in Moscow on US-Soviet accomodation while reducing Moscow's freedom of action against the PRC, Brzezinski maintained that the visit greatly increased the PRC's international prestige, particularly in Asia, sowed confusion in Japan, and it maximized insecurity in Taiwan. Moreover, US-PRC rapprochement strengthened Peking's position in the Sino-Soviet conflict. In his words: "the foregoing is consistent with the Chinese Communists' commitment to a long-range revolutionary process."[100] In short, like the USSR, the PRC is still committed to a world-wide communist expansion.

IMAGE OF ALLIANCES

Brzezinski's belief that conflict is inherent in international relations was also evident in his image of alliances. Unlike Kissinger, who studied NATO, Brzezinski concentrated primarily on the Soviet bloc, focusing on US relations with Western Europe and Japan during the Nixon and Ford administrations. Nevertheless, Brzezinski's beliefs regarding alliances can be ascertained from his writings regarding relations between the superpowers and their allies.

In 1965, in *Alternatives to Partition* (the same year Kissinger's *The Troubled Partnership* was published), Brzezinski provided the most lucid manifestation of his beliefs regarding alliances. His brief examination of US-West European relations reveals that for Brzezinski, as for Kissinger, conflict within NATO was caused "by contradictory national priorities," not by General de Gaulle. Sharing Kissinger's view that de Gaulle's tactics intensified intra-alliance disputes, Brzezinski, like Kissinger, argued that these stemmed from the decline in West European insecurity and the West European economic recovery (both testifying to the success of US policy).[101] As a result of these developments the earlier automatic congruity of national interests became obscured by contradictory national priorities.[102] In his view, the divergent US-West European interests were most evident in the different perceptions regarding the Atlantic partnership and in the alternative conceptions of military strategy. Brzezinski argued:

> The American emphasis on the Atlantic partnership meant continued American leadership to the French and continued partition to the Germans. It presumed an identity of interests without an identity of goals. Yet, as Hans Morgenthau rightly observed, "Such identity of interests is rare in peace and cannot even be taken for granted in war. It exists among the members of the Atlantic alliance only on the most general plane: the Atlantic alliance is united in its opposition to communist aggression and subversion. But this interest is not a policy in itself: it must be implemented by common policies. Such policies, to which all members of the alliance are committed, do not at present exist.[103]

In short, like Kissinger, Brzezinski believed that US and West European interests are not identical in all cases, and that the range of divergence is likely to increase as the West European preoccupation with security declined, irrespective of any changes in Soviet ambitions and behavior.[104] However, it should be noted that in his critiques of the

Nixon-Kissinger NATO policy, Brzezinski implied that the disputes were caused by Kissinger and not divergent national priorities.

Convinced that "national sovereignty" influences the foreign policy of all states,[105] Brzezinski explained:

> (. . .) on both sides of divided Europe the lessened fear of war made particular national priorities more important in defining the attitude of each member state either toward NATO or toward the Warsaw Treaty.
>
> The words "national sovereignty" were thus invoked with equal solemnity by General de Gaulle and First Secretary Gheorghiu-Dej, and by both with a feeling of security. They accurately perceived that while United States and Soviet military power had not declined, the two superpowers could not use it in any other way except to check each other. The French leader's criticism of the Atlantic Community as posing a threat to European independence – to the "very soul" of Europe – were matched by the Rumanian insistence that "socialist division of labor" was incompatible with the country's sovereignty.[106]

In Brzezinski's view, developments within the Soviet bloc have refuted the 1952 Soviet claim that as a result of the common ideological outlook "'a new, socialist type of international relations arose with the formation of the commonwealth of socialist states'." He asserted that a common ideology does not guarantee, as the Soviets alleged, the utmost respect for the sovereignty of the smaller East European states while assuring a common foreign policy.[107] Brzezinski believed that the Soviet efforts to create a united and stable interstate system in Eastern Europe based on the acceptance of Soviet leadership failed because "what the Soviet leaders had not foreseen was that stable and popularly accepted regimes, even though communist, would tend to become nationalistic."[108] This was evident in the case of Yugoslavia, Albania, and Rumania. For Brzezinski, then, as for Kissinger, in all states considerations of national sovereignty dominate the conduct of foreign policy.[109]

The belief that nationalism undermined Marxism-Leninism was manifest in Brzezinski's argument that by the late 1950s international politics returned to Eastern Europe as a result of the declining Soviet predominance and the need to base unity on diversity.[110] The shift from integral to international relations among the Communist states was the result of the following factors:

1. The new ruling Communist elites in Eastern Europe gradually became more confident of their ability to build "socialism", especially if they were permitted to make some domestic adjustments;
2. The indigenous and independent Communist regime in China "objectively" strengthened the case of those within the ruling elites who felt that Stalinism should be viewed as a transitional phase leading to a more genuine Communist internationalism rather than as an enduring prescription;
3. The accumulated tension of popular, national reaction against Soviet domination which Communist leaders could not afford wholly to ignore;
4. The ideological neutrality of the technological revolution which merged with the increased preoccupation of the East European elites with national economic growth and industrial development.[111]

In his view, the impact of these factors was intensified by the post-Stalin crisis in the Communist world and, specifically, by the exacerbation of the Sino-Soviet conflict. However, Brzezinski also believed that "the ruling communist elites have no interest in becoming absorbed by the West, even though pushed in that direction by economic and popular pressures." This was demonstrated by the actions of Yugoslavia and Poland which moved closer to Moscow once the more objectionable aspects of their relationship with the USSR were eliminated.[112]

The Sino-Soviet conflict, according to Brzezinski, made East European support for Moscow so important that it "has increasingly tended to restrict Soviet freedom of action in Central Europe," while enlarging the scope for maneuver and self-assertion by the East Europeans. However, while believing that the increasing impact of nationalism in the definition of Eastern European domestic and foreign priorities "contributed to a gradual erosion of communist ideological militancy,"[113] he acknowledged, that "nationalism is not only and in every case directed against the Russians . . . " since in the multi-ethnic East European states ethnic tensions "weaken its effectiveness as a basis for opposition to Soviet domination."[114] In addition, the negative impact of nationalism in Soviet-East European relations is limited by the strongly held communist view that 'ideological coexistence' is by definition counter-revolutionary.[115] Moreover, he argued that the shared ideological assumptions make any political decision related to them necessarily relevant to those made by other communist regimes. Therefore, a policy by one regime either validates the policy of another regime or, if at variance with it, threatens its legitimacy and ideological orthodoxy. Accordingly, the traditional principle of noninterference in the domestic political affairs of one sovereign state by another became inapplicable to relations among Communist states. Brzezinski maintained that since communist regimes come under great domestic pressure to adjust to domestic circumstances, "only a continuous 'consultation' between the ruling parties can maintain the cohesion so essential to universal victory."[116] Therefore, following Moscow's lead, East European leaders placed limits on the free flow of ideas and cultural contacts while preaching "economic peaceful coexistence" which they believed to be essential to the survival of their economic system.[117]

For Brzezinski, the return of international politics to Eastern Europe, meant a transformation of the relations among Communist states, not a total separation. They still prefer to associate with each other since their leaders subscribe to certain common ideological assumptions, had similar operational and ideological training, and share a self-righteous hostility toward capitalism. Therefore, even if ideology does not always influence their policy, there is a common and explicit faith linking the leaders of these states. Seeing a parallel development in NATO, Brzezinski pointed out, "the Rumanians, like De Gaulle in the West, were setting their national interest above the broad 'common' interest of other like-minded states. They most certainly were not defecting to the other side, unless pushed there by excessive reactions from the dominant power of their bloc."[118] In his view, the change in the Soviet bloc manifested the revival of the supremacy of states and the collapse of the old communist dream of one united communist state."[119] Brzezinski concluded, however, that while Eastern Europe is no longer subject to monolithic communism, it is not dominated by pure and simple nationalism. He argued that it "is governed by an unsteady combination of nationalism and communism,"[120] which is reinforced by the East European and Soviet fear of a rearmed self-assertive Germany.[121] Brzezinski believed that Soviet power and the overriding sense of dependence on the USSR for protection against Germany inhibit any East European initiatives that deviate from the Soviet general line.[122] Moreover, he was convinced that the communist element inclined East European leaders "to give the Soviet Union the benefit of the doubt on international issues."[123]

Brzezinski believed that the inability of the communist economies to meet rising consumer demands and the ideological neutrality of the technological revolution further undermine the unity of the Soviet bloc.[124] In his view, the inevitable decline of ideology and of the fear of a resurgent Germany, will increasingly compel Moscow to provide more economic assistance to demonstrate the "objective" benefits of its alliance system.[125] But Moscow could not provide it without expanding trade with the West.

Moreover, the increasingly widespread realization in Eastern Europe that internal investment needs are not likely to be met within the Council of Economic Mutual Assistance (CEMA), and that tighter integration in CEMA could eventually limit national independence by becoming a control lever for Moscow, also undermined the Soviet ability to prove the "objective" benefits of the Soviet-East European relationship.[126] The division of Europe – and the Iron Curtain – was justified by the arguments that it was essential for the industrialization of East Europe and its liberation from economic dependence on the West, and that the communist model of industrialization is historically superior, i.e., more rapid. Acknowledging that East European industrialization has been impressive, he stressed that the lack of a clear-cut superiority in this field and the comparative failures in agriculture and in personal consumption were undermining the ideological underpinnings of the communist position in Eastern Europe.[127] In his view, the East European preoccupation with domestic economic growth is already undermining the communist bloc orientation. However, warning that "it would be dangerous to underestimate the degree to which certain basic ideological prejudices have become imbedded in the social fabric, existing institutions, personal perspectives, [and] vested interests," Brzezinski concluded that the trend strongly favors a more domestically oriented ideological perspective – in brief domesticism not universalism, relativism not absolutism.[128]

In Brzezinski's view, however, much more important than the impact of nationalism in the two alliances was the divergent thrust in their historical development.[129] He claimed that the EEC and the Franco-German accord indicated that, despite internal conflicts, "the broad thrust of Western European development is toward increasing cooperation and – much more important – toward a European consciousness," especially among the younger generations which already see Western Europe as an entity in all but the political field. Claiming that the technetronic revolution accelerated West European cooperation, but recognizing that "a positive regionalism is yet to mature," Brzezinski argued, that the new consciousness provides the needed psychological basis for a new Europe.[130] Hence, while sharing Kissinger's belief in the importance of nationalism in relations among states, Brzezinski, unlike Kissinger, de-emphasized its vitality in Western Europe. In Japan, however, which lacks the external outlet that unification provides for West Europeans, the technetronic revolution, according to Brzezinski, sharpened internal political conflicts, and it could lead to a revival of nationalism or ideological radicalism if no effort is made to forge a community of the developed nations that would provide an outlet.[131] But Eastern Europe, in Brzezinski's view, is becoming less united as a result of: (a) the reliance on narrow nationalism (often a substitute for either internal legitimacy or for external Soviet support) in resisting Soviet domination; and (b) the inherent inclination of the communist system to escalate differences into matters of ideological principle thus inhibiting the resolution of conflicts and in turn cooperation.[132] He believed that Moscow will not succeed in strengthening CEMA and the Warsaw Pact Treaty Organization (WTO) since the efforts to do so came at a time (early 1960s) when the East European elites were becoming more sensitive about their sovereignty and, given the Stalinist legacy, feared that any multilateral political organization was essentially a design for perpetuating Soviet hegemony. The Sino-Soviet conflict precluded the use of sanctions against them since Moscow needed their support to counter the PRC.[133] Brzezinski believed that, despite the different approaches of the superpowers toward their allies, the Europeans, both Eastern and Western, have not accepted the division of Europe.[134] Moreover, like Kissinger, Brzezinski believed that neither superpower could easily impose sanctions against its allies.

Brzezinski, like Kissinger, believed that America's allies were vital to the creation of a new international system. In 1970 he wrote:

> From an American standpoint, the more important and promising changes in the years to come will have to involve Western Europe and Japan. The ability of these areas to continue to grow economically and to maintain relatively democratic political forms will more crucially affect the gradual evolution of a new international system than will likely changes in American-Soviet relations. Western Europe and Japan offer greater possibilities for initiatives designed to weave a new fabric of international relations, and because, like America, they are in the forefront of scientific and technological innovation, they represent the most vital regions of the globe.[135]

This belief led Brzezinski to advocate trilateral cooperation among the US, Western Europe, and Japan.[136] By 1976, however, he recognized that "neither Europe nor Japan are prepared to play a major role" in resolving the traditional or the new global problems,[137] a view advanced by Kissinger in the 1960s.

Yet, aware of the limits imposed by national sovereignty, Brzezinski stressed that "the movement toward a larger community of the developed nations will necessarily have to be piecemeal," and it will not lead to the disintegration of the Eastern and Western alliance systems. Underlining his proposal for a broader structure of cooperation was his conviction that "such a structure would not sweep aside United

States-Soviet nuclear rivalry, which would remain the axis of world military might."[138] Brzezinski believed that "America and Russia will not abandon Europe, for neither could be certain that its departure would not mean the extension of the power of the other – no matter what formal guarantees were provided."[139] In his view, the partition of Europe "can only be ended if the American-Soviet confrontation in Europe is gradually transformed into cooperation," an unlikely possibility in the foreseeable future.[140]

IMAGE OF THE NEW STATES

Brzezinski believed that "the Third World is a victim of the technetronic revolution." In his view, regardless of the rate of development in the less developed countries, "many of them will continue to be dominated by intensifying feelings of psychological deprivation." Convinced that in an electronically intermeshed world as the gap between developed and less developed countries increased "absolute or relative underdevelopment will be intolerable," he argued that today the Third World confronts not just a revolution of rising expectations, but "the specter of insatiable aspirations." The major problem in the new states, according to Brzezinski, "is not the absence of change," but "an intensifying feeling of relative deprivation of which they are made more accutely aware by the spread of education and communications."[141] Believing that the subjective revolution in the new states is preceding change in the objective environment thus creating a state of unrest, uneasiness, anger, and outrage,[142] Brzezinski feared that "passive resignation may give way to active explosions of undirected anger."[143]

For Brzezinski, the US unconsciously promotes Third World instability, impatience, and frustration because despite its efforts to prevent revolutionary upheavals and establish international stability, its social impact on the world is unsettling, innovative, and creative. He argued that while it provokes violent anti-Americanism, the US triggers expectations which are measured by US standards but cannot be met in most countries until well into the next century. This intensifies social contradictions and conflict between the generations thus making social fragmentation the principal problem. The US, however, also accelerates the unification of other societies, not only by promoting regionalism, but because other states see unification as the best means for combating American influence. In short, he believed that as the first global society, the US "unifies, changes, stimulates, and challenges others – often against its own immediate interests."[144]

Third World instability according to Brzezinski has been accelerated by the "new" nationalism – "a radical, changing force creatively mobilizing community feelings but also prompting ethnic exclusiveness and conflicts." He argued that "as the nation-state is gradually yielding its sovereignty [to international banks and multinational corporations] the psychological importance of the national community is rising, and the attempt to establish an equilibrium between the imperatives of the new internationalism and the need for a more intimate national community is the source of friction and conflicts." [145] In the Third World the conflicts are intensified by the lack of clear national identities and the efforts by some new states to acquire highly destructive weapons. Brzezinski feared that in their efforts to create national unity some states may be able and tempted to use modern weapons in "underworld" wars among themselves which could involve the superpowers. [146] As he explained:

> Growing anarchy in the Third World would very likely involve racist and nationalist passions. At the very least, this would create major pockets of disruption and chaos in the world; at worst, Third World instability could draw the more developed nations into potentially antagonistic forms of involvement that could have the same effect on American-Soviet relations as Balkan conflicts had on the European order prior to World War I. [147]

In short, like Kissinger, Brzezinski was primarily concerned with the impact of Third World instability on US-Soviet relations.

Brzezinski believed that Third World communism is closely linked to nationalism and racism. He argued that:

> Communism came to the Third World masses before their political awakening, and it has succeeded only where it has become both the external expression and the internal content of the new sense of national identity. Focusing on industrialization as the way in which to fulfill popular aspirations on both external and domestic levels, communism galvanized feelings of inferiority toward the more advanced West. Indeed, because of this, communism in the Third World has been especially vulnerable to the racism that – given the bitter legacy of the white man's imperialism – inevitably infected the new nationalism. [148]

For Brzezinski, this linkage deprived communist ideology of both its universality and its rationality. He maintained that Third World communist parties by "embracing racism and intense nationalism . . . are capitulating to reality rather than reshaping it." [149]

In Brzezinski's view, "global politics are becoming egalitarian rather than libertarian," with Third World demands "focusing predominantly on material equality rather than on spiritual or legal liberty." He maintained that the passion for equality motivates the new states in their struggle against the developed world,[150] and specifically the US whose wealth has become the focal point of envy. He argued that in the new states

(. . .) the difficulty in defining equality is compounded by the fact that in most cases complaints result not only from immediate social inequities but from an acute sense of deprevation vis-à-vis the developed world. The small size of many of the new states further intensifies their feeling of impotence and complicates the task of redress. Their economic dependence on unstable commodity markets and foreign capital means that their liberty is highly relative and tenuous. The result is a condition in which liberty seems threatened by the absence of international equality.[151]

Brzezinski believed that the desire for equality leads most Third World leaders to embrace socialism which they see as a vehicle for establishing a national identity, promoting economic development, and gradually erasing internal and external inequality. He was hopeful, however, because, despite their preoccupation with economic development and their use of undemocratic political means and Marxist-Leninist terminology, Third World leaders stressed nationalism and the spiritual importance of the human being.[152]

In 1973, those beliefs led Brzezinski to criticize Nixon's and Kissinger's "implicit indifference . . . to the problems of the less-developed nations." He wrote:

The problem of the less-developed nations is the moral problem of our time . . . today subjective change is much more rapid than objective change. Access to literacy, circulation of newspapers, the impact of mass communications, increased political participation are more rapidly transforming the way people think than economic growth is transforming the way people live. The consequence is a heightened awareness of global inequality and an increased determination to erase it. Intensified social strife and global animosity are bound to be the consequence of mankind's failure to tackle the problem of global inequality.[153]

In late 1976, just prior to becoming National Security Adviser, Brzezinski reiterated those beliefs in another critique of Kissinger's policies.[154]

For Brzezinski, economic aid is a partial response for closing the widening gap between mass consciousness and material reality, and for reducing the animosity between the Third World and the developed world. In his view, a major problem is the lack of Third World leadership that knows how to mobilize the masses and how to utilize foreign aid intelligently. He realized, however, that such leadership tends to be unresponsive to foreign interests and advice, thus stimulating foreign resentment. Brzezinski believed that even if Third World leaders were committed to social change they confronted a dilemma:

> To admit the reality of the slowness of change is to deprive themselves of the support of the masses and to yield the political initiative to radical demagogues; to mobilize the masses on behalf of unattainable goals is to court an eventual explosion – unless that mobilization becomes a vehicle for subordinating the masses to centralized, bureaucratic control of the sort that communist leaders provide most effectively.[155]

Moreover, if they sought the support of the propertied and the educated groups little, if anything, would change since that support depended on the maintainance of the traditional social order. In short, Brzezinski believed that structural limitations prevent the Third World from moving closer to the developed world economically or politically.

Brzezinski believed that the real values, not the rhetoric, of the Third World elites will be shaped by the domestic changes in the more advanced world; changes directly and personally visible to them through travel, study, and the global mass media. He maintained that "this intimacy with life abroad will further reduce the importance of integrative ideologies, which had previously provided a substitute for clear vision of the future and the outside world." For Brzezinski, "proximity and global congestion now dictate revolutionary diversity"[156] which, while reducing the appeal of Communism, is further undermining the creation of a new global consensus; the sine qua non of global stability.

EVENTUAL REALIZATION OF FUNDAMENTAL POLITICAL VALUES: OPTIMISM/PESSIMISM

What are the prospects for the eventual realization of one's fundamental political values and aspirations? Can one be optimistic or pessimistic on this score; and in what respects the one and/or the other?

Brzezinski was essentially optimistic about the eventual establishment of a community of the developed nations and the creation of a new international order. His optimism stemmed primarily from his belief that the US despite its shortcomings "remains the globally creative and innovative society," which "still provides to most people in the world the most attractive social condition (even if not the *model* and that remains America's special strength" (his italics). In his view the "Soviet Union is not even a rival in this respect."[157] Conceding the gravity of America's problems Brzezinski declared: "my view of America's role in the world is still an optimistic one . . . I truly believe that this society has the capacity, the talent, the wealth, and, increasingly, the will to surmount the difficulties inherent in this current historic transition."[158] On the whole, Brzezinski appeared more optimistic than Kissinger about America's potential to shape the future of the international system.

The global impact of the technetronic revolution reinforced Brzezinski's optimism. Recognizing the possibility for international chaos, he stated: "Yet it would be wrong to conclude that fragmentation and chaos are the dominant realities of our time," since a new global consciousness is emerging for the first time. In his view, this revolution by increasingly making possible global responses to such contemporary dilemmas as disease, famine, poverty, pollution, and overpopulation advances the emergence of this new consciousness. He argued that "the availability of the means to cooperate globally intensifies the sense of obligation to act." Moreover, "the sense of proximity, the immediacy of suffering, the globally destructive character of modern weapons all help to stimulate an outlook that views mankind as a community." The existence of a rudimentary framework of global social and economic institutions, and the emergence of new yardsticks by which the public measures international competition, fed Brzezinski's optimism regarding the eventual establishment of a new international system.[159]

In Brzezinski's view, the gradual evolution of a new international system will be preceded by the development of a community of the developed nations. Admitting that this community is "at best a distant objective" and that its creation "involves a long and gradual process," he was optimistic about its eventual formation,[160] given the common political values of the US, Western Europe, and Japan, and the fact that they were in the forefront of scientific and technological innovation. But more importantly, Brzezinski maintained that "under the pressures of economics, science, and technology, mankind is moving steadily toward large-scale cooperation" and "despite periodic reverses, all human history clearly indicates progress in that direction."[161] However, convinced that optimism is not a self-fulfilling prophecy while pessimism tends to be and that pessimism is incompatible with democracy, he was greatly concerned with the decline in Western optimism and confidence and with the increasing uncertainty and pessimism within the new states. This was evident in his warning that if pessimism becomes the dominant mood it will paralyze effective responses and needed reforms.[162]

Yet, conditional pessimism tinged Brzezinski's optimism regarding the foreseeable future. He qualified his basic optimism by stating: "my view of America's role in the world is still an optimistic one. I say 'still' because I am greatly troubled by the dilemmas we face at home and abroad, and even more so by the social and philosophical implications of the direction of change in our time . . . I do not mean to minimize the gravity of America's problems – their catalogue is long, the dilemmas are acute, and the signs of a meaningful response are at most ambivalent."[163] His analysis of the international environment fed his pessimism. He noted:

> The new global consciousness . . . is only begining to become an influential force. It still lacks identity, cohesion, and focus. Much of humanity – indeed, the majority of humanity – still neither shares nor is prepared to support it. Science and technology are still used to buttress ideological claims, to fortify national aspirations, and to reward narrowly national interests . . . The new global unity has yet to find its own structure, consensus, and harmony.[164]

In other words, while "a new pattern of international politics is emerging" the "real unity of mankind remains remote."[165] For Brzezinski, then, despite America's potential and the emerging global consciousness of mankind as a community, today there is an ever-present danger of international chaos. In his view, statesmen had to be constantly aware of this possibility and to avoid contributing to its actualization by defective calculations and inept political behavior.

PREDICTABILITY OF THE POLITICAL FUTURE

Is the political future predictable? In what sense and to what extent?

Brzezinski, like Kissinger, believed that the political future, and particularly the foreseeable future, can be predicted with considerable accuracy.[166] His analysis of the forces of change in the world today demonstrates his willingness to predict international developments. Brzezinski's belief in

America's potential led him to predict that "at the end of the century America will still be a significant force for global change, whether or not the dominant subjective mood is pro-or anti-American." [167]

The study of America's main adversaries, and specifically the USSR, led Brzezinski to predict in 1970, that "in the short run, development toward a pluralist, ideologically more tolerant system does not seem likely." [168] Predicting that there will be slow change, Brzezinski argued, that "th[e] combination of eroding ideology and intensifying nationalism makes it unlikely that the Soviet Union will soon become involved either in militantly advancing the cause of world revolution or in actively promoting a policy of global cooperation." In that context, "its attractiveness as the socio-economic model for contemporary communism . . . will probably continue to decline." [169] In his view, "American-Soviet rivalry is hence likely to become less ideological in character, though it may become more extensive geographically and more dangerous in terms of the power involved." [170] To Brzezinski, "close [US-Soviet] cooperation seem[ed] a very unlikely prospect in the coming decade." [171] He maintained that "the Soviet Union will in the foreseeable future remain too strong externally not to be a global rival to the United States but too weak internally to be its global partner." [172] Hence, Brzezinski predicted that "there will be no global security arrangement in the foreseeable future." [173]

Believing that communications and education cannot be contained, Brzezinski "expected that political tensions will mount as purely parochial, traditional attitudes yield to broader global perspectives." [174] He predicted that, given America's impact on the world, "many of the upheavals in the Third World will unavoidably have a strong anti-American bias . . . particularly . . . where American presence and power has traditionally been most visible." However, "in areas near the Soviet Union and China . . . anti-Soviet and anti-Chinese attitudes are likely to predominate in the long run, irrespective of the character of the internal reforms and of the external complexion of the regimes." [175] In Brzezinski's opinion, "the prospect is that feelings of intensive resentment will most likely grow as the gap between the Third World and the developed world widens. Indeed, they will probably intensify . . . " as by the year 2000 the world will be divided into post-industrial technetronic states, mature-industrial states, early-industrial states, pre-industrial states, and those remaining still in extremely primitive conditions. He declared that the third and fourth groups of states "will in all likelihood be the centers of volatile political activity, resentment, tension, and extremism." [176]

The conditions in the Third World led Brzezinski to conclude that "it is quite possible that in the years to come individual, highly nationalistic, perhaps even racist communist parties will come to power in some Asian, African, or Latin American countries by appealing both to populist nationalism of the masses and the statism of impatient intellectuals." He asserted, however, that it is "unlikely that seizures of power will be effected by the orthodox and formal communist parties . . . " In his view, "the successful [Third World] revolutionaries, though . . . labeling themselves communists, will probably be loosely organized coalitions of impatient middle-class intellectuals, younger officers, and students . . . more likely to be motivated by a vaguer and more volatile combination of radicalism, nationalism, and more even some racism." Therefore, Brzezinski maintained that "the revolutions to come will . . . neither signify an automatic addition of strength to 'international communism' nor represent a step forward toward the intellectual unity of mankind."[177] He argued that "the revolutionary process as such will not necessarily determine the foreign policy stance of the new elites, which is more likely to be shaped by a combination of traditional antipathies, current fears, and domestic political needs." Nevertheless, like Kissinger, Brzezinski was convinced that international stability would be threatened because Third World "regimes will be assisted and exploited by the Soviets and the Chinese," even though "it will still be more a matter of tactical cooperation than of actual control and a common strategic policy."[178]

But like Kissinger, Brzezinski believed that, although the general outlines of future political developments are predictable, the consequences of specific policies and events are unpredictable. This was evident in his declaration that policy-planning "should be highly contingent . . . It must be based on the realization that any assessment of reality is, at the very best, only a partial approximation."[179] In 1961, discussing the prospects of ideological erosion and the sources of ideological vitality in the USSR, Brzezinski concluded: "The final outcome of these clashing tendencies depends on too many variables to be safely predicted, but uncertainty about the outcome should not obscure the certainty about conflicting pressures."[180] In 1967, rejecting the possibility of a Sino-Soviet conflict, he stated: " . . . it appear[s] highly unlikely that the division would be deep enough to make one of the units take the ultimate initiative of splitting, or eventually even siding with the 'historically doomed' enemies." He acknowledged, however, that "unforeseen factors can intervene in any of these hypothetical projections." In his view, "clumsy responses by either side" on the issues in dispute and "the succession problem" in each power constitute unpredictable factors.[181] Brzezinski's beliefs regarding the predictability and unpredictability of the political future were evident in his policy recommendations which were based on the more predictable general trends of future political developments than on the less predictable outcomes of specific events.

CONTROL OF HISTORICAL DEVELOPMENT

How much "control" or "mastery" can one have over historical development? What is one's role in "moving" and "shaping" history in the desired direction?

Like Kissinger, Brzezinski believed that man within limits can shape historical development. In 1961, recommending actions that the West should take in its relations with the communist camp, Brzezinski declared, that "the time has now come for the West to prod history along." [182] The basis of this belief is most evident in Brzezinski's discussion of Christianity, nationalism, and especially Marxism as a system of thought, as well as his focus on statesmen. His discussion emphasized that, man progressed from the view that human endeavor was futile and the acceptance of events with fatalism, to a belief that he can both understand and shape his reality. [183] Stressing "the enslaving effect of institutionalized Marxism," Brzezinski declared:

> Marxism is simultaneously a victory of the external, active man over the inner, passive man, and a victory of reason over belief: it stresses man's capacity to shape his material destiny – finite and defined as man's only reality – and it postulates the absolute capacity of man to truly understand his reality as a point of departure for his active endeavors to shape it. [184]

For Brzezinski, "Marxism appealed simultaneously to man's ethical, rational, and Promethean instincts." Turning to the third instinct, he stated, that "the Promethean stood for 'man's faith in his powers, for the notion that history is made by the people and that nothing can hem in their advance to perfection'." "In this sense," according to Brzezinski, "Marxism has served as a mechanism of human 'progress', even if its practice has often fallen short of its ideals." This view led him to criticize Teilhard de Chardin's study *The Phenomenon of Man*, for omitting to point out that "for many outside the immediate influence of the West and its Christian tradition it has been Marxism that has served to stir the mind and to mobilize human energies purposefully." [185] Focusing on the activistic nature of Christianity, nationalism, and Marxism, Brzezinski stated: "Given the dominant role of the activist West in shaping the outlook of our times, now, in the second half of the twentieth century, almost everyone – often without knowing it – is to some extent a Christian, a nationalist, and a Marxist."[186] For Brzezinski, as for Kissinger, then, man can both understand and move history in the direction he desires.

The belief that man can shape history was evident in Brzezinski's focus on political leaders who tried to control historical development. In examining the political history of the USSR and the PRC, Brzezinski concentrated on Lenin, Stalin, Khrushchev, and Mao, and on their impact on the international communist movement and on East-West relations. In the West, he centered primarily on Nixon and Kissinger. Discussing their roles, Brzezinski stated: "the central question here is the extent to which the Administration has succeeded in fashioning a foreign policy that will shape the *future* and not resolve mainly the legacies of the past" (his italics).[187] By basing his grading of the Nixon-Kissinger policies on their impact in shaping the future, Brzezinski underlined his belief that individuals can influence historical development. However, recognizing that man's control of history is limited, he declared: "this country's commitment to international affairs on a global scale has been decided by history. It cannot be undone, and the only remaining relevant question is what its form and goals will be."[188] He claimed that on certain issues the Administration "has been the prisoner of . . . history,"[189] and stressed, that his criticisms of its policies "concentrate[d] only on matters for which our foreign policy principals can be justifiably seen as accountable,[190] that is, the concentration of policymaking in the White House, and the use of secretive personal diplomacy and suprise.

Brzezinski's belief regarding man's role in shaping history is evident in his critiques of political leaders and, especially of Nixon and Kissinger. Sharing Kissinger's belief that statesmen must have a vision of the future, Brzezinski attacked the Nixon Administration for its "static vision of the world" and its "predilection for the acrobatic over the architectural." More specifically, for Brzezinski, "the Nixon Doctrine [was] most deficient" because it lacked "a common vision and framework" as it applied to America's relations with its allies and the new states.[191] Attacking the Nixon-Kissinger "secretive and personal style," Brzezinski approvingly quotes Spengler stating that "the central task of a true statesman is 'to create a *tradition*, to bring on others so that one's work may be continued with one's own pulse and spirit, to release a current of like activity that does not need the original leaders to maintain it in form'" (his italics). Hence, he denounced "the Administration's failure to articulate fully and explicitly its concepts and aims" and to "engage in collective consultations and in open conceptualization," in order to build enduring public support for its foreign policy.[192] In other words, he shared Kissinger's conviction that a statesman must be an educator. Moreover, like Kissinger, Brzezinski believed that statesmen must implement their vision.[193] Arguing for planning in foreign policy he stressed, that recognition of "what is likely and what is desirable results in the formulation of the deliberately attainable."[194] In his words: "the future can and must be planned, that unless there is a modicum of deliberate choice, change will result in chaos."[195]

CHANCE (AND TRAGEDY) IN HUMAN AFFAIRS

What is the role of "chance" in human affairs and in historical development?

Unlike Kissinger, Brzezinski did not deal directly with the role of chance (and tragedy). However, like Kissinger, he believed that chance, which he equated with "unforeseen developments," can never be completely eliminated from historical development and that the statesman's task is to reduce it to a minimum. In his predictions Brzezinski always raised the possibility that "unforeseen developments" could affect the direction of history. Essentially optimistic about America's potential, in 1970 he stated that "unless there is major scientific and economic stagnation or a political crisis, at the end of the century America will still be a significant force for global change."[196] Predicting that "the Soviet economy will continue to grow in the years ahead," he noted, "but it does appear likely that, barring some unforeseen development in either the United States or the Soviet Union, the absolute gap between the two countries will widen even further."[197] Believing that to most people in the world the US is the most appealing "model," Brzezinski declared: "nor is it certain, as has been occasionally argued that in the years to come communism will offer to the Third World an attractive model combining sustained economic development and social modernization with political stability."[198] The element of uncertainty evident here indicates Brzezinski's belief that chance can intervene and modify in an unpredictable way America's leading role in the world and the declining appeal of communism.

Brzezinski's belief in the role of chance did not stop him from urging statesmen to act deliberately in order to reduce it. In his view, world stability is threatened not so much by chance as by the misunderstanding regarding the nature of adversaries, the thrust of change in our time, and America's role in the world. Brzezinski argued that comprehensive policy-planning would provide statesmen with a conceptual framework and, in turn, the intellectual confidence which can supply the necessary staying power in the face of adversity and the confident feeling that efforts to attain certain broad goals are historically relevant. He maintained that a conceptual framework, by defining the meaning of international reality, could preclude reactive policymaking in response to a myriad of specific – and seemingly unconnected – events, hence, undermining the conviction that the primary obstacle to man's endeavors to shape history is the role played by chance.[199]

CONCLUSION

This analysis indicates that like Kissinger, Brzezinski believed in the conflictual nature of politics. The conflict emanates from man's inherent aggressiveness and the rivalry between nations operating without a global political consensus. For him, as for Kissinger, international conflict has been intensified by the injection of Communist ideology which stresses the continuation of conflict until socialism becomes a world system. Indeed, he agreed with Kissinger that the pursuit of this absolute objective by the USSR and the PRC makes them revolutionary powers and that since the USSR can back its ideological foreign policy with overwhelming military power it should be the focus of US policy. However, unlike Kissinger, he also believed that the US – the model technetronic society – unconsciously and unintentionally promotes the revolutionary forces by setting standards of modernization that most states cannot meet while the process of modernization disrupts the traditional institutions and focuses resentment on the US. For Brzezinski, while the conflict generated by Moscow's and Peking's ideological foreign policy is "bad" since its purpose is to change the international system, that resulting from America's social impact is "good" since it is unintentional. In Brzezinski's view, the linkage of nationalist and ideological conflicts with the accelerating pace of change brought about by the technetronic revolution increased the possibility of international chaos. Despite the emerging global consciousness, Brzezinski believed that the real unity of mankind remains remote and that concentrated humanity is increasingly characterized by the routinization of conflict.

Like Kissinger, Brzezinski did not change his view that the USSR and the PRC are revolutionary powers. Brzezinski shared Kissinger's belief that while Moscow no longer declares that war is inevitable and is willing to cooperate in reducing the risk of a mutually destructive nuclear war, it has not abandoned its commitment to a world-wide communist society since it views peaceful coexistence as an ideological offensive to change the international system by means short of nuclear war. In his view, this was also demonstrated by the Soviet concept of détente which stresses intensified ideological hostility. Yet, while concerned with Moscow's military capabilities and its willingness to use it, he believed that the danger to stability from the ideological offensive alone has been reduced since the CPSU has turned Soviet ideology into a dull social and political orthodoxy. He did not believe that the increasing ideological diversity within the Soviet bloc would undermine the USSR's revolutionary nature since the gradual erosion of certain ideological aspects is balanced by the sources of ideological vitality, especially Moscow's foreign policy achievements which demonstrate the correctness of Soviet ideology and revitalize it thus precluding the Party's decay. Moscow's reassertion of ideological orthodoxy and more vigorous ideological indoctrination, led Brzezinski to reject the thesis that liberalization or democratization of the USSR was taking place and the inference that Moscow would abandon its goal. For Brzezinski, the convergence of East and West in terms of contemporary styles and values of mass culture did not reduce political differences. Rejecting the theory of convergence for predicting a revolutionary change in the USSR and the US, he maintained that their evolution is more likely since each has been successful in its own way. In his view, even if the US and the USSR became more alike their rivalry would continue given the incompatibility of their national interests. Moreover, despite the Sino-Soviet split, he believed that the USSR and the PRC differed only in tactics and timing, not in their commitment to change the international system. For Brzezinski, Peking's efforts to undermine US-Soviet cooperation to reduce the risk of nuclear war made the PRC the most immediate threat to peace but he was not concerned since the PRC was militarily weak and its racial and cultural distinctiveness made its model more difficult to export. Moreover, he believed that while US-PRC rapprochment placed higher premium in Moscow on US-Soviet accomodation, for Peking it was an expedient arrangement to strengthen its position in the Sino-Soviet conflict and to reduce Moscow's freedom of action against it.

For Brzezinski, as for Kissinger, the conflictual nature of politics is also evident in intra-alliance disputes which are caused by contradictory national priorities and not individuals such as de Gaulle. In his view, as the US allies become less preoccupied with security the divergence between the US and their interests will increase thus intensifying the disputes. But despite the disputes, he argued that Western Europe and Japan, being in the forefront of the scientific and technological revolution and sharing the same values, offer greater possibilities for joint initiatives to create a new inter-national system. Yet, in 1976, he recognized that they were not prepared to play a global role. Brzezinski believed that national sovereignty influenced relations even among socialist states, but argued that in the multiethnic East European societies ethnic tensions weaken nationalism's effectiveness as a basis for opposing Moscow, as do the shared ideological assumptions and the view that peaceful coexistence is counter-revolutionary. He also believed that Moscow's inability to provide economic assistance and the neutrality of technological revolution further undermined the unity of the Soviet bloc. In his view, the return of international politics to Eastern Europe did not indicate that the Communist elites were interested in being absorbed by the West. For Brzezinski, Eastern Europe is governed by an unsteady combination of nationalism and communism which is reinforced by the fear of a rearmed self-assertive Germany. Moreover, while convinced that both East and West Europeans have not accepted the division of Europe, he maintained that while Western Europe is developing a European consciousnes, Eastern Europe is becoming less united.

Seeing that the Third World is a victim of the technetronic revolution, he argued that the subjective revolution which is preceding change in the objective environment will further intensify international conflict. In his view, the US unconsciously promotes Third World instability through its social impact which triggers expectations which are measured by US standards but cannot be met in most societies. This instability is accelerated by the efforts of new states to establish an equilibrium between internationalism and national unity. Like Kissinger, Brzezinski feared that efforts to create national unity by using modern weapons could involve the superpowers thus intensifying international conflict. For Brzezinski, the desire for material equality motivates the Third World hostility against the developed world and leads its leaders to embrace socialism convinced it is a vehicle for promoting national unity, economic development, and erasing internal and external inequality. However, he believed that Third World socialism would not automatically strengthen international communism since ideological considerations do not necessarily determine the foreign policies of Third World socialist regimes. Moreover, since Third World communism is closely linked to nationalism and racism it deprives the revolutionary ideology of its universality. For Brzezinski, the real values of the Third World elites are shaped by the domestic changes in the advanced societies, thus further reducing the importance of Communist ideology as a unifying force. Nevertheless, like Kissinger, Brzezinski feared that global stability is threatened because Third World regimes are assisted and exploited by Moscow and Peking even though it is more a matter of tactical cooperation than of actual control and a common strategic policy.

Brzezinski's belief in America's positive role in the world and the emergence of a global consciousness for the first time due to the impact of the technetronic revolution made him more optimistic than Kissinger about eventual establishment of a community of the developed states and the creation of a new world order. But he was concerned with the increase of pessimism in the West, and particularly in the Third World, since he viewed pessimism as a self-fulfilling prophecy that paralyzes effective responses. He was also pessimistic regarding the foreseeable future since the emerging global consciousness lacks identity, cohesion, and focus. Sharing Kissinger's belief that, despite the unpredictability of specific events, the foreseeable future is predictable, Brzezinski predicted that the US will continue to influence the world while the appeal of the USSR as a model will increasingly decline, that the US-Soviet rivalry will go on, and that Third World instability will increase as traditional attitudes yield to global perspectives. Like Kissinger, he believed that while man's control of historical development is limited, a statesman can shape history by providing a vision of the future, by implementing it, and by educating his nation. Moreover, like Kissinger, he believed that while chance can never be completely eliminated from historical development the task of a statesman is to reduce it to a minimum.

4 The Instrumental Beliefs of Henry Kissinger

INTRODUCTION: NOTIONS OF CORRECT STRATEGY AND TACTICS

In the spring of 1974, in "The Deceptive Structure of Peace," Brzezinski succinctly outlined what he believed to be the "matters for which our foreign policy principals [Nixon and Kissinger] can be justifiably seen as accountable." He grouped these under three categories: (a) The Predilection For The Personal Over The Politic; (b) The Predilection For The Covert Over The Conceptual; (c) The Predilection For The Acrobatic Over The Architectural.[1] These matters he argued, contributed to the Administration's failure to fashion a foreign policy that will shape the future. The matters discussed by Brzezinski focused primarily on Kissinger's instrumental beliefs, that is, beliefs regarding the different approaches to calculating political strategy and tactics.

Kissinger's notions of correct strategy and tactics in the context of political action were evident in his analyses of nineteenth century European diplomacy and, particularly, his critiques of US national security policy. An understanding of Kissinger's instrumental beliefs is essential in explaining his design of the National Security Council (NSC) and his view of the role of the National Security Adviser, as well as his impact on US national security policy. This chapter examines Kissinger's beliefs regarding strategy and tactics for achieving national goals. The content of his beliefs is presented quite frequently in Kissinger's words.

BEST APPROACH FOR SELECTING GOALS FOR POLITICAL ACTION

What is the best approach for selecting goals or objectives for political action?

For Kissinger, goals or objectives for political action should be selected on the basis of: (a) the power-realist approach; (b) the strategic long-term approach; (c) a non-ideological/non-moralistic approach; and (d) a conceptual approach.

Kissinger's belief in the power-realist approach is evident in all of his writings whose main focus was power, particularly military power, and its uses for the achievement of national objectives. Although Kissinger did not define his concept of power, by identifying its components he revealed that he perceived it as a contextual, psychological relationship between those who exercise it and those over whom it is exercised. In his words, "until power is used, it is . . . what people think it is."[2] He always stressed the importance of the psychological components of national policy and the necessity to relate the physical to the psychological balance of international relations[3] since nuclear technology makes it possible to change the global balance of power through developments within one's territory.[4] For Kissinger, military power is the most important component of national power, but not the only one. Convinced that a political situation reflected a combination of political, economic, psychological, and military factors, he warned that "the emphasis on any one of these factors to the exclusion of the others was self-defeating . . . superiority in one category of power would be compensated by a manipulation of the others."[5] Kissinger's recognition of the importance of all the components of national power was evident in his argument that "to the extent that we succeed in seeing policy as a unity in which political, psychological, economic, and military pressures merge, we may actually be able to use Soviet theory [of ambiguity] to our advantage."[6]

Reliance on the power-realist approach reflects Kissinger's belief that "no international order is ever stable *solely* because it is considered legitimate by its component states" (his italics).[7] Criticizing the US reluctance to think in terms of power and equilibrium he stated that "foreign policy cannot be conducted without an awareness of power relationships."[8] He believed that "No statesman can make the survival of his country entirely dependent on the assumed good will of another sovereign state, because one of his most effective guarantees for this will remaining good is not to tempt it by too great a disproportion of power."[9] Moreover, the USSR's and the PRC's commitment to transform the international system convinced him that without an equilibrium of power between the US and the Soviet bloc, "we will have no chance to undertake any positive measures."[10] He was unwilling to upset the strategic balance between the superpowers even in the name of allied unity or the support of the new states since he believed that without it cooperation with them would not be possible.[11] His preoccupation with the superpower balance reflected his conviction that the elements of stability characterizing the nineteenth century international system (stable military technology, limited claims, the multiplicity of major powers), cannot be recreated today. For Kissinger, however, this equilibrium is dynamic and changing, not permanent; a view consistent with his belief that the foundation of a stable international system is the relative security and thus relative insecurity of its members. He maintained that the balance of power only limits the scope of aggression, it does not prevent it; therefore a doctrine of legitimacy must be established. Moreover, recognizing the limits of power, he stressed that although "a new international order is inconceivable without a significant American contribution . . . political multipolarity makes it impossible to impose an American design." [12]

Kissinger recognized, however, that the power-realist approach presented a dilemma because the destructive power of nuclear weapons had made the thought of war repugnant and increased the reluctance to use them, thus depriving statesmen of a tool that historically had been used to achieve national objectives. The US reluctance to use its power distressed Kissinger because to the USSR and the PRC, "policies unrelated to a plausible possibility of employing force seem either hypocrisy or stupidity." Believing that "our only possibility for affecting their actions resides in the possession of superior force," he declared, "no more urgent task confronts American policy than to bring our power into balance with the issues for which we are most likely to have to contend." [13]

In Kissinger's view, the power-realist approach necessitates the related strategic long-term approach to policymaking. He was greatly concerned with the powerful American tendencies to identify foreign policy with the solution of immediate issues,[14] and to deal with them as they arise which meant that emerging crises usually settle disputes about priorities.[15] He was also troubled by the bureaucratic-pragmatic nature of American leadership and its *ad hoc* approach to policy.[16] Bureaucratic procedures for resolving policy problems, according to Kissinger, "neglect the long-range because the future has no administrative constituency," [17] and as a result, "[US] policy is . . . geared to dealing with emergencies; it finds difficulty in developing the long-range program that might forestall them." [18] Only the long-term approach could preclude crises, he argued, and that required a strategic doctrine. Kissinger maintained that "whatever the problem . . . whether it concerns questions of military strategy, of coalition policy, or of relations with the Soviet bloc, the nuclear age demands above all a clarification of doctrine." For Kissinger,

> Strategic doctrine transcends the problem of selecting weapons systems. It is the mode of survival of a society, relating seemingly disparate experiences into a meaningful pattern. By explaining the significance of events in *advance* of their occurrence it enables society to deal with

most problems as a matter of routine and reserves creative thought for unusual or unexpected situations. The test of a strategic doctrine is whether it can establish a pattern of response – a routine – for the most likely challenges. (his italics)[19]

In his view, "the basic requirement for American security is a doctrine which will enable us to act purposefully in the face of the challenges which will inevitably confront us. Its task will be to prevent us from being continually surprised."[20] Kissinger argued that "whether the goals of a state are offensive or defensive, whether it seeks to achieve or to prevent a transformation, its strategic doctrine must define what objectives are worth contending for and determine the degree of force appropriate for achieving them."[21] In short, "power must be related to the purpose for which it is to be used."[22]

Kissinger rejected the ideological/moralistic approach to decision-making characterizing revolutionary powers, since its insistence on absolutes prevents the establishment of both the equilibrium of forces and legitimacy, the prerequisites of stability.[23] Historically, this approach led the US to transform all wars into crusades and to apply its power in the most absolute terms. Criticizing the American reluctance to think in terms of power and the view that "peace is the 'normal' pattern of relations among states,"[24] he concluded: "because our strategic doctrine recognized few intermediate points between total war and total peace, we have found it difficult, during periods of Soviet belligerency, to bring the risks of resistance into relationship with the issues which have actually been at stake."[25] Kissinger defined the "[US] dilemma as the conflict between the quest for absolute answers and the risks of the nuclear age," and feared, that "the fact that every problem has found a final solution in the past may stand in the way of the realization that henceforth only partial remedies are possible."[26] Convinced that "the contemporary dilemma is that there are no total solutions,"[27] he feared that "the insistence on absolutes, either in assessing the provocation or in evaluating possible remedies, is a prescription for inaction."[28] Moreover, while recognizing the need to identify the US with the aspirations of humanity since for the major part of it the present can be endured only through a vision of the future, he believed that such an approach with its emphasis on total solutions could not succeed given "the inherent impossibility of fulfilling the expectations aroused by revolutionary slogans."[29] For Kissinger, then, only a non-ideological/non-moralistic national security policy would lead to the achievement of limited US objectives within the existing international system.

For Kissinger, the power-realist approach and the related strategic approach required a conceptual approach to decision-making. Believing that statesmanship involves in part the problem of conception,[30] he questioned the adequacy of US leadership groups to deal with the challenges America is likely to confront, since by training they are better prepared to deal with technical and economic issues than with conceptual and political problems. In his view, "the absence of a conceptual framework makes it difficult for them even to identify our problems or to choose effectively among the plethora of proposals and interpretations produced by our governmental machinery." These problems are compounded by the American cult of the expert and the premium on specialization. Kissinger argued that the inability of US leadership groups to think conceptually in political and in strategic terms "explains many postwar Soviet successes . . . [since] whatever the qualities of Soviet leadership, its training is eminently political and conceptual."[31] In short, Kissinger believed that conceptualization is a lonely act inherent in leadership.[32]

Believing in the conceptual approach to decision-making, Kissinger strongly opposed the selection of goals by bureaucratic means. In his view, "there is an inherent tension between the mode of action of a bureaucracy and the pattern of statesmanship."[33] In *A World Restored*, he explained:

> For the spirit of policy and that of bureaucracy are diametrically opposed. The essence of policy is its contingency; its success depends on the correctness of an estimate which is in part conjectural. The essence of bureaucracy is its quest for safety; its success is calculability. Profound policy thrives on perpetual creation, on a constant redefinition of goals. Good administration thrives on routine, the definition of relationships which can survive mediocrity. Policy involves an adjustment of risks; administration an avoidance of deviation. Policy justifies itself by the relationship of its measures and its sense of proportion; administration by the rationality of each action in terms of a given goal. The attempt to conduct policy bureaucratically leads to a quest for calculability which tends to become prisoner of events. The effort to administer politically leads to total irresponsibility, because bureaucracies are designed to execute, not to conceive.
>
> The temptation to conduct policy administratively is ever present . . . But the concern with technical problems in foreign affairs leads to a standard which evaluates by mistakes avoided rather than by goals achieved, and to a belief that ability is more likely to be judged by the pre-vision of catastrophes than the discovery of opportunities.[34]

Convinced that in this revolutionary period when conceptualization is vital, complex technical problems have seized the attention of US leaders, Kissinger stressed, that, "we will never be able to contribute to building a stable and creative world order unless we first form some conception of it."[35] But he did not believe that such a conception can come from planning staffs since he viewed planning as the projection of the familiar into the future and the staffs as bureaucratic structures in a quest for predictability and objectivity, both of which reduce creativity.[36] Concluding that the complexities of contemporary life inhibit the establishment of a balance between the requirements of organization and the need for inspiration on which a society's vitality depends, and concerned with the shortcomings of US leaders, Kissinger emphasized inspiration over organization.[37] These beliefs were manifest in Kissinger's criticism of American empiricism which "in foreign policy leads to a penchant for *ad hoc* solutions,"[38] and of the resistance to the hypothetical cases inherent in conceptualization (his italics). Kissinger specifically criticized the National Security Council for focusing on "administrative efficiency than . . . the elaboration of national objectives." For him, its conclusions "reflect the attainable consensus among sovereign departments rather than a sense of direction."[39]

MOST EFFECTIVE PURSUIT OF GOALS

How are the goals of action pursued most effectivelly?

Kissinger's answer can be summarized in 8 maxims: (1) assume the responsibilities of leadership; (2) control all factors essential to survival by not aiming at peace directly as a goal of policy; (3) maintain an adequate relatiatory force; (4) establish a relationship between power and the will to use it; (5) harmonize political and military objectives; (6) define the strategic transformations to be resisted; (7) utilize the linkage of issues; and (8) generate coalitions of shared purposes.

For Kissinger the effective pursuit of goals requires the assumption of the responsibilities of leadership, which means a willingness to stand alone if the situation requires it. His belief in leadership is related to his notion of statesmanship and his belief in power. He explained his refusal to subordinate the requirements of the over-all strategic balance to the policy of alliances and to efforts to win over the uncommitted by stating:

> In some situations, the best means of bringing about a common purpose is by an act of leadership which overcomes fears and permits no further

equivocation. The price of our power is leadership. For what else is leadership except the willingness to stand alone if the situation requires? The failure to assume these responsibilities will not result in a consensus of humanity; it will lead to the creation of a vacuum.[40]

Moreover, Kissinger believed that "leadership is the refusal to confine action to average performance; it is the willingness to define purposes perhaps only vaguely apprehended by the multitude." He constantly stressed that "a statesman must act as if his inspirations were already experience, as if his aspiration were 'truth'."[41] In *The Necessity for Choice*, he wrote that "the test of statesmanship is the adequacy of its evaluation *before* the event. A democracy, to be vital, requires leaders willing to stand alone" (his italics). But more importantly, he believed that in an age of revolution "creativity presupposes a willingness to alter even the seemingly successful."[42] Believing that "the thrust of Soviet aggression will always be directed at the weak points in our armor and to the issues in which our psychological inhibitions are at a maximum," he stated: "to deal with problems of such ambiguity presupposes above all a moral act: a willingness to run risks on partial knowledge and for a less than perfect application of one's principles."[43]

In Kissinger's view, "peace . . . cannot be aimed at directly" as a goal of policy since "it is the expression of certain conditions and power relationships," that is, an equilibrium of forces and an agreement about the permissible aims and methods of foreign policy. He believed that "it is to these relationships – not to peace as such – that diplomacy must address itself." For Kissinger, "no idea could be more dangerous" than to conceive peace as the avoidance of war and to make it the state's primary objective since that would place the international system at the mercy of the revolutionary states which are willing to forego peace. He claimed that, "to entrust the fate of a country entirely to the continued good will of another sovereign state is an abdication of statesmanship; it means that survival is completely dependent on factors outside one's own control."[44] And to Kissinger, "a wise policy will keep under its own control all factors essential to survival."[45]

For Kissinger, "the key to survival is the possession of an adequate retaliatory force," because "without [it] no other measures are possible,"[46] since the US "would be at the mercy of the Soviet rulers"[47] who explicitly reject harmony between different social systems. However, questioning the ability of the US to develop a strategy for using such a force, Kissinger declared: "to seek safety in numerical superiority or even in superior destructiveness may come close to a Maginot-line mentality – to seek in numbers a substitute for conception."[48] His rejection of numerical superiority emanated from his conviction that in the future its strategic and political significance "is certain to diminish."[49]

Kissinger believed that "in the relations among states, strength of will [to resist aggression] may be more important than power."[50] Convinced that "a power can survive only if it is willing to fight for its interpretations of justice and its conception of vital interests,"[51] he stressed that the "maximum development of power is not enough" since "with modern technology such a course must paralyze the will."[52] In his view, it was imperative "to establish a reasonable relationship between power and the willingness to use it; between the physical and the psychological components of national policy."[53] Kissinger repeatedly declared that "we cannot base all our plans on the assumption that war, if it comes, will be inevitably all-out. We must strive for a strategic doctrine which gives our diplomacy the greatest freedom of action" by "creat[ing] alternatives less cataclysmic than a thermonuclear holocaust." For Kissinger, then, "mastery of the challenges of the nuclear age will depend on our ability to combine physical and psychological factors, to develop weapons systems which do not paralyze our will; and to devise strategies which permit us to shift the risk of counteraction to the other side."[54]

In Kissinger's view, it is essential to harmonize the political and military objectives of the United States.[55] He declared: "we must learn that there are no purely political solutions any more than purely military solutions."[56] He claimed that the US will achieve a strategic transformation in its favor only if it overcomes the notion that war and peace, military and political goals, were separate and opposite, and adjusted its political objectives to the risks of the nuclear period.[57] He argued that the growth of the Soviet nuclear power while increasing "our reluctance to engage in war even more has not . . . changed the fundamental question of how our political and military doctrines can be harmonized, how our power can give impetus to our policy rather than paralyze it."[58] Kissinger feared that "an all-or-nothing military policy will . . . play into the hands of the Soviet strategy of ambiguity which seeks to upset the strategic balance by small degrees and which combines political, psychological, and military pressures to induce the greatest degree of uncertainty and hesitation in the minds of the opponent."[59] Acknowledging the mutual fear of all-out war, he explained:

> But though each side may be equally deterred from engaging in all-out war, it makes all the difference which side can extricate itself from its dilemma *only* by initiating such a struggle. If the Soviet bloc can present

its challenges in less than all-out form, it may gain a crucial advantage. Every move on its part will then pose the appalling dilemma of whether we are willing to commit suicide to prevent encroachments, no one of which seems to threaten our existence directly but which may be a step on the road to our ultimate destruction. (his italics)[60]

In Kissinger's view, the policy of containment, based on the assumption that military strategy and diplomacy represented successive phases of national policy, had permitted the Soviet leaders to implement this strategy to expand the Soviet orbit, while the increasing Soviet nuclear capability increased the US reluctance to engage in all-out war. For Kissinger "[US] insistence on divorcing force from diplomacy caused [its] power to lack purpose and [its] negotiations to lack force,"[61] while the "[US] announced reluctance to engage in all-out war gave the Soviet bloc a psychological advantage"[62] and "removed the Soviet leader's inhibitions against expanding their influence."[63]

For Kissinger, the necessity to combine the physical and psychological components of power and to harmonize political and military objectives, makes the linkage of issues indispensable to effective pursuit of goals. Hence, he rejected decision-making by *ad hoc* committees and the handling of issues by experts who focused on their technical rather than their political aspects. Criticizing the refusal to link political and military objectives, he declared: "the attitudes of our high officials and their method of arriving at decisions inevitably distort the essence of policy. Effective policy depends not only on the skill of individual moves, but even more importantly on their relationship to each other. It requires a sense of proportion and a sense of style." In his view, "all these intangibles are negated when problems become isolated cases."[64] For Kissinger, linkage was inherent in the strategic approach to policymaking; an understanding of the relationships between seemingly discrete events is vital for imposing conceptual order on policy.[65]

Kissinger maintained that "as a status quo power, the basic strategic problem for the United States is to be clear about what strategic transformations [it is] prepared to resist." Arguing that the destructiveness and speed of modern nuclear weapons and the polarization of power have ended America's historic invulnerability and margin of safety, Kissinger stressed that US policymakers must overcome the purist and abstract doctrine of aggression that traditionally had allowed the US to let a threat take unambiguous shape before engaging in war. The US inability "to define a *casus belli* which would leave no doubt concerning [its] moral justification for using force"[66] distressed Kissinger who feared that "in the nuclear age, by the time a threat has become unambiguous it may be too late to resist it" (his italics). In his view, "resistance to aggression . . . depends not only on our strength, but also on our ability to recognize aggression." Realizing that "nuclear technology makes it possible, for the first time in history, to shift the balance of power solely through developments *within* the territory of another sovereign state" and that "the forms of attack have multiplied," i.e., internal subversion, intervention by "volunteers", and domination through political and psychological warfare (his italics), Kissinger stated: "the crucial test of our strategic doctrine is . . . what it defines as a threat."[67]

Kissinger's belief that "political multipolarity makes it impossible to impose an American design" and that the change in the nature of power has eroded its relationship to policy so that military superiority does not confer influence automatically,[68] led to his conclusion, that "to act consistently abroad we must be able to generate coalitions of shared purposes." In his view, only when the US had acted in concert with others and gained a reputation as a member of such a concert, had it been able to gain influence and in turn achieve its goals most effectively. For Kissinger, this meant that the US must be concerned more with the overall framework of order while regional groups of states supported by the US will be responsible for the balance of power in their immediate areas.[69] Convinced that West Europeans would not play a global role, he argued that US-West European cooperation "must concentrate on issues within the Atlantic area."[70] He specifically urged the creation of an Atlantic community which he considered vital to maintain the West's relevance to the rest of the world.[71] For Kissinger, the need for US leadership to preclude the creation of vacuums and the necessity for coalitions of shared purposes complemented each other.

CALCULATION, CONTROL, AND ACCEPTANCE OF RISKS

How are the risks of political action calculated, controlled and accepted?

The following principles summarize Kissinger's beliefs regarding risks: (a) acceptance and willingness to run risks is inherent in leadership and policymaking; (b) the ultimate risk of thermonuclear war must be avoided, except as a last resort, but it can be calculated and controlled; (c) develop a wide array of military capabilities to reduce dependence on the strategy for all-out war to prevent limited aggression; (d) strengthen the credibility of the US deterrent to preclude the deterioration of America's international position; and (e) increase the flexibility of both strategy and diplomacy.

For Kissinger the acceptance of risks is inherent in leadership and policymaking since "policy involves an adjustment of risks,"[72] "for only the risks are certain; the opportunities are conjectural."[73] In rejecting policymaking by bureaucratic means he explained:

> The basic motivation of a bureaucracy is its quest for safety; its preference is in favor of a policy of minimum risk. . . . The inclination of a bureaucracy is to deny the possibility of great conception by classifying it as "unsound," "risky" . . . It is no accident that most great statesmen were opposed by the "experts" in their foreign offices, for the very greatness of the statesman's conception tends to make it inaccessible to those whose primary concern is with safety and minimum risk.[74]

In short, for Kissinger, leadership requires a willingness to take risks.

The willingness to run risks was balanced by Kissinger's belief that "thermonuclear war must be avoided except as a last resort," when national survival is directly threatened.[75] In his view, "an all-out attack is the least likely form of Soviet strategy, either politically or militarily,"[76] but the gratest danger of an all-out war lies in miscalculation. He believed, however, that this is the only war that can be avoided if we leave no doubt concerning our capabilities and our determination.[77] But, he warned, "this 'avoidable' war may break out if the other side becomes convinced that we cannot interfere locally and that our threats of all-out war are bluff."[78] In his view, the side which can convince its opponent of its greater readiness to risk an all-out war is in the stronger position.[79] For Kissinger, "the refusal to run any risks would amount to handing the Soviet leaders a blank check."[80] Indeed, he was convinced that in the postwar period many of the Soviet gains, not justified by the relation of forces, have been due in large part to a greater moral toughness and a greater readiness to run risks, both physical and moral, than the West.[81] According to Kissinger, the Western tendency to see even opportunities as risks has given the USSR the fundamental advantage despite the bankruptcy of its social system and the instability of its leadership structure.[82] In short, he believed the risk of an all-out war can be calculated and controlled by ensuring that the USSR does not achieve a clear superiority in its capability to conduct an all-out war,[83] and more importantly, by convincing the USSR that the US is willing to risk an all-out war.

Kissinger distinguished not only the magnitude of risks but also between risks that are immediate and those which are more remote. In his words, "the likelihood of a continuing revolutionary conflict should not be confused with the imminence of an all-out showdown."[84] He argued that a greater, long-term, indirect risk existed as a result of the US exclusive dependence on a strategy for all-out war since it "obscured the most likely security problem: the attempt by the Soviet leaders to upset the strategic balance, not at one blow, but piecemeal."[85] In his view, "limited aggression . . . is a threat which jeopardizes survival *ultimately* (his italics).[86] Kissinger's constant preoccupation with the Soviet strategy of ambiguity reveals the importance he attached to the control of this risk.[87] He feared that "if all-out war is our only possible response to aggression of any type, more and more challenges will begin to appear as indirect threats only."[88] He stressed that an all-or-nothing military policy gave the Soviets "an opportunity to . . . neutralize the [US] psychologically by so graduating their actions that the provocation would never seem 'worth' an all-out war."[89] Believing that "all-out war . . . comes about through the abdication of political leadership,"[90] and seeking to control this risk, Kissinger advocated the necessity of a strategy for limited war, including limited nuclear war, which he considered "not . . . a matter of choice but of necessity . . . result[ing] from the impossibility of combining both maximum force and the maximum willingness to act."[91] For Kissinger, "whatever the validity of identifying deterrence with maximum retaliatory power, we will have to sacrifice a measure of destructiveness to gain the possibility of fighting wars that will not amount to national catastrophe." In his view, "policy . . . is the science of the relative. The same is true of strategy, and to understand this fact, so foreign to our national experience, is the task history has set our generation."[92]

The strengthening of US credibility was, according to Kissinger, indispensable for the control of risks. In his view, US credibility was undermined by (a) the exclusive dependence on the threat of all-out war as a deterrent to all forms of aggression; (b) the increasing destructiveness of nuclear weapons which reinforces the reluctance to use force; (c) the ever increasing gap between the policy of deterrence and the strategy for fighting a war in case deterrence fails; and (d) the failure to resort to force in the face of a considerable number of Soviet challenges. The enhancement of US credibility required, according to Kissinger: (a) convincing an aggressor of the decision to resist; (b) insuring that the penalties of aggression outweigh the benefits; and (c) developing a reputation for ruthlessness and/or for a greater willingness to run risks. In his view, these requirements are "importantly affected by *the experience of the last use of force*" (his italics).[93] Kissinger was convinced that "a threat is effective only if it is believed, and a threat which cannot be brought to bear on the issues at stake loses its credibility."[94] He warned however, that "while the deterrent threat must be credible, the quest for credibility must not lower the penalties to a point where they are no longer unacceptable."[95] Kissinger also acknowledged that the requirements necessary for credibility "imply a combination of readiness and subtlety almost impossible for a peaceful status quo country to achieve – much less for a coalition of such countries."[96]

For Kissinger, the control of risks also required tactical flexibility in both diplomacy and strategy. The importance he attached to flexibility was evident in his unrelenting reiteration of the need to establish a relationship between force and diplomacy, between power and the willingness to use it. He constantly stressed that only superior flexibility can control risks generated by the Soviet strategy of ambiguity which is characterized by highly tactical flexibility and brutal consistency. In his view, the first requirement of flexibility in diplomacy was the development of a maximum number of military capabilities which will enable the US to achieve the entire spectrum of deterrence.[97] The second requirement of flexibility was the reduction of bureaucratic control of foreign policy. This reflected Kissinger's belief that "there is an inherent tension between the mode of action of a bureaucracy and the pattern of statesmanship."[98] He concluded his analysis of the bureaucratic impact on foreign policy by stating that "the very nature of the governmental structure introduces an element of rigidity which operates more or less independently of the convictions of statesmen or the ideology which they represent." Kissinger accepted "an institutionalization of decision-making [as] an inevitable by-product of the risks of international affairs in the nuclear age," yet, he argued, the bureaucratic quest for predictability and objectivity ensures increased control over the domestic environment "at the price of loss of flexibility in international affairs."[99]

Convinced that efforts to reduce the rigidity in foreign policy by improving the bureaucratic structures responsible for it only absorbs the energies of top executives, he wrote favorably of extra-bureaucratic means of decision such as reliance on special emissaries or personal envoys. He argued that "their status outside the bureaucracy frees them from some of its restraints." In Kissinger's view, "international agreements are sometimes possible only by ignoring safeguards against capricious action . . . [and] impasses [resulting from the search for objectivity and calculability] . . . can be overcome only by essentially arbitrary decisions." He maintained that conducting foreign policy bureaucratically "becomes especially dangerous in a revolutionary period" because "the issues which are most significant may not be suitable for administrative formulation and even when formulated may not lend themselves to bureaucratic consensus." He stressed that "when the issue is how to transform the existing framework, routine can become an additional obstacle to both comprehension and action." [100] In short, he believed that the reduction of bureaucratic control of foreign policy is essential to increase flexibility which is imperative for controling risks.

THE BEST "TIMING" OF ACTION

What is the best "timing" of action to advance one's interest?

Kissinger's answer to this question is related to his short-term pessimism and long-term optimism and to his belief that the continuing revolutionary conflict will be protracted. The following precepts outline his beliefs regarding timing: (a) be willing to fight indefinitely the protracted conflict with the USSR; (b) avoid the quest for quick military and diplomatic victories; (c) develop the ability to apply the elements of one's superiority more rapidly than the opponent; and (d) implement a policy of precaution.

For Kissinger, "effective action against the Soviet threat . . . must presuppose that the contest with the Soviet bloc is likely to be protracted." He insisted, that this is "a fact from which we cannot escape, because the Soviet leaders insist on it." Believing that the doctrine of protracted conflict is "the great advantage of communism" he criticized US policymakers for "conduct[ing] our relations with the Soviet bloc, whether military or diplomatic, as if it were possible to conceive of a terminal date to the conflict." [101] The belief that "the only safe United States policy is one which is built on the assumption of a continued revolutionary struggle," [102] led Kissinger to declare: "both in our diplomacy and in our military policy we must be able to gear firmness to patience and not to be misled by Soviet maneuvers or by our preference for absolute solutions." [103]

Kissinger rejected the quest for quick military or diplomatic victories because "is considered a sign of weakness [by the Sovie bloc] to be exploited" by the strategy of ambiguity and the doctrine of protracted conflict.[104] This conviction is evident in his statement that "the side least eager for peace has the negotiating advantage because it can outwait, if not outfight, its opponent." This belief led Kissinger to warn that as a result

in any conflict with Communist powers it is important, above all, to be clear at the outset about the precise objectives of the war. *And no conditions should be sought for which one is not willing to fight indefinitely and no advance made except to a point at which one is willing to wait indefinitely. The side which is willing to outwait its opponent – which is less eager for a settlement – can tip the psychological balance, whatever the outcome of the physical battle.* (his italics) [105]

Concerned that "our impetuosity . . . transform[s] time into an enemy ally," Kissinger stressed, "patience and subtlety must be as important components of our strategy as power." [106]

While rejecting the quest for quick victories, Kissinger considered the rapid application of one's power vital for achieving one's objectives. In his words: "the key to a proper doctrine is the correct understanding of the elements of one's superiority and the ability to apply them more rapidly than the opponent." [107] Kissinger argued that the destructiveness and speed of modern nuclear weapons and the polarization of power have ended America's historic invulnerability and reduced its traditional margin of safety. The US can no longer depend on other countries to hold the line while it assesses events and organizes its defenses since they have lost either the power or the will to resist aggression. Convinced that resistance to aggression depends on both strength and the ability to recognize it, he stated: "in the nuclear age, by the time a threat has become unambiguous it may be too late to resist it." [108] Kissinger insisted that timing would be improved by reducing the bureaucratic influence on foreign policy since the bureaucracy's search for certainty undermines it by making it very difficult to arrive at decisions on time, to change established policy, and to recognize crucial problems for a long time. [109]

Kissinger rejected the tendency to await developments, believing that "delay might result in irretrievable disaster." [110] He was convinced that "the Soviet strategy of ambiguity can ultimately be countered only by a policy of precaution, by attempting to nip Soviet moves in the bud before Soviet prestige becomes so deeply engaged that any countermeasures increase the risk of war." He realized however, that "a policy of precaution is the most difficult of all for status quo powers to implement" since "all their preconceptions tempt them to wait until the Soviet threat has become unambiguous and the danger has grown overt, by which time it may be too late." [111]

UTILITY OF DIFFERENT MEANS FOR ADVANCING ONE'S INTERESTS

What is the utility and role of different means for advancing one's interests?

For Kissinger, the answer to this question flows from his belief that it is essential to establish a relationship between power and the willingness to use it, between force and diplomacy. It can be summarized by the following principles: (a) All-out war has ceased to be an instrument of policy, except as a last resort; (b) the use of force in the context of limited wars is essential to achieve limited objectives; (c) diplomacy would not resolve the fundamental problems but it is imperative in order to keep conflicts limited and to identify the US with the aspirations of humanity; (d) summits could be useful for breaking a deadlock, charting a new course, and ratifying agreements; (e) arms control is useful only for reducing the instability caused by the volatile weapons technology; (f) consultation is better for implementing a consensus than for creating it; and (g) the education of domestic and world opinion about the realities of the nuclear age facilitates the advancement of national interests.

For Kissinger, "all-out [nuclear] war has . . . ceased to be a meaningful instrument of policy" for three reasons. First, world opinion precludes its use against the minor powers, as does the complexity of its strategy which makes it unsuitable for wars of limited objectives; the only type of war Kissinger considered acceptable for resolving disputes among nations while maintaining stability. Second, against the major powers all-out war can be used only for negative ends, such as preventing the aggressor from achieving victory. Third, given the nuclear stalemate, all-out war between the superpowers entails the risk of national destruction for both sides.[112] Those reasons and his conviction that "an all-out attack is the least likely form of Soviet strategy, either politically or militarily,[113] led Kissinger to conclude that "an all-out war which starts as an all-out war is the least likely contingency."[114] Nevertheless, he acknowledged that all-out war "is likely to be employed . . . only as a last resort: an act of desperation to be invoked only if national survival is unambiguously threatened."[115] Kissinger feared, however, that as the risks of all-out war become better understood the definition of an unambiguous threat will become more rigid. He considered this a dangerous development given the Soviet strategy of ambiguity, and the fact that the nuclear stalemate has encouraged other forms of conflict short of all-out war. However, while rejecting all-out nuclear war as an instrument for achieving positive objectives, Kissinger declared that "we must maintain at all times an adequate retaliatory force and not shrink from using it if our survival is threatened."[116] Otherwise "no other means are possible."[117] He never wavered in his belief that war between nuclear powers "has to be planned on the assumption that it is likely to be a nuclear war."[118] Hence, he opposed the renunciation of the first-use policy, explaining that "if we concede the first nuclear blow, we can be certain that nuclear weapons will be used against us at a moment we are most vulnerable, either physically or psychologically." [119]

The belief that all-out war is no longer a conceivable instrument of policy compelled Kissinger to seek other ways that would make the use of force an effective means for achieving national goals in the international system. He was driven by the conviction that "to the extent that recourse to force has become impossible, the restraints of the international order may disappear as well." In his view, the use of force was particularly necessary given the belief in the USSR and the PRC, that policies unrelated to the use of force are irresponsible and reckless. Kissinger feared that the inability and/or unwillingness of the US to use force would create a power vacuum to be filled by the USSR. [120]

For Kissinger, limited war, including limited nuclear war, was the instrument of policy that would establish a relationship between power and the will to use it. Noting the greater risks inherent in limited nuclear war, he argued that "against a nuclear power conventional war carries with it almost the same risks as nuclear war." [121] His support for limited war reflects his rejection of absolutes and his view that political and military objectives must be harmonized. In his words, being "essentially a political act, its distinguishing feature is that it has no 'purely' military solution." [122] Recognizing the difficulty in keeping wars limited in a period which lacks both stable power relationships and an international agreement about the permissible aims and methods of foreign policy, Kissinger declared that those shortcomings may be outweighed "by the common interest in avoiding a thermonuclear war." Conceding that the risk of escalation into an all-out war existed, he argued that "in reality both sides will probably grasp at every excuse, however illogical, to keep a thermonuclear holocaust from occurring." For Kissinger, then, the fear of an all-out war between the superpowers "offers an opportunity to set limits to both war and diplomacy." [123]

A strategy of limited war, according to Kissinger, is essential for three reasons: (a) it is the only means for preventing the Soviet bloc, at an acceptable cost, from overrunning the peripheral areas of Eurasia; (b) its wide range of military capabilities may spell the difference between defeat and victory even in an all-out war; and (c) intermediate applications of power offer the best chance to bring about strategic changes favorable to the West. [124] In his view, such a strategy required that

> (1) the limited war forces must be able to prevent the potential aggressor from creating a fait accompli; (2) they must be of a nature to convince the aggressor that their use, while involving an increased risk of all-out

war, is not an inevitable prelude to it; (3) they must be coupled with a diplomacy which succeeds in conveying that all-out war is not the sole response to aggression and that there exists a willingness to negotiate a settlement short of unconditional surrender.[125]

In short, Kissinger believed that "its merit is precisely that it may open the way to a political solution."[126]

In Kissinger's view, the prerequisites for a strategy of limited war are: a doctrine and a capability. The doctrine must be based on the realization that "it is no longer possible to impose unconditional surrender at an acceptable cost" because an attempt to do so "would surely lead to all-out war."[127] In addition, it must define the objectives worth fighting for and determine the degree of force appropriate for achieving them.[128] Turning to capability, Kissinger challenged the prevailing view that by building forces for deterring all-out war the US was also developing the capability for fighting limited wars. He argued that "to use the strategic striking force as a dual-purpose force would weaken the deterrent to all-out war at the precise time when it should be strongest." In his view, "to the extent that our retaliatory force declined in strength [by being used in a limited war], our ability to deter all-out war would decline and therewith the sanction for keeping the war limited."[129] Kissinger also opposed the use of the strategic forces in limited wars because they were designed to cause the maximum destruction in the shortest time. He maintained that forces for limited war must be "flexible and discriminating" since "neither the locale of the conflict nor the targets can be determined in advance," as they are in the case of all-out war. The flexible and discriminating nature of these forces makes possible both the graduated application of force to achieve limited objectives and the essential breathing spaces for political contacts.[130] Kissinger specifically recommended the creation of forces with high mobility and considerable firepower which can be quickly deployed in the trouble spots and use force with discrimination to prevent faits accomplis. Convinced that "the capacity for rapid deployment is crucial," he pointed out that "the ability to get into position rapidly even with relatively small forces can serve as a gauge of the determination to resist and contribute to the re-establishment of an equilibrium before either side becomes too heavily committed."[131] In short, a demonstration of the capability for limited war and the willingness to use it to defend one's interests would make aggression less likely. Ideally, for Kissinger, the limited war capability should consist of both large-scale conventional forces and tactical nuclear weapons.[132]

In response to those opposed to the concept of limited war, Kissinger stated: "no responsible person advocates *initiating* limited war. The problem of limited war will arise only in case of Communist aggression or blackmail. In these circumstances, if we reject the concept of limited war, our only options will be surrender or all-out war" (his italics). For Kissinger then, limited war "is preferable not to peace, but to surrender or all-out war." [133]

Despite his belief that "diplomacy . . . the adjustment of differences through negotiation, is possible only in 'legitimate' international orders," [134] Kissinger assigns it an important role in the present revolutionary period. Recognizing that its effectiveness for settling disputes among nations was drastically reduced by the USSR's and the PRC's commitment to transform the existing international system, by the polarization of power, and by the inhibitions regarding the use of force, he argued that diplomacy can still perform the following functions: (a) provide a forum for the settlement of disputes which have become unprofitable for both sides; (b) keep open the channels of information; and (c) enable each side to convey its intentions to the other. He considered the third function as the most important because he believed that while neither side wanted an all-out war, such a war "is more likely to arise out of a misunderstanding of the opponent's intentions than out of conviction in an ability to destroy the opponent at acceptable cost." For Kissinger, "to prevent such miscalculation or misinterpretation of our intentions by the Soviet Union should be a principal task of our diplomacy." [135] In short, the use of limited war "is impossible unless our diplomacy succeeds in conveying our intentions to the other side." [136]

However, Kissinger's belief that "it is futile to deal with a revolutionary power by 'ordinary' diplomatic methods" [137] was counterbalanced by the conviction that "the contemporary revolution cannot be managed by force alone." Stressing the symbolic role of diplomacy he stated, "it requires a consistent and bold program to identify ourselves with the aspirations of humanity." [138] He argued that the ideological aspect of the East-West conflict and the revolution of the newly independent states demanded a greater focus on the psychological aspect of negotiations in order to capture the symbols which move humanity, thus depriving the USSR and the PRC of opportunities to subvert the West, and in turn the existing international system. [139] Criticizing the false premises of Western diplomatic efforts he stated: "they enable the Soviet spokesmen to define the moral framework of most disputes and to shift the debate to issues of maximum embarrassment to us." [140] Kissinger insisted that diplomatic relations with the USSR and the PRC must be conducted on the following bases: (a) the transformation of their domestic systems should not be a precondition to negotiations; (b) negotiations must not be viewed as an end in themselves; (c) negotiations must be based on concrete programs which define a settlement consistent with Western values and security interests; (d) concessions should not be used to assuage feelings of insecurity since they are seen as needless surrender; (e) conciliatory statements should be avoided because they appear as hypocrisy or stupidity, ignorance or propaganda; (f) proposals must be framed with a maximum of clarity and simplicity, for their major utility is their symbolic content; (g) strategic opportunities must be used lest the image of weakness and not of moderation is generated; (h) détente or peaceful coexistence should not be viewed as equivalent to peace; and (i) the most soluble issues must not be the focus of negotiations because they become a means for Communist leaders to liquidate unprofitable disputes and shift all points of tension to the West.[141]

Summitry, for Kissinger, embodied the worst features of diplomacy. Rejecting the view that, peace being the normal condition, conflicts are caused by the shortsightedness of statesmen and thus can be resolved only by their change of heart, he argued that without a unified strategy and a specific program, the reliance on personalities and the implication that all problems can be settled with a summit permit the Soviet leaders to use summit meetings to demoralize the West. Kissinger insisted that "it is in the Soviet interest to turn all disputes into clashes of personalities" therefore making it very difficult for the West to raise the need for the settlement of concrete issues.[142] Yet, after assessing the utility of summits, he concluded that they are useful for breaking a deadlock, charting a new course, ratifying agreements and giving general guidelines for futher detailed negotiations, and declared, "they should be used for these purposes with courage and conviction." For Kissinger, summits "should be held only when there is some clear, substantive advantage in prospect", and only on the basis of a concrete program or purpose.[143]

Believing that the inhibitions with respect to the use of force have transformed the East-West revolutionary struggle into an armaments race,[144] Kissinger advocated arms control as a means for enhancing stability. He rejected the popular notion that general disarmament would reduce the possibility of war, and stressed that the utility of arms control is limited to reducing the instability caused by the rapid change in weapons technology. Therefore, "it must not be approached with the attitude that without it all is lost" because the Soviets would use arms control negotiations primarily for psychological warfare to demoralize the West.[145] He constantly insisted that its goals should be to reduce the risks of surprise attack, accidental war, and the proliferation of nuclear weapons. Kissinger's belief that armaments are the reflection of conflict rather than the cause, and that stability required the removal of the causes of political conflict, led to his constant reiteration that "until progress is made towards solving these more fundamental problems, measures of arms control can ameliorate but not remove the existing climate of distrust."[146] Rejecting the argument that arms control should be pursued in order to free resources for economic competition, he stressed that "the purpose of arms control is to enhance the security of *all* parties" (his italics), and warned that "any attempt to achieve a unilateral advantage must doom arms control."[147] Since the need for arms control was produced by technological factors, Kissinger maintained that "effective schemes required careful, detailed, dispassionate studies and the willingness to engage in patient, highly technical negotiations."[148] In addition, he insisted that because "their rate of obsolescence is as rapid as the rate of technological change . . . [they] must . . . have a built-in mechanism for adaptation and review."[149] Moreover, convinced that the control of nuclear weapons "without restoring the balance of conventional forces is sheer irresponsibility,"[150] he argued that "no real progress is possible in the field of arms control until we achieve agreement within our military establishment and within the Western alliance about the elements of security.[151]

In Kissinger's view, the lack of consensus within the Atlantic Alliance about the international situation and the requirements of stability, undermined the utility of negotiations, arms control, and limited war.[152] Challenging the widespread notion that more extensive consultation within the existing alliance framework would create the necessary consensus by resolving the central issues, he stated, "consultation . . . is far from a panacea. It is least effective when it is most needed: when there exist basic differences of assessment or of interest. It works best in *implementing* a consensus rather than in *creating* it" (his italics).[153] However, convinced that improved consultation can alleviate intra-alliance tensions by resolving some of the peripheral issues, Kissinger urged the improvement of the consultative process within the US alliance system in order to enhance its unity and thus facilitate the use of other means in dealing with the USSR and the PRC. He understood, however, that consultation could also be used by allies to limit America's freedom of action in the international system.[154]

Believing that next to the physical balance of power "there exists a psychological balance based on intangibles of value and belief,"[155] and that the ideological struggle aimed at the political loyalties of humanity, Kissinger urged statesmen to educate public opinion about the realities of the nuclear age.[156] The importance he attached to education as a means for advancing national interests reflected his conception of the statesman as an educator who must bridge the gap between a nation's experience and his vision. According to Kissinger, a public fully aware of revolutionary threats, strategies and tactics, and the dangers of seeking absolute objectives by total means, will be better prepared to support a more flexible foreign policy to prevent revolutionaries from subverting the international system. While believing that "the stability of an international order depends on self-limitation, on the reconciliation of diffent versions of legitimacy," he also recognized that in a revolutionary period the competing systems of legitimacy not only make it extremely difficult to agree on the nature of "just" demands, but more importantly, they make it nearly impossible to legitimize the attainable international consensus domestically. The importance Kissinger attached to the reduction of ignorance regarding power relationships in order to facilitate the statesman's difficult, if not impossible, task of legitimizing his policies domestically is evident in the statement that "nations learn only by experience; they 'know' only when it is too late to act." [157]

CONCLUSION

This examination reveals that for Kissinger the goals for political action should be selected on the basis of four interrelated approaches. First, believing that an equilibrium of power is a prerequisite to stability, he insisted on the power-realist approach. He maintained that the USSR's and the PRC's commitment to transform the international system and their belief in using power makes the possession of superior force vital to influencing their actions. Kissinger was unwilling to upset the strategic balance between the superpowers even for the sake of allied unity or the support of the new states. However, while conceiving power as a contextual psychological relationship in which military capability is its most important component, he warned that the exclusion of its other components is self-defeating. Second, believing that nuclear weapons have increased the reluctance to use force, Kissinger advocated the related strategic long-term approach to develop a strategic doctrine which defines the objectives worth fighting for and determines the degree of force appropriate for achieving them. Third, Kissinger rejected the ideological/moralistic approach characterizing revolutionary powers since its insistence on absolutes prevents the establishment of both the equilibrium of forces and legitimacy; the prerequisites of stability. Convinced that the present dilemma is that there are no total solutions, he viewed the insistence on absolutes as a prescription for inaction. Fourth, for Kissinger, the power-realist and strategic approaches rested on a conceptual approach to decision-making. Indeed, believing that conceptualization is inherent in leadership, he stressed that we can create a stable international order only if we first form some conception of it.

For Kissinger, the goals of action can be pursued most effectivelly by observing the following requirements. First, by leadership which is a willingness to stand alone if the situation requires it since without it the result will be not a consensus but a vacuum to be exploited by opponents. Second, by controlling all factors essential to survival, that is, not making peace – the avoidance of war – the direct objective of policy because that would place the international system at the mercy of revolutionary states which are willing to forego peace. Third, by possessing an adequate retaliatory force, not numerical superiority, which in the nuclear age is the key to survival since without it no other measures are possible. Fourth, by establishing a relationship between power and the will to use it. Recognizing that nuclear power has increased the reluctance to use force, Kissinger stressed that the strength of will to resist aggression may be more important than power. Fifth, by combining the physical and psychological factors of power and by harmonizing political and military objectives to strengthen the will to resist. Sixth, by using the linkage of issues which is essential for meeting the fourth and fifth requirements. For Kissinger, the linkage of issues is inherent in the strategic approach to policymaking. Seventh, by clearly defining the strategic transformations one is prepared to resist since today, by the time a threat becomes unambiguous it may be too late. Finally, by creating coalitions of shared purposes since military superiority does not confer influence automatically and political multipolarity makes it impossible to impose an American design.

The following maxims summarize Kissinger's beliefs regarding the calculation, control, and acceptance of risks. First, he believed that the acceptance and willingness to run risks is inherent in leadership since policy involves an adjustment of risks which are certain; the opportunities are conjectural. Second, for Kissinger, the ultimate risk of thermonuclear war must be avoided except as a last resort when one's survival is directly threatened. However, he believed that this risk can be calculated and controlled by leaving no doubt about one's capabilities and determination to use them. Third, he also believed that it is just as important to develop a strategy for limited war, including limited nuclear war, to control the greater, long-term, indirect risks to survival, namely, the attempts to upset the strategic balance piecemeal by limited aggression. Fourth, a strong credibility was, according to Kissinger, indispensable for the control of risks, and it depended above all on a reputation for ruthlessness and/or for a greater willingness to run risks. Finally, believing that the control of risks required tactical flexibility in both diplomacy and strategy, he insisted on the establishment of a relationship between force and diplomacy and between power and the willingness to use it, and on the reduction of bureaucratic control of foreign policy.

Kissinger's beliefs regarding the best timing of action to advance one's interests are related to his short-term pessimism and long-term optimism and to his belief that the revolutionary conflict will be protracted. In his view, the nature of the conflict dictates that one must be willing to fight indefinitely since opponents insist on it, and to avoid the quest for quick military and diplomatic victories. For Kissinger, the side which is willing to outwait its opponent can tip the psychological balance whatever the outcome of the physical battle. However, he considered the rapid application of one's power vital since in the nuclear age by the time a threat becomes unambiguous it may be too late. Indeed, Kissinger believed that the Soviet strategy of ambiguity can ultimately be countered only by a policy of precaution.

For Kissinger, the utility of different means for advancing one's interests depended on their usefulness for maintaining the equilibrium of power and legitimacy – the prerequisites to a stable international order. Believing that all-out nuclear war has ceased to be an instrument of policy, except as a last resort, he insisted on the need to develop a wide array of military capabilities, including that for limited nuclear war, to prevent limited aggression, for him the most likely contingency. His advocacy for limited war issued from his rejection of absolutes and his belief in harmonizing political and military objectives. In his view, the fear of nuclear war offered the opportunity to set limits to both war and diplomacy. For Kissinger, if recourse to force becomes impossible the restraints of the international system will disappear. Believing that traditional diplomacy is possible only in a legitimate international order, he maintained that it would not resolve the present international conflicts since the revolutionary powers reject the system itself. Nevertheless, it could be most useful for conveying one's intentions to opponents thus preventing all-out war by miscalculation and for identifying the US with the aspirations of humanity. For Kissinger, summitry embodied the worst features of diplomacy, yet, he argued that when based on a concrete program or purpose it is useful for breaking a deadlock, charting a new course, and ratifying agreements. Convinced that arms control is useful only for reducing the instability caused by the weapons technology, he warned that it must not be approached with the attitude that without it all is lost. Kissinger believed that consultations work best in implementing a consensus rather than in creating it, and that the creation of a consensus required statesmen to educate public opinion about the realities of power in a revolutionary age.

5 The Instrumental Beliefs of Zbigniew Brzezinski

INTRODUCTION: NOTIONS OF CORRECT STRATEGY AND TACTICS

Brzezinski's notions regarding correct strategy and tactics vis-à-vis political adversaries, allies and the less-developed states were evident in his critiques of US foreign policy and, in particular, in those regarding its conceptualization and execution by the Nixon and Ford Administrations. While admitting that it "is an almost superhuman task" to shape and conduct a global foreign policy with long-term objectives clearly in sight in a setting of unprecedented domestic changes and a highly unpopular war,[1] in the summer of 1976 he declared:

> The attendant danger of a philosophical isolation without precedent in American history has been accentuated by the new style and substance of U.S. foreign policy, especially as pursued by the Nixon administration . . . Covert, manipulative, and deceptive in style, it seemed committed to a largely static view of the world, based on a traditional balance of power, seeking accommodation among the major powers on the basis of spheres of influence, and more generally oriented toward preserving the status quo than reforming it. This further widened the gap that was opened already during the Vietnam war . . . and provided the emotional underpinnings for an increasingly hostile attitude abroad toward U.S. foreign policy.[2]

Acknowledging that Nixon's foreign policy "involved an admirably intelligent application of the power-realist approach," Brzezinski stressed that the policy "is open to several criticisms, on the operational level as well as on the broader level of historical pertinence.[3] For Brzezinski, Kissinger was "an able Special Assistant," and one "of the two key architects" of US national security policy, but Nixon was "to a greater extent the conceptual architect of his Administration's policy."[4]

Brzezinski acknowledged that the national security policy void resulting from the disintegration of the foreign policy consensus and the breakdown of WASP domination of foreign affairs "was filled largely by

Kissinger," but argued, that "his 'spectaculars' deflected debate from the more basic issues . . . and the secretive style and the manipulative character of Kissinger's stewardship had the effect of accelerating Congressional entry into direct foreign policy making."[5] Unlike Kissinger, however, Brzezinski did not deal in detail with the nature of strategy and tactics for achieving national goals. Nevertheless, noting his statement that his description of Kissinger's style as personal, covert, and acrobatic was "an overstatement, a product of the campaign,"[6] this chapter examines Brzezinski's beliefs regarding correct strategy and tactics which provided the bases for his evaluation of the Nixon-Kissinger approach to decision-making and foreign policy. The content of his beliefs is presented quite frequently in Brzezinski's words.

BEST APPROACH FOR SELECTING GOALS FOR POLITICAL ACTION

What is the best approach for selecting goals or objectives for political action?

Brzezinski believed that the goals for political action must be chosen on the bases of: (a) the power-realist approach; (b) the planetary humanist approach; (c) a combination of both approaches; (d) a conceptual approach; (e) an architectural approach; and (f) a non-ideological, yet moral approach.

Brzezinski's belief in power realism is manifest in all of his writings. Although his notion of power was never explicitly defined, his discussion of its various elements indicates that for him, as for Kissinger, it was a contextual, psychological relationship in which military power is the most vital element. Convinced that "there will be no global security arrangement in the foreseeable future," and concerned about the ever increasing military power of the USSR,[7] Brzezinski declared, that "for the foreseeable future it is . . . absolutely essential to maintain American military superiority over the Soviet Union." He rejected parity, arguing that it would lead to Soviet nuclear blackmail and reignite the increasingly dormant revolutionary tendencies in the USSR. He viewed US military superiority as an essential precondition for the Soviet commitment to peaceful coexistence and as the basis of political steps to encourage the USSR toward a grand reconciliation with the Western world.[8] Brzezinski's belief in military "superiority" led him to criticize SALT and its intellectual underpinnings, Kissinger's concept of "sufficiency." He saw SALT as a Soviet tactic to prevent the improvement of the US defense capabilities, and was convinced that the Soviet leadership, and particularly the military, were exploiting it to attain military "superiority" over the US which, while meaningless in war, is relevant in a major showdown.[9] Rejecting the argument that the concession of numerical superiority to the USSR in the SALT agreements was compensated for by American technological superiority, Brzezinski stressed that when Soviet technological inferiority was erased the USSR will accept real parity only when faced with a massive and very costly US arms program, in his view, a highly unlikely course.[10] His belief in military superiority was also manifest in the high grade (B-) he gave to the Nixon Administration for resisting cuts in defense which, in his judgment, would have suddenly destabilized the nuclear balance and thus "jeopardiz[e] nothing less than national survival."[11] Moreover, despite his criticism of Kissinger, Brzezinski shared Kissinger's view that the US defense efforts must be on a scale capable not only of insuring American safety but also the safety and independence of its allies and friends.[12]

However, while accepting the power-realist approach as essential in dealing with the Communist world which he viewed as the key problem for US national security policy, Brzezinski founded it inappropriate for managing relations with the Third World and the advanced countries because of the shift from international politics in which political, security, and economic issues were relatively compartmentalized, to a new global politics in which they were linked, thus making the distinction between domestic and foreign policy irrelevant.[13] He did not reject the power-realist approach, but felt that since the Nixon Administration had applied it effectively and made the competitive US-Soviet relationship more stable, relations with the Communist world "may no longer represent the central problem."[14] This view led Brzezinski to advocate the planetary humanist approach for selecting goals regarding the Third World, arguing that it is essential given humanity's common problems (nutrition, ecology, development, social justice, and equality). He saw no conflict between power-realism and planetary humanism since both started with the same basic premise, namely, that global interdependence is the inescapable reality of our time.[15] Regarding the two approaches as complementary and believing that "policy is a matter of emphasis," for Brzezinski the issue was whether priority is given to political stability or to social change.[16] Moreover, he maintained that, being complementary, the two approaches should be combined when dealing with the advanced countries.[17] However, unlike Kissinger who explicitly advocated the power-realist approach, Brzezinski recommended all three depending on the issue in question. Nevertheless, his preoccupation, if not obsession, with the ever growing military power of the USSR indicated a preference for the power-realist approach, and in that sense he was closer to Kissinger in favoring military security and stability over social change.[18] He constantly warned that despite the partial codification of the competitive US-Soviet relationship by SALT I "the problem of security remains . . . a high-priority item"[19] because the expansion of Soviet military power has a momentum of its own not subject to occasional periods of détente.[20]

Brzezinski, like Kissinger, believed in a conceptual approach to policymaking. He constantly stressed that the scope of America's global involvement "requires, above all else, a self-conscious intellectual effort to understand and to define the meaning of our reality; it calls for a conceptual rather than a purely pragmatic – and hence essentially reactive – approach."[21] Recognizing that in a policy operating on a global scale it is extremely difficult to combine deliberate action with sustained forethought because of the lack of precise measurements of success and failure and of acceptable and enduring priorities, as well as clear-cut formulas, Brzezinski argued that only a conceptual framework would permit policymakers to focus on the centrally important issues and to integrate into a meaningful whole the enormously varied and countless specific programs, policies, and objectives the US is pursuing daily all over the globe.[22] He feared, however, that the conceptual clarity may be precluded by the shift to a new global politics which blurred the distinctions between issues.[23] Sharing Kissinger's view that US policymakers were ill-prepared to deal with a foreign policy that is global in scope given their preference for the problem-solving approach and suspicion of conceptual thought, Brzezinski was also concerned by the fact that communist leaders were freed from many dilemmas confronting US policymakers by their relatively limited global involvement and the analytical framework provided by Marxism-Leninism which, while flawed, permits them to act with conviction.[24]

The belief in the conceptual approach made Brzezinski a strong advocate of comprehensive policy planning which had been rejected by Kissinger as the projection of the familiar into the future in the quest for objectivity.[25] In Brzezinski's view, policy planning would develop the essential conceptual framework that defines the meaning of contemporary international reality, thus facilitating the deliberate and coherent selection of goals and even the introduction of moral considerations into the formulation of policy. Moreover, by strengthening the policymaker's intellectual confidence that efforts to achieve certain broad goals are historically relevant, it can provide the necessary staying power in the face of adversity. Arguing that policymaking without a conceptual framework is essentially a reactive process of managing crises and the countless specific, and seemingly unrelated issues, Brzezinski stressed the need for focusing on architectural questions and for reducing bureaucratic obstacles to the translation into policy of intellectual insight. He suggested that conceptualization would be improved by restructuring the Policy Planning Council and by creating a new body, tied to the President's office.[26]

However, while Kissinger viewed conceptualization as a lonely act inherent in statesmanship, Brzezinski assigned this task to policy-planners whom he characterized as visionaries and prophets; terms Kissinger used to describe statesmen. In his view, this task required the qualities of a prophet who is sensitive to the broad sweep of history, of a strategist with the capacity to define historically relevant concepts and goals, and of a gadfly who stresses the need for a continuous review of current policies and tactics to ascertain if current actions are consistent with broader objectives when history takes a turn. Moreover, while Kissinger believed that statesmen must implement their vision,[27] Brzezinski argued that the impact of planners in the selection of goals rests on the organization and staffing of the planning structure and on its close connection to the actual exercise of power. In his view, the planner's influence on policy would be greater if he had physical access to the top policymakers and at the same time had their personal confidence. Speech-writing, however, was viewed by Brzezinski as a direct channel to the top policymakers since their need for "new ideas" gives the planner the opportunity to bypass the bureaucratic opposition to recommended departures from established policies.[28] His belief in the conceptual approach was evident in his attacks on the Nixon-Kissinger team for emphasizing the need for a conceptual framework, yet, in Brzezinski's view, failing to articulate it fully and explicitly. In his words, the Administration had a "predilection for the covert over the conceptual." Acknowledging that a secretive and highly personal approach heavily reliant on suprise, maneuver and even deception "is admirably suited to handling adversary relationships,"[29] Brzezinski argued that in a democracy knowledge of the conceptual framework is essential to provide a basis for enduring public support for foreign policy, and that required collective consultation and open conceptualization.[30] In short, his conception of policy-planning and his critiques of the Nixon-Kissinger style of policymaking indicates that while sharing Kissinger's belief regarding the need for a conceptual approach, Brzezinski had a different view of it. Kissinger saw the development of a conceptual framework and its implementation as the solitary tasks of the statesman[31] while Brzezinski conceived it as an open collegial task and separated it from the responsibility of execution.

Brzezinski's view of the conceptual approach was consistent with his perception of the architectural approach which he also considered as essential to policymaking. In his view, "the essence of architecture . . . involves cooperation, joint planning, and consultation."[32] Maintaining that "only acrobatics . . . involve solo feats of great individual accomplishment, rampant performance, and short duration," Brzezinski stressed that in the present era "no major architectural structure can be the creation of a single individual, even though one individual may infuse it with . . . creative insight."[33] In other words, neither the Nixon-Kissinger team nor the US alone can establish a stable international order, a view shared by Kissinger.[34] Brzezinski's belief in the architectural approach was manifest in his severe criticism of the Administration for its "predilection for the acrobatic over the architectural." However, a closer analysis indicates that the real focus of Brzezinski's critiques was the Administration's misinterpretation of the present era which he acknowledged to be a subjective matter, since "one man's historical relevance is another's intellectual impertinence."[35]

Believing that the bureaucratized Soviet doctrine has lost its appeal, thus reducing the ideological threat to international stability, Brzezinski, like Kissinger, insisted on a non-ideological approach to foreign policy. He criticized US policymakers for reducing international problems to an ideological confrontation and for identifying radical change as contrary to US interests,[36] arguing that since "the problems of the 1970's will be less overtly ideological, more diffuse,"[37] the US should emphasize ecology rather than ideology to benefit from the unprecedented public preoccupation with ecological issues.[38] In his view, America's global isolation increases when its foreign policy is guided by the ideological claim that the present world struggle is between liberal democracy and various forms of despotic statism. Brzezinski argued that since states will continue to differ greatly in the foreseeable future, by not making liberal democracy the key issue the US can exploit its commitment to pluralism to prevent the creation of a doctrinal coalition against it.[39] Moreover, he claimed, "a less ideological perspective will reduce the American-Soviet relationship to its proper proportions."[40] Brzezinski's belief in the non-ideological approach was manifest in his declaration that the community of the developed states must not become a new anti-communist alliance. He argued that while recognizing the USSR's and the PRC's insensitivity to global issues, the community, by inviting the Communist states to cooperate in international efforts to assist the less developed countries, would reduce the temptation of Moscow and Peking to exploit national rivalries thus helping to end gradually the ideological civil war.[41]

However, unlike Kissinger, who also refused to introduce moral considerations into foreign policy, Brzezinski maintained that a moral approach to policymaking would complement the planetary humanist approach, and together they will tap the moral resources of the American people. He stressed that "America's relationship with the world must reflect American domestic values and preocupations" because today in a democracy, a profound discrepancy between internal norms and external behavior will be quickly exposed by the mass media, thus undercutting the public support needed for its foreign policy.[42] Concerned with what he perceived to be the Nixon-Kissinger disregard of moral imperatives and the resultant decline of US moral authority, he insisted that, given the US traditional role, as moral considerations become a more compelling force than ever before, "a morally indifferent America is automatically a weaker America; an amoral America is also likely to become a lonely America."[43] In short, America's domestic commitment to social justice must be extended in its external conduct. Moreover, he argued that in situations where power limitations make it impossible to exercise any political influence, neutrality and moral indignation can be a substitute for political impotence.[44] Brzezinski's depiction of the Nixon-Kissinger foreign policy as Machiavellian and deceptive reflected those convictions.[45]

MOST EFFECTIVE PURSUIT OF GOALS

How are the goals of action pursued most effectively?

Brzezinski believed that the effective pursuit of goals requires: (a) prudent leadership; (b) resort to bold initiatives; (c) the demonstration of political will; (d) the linkage of issues; (e) the institutional and political reorganization of the policymaking process; (f) trilateral cooperation; (g) comprehensive reciprocity; and (h) political dramatization.

Brzezinski, like Kissinger, believed that leadership is essential to the effective pursuit of goals. However, while Kissinger viewed it as the lonely task of the statesman and the price of power, Brzezinski conceived it as an open collegial task involving cooperation, joint planning, and consultation. This conception is implicit in his definition of architecture which "means the enlisting of others in a common effort. It does not mean dictation and overt leadership."[46] Brzezinski's conception emanated from the belief that as a result of the unprecedented complexity of modern problems and the global scope of US foreign policy, "no one individual, however intellectually inclined, can alone formulate and integrate the necessary responses."[47] Attacking the Nixon/Ford-Kissinger team for its unprecedented concentration of decision-making power and its "repeated grand-stand acts of personal leadership," he argued that the difference between "responsible leadership" and "ambitious leadership" lies in the recognition that in an alliance unilateralism by the dominant state is both more contagious and more destructive than unilateralism by the smaller members.[48] Viewing US public opinion as ambivalent but constructively malleable, Brzezinski concluded that in the absence of national leadership capable of defining politically and morally compelling goals to which the public can respond positively, there is a risk that isolationism could become the dominant mood. This risk, he maintained, heightens the centrality of leadership in America and makes more dangerous appeals intended to exploit American disenchantment with world affairs. Brzezinski warned that "if the leadership needed to translate [America's] potential into reality fails to materialize" it "would be disastrous not only for America but even more so for the world."[49] Believing that "the basic reality of international affairs is that some leadership is needed, that only America can provide it, and that even our friendly foreign critics expect it," he criticized the Nixon Doctrine for "offer[ing] little leadership and historical direction."[50]

Brzezinski's conception of prudent leadership as a collegial task did not preclude the taking of bold initiatives, and in this sense he implied a qualified acceptance of Kissinger's belief that at times unilateralism is preferable to inaction in order to prevent the creation of a vacuum.[51] Sharing de Gaulle's view that great leaders are remembered "for the sweep of their endeavors", Brzezinski claimed that this "is true of great nations as well" since "leadership is measured not only by their power but also by the scope of their goals." The view that "leadership is a dynamic . . . condition" and that "it expands with the tasks undertaken," led Brzezinski to conclude that a US commitment to a grand goal can attract and mobilize adherents.[52] His repeated calls for US initiatives stemmed from the following convictions: (a) the USSR would not help in the creation of a new global community; (b) the US cannot shape the world single-handed but it may be the only state capable of stimulating common efforts to do so; (c) the US, as the first global society, is saddled with major responsibility for shaping the framework for change although world conditions do not call for a Pax Americana; and (d) the absence of a constructive US initiative would at the very least perpetuate the present drift in world affairs given the old divisions in the advanced countries and the weakness and parochialism of the developing states.[53] Rejecting the fashionable view that disengagement is the answer to US problems, Brzezinski stressed that America "will have to take the lead" in giving a positive direction and expression to the accelerating pace of change, otherwise it could lead to chaos and eventually threaten American democracy.[54] Brzezinski's belief in the necessity for US initiatives was evident in all of his proposals. In his view, "much of the initiative and impetus for the [creation of a community of the advanced nations] will have to come from the United States."[55] His proposal for ending the partition of Europe depended on creative US initiatives and the definition of new objectives behind which both America and Europe can join. He declared that "A common venture infuses new unity."[56] However, unlike Kissinger who was willing to act unilaterally in the case of disagreement about the new objectives, Brzezinski did not answer the question: What happens if as a result of divergent national interests the other states do not accept the US definition of the new goals? In most cases he argued that joint initiatives by the advanced countries would resolve such problems,[57] a view consistent with his conception of leadership as a collegial task. When the West Europeans and the Japanese rejected what he termed "Kissinger's important and thoughtful speech" calling for a "new Atlantic Charter", this lack of clarity regarding the source of the needed initiatives led him to criticize it on technical grounds, that is, lack of consultations and the fact that Japan was invited to join after the strengthening of Atlantic ties.[58] For similar reasons he also criticized the Trilateral Energy proposal.[59] Brzezinski's unwillingness to stand alone, as Kissinger did, led him to advocate a less overt and assertive leadership based on greater equality even though he never accepted the other advanced states as equal to the US.[60]

Brzezinski, like Kissinger, recognized the vital relationship between power and the will to use it, and repeatedly stressed that the demonstration of political will is essential to the effective pursuit of goals. In his view, the US reaction to events in the German Democratic Republic (GDR) in 1953, in Hungary in 1956, and in Czechoslovakia in 1968, had manifested that "the West did not have the will to use force."[61] His belief in the necessity of political will was most evident in his critique of Kissinger's concept of "sufficiency" which provided the intellectual underpinnings of the new US defense posture. Since sufficiency called for enough force to influence the enemy's intentions while preventing the crumbling of Western determination, for Brzezinski, "will became the crucial variable." Noting that the US defense posture rested on psychological intangibles and the Western reluctance to use force, he advocated "superiority," explaining that since national will is both a matter of dedication and confidence, "it is very much affected by whether a nation feels itself stronger or weaker."[62] The relative parity of the early 1970s, according to Brzezinski, made political will vital to the outcome of crises by determining whether a government panics or overreacts.[63] His belief in the importance of political will for the effective pursuit of goals was also evident in his criticisms of the failure of the advanced countries to deliberately synchronize their international economic policies and jointly undertake long-term programs to decrease their dependence on oil. He constantly declared that given the politicization of international economics such objectives "will require a major act of political will." Otherwise, the increasing unilateralism emanating from domestic demands will lead to a desperate scramble for resources and intensifying conflicts among the allies.[64] Unlike Kissinger, Brzezinski did not see unilateralism as a demonstration of political will. On a broader level, Brzezinski was concerned that America's will to play a positive world role was being undermined by the shattering of the foreign policy consensus, the increasing pessimism within the West, and the temptation to escape a hostile world in the guise of "isolated self-righteousness."[65]

For Brzezinski, as for Kissinger, the linkage of issues is vital to the effective pursuit of goals. He argued that linkage has become essential given the shift from international politics, in which issues were relatively compartmentalized, to a new global politics, in which they are intermeshed and in which the distinction between their domestic and foreign aspects is becoming increasingly blurred. In Brzezinski's words, "this linkage is not an artificiality – it is a fact. It is a fact because the human condition is an interrelated fact."[66] His advocacy for combining the power-realist and the planetary humanist approaches and his attacks on the Nixon-Kissinger "passive" approach to détente reflected his desire to utilize this linkage.[67] Viewing détente itself as "a welcomed development,"[68] he argued that the Nixon-Kissinger approach to it lacked the necessary linkage between the expansion of US-Soviet political and economic ties and the reduction of Soviet restraints on more extensive cultural and social contacts. He insisted that "only an active détente [which in his view the Soviets did not want] . . . represents the best hope for stable peace. And an active détente means a linkage between economic, political, and cultural negotiations."[69] He stressed that "to separate one set of issues for resolution ahead of all others is impossible, especially if the resolution of only one set of issues is more profitable to some parties and less to others."[70] In his view, the active approach to détente with its stress on linkage was the only means for ending peacefully the European partition.[71] In short, Brzezinski criticized not linkage as such but Kissinger's particular use of it.

Brzezinski believed that the effective pursuit of goals requires the institutional and political reorganization of the policymaking process. This belief issued from his conviction that the US "is presently not equipped institutionally or personally to undertake [the necessary program]" for achieving its objectives. For Brzezinski, the Nixon/Ford-Kissinger approach to policymaking demonstrated that the "policy-making process is too narrow, too personal, and conceptually too anachronistic."[72] Criticizing the existing division of labor between the Secretary of State and the Secretary of the Treasury, given the former's exclusive preoccupation with traditional diplomatic issues (a criticism of Kissinger) and the latter's minimal international political sensitivity, Brzezinski urged the speedy creation of a joint economic-political machinery preferably headed by the Vice-President (if he is interested and knowledgeable about foreign affairs). He claimed that this "special supra-departmental organ," focusing especially on the new global problems, could develop the needed US policy initiatives on global issues, provide the necessary interdepartmental coordination, and stimulate a bipartisan effort.[73] This idea, which Kissinger would have viewed as another bureaucratic structure that would place constraints on statesmen, reflected Brzezinski's belief that no one individual alone can formulate and integrate the necessary responses to current problems; a belief not shared by Kissinger.[74]

The belief that the US alone cannot mount the needed responses to contemporary global problems even though it is the only state capable of initiating common efforts to do so,[75] made Brzezinski an ardent advocate of trilateral cooperation. He attacked both the Nixon Doctrine and the Year of Europe speech for failing to call for a larger community of the developed nations. In 1973, he declared *"the active promotion of such trilateral cooperation must now become the central priority of U.S. policy"* (his italics).[76] In Brzezinski's view, "Failure to do so would be very costly for the future of mankind."[77] He insisted however, that the underlying motivation of such cooperation should not be even implicitly derived from security fears stimulated by the USSR.[78] His criticism of what he called Kissinger's "important and thoughtful speech" regarding a new Atlantic Charter indicated that Brzezinski regarded the Atlantic framework as too narrow to respond effectively to the problems confronting mankind. The inclusion of Japan in the new charter did not alter his opinion about Kissinger's initiative because it stressed the strengthening of Atlantic ties and then invited Japan to come in. According to Brzezinski, "Japan must be included in any new initiative from the very start." In his view, the closer cooperation among the US, Western Europe, and Japan would help to create a stable core for global politics on the basis of which the traditional threats of war and the new global issues can be effectively addressed.[79] Brzezinski was convinced that trilateral cooperation was possible because the advanced countries share both common security concerns and certain political-philosophical assumptions, and have the needed economic and technological resources. Hence, they should shape, though not necessarily coordinate, their policies with broader concerns in mind than the dictates of national interest alone.[80] Such cooperation appealed to Brzezinski because he felt that Soviet opposition to it could neither prevent it nor exploit it.[81] By 1976 he recognized, however, that neither Europe nor Japan are prepared to play a major global role despite the availability of resources[82] – a view advanced by Kissinger in the 1960s. In short, Brzezinski, like Kissinger, believed that the effective pursuit of goals requires the creation of coalitions of shared purposes, but they differed about their nature and scope.[83] Unlike Kissinger, however, Brzezinski failed to recognize soon enough the limitations impeding trilateral cooperation.

Believing that the effective pursuit of goals dictates reciprocity of treatment, Brzezinski stressed that this is especially necessary in relations with adversaries, and particularly with the USSR. He maintained that to induce cooperation and limit hostility the US must pursue an intricately nuanced balance between courtship and reciprocity, declaring that reciprocity "is a necessary component, lest a premium be put on uncooperative behavior," thereby strengthening the case of the more dogmatic Soviet leaders who believe that a hostile policy toward the West involves few, if any, costs. Yet, he recognized that to be educational rather than escalatory, the reciprocal actions must duplicate as exactly as possible the actions to which they are a response, and must be taken as regrettable reactions to unilateral hostile actions.[84] This belief was evident in Brzezinski's attacks on the Nixon-Kissinger approach to détente. Stressing that the Soviet unwillingness to reciprocate "is a basic violation of the concept of détente," he asserted, "comprehensive reciprocity in U.S.-Soviet relations – political, strategic, and social – is the only solid base for an enduring détente." For Brzezinski, until the USSR reciprocates, the US must cultivate détente prudently, and not allow the economic relationship, whose only beneficiary is the USSR, to become its primary blossom.[85]

For Brzezinski, the contemporary challenge "may require some political dramatization if the needed responses are to be generated." In his view, the need to dramatize proposed policies stemmed from the lack of political will in the West to undertake the necessary programs and the fact that democracies are generally unresponsive to crisis situations until the crisis becomes severe. Brzezinski argued that unless the Western publics can be convinced of the gravity of the challenge it is unlikely that the needed programs will be forthcoming. He suggested that the publics can be persuaded by a heads-of-government meeting on the *state of social emergency* (his italics), by the personal involvement of the Vice President who has been placed in charge of the new global problems, and by presidential speeches which he considered the best vehicle for imposing a doctrine or for launching an initiative.[86]

CALCULATION, CONTROL, AND ACCEPTANCE OF RISKS

How are the risks of political action calculated, controlled and accepted?

While Brzezinski did not answer this question explicitly, he seemed to share Kissinger's belief that the acceptance of risks is vital to their calculation and control.[87] Unlike Kissinger, however, his acceptance of risks was limited by a certain reluctance to take them alone. For Brzezinski, the US was confronted with the major risks of nuclear war by miscalculation, of isolation in the world, and of escalating international anarchy, all of which could be calculated and controlled by: (a) strengthening the credibility of the US deterrent; (b) maintaining Western military strength and vigorously protecting Western interests; and (c) prudent leadership, joint initiatives, and trilateral cooperation.

For Brzezinski, as for Kissinger, the major risks would arise from miscalculation, but these could be controlled by strengthening the credibility of the US deterrent. Believing that the USSR and the PRC were seeking absolute security, he insisted that this could be achieved only by maintaining military "superiority" over the USSR. He was convinced that, given the highly dynamic nature of the nuclear equation, even parity, if artificially contrived, could lead to a false sense of calculable certainty which would stimulate Soviet risk-taking on the assumption that the West is more likely to yield to nuclear blackmail.[88] Recognizing that "superiority" is meaningless if a war is actually fought, he stressed that in a major showdown it becomes relevant, and that the Soviet leaders "instinctively appreciate [this] better than we."[89] The partial codification of the competitive US-Soviet relationship by the 1972 Moscow agreements did not change Brzezinski's belief regarding the necessity of US military "superiority". He insisted that risks by miscalculation had increased since the US had conceded numerical superiority to the USSR. Brzezinski feared that Moscow might be tempted to exploit its imagined margin of superiority to get under the threat of war significant political gains.[90]

Brzezinski believed that the strengthening of credibility dictates that *"Western military strength must be maintained and Western interests vigorously protected"* (his italics). He stressed that due to the increasing East-West cooperation "it is important that there be no uncertainty on the other side as to the West's determination to protect its interests." For Brzezinski, the Western position can be undermined by failure to resist even limited Soviet pressure in Berlin.[91] Convinced that the control of risks requires the repetition of the historical lesson of the Cuban missile crisis which deflated Moscow's confidence in its ability to get concessions from the West by military threats, he declared, "we must never allow them to think they can."[92] He argued that, in a setting of nuclear parity and increasing anarchy in the Third World, this was vital because the USSR encouraged by a false sense of calculable certainty might abandon its strategy of risk reduction which had guided its external behavior in a setting of US superiority.[93]

Brzezinski's fear of stimulating Soviet risk-taking derived from his conviction that "the communist system was created as an institution of revolution and conflict and hence in some ways is less threatened by international tensions than by protracted international harmony."[94] For him this was demonstrated in the Indo-Pakistani war, the first crisis conducted in the context of nuclear parity, where Soviet behavior manifested that under certain circumstances Moscow's interests are better served by continued hostilities.[95] Moreover, believing that the success of revolutionary movements revive Soviet revolutionary expectations, Brzezinski recommended the use of force in areas where local power could not stop communist force, terrorism, and/or guerrilla warfare. He saw no contradiction between peaceful engagement toward some Communist states and a forcible stand against violence by others.[96] For Brzezinski, then, as for Kissinger, the calculation and control of risks requires the total elimination of opportunities that could be exploited by adversaries.

The reluctance to take risks alone is mostly evident in Brzezinski's calls for prudent leadership, joint initiatives, and trilateral cooperation to control risks emanating from the impact of divergent national interests in relations among the advanced states, and from the exploitation of such risks by the USSR, the PRC, and the less developed states. This reluctance is reflected in both his conception of prudent leadership which, although not explicitly defined, implies caution as to danger and risk, and his description of the USSR as prudent, in the sense that it pursues a strategy of risk reduction by seeking the rapid containment of warfare.[97] Brzezinski's emphasis on joint initiatives and his criticism of Kissinger's Year of Europe also manifests an unwillingness to take risks by acting unilaterally in situations where joint initiatives are not possible. Finally, his advocacy of trilateral cooperation was seen as a means to make joint responses to global problems possible and to identify the US with a larger goal, thus reducing the risk of America's isolation in the world.[98]

THE BEST "TIMING" OF ACTION

What is the best "timing" of action to advance one's interest?

Brzezinski's answer to this question is consistent with his short-term pessimism and long-term optimism, and it can be summarized by the following maxims: (a) the ability to react quickly to numerous diverse situations is vital to global involvement; (b) immediate action is needed to preclude global economic and energy crises; and (c) the immediate responses must be taken in the context of long-term goals.

Brzezinski believed that the ability to react quickly to numerous diverse and often unique situations is vital to global engagement.[99] Sharing Kissinger's view that bureaucracies have a negative impact on timing he argued that comprehensive policy-planning and the reorganization of the policymaking process and the foreign relations machinery would reduce delays thus permitting the US to apply elements of its superiority more rapidly than its adversaries. In this respect he was greatly concerned with Congressional involvement into direct foreign policymaking since it denies the executive the necessary flexibility and the freedom of timing. Brzezinski asserted that Congress is slow in recognizing changes in the world, "whereas promptness in responding to change and to opportunity is of the essence." [100] For Brzezinski, Kissinger's secretive and manipulative style had a negative impact on timing since it accelerated the Congressional entry into direct foreign policymaking thus further reducing the executive's ability to act rapidly with tactical flexibility.[101]

Brzezinski's insistence that the economic and energy problems "require most immediate responses" because "they pose the most urgent danger to international stability" was based on his conviction that the available time for taking effective action is limited.[102] He repeatedly stressed the need to act rapidly because by the time risks become self-evident "it might be too late." [103] In this sense, though not explicitly, Brzezinski, like Kissinger, was advocating a policy of precaution. Brzezinski's sense of timing was also evident in his assessment of the threats posed by the USSR and the PRC. He insisted that responses to them "must be based on the distinction between the immediate threat and the long-range problem." He believed that the USSR was a more immediate threat than the PRC because its national ambitions were backed by overwhelming military power. The military impotence of the PRC made it less of an immediate threat but a greater long-range threat to peace. However, due to the conditions of underdevelopment and socioeconomic crisis in the Third World which feed revolutionary Communism, the PRC is the most immediate concern.[104]

For Brzezinski, however, responses to immediate threats must be taken in the context of long-term goals. This belief emanated from his conviction that the major problems both within the US alliance system and in the East-West relationship would not be resolved in the foreseeable future. In his view, immediate action was necessary to prevent crises which could preclude the needed long-term programs. Recognizing that the present international system needs to be significantly reformed, Brzezinski asserted that systems "do not appear all of a sudden, through a single act of creation . . . they require patient efforts."[105] Moreover, he saw the creation of a community of the developed states as "a long and gradual process."[106] These views led him to criticize the Nixon Administration for its impatient policies toward allies and adversaries and to stress that US policy toward both "must be more patient." US policies must be based on the recognition that the existing differences are deeply embedded in institutions, bureaucracies, vested interests, and even human psyches and "are not going to disappear rapidly."[107]

UTILITY OF DIFFERENT MEANS FOR ADVANCING ONE'S INTERESTS

What is the utility and role of different means for advancing one's interests?

Brzezinski, unlike Kissinger, did not examine in detail the utility of the different means for advancing one's objectives. However, he shared Kissinger's belief that the achievement of national goals requires an effective relationship between power and the will to use it, and it is in this context that he assessed rather briefly the usefulness of various means. In brief, Brzezinski believed that the advancement of national interests requires: (a) the avoidance of an all-out nuclear war but at certain times and in certain places the use of force to defend concrete US interests; (b) collective consultations with allies; (c) arms control; (d) diplomacy; (e) summits to permit the personal exchange of views thus reducing wrong impressions and false expectations; and (f) education of domestic and world opinion to facilitate international cooperation.

Brzezinski shared Kissinger's belief that in certain places and at certain times the achievement of world order requires the use of force. He declared that international chaos will not be prevented if the US is unwilling to use its military power in areas where local military forces are unable to meet the challenges of communist force, terrorism and/or guerrilla warfare.[108] Brzezinski insisted, however, that active US intervention is imperative primarily for defending concrete US interests or for responding to overt hostile acts by the USSR and the PRC.[109] But his willingness to use force was balanced by his conviction that war between the superpowers has lost its utility as an instrument of policy given the destructiveness of nuclear weapons. In his view, war is a luxury that only weak states can afford. This belief, however, did not stop him from advocating the maintainance of the capability for a nuclear war to neutralize the nuclear forces of the USSR and the PRC. Moreover, Brzezinski believed that a war against a weak state is not really effective for advancing a superpower's interests since the superpower's military power is offset by the other superpower and the weak state can undertake an all-out effort that advanced states cannot match spiritually.[110] For Brzezinski, as for Kissinger, then, nuclear war has lost its utility as an instrument of policy but the use of limited force is essential for advancing national interests.

For Brzezinski, collective consultations were the cure-all for the dilemmas confronting the US alliance system, a view rejected by Kissinger. Trilateral cooperation, he stressed, requires "nothing less than deliberate, closer and more institutionalized political consultation" among the US, Western Europe, and Japan.[111] Yet, he criticized the Nixon Administration for insisting on formal consultations with the European Economic Community (EEC).[112] Rejecting Kissinger's argument that improved consultation could only improve the implementation of a consensus rather than create it, Brzezinski maintained that real consultations (not defined) among these three power centers would develop "some genuine consensus" regarding the international situation on the basis of which joint longer-term policies can be formulated to deal with the global problems.[113] His belief in consultation was manifest in his conception of the architectural approach in which it was one of its three key elements,[114] and in his praise of the Nixon Administration for consulting the European allies about the highly sensitive SALT I negotiations.[115] At the same time, it led to his criticism of the Administration for consulting neither the West Europeans prior to the Year of Europe speech and during the Yom Kippur War, nor the Japanese and the Australians regarding the initiative toward Peking.[116] Consultation within the US policymaking circles was also seen by Brzezinski as a useful means to create the domestic consensus that will provide enduring public support for US foreign policy.[117]

The belief that it is improbable that an effective system of US-Soviet arms control can be mutually agreed upon in the foreseeable future,[118] did not stop Brzezinski from endorsing arms control as a useful means for improving world stability. In his view, it was dictated by the increasing risk of an accidental nuclear war due to the great numbers and complexity of modern weapons and by the destructiveness of such a war. Convinced that this risk still existed despite the partial codification of the competitive US-Soviet relationship by SALT I, he declared that "efforts to codify and expand the developing U.S.-Soviet arms control arrangements must be continued." He believed that "the vigorous pursuit of SALT II is the logical conclusion."[119] Brzezinski, however, suspected that for the USSR arms control was a tactical move that would permit it to achieve military superiority over the US.[120] He argued that as long as the political enmity between the superpowers exists, it is in the interest of the weaker side to use arms control to get both greater equality in power and even the opportunity to deceitfully change the balance of power.[121] Despite his recognition that SALT I was concluded at a time when the US Congress was unwilling to match the massive Soviet military buildup, this view led him to attack Nixon and Kissinger for conceding numerical superiority to the USSR. Rejecting the view that US technological superiority could offset the Soviet quantitative superiority, Brzezinski warned that it will be very difficult to undo this asymmetry once the USSR erased its technological inferiority. He maintained that a more patient, tough, and forward approach could have eventually produced a more advantageous agreement for the US or established whether the Soviets were exploiting SALT primarily to improve their military position.[122] In short, like Kissinger, Brzezinski believed that arms control is useful for reducing the instability caused by the escalating arms race but it should not be pursued with the attitude that without it all is lost.

Brzezinski, like Kissinger, believed that the USSR's and the PRC's commitment to a world-wide communist society reduced the utility of traditional diplomacy for settling concrete political issues. Yet, he endorsed diplomacy as a means for exploring the intentions of adversaries. His denunciation of the Nixon-Kissinger personal and secretive diplomacy, however, implied that for him, national interests are best advanced by "open, formal" diplomacy. His criticism of the Nixon-Kissinger emphasis on good personal relations with the Soviet and the Chinese leaders indicated that Brzezinski shared Kissinger's fear that the Western reliance on personalities would permit adversaries to use summit meetings to demoralize the West without making important political concessions.[123] Convinced that negotiations with the East must be seen as a long-term process that would not bring immediate results, Brzezinski attacked the Nixon-Kissinger impatience in negotiating with Moscow.[124] Moreover, he criticized the Administration for its timid approach in pursuing multilateral negotiations, as a complement to the bilateral US-Soviet talks, to resolve some of the major issues in the East-West European relationship, thus reducing the allied fear of a US-Soviet condominium.[125] For Brzezinski, then, diplomacy can be useful for advancing national interests if it is conducted openly with flexibility, patience, toughness, and on the principle of reciprocity of treatment.

Brzezinski's criticism of Nixon's and Kissinger's personal diplomacy did not manifest an outright rejection of summitry. In 1968, he suggested annual two-day informal summits between the American and the Soviet heads of governments in addition to regular meetings with the leaders of the allied and friendly states. However, unlike Kissinger who insisted on a concrete program for negotiation, Brzezinski argued that summits need not always have a formal agenda. He saw summits as "a useful device – both symbolically and practically" – because they would provide the leaders with "a regular opportunity for personal exchange of views and for the maintenance of personal contact." His emphasis on personalities appears inconsistent with his attacks on Nixon and Kissinger. Yet, it is not if one takes into account Brzezinski's conviction that "it would be best to hold [summits] in places that minimize public exposure and avoid fanfare." Brzezinski criticized them not for going to Moscow and Peking, but for publicizing the summits thus generating the false expectation that those meetings would produce "a generation of peace." His denunciation of the Moscow agreements did not stop him from welcoming the summit as "a major step in building a framework of U.S.-Soviet cooperation."[126] He argued, however, that the accommodation with adversaries could have been achieved by high-level talks by the Secretary of State.[127] Brzezinski maintained that, if held regularly, even at times when there is a disagreement over a major issue, summits would preclude the generation of false expectations and miscalculations, while gradually stimulating a sense of mutual involvement in world affairs and a new more mature pattern in the relationship between the world's major adversaries.[128] In short, for Brzezinski, as for Kissinger, summits would not settle the East-West conflict but they could advance the national interests by clarifying intentions and reducing the risk of miscalculation.

The "education" of domestic and world opinion about the realities of the nuclear age and the basic principles and goals of US foreign policy, according to Brzezinski, can facilitate the achievement of national objectives. He felt that the lack of a consensus both domestically and internationally about the meaning and thrust of change in the technetronic age makes "education" a useful means for giving the emerging global consciousness the identity, cohesion and focus it needs, and thus helping international cooperation. Brzezinski did not explicitly discuss "education" as an instrument of foreign policy, but his belief in it is reflected in his criticism of the Nixon Administration for its failure to clarify its conceptions and aims and in his demands that economic ties with the East be linked to more extensive cultural and social contacts.[129] Indeed, since the 1960s he had urged Western leaders to try and shape East European public opinion as the Soviets cultivated Western public opinion, and not to be too concerned about damaging relations with East European governments since they were becoming more responsive to public attitudes. For this task he viewed Radio Free Europe and Radio Liberty as indirect but useful means and opposed any restrictions on their freedom.[130] Brzezinski argued that Nixon and Kissinger heeded Spengler's maxim that to influence events a statesman must command the Press, which has the power to define the "truth," and through their off-the-record briefings, press conferences, etc., manipulate it to deliver only their version of the truth. But their closed and highly personal system of policymaking, in his view, made it impossible to accomplish what Spengler perceived to be the central task of a true statesman, that is, create a tradition and involve others so that their policies will be continued in the same spirit once they left office.[131] For Brzezinski, the creation of a tradition is vital in democracies where foreign policy must generate belief in order to get the necessary public support. His conviction that a true statesman must create a tradition parallels Kissinger's belief that a statesman must be an educator and legitimize his policies domestically. Unlike Kissinger, however, Brzezinski did not believe that in this task the statesman's possibilites are limited.[132] His criticism of the Nixon-Kissinger approach to policymaking implied that a tradition can be created by open debate, collective consultations, open conceptualization, shared political responsibility, and reciprocity of treatment when dealing with adversaries.[133] In short, while sharing Kissinger's belief that "education" through words and actions can facilitate the advancement of national interests, Brzezinski did not perceive the limitations inherent in this task.

CONCLUSION

This analysis indicates that like Kissinger, Brzezinski believed in the power-realist approach to decision-making. Yet, although sharing Kissinger's conception of power, he placed greater emphasis on military capabilities than Kissinger did. However, convinced that Nixon and Kissinger had applied this approach effectively in dealing with the Communist world where its use is essential, he advocated the need for a planetary humanist approach for selecting goals regarding the Third World. Viewing these two approaches as complementary, Brzezinski insisted that they should be combined when dealing with the advanced states. While not advocating the power-realist approach as explicitly as Kissinger did and despite his recommendation that all three approaches be used depending on the issue, Brzezinski's preoccupation, if not obsession, with Soviet military capabilities indicated a preference for the power-realist approach. In this sense he was closer to Kissinger in favoring military security and stability over social change. He also shared Kissinger's belief in the conceptual approach to policymaking, and like Kissinger stressed the need for a conscious intellectual effort to understand and define the present international reality to avoid policy by reaction. In his view, only a conceptual framework can facilitate the deliberate selection of goals and strengthen one's intellectual confidence thus permitting one to act with conviction in the face of adversity. However, unlike Kissinger, for whom the development of a conception and its implementation were inherent in leadership, Brzezinski viewed the development of a conceptual framework as an open collegial task and separated it from the responsibility of execution. For Brzezinski, another needed approach is the architectural which requires cooperation, joint planning, and consultation. Believing that the bureaucratized Soviet doctrine has lost its appeal (thus reducing the ideological threat to stability), he, like Kissinger, insisted on a non-ideological approach to foreign policy. But, unlike Kissinger, he advocated a moral approach to policymaking to complement the planetary humanist approach and together to tap the moral resources of the American people and world opinion.

While sharing some of Kissinger's beliefs regarding the requirements for the effective pursuit of goals, Brzezinski conceived them differently. Like Kissinger, Brzezinski believed in the need for leadership, but he conceived it as an open collegial task involving joint planning and consultation, not as the lonely task of statesmen. However, he also believed in the need for bold initiatives, and in this sense he implied an acceptance of Kissinger's conception of leadership as the willingness to stand alone to prevent the creation of a vacuum. His two conceptions of leadership led him to advocate both US prudent leadership and trilateral cooperation as the central priority of US foreign policy, the latter being similar to Kissinger's belief in the need to generate coalitions of shared purposes. Agreeing with Kissinger that the establishment of a relationship between power and the will to use it is an essential requirement, he stressed that its achievement dictated the demonstration of political will. He also shared Kissinger's belief that the linkage of issues is vital to the effective pursuit of goals. However, while Kissinger believed that the exclusion of the bureaucracy is vital, Brzezinski insisted only on the institutional and political reorganization of the policymaking process. Moreover, Brzezinski was convinced that the effective pursuit of goals in relations with adversaries dictates reciprocity while the decline of optimism and political will in the West make the political dramatization of initiatives necessary.

Unlike Kissinger, who viewed the willingness to take risks as inherent in leadership, Brzezinski was less prepared than Kissinger to take risks alone and advocated prudent leadership and joint initiatives in order to reduce risks. However, like Kissinger, Brzezinski believed that the major risks arise from miscalculation but they can be controlled by maintaining military superiority over the USSR to enhance US credibility and by vigorously protecting Western interests. Convinced that the communist system is better suited to revolution and conflict than to protracted international stability, he insisted that the control of risks requires the total elimination of opportunities that could be exploited by adversaries.

As in the case of Kissinger, Brzezinski's beliefs regarding the best timing of action issued from his short-term pessimism and long-term optimism and his belief that the East-West conflict will be protracted. Agreeing with Kissinger that the ability to react quickly to numerous diverse situations is vital to global involvement and convinced that the US lacked that ability, he advocated institutional changes that would permit the US to apply elements of its superiority more rapidly than its adversaries. Moreover, sharing Kissinger's conviction that by the time risks become self-evident it is usually too late, Brzezinski insisted on distinguishing the immediate from the long-range threats and on focusing on those that are immediate. However, his belief in the protracted nature of the revolutionary threat led him to warn that responses to immediate threats must be taken in the context of long-term goals.

For Brzezinski, as for Kissinger, all-out nuclear war between the superpowers has lost its utility as an instrument of policy, but the use of limited force to defend concrete US interests is still vital. Rejecting Kissinger's view that consultations could only alleviate the intra-alliance disputes, Brzezinski believed that collective consultations could both create and implement a consensus, thus resolving the dilemmas in relations with allies. He also viewed consultations as useful for creating a domestic consensus regarding America's role in the world. But he shared Kissinger's belief that the utility of arms control is limited to reducing the instability caused by the escalating arms race. Therefore, he too warned that it should not be approached with the view that without it all is lost. He also shared Kissinger's belief that the USSR's and the PRC's commitment to create a world-wide communist society has reduced the utility of traditional diplomacy. Nevertheless, he also endorsed it, especially when it is open and formal, as useful for exploring the intentions of adversaries. Moreover, while agreeing with Kissinger that summits can be useful, he, unlike Kissinger, did not insist that they always have a concrete agenda, only that they must be informal and regular. Finally, like Kissinger, Brzezinski believed in the utility of education for advancing national interests but he did not perceive the limitations inherent in the task of educating domestic and world opinion about the realities in the nuclear age.

6 Kissinger Organizing Power for Decision-Making

The selection of the National Security Adviser depends in large part on the compatibility of views about the basic premises of national security policy and on the congruence of operating styles. By serving at the President's pleasure the adviser is an extension of him in the policymaking process, hence the President's choice has a direct impact on how other questions about the control of that process will be answered. As Nixon stated: "I planned to direct foreign policy from the White House. Therefore I regarded my choice of a National Security Adviser as crucial. Considering the importance I placed on the post, I made my choice in an uncharacteristically impulsive way."[1] This chapter examines the correspondence between Nixon's and Kissinger's beliefs regarding world politics and strategy and tactics for achieving national goals, the definitions of their roles by the principal policymakers, and the impact of these on the organization of the formal and informal policymaking structures which could have affected the consistency between Kissinger's beliefs and his policy preferences and/or actions while in office. In addition, it examines whether these structures manifested any of Kissinger's beliefs.

NIXON/FORD AND KISSINGER: A SHARED PERSPECTIVE

In acknowledging that his major foreign policy achievements were inextricably linked to Nixon, Kissinger admitted the existence of a special relationship between them based on compatible operating styles and perceptions.[2] He confessed, however, that prior to their meeting on November 25, 1968, he shared Nelson Rockefeller's view that Nixon was "an opportunist without the vision and idealism needed to shape the destiny of [the US]."[3] Noting the congruence of their beliefs Nixon also admitted that many of his foreign policy successes depended heavily on Kissinger,[4] and attributed Kissinger's negative image of him prior to the election to politics.[5] This section outlines Nixon's conceptions regarding national security policy as he expressed them in speeches, statements, and interviews during the campaign and points out their correspondence with Kissinger's operational code.

Nixon, like Kissinger, believed that the USSR and the PRC are revolutionary powers committed to a world-wide communist society but recognized that their policies toward the West differed.[6] In the late 1960s, he also realized that the intensifying Sino-Soviet tensions and the approaching nuclear parity with the US increased Moscow's willingness to reach some accommodation with the West. For Nixon, "[this] change of the head, not of the heart" resulted primarily from the economic and military strength of NATO, Moscow's fear of the PRC, and the Cuban missile crisis which convinced Soviet leaders that a superpower confrontation would lead to nuclear war and mutual destruction.[7] Sharing Kissinger's view that peaceful coexistence was a Soviet ideological offensive, Nixon rejected it as "completely inadequate and negative" basis for East-West relations,[8] but the risk of nuclear war led him to declare that for the superpowers "there is no acceptable alternative to peaceful negotiation."[9] Peking's continued hostility, however, led Nixon to declare in 1968 that the PRC is "the greatest threat to peace." He feared that unless the US created conditions that will force it to turn inward and recognize the dangers of a world conflict, Peking will eventually export to the Third World not only revolution but nuclear weapons as well, thus increasing the risk of nuclear war.[10] For Nixon, US policy towards the PRC should be "containment without isolation," in the short-run, a policy of firm restraint, of no reward, and of creative counterpressure to convince Peking that its interests can be served only by accepting the basic rules of international conduct; in the long-run, pulling the PRC into the world community.[11] But he rejected the view that a US-Soviet coalition against the PRC would serve US interests.[12] Nixon's willingness to negotiate, however, did not alter his belief that "where the battle against Communism is concerned, victories are never final so long as the Communists are still able to fight."[13]

For Nixon, as for Kissinger, relations with adversaries required a unified and strengthened US alliance system. Seeing the resolution of Atlantic disputes as a top priority, he stressed the need for more consultations and the necessity for "work[ing] on the problem of de Gaulle" and for "find[ing] a way to get Britain into Europe."[14] Convinced that the Asian allies were a "buffer" between the US and the PRC he urged the development of a regional pact with US economic and military assistance to contain the PRC. For Nixon, the Vietnam war demonstrated that the US cannot continue to be a world policeman without more support from other states which have an equal stake in freedom. Believing that US military intervention to defend small states increased the risk of superpower confrontation, he advocated the establishment of regional pacts with US assistance which would be responsible for containing aggression in the immediate area.[15] He accepted the need for US military intervention in cases where the pacts failed, but only if there was an explicit request by the threatened states which would automatically become allies in whatever response Washington considered necessary. Convinced that the US can no longer carry the burden alone, Nixon declared that "the time has come for other nations in the free world to bear their fair share of the burden of defending peace and freedom around the world."[16] Moreover, sharing Kissinger's conviction that not all states were vital to US interests, he promised "the complete reappraisal of American policies in every section of the world," starting with Vietnam,[17] which he saw as "a small country on the rim of the continent" that "does not fill the map."[18]

Nixon's attacks on President Johnson's efforts to impose a purely military solution in Vietnam indicated that he shared both Kissinger's conception of power as a contextual psychological relationship dependent on a combination of military, political, economic, and psychological factors, and his belief that reliance on a single factor is self-defeating.[19] Nixon's belief in power-realism was manifest in his statement that "because this will be a period of negotiations we shall restore the strength of America so that we shall always negotiate from strength and never from weakness,"[20] and his advocacy for developing the military potential of US allies.[21] Sharing Kissinger's belief that foreign policy should be non-ideological, Nixon repeatedly stated: "we do not seek domination over any other country. We believe deeply in our ideas but we believe they should travel on their own power and not on the power of our arms."[22] Moreover, recognizing that many Third World states, where the ideological conflict had shifted, rejected the US as a model, Nixon warned Americans not to seek to impose upon them the Western ideal of democracy since it may not be best for them given their different traditions and state of development. He argued that what mattered was the conscious and deliberate efforts of governments to make their systems more democratic.[23]

Nixon and Kissinger also agreed that the effective pursuit of national goals required leadership, credibility, linkage, power and the will to use it, and the rejection of the quest for quick military and diplomatic victories. For Nixon, as for Kissinger, inherent in leadership is the willingness to take risks. In *Six Crises*, Nixon wrote that a crisis involves both danger and opportunity and what counts is using the opportunity.[24] Convinced that "leadership in foreign policy flows today from the President or it does not flow at all,"[25] Nixon criticized Johnson and declared, "it's time for new leadership to restore respect for the United States."[26] Moreover, believing that leadership is inherent in power, Nixon argued that states possessing great power "have the responsibility of decision" and only the weak "can indulge in the luxury of criticism of others."[27] Nixon's charge that Kennedy and Johnson fostered "a gravely and serious security gap", his rejection of parity as the concept meaning superiority for potential enemies, and his promise to restore an aggregate "clear cut military superiority", manifested his agreement with Kissinger's belief that the US must maintain the credibility of its deterrent. In addition, his statement that "to let [the USSR] a weaker but . . . expansionist nation achieve parity indicates an erosion of our commitment and will", indicated that for Nixon, as for Kissinger, the will to resist aggression is as important as power.[28] His pledge to bring "an honorable end" to the Vietnam war, and his declaration that "I certainly do not seek the Presidency for the purpose of presiding over the destruction of the credibility of American power throughout this world,"[29] manifested his belief in the importance of credibility. For Nixon, Vietnam did "not exist in isolation,"[30] therefore it had to be linked to the other issues in superpower relations that had to be resolved in order to achieve world stability. Criticizing Johnson for focusing exclusively on Vietnam, he maintained, "I did not feel that there should be any single foreign policy priority. There were many priorities, moving in tandem, each affecting the others."[31] Moreover, Nixon argued that although the Vietnam war must be ended honorably, the negotiated settlement must be consistent with US limited objectives and the long-term requirements of stability in Asia, and declared, that "this will require patience."[32] His emphasis on the need for patience indicated agreement with Kissinger's belief that the quest for quick military and diplomatic victories must be avoided in order to demonstrate US resolve to fight indefinitely the protracted conflict with revolutionary powers.

President Ford's willingness to keep Kissinger as both National Security Adviser and Secretary of State indicated that he agreed with the premises that had guided national security policy since 1969, as well as Kissinger's notions of correct strategy and tactics.[33]

THE QUESTION OF ROLES: THE ADVISER AND THE SECRETARIES OF STATE AND DEFENSE

The appointment of Kissinger before the selection of the Secretaries of State and Defense demonstrated Nixon's determination to conduct foreign policy personally. By strengthening the role of the Assistant and the NSC staff, Nixon could guarantee his control of the policymaking process since their influence derived from his confidence in them and not from administrative arrangements. The importance Nixon attached to

Kissinger's role was not evident on December 2, 1968, when he stated that Kissinger's role would be to restore the functions of the NSC system, to focus on long-range planning, and to present him the widest range of policy options. Kissinger's appointment, however, reflected Nixon's belief that "lawyers in politics need non-lawyers around them [who approach a problem on the basis of "how to do it" rather than "how not to do it."][34] To reassure the Departments of State and Defense that the revitalization of the NSC system would not undermine their prerogatives, Nixon emphasized that Kissinger would not become "a wall" between him and their Secretaries. Refusing to state his foreign policy views to the press, Kissinger reinforced Nixon's reassurance by arguing that his position "is inconsistent with making public statements on substantive issues."[35]

Nixon's declaration that he "intend[ed] to have a very strong Secretary of State"[36] was not in conflict with his resolve to direct foreign policy himself since the strength he was seeking in the Secretary was not in policymaking but in administration. William Pierce Rogers, a close friend of his in the Eisenhower years, was appointed by Nixon for the following reasons: (a) Rogers' ignorance of foreign policy guaranteed that he through Kissinger would control policy; (b) Rogers was a strong executive who could manage the State Department and assure support for his policies; (c) Rogers' good reputation on Capitol Hill would facilitate relations with an increasingly isolationist Congress; and (d) Rogers was a resourceful negotiator and would be of great help in the "era of negotiations."[37] For Secretary of Defense Nixon chose Melvin Laird, a former member of the House of Representatives with expertise on defense appropriations and influential friends in Congress. Nixon's commitment to restore US military superiority over the USSR and the anti-defense sentiment in Congress dictated that Laird's primary role would be to guide the defense programs through Congress and to manage the Pentagon.[38] In short, by defining the roles of Rogers and Laird as administrative rather than policymaking, Nixon ensured that he and Kissinger would set the direction of foreign policy.

Rogers' resignation on August 22, 1973, and Kissinger's appointment as Secretary of State in September, did not alter Kissinger's dominant role in the policymaking process since he retained his NSC position which he viewed as vital to achieving his foreign policy goals. But by giving priority to his role as Secretary in order to maintain the continuity of policy during the Watergate affair, Kissinger reduced his direct involvement in the NSC system. Ford's reluctance to take the initiative in foreign policy and his tendency to deal with issues brought before him by world events and his

Secretary of State, guaranteed Kissinger's role as the architect and executor of US foreign policy.[39]

THE NATIONAL SECURITY COUNCIL SYSTEM

In a radio speech on October 24, 1968, Nixon attributed most US foreign policy failures since 1960 to the abandonment of the NSC by Kennedy and Johnson, and promised to "restore [it] to its preeminent role in national security planning."[40] His desire for a more formal approach to policymaking was shared by Kissinger who had criticized ad hoc policymaking, the lack of long-term planning, and the absence of an agency to monitor the execution of decisions. The NSC system envisioned by Nixon and organized by Kissinger consisted of the NSC staff, the Interdepartmental Groups (IG), and the Senior Review Group (SRG). The NSC staff was divided into the front office, consisting of Kissinger's closest aides, a crisis center, a planning group, a research contingent, an analysis section, and the operational experts for regional and functional areas. The NSC staff's main tasks were to supervise studies on a wide range of policy issues, and to prepare, under Kissinger's supervision, detailed outlines for the President's foreign policy statements and speeches.[41] The IGs were chaired by the Assistant Secretary of State for the area under consideration and included the Assistant Secretaries from Defense, Commerce, Treasury and other related departments or their deputies, and an NSC staff member (with de facto Assistant Secretary rank). The IGs' function was to produce a policy study with the full range of options for NSC consideration. The IG studies would be clarified or refined by the NSC staff before being forwarded to the SRG chaired by Kissinger, and consisting of the Under Secretary of State, the Deputy Secretary of Defense, the Director of the Central Intelligence Agency (CIA), and the Chairman of the Joint Chiefs of Staff (JCS) or their deputies, depending on the issue under review. The task of the SRG was to insure that all realistic alternatives were presented to the President. The execution of decisions was monitored by the Under Secretaries Committee (USC), chaired by the Under Secretary of State, and consisting of the Deputy Secretary of Defense, the Director of the CIA, the Chairman of the JCS and Kissinger. The USC also considered issues referred to it by the SRG.[42]

The policymaking process began with a National Security Study Memorandum (NSSM) ordering the preparation of a specific policy review by a specific date. The NSSM originated by Kissinger was approved by Nixon, and was assigned to the appropriate IG over Kissinger's signature.

The NSC staff member within the IG would make sure that the study reviewed all the options and then present the study to Kissinger by the due date. Another member of the NSC staff would review these options independently of the area staff member before they were presented to the SRG. The SRG considered whether the study had dealt with all the options and either returned it to the IG for redrafting or scheduled it for formal NSC consideration. However, unless Kissinger considered a policy option realistic, it would not be presented to the President. At the NSC regularly scheduled meetings Kissinger presented the various options. Once a decision was made by Nixon, but never in the meeting, it would be relayed back to Kissinger who in turn relayed it to the Under Secretaries Committee. The authority to originate and sign the NSSMs permitted Kissinger to determine the context of policy review, the questions to be asked, and the calendar of discussion. In addition, as Chairman of the SRG, he could veto, order redrafting, insert amendments, and generally shape the content and tone of the study. Moreover, his cover memo (not part of the formal NSC system) accompanying the studies into the Oval Office, analyzing, often attacking the bureaucratic options, and presenting for Nixon's eyes only his own recommendation, enhanced Kissinger's control of the policymaking process.[43]

The fact that Nixon asked Rogers and Laird for their views on Kissinger's NSC structure proposal the day after he approved it, provided another indication of his determination to control the policymaking process himself. The Secretaries raised no objections to the NSC proposed structure at the Key Biscayne, Florida, meeting on December 28, 1968, where the four discussed it. Rogers' subsequent efforts (with the encouragement of his subordinates) to defend the preeminence of the State Department failed given Nixon's distrust of it and Kissinger's opposition to policymaking by bureaucratic means.[44] The only change in the proposed structure was the inclusion of the CIA which originally was excluded because of Nixon's belief that it was staffed by liberals opposed to him. The CIA's limited role to providing the NSC intelligence briefings was expanded on Laird's request. Its Director was permitted to participate in the NSC meetings and to propose the initiation of studies – minor concessions that did not threaten Kissinger's control of the process.[45] National Security Decision Memorandum (NSDM) 2, signed on January 19, 1969, created the NSC system, and Kissinger's victory in the contest over its structure established his authority as Nixon's senior adviser on national security policy. The rationale for the NSC system provided in the annual foreign policy Reports to Congress reiterated the following of Kissinger's instrumental beliefs: (a) the need for a conceptual framework to preclude ad hoc decision-making in response to crisis; (b) the necessity to avoid making policy bureaucratically; (c) the need to relate political and military objectives; and (d) the importance of controlling implementation.[46]

The four Presidential Reports to Congress became an issue of contention between Kissinger and Rogers who sought to become the Administration's foreign policy spokesman by publishing three reports of his own. The first ever Presidential Reports on foreign policy, introduced on Kissinger's recommendation and written by him and his staff, reflected his belief that to shape history a statesman must be an educator.[47]

The 37 NSC meetings and the 85 NSSMs in 1969 fulfilled Nixon's campaign promise to revitalize the NSC system. But the number of both meetings and NSSMs decreased in the following years. The NSC met 21 times in 1970 and 10 in 1971 (through September) while Kissinger assigned only 26 NSSMs in 1970 and only 27 during the first nine months of 1971.[48] The original system evolved as key individuals in Kissinger's original staff resigned while the staff itself increased in size, and as new groups were established to deal with crucial issues. The new groups were chaired by Kissinger thereby further enhancing his control of the policymaking process. These were: The Washington Special Actions Group (WSAG) formed in April 1969 to oversee crisis management and contingency planning; the Verification Panel set up in July 1969 to direct arms control strategy; the Vietnam Special Studies Group (VSSG) to check intelligence and trends in the war; the Defense Program Review Committee (DPRC) to keep the defense budget in line with foreign policy objectives; and the 40 Committee to supervise covert intelligence operations. Their membership was often the same. In addition, from time to time, Kissinger formed NSC ad hoc groups to deal with special issues.[49] Kissinger admitted that the NSC system made Presidential control of policy easier; its studies revealed both the range of options and which ones were supported by the departments, and made it possible to delay decisions. The President's decisions, however, were implemented through informal channels.[50] Kissinger's extensive use of these channels reflected his belief that it is dangerous to separate planning from execution.

Under President Ford the number of both NSC meetings and NSSMs increased. By April 1976, the NSC met 31 times while 35 studies were assigned in the first 21 months of the Administration. The NSC staff continued to operate under the direction of Kissinger's deputy, Major General Brent Scowcroft, but it became less influential with the departure of key individuals who followed Kissinger into the State Department. In November 1975, Ford appointed Scowcroft as his National Security Assistant, but despite the re-establishment of the staff's formal neutrality vis-à-vis the departments it did not regain its power because the President did not take the initiative in foreign policy and did not use Scowcroft to reduce his dependence on Kissinger.[51]

INFORMAL STRUCTURES: THE "BACKCHANNEL" SYSTEM

The development of the backchannel system began the day after Inauguration and although Nixon and Kissinger differ as to which one suggested it, it is consistent with their belief that policy should not be made bureaucratically.[52] Over the years Kissinger established a number of backchannels with foreign leaders and within the bureaucracy. As policies were established and Kissinger's power widened the most important decisions were made outside the NSC system in intimate discussions between Nixon and Kissinger. Nixon's operating style (that is, his tendency to work with and through a handful of people, his preference for making decisions in private, and his desire to maintain his flexibility), the congruence of their beliefs, and Kissinger's access to Nixon, facilitated this shift which was inconsistent with Nixon's campaign pledge not to make policy by "catch-as-catch-can talkfests" outside the NSC system.[53] Between 1969 and the end of 1970, before each backchannel meeting, Kissinger submitted for Nixon's approval an outline of his talking points which Nixon rarely changed. After that period Nixon approved the strategy, usually orally, and almost never intervened in its day-to-day execution. However, after each meeting Kissinger submitted his report and analysis to assure him that his orders were carried out.[54] Kissinger admits that "the NSC machinery was used more fully before my authority was confirmed, while afterwards [end of 1970] tactical decisions were increasingly taken outside the system in personal conversations with the President."[55]

For implementing tactical decisions Nixon and Kissinger depended on the backchannel system which directly linked the White House to the field without going through the Departments of State and Defense. Many times, to avoid endless confrontations with the bureaucracy, Nixon asked Kissinger to deal with key foreign leaders through "backchannels," thus disassociating himself from the foreign policy ventures of the Departments of State and Defense. Acknowledging that this practice increased his role, Kissinger admitted that it created problems when policies were implemented.[56] The backchannel system, while contradicting Nixon's campaign pledge not to permit Kissinger to interfere with the operations of the State Department by spending too much time going through cables in the Situation Room,[57] was consistent with Kissinger's beliefs that a statesman must personally implement his vision and that sometimes international agreements are possible only by acting through special emissaries or personal envoys, which make it possible to increase flexibility by bypassing the bureaucratic rigidity.[58] The impact of those beliefs was also manifest in Kissinger's use of Soviet and Chinese interpreters for maintaining the integrity of those backchannels.[59]

CONCLUSION

This examination reveals a correspondence between Nixon's and Kissinger's beliefs and a consistency between their beliefs and the formal and informal policymaking structures they established. Nixon shared Kissinger's belief regarding the revolutionary nature of the USSR and the PRC and the recognition that their strategies toward the West differed. They both agreed that while the Soviet acceptance of the risk of nuclear war and concern with the PRC made US-Soviet negotiations for reaching some accommodation possible, peaceful coexistence was a Soviet ideological offensive in the protracted East-West conflict. For Nixon, however, the PRC's insistence that nuclear weapons can be used and on exporting revolution to the Third World made it the greatest threat to peace. He insisted on containment without isolation to convince Peking to accept the rules of international conduct and then to pull it into the world community. But like Kissinger, he rejected the view that a US-Soviet coalition against it can serve US interests. Nixon and Kissinger agreed that since the US could no longer impose its design on the world or defend all threats to global stability alone, a united and strengthened US alliance system was essential to relations with its adversaries.

Nixon, like Kissinger, believed in the power-realist and the non-ideological approaches to foreign policy. He also advocated the need to restore US and NATO military strength and the willingness to use force and, sharing Kissinger's conception of power, he also warned that a reliance on a single component of it is self-defeating. Nixon's belief in a non-ideological approach to foreign policy led him to warn against trying to impose the Western ideal of democracy in the Third World where the ideological conflict has shifted. Nixon and Kissinger also agreed on the requirements for the effective pursuit of goals. First, he shared Kissinger's belief in the need for leadership and his view that inherent in leadership is the willingness to take risks. Second, he and Kissinger agreed that credibility is vital, and that its enhancement required an aggregate clear-cut military superiority and the demonstration of political will. Third, they concurred on the need to establish a relationship between power and the will to use it since the will to resist aggression is as important as power. Fourth, they agreed that political will can be demonstrated by avoiding the quest for quick military and diplomatic victories. Finally, they both believed that the linkage of issues is vital.

Nixon's belief in leadership was manifest in the appointment of Kissinger as National Security Adviser and the organization of the NSC, and in his definition of Rogers' and Laird's roles as administrative rather than policymaking. Since the influence of Kissinger and the NSC staff derived from his confidence in them he could ensure that leadership in foreign policy flowed directly from him and not from administrative arrangements. The official rationale for the NSC system which gave Kissinger control of the foreign policymaking process was consistent with a number of Nixon's and Kissinger's beliefs, especially in the need for both a conceptual and a strategic approach to policymaking to preclude ad hoc decisions in response to crisis, in the need to harmonize political and military objectives, in the need to avoid making policy bureaucratically, and in the importance of controlling the implementation of one's vision. The establishment of the backchannel system and Nixon's rejection of the State Department's efforts to defend its preeminence in foreign policy reflected their belief that policy should not be made by bureaucratic means. Kissinger's extensive use of backchannels for implementing presidential decisions was consistent with his belief that to shape history a stateman must both provide a vision and implement it. It also reflected his conviction that sometimes international agreements are possible only by acting through special envoys which being outside bureaucratic control increase flexibility which is essential for controlling risks and exploiting opportunities. Moreover, the first ever Presidential Reports on foreign policy introduced by Kissinger also reflected his belief that to shape history a statesman must be an educator. In short, the examination of the NSC and the backchannel systems reveals that their structure, their rationale, and their use was consistent with a number of beliefs which Nixon and Kissinger shared.

7 Brzezinski Organizing Power for Decision-Making

The appointment of Brzezinski as National Security Adviser, unlike Kissinger's, was not totally unexpected for two reasons: (a) Brzezinski and Jimmy Carter, unlike Nixon and Kissinger, were personally close since 1973 when Carter joined the Trilateral Commission which Brzezinski directed; and (b) by the end of 1975 Brzezinski emerged as Carter's principal foreign policy adviser.[1] In announcing Brzezinski's appointment Carter described him as "the key adviser for me" in international affairs while admitting that "I've been an eager student in the last two or three years."[2] This chapter examines Carter's beliefs regarding world politics and strategy and tactics for achieving national goals and their congruence with those of Brzezinski, the definitions of their roles by the principal policymakers, and the impact of these on the organization of the formal and informal policymaking structures which could have affected the consistency between Brzezinski's beliefs and his recommendations and/or actions while in office. In addition, it examines whether these structures reflected any of Brzezinski's beliefs, and notes the similarities and differences with the structures established by Nixon and Kissinger.

CARTER AND BRZEZINSKI: A SHARED PERSPECTIVE

Carter's admission that Brzezinski was his "teacher" in international affairs suggests that some of his views in this area might be similar to Brzezinski's. This section examines Carter's conceptions about national security as he outlined them in speeches, debates, and news conferences during the campaign and their congruence with Brzezinski's operational code.

For Carter, as for Brzezinski, a stable world order "cannot be built on a preoccupation with the old strategic issues which have dominated East-West and North-South relations." Sharing Brzezinski's belief that "in the near future . . . issues of war and peace will be more a function of economic and social problems than of the military security problems,"[3] Carter stressed the need to resolve the new global problems, i.e., pollution, depletion of energy, food shortages, over-population, etc.[4] Like Brzezinski,

Carter, was greatly concerned with the military buildup of the USSR in the 1970s,[5] yet, during the campaign he de-emphasized US-Soviet relations – a stand reflecting Brzezinski's criticism of the Nixon/Ford-Kissinger excessive preocupation with adversaries.[6] Rejecting calls for a return to cold war, Carter stated "I support the objectives of détente," but "I cannot go along with the way it has been handled by Presidents Nixon and Ford" because Kissinger "[is] giving up too much and asking for too little."[7] In his view, the absence of clearly defined US goals made it difficult to compete with the USSR "on an equal basis," therefore, by accepting the Soviet concept of détente the US had "been outtraded in almost every instance."[8] Agreeing with Brzezinski (and Kissinger) that "to the Soviets, détente is an opportunity to continue the process of world revolution without running the threat of nuclear war,"[9] Carter warned Moscow that indirect challenges by proxy must stop since they are "potentially more dangerous than face to face disagreements, and . . . they make a mockery of the very concept of détente."[10] He also reiterated Brzezinski's view that détente must become "broader and more reciprocal."[11] Moreover, arguing that the Sino-Soviet conflict and the US withdrawal from Southeast Asia increased the opportunity for improving the US-PRC relationship, Carter criticized Ford for not doing so and promised to pursue the normalization of relations with the PRC that began with Nixon's trip to Peking.[12]

Accepting Brzezinski's view that trilateral cooperation must become the central priority of US foreign policy, Carter attacked Kissinger for neglecting America's allies and for keeping them separate in order to dominate them.[13] He repeatedly stressed that *"the time has come for us to seek a partnership between North America, Western Europe, and Japan"* (his italics) based on the common economic, political, and security concerns of the three regions. The impact of Western Europe and Japan on the world led Carter to advance the pre-1976 Brzezinski view that "they [were] prepared to play even larger global roles in shaping a new international order." In addition, like Brzezinski, Carter advocated increased unity and consultation with other states which shared America's democratic values and political and economic concerns, such as Israel, Australia, and New Zealand.[14] For Carter, as for Brzezinski, the unity of the advanced democracies offers greater possibilities for shaping a more stable and just world order.[15] Moreover, Carter promised to pay more attention to the developing states than Kissinger had, and to widen the opportunities for genuine North-South consultations so that they can participate in shaping the policies that affected them.[16]

For Carter, as for Brzezinski, the foreign policy of Nixon and Ford "[had] been almost all style and spectacular, and not substance."[17] In his view, their "balance of power politics" with its exclusive focus on superpower relations demonstrated that they had no vision of the future.[18] Despite the rhetoric, however, Carter, like Brzezinski, did not reject balance of power politics outright, but promised a foreign policy based on a creative blend of power-realism and planetary humanism. In his words: "The time has come . . . to supplement balance of power politics with world order politics."[19] Reiterating Brzezinski's belief that one of the greatest threats to global stability lay in the disintegration of the international order as a result of world congestion, increasing impatience with global inequities, and political awareness through instant communications, Carter called, as Brzezinski had, *"for a new architectural effort, with creative initiative by our nation, with growing cooperation among the industrial democracies as its cornerstone, and with peace and justice its constant goal"* (his italics).[20]

Carter, like Brzezinski, believed that the US approach to the world must be non-ideological. Sharing Brzezinski's view that the establishment of "a more stable and just world order" dictated a commitment to pluralism, Carter declared: "we must respect the results of democratic elections . . . we must learn to live with diversity." However, he made US cooperation with regimes whose ideologies are not shared by most Americans conditional upon their support of the democratic process and existing international commitments and their independence from external political direction (implying from the USSR and the PRC).[21] Carter's belief in the non-ideological approach was also manifest in his arguments that violations of human rights "are not limited to any one country or one ideology" and that a common response to global dilemmas was needed despite ideological differences.[22] However, Carter, like Brzezinski (and Kissinger), stressed that US support for global diversity did not imply acceptance of Soviet or Chinese direction and control of regimes that do not share American ideals.

But Carter, like Brzezinski, believed that a non-ideological foreign policy could be strengthened if injected with moral integrity. Charging that "moral decay has weakened our country" as a result of the neglect of values in pursuing foreign policy objectives, Carter insisted that "it is time for America to move and speak not with boasting and belligerence but with a quiet strength, to depend in world affairs not merely on the size of an arsenal but on the nobility of ideals." This was not a call for an ideological foreign policy, but for one that reflected America's domestic values and preoccupations, i.e., commitment to freedom, equality, liberty, and basic human rights.[23] Attacking Ford for supporting dictatorships while ignoring human rights, and for not pressuring the USSR to observe basket three of the Helsinki Accords, Carter stressed that protesting the violations of human rights in the USSR was not enough since "such violations are not limited to any one country or one ideology." Convinced that an amoral foreign policy weakens the US, he declared that the US and its allies by their example, utterances, and various forms of economic and political persuasion "can take the lead in establishing and promoting basic global standards of human rights."[24]

Convinced that in foreign policy Kissinger "has been the President," Carter, like Brzezinski, leveled his most vehement denunciations at Kissinger's excessively personal and secretive diplomatic style. Carter and Brzezinski concurred that the effective pursuit of national objectives required leadership, strength, open consultations, negotiations, and the reduction of nuclear weapons. Sharing Brzezinski's view that the Nixon/Ford-Kissinger team had neither a vision of the future nor "a comprehensive, understandable foreign policy that deals with world problems or even regional problems,"[25] Carter charged, that the US "[had] been adrift too long . . . without leadership too long."[26] In his view, the US had to reassert its leadership in the world since "a lot of the other nations are looking to the United States . . . [to] assume a leadership role."[27] For Carter, however, this meant "joint policy making," not unilateralism. Agreeing with Brzezinski's conception of leadership as a collegial task, Carter stated: "we . . . *must* have an *international policy of democratic leadership*" (his italics), explaining that we must reestablish a spirit of common purpose among democratic nations.[28] For Carter, the failure of leadership was also evident in Ford's inability to realize America's potential strength. Declaring that the "[US] is not strong anymore . . . not respected anymore," Carter pledged "a defense capability second to none." He agreed with Brzezinski, however, that while "a defense capability . . . a fighting capability" was dictated by the enormous military power of the USSR, it is not the only measure of national strength. Reiterating Brzezinski's argument that America's special strength derived from its commitment to principles, its moral integrity, its national unity, the respect of allies and friends, and bi-partisanship in foreign policy, Carter insisted, that "in those respects, we're not strong," as a result of the secrecy and exclusion that characterized policymaking under Nixon and Ford.[29] To realize America's special strength Carter promised "aggressive leadership"[30] and "to involve the American people and the Congress in the shaping and conduct of our foreign policy." Attributing policy failures in Vietnam, Cambodia, Chile, Pakistan and Angola to Kissinger's "Lone Ranger-type" diplomacy, he declared, "every time we've made a serious mistake in foreign affairs, it's been because the American people have been excluded from the process."[31]

For Carter, Congressional involvement would be assured through wider and genuine consultations while the participation of the public could be achieved by the restoration of the fire-side chats and press conferences.[32]

Carter agreed with Brzezinski that genuine, regular consultations was a panacea for resolving the dilemmas of the US alliance system and the conflicts with the developing states. Convinced that the dilemmas and conflicts resulted from Kissinger's "Lone Ranger" diplomacy and not from the divergent conceptions of national interests as Kissinger argued, Carter advocated "more frequent consultations on many levels" and the avoidance of unilateral acts. He also advanced Brzezinski's view, that "periodic summit conferences and occasional meetings" of Western leaders would help alliance relations if contacts are established at all levels.[33] But he recognized the limited utility of summitry for settling the East-West conflict. Despite his denounciations of secrecy, however, Carter indicated that he was prepared to hold unpublicized meetings with Soviet leaders to find a solution in the Middle East.[34] In short, while rejecting personal and secret negotiations, he viewed negotiations and summitry as useful means for achieving national objectives. However, he insisted on more multilateral diplomacy and on the need to focus on economic and scientific issues as well as on the military and political problems.

For Carter, the nuclear engineer, the proliferation of nuclear weapons was a subject of deep personal concern. He viewed arms control as a useful means for reducing the instability emanating from the arms race between the superpowers and the proliferation of nuclear weapons. He agreed with Brzezinski, however, that the SALT I agreements "succeeded largely in changing the buildup in strategic arms from a 'quantitative' to a 'qualitative' arms race."[35] Convinced that "the core of détente is the reduction in arms,"[36] Carter criticized both the Vladivostok Agreement for its high ceilings on strategic arms and Ford for the lack of progress on SALT II. He maintained that the SALT talks "must seek significant nuclear disarmament."[37] Moreover, fearing that the proliferation of nuclear weapons increases the risk of nuclear war, he called for "an alliance for survival . . . transcending regions and ideologies," that would seek to meet the energy needs of all states thus reducing reliance on nuclear energy, make the spread of peaceful nuclear power less dangerous, and limit the spread of nuclear weapons.[38] Carter repeatedly attacked Ford for pressuring Congress to hold up on non-proliferation legislation,[39] and specifically advocated a "voluntary moratorium on the national purchase or sale of enrichment or reprocessing plants."[40] Moreover, greatly concerned that the US contrary to its beliefs and principles had become the world's leading arms merchant,[41] he pledged to work with the allies and the

USSR in order "to limit the *flow of arms into the developing world*" (his italics).[42]

THE QUESTION OF ROLES: THE ADVISER AND THE
SECRETARIES OF STATE AND DEFENSE

During the campaign Carter defined his Presidential role as "the primary focal point for the evolution of policy,"[43] and saw no conflict between controlling policy personally and his pledge to end the centralization and abuse of power by the White House since he did not intend to make his Cabinet subordinate to his staff. This was evident in the selection of Cyrus Vance for Secretary of State before the appointment of Brzezinski as the National Security Adviser. In announcing Vance's appointment on December 3, 1976, Carter described him as "a superb adviser and negotiator – a level-headed, competent good manager" and, after citing Vance's experience in the national security field, he declared: "he will be working with me as a top foreign affairs officer."[44] Important here is Carter's stress on management rather than policymaking and his definition of Vance's role as "a top" rather than "the top" foreign affairs officer. Vance's reputation as a technocrat with an incisive executive mind who can implement Presidential policy and the fact that, unlike Kissinger and Brzezinski, he had no public record of strong personal views on national security policy, could make it easier for Carter to lead and Vance to maintain a low profile. Moreover, his willingness to get along with Congress reassured its members who were seeking, and had been promised, a greater role in policymaking. In defining his own role Vance indicated that, unlike Kissinger, he did not believe in dominating both the making and the execution of policy.[45] In his words, the Secretary of State "must be involved in the question of determining the principles and the policies which are used, together with the President, and where necessary the Secretary should play a part." Vance did not see himself as a personal negotiator. Negotiating, he maintained, "could and would be done by the people who have been picked as negotiators, and that it would be unnecessary for the Secretary of State to get involved," except when his participation could break a deadlock. Moreover, his unwillingness after the announcement of his appointment to go beyond the reiteration of Carter's statements in stating his views on the major issues, displayed a hesitation to be the Administration's spokesman – an essential task given Carter's pledge to involve the people in the making of national security policy.[46]

The definition of the Adviser's role as a coordinator, and not as a policymaker, was consistent with Carter's and Brzezinski's criticism of Kissinger's role. Announcing Brzezinski's appointment on December 16, 1976, Carter stated: "this position is one that ties together in the most effective way the President [and the Secretaries of Treasury, State and Defense]." Following the President-elect, Brzezinski declared: "I see my responsibility as being primarily that of enhancing the decision-making process involving the President and first of all and above all his primary adviser on foreign affairs, the Secretary of State, as well as the Secretaries of Defense, Treasury and others." He stressed that he would recommend policy changes to Vance and Carter if asked, explaining, "I don't envisage my job as a policymaking job. I see my job essentially as heading the operational staff of the President, helping him to integrate policy, but above all, helping him to facilitate the process of decision-making in which he will consult closely with his principal Cabinet members." Brzezinski's deference to the Secretaries demonstrated a willingness to follow Carter's pledge that the Cabinet would not be subordinate to the White House staff. However, unlike Vance, Brzezinski publicly reiterated his views on détente, SALT, and trilateral cooperation, thereby demonstrating that, given the public knowledge of his strong personal views on policy issues, Carter's agreement with some of them and the campaign promise to involve the American people, he might be "forced" to act as the Administration's spokesman if Vance did not fulfill this role.[47]

For Secretary of Defense, Carter appointed Harold Brown who knew the President-elect as well as Vance and Brzezinski. Brown met Carter in 1973 when he joined the Trilateral Commission directed by Brzezinski, and Vance in the 1960s when both served in the Department of Defense; Vance as Deputy Secretary of Defense and Brown as Secretary of the Air Force. Brown fitted neatly into the role Carter defined for the Secretaries in the national security area, namely, an individual without strong ideological indentification, but with extensive practical and managerial experience. Indeed, in introducing Brown, Carter described him as "a distinguished scientist, a top-flight manager."[48]

THE NATIONAL SECURITY COUNCIL SYSTEM

Carter's promises to avoid "Lone Ranger" diplomacy, to direct national security policy personally, and to reduce the number of agencies, and Brzezinski's desire to influence policy without appearing to do so, were manifest in the structure of the NSC system. Rejecting Brzezinski's original proposal for NSC reorganization because it had "too many committees,"[49] Carter and Brzezinski agreed that the NSC be organized into two committees, the Policy Review Committee (PRC) and the Special Coordination Committee (SCC). The PRC, chaired by the appropriate Secretary depending on the issue considered (but in practice mostly by Vance) dealt with foreign, defense, and international economic issues. The SCC, chaired by Brzezinski, was responsible for arms control, intelligence issues and crisis management, and monitored the implementation of Presidential decisions regarding national security. It should be noted that the SCC retained control of the issues that Brzezinski had in the original NSC proposal assigned to the three committees to be chaired by him.[50] The members of these committees were the statutory members of the NSC or their representatives, the National Security Adviser, and other senior officials as appropriate. The PRC met more frequently at the beginning of the Administration while the SCC became more active later on. In addition, existing NSC IGs, chaired by a senior departmental official, were to continue as needed under the direction of the PRC. Their membership included the agencies represented in the PRC and other agencies depending on the issue under consideration. Moreover, NSC ad hoc groups could be appointed to deal with particular problems. Presidential Directive (PD)/NSC-2, signed on January 20, 1977, codified this structure and reiterated Carter's promise "to place more responsibility in the departments and agencies while insuring that the NSC, with my Assistant for National Security Affairs, continues to integrate and facilitate foreign and defense policy decisions." However, while Brzezinski was to be an integrator and a facilitator and not a policymaker in the process, PD/NSC-2 gave him the power, under Carter's direction and in consultation with the Secretaries, to determine the agenda of NSC meetings. Moreover, Carter at the very first Cabinet meeting gave Brzezinski Cabinet status.[51]

The policymaking process began with the request for a Presidential Review Memorandum (PRM) or a more simple option paper prior to a PRC or SCC meeting. For issues controlled by the PRC, the department whose Secretary would chair the meeting supervised the preparation of the papers; for issues dealt in the SCC, the NSC staff took the lead. On issues that did not require Cabinet-level attention a "mini-PRC" or "mini-SCC" met under the chairmanship of the appropriate department Under Secretary or David Aaron, Brzezinski's deputy. The meeting of the PRC or the SCC produced: (a) either a unanimous recommendation for a Presidential decision or a report on alternative policy options; or (b) options papers for a formal NSC meeting. However, the reports of the PRC and SCC meetings to Carter were prepared by the NSC staff and submitted to him by Brzezinski. Carter's decision was transmitted to the departments in the form of a PD, in the case of important decisions, or by a decision memo from Brzezinski, reflecting the President's views on the report. Some of the PDs were signed by Brzezinski once Carter had approved their text. PD/NSC-1 established the system of PRM and PD replacing the system of NSSM and NSDM of the Nixon and Ford Administrations.[52]

The fact that Carter did not consult Vance and Brown before deciding on the final NSC structure indicated his determination to control national security policy personally, and permitted Brzezinski to oppose successfully changes sought by the Secretaries and Stansfield Turner, the Director of the CIA. Maintaining that he had not been consulted Vance objected to Brzezinski regarding the SCC control of SALT and crisis management. Brzezinski defended his control of SALT by arguing that under Carter's instructions, if SALT was assigned to the PRC, Brown, not Vance, must chair the meetings. Regarding crisis management Brzezinski stressed that serious crises called for the President's attention and since vital communications were located in the Situation Room, only he could coordinate crisis management until Carter took control of the situation. Brzezinski's efforts to control SALT and crisis management reflected his belief that the USSR was the most immediate threat to world stability. Control of SALT meant that he, like Kissinger through the Verification Panel, could have a major impact on Carter's Soviet policy, while control of crisis management would permit him, as the WSAG allowed Kissinger, to shape the agenda thus influencing decisions in major crises which in all probability would involve the USSR. Vance also opposed Brzezinski's proposal to submit the reports of the PRC and SCC meetings to Carter before they were reviewed by the Secretaries since that gave Brzezinski the power to interpret the policy recommendations of the Departments. However, Carter's fear of leaks resolved the matter in Brzezinski's favor by putting the burden on those wishing to review the reports in draft to go to the White House in order to do so; an unrealistic option given the pressures on their time.[53] The Secretary of the Treasury, Michael Blumenthal, and the Chairman of the Council of Economic Advisers, Charles Schultze, encouraged by Carter's pledge to involve them in the making of national security policy, challenged Brzezinski's control of international economic issues. He succeeded, however, in controlling international economic matters which have a large political/strategic dimension by invoking the President's name and by persuading Carter, later on, to appoint Henry Owen as Ambassador-at-Large, associated with the NSC and reporting to him through Brzezinski, to coordinate the preparation for the annual economic summits. Another challenge to Brzezinski came from Turner who tried to have a CIA officer present when he gave the morning intelligence briefing to Carter. But by changing the name to the "national security briefing" Brzezinski eliminated this threat to his control of policymaking. Moreover, Turner always briefed Carter with Brzezinski in attendance.[54] The appointment of Senator Edmund S. Muskie as Secretary of State on April 29, 1980, reopened some of the procedural questions regarding the NSC system, but Carter rejected Muskie's efforts to change the existing structure.[55]

Despite the formal enhancement of the Secretaries' roles and Brzezinski's criticism of Kissinger's role, Carter's desire to direct policy personally allowed Brzezinski to control policymaking. Unlike Kissinger, however, who controlled policy by chairing all of the key committees, Brzezinski established his dominance by the following means: (a) he was one of three assistants with direct access to Carter at any time (and continuous contact several times a day); (b) he succeeded on being the only one to give Carter the morning "national security briefing"; (c) he interpreted Carter's annotations to NSC reports as the basis for written and oral instructions to the Secretaries; (d) he initiated a weekly NSC report for Carter alone; (e) policy disagreements in the PRC or the SCC, originally resolved by Carter, were eventually solved by Brzezinski who announced his interpretation of the consensus at SCC meetings thus putting the burden on the dissenters to appeal to the President; (f) he exploited the scheduling of the formal but relatively infrequent NSC meetings by giving Carter broader strategic memos on the eve of such meetings; (g) he opened the NSC meetings by presenting the agenda, he posed the key questions on which decisions were needed, and he summarized the decisions of the meetings in PDs or in directives he signed interpreting Carter's decision; (h) he controlled the clearance of all major cables with policy implications before they were sent out, and of talking points for major foreign policy discussions by the Secretaries of State and Defense; (i) he directed the preparation of major Presidential speeches on national security policy; (j) he cleared foreign travel by the Cabinet; (k) he had his own NSC press spokesman; and (l) he limited the participation of domestic political advisers in discussions of national security policy.[56] The preceding procedures, justified in the name of policy coordination, were inconsistent with Brzezinski's and Carter's calls for open policymaking and true collegiality. However, they reflected Brzezinski's beliefs in the importance of continuous informal access to the top decision-maker and in the power of Presidential speeches and statements for imposing a doctrine or for launching an initiative.[57]

INFORMAL STRUCTURES: "FRIDAY PRESIDENTIAL
BREAKFAST" AND "V-B-B"

Carter's preference to use formal NSC meetings for major issues, i.e., the
definition of the basic position on SALT, the US responses to the Soviet
invasion of Afghanistan and to the revolution in Iran, etc., generated the
need for supplementary mechanisms which involved him in policymaking
personally, or indirectly through Brzezinski. As a result two informal
structures emerged early in the Administration: the Friday Presidential
Breakfast; and the Vance, Brown, Brzezinski (V-B-B) luncheon (later
M-B-B for Muskie). The weekly Friday Presidential breakfast was initiated
by Carter on June 25, 1977, in order to give Vance more personal contact
and thus permit more substantive discussion of the issues. Its original
participants were Carter, Mondale, Vance and Brzezinski, but when the
hour and a half sessions evolved into important executive meetings,
Jordan, Brown, and Powell were added. Occasionally, one or two others would join depending on the issues being considered. When Carter
rejected Brzezinski's suggestion to develop an agenda for each breakfast,
Brzezinski did so indirectly by suggesting to the President at the morning
national security briefing (held before the breakfast) possible discussion
topics. However, while the informality and confidentiality permitted a more
candid exchange of views, problems developed with the way the decisions
were made and interpreted since each participant used his own notes as
guidance for implementation. To resolve those problems Carter allowed
Brzezinski to provide an authoritative interpretation of his decisions as
guidance for the other participants after the UN fiasco regarding the vote
on Jerusalem.[58]

The V-B-B (later M-B-B) luncheon was initiated by Brzezinski in early
March 1977, to resolve problems that he, Vance, and Brown felt did not
require a formal SCC or PRC meeting. Each of the participants acted
sequentially as the host. The luncheon's agenda was prepared by their
respective staffs but no aides attended. After the meeting Brzezinski
prepared the memorandum listing the decisions reached either as a direct
recommendation to Carter or as a common position for the PRC or the
SCC meetings. He forwarded copies to the Secretaries and a report to the
President who insisted on immediate reporting. Carter's desire to direct
policy personally enhanced Brzezinski's role by making NSC coordination
possible, but it generated problems regarding the delegation of authority to
the Departments. Brzezinski admitted that he resolved them by acting on
Carter's behalf "without his direct knowledge" since Carter viewed efforts
to relieve him of excessive detail as an usurpation of authority.[59]

Moreover, while Brzezinski rejected Dobrynin's hints about establishing a backchannel similar to Kissinger's, he did have frequent consultative meetings with Dobrynin and the head of the PRC's Liaison Mission. This arrangement reflects both his belief in collegiality, since he rejected Dobrynin's offer by arguing that Vance would be the negotiator, and his belief in controlling the policymaking process.[60] Indeed, despite his belief in true collegiality this channel was used a number of times by Brzezinski, as it had been used by Kissinger, to initiate negotiations with the USSR and the PRC.[61]

CONCLUSION

This analysis reveals both similarities and differences between Carter's and Brzezinski's beliefs regarding world politics and strategy and tactics for achieving national goals, as well as consistency and inconsistency between their beliefs and the formal and informal policymaking structures they established. Sharing Brzezinski's belief that in the near future war and peace will be dominated more by economic and social problems than security issues, and his concern with the Soviet military buildup, Carter agreed with Brzezinski that foreign policy goals should be selected on a creative blend of power-realism and planetary humanism. However, Carter deemphasized US-Soviet relations as the central priority for US policy much more than Brzezinski and was not as preoccupied with the Soviet military buildup, indicating a preference for social change over political stability. Like Brzezinski, Carter supported the objectives of détente and opposed the way it was pursued by Nixon and Ford. Agreeing with Brzezinski that for Moscow détente was an opportunity to change the international system without running the risk of nuclear war, he, too, insisted that détente must become reciprocal and comprehensive. However, Carter did not share Brzezinski's view that US-PRC rapprochement was an expedient arrangement for Peking, and promised to pursue the normalization of US-PRC relations. Moreover, agreeing with Brzezinski on the need for a non-ideological, yet moral approach to foreign policy, Carter advocated support for human rights in both Communist and non-Communist states alike. However, despite their belief in the non-ideological approach to foreign policy, both made US cooperation with regimes whose ideologies are not shared by Americans conditional upon their support for the democratic process and independence from Soviet and Chinese direction or control. Like Brzezinski, Carter also advocated trilateral cooperation as the central priority of US foreign policy since the unity of the advanced democracies offers greater possibilities for joint initiatives to shape a new international order. But unlike Brzezinski, Carter did not recognize that Western Europe and Japan were not prepared to play a larger global role.

Carter and Brzezinski concurred on the requirements for the effective pursuit of national goals. Carter, like Brzezinski, believed in the need for leadership and conceived it as joint policymaking. The conception of leadership as a collegial task led him to reiterate Brzezinski's belief in the need for open, regular consultations to reestablish a domestic consensus and a common purpose among democratic nations and to resolve conflicts with the developing world. He and Brzezinski also agreed that while open diplomacy and summitry could not resolve the East-West conflict, they are useful for achieving national objectives. However, while agreeing with Brzezinski that arms control is useful for reducing the instability emanating from the arms race, Carter, unlike Brzezinski, viewed the reduction of arms as the core of détente and stressed that significant nuclear disarmament must be the goal of SALT.

The definition of the roles of Vance and Brown as managerial and of Brzezinski as a coordinator was consistent with Carter's beliefs in controlling policy personally and in open, joint policymaking, which he saw as compatible since he did not intend to make his Cabinet subordinate to his staff. The acceptance of Brzezinski's proposed NSC structure without prior consultation with Vance and Brown also reflected his belief in controlling policy personally, but it was inconsistent with his advocacy for open, joint policymaking. This inconsistency was also evident in Brzezinski's efforts to control the policymaking process despite his attacks on Kissinger's role. However, Brzezinski's efforts to retain control through the SCC of issues related to SALT, intelligence, and crisis management, were consistent with his beliefs that the increasing Soviet military capabilities make the USSR the greatest threat to peace, that the major crises result mainly from Moscow's and Peking's efforts to exploit Third World instability, and that SALT should not be the primary goal of détente. Moreover, consistent with his beliefs in the importance of continuous access to top policymakers and of Presidential speeches for imposing a doctrine and for launching new initiatives, Brzezinski through procedural means tried to be the only one with such access to Carter and to control the drafting of Carter's speeches. His actions, however, were inconsistent with his advocacy for collegiality. In addition, while Carter's and Brzezinski's belief in collegiality was manifest in the Friday Presidential breakfast and the V-B-B (and later M-B-B) luncheon, Brzezinski's consultative meetings with Dobrynin and the Chinese were inconsistent with his attacks on Kissinger's backchannel initiatives.

Brzezinski's efforts to control the issues regarding US Soviet policy through the SCC indicate that he was more of a power realist than a planetary humanist, while his use of procedural means to control the policymaking process manifests that despite his advocacy for collegiality he accepted Kissinger's conception of leadership.

8 Kissinger and the Adversaries: the USSR and the PRC

Kissinger's advocacy for a strategy that would define the national goals worth fighting for and determine the degree of force appropriate for achieving them led many observers to hope that the Nixon Administration would develop and implement a global strategy that would achieve peace. But when that strategy was not immediately and explicitly outlined they charged that none existed. The Administration's major policies – US-PRC rapprochement, US-Soviet détente, the Vietnam negotiations – appeared more as a brilliantly executed series of improvisations than a mosaic in which each of its parts is integral to the whole conception. Brilliant improvisations, however, can only emerge from a concept underneath the apparent spontaneity and this appears to be the case with Kissinger's most important actions.[1] This chapter examines Kissinger's impact on US policy toward the PRC and the USSR by analyzing the consistency between his beliefs regarding world politics and strategy and tactics for achieving national goals, and his policy preferences and/or actions as it became manifest in the rationale of policies in his memorandums to Nixon, in official statements, in his approach to issues, and in the agreements he negotiated with the PRC and the USSR. The impact of those beliefs on Kissinger's behavior is also ascertained by examining their consistency with his policy recommendations since January 20, 1977.

THE NEED FOR STRATEGY

Nixon's 1970 Report to Congress subtitled *A New Strategy for Peace*, declared: "This first annual report on US foreign policy . . . is this Administration's statement of a new approach to foreign policy, to match a new era of international relations."[2] The analysis of the international and domestic situations and the outline of the new approach in this report, and the three that followed, reiterated the philosophical and intrumental beliefs of their principal author, Kissinger. The developments regarding

America's adversaries "which made a new policy . . . necessary" were: (a) the disintegration of the Communist bloc and the intensifying conflict between the USSR and the PRC; (b) the replacement of US superiority in strategic weapons with a new strategic balance in which the US and the Soviet nuclear forces are comparable; (c) the Soviet recognition that there can be no gain from a nuclear war; and (d) the transformation of the Communist challenge from the threat of military invasion to a more subtle mix of military, psychological, and political presures. Domestically the situation was characterized by a nascent isolationism in reaction to the Vietnam war and the growing conviction that "the time had come for other nations to share a greater portion of the burden of world leadership."[3] For many these developments revealed a foreign policy in crisis, but for Nixon and Kissinger, inherent in this crisis were "new opportunities" for building a durable peace.[4]

The Administration's definition of durable peace was outlined in the 1970 Report which declared: "Peace must be far more than the absence of war. Peace must provide a durable structure of international relationships which inhibits or removes the causes of war." It stressed that a lasting peace is possible only "when *all* nations will have a stake in peace, and will therefore be partners in its maintenance" (his italics).[5] The Reports that followed stressed that "there could be no stable world order if one of the major powers remained outside it and antagonistic toward it."[6] These statements reiterated Kissinger's conceptions of peace and legitimacy, the foundations of his models for stable and revolutionary international systems. Moreover, in stating the key premises of the new approach to foreign policy the Reports repeated Kissinger's notions of correct strategy and tactics in a slightly altered form. The reports stressed: (a) that a leading American role is indispensable to world peace and progress; (b) the need for a conceptual approach to break the cycle of reaction to recurrent crises; (c) the necessity for partnership with allies and for maintaining US commitments (see Chapter 10 on relations with allies); (d) the need for strength since peace cannot be gained by goodwill alone; (e) the willingness to negotiate without illusions about the enduring ideological conflict; and (f) the need for enhancing security through arms control.[7] The Reports left no doubt that the new approach was based on the belief that the USSR and the PRC were revolutionary powers. According to the 1970 Report, "if some nations define their security in a manner that means insecurity for other nations, then peace is threatened and the security of all is diminished."[8] This, Kissinger believed, was the distinguishing feature of a revolutionary power. Moreover, reflecting Kissinger's belief that the East-West conflict will be protracted, it warned against expectations of rapid, extravagant progress, and the illusion that Communists have already given up their ideological beliefs or are about to do so in the negotiations.[9]

A basic postulate of the Administration's new approach was the concept of linkage which Kissinger equated with the strategic/conceptual approach to policymaking. His belief in linkage was evident in a letter he drafted which Nixon sent to Rogers, Laird, and Helms on February 4, 1969, declaring linkage the official policy.[10] Departmental opposition to it and the strong public and Congressional criticism did not alter Kissinger's and Nixon's belief in it.[11] The 1970 Report to Congress declared:

> The central fact [in successful negotiations] is the inter-relationship of international events. We did not invent the interrelationship; it is not a negotiating tactic. It is a fact of life. This Administration recognizes that international developments are entwined in many complex ways: political issues relate to strategic questions, political events in one area of the world may have a far-reaching effect on political developments in other parts of the globe.[12]

Kissinger repeatedly explained that "we saw linkage . . . as synonymous with an overall strategic and geopolitical view. To ignore the interconnection of events was to undermine the coherence of *all* policy" (his italics).[13]

However, in the absence of any agreements, until Kissinger visited Peking in 1971, SALT I in 1972, and the Paris Agreement on Vietnam in 1973, commentators viewed the promised structure of peace and its intellectual underpinnings as catchy slogans and speculated that the Administration wanted to reinstitute the pentagonal balance of power Kissinger had written about in *A World Restored*. Nixon's statements, that it would be a safer, better world if a strong United States, Europe, Soviet Union, China and Japan were balancing each other, supported this thesis.[14] Few noticed that since *A World Restored* Kissinger had not advocated a pentagonal balance – a stand consistent with his belief that only the US and the USSR could transform the global balance of power and his conviction that today many of the elements of stability characterizing the nineteenth century international system cannot be recreated.[15] Yet, the Reports indicate the outlines of a strategy that would: (a) end the Vietnam war in a way that would preclude a return to a new isolationism thus maintaining US credibility abroad; (b) redefine the national interests to avoid the depletion of US resources in the pursuit of idealistic goals peripheral to the central balance of geopolitical power; (c) formulate a concept of international order consistent with US national interests but acceptable to most states as a standard of international legitimacy; and (d) permit dramatic initiatives on global issues to retain America's leadership in the world. Nixon and Kissinger were convinced that by meeting those requirements the Administration could restore US power and in turn enhance global stability. Evident here are Kissinger's beliefs (shared by Nixon) in credibility, balance of power, legitimacy, leadership, and in a non-ideological approach to foreign policy.

But what was Kissinger's design of the structure of peace if not a pentagonal balance?

A TRIANGULAR BALANCE: THE OPENING TO THE PRC

Kissinger answered the question indirectly in the speeches he wrote for Nelson Rockefeller in 1968. The Presidential candidate declared: "I would begin a dialogue with Communist China. In a subtle triangle of relations with Washington, Peking, and Moscow, we improve the possibilities of accommodations with each as we increase our options toward both." He stressed that "in such a framework we can talk with Soviet leaders with new purposefulness and hope about a basic settlement."[16] Evident here is Kissinger's belief that the USSR was the greatest threat to peace. But his theoretical interest in a triangular balance (and Nixon's desire to pull the PRC into the world community) was not manifest on March 14, 1969, when Nixon's rationale for the "Safeguard" ABM program was a defense against a Chinese nuclear attack in the 1970s.[17] But while reflecting Nixon's belief that the PRC was the greatest threat to peace and domestic political considerations, this rationale, by implying a common US-Soviet interest in containing the PRC, appeared inconsistent with his and Kissinger's desire for a dialogue with Peking.

By June, however, this inconsistency disappeared and the triangular balance began to emerge as Kissinger's strategy in his reports to Nixon and in his arguments in the SRG and in the WSAG.[18] Greatly concerned with the continuation of the Sino-Soviet clashes in areas militarily favoring the USSR and with Soviet hints about removing the threat posed by the PRC, Kissinger proposed, and Nixon approved, unilateral steps, declarations, and the use of intermediaries as means to signal Peking the Administration's willingness to negotiate. On July 21 the Administration began to ease trade and travel restrictions to the PRC, while in August, Nixon in his trip around the world rejected Brezhnev's proposal for an Asian collective security system and through Presidents Yahya Khan of Pakistan and Nicolae

Ceauşescu of Romania conveyed his opposition to Soviet efforts to isolate the PRC. Rogers, Under Secretary Elliot Richardson and CIA Director Richard Helms repeated the signal,[19] which was made official in the 1970 Report to Congress. Nixon declared: "The Chinese . . . should not remain isolated from the international community. In the long run, no stable and enduring international order is conceivable without the contribution of this nation of more than 700 million people,"[20] and stressed:

> Our desire for improved relations is not a tactical means of exploiting the clash between China and the Soviet Union. We see no benefit to us in the intensification of that conflict, and we have no intention of taking sides. Nor is the United States interested in joining any condominium or hostile coalition of great powers against either of the large Communist countries. Our attitude is clear cut – a lasting peace will be impossible so long as some nations consider themselves the permanent enemies of others.[21]

Nixon's rationale for the opening to Peking reflected Kissinger's conception of a stable international order while his emphasis on equidistance was consistent with Kissinger's belief that the US must take advantage of the Sino-Soviet split without promoting it as a policy. Indeed, he explained that the "1 1/2 war" strategy, adopted on Kissinger's recommendation,[22] was based on the premise that "the prospects for a coordinated two-front attack on our allies by Russia and China are low both because of the risks of nuclear war and the improbability of Sino-Soviet cooperation."[23]

The policy discussions and Kissinger's reports to Nixon reveal that his main fear was that a Soviet attack on the PRC would upset the geopolitical balance of power and permit Moscow to use all its military capabilities against the West. If ignored by the US, such a demonstration of Soviet dominance and US impotence (or indifference – the result would be the same) would lead to the accommodation to Soviet demands by allies and smaller states thus undermining US foreign policy. Kissinger showed no interest in the ideological dispute but sought to take advantage of Peking's challenge to Moscow's geopolitical ambitions to get concessions in Vietnam and other issues of concern to the Administration.[24] Evident in his calculations were his beliefs in maintaining the strategic balance (by defending the PRC) and in taking risks (by confronting the USSR to do it). The opening to the PRC gave tangible expression to Kissinger's beliefs in a non-ideological approach to foreign policy and in the need to base it on the emerging political multipolarity despite the military bipolarity of the international system. Indeed, it was justified

as such in the 1973 Report to Congress.[25] Moreover, the opening to
the PRC provided the dramatic initiative he viewed as essential for
maintaining America's leadership in the world. Peking's desire to use
the US as a counterweight to Moscow facilitated the opening to the
PRC.[26]

For Kissinger, State Department opposition to the PRC initiative proved
that conducting foreign policy bureaucratically leads to rigidity and loss
of opportunities. The interagency studies he ordered and the discussions
by the SRG and the WSAG revealed that the bureaucracy could perceive neither the global implications of the Sino-Soviet clashes nor the
opportunity for establishing a triangular relationship that would increase
US policy options toward its adversaries. Believing in a non-ideological
approach to foreign policy he opposed the State Department's insistence
that the US await the change in the PRC's militant ideology before it
seeks to improve relations with it and stressed the PRC's impact on
the global balance of power.[27] The State Department's obsession with
bilateral issues, i.e., Taiwan, trade, travel, PRC admission to the UN,
evident in the studies and in the Kissinger/Rogers controversy over the
content of the reconvened Warsaw talks, reinforced Kissinger's belief in
its inability to deal with policy conceptually.[28] Rejecting the Department's
view that the improvement of US-PRC relations without prior progress on
the bilateral issues implied a US concession, Kissinger maintained that
these were peripheral to Peking's fear of Soviet expansion.[29] Moreover,
dismissing warnings from Rogers that rapprochement with the PRC would
undermine the improvement of US-Soviet relations and his proposal that
the Soviets be informed of all US-PRC contacts,[30] he stressed, in his
reports to Nixon, that Moscow's growing preoccupation with the PRC
would make the USSR more flexible on East-West issues. In October
1971, he wrote: "The beneficial impact on the USSR is perhaps the
single biggest plus that we get from the China initiative."[31] In addition, Kissinger, unlike the State Department, was not greatly concerned
with the negative impact on relations with allies, and specifically with
Japan, since Prime Minister Eisaku Sato, on January 22, 1971, had
publicly proposed to increase trade and press contacts with Peking and
to initiate talks at the governmental level. His refusal to sacrifice the
Peking initiative to allied unity and thus undermine US foreign policy
reflected his beliefs that disagreements on peripheral issues, the right
to be consulted, is the price for unity on issues that really matter –
the geopolitical balance – and that consultation permits allies to either
preempt or thwart US policies without resolving the issue of America's
global role.[32]

In short, Kissinger's beliefs in maintaining the strategic balance, in a non-ideological foreign policy and in linkage, collided with the State Department's obsession with bilateral issues, opposition to linkage, allied reactions, and injection of ideological considerations. This led to his suggestion in January 1970 for high-level talks between special emissaries in Peking; a suggestion reflecting his belief that international agreements are sometimes possible only by extra-bureaucratic means. In his view, the border clashes made 1969 such a time. Rogers' insistence that the issue of emissaries be discussed only after Peking yielded on the bilateral issues reinforced Nixon's negative opinion of the State Department and led to Kissinger's secret visit to Peking in July 9, 1971.[33] The 1972 Report to Congress conceded the negative impact of the secret trip on allied unity but stressed that there were "overriding reasons" for it and that "the price . . . was . . . unavoidable."[34] In short, it reiterated Kissinger's belief that disputes with allies on peripheral issues are acceptable when the goal is to maintain the global balance of power.

Kissinger's calculations proved correct. Chou En-lai and Mao Tse-tung, in discussions with Kissinger and Nixon, stressed the need to remove the Soviet threat to global stability and not the bilateral issues, i.e., Taiwan, membership in the UN, etc.[35] Indeed, on February 28, 1972, the Shanghai Communique, negotiated by Kissinger and Chou En-lai, with minor revisions demanded by Rogers and accepted by Nixon as protection against conservative attacks, revealed that US-PRC rapprochement resulted from their common opposition to Moscow's geopolitical ambitions.[36] Kissinger's acceptance of Chou En-lai's proposal that the Communique state the US-PRC differences rested on his recognition that this would reassure the allies and friends of both, while it would give credibility to common positions without raising expectations. The Communique declared that the US and the PRC would seek to normalize relations, would not enter into agreements directed at other states, and would oppose efforts to establish hegemony in the Asian-Pacific region.[37] The commitment to oppose hegemony (a euphemism for Soviet expansionism) was introduced by Kissinger and while it satisfied Peking's needs for entering the relationship, it reflected his belief that the USSR was the greatest threat to peace. The commitment to avoid collusion with any major power against another (also expressed in the Reports to Congress) manifested his conviction that only equidistance between Moscow and Peking would increase US options toward both the USSR and the PRC.[38] The agreement to normalize relations was given tangible expression in 1973, following the Vietnam settlement, when Liaison Offices were established in Washington and Peking. The Shanghai Communique guided US-PRC relations, without a dispute over its interpretation, until the establishment of diplomatic relations in 1979.[39]

The beliefs that led Kissinger to pursue US-PRC rapprochement were manifest in his criticism of his successors. Convinced that only implicit linkage can be effective he found Vance's opposition to it and his exclusive focus on US-Soviet relations just as damaging as Brzezinski's explicit use of the "China card" against the USSR. The Carter Administration, he argued, must base its Soviet and PRC policies on geopolitical considerations and not on the fluctuations of US relations with either adversary.[40] For Kissinger, Reagan's anti-Soviet rhetoric which appeared to freeze the US into rigid hostility toward the USSR, thus freeing the PRC to adopt, at little risk, a militant Third World posture, reflected a disregard for linkage. His conviction that the triangular relationship is vital to the geopolitical balance of power led him to criticize members of the Reagan Administration whose statements on Taiwan implied a reversal of policy as stated in the Shanghai Communique and the accord on normalization of 1979. Kissinger's belief that bilateral issues should not be allowed to undermine the US-PRC political relationship was evident in his advice to the Secretary of State, George Shultz. Kissinger suggested that Shultz on his visit to Peking must focus, as he had, on harmonizing the US and PRC views of their global roles and not on Taiwan, trade, or technology, since the bureaucratic inertia that precludes progress on those issues can be overcome only by giving priority to the political aspects of the relationship.[41] He censured both Carter and Reagan for reneging on promises to transfer technology because they raised doubts in Peking about the strategic parallelism of interests. Kissinger supported technology transfer since the PRC "could not represent a *military* threat to American interests for the rest of this century, by which time current technology will be superseded" (his italics).[42] Urging the PRC's rearmament, Kissinger stressed that "a threat to its security would undermine the global equilibrium as surely as Soviet domination of Europe."[43] Moreover, convinced that US willingness to defend the global equilibrium must be continuously demonstrated to prevent the PRC from moving toward Moscow if only to gain time, he supported a tougher US stand on Angola, Ethiopia, Iran, and Afghanistan and recommended acting in concert where interests converge, i.e., Afghanistan and Indochina.[44] Evident in his recommendations to Carter and Reagan was his belief that the military power of the USSR makes it a greater threat to global stability than the PRC.

US-SOVIET RELATIONS: FROM CONFRONTATION TO DETENTE

For Kissinger, military bipolarity made the US-Soviet relationship vital to the establishment of a stable international order.[45] His primary objective, however, was not to bring about the domestic transformation of the USSR but to adjust its external goals to the imperatives of a stable international system. The 1971 Report to Congress stated: "the internal order of the USSR, as such, is not an object of our policy, although we do not hide our rejection of many of its features. Our relations with the USSR . . . are determined by its international behaviour."[46] Kissinger repeatedly stressed that:

> Détente is not rooted in agreement on values; it becomes above all necessary because each side recognizes that the other is a potential adversary in a nuclear war. To us détente is a process of managing relations with a potentially hostile country in order to preserve peace while maintaining our vital interests. In a nuclear age, this is in itself an objective not without moral validity – it may indeed be the most profound imperative of all.[47]

Kissinger's objectives and rationale for détente were consistent with his belief in an non-ideological approach to foreign policy and his conception of legitimacy. For Kissinger US-Soviet détente rested on two pillars: (1) resistance to Soviet expansionism; and (2) a willingness to negotiate on concrete issues.[48] The first was manifest in his support for new strategic programs and in taking risks to defeat the Soviet strategy of ambiguity, and the second in SALT and in economic cooperation.

Maintaining the Military Balance

For Kissinger, an equilibrium of military power is the first structural imperative of a stable international order. A rough equilibrium in strategic nuclear weapons was most desirable in Kissinger's view, since superiority by either side would be destabilizing and exact parity might be impossible to attain, given the differences in US and Soviet strategic weapons systems. The concept of sufficiency advanced by Kissinger incorporated both concepts, superiority and parity, and was supported by Nixon despite his 1968 call for superiority and Laird's opposition to it.[49] The 1971 Report to Congress declared:

The concept of sufficiency is . . . in part a political concept, and it involves judgments whether the existing and foreseeable military environment endangers our legitimate interests and aspirations.

In its narrow military sense, it means enough force to inflict a level of damage on a potential aggressor sufficient to deter him from attacking.

In its broader political sense, sufficiency means the maintenance of forces adequate to prevent us and our allies from being coerced. Thus the relationship between our strategic forces and those of the Soviet Union must be such that our ability and resolve to protect our vital security interests will not be underestimated . . . It would be inconsistent with the political meaning of sufficiency to base our force planning solely on some finite – and theoretical – capacity to inflict casualties pressumed to be unacceptable to the other side.

The United States and the Soviet Union have now reached a point where small numerical advantages in strategic forces have little military relevance.[50]

Evident here is Kissinger's belief that while the US must maintain an adequate retaliatory force, it must not seek safety in numerical superiority since its strategic and political significance is diminishing.

However, as conceived by Kissinger, the doctrine of strategic sufficiency permitted the US to deploy strategic weapons in order to sustain the credibility of its deterrent. The 1971 Report to Congress declared:

But sufficiency also means numbers, characteristics, and deployments of our forces which the Soviet Union cannot reasonably interpret as being intended to threaten a disarming attack. Our purpose, reflected both in our strategic programs and in our SALT proposals, is to maintain a balance, and thereby reduce the likelihood of nuclear war.[51]

Moreover, it made it possible to relate strategic planning to the destruction not only of civilians but of military targets as well. Concerned that strategic parity might lead to the use of strategic forces in less than an all-out attack, Kissinger urged Nixon in June 1969 to order the Pentagon to develop a more discriminating strategy for all-out nuclear war and strategies to meet contingencies other than all-out war.[52] The rationale of Kissinger's recommendation appeared in the 1972 Report to Congress which stated:

Our forces must also be capable of flexible application. A simple "assured destruction" doctrine does not meet our present requirements for a flexible range of strategic options. No President should be left with only one strategic course of action, particularly that of ordering the mass destruction of enemy civilians and facilities. Given the range of possible political-military situations which could conceivably confront us, our strategic policy should not be based solely on a capability of inflicting urban and industrial damage presumed to be beyond the level an adversary would accept. We must be able to respond at levels appropriate to the situation. This problem will be the subject of continuing study.[53]

This statement reflects Kissinger's belief in the need to develop a strategy that relates power to diplomacy and the will to use it. But translating these conceptual innovations into operational strategic options proved very difficult and, although the flexible strategic options objective received greater articulation and emphasis under Secretaries of Defense James R. Schlesinger (1973–75) and Harold Brown, this objective has not yet been achieved.[54]

To maintain the strategic balance, Kissinger, despite the Congressional and bureaucratic opposition to new weapons programs and pressures to cut the defense budget, supported the antiballistic missile defense system (ABM), the MIRV, the B-1 bomber, the Trident submarine and missile, the MX ICBM, the cruise missile, and strengthened conventional forces.[55] His rationale for supporting the new strategic programs was manifest in a report to Nixon on June 17, 1969 and was reiterated in the 1971 Report to Congress which stated: "sharp cutbacks could not permit us to satisfy our sufficiency criteria and were unwarranted in view of the continuing growth of Soviet forces. Unilateral reductions could . . . eliminate any Soviet incentives for an agreement to limit strategic arms. They would also raise serious concerns among our allies, particularly in NATO."[56] Kissinger strongly supported the highly controversial "Safeguard" ABM and MIRV programs; the ABM because he viewed it as a major Soviet incentive for a SALT agreement since Moscow announced its interest in strategic talks shortly after Johnson's decision to deploy the "Sentinel" ABM system, and the MIRV because, as he wrote to Nixon on May 23, 1969, acceding to a moratorium on MIRV testing "might create pressures to halt Minuteman III and Poseidon programs . . . thus further unravelling the U.S. strategic program." Kissinger's opposition to unilateral cuts of defense programs reflected his belief that the USSR's search for absolute security precluded the possibility that it will reciprocate.[57] His declaration that "Détente could never replace a balance of power; it would be the result of equilibrium, not a substitute for it,"[58] manifested his belief that the strategic balance is a prerequisite to pursuing positive objectives such as arms control and increased trade.

Kissinger rejected the view that new strategic programs would endanger the arms limitation objective of the Administration because as the 1972 Report to Congress explained:

> Our actions have been designed primarily to guarantee the continuing survivability of our retaliatory forces . . . improvements in our existing forces and the development of new programs are not incompatible with negotiations to limit strategic arms. They complement the broad effort of this Administration to guarantee the security of the United States while moving toward a structure of greater international stability and restraint. We have been conscious of the opportunities provided in the Strategic Arms Limitation Talks to add a vital dimension of stability to our competitive relationship with the USSR.[59]

This view led to disputes between Kissinger, and Rogers, Smith and others who maintained that the deployment of ABMs and MIRVs would preclude an agreement on arms limitation.

Arms Control: SALT I and SALT II

Parallel to his efforts to maintain the strategic balance by new weapons programs, Kissinger used SALT to reduce the instability generated by technology and thus by stabilizing the strategic arms race to free resources for building conventional and regional forces where greater imbalances existed.[60] In 1975, asked what he considered to be his most significant political achievement up to that time, Kissinger responded, "SALT, without a question, SALT."[61] Kissinger's approach to SALT was consistent with his ultimate goal, the establishment of a stable international system, since it would help produce one of its two structural imperatives – an equilibrium of military power.[62] His approach to SALT reflected his belief that despite its revolutionary nature the USSR might cooperate in arms control given its fear of nuclear war. In addition, it reflected his beliefs regarding linkage, the utility of arms control, and the utility of summits.

The Soviet offer on January 20, 1969, to start the SALT talks immediately was rejected by Kissinger who supported Nixon's insistence that SALT be linked to Soviet restraint in Vietnam, Berlin, and the Middle East.[63] But his efforts to delay the talks until the Administration developed its strategy and defined its goals failed. Under Congressional and bureaucratic pressures to reject linkage and exploit the opportunity offered by Moscow,[64] Nixon (on June 11) authorized Rogers to inform Moscow that the Administration was ready to start exploratory talks on November 17, 1969. The lack of bureaucratic consensus, however, permitted Kissinger to take control of the talks.[65] This was evident both in the conception and execution of SALT. His conceptual contribution was manifest in the selection of options to be presented to the Soviets. The options were selected from those proposed by the Departments and reflected the bureaucratic and political considerations of the issue, but common to all options was the linkage between ABM and offensive weapons limitations.[66] Convinced that Moscow pursued the mere fact of SALT talks to kill ABM and other strategic programs thus avoiding the negative economic impact of a new arms race, Kissinger insisted on negotiating defensive and offensive limitations simultaneously. Hence, he opposed efforts by Rogers and Smith to negotiate an ABM ban only simply because Moscow indicated that such an agreement was possible,[67] and supported the deployment of Phase II of "Safeguard." At the NSC meetings on January 23, 1970 and January 27, 1971, he argued that Moscow would have no incentive to negotiate after construction stopped since Congress was ready to kill the ABM program.[68] Moreover, in April 1970, when Nixon hoping to influence the Congressional elections seemed ready to trade an ABM ban only for a summit in Moscow, Kissinger advised against it given the lack of progress in SALT and Vietnam on which Nixon had insisted since 1969.[69] For Kissinger, Moscow's interest in stopping "Safegard" made "ABM . . . the heart of . . . SALT."[70] By agreeing to limit "Safeguard" while stopping Congress from killing the program he hoped to induce Moscow to limit its offensive strategic programs – his main objective in SALT – [71] thus, preserving an adequate retaliatory capability in the face of domestic opposition to new strategic programs.

The linkage of SALT to political issues reflected Kissinger's belief that stability required the resolution of political conflicts. Believing that the utility of arms control is limited to reducing the instability caused by nuclear technology he, unlike Rogers and Smith, did not approach SALT as if without it all was lost.[72] Kissinger's willingness to wait until Moscow accepted simultaniety in defensive and offensive limitations reveals his belief that in the protracted conflict with the USSR patience is as an important component of strategy as power since the side least eager for a settlement can tip the psychological balance thus gaining the negotiating advantage. Indeed, Moscow, having failed to exploit the disputes between the SALT delegation and Kissinger, accepted simultaneity in negotiating defensive and offensive limits on May 12, 1971;[73] and in April 1972, during Kissinger's secret trip to Moscow, Brezhnev agreed to include SLBMs in the offensive freeze.[74] The SALT I agreements confirmed those two breakthroughs.

The SALT negotiations culminated in the ABM treaty and the Interim Agreement on the limitation of strategic offensive arms – signed on May 26, 1972, by Nixon and Brezhnev. The ABM treaty, being of unlimited duration, limited ABM deployment to two sites in each country, one to protect the national capital and the other to protect an ICBM field, and each site was limited to 100 ABM launchers and 100 interceptor missiles. The site area was limited to a radius of 150 kilometers. The capital site was limited to 6 radar complexes and the ICBM site to 2 large phased-array radars and 18 smaller radars. But the deployment of radars for early warning of strategic ballistic missile attack was not permitted nor was the testing of other missiles, launchers, or radars in an ABM mode. Although modernization and replacement of ABM systems was allowed, the treaty prohibited the development, testing, and deployment of sea-based, air-based, space-based, or mobile land-based ABM systems and the modification of launchers that would increased their launching capability. In addition, no ABM systems could be deployed or transferred outside the national territory.[75] The Protocol to the ABM treaty signed at the Moscow summit on July 3, 1974, limited each country to one ABM site.[76] For Kissinger, since neither country had built the second site, the agreement was more advantageous to the US since the Congress was unlikely to appropriate the funds for the second permitted site.[77]

The Interim Agreement placed a five-year freeze on strategic offensive launchers with strict limits on numbers and replacement procedures. The USSR was limited to 1618 ICBMs, 950 SLBMs, and 62 submarines, while the US was confined to 1054 ICBMs, 710 SLBMs, and 44 submarines.[78] The numerical inequality in launchers accepted by Kissinger reflected his view that given Johnson's decision to respond to the Soviet buildup by deploying MIRVs, and not by increasing the number of launchers, without the freeze the Soviet advantage in launchers would have continued to grow. He argued that since the US had no strategic programs that could be deployed during the five-year freeze the agreement did not affect the US at all while it limited Soviet deployments of offensive weapons.[79] Moreover, he felt that the Soviet advantage in launchers was counterbalanced by the US superiority in bombers, technology, accuracy, and MIRVs.[80] Kissinger's acceptance of inequality in launchers is consistent with his belief that security must not be sought in numerical superiority. The Interim Agreement clearly demonstrated that Kissinger was more interested in the psychological benefits, that would be derived from it, which would facilitate actual disarmament agreements in the future.

The SALT agreements fulfilled Kissinger's criteria for a sucessful summit, that is, that it produce concrete agreements. The ABM treaty and the Interim Agreement were made possible by Kissinger's ability to cater to the USSR's analogous political needs and to make these even more intense by the acceleration of the US-PRC rapprochement.[81] It was more than coincidental that after Nixon's July 15, 1971, announcement that he would visit the PRC, the USSR began to make concessions that produced the outlines of an ABM treaty in early 1972. In addition, the US-Soviet negotiations produced agreements on measures to reduce the risk of accidental nuclear war and on procedures to modernize the "hot line" between Washington, and Moscow.[82]

Kissinger's approach to SALT II was another manifestation of his belief that security must not be sought in numerical superiority alone. The inequality in launchers he accepted in the Interim Agreement became the focus of the debate regarding détente and led the Defense Department to demand "equal aggregates," that is, equality in every weapons system – ICBMs, SLBMs, and heavy bombers. In Kissinger's view, "this was a symbolic objective that reflected domestic pressures, not a political or strategic analysis,"[83] since (a) even if Congress funded the highly controversial Trident and B-1 programs the US could not achieve numerical equivalence; and (b) the Defense Department, without any reference to SALT, continued to reduce US forces by administrative decisions.[84] Moreover, he was greatly concerned with the readiness of the JCS to abandon all MIRV limitations for exact equivalence in launchers and the State Department/ACDA proposal for a moratorium on all MIRV testing and deployment[85] because without limits on MIRVs numerical ceilings on launchers would be meaningless since US ICBMs, being fixed targets, would become vulnerable to the increasing number of Soviet warheads,[86] and the moratorium would have killed the Trident, the only new US missile under development. Kissinger's objective in SALT II was to retain the invulnerability of US ICBMs by limiting the MIRVing of Soviet ICBMs.[87] But since no US weapons program generated an incentive for Moscow as ABM had done in SALT I, he sought to create one by: (a) insisting (in July 1973) that the Pentagon develop the long-range cruise missile which it was ready to abandon in order to save the B-1; (b) pushing for research on an airborne ICBM; and (c) appealing to Nixon (in January 1974) to stop the Pentagon from reducing the rate of Trident submarine production from three a year to one a year.[88] Indeed, in his meeting with Brezhnev at Zavidovo in May 1973, Kissinger hinted that the US would not develop a cruise missile with a range of more than 3000 kilometers if the USSR promised not to MIRV its heavy ICBMs. But Brezhnev would not discuss any MIRV limits prior to the completion of the Soviet MIRV testing program.[89]

Constrained by domestic pressures from choosing either of the two options that made strategic sense, a massive buildup to ensure Soviet restraint by the threat of a counterforce capability, or freezing the status quo with the US edge in warheads, Kissinger, at the NSC meeting on March 21, 1974, proposed the extension of the Interim Agreement for three years – with its inequality in missile launchers – provided the Soviets accepted a reciprocal inequality in MIRVed land-based ICBMs comparable to their advantage in the total number of launchers.[90] He saw no harm in accepting by agreement a ceiling that the Pentagon had established in its published five-year projection. But Brezhnev while accepting the principle of unequal MIRV aggregates during Kissinger's visit in Moscow on March 24, rejected Kissinger's demand that a ceiling on MIRVs must contain a sublimit on land-based ICBMs.[91] Brezhnev's rejection of an ICBM sublimit, Senator Jackson's and Secretary Schlesinger's open opposition to SALT, conflicting demands by the agencies, and Nixon's increasing involvement in Watergate, led to a stalemate in SALT by early June 1974.[92] However, in November 1974 at Vladivostok, Ford pressed for equal aggregates and Brezhnev agreed to an accord limiting each side to 2400 delivery vehicles of which 1320 could be MIRVed. The Defense Department, however, which had insisted on equal aggregates, did not propose programs to build up to the permitted level.

The consistency between Kissinger's beliefs and his actions is also evident in his critiques of the Carter and Reagan policies. In a statement before the Senate Committee of Foreign Relations regarding SALT II he reiterated that "SALT cannot be considered in isolation. It is one element in our overall national security policy. It must be viewed in the context of the global balance that it reflects, or purports to affect."[93] Arguing that the ominous shift in the military balance against the US and the unprecedented Soviet use of proxy forces in Africa, the Middle East, and Southeast Asia, demonstrated that US national security and the global equilibrium were in grave danger,[94] he urged the Senate not to deal with the SALT II treaty in a vacuum but to simultaneously seek to restore the military and geopolitical balance.[95] In his view, since the sharp shift in the military balance resulted not from SALT but from unilateral cuts of US weapons programs it can be altered.[96] Kissinger criticized Carter for systematically deprecating the role of power, for rejecting the linkage between SALT and Soviet political conduct, for using the whole defense budget as a bargaining chip to win approval for SALT,[97] and specifically, for cancelling the B-1, for delaying the MX, and for slowing down the Trident and the cruise missile programs[98] which he had defended as essential to maintain the strategic balance. Moreover, Carter's declarations indicating a return to the strategic doctrine of assured destruction led Kissinger to reiterate his belief that dependence on it will gradually lead to strategic and eventually geopolitical paralysis.[99] Those concerns led Kissinger to make his support for the ratification of the SALT II treaty *"entirely conditional"* (his italics) on Presidential and Congressional support for the development of a new defense program and doctrine and the explicit linkage between SALT and Soviet geopolitical restraint.[100]

For Kissinger, Reagan put the US on the right track by pushing a rearmament program that will in time balance the Soviet buildup, and by stressing the need for restraint in Soviet geopolitical conduct.[101] Indeed, he argued that the Strategic Defense Initiative (SDI) "may be [Reagan's] greatest contribution to strategic theory," but stressed the need for some conceptual definition of it.[102] Moreover, criticizing the Reykjavik framework which sought a zero option on INF, 50 percent reduction in US and Soviet strategic forces and limitations on SDI, Kissinger declared its adoption would undermine the credibility of the US nuclear deterrent and urged its rejection.[103]

Searching for Legitimacy: Basic Principles and the Agreement on the Prevention of Nuclear War

Believing that arms control by itself could not alleviate conflicts between the superpowers but becomes a safety valve for Soviet expansionist designs, Kissinger linked it to restraint in geopolitical competition. On May 29, 1972, at the Moscow summit Nixon and Brezhnev signed the Basic Principles of US-Soviet Relations and on June 22, 1973, at the Washington summit, they signed the Agreement on Prevention of Nuclear War (APNW). Kissinger pursued the Soviet proposals for those agreements in order to create incentives for Moscow to reciprocate on issues of concern to the US and establish a yardstick by which to measure Moscow's compliance with what he considered to be the permissible goals and methods of foreign policy. Soviet compliance would reduce tensions while violations would undermine Moscow's peace offensives and provide domestic support for opposing Soviet aggression.[104] Moreover, he viewed Soviet adherence to those agreements as a first step toward the achievement of the second structural imperative of a stable international system – the acceptance of its framework by all major powers. Indeed, according to the Shanghai Communique, similar principles were to govern US-PRC relations.[105]

The proposal for the Basic Principles came from Moscow on January 21, 1972, through the Kissinger/Dobrynin channel and it was negotiated by Kissinger and Gromyko during Kissinger's secret trip to Moscow in April.[106] But the final agreement was based on a Sonnenfeldt/Kissinger draft.[107] The Basic Principles declared:

> . . . the improvement of US-Soviet relations . . . without in any way prejudicing the interests of third countries . . . will proceed from the common determination that in the nuclear age there is no alternative to conducting their mutual relations on the basis of peaceful coexistence. Differences in ideology and in the social systems of the United States and the Soviet Union are not obstacles to the bilateral development of normal relations based on the principles sovereignty, equality, non-interference in internal affairs, and mutual advantage.[108]

They committed the superpowers on a "long-term basis": (a) to "do their outmost to avoid military confrontations and to prevent the outbreak of nuclear war . . . " "and always exercise restraint in their mutual relations, and . . . to negotiate and settle differences by peaceful means . . . in a spirit of reciprocity . . . "; (b) to refrain from "efforts to obtain unilateral advantage at the expense of the other, directly or indirectly" and to "[renounce] the use or threat of force"; (c) to summitry to exchange views on problems of mutual interest; (d) to pursue bilateral and multilateral arms limitations and specifically to special efforts to limit strategic weapons; (e) to "actively promote the growth" of commercial and economic ties; and (f) to "make no claim for themselves, and not recognize the claims of anyone else, to any special rights or advantages in world affairs." The Basic Principles clearly demonstrated not only Kissinger's belief in a non-ideological foreign policy but his efforts to get Moscow to pursue its interests in a similar manner, in short, to relinquish its revolutionary goals. His acceptance of the term "peaceful coexistence" in the agreement appears inconsistent with his belief in maintaining the geopolitical balance since he believed that it was a Soviet offensive tactic to subvert that balance. But the inconsistency disappears in view of the obligations undertaken and the realization that, on Kissinger's insistence, the Basic Principles declared that they "do not affect any obligations with respect to other countries earlier assumed", and are "not directed against third countries and their interests."[109] By reassuring US allies and the PRC and by taking risks (before and after the signing of the Basic Principles) to stop Soviet encroachments in the international system Kissinger was convinced Moscow's tactic would not succeed.

The proposal for the APNW came from Brezhnev during Kissinger's secret trip to Moscow in April 1972 and was negotiated in the back-channel.[110] Kissinger rejected a number of Soviet drafts proposing the bilateral renunciation of the use of nuclear weapons because their acceptance would have undermined NATO's defense, raised doubts about the US credibility among friends that had no formal treaties with the US, and destroyed US-PRC rapprochement by proclaiming, in effect, a US-Soviet military alliance against Peking. Indeed, to prevent this from happening he briefed both the PRC and the major European allies about the Soviet proposal.[111] But he accepted Brezhnev's proposal in order to give Moscow an additional incentive for acquiescing to US policy in Vietnam – a linkage evident in his refusal to pursue it until the Vietnam Peace Agreement had been reached.

Kissinger's first counterdraft was given to Brezhnev at the Moscow summit but the APNW was finalized by them at Zavidovo in May 1973 on the basis of a US draft. The APNW stated that US and Soviet foreign policies and actions will be "guided by the objectives of strengthening world peace and international security" and, specifically, the objective "to remove the danger of nuclear war and of the use of nuclear weapons." To realize this objective "each Party will refrain from the threat or use of force against the other, against the allies of the other . . . and against other countries, in circumstances which may endanger international peace and security." It committed the US and the USSR to "urgent consultations with each other . . . to avert" the risk of nuclear war resulting from their bilateral or third country relations. Once again, at the insistence of Kissinger, the agreement stipulated that it "shall neither affect or impair the inherent right of individual or collective self-defense nor the obligations undertaken by either party towards its allies or other countries in treaties, agreements, and other appropriate documents."[112] To avoid misinterpretations, in a press briefing after the signing, Kissinger stated: "Each side has now set down in precise form its willingness to practice self restraint not only in relations with each other but with *all* other countries" (his italics).[113] In short, Kissinger had negotiated an agreement that did not imply a US-Soviet condominium or permit a nuclear war against third states while it ruled out such a war between the superpowers. Moreover, it did not suggest, in ruling out nuclear war, that conventional war was acceptable. Indeed, those themes were evident in all of his responses to Moscow's proposals on this issue.[114] For Kissinger:

> The Agreement on the Prevention of Nuclear War reflected our belief that control of arms presupposed restraint in international conduct;

that coexistence between the superpowers would ultimately depend on adherence to standards of behavior by which they would learn not to threaten each other's vital interests.[115]

In summary, the Basic Principles and the APNW reflected Kissinger's belief that peace/stability depends on limiting conflicts within the existing international system by adjusting differences through negotiation. By combining incentives and penalties he sought to restrain Soviet international conduct by convincing Moscow to accept the existing international order and what he considered to be the permissible aims and methods of foreign policy, in brief, to persuade Moscow to abandon its revolutionary goal of creating a global communist society. This was most evident in Kissinger's substitution of the Soviet proposal of banning nuclear weapons in war with renouncing the threat of force in peacetime. His rejection of Moscow's proposal to undertake an obligation to concert US-Soviet actions toward the PRC also reflected his belief that the essential equilibrium of power could not be achieved without the PRC. The fact that he negotiated both agreements himself manifested Kissinger's belief that a statesman must personally implement his vision.

Trade in US-Soviet Relations

For Kissinger and Nixon expanded economic relations was the second element in US-Soviet cooperation and a manifestation of their belief in linkage. Believing that only improved political relations could lead to increased trade, they linked increased trade to Soviet restraint in Vietnam, Berlin and the Middle East, and made this explicitly clear to Moscow. In Kissinger's view, since the USSR could do very little for the US economically, "given Soviet needs, expanding trade without a political quid pro quo was a gift."[116] The Soviet desire for expanded trade facilitated this linkage.[117]

Kissinger's belief in the primacy of politics was evident in his recommendations which stressed that economic concessions are a political instrument to be used as incentives for Soviet restraint in world affairs. East-West trade was formally addressed in the NSC meeting on May 21, 1969, in the face of Congressional and bureaucratic pressure to liberalize trade to improve the political atmosphere. Here Kissinger opposed the expansion of trade without a political quid pro quo, and specifically suggested the approval of only one out of three requests for licenses to sell products to the USSR. He felt that by approving the license for an oil extraction plant the long lead time for its contruction would give the US continuing leverage since items could be withheld in times of Soviet adventurism. Moreover, to preclude the loss of business to the allies without affecting Soviet conduct he also recommended that the US export control list be brought into line with the less restrictive list of the Co-ordinating Committee on Export Controls (COCOM). Nixon, however, incensed with Moscow's continuing support for Hanoi, rejected Kissinger's proposals and ordered opposition to all legislative efforts to liberalize trade.[118] In executing Nixon's decision Kissinger repeatedly disapproved requests by the Departments of State, Commerce and Agriculture which sought to expand trade by administrative fiat without any political reciprocity.[119]

The timing of Kissinger's approval for the expansion of trade is another manifestation of his beliefs in linkage and in the primacy of politics. He delayed until April 1971 a trip to Moscow by Agriculture Secretary Earl Butz to discuss grain sales;[120] and in May when Moscow accepted his proposal to deal with offensive and defensive arms limitations simultaneously, Kissinger approved the sale of US machinery for the Kama river truck plant – a sale he had opposed in the NSC meeting in 1969 despite Congressional and bureaucratic pressures. However, he withheld approval for other projects related to the plant until the Berlin breakthrough in July. He also withheld part of the project during the India-Pakistani crisis when he felt that Moscow was encouraging Indian aggression against Pakistan. In the wake of the opening to Peking Soviet actions would have demonstrated the futility of reliance on Washington thus damaging US credibility.[121]

Kissinger's insistence that trade be linked to improved political relations continued even after the Soviets accepted his proposals about SALT and Berlin. During his secret trip to Moscow in April 1972, he responded to Brezhnev's suggestions about joint ventures in Siberia, the granting of MFN status to the USSR and credits, by stating that political progress at the summit could lead to a general agreement on economic relations to be made concrete in the summer. Kissinger admits, however, that Brezhnev did not reveal his real need – grain – which soon became a controversial issue in US-Soviet détente.[122] Grain sales were not directly linked to Soviet restraint by Kissinger due to his lack of knowledge about the real Soviet need for grain and the fact that during the summit Brezhnev and Kosygin feigned little interest when Nixon, seeking to benefit from such sales during the campaign, raised the issue several times. Indeed, he considered Kosygin's offer to Rogers to buy $150 million of grain too insignificant and advised against its inclusion in the summit communique.[123] But progress on a number of bilateral commercial negotiations at the lower levels of government placed economic relations on the summit agenda. However, as Kissinger had told Brezhnev, while article seven of the Basic Principles declared that "the USA and the USSR regard commercial and economic ties as an important and necessary element in the strengthening of their bilateral relations and thus will actively promote the growth of such ties," no specific projects were agreed upon.[124] In July, however, Commerce Secretary Peter Peterson visited Moscow and reached agreement on repayment of the Soviet lend-lease debts, the extention of MFN status, the establishment of commercial facilities in Moscow and Washington, and on a three-year sale of US agricultural products and US credits to finance them. Here, Kissinger's role was limited to negotiating with Brezhnev during his September trip to Moscow the final figures of the lend-lease agreement.[125] However, after the US-Soviet grain deal, negotiated by Butz and Peterson in June, led to attacks on détente due to the dramatic rise in US food prices,[126] Kissinger sought to control all commercial transactions with the USSR by treating them as foreign policy matters. In 1975, in negotiating a five-year agreement to sell the Soviets grain, Kissinger linked grain with oil in an attempt to drive a wedge between Moscow and the Arabs, but the linkage failed because the Soviets agreed to sell only small amounts of oil at prices below those of OPEC.[127]

The consistency between Kissinger's beliefs and his actions was manifest not only in his efforts to link trade to the improvement of political relations but in his efforts to keep this linkage implicit. His attempts to defeat Senator Henry M. Jackson's amendments explicitly linking the granting of MFN status to the USSR with increased Jewish emigration and the handling of political dissidents reflected his belief that national goals should be selected on the basis of an non-ideological/non-moralistic approach.[128] In statements to Senatorial committees Kissinger reminded his listeners that the "overriding objective [of détente] must remain . . . the prevention of nuclear war." He declared: "we cannot accept the principle that our entire foreign policy – or even an essential component of that policy such as the normalization of our trade relations – should be made dependent on the transformation of the Soviet domestic structure." Reminding the Senators that the Administration had been criticized for depriving US business of lucrative contracts by linking trade to international developments, Kissinger stated: "the issue is not whether we condone what the USSR does internally; it is whether and to what extent we can risk other objectives – and specifically the building of a structure for peace – for these domestic changes." For him, "the major impact of . . . denial of MFN status to the Soviet Union would be political, not economic . . . [it] would call into question our intent toward an improved relationship."[129] Kissinger feared that this "ex post facto form of linkage . . . casts doubt on our reliability as a partner" without improving human rights in the USSR – a fear consistent with his belief that credibility is vital in pursuing national objectives. Urging the Senators to maintain a sense of proportion about the leverage trade gives US diplomacy with Moscow, he stressed that economic incentives alone could not substitute for an equilibrium of power.[130] Kissinger's private overtures to Moscow to ease Jewish emigration in order to improve the atmosphere of US-Soviet relations succeeded in increasing the number of individuals from 400 a year in 1968 to 35 000 in 1973; an increase corresponding to the improvement in political relations. Indeed, in 1974, private diplomacy led to an informal Soviet agreement to a 45 000 a year target but the Jackson/Vanik amendment made it impossible for Moscow to be more forthcoming and in January 1975 it rejected the entire trade agreement.[131]

The belief that the West should insist on a political quid pro quo for increased trade led Kissinger to criticize both Carter for refusing to link the sale of grain (prior to 1979) to Soviet restraint,[132] and Reagan for avidly encouraging Soviet grain purchases.[133] His opposition to tying sanctions to Poland to the recognition of Solidarity, however, was consistent with his belief in a non-ideological foreign policy, that is, trade must be linked to foreign and not domestic changes.[134] For Kissinger, the Soviet-Cuban intervention in Angola, in Ethiopia and in South Yemen, the invasion of Afghanistan, and the suppression of Solidarity in Poland, destroyed the pro-trade thesis since they occurred in the period of increased East-West economic cooperation. But he also rejected the anti-trade thesis. Acknowledging that any trade will indirectly help Moscow's military buildup, he reiterated that a prudent trade and credit policy "is bound to create vested interests that can act as an incentive" for Soviet restraint.[135] Kissinger noted, however, that such policy is undermined by the increased trade between the USSR and the other industrial states. In his view, the Soviet gas pipeline demonstrated that in the 1980s "economic relations . . . have done much more to induce *Western* restraint" in the face of the Soviet assault on the geopolitical balance (his italics). The handling of this issue led him to attack the western leaders for seeking immediate gains without regard to the political risks in strengthening "a hostile and aggressive political system."[136] Western economic power can still be used according to Kissinger to maintain the geopolitical balance but it is essential to muster the political will and agree on the following: (1) that East-West trade must be subject to some political control and some political conditions; (2) that these controls promote clear-cut and attainable objectives; (3) to modernize the COCOM list of prohibited strategic exports and to stick to it; (4) to tie credits to specific projects; (5) the projects should be long-term so that there is a serious penalty in their termination; and (6) to end all government subsidies and guarantees for private bank credits to Eastern Europe.[137] In short, his recommendations in the 1980s are consistent with those in the early 1970s.

FORCE AND DIPLOMACY: DÉTENTE TESTED

For Kissinger détente was not incompatible with geopolitical competition since he believed that for Moscow peaceful coexistence was an offensive tactic to change the international system by means other than all-out war. Hence, his focus on US-Soviet relations did not prevent him from challenging Soviet encroachments in Jordan and Cienfuegos in 1970, in the October War in 1973, and in Angola since 1974. In his words: "they all represented – or seemed to us to represent – different facets of a global Communist challenge. None could have succeeded without Communist impetus or encouragement."[138] His response to these challenges was consistent with his belief that the Soviet strategy of ambiguity designed to overturn the global equilibrium by marginal changes can be defeated only by a policy of precaution; by nipping the Soviet moves in the bud before Soviet prestige became so deeply engaged that any US counter-measures increase the risk of war. Kissinger's actions in every crisis also demonstrated his beliefs in establishing a relationship between diplomacy and power and in taking risks.[139]

For Kissinger, the civil war in Jordan in September 1970, soon after the establishment of a Soviet combat presence in Egypt, was a Soviet attempt to alter the regional balance of power by radicalizing the Middle East through its encouragement of Iraqi and Syrian intervention on the side of the Palestinian guerrillas against King Hussein.[140] The Kissinger/Rogers controversy over the US response to the crisis revolved around the possible risks of Soviet reaction. In the NSC and WSAG meetings he opposed Rogers' suggestion that no military action be taken to support Hussein since it could lead to US-Soviet confrontation and pressed for the rapid buildup of the Sixth Fleet off the coast of Lebanon. Moreover, Kissinger rejected Rogers' demand that Nixon's pledges of support for Israeli action in support of Hussein be formally revoked when it appeared that the crisis was over and insisted on the continued buildup of the Fleet.[141] Kissinger prevailed since Nixon agreed that US credibility dictated support for Hussein.[142] The 1971 Report to Congress captured the essence of the controversy by declaring: "The discreet projection of American presence in the Mediterranean during the Jordanian crisis did not increase the chances of outside intervention. Rather it served as a reminder that outside intervention carried great risks." [143] Evident here is Kissinger's beliefs in using power and in taking risks.

The simultaneous Soviet attempt to construct a submarine base at Cienfuegos, despite the exchange of assurances in August that the 1962 Kennedy-Khrushchev understanding was in force, was also seen by Kissinger as a manifestation of Moscow's strategy of ambiguity. In his words: "I saw the Soviet move as going beyond its military implications; it was part of a process of testing under way in different parts of the world . . . I strongly favored facing the challenge immediately lest the Soviets misunderstand our permissiveness and escalate their involvement to a point where only a major crisis could remove the base." [144] But Nixon, fearing another Cuban crisis during the Congressional election, accepted Rogers' suggestion for quiet diplomacy to avoid a US-Soviet confrontation. [145] For Kissinger, acquiescence to the original installation only increased the risks in opposing its expansion. Press reports, however, following a Pentagon disclosure about the situation, forced Nixon to accept Kissinger's suggestion to challenge Moscow before the election. But while rejecting Laird's proposal for a public confrontation, Kissinger through warnings in the backchannel achieved the dismantlement of the installation and stoped subsequent Soviet efforts to service submarines from Cuban ports. [146]

The October War of 1973 demonstrated that the Basic Principles and the APNW did not change Kissinger's belief regarding the Soviet strategy of ambiguity since he considered the Soviet persistence in achieving them as an integral part of that strategy. His main objective during the war was to maintain US credibility by defending regional stability. Kissinger, fearing a Soviet-Arab collusion as in the 1970 Jordanian crisis, was determined to preclude an Arab victory with Soviet arms in order to convince the Arabs that the US was the key to peace. [147] In his words: "I never doubted that a defeat of Israel by Soviet arms would be a geopolitical disaster for the United States." [148] For Kissinger, because of the attack on the Presidency "we would need to show that we were determined to prevent Soviet intervention, but we had to do so in a low-key way conveying confidence without weakness." [149] Indeed, his belief that credibility requires a demonstration of power and will was manifest in his recommendations to the WSAG on October 6 to provide military aid to Israel and to move the US Sixth Fleet into the eastern Mediterranean. The fact that Kissinger tailored both actions to increased Soviet support for the Arabs reflects his belief that in the Middle East the USSR was the threat to peace. [150] Kissinger prevailed over efforts of the Departments of State and Defense which sought to delay the shipments to Israel to retain Arab goodwill and the supply of oil by asking at the WSAG meeting on October 13 for the resignations of the opponents of the airlift.[151] In addition, Kissinger pressured Portugal to get transit rights at Lajes airbase in the Azores to facilitate the airlift. On October 24, however, when Brezhnev's note to Nixon threatened to move troops in the Middle East unilaterally in response to Sadat's request for a joint US-Soviet force to stop the Israeli offensive and Moscow alerted its airborne troops and increased its ships in the area, Kissinger recommended to Nixon that the US forces be placed on alert.[152] On the same day WSAG ordered US forces to increase alert status to DEFCON 3 and to send two more carriers to eastern Mediterranean.[153] Rejecting the idea of a joint US-Soviet force because it would have a devastating impact on US relations with the PRC, the European Allies, and the moderates in the Middle East, all of whom feared a superpower condominium, Kissinger stated before the WSAG: "we were determined to resist by force if necessary the introduction of Soviet troops into the Middle East regardless of the pretext under which they arrived."[154] Publicly he warned Moscow that "we shall resist aggressive foreign policies. Détente cannot survive irresponsibility in any area, including the Middle East."[155] In his view, the demonstration of US power and will was vital since this was the first time Moscow threatened to introduce troops in a region not contiguous to the USSR and for reasons unrelated to the survival of a socialist regime. Indeed, the War Powers Act, passed on October 12, did not affect the consistency between Kissinger's beliefs and his recommendations.

Kissinger's actions in the Angola situation were also driven by the same beliefs. From 1974 to November 1975 he showed a relative lack of concern in Angola although through the 40 Committee he recommended, and Ford approved, covert military aid for FNLA and later UNITA.[156] Publicly he maintained that no US strategic interests were threatened by a purely internal struggle for power.[157] But between November 1975, when the Soviets began the airlift of arms and Cuban troops, and December, when the Senate banned covert aid for Angola, Kissinger began to see Angola as part of the US-Soviet geopolitical struggle and to warn Moscow publicly and in the backchannel that its actions, being incompatible with the Basic Principles, could threaten détente.[158] For Kissinger, Moscow's resumption of the airlift (suspended during the Congressional debate over covert aid) two days after the ban demonstrated the risks of the US refusal to intervene. His real fear was that Angola, being the first demonstration of US unwillingness to respond to Moscow's first attempt to impose militarily a Communist regime outside the immediate Soviet orbit, would set a precedent that "would have the gravest consequences for peace and stability,"[159] since it would undermine US credibility, the foundation of global stability. Declaring that: "the question is whether America still maintains the resolve to act responsibly as a great power – prepared to face a challenge when it arises," he warned: "the failure of the United States to respond effectively will be regarded in many parts of the world as an indication of our future [lack of] determination to counter similar Communist interventions."[160] In his view, "if the pattern is not broken now, we will face harder choices and higher costs in the future."[161]

Kissinger's beliefs regarding the Soviet strategy of ambiguity, the need to take risks, the need to establish a relationship between power and diplomacy, and the need to maintain the strategic balance were also evident in statements after January 20, 1977. Reiterating his view that Angola represented not a direct threat to US security, but an indirect long-term danger since the Soviets were permitted to intervene globally to change the local balance of power, he stressed; "we can no longer wait for dangers to become overwhelming, they will appear ambiguous when they are still manageable."[162] Kissinger maintained that "[h]ad we succeeded in Angola, there would have been no Ethiopia,"[163] and attributed the two invasions of Zaire, the establishment of a Soviet base in South Yemen, the invasion of Afghanistan, the Vietnamese occupation of Cambodia, the Soviet support of terrorist groups, and the massive delivery of Soviet arms to Central America, to the unwillingness of Congress to resist Moscow's intervention in Angola,[164] and Carter's pursuit of arms control without linkage to political issues.[165] Moreover, he warned that Soviet successes in Angola, Ethiopia, Iran, and Afghanistan are undermining the PRC's view of the US as the guardian of the global equilibrium and tempt it toward Moscow, if only to gain time, thus undermining the triangular balance and in turn global stability.[166] For Kissinger, Brezhnev's reiteration of the Soviet commitment to support struggles of liberation while negotiating arms limitations revealed the need to demonstrate US power and will to prevent Moscow from exploiting opportunities inherent in local conflicts to undermine the geopolitical equilibrium.[167] Indeed, he made his support for the ratification of SALT II conditional on the Senate's and Carter's explicit linkage of arms control to Soviet political restraint.[168]

In short, from 1969 to 1977, Kissinger's actions indicated that with a policy of precaution and the demonstration of power and will he sought to defeat Moscow's strategy of ambiguity designed to change the international system incrementally by avoiding all-out provocation (Cienfuegos) and by inducing lesser powers to do its fighting (Jordan, the October War, Angola). The Congressional ban on covert aid, however, revealed that he could not overcome the Western tendency to wait until the danger has grown overt; a tendency he believed had permitted Moscow to make political gains (Angola, Ethiopia, Afghanistan) unjustified by the relations of forces but made possible by the inward Western uncertainty as to whether these marginal changes in the geopolitical balance were worth the risk of an all-out war. Kissinger continues to reiterate his beliefs that US credibility is essential to global stability and that only the demonstration of US power and will to take risks can preclude the marginal changes in power that could eventually threaten Western survival.

CONCLUSION

This examination indicates that Kissinger's recommendations and/or actions while in office regarding US policy toward the USSR and the PRC were consistent with his beliefs as were his policy recommendations after 1977. The consistency was evident in the Administration's new approach to foreign policy. As outlined in the annual Reports to Congress the "New Strategy for Peace" reiterated Kissinger's beliefs: (a) that peace/stability was more than the absence of war, it must be based on an equilibrium of power and legitimacy; (b) that a stable order is not possible if a major power rejects it and pursues a revolutionary foreign policy in order to change it; (c) that the USSR and the PRC are revolutionary powers; (d) that Moscow's acceptance of the risk of nuclear war could lead only to limited cooperation to reduce it; and (e) that the real threat to stability emanates from the Soviet strategy of ambiguity and not from a Soviet nuclear attack. The Reports also reasserted his belief in the need to base the new strategy on the power-realist, the conceptual, the strategic, and the non-ideological/non-moralistic approaches, and in the need for strength, linkage, leadership, partnership, negotiations, and arms control. Moreover, consistent with Kissinger's belief that the East-West conflict will be protracted, the Reports, while noting the changes in the Communist bloc, warned against expectations of rapid progress and the illusion that the Communists have or are about to abandon their commitment to change the international system.

By focusing mainly on US-Soviet détente and then on US-PRC rapprochement, Kissinger was acting consistently with his beliefs that Soviet military power makes the USSR a greater threat to global stability than the PRC and that a stable international order requires both an equilibrium of power and legitimacy. To achieve the equilibrium of power he: (a) conceived of sufficiency which permitted him to support both new strategic programs to balance some of the military capabilities of the USSR and SALT to slow down the Soviet military buildup given the domestic opposition to new US weapons programs; and (b) strongly supported US-PRC rapprochement only after he realized that Moscow was intending to attack the PRC which he viewed as a counterbalance to the USSR in the Far East. Kissinger's search for an equilibrium of power was consistent with his belief in the power-realist approach. His insistence that the objective in both US-Soviet détente and US-PRC rapprochement was to adjust Moscow's and Peking's external goals and not to change the internal system of the PRC and the USSR reflected his belief in the non-ideological/non-moralistic approach to politics. As a power-realist he insisted that the Shanghai Communique declare that US-PRC rapprochement resulted from the common opposition to Moscow's geopolitical ambitions, a declaration also consistent with his belief that the USSR is a greater threat to peace than the PRC. His pursuit of US-PRC rapprochement before ideological changes in Peking and his opposition to publicly linking US-Soviet trade to the improvement of human rights in the USSR gave tangible expression to his belief in the non-ideological/non-moralistic approach to politics. Since 1977 Kissinger's recommendations have also been consistent with those beliefs. As a power-realist he advised both Carter and Reagan to base their policies toward the USSR and the PRC on geopolitical considerations and not on the fluctuations of US relations with either adversary and advocated the rearmament of the PRC to counterbalance the USSR. His advice that Reagan end his hostile rhetoric regarding the USSR was consistent with his belief in the non-ideological/non-moralistic approach to politics.

The rationale of Kissinger's recommendations and actions in support of new strategic weapons programs and his approach to SALT were also consistent with his other beliefs. His pursuit of strategic sufficiency demonstrated his belief that an adequate retaliatory force, not numerical superiority, is the key to peace – a belief also evident in his acceptance of inequality in launchers in SALT I and opposition to Defense Department's demands for "equal aggregates" in SALT II. Kissinger's insistence that SALT be linked to Soviet restraint in Vietnam, Berlin, and the Middle East and that ABM be linked to offensive weapons limitations, was consistent with both his beliefs in linkage and in the limited utility of arms control. The linkage of SALT to political issues also reflected his belief that Moscow's willingness to cooperate in arms control emanated from its acceptance of the risks of nuclear war and not from its abandonment of its revolutionary goal since it views peaceful coexistence as an offensive tactic to subvert the international system by means short of an all-out nuclear war. While Kissinger's requests that the Pentagon develop a more discriminating strategy for all-out nuclear war reflected his belief that such a war has ceased to be an instrument of policy, except as a last resort, his requests for developing strategies and capabilities to meet contingencies other than all-out nuclear war were consistent with his belief that only by establishing a relationship between power and the will to use it can the US defeat the more likely incremental threats to peace. Kissinger's willingness to slow down SALT until Moscow accepted the linkage between SALT and political restraint and simultaniety in offensive and defensive weapons was consistent with his belief in the need to avoid the quest for quick military and diplomatic victories in the protracted conflict with the USSR. His advice to Nixon not to trade ABM for a summit until Moscow accepted simultaniety and demonstrated restraint in Vietnam, and his own demands in his meetings in Moscow and Peking, were consistent with his belief that summits should be held only on the basis of a concrete program in order to break a deadlock, chart a new course, and ratify agreements. Kissinger's recommendations since 1977 reiterate some of the preceding beliefs. Reasserting the need to maintain the equilibrium of power, he made his support for the ratification of the SALT II treaty *entirely conditional* on the development of new defense programs and the explicit linkage between SALT and Soviet geopolitical restraint, and supported Reagan's insistence on linkage and his rearmament progam. However, he rejected the Reykjavik framework for resting global stability exclusively on arms control.

As a first step toward achieving legitimacy – the second structural imperative of a stable international system – Kissinger accepted the Soviet proposals which led to the agreements on the Basic Principles and the APNW. While his belief in linkage was evident in the fact that he pursued them only after progress was made in SALT and in the negotiations in Vietnam, his belief in maintaining the equilibrium of power was manifest in his insistence that these agreements include provisions for protecting US allies and the PRC. The agreements established a yardstick by which to measure Moscow's compliance with what he considered to be the permissible goals and methods of international conduct. But believing that stability does not depend on goodwill alone Kissinger tested the Soviet commitment to détente in Jordan, Cienfuegos, the October War, and in Angola. His willingness to use force reflected his belief that for Moscow peaceful coexistence is an offensive tactic to subvert the international system by means other than all-out nuclear war. His readiness in every crisis to both negotiate and use force were also consistent with his beliefs in the need to establish a relationship between diplomacy and power, that credibility requires a demonstration of power and political will, and in taking risks. Since 1977 the Western unwillingness to resist Moscow's expansionism has led Kissinger to reiterate those beliefs.

Moreover, consistent with his belief that to shape history a statesman must both provide and implement a vision, Kissinger personally undertook the opening to Peking and negotiated the major breakthroughs in SALT I and SALT II, the Basic Principles and the APNW, and the Shanghai Communique. His task of implementing his vision was facilitated by the fact the Nixon shared his beliefs regarding the USSR and the PRC and his notions regarding correct strategy and tactics.

9 Brzezinski and the Adversaries: the USSR and the PRC

Brzezinski's appointment led many to believe that the Carter Administration would focus less on the USSR and the PRC and more on trilateral cooperation, the Third World, nuclear non-proliferation, and the moral dimension of foreign policy. This belief rested on Brzezinski's criticism of the Nixon-Kissinger strategy for its excessive preoccupation with relations with adversaries, for its neglect of US relations with allies, and for its indifference to the less-developed countries and to moral imperatives and on Carter's reiteration of those criticisms during the campaign. But soon it became evident that Carter's national security policy was dominated by internal conflicts over its focus and, eventually, despite the campaign pledges, with America's Communist adversaries – the USSR and the PRC. Moreover, it appeared that normalization of US-PRC relations, US-Soviet relations, trilateral cooperation, and US-Third World relations were simply a series of badly executed improvisations that lacked an overall strategic conception. This chapter examines Brzezinski's impact on US policy toward the PRC and the USSR by analyzing the consistency between his operational code beliefs and his policy preferences and/or actions as it manifested itself in the rationale of policies in his memorandums to Carter, in official statements, in his approach to issues, and in his initiatives toward the PRC and the USSR. The impact of those beliefs on Brzezinski's behavior is also ascertained by examining their consistency with his policy recommendations after January 20, 1981. This chapter also underlines the similarities and differences between Brzezinski's proposals and/or actions and those of Kissinger.

THE NEED FOR ARCHITECTURE

In 1977, Carter came into office without a comprehensive, coherent strategy for conducting relations with the USSR and the PRC but with the determination to pursue SALT and, what Brzezinski called, a more comprehensive and reciprocal détente.[1] He believed that the improvement of the US-Soviet relationship was essential for facilitating the pursuit of his other goals, namely, achieving peace in the Middle East, advancing human rights, nuclear and conventional nonproliferation and arms reductions, promoting allied unity and cooperation, reactivating MBFR, and achieving a comprehensive test ban (CTB).[2] The Administration's efforts to develop a comprehensive national security strategy became evident in a number of speeches Carter gave in the spring and summer of 1977. The most definite outline of that strategy was presented by Carter in a speech at Notre Dame University on May 22, 1977. Declaring his belief in the appeal of democracy, Carter stressed: "I believe we can have a foreign policy that is democratic, that is based on fundamental values, and that uses power and influence . . . for humane purposes." Noting that "democratic methods are the most effective," he stated that improper tactics will not be used at home or abroad and that the foreign policymaking process will be open to the American people. Confident in US strength, he expressed the determination to seek "substantial mutual reductions in the nuclear arms race." Declaring his confidence in America's future, Carter stressed: "we are now free of that inordinate fear of communism which once led us to embrace any dictator who joined us in that fear," and led the US "to adopt the flawed and erroneous principles and tactics of our adversaries, sometimes abandoning our own values for theirs." Rejecting the "covert pessimism" of previous US leaders which had intensified the moral crisis produced by the Vietnam war, Carter reiterated the return of American confidence and optimism. But he also noted that while the fear of US-Soviet conflict had diminished, the competition has become more extensive. Emphasizing that "the world is still divided by ideological disputes, dominated by regional conflicts, and threatened by the danger that we will not resolve the differences of race and wealth without violence or without drawing into combat the major military powers," Carter stressed that we can no longer separate the traditional issues of war and peace from the new global questions of justice, equity, and human rights." For Carter, the US should not fear this new world, but should help to shape it by a new foreign policy "based on constant decency in its values and on optimism in our historical vision." The US must respond to the new reality of a politically awakening world by inspiring, persuading, and leading. Carter expressed his determination to "shape an international system that will last longer than secret deals" by an open, non-manipulative policy resting on five cardinal principles: (a) commitment to human rights; (b) joint efforts with Western democracies to "shape the wider architecture of global cooperation"; (c) working with the USSR to halt the strategic arms race and "produce reciprocal stability, parity, and security," and undertake joint efforts to aid the developing world; (d) commitment to achieving lasting peace in the Middle East; and (e) reducing the worldwide spread of nuclear and conventional weapons. Moreover, Carter revealed his desire to normalize relations with the PRC since it is "a key force for global peace."[3]

However, unlike Kissinger who controlled the writing of the foreign policy Reports to Congress, Carter's determination to control foreign policy personally and his commitment to collegiality made it much more difficult for Brzezinski to insert his beliefs in Carter's speeches without modifications despite his efforts to do so. Therefore, the Notre Dame and the other speeches reflected beliefs shared by all the principal policymakers. Nevertheless, the strategy outlined by Carter is notable: (a) for emphasizing Carter's and Vance's conviction in the necessity for stabilizing and improving US-Soviet relations through arms control and their reluctance to use force – a means Brzezinski believed to be essential for maintaining peace; and (b) for reiterating Brzezinski's beliefs in the moral and architectural approaches to foreign policy, in reciprocity as the bases of the US-Soviet relationship, and in the protracted nature of the East-West conflict. As Carter repeatedly warned: the differences in the competitive US-Soviet relationship "will not be solved easily. They will not be solved quickly."[4]

By the spring of 1978, however, Soviet intervention in Africa and the resulting criticism at home, compelled Carter to dispel, in his words, the myths that the US is unwilling to build its military strength and to use it to defend its friends and its global interests. On March 17, at Wake Forest University, in a major speech drafted under Brzezinski's direction, Carter strongly criticized Moscow's continuous buildup of strategic and conventional forces and "ominous inclination . . . to use its military power – to intervene in local conflicts, with advisers, with equipment, and with full logistical support and encouragement for mercenaries from other Communist countries." Emphasizing that functional equivalence in strategic forces allows Moscow to use its massive conventional forces for political blackmail to threaten US vital interests he declared: "We will match, together with our allies and friends, any threatening power through a combination of military forces, political efforts, and economic programs. We will not allow any other nation to gain military superiority over us." Reiterating his desire for cooperation with the USSR and other states for reducing regional conflicts, Carter noted his desire not to intervene militarily in other states as well as his determination to "oppose intervention by others." He announced that he will counterbalance Moscow's military power by: (a) "maintaining the strategic nuclear balance," stressing "our strategic forces must be – and must known to be – a match for the capabilities of the Soviets";

(b) "working closely with our NATO allies to strengthen and modernize our defenses in Europe"; and (c) "maintaining and developing forces to counter any threats to our allies and friends in our vital interests in Asia, the Middle East, and other regions of the world." However, once again, but less emphatically, he expressed the desire to "seek security through dependable, verifiable arms control agreements wherever possible."[5] The term détente was not used but US-Soviet cooperation was made conditional on restraint in the Soviet military buildup and international conduct.

In another speech at the Naval Academy on June 7, Carter reaffirmed his commitment to maintain the US nuclear and conventional strength and focused on Soviet intentions. Declaring that "our long-term objective must be to convince the Soviet Union of the advantages of cooperation and of the costs of disruptive behavior," he reasserted Brzezinski's beliefs that "efforts to cooperate do not erase the significant differences between us" because "To the Soviet Union, détente seems to mean a continuing aggressive struggle for political advantage and increased influence in a variety of ways. The Soviet Union apparently sees military power and military assistance as the best means of expanding their influence abroad." Stressing that "for a long-time" the US-Soviet relationship "will be competitive," Carter made an effort not to oversell détente. Moreover, reiterating Brzezinski's belief that "détente must be broadly defined and truly reciprocal" he offered Moscow "either confrontation or cooperation" since the US "is adequately prepared to meet either choice."[6] While Brzezinski maintained that the speech "was largely Carter's own handiwork" and that he only inserted his beliefs in reciprocity and the need for restraint, it is difficult not to note that Carter's definition of the Soviet view of détente was a reiteration of Brzezinski's conception of peaceful coexistence.[7]

Despite the reiteration of Carter's desire, although less emphatically, to pursue arms control and not use force, evident in Carter's speeches are Brzezinski's beliefs that Soviet military power and its use in regional conflicts is the greatest threat to peace, that Moscow's actions dictated an active US role and a willingness to match Soviet military power and to use force, and that the US must insist on a reciprocal and comprehensive détente.[8]

In summary, the shift in the Administration's strategy from emphasis on arms control and a reluctance to use force in 1977 to a greater willingness to match Soviet military power and use it to oppose Moscow's intervention in regional conflicts in 1978, reflects Carter's greater acceptance of Brzezinski's recommendations – an acceptance resulting from Moscow's intransigence in arms control and continuous use of its military power in the Third World. Nevertheless, the Vance/Brzezinski disputes emanating from Brzezinski's insistence and Vance's refusal to insert in Carter's elaboration of the Administration's strategy the code words reciprocal and comprehensive, reflect Brzezinski's conception of détente as being wider than arms control and his belief in the importance of Presidential speeches as a means for setting priorities and undertaking new initiatives. But despite the consistency in Brzezinski's recommendations, the strategy outlined by Carter reflected acrobatics rather than architecture.[9]

US-SOVIET RELATIONS: FROM DETENTE TO CONTESTATION

The evolution of US-Soviet relations under Carter from détente to contestation reveals that Carter approved a greater number of Brzezinski's recommendations due to Moscow's intransigence in the arms control negotiations and in particular its increasing military intervention in Third World conflicts. However, this was not evident in Carter's first letter to Brezhnev which outlined the basis on which he intended to approach the broad improvement of US-Soviet relations. The idea for the letter came from Brzezinski who, despite his criticism of the Nixon-Kissinger personal diplomacy, recognized Carter's desire for it and suggested that Carter pursue it by initiating private correspondence with Brezhnev and other world leaders. The letter, based on a draft from Vance, incorporated a number of Brzezinski's recommendations. Stressing that Carter was committed to the improvement of US-Soviet relations on "the basis of reciprocity, mutual respect and benefit," the letter assured Brezhnev that Carter shared his determination not to seek superiority in arms and emphasized three areas where progress could be made toward this goal: (a) the rapid conclusion of SALT; (b) an adequately verified comprehensive ban on nuclear tests, accompanied by greater openness about the respective strategic policies (inserted on Brzezinski's insistence); and (c) renewed efforts in MBFR. Declaring Carter's intention to actively seek a peaceful settlement to the Middle East and southern African conflicts, it stated his belief that Moscow can contribute to the achievement of progress toward peace in both of these critical areas. Moreover, it expressed Carter's hope for an early summit meeting. While the desire for an early summit and emphasis on arms control manifest Carter's faith in personal diplomacy and in arms control as "the best tool for improving [US-Soviet] relations" (a view shared by Vance), the insistence on reciprocity, on assistance in resolving regional conflicts, and on greater openess about strategic policies, manifests Brzezinski's beliefs that comprehensive détente dictates the linkage of Soviet geopolitical restraint to arms control and that secrecy on strategic matters hides Moscow's real objective to acquire military superiority with which to pursue its ultimate goal of a world-wide communist society. Indeed, Brzezinski reiterated those beliefs in preparing Carter for his first meeting with Dobrynin on February 1, and in his draft of the response to Brezhnev's reply.[10]

However, in 1980, Carter's desire for arms control had been reduced to abiding by the SALT II treaty's terms as long as Moscow did so and a promise to seek its ratification at the earliest opportune time.[11] His commitment not to seek military superiority had been replaced by the determination to do so. As he explained: "We must pay whatever price is required to remain the strongest nation in the world. That price has increased as the military power of our major adversary has grown and its readiness to use that power been made all too evident in Afghanistan."[12] Stating that "the Soviet invasion of Afghanistan is a threat to global peace, to East-West relations, and to regional stability and to the flow of oil," Carter declared: "we must have both the military power and the political will to deter our adversaries and to support our friends and allies."[13] Indeed, the declaration of the Carter Doctrine revealed that Carter's reluctance to use force had also been superseded by the determination to do so.[14] Moreover, Carter insisted that "Détente with the Soviets remains our goal, but détente must be build on a firm foundation of deterrence. The Soviets must understand that they cannot recklessly threaten world peace. They cannot commit aggression, and in doing that they must realize that they cannot still enjoy the benefits of cooperation with the West, and specifically with us."[15] In short, by 1980 Carter's declarations regarding US-Soviet relations revealed a greater acceptance of Brzezinski's recommendations regarding military power, the use of force, credibility, linkage, and détente.[16] But did Brzezinski's beliefs affect the evolution of the US-Soviet relationship beyond declaratory policy? To this question I now turn.

Maintaining the Military Balance

Carter's confidence in US military strength and his assurance to Brezhnev not to seek military superiority were inconsistent with Brzezinski's belief that such superiority is vital for preventing Moscow from blackmailing the US and its allies and for keeping dormant its revolutionary tendencies which could be reignited by foreign policy successes. On January 20, 1977, Carter approved Brzezinski's request for a comprehensive assessment of the US-Soviet strategic balance. PRM-10, issued on February 18 and completed in June under Brzezinski's guidance, reiterated his belief that while the US can compete with the USSR politically, economically, and ideologically, the momentum and character of Moscow's military buildup and its growing willingness to project its military power in the Third World makes the pursuit of a reciprocal and comprehensive détente impossible without first reversing the deteriorating strategic and conventional military balance. Indeed, Brzezinski's efforts to reverse that balance were manifest in PD-18, signed on August 24, 1977. Rejecting State's proposals that the US strategic forces be limited to an assured destruction capability, that reduction of US forces in Europe and Korea be considered, and that the uncertain military balance in the Indian Ocean-Persian region be addressed through arms control with Moscow, Brzezinski, with Brown's support, got Carter to direct in PD-18 that the US maintain "essential equivalence" in strategic forces, reaffirm NATO's strategy for forward defense, and maintain a "deployment force of light divisions with strategic mobility" for global contingencies in regions like the Persian Gulf and Korea; the latter being the NSC initiative for the Rapid Deployment Joint Task Force (RDJTF), better know as the Rapid Deployment Force (RDF).[17] PD-18 did not direct the reversal of the military balance but Brzezinski's recommendations reflected his belief that the US must maintain military superiority in order to pursue détente with the USSR.

Brzezinski's belief in military superiority was also evident in the debates regarding SALT II. He strongly urged Carter to approve the deployment of the new MX missile before the signing of SALT II. He maintained that without the deployment of new strategic weapons programs that would bring US forces to the level permitted by SALT I, Carter was placing the US at a strategic disadvantage given the growing accuracy of Soviet ICBMs. Indeed, in the fall of 1977, Brzezinski's cover memos reiterated views he advanced in his attacks of SALT I, namely, that in a protracted crisis Moscow could force the US to make significant political concessions. But Carter's decision on the MX was delayed by disputes over its basing mode which raised the issue of verification and in turn the possibility of not reaching an agreement in arms control. Moscow's rejection of the MX multiple aim point (MAP) basing proposal and opposition to the cruise missile reinforced Brzezinski's conviction that Moscow used SALT to lull the West in order to achieve military superiority. Hence, in August 1978, he sought to force a decision on the MX by using the Defense budget process to examine the viability of the strategic triad and to force some form of a budget decision by early 1979, and by undertaking an effort to refine the US strategic doctrine to include war-fighting as a necessary element of deterrence.[18] Brzezinski's efforts, however, to get support for the MX were hampered: (a) by Carter's uncertainty as to whether the US still needs a triad and his feeling that Brzezinski was partly responsible for creating the perception of Soviet superiority; and (b) by State's slight preference for a dyad over the triad and fear that any MX basing mode will complicate verification thus undermining SALT II.[19] Carter approved Brzezinski's recommendation, supported by Vance and the JCS, to develop the ten-warhead MX for ground mobile deployment since it increased the chances of SALT II ratification. The Administration could maintain that it offset to some extent the largest Soviet ICBM and gave the US the largest number of reentry vehicles allowed under SALT II, thereby enabling the US to retain its margin in overall deliverable nuclear weapons.[20] Brzezinski's efforts to get Carter's approval for the MX was consistent with his criticism of SALT I which in his view conceded numerical superiority to the USSR while dismissing the possibility that once the Soviets overcame their technological inferiority it will be difficult for the US to undo the asymmetry without a massive and very costly arms program.

Brzezinski's belief that the growing military power of the USSR made it the greatest immediate threat to global stability was manifest in his efforts to redefine US defense strategy. Having succeeded in 1977 in getting Carter's approval in PD-18 for what became the RDF, Brzezinski pressed the issue with the Pentagon. But having no success, in 1979 he sent Brown a number of Presidential requests for reports on the RDF's progress and returned them to Brown with Carter's marginal notes expressing dissatisfaction with the rate of progress. Brzezinski's pushing and Brown's support led (in March 1980) to the establishment of the RDF which, in his view, would permit the US to project its power rapidly into vital regions thus preventing Moscow from exploiting local conflicts to undermine the global equilibrium.[21] His support for the RDF reflected his belief that the ability to react quickly to numerous diverse situations to preclude faits accomplis is vital to global engagement

Moreover, concerned with the USSR's massive buildup of a conventional war-fighting capability, its development of a long-range deployment capability which it increasingly used in the Third World, and its movement toward a genuine nuclear-war fighting capability and doctrine, Brzezinski tried to get the Defense Department to review the US strategic doctrine and to interest Carter in it by asking Brown on March 31, 1977, for statements on US nuclear war doctrine, on the procedures for conducting war beyond the initial stage, and on the basic objectives to be achieved through limited nuclear options. To facilitate doctrinal innovation, in mid-1978 he strengthened the NSC staff dealing with military issues. The result was a series of PDs between September 1978 and July 1980 dealing with mobilization, defense, command and control for a protracted conflict, and with flexible use of US strategic and conventional forces for achieving objectives selected as the US engaged in conflict. Brzezinski's efforts reflected his beliefs that the greatest threat to peace is Soviet military power and that effective deterrence requires a doctrine which takes into account both the capabilities as well as the psychological-political predispositions and war doctrine of potential adversaries. In short, like Kissinger, Brzezinski through the PDs tried to give the US the capability and doctrine, at least theoretically, to manage a prolonged conflict with the USSR.[22]

In the 1980s, Brzezinski reasserted his belief that the historically enduring US-Soviet contest is not susceptible to a broad and quick resolution. Like Kissinger, Brzezinski continued to insist that for this contest the US needs a long-term strategy responsive to geostrategic needs and above all to maintain the US-Soviet strategic military balance – the prerequisite to peace. Noting the existence of an ambiguous strategic equivalence, Brzezinski reaffirmed his belief that since military power is the sole basis of the USSR's status as a global power the possibility exists that by the mid-1990s the continuation of the massive Soviet buildup in both offensive and defensive strategic forces might drastically alter the balance to the disadvantage of the US. He feared that vulnerability of US land-based strategic systems, communications, and command centers could lead to geostrategic paralysis in the US, thereby undermining the stability of the US-Soviet relationship.[23] Reasserting that in all other aspects of power the USSR is not even a truly competitive rival of the US, Brzezinski stressed that, once Soviet military power is checked, the USSR ceases to be a historically threatening rival. In his view, to neutralize Soviet military power the US "must maintain an integrated military capability for surface, sea, and space combat as the central point of departure for the waging of an enduring and consuming political contest for earth control."[24] In short, in a slightly altered form, he reiterated his belief in the need for military superiority to prevent the USSR from achieving a world-wide communist society. For Brzezinski, mutual strategic security should be both the US and the Soviet goal. To achieve this he recommended, among other things, the deployment of a prudent mix of offensive and defensive strategic systems and especially the deployment of a limited space-based strategic defense and, to permit it, he argued for the renegotiation of the ABM treaty and, if Moscow refused, its abrogation. Indeed, he supported SDI since it would permit the US to deny space control to Moscow, and stressing the centrality of technological superiority, he maintained that at the very least the US must maintain a technological edge sufficient to nullify Moscow's numerical advantage in weaponry. He continues to insist that the best deterrence to a nuclear war at any level is the development of a strategic doctrine and deployment of forces to insure greater flexibility in war-fighting options. He also repeated his recommendations for strengthening the RDF to defend the vulnerable southwestern strategic front. In short, his call for an integrated strategy combining mutual strategic security with conventional global flexibility to maintain extended deterrence, to deny Moscow a quick conventional victory in any Eurasian theater, and to ensure a conventional Soviet military defeat in a non-Eurasian conflict,[25] manifests Brzezinski's beliefs that military superiority and the will to use force are the prerequisites to American leadership in the world which he still sees as "the only alternative to . . . global anarchy and international chaos."[26]

Arms Control: SALT II

Carter's determination to pursue SALT II was shared by Vance and Brzezinski but for different reasons. Vance viewed SALT as a means for stabilizing US-Soviet relations and reaching a wider US-Soviet cooperation; thus he was prepared to make concessions to avoid a stalemate in the negotiations. He and Carter also agreed that SALT should not be linked to other issues in the relationship. Brzezinski, however, believing that SALT should be used as a means to reduce the momentum of the Soviet strategic buildup which permitted Moscow to exploit opportunities in the Third World, urged a slower pace and opposed the granting of concessions to bring Moscow into the negotiations – recommendations reflecting his belief in demonstrating political will. Moreover, convinced that détente should be reciprocal and comprehensive, he insisted on linking SALT to Soviet geopolitical restraint.[27] In his first on-the-record briefing on the US SALT proposal, on April 1, Brzezinski noted that if or when accepted, it could lead to a more stable and eventually more cooperative US-Soviet relationship, and stressed its strategic and political intentions and the fact that it was linked to a number of "other proposals designed to place the American-Soviet relationship not only on a more stable basis but to make the cooperative elements in [it] more comprehensive."[28]

In the NSC and SCC meetings, and in his policy recommendations in cover memos and reports to Carter, Brzezinki tried to convince both Carter and Vance to stand firm and not make concessions in the face of Soviet rejections. He feared that given Vance's desire to move fast on SALT and used it as a basis for a wider US-Soviet accommodation, he would make concessions in the negotiations.[29] Indeed, at the NSC meeting on March 22 to decide the US negotiating position, Vance was instructed to put forth the two US SALT proposals and remain firm in the case of Soviet rejection.

Convinced that Moscow would reject Carter's proposal for comprehensive deep cuts below 2000, Brzezinski did not support it. For him, however, Moscow's acceptance of Carter's proposal would have been a turning point in the US-Soviet relationship since it would have reduced the arms race and could have led to political and strategic stability. But he felt that to succeed Moscow had to be convinced by the US refusal to retreat to its fallback option that Carter was prepared to stand fast and, if necessary, to engage in an arms race.[30] Indeed, when Moscow rejected the US proposals in March and Vance, from Moscow, urged the submission of the fallback option, on Brzezinski's and Mondale's recommendation Carter rejected Vance's suggestion.[31] Brzezinski's efforts, supported by Brown and Hamilton Jordan, to convince Carter of the need to demonstrate political will by slowing down the pace of the negotiations and by rejecting Vance's and Paul Warnke's push for a more conciliatory approach never stopped.[32] Indeed, in his first news conference on SALT he stressed the need for "patience" and "persistence" – a suggestion reflecting his belief that the protracted East-West conflict makes negotiations a long-term process that would not bring immediate results in the reduction of tensions.

Brzezinski's suggestion that the US must seek modest cuts since Moscow was not likely to accept more than that, was accompanied by his advocacy of an NSC initiative for an ICBM freeze as a SALT option. In the SCC meetings he argued that while an early agreement on modest cuts would eliminate the Soviet quantitative superiority, an ICBM freeze would limit the momentum of Soviet ICBM modernization thus preventing the achievement of Soviet qualitative superiority. The proposed freeze at the current US level of 550 MIRVed ICBMs would have stopped the MX program which he supported but it would have slowed the Soviet deployment of SS-17s, SS-18s, and SS-19s (being below that level Moscow would have been allowed to build up to). His preferred options reflected his criticism of SALT I. Nixon and Kissinger, he had argued, conceded numerical superiority to the USSR on the spurious argument of US technological superiority and had stressed that this asymmetry could not be undone once Moscow erased its technological inferiority. For Brzezinski, the objective in SALT II was to stop the USSR from achieving both quantitative as well as qualitative superiority. Indeed, in his first news conference on SALT he stated that an ICBM freeze would reduce the level of competition both "qualitatively and quantitatively."[33] This he had argued was the problem with the Vladivostok accord negotiated by Kissinger and this was the reason he gave here in explaining Carter's rejection of that accord.

Carter, however, went for the comprehensive deep-cut option. Moscow's rejection of the US proposals at the Moscow talks on March 28–30, 1977, and refusal to table a counterproposal, generated widespread domestic and allied concern that détente was coming to an end; and Brzezinski feared that Carter's and Vance's public commitment to SALT might lead them to make concessions in order to save SALT and détente. In his view, only by waiting for Moscow's counterproposal would Carter convince Moscow that the US would not accept its concept of détente which permitted expansionism by proxy in the Third World just for an agreement on SALT.[34]

Brzezinski's belief that East-West negotiations must be approached with persistence and patience came into conflict with Carter's desire for an early summit to complete the SALT II negotiations; a desire Carter expressed repeatedly to the Soviets. But Brezhnev refused to commit himself to a summit until a SALT agreement was reached. Moscow's rejection of the US SALT proposal did not stop Carter from repeating his interest in a summit despite Brzezinski's suggestion not to do so. On Brzezinski's recommendation, however, on June 9, Carter proposed a less formal meeting in Alaska (similar to the Ford-Brezhnev meeting in Vladivostok). The idea for a meeting in Alaska had been suggested by Brzezinski repeatedly in 1968, in 1976, and publicly with Carter's approval in mid-April 1977, and it reflected his belief that regular, informal annual consultative meetings not tied to specific agreements make serious discussion of contentious issues possible without generating public expectations for a wide-ranging agreement. Indeed, this belief had led him to attack Nixon and Kissinger for using formal summits which led to the oversale of détente.[35] In July 1977, Carter, to generate greater momentum in US-Soviet relations, undertook another initiative through Averell Harriman. Harriman with Vance's encouragement, in a draft letter from Carter to Brezhnev, again raised the issue of a summit, perhaps at Camp David. Brzezinski, however, prevailed on Carter to redraft the letter into a proposal from Harriman himself to prevent the impression that a US-Soviet summit was a Soviet concession, thus intensifying the pressure on Carter to reciprocate. Brezhnev's rejection of the summit proposals, however, did not help Brzezinski in convincing Carter and Vance from raising the issue again.[36] In short, while Brzezinski's belief that détente must not be oversold led him to oppose Carter's repeated offers for a summit, his specific proposal for it reiterated his belief that regular informal meetings can be useful for clarifying intentions and reducing the risks of miscalculation.

In preparation for the Vienna summit on June 15–18, Brzezinski's recommendations to Carter reiterated his belief that détente to be reciprocal and comprehensive must not be limited to SALT. Dismissing Dobrynin's insistence that the summit be confined to SALT and rejecting Vance's view that the primary topic in the Carter-Brezhnev talks should be SALT the mutual acceptance of the status quo in the developed world and avoidance of confrontation in dealing with the Third World, Brzezinski urged Carter very strongly to discuss the state of the US-Soviet relationship as a whole, and stress the negative impact on détente of the continued Soviet military buildup and especially of Soviet direct or indirect military involvement in the Indian Ocean region. Consistent with his opposition to overselling détente, he emphasized to Carter that "the summit would be worthless" unless the Soviets understood the importance Americans placed on those issues and agreed to follow-up consultations on them. However, in view of Vance's reluctance to engage the Soviets on a broader dialogue that stressed that Moscow's military intervention in the Third World was incompatible with détente, Brzezinski hinted to Carter that he could undertake such a talk. Moreover, concerned with Carter's desire to push for concrete agreements on a large number of issues, Brzezinski urged him to limit the summit talks to regional restraint and arms control to prevent the overselling of détente. He also thwarted a plan by Blumenthal and Kreps to attend the summit fearing that their presence would generate expectations for a trade agreement which if not reached would have undermined domestic support for the SALT II Treaty. At the summit Carter reiterated Brzezinski's belief that Soviet geopolitical restraint must be linked to arms control in order to develop a reciprocal and comprehensive détente. But Brezhnev, rejecting linkage, refused to engage in such a dialogue.[37]

For Brzezinski the SALT II agreement was a success for imposing stricter limits on the USSR thus slowing the momentum of its military buildup. Under SALT II each side was limited to 2250 launchers both missiles and heavy bombers, 1320 being ALCM carriers and MIRVed missiles, 1200 being MIRVed missiles, 820 being MIRVed ICBMs, with 308 modern heavy missiles for the USSR only. Publicly Brzezinski stressed the fact that SALT II set equal ceilings, thus depriving the USSR of the numerical superiority it was granted under SALT I. In his words: "This negotiated principle of equality will require an actual reduction in the Soviet Union's intercontinental Forces." He also emphasized the fact that the limit on the number of warheads on each MIRVed ICBM simplified strategic planning and military projections, and that the treaty permitted each side to develop and deploy one new ICBM – for the US the MX which he strongly supported to reduce the growing vulnerability of the US ICBM force. For Brzezinski, "the SALT II treaty is not an agreement based on trust. It stands on its own merits based on common interest," reducing the risk of a nuclear holocaust. He repeatedly stressed that "the SALT II treaty will . . . not signal the end of the East-West competition. Where our interests are threatened, we shall defend them. And where we can broaden détente and achieve new forms of cooperation with the Soviet Union, we shall seek to do so as well. SALT II is not the end of military competition with the Soviet Union even in strategic arms." [38] To disarm the treaty's critics Brzezinski was publicly claiming that SALT II was not linked to the internal and external actions of the USSR, [39] but his support of Carter's decision on January 3, 1980, to postpone the treaty's ratification since the Soviet invasion of Afghanistan had killed the Senate's support reflected his belief that a reciprocal and comprehensive détente dictates above all the linkage of Soviet geopolitical restraint to arms control. Moreover, on being told of Carter's decision he reassured him that since the invasion was "the most direct case of Soviet military aggression since 1945" a broader strategic response was required, and tried to convince him, repeatedly after that, that "you first have to be a Truman before you are a Wilson" – a reflection of his belief that Soviet military interventionism dictates the enhancement of US credibility by demonstrating political will.[40]

In the 1980s, like Kissinger, Brzezinski continued to warn that since Moscow is using arms control as a political tool to promote US strategic impotence, it should not be viewed in isolation but as an integral part of US national defense policy which seeks to deny Moscow a politically decisive military edge and it should be linked to Soviet geopolitical restraint. He reasserted that future comprehensive arms control agreements must shift from quantitative reductions to qualitative limitations. However, seeing this as an unattainable goal since a truly historical transformation of the US-Soviet relationship is unlikely, he declared that the US must seek narrowly focused, highly specific interim agreements, especially on first-strike systems. Insisting on genuine verification, including some form of on-site inspection for mobile missiles, he repeated his suggestion that the US must publicly insist on the lifting of Soviet strategic secrecy since it is incompatible with genuine and confidence building arms control. For Brzezinski, as for Kissinger, the main obstacle to a genuine arms control agreement is the lack of US strategic arms programs with which to bargain with the USSR.[41] Indeed, he views SDI as "a major source of leverage" and "the principal catalyst" for the limited progress on START made at Reykjavik and opposes the Democratic Party's advocacy for a nuclear freeze. His belief in linkage and in summits without fanfare led him to criticize the Reykjavik summit because: (a) it did not link Soviet geopolitical restraint to START; and (b) Reagan took the Soviet bait and engaged in a competition of "non-nuclear visions of the future" which are unrealistic as long as the political conflict persists. Brzezinski still insists on linkage and on summit meetings scheduled well in advance to routinize the process thus preventing excessive expectations in US-Soviet relations.[42]

Human Rights and US-Soviet Trade

Carter's campaign pledge to promote human rights was reiterated in his speeches in 1977 but it was not explicitly linked to US-Soviet relations. The speeches stressed that the human rights policy was universal in application and called for the strengthening of the international machinery responsible for human rights.[43] In policy debates, however, Brzezinski repeated his belief that the appeal of American democracy and the declining appeal of Communism made active support for human rights a vital asset for mobilizing world opinion thus focusing global attention on the glaring internal weakness of the Soviet system. His reports to Carter suggested that insistence on human rights be part of the ideological/moral competition and "an opportunity to put the Soviet Union ideologically on the defensive."[44] These suggestions reflected his belief in the moral approach in foreign policy and his criticism of Kissinger for refusing to publicly insist on the improvement of human rights in the USSR. Carter, however, in speeches and letters to Brezhnev, reassured Moscow that his commitment to human rights was not an attempt to interfere in its internal affairs, and expressed the hope that Moscow would observe the Helsinki accords.[45] For further reassurance Carter wrote Brezhnev that we "welcome private, confidential exchanges" on human rights in the hope of achieving results – an action inconsistent with his and Brzezinski's criticism of Kissinger's pursuit of human rights by quiet diplomacy but consistent with Vance's desire for this approach.[46] But efforts to reassure Moscow failed when Carter felt compelled, having criticized Ford's refusal to meet Alexander Solzhenitsyn, to respond to a letter from Andrei Sakharov which drew attention to the human rights violations in the USSR. The fact that Carter's response stressed the global character of the human rights policy did not convince Moscow which saw Carter's personal pledge to Sakharov to promote human rights in the USSR as interference in its internal affairs and stepped up the suppression of human rights activists.[47] Carter's efforts to reassure Moscow stopped in June 1978 when he publicly attacked Moscow for violating human rights despite its signing of the Helsinki accords.[48]

Brzezinski's fear that Moscow was achieving selective détente due to Carter's and Vance's refusal to link SALT II to Soviet intervention in the Horn, to US-Soviet trade, and to human rights was evident in his February 17, 1978, weekly report which urged linkage and, specifically, "continued insistence on human rights as part of the ideological competition." [49] In July 1978, however, to remove a needless irritant in US-Soviet relations created by the imprisonment of some leading human rights activists, Brzezinski sought and obtained Carter's approval for initiating exploratory talks with Dobrynin regarding the possible exchange of two Soviet UN employees charged with espionage for leading human rights activists. By April 1979, in their consultative meetings, he and Dobrynin agreed to exchange the two Soviet spies for five human rights activists. In this case, his approach was inconsistent with his attacks on Kissinger for dealing with human rights through backchannel initiatives. However, prior to this agreement, Brzezinski, despite Soviet appeals to postpone the trial of the two UN employees, convinced Carter to reject State's preference not to convict them for fear that Soviet reprisals would undermine the US-Soviet relationship. He maintained that only by insisting on issues such as human rights could the US achieve a comprehensive détente. Brzezinski's advice reflected his beliefs in reciprocity and in the need to demonstrate political will. [50]

Moreover, in the summer of 1978, Moscow's decision to put on trial Anatoly Shcharansky and Aleksander Ginzburg permitted Brzezinski to explicitly link human rights to US-Soviet trade. This action provoked widespread public outrage and Carter's domestic advisers urged him to personally take the lead in responding. On July 8, a meeting chaired by Brzezinski recommended the adoption of some restraints on technology transfer. But Vance, Blumenthal, and Commerce Secretary Juanita Kreps, while agreeing to criticizing Moscow's action, opposed any trade restraints. Brzezinski, supported by Brown and the domestic advisers, prevailed on Carter to impose restraints on the transfer of technology on July 18. [51] He strongly opposed attempts by the Departments of the Treasury, Commerce, and State to undermine Carter's decision by administrative fiat and by new trade initiatives. Carter's belief in collegiality, however, made his efforts to use linkage much more difficult than Kissinger's, and he would not have succeeded without the support of Schlesinger and Brown who maintained that national security dictated a revision of the decision by Commerce to approve the Dresser licenses applications for a drill-bit factory and an electron-beam welder that Carter's decision had deferred. Brzezinski also prevailed on Carter to reject a request by Vance, Blumental, and Kreps, on November 18, for an NSC meeting to review the policy on US-Soviet trade and examine means to enhance the scope of economic cooperation. [52] Moreover, in March 1979, Brzezinski opposed a proposal by Vance and Blumenthal to simultaneously grant MFN status to the PRC and the USSR. Here, his efforts were facilitated by the Senate's insistence on linking MFN status to the human rights in the USSR and Moscow's rigidity in SALT, its support of military actions by Vietnam, and its exploitation of anti-Americanism in Iran and increasing military intervention in Afghanistan.[53] Brzezinski's efforts to link human rights to trade restraints was consistent with his belief that trade must be increased only in the context of a genuinely improving overall US-Soviet relationship since increased trade by helping the Soviet economy reduces pressures for reforms thus buttressing the Soviet political system.

In the 1980s, Brzezinski's obsession with Soviet military power has not been matched by an equal insistence for reducing human rights violations. An indication that while he sees the issue as a useful means in the US-Soviet ideological contest due to the convergence of increasing global demands for equity and human rights with the decline in the appeal of Soviet ideology and increasing public knowledge of Soviet human rights violations, he still believes that the prerequisite to using any other means in the US-Soviet rivalry is the maintenance of the global military equilibrium. Nevertheless, he criticized Reagan's agenda for the summit at Reykjavik since it failed to explicitly link arms control to human rights initiatives.[54]

FORCE AND DIPLOMACY: DETENTE TESTED

Brzezinski's beliefs that a reciprocal and comprehensive détente requires Soviet geopolitical restraint, and that this can be achieved only by the use of linkage and by the demonstration of power and political will to defend vital US interests, were manifest in his recommendations and actions regarding the response to the Soviet-Cuban intervention in the Horn of Africa, the Soviet brigade in Cuba, and the Soviet invasion of Afghanistan.

In the summer of 1977, Soviet efforts to exploit through Cuban proxy the territorial conflict in the Horn of Africa led to a Vance/Brzezinski dispute about the US approach to US-Soviet relations. Rejecting Vance's view that the Somali-Ethiopian conflict was a purely local issue that required a US-Allied collective diplomatic response and that in the long-run the Ethiopians would oust the Soviets as Egypt and Sudan had done, Brzezinski, in view of the Soviet-Cuban intervention in Angola and expansion of the Soviet military presence in South Yemen, maintained that Moscow's support of Cuban activities in Ethiopia presented a major threat to vital US interests in the Arabian peninsula.[55] At the end of the summer, with increasing evidence of Soviet intervention he promoted, despite Vance's objections, a State-chaired PRC meeting on the issue which recommended, and Carter approved, to accelerate steps to reassure and strengthen Sudan and Kenya and to explore means of convincing African leaders to condemn the Soviet-Cuban military presence. To warn the Soviets he briefed the press on the dangers of expansionism for détente and he prevailed on Carter to direct Andrew Young on November 22 to condemn the Soviet-Cuban intervention in Africa in the UN. The growing airlift of Cuban troops and Soviet arms into Ethiopia led Brzezinski, on December 14, to personally warn Dobrynin that its continuation would force the US to stop restraining regional powers from sending in their troops. Indeed, he supported Sadat's offer to deploy Egyptian troops in Somalia, which did not happen perhaps due to the US reluctance to provide logistical and financial support. Moreover, he opposed Gromyko's suggestion for a joint US-Soviet mediation fearing that it would create the impression of a condominium while legitimizing the Soviet presence in the Horn. Instead, he proposed that greater efforts be made to get regional leaders to call for a withdrawal of all foreign troops and for mediation by African states alone.[56]

In mid-January 1978, with the increasing Soviet involvement in Ethiopia, Brzezinski started to convene frequent SCC meetings on the grounds that the issue was gradually escalating into a crisis to convince the Administration of the seriousness of the situation. He argued that it was necessary to make the war increasingly costly both politically and militarily to convince Moscow that, unlike Angola, a more conciliatory attitude later would not lead to US adjustment to the consolidation of the Soviet presence.[57] To do this Brzezinski urged the deployment of an aircraft carrier task force near Ethiopia to signal the US willingness to defend its vital interests and thus maintain its credibility in the region and the encouragement of friendly states to supply Somalia with non-US origin weapons. But Vance and Brown opposed the use of the task force fearing that the unwillingness to use it if Ethiopia invaded Somalia would damage the credibility of such a force in a future crisis and Carter rejected Brzezinski's suggestion.[58] He insisted that Moscow be "unambiguously but quietly advised" of the destructive impact its intervention would have on US-Soviet relations and reminded that the US had restrained its actions in areas of concern to it, namely, the transfer of military technology to the PRC because Carter wanted to develop "a genuinely comprehensive détente."[59] The rationale for his proposals to threaten the use of force and to transfer technology to the PRC was evident in his weekly reports to Carter on February 9 and 17. The first, entitled "Strategic Deterioration," warned that Moscow's success in the Horn would be dangerous to US-Soviet relations because: (a) it would demonstrate the USSR's capacity and will to assert itself in the Third World; and (b) it would encourage Libya, Algeria, and Cuba to act more aggressively. It stressed that through Angola and Ethiopia, Moscow "will be demonstrating that containment has now been fully breached." The second report emphasized that since Carter came into office Moscow has been cooperating in those functional areas likely to cement a parity relationship with the US, but has not been accommodating in ideological and political areas; in fact it is quite prepared to exploit regional conflicts. It concluded, that the USSR "is seeking, and apparently has had some success in obtaining, a selective détente." To prevent further Soviet successes it suggested continued insistence on human rights as part of the ideological competition, countercampaigns on interventionism, and more affirmative political initiatives toward the PRC.[60] In short, it reiterated his belief that Nixon and Kissinger should have linked SALT I and functional cooperation to human rights and other issues to achieve a reciprocal and comprehensive détente.

Concerned that the situation in the Horn and the failure to exploit politically the US favorable position in the US-Soviet-PRC triangle would further deteriorate the US global position, Brzezinski warned Carter he could lose SALT II and the ability to deal with other issues. Indeed, on March 1, he publicly linked the Soviet military involvement in Ethiopia to the wider US-Soviet relationship, and especially to SALT II, by declaring: "We are not imposing any linkage, but linkages may be imposed by unwarranted exploitation of local conflict for larger international purposes" – a reiteration of his belief that by indirect expansion Moscow was trying to achieve a world-wide communist society. On March 2, Carter reiterated that linkage by stating that Soviet intervention and SALT II "are linked because of actions by the Soviets. We don't initiate the linkage." But Vance, fearful of losing SALT, on the same day, declared before the Senate Foreign Relations Committee: "There is no linkage between the SALT negotiations and the situation in Ethiopia."[61] Carter, however, despite his initial rejection of linkage and Vance's strong opposition to it, in his speeches began to reiterate Brzezinski's recommendations.[62]

The "discovery" of a Soviet brigade in Cuba in late July 1979 led Brzezinski to reiterate his beliefs that a reciprocal and comprehensive détente required Soviet geopolitical restraint not arms control alone, and that this could be achieved only by demonstrating US power and political will. Initially, Brzezinski concluded that the brigade did not violate previous US-Soviet understandings, but warned Carter of the negative impact it would have on SALT and reiterated his recommendation to increase pressure on Cuba and the USSR and to stress the incompatibility of their global expansionism with a stable détente. But like Kissinger in the Cienfuegos issue in 1970, Brzezinski seeing no immediate strategic threat deemphasized the brigade issue itself. Indeed, since control of the issue by SCC would have implied a crisis, he let it be handled by the Policy Review Committee. Convinced that Moscow would not accept a public defeat as it did in 1962, to preclude a crisis in US-Soviet relations he proposed that Vance quietly resolve the issue with the Soviets. Once the issue became public, however, and Senators linked the brigade's withdrawal to SALT ratification, Vance called for its immediate withdrawal but insisted in confining the issue to Cuba itself. In his view, a tough public posture without linkage would satisfy the Senators' demands and thus save SALT II. He also strongly opposed Brzezinski's proposal to establish military ties with the PRC. But Brzezinski felt that only by focusing attention on world-wide Soviet expansionism by Cuban forces would Carter be able to deemphasize the brigade issue itself and save SALT. Indeed, he urged Carter to stress the need for defense increases without any reference to SALT, to condemn the Soviet-Cuban activities in the Third World, to intensify worldwide US efforts to ostracize Cuba, especially by pressuring the West Europeans, to develop a dialogue with Peking on technology transfer and military issues, and to increase Voice of America broadcasts to Soviet minorities.[63]

Convinced that US credibility would suffer as a result of combining public demands for withdrawal with the unwillingness to act, Brzezinski declared that the brigade issue was analogous to the Berlin Wall crisis of 1961. Hence, since Moscow would not withdraw the brigade the US must indicate that while it was unacceptable the US could live with it. Moreover, believing that credibility dictated the demonstration of political will, Brzezinski opposed Vance's recommendation to convene a group of senior statesmen to advice Carter on the issue which, in his view, provided an opportunity to establish Carter's credentials as a tough-minded Truman-type leader by focusing world attention on Moscow's use of Cuban forces to promote Soviet strategic objectives in the Third world.[64] But Carter, sharing Vance's fear of losing SALT II, in an address on October 1, 1979, while noting that Moscow "must take" responsibility for escalating Cuban military actions abroad, stressed the "overwhelming mutual concern in preventing a nuclear war" and urged ratification of SALT II. Emphasizing his "determination to give a measured and effective response to Soviet competition and to Cuban military activities around the world," Carter outlined steps taken to defend US interests, but declared: "the brigade issue is certainly no reason for a return to the cold war."[65] For Brzezinski, Carter's refusal to link SALT to Soviet geopolitical restraint demonstrated his lack of political will and led him to consider resignation[66] – a reflection of his beliefs that détente

must not be limited to SALT alone and in the need to demonstrate
political will.

Brzezinski's efforts to commit the US to a tougher and a wider response
to Soviet expansionism in the Third World was also manifest in his
suggestions regarding the US reaction to the increasing Soviet military
intervention in Afghanistan. In the spring of 1979, in the morning national
security briefings, he repeatedly warned Carter that, given Moscow's
historical push to the south, Soviet dominance in Afghanistan would
permit Moscow to promote a separate Baluchistan, which would give
it access to the Indian Ocean while dismembering Pakistan and Iran.
Carter's response was to instruct Vance to brief Afghanistan's allies on
the situation which Vance did reluctantly. Vance's reluctance to formally
register US concern over the Soviet intervention and to aid the resistance
in Afghanistan, and Moscow's disregard of warnings that its actions would
damage détente, led Carter to permit Brzezinski himself to publicize the US
concern. He also asked Brzezinski to prepare contingency options in the
event of an overt Soviet military intervention.[67] Concerned that Vance's
inaction was undermining US credibility, Brzezinski in his weekly report
on September 13, entitled "Acquiescence vs Assertiveness," criticized the
State Department for the misperception that in the US-Soviet relationship
the USSR was the more assertive power and recommended that the US
defense buildup be publicly justified as essential in view of the Soviet
military buildup, not as an attempt to save SALT II. He also proposed that
the US explicitly and strongly condemn the Soviet-Cuban expansionism,
ostracize Cuba and widely share intelligence about its activities, transfer
sensitive technology to the PRC and develop a US-PRC military dialogue,
expand broadcasts to the Moslems and Ukrainians in the USSR, and
initiate a wider US-Soviet dialogue which stressed the need for "reciprocal
restraint." But despite Carter's orders Vance opposed Brzezinski's efforts
to publicize Moscow's expansionism in order to mobilize the Islamic world
and his attempts to assist the resistance in Afghanistan.[68] The invasion
of Afghanistan on December 25, while permitting Brzezinski to bypass
a Policy Review Committee scheduled meeting and take control of the
issue through the SCC, which was also dealing with the crisis in Iran,
did not end Vance's opposition to linkage to save SALT II and détente.
On December 26, Vance and Christopher opposed Brzezinski's proposal
that an urgent Presidential message to Brezhnev declare that the invasion
jeopardized SALT II and affected the scope of the US-PRC relationship.
For Brzezinski the invasion had initiated "a regional crisis of strategic
significance" and presented an opportunity to demonstrate Carter's political will thus strengthening US credibility. Therefore, he called Carter

at Camp David and recommended an NSC meeting to deal with it. At the NSC meeting on December 28, Carter toughened Brzezinski's proposed message to Brezhnev. Calling the invasion "a clear threat to the peace," he decided to reassure Pakistan despite disagreements over nuclear nonproliferation, and to increase cooperation with Saudi Arabia and Egypt regarding Afghanistan.[69]

Brezhnev's assertion that the Soviets were invited into Afghanistan, led Carter to accept Brzezinski's recommendation for a wider response to the strategic challenge in the Persian Gulf. In a series of NSC meetings between December 30 and January 3 to decide the US response, Brzezinski urged the transfer of technology or even defensive arms to the PRC, tougher controls on technology transfer to the USSR and a large aid package for Pakistan while Vance proposed reinstating the draft and a deep cut in US grain deliveries to the USSR. Vance, Christopher, and Cutler opposed Brzezinski's recommendations while Mondale opposed the grain cut fearing it would damage Carter in the forthcoming Iowa primary. Vance also opposed Mondale's proposal to withdraw from the Summer Moscow Olympics.[70] On January 4, in an address to the nation, Carter reiterated most of Brzezinski's recommendations. Stating that "this invasion is an extremely serious threat to peace – because of the threat of further Soviet expansion into neighboring countries in Southwest Asia, and also because such an aggressive military policy is unsettling to other people, throughout the world," he declared "we must recognize the strategic importance of Afghanistan to stability and peace. A Soviet-occupied Afghanistan threatens both Iran and Pakistan and is a stepping stone to possible control over much of the world's oil supplies." Carter maintained that if Moscow dominated Afghanistan and adjacent states "the stable, strategic and peaceful balance of the entire world will be changed." Therefore, he announced that he asked the Senate to defer the ratification of SALT II, and decided to severely restrict trade with the USSR by stopping the sale of high technology and other strategic items, by curtailing fishing privileges in US waters, and by not delivering 17 million tons of grain. He also announced that all US-Soviet official exchanges were suspended, that the US might not participate in the Moscow Summer Olympics if Moscow's aggression continued, that military and other aid will be given to Pakistan, and that other states in the region would be assisted in a similar way.[71]

In the State of the Union address on January 23, Carter declared:

Let our position be absolutely clear: An attempt by any outside force to gain control of the Persian Gulf region will be regarded as an assault on the vital interests of the United States of America, and such an assault will be repelled by any means necessary, including military force.[72]

Carter also declared that "we are prepared to work with other countries in the region to share a cooperative security framework that respects differing values and political beliefs, yet which enhances the independence, security, and prosperity of all."[73] Carter's declarations were Brzezinski's recommendations. He specifically urged Carter to emulate Truman's response to the Soviet threat to Turkey and Greece since a declaration of US willingness to intervene would enhance US credibility thus strengthening the determination of states to oppose Soviet intervention.

The Carter Doctrine, (as the declaration became known), reflected Brzezinski's belief that continuous US involvement in the world was essential for peace. Moreover, it formally recognized his belief that US security was interdependent with the security of three central and interrelated strategic zones, namely, Western Europe, the Far East, and the Middle East-Persian Gulf area. For Brzezinski, Soviet control of the oil around the Gulf would permit Moscow to blackmail both Western Europe and the Far East.[74] Following Carter's addresses, Brzezinski, in confidential meetings with allied and friendly governments, tried to prevent the impression that the US might reconsider its actions thus maintaining support for the sanctions, and strongly opposed Vance's suggestions for reviving détente. However, to reduce tension he also proposed that an international force from neutral Islamic states replace the Soviets in Afghanistan to give Moscow a way out.[75]

In the 1980s, the US-Soviet contest has been Brzezinski's main preoccupation. Like Kissinger, he insists that the US must respond effectively to key regional crises that provide opportunities for Moscow's intervention. Consistent with his beliefs that Moscow is still committed to achieve a world-wide communist society and that external defeats are the greatest stimuli for promoting significant change within the USSR, he declared: "it is critically important that each [US] initiative be carefully designed to promote the central American objective of checking the outward thrust of Soviet power and of gradually altering the manner in which the Soviet Union conducts the rivalry." The USSR must be convinced that "instead of trying to recast the world in its own image, [it] should increasingly join in coping with the world as it actually is."[76] To deal with the third central strategic front – southwest Asia – Brzezinski reiterated that the US must reinforce the resilience against Soviet advances by giving more military aid to Pakistan, by gradually improving relations with Iran, by assisting the resistance in Afghanistan while probing for Soviet willingness to withdraw, by diplomatically pushing forward the Arab-Israeli peace process, and particularly the resolution of the Palestinian problem, and by stimulating a more distinctive political consciousness among Soviet Muslims through radio broadcasts and other means as a deterrent to further Soviet absorption of Islamic peoples.[77] For dealing with the Central American crisis emanating from the antiquated social and political structures and from the entrance of "an alien ideological power" – the USSR – through the Cuban and Nicaraguan revolutions, he suggested that the US must: (a) advance regional economic development and a more solid base of political democratization; (b) exert every effort, including the use of force, to obtain the external neutralization and internal self-determination of Nicaragua; and (c) be ready to apply force immediately if the Soviets or Cuba intervened militarily to suppress the opposition in Nicaragua. Brzezinski was especially concerned that a merger of the wider crisis in Central America with a crisis in Mexico would be exploited by Moscow thus opening up a fourth central strategic front.[78] But he criticized the new doctrine of an anti-Communist liberation struggle because it links two conflicts directly involving the interests of the superpowers – Afghanistan and Nicaragua – with peripheral conflicts – Angola and Kampuchea – thus diverting public attention from the important foci of the long-term US-Soviet confrontation.[79] To deprive Moscow of opportunities to expand its influence, he also stressed the need to intensify efforts to accelerate a racial accommodation in South Africa,[80] and to actively intervene to promote long-term economic and political stability in the Philippines.[81] However, believing that the US-Soviet conflict is protracted, Brzezinski emphasized that the US must take a long-term approach and pursue its objectives steadily over several decades. On the whole, while accepting the need for diplomatic and economic means in dealing with the causes of regional conflicts, like Kissinger, Brzezinski continues to insist that Soviet geopolitical restraint can be induced only with the demonstration of US power and political will.

A TRIANGULAR BALANCE: NORMALIZATION OF US-PRC RELATIONS

The normalization of relations with the PRC became a key strategic goal of Brzezinski since it would have greatly enhanced the stability of the Far East thus helping the US in the global US-Soviet contest. This, however, was not evident in the pre-inaugural "informal" NSC meetings where he was pre-occupied with the US-Soviet relationship. Indeed, Vance, not Brzezinski, asked for a study on US-PRC normalization shortly after the inauguration and on April 15, in a memo to Carter, argued that "in terms of our strategic position, normalization is highly desirable." However, stressing that "we should do more" on this issue,[82] Vance warned that establishing a security relationship with Peking as Brzezinski and Brown were suggesting "would pose real risks" in relations with Moscow and Tokyo.[83] Despite his initial disinterest in normalization, Moscow's exploitation of local conflict in Angola, Ethiopia and Yemen led Brzezinski to urge rapid normalization and gave it a great deal of personal attention to make Moscow "understand the value of restraint and reciprocity." Rejecting Vance's view that there be no linkage between SALT and Soviet geopolitical restraint, he maintained that the US should not be excessively deferential to Moscow's concern about US-PRC collaboration. Indeed, Brzezinski admitted that in dealing with US-PRC normalization he thought "a great deal" of the Soviet dimension despite public statements that it had nothing to do with US-Soviet rivalry and that the timing of it was "definitely influenced by the Soviet dimension"[84] – an admission reflecting his belief that the USSR was a greater threat to global stability than the PRC.

Brzezinski's initial hesitation in urging normalization reflected his belief that the PRC was a long-range threat to peace; a belief that had led him to attack Nixon for neglecting the revolutionary nature of the PRC and focusing exclusively on the anti-Soviet aspect of the opening to Peking. Indeed, he wondered whether a strategic connection could be promoted without normalization, convinced Moscow would reduce its expansionism for fear of driving the US into a greater security cooperation with Peking.[85] In the spring of 1977, however, Brzezinski began to reiterate Kissinger's belief that a strong and secure PRC was in the US interest since it helps to maintain the global equilibrium, a requisite of peace. On his recommendation, Carter reiterated this belief in the Notre Dame speech on May 22, 1977, by declaring:

> It is important that we make progress toward normalizing relations with the People's Republic of China. We see the American-Chinese relationship as a central element of our global policy, and China as a key force for global peace. We wish to cooperate closely with the creative Chinese people on the problems that confront all mankind, and we hope to find a formula which can bridge some of the difficulties that still separate us.[86]

Responding with an invitation to dinner for Brzezinski, which Carter approved, the PRC began a closer personal relationship with him.[87]

Endorsing as a point of departure the reaffirmation of Nixon's five points as a "pledge" to Peking, Brzezinski recommended that the relationship involve: (a) the expansion of bilateral contacts; (b) quiet consultations to further the common strategic objective of discouraging Soviet expansionism; and (c) normalization to be moved forward whenever opportune.[88] However, sharing Kissinger's belief that US credibility is vital in dealing with Peking, Brzezinski urged Carter to enhance it by demonstrating his political will in policies toward Cuba, Vietnam, Korea, Iran, Turkey, and southern Africa. Concerned that Vance's trip to Peking in August might not make any progress toward normalization, he suggested that the PRC's receptivity for a strategic dialogue be tested by proposing a visit by Brown in the late spring of 1978. To improve bilateral relations, Brzezinski urged the creation of an ad hoc committee to be chaired by him and Frank Press, Carter's science and technology adviser, to examine the granting of four out of thirty pending export licences to Peking – an action inconsistent with his criticism of Nixon and Kissinger for excluding Rogers from the opening to Peking. Although pledges of collegiality by Carter and him made Vance's total exclusion impossible, like Kissinger, he sought to limit Vance's impact on policy toward Peking by creating a new committee under his control to direct initiatives. He also encouraged trade, as Nixon and Kissinger did, to convince Peking the US was interested in a strategic relationship. But Carter and Vance were reluctant to move faster on normalization as Brzezinski was urging by the end of June. Vance argued that moving closer to Peking could only damage US-Soviet relations and antagonize supporters of Taiwan, and Carter felt that " . . . we 'should not ass-kiss them the way Nixon and Kissinger did'."[89]

Brzezinski's desire for rapid normalization was evident in his proposed cable to Vance who was in Peking to use "any opportunity" to normalize relations; a proposal rejected by Carter after a warning from Mondale about a possible negative Senate reaction. Vance's unwillingness to go for normalization despite the fact that he took a draft agreement with him and his and Carter's preoccupation with SALT, the Middle East, and the Panama Canal treaty permitted Brzezinski to take the initiative in pursuing normalization. In mid-October Brzezinski decided to focus more on a politically consultative relationship and less on normalization, and he quietly encouraged the Chinese to invite him to Peking – an action inconsistent with his belief that the Secretary of State must pursue accommodation with adversaries. Peking's invitation in early November led to a dispute with Vance who wanted to control negotiations with the PRC, but it allowed Brzezinski to pressure the bureaucracy to expand bilateral relations through greater scientific contacts and a more favorable attitude toward the transfer of militarily sensitive technology to the PRC. With Brown's support, he overcame Vance's objections and by early February 1978 he devised an interagency system to handle Peking's requests in a more positive manner. Also, on his own authority he arranged for Peking to get a NATO briefing on the global strategic problem, thereby initiating, as Kissinger had done through his briefings to the Chinese, a tacit security relationship with the PRC. In addition, he began to hold regular consultative meetings with Ambassador Han Hsu to brief him on US foreign policy initiatives – an approach inconsistent with his and Carter's attacks on Kissinger's secretive and personal diplomatic initiatives.[90]

Vance strongly opposed Brzezinski's visit, fearing his closeness to Carter implied normalization thus endangering SALT and the improvement of US-Soviet relations, and that it would undermine his role as the foreign policy spokesman of the Administration. To stop Brzezinski, he proposed that Mondale visit Peking as part of his scheduled trip to the Far East.[91] From November 1977 to March 1988, with the support of Brown and Mondale, Brzezinski sought Carter's approval go to Peking, arguing that his reputation as a hardliner gave him greater credibility in the PRC which shared his views about Moscow and that his visit would improve the US position against the USSR which was misusing détente to improve its geopolitical position in the Persian Gulf and the Horn of Africa. To overcome Carter's fears of undermining Vance he stressed his trip's consultative purpose while arguing that Mondale's visit would generate expectations that the US and the PRC were on the verge of normalizing relations. In addition, like Kissinger, he stressed the importance of maintaining better relations with both Moscow and Peking than either of them had with each other.[92] However, unlike Kissinger, who was assisted by Nixon in excluding Rogers from major policy initiatives, Carter's belief in collegiality, manifest in his reluctance to bypass Vance, and his need to personally control major initiatives, forced Brzezinski to form alliances with Brown and Mondale in order to pursue his initiatives toward the PRC. While the alliances with Brown and Mondale could have been a reflection of Brzezinski's own belief in collegiality, it is more likely that they manifested a tactical move to pursue rapid normalization with the PRC in the face of Vance's opposition to it. Brzezinski's pursuit of rapid normalization, however, was consistent with his beliefs in taking bold initiatives and that the PRC could assist the US in counterbalancing the Soviet threat to peace.

Carter's decision in March 1978 to send Brzezinski to Peking did not end the Vance/Brzezinski conflict regarding US policy toward Moscow and the PRC. To reassure Moscow, Vance: (a) gave the Soviet Embassy advance word about Brzezinski's visit despite his agreement with Brzezinski that it would be publicly announced after his return from a scheduled trip to Moscow for further SALT negotiations; and (b) prior to Brzezinski's departure proposed that Gromyko be invited to the White House while Brzezinski was in Peking. But Carter rejected Vance's proposal convinced by Brzezinski that an invitation to Gromyko would undermine his visit domestically and in Peking by demonstrating a major policy split. To enhance US credibility in Peking, which he believed had been damaged by the neutron bomb "indecision," Brzezinski urged Carter to give the PRC preferential treatment over the USSR on technology transfer, personally briefed the Chinese fully on the SALT negotiations, and included the Deputy Assistant Secretary for Defense Morton Abramowitz in his delegation to brief the Chinese on the strategic situation.[93] Moreover, to demonstrate Carter's political will, prior to his departure he arranged for US planes to provide support to a French airdrop in Zaire in response to unrest fomented indirectly by Moscow through Angolan and Cuban assistance.[94]

With Carter's decision to proceed toward normalization Brzezinski drafted instructions for himself stressing that the central purpose of the trip was to reach a strategic understanding with Peking and second to reassure it that Carter was committed to normalization. Carter's revision of the instructions could not hide the fact that they were a reiteration of Brzezinski's beliefs. Regarding the strategic understanding Brzezinski was told to declare: (a) that relations with the PRC were "a central facet of US global policy" given the common interests and parallel long-term strategic concerns, especially "our common opposition to global or regional hegemony by any single power"; (b) Carter's determination to seek peace with the USSR, while competing with it, and deterring its military challenge and proxy expansionism around the world; (c) to stress the enduring competitive nature of the US-Soviet relationship and the US determination to compete as long as necessary while noting its cooperative aspects, especially in arms control; (d) to emphasize that the Soviet threat results from a combination of increasing Soviet military power, political shortsightedness, big-power ambitions, and the desire to exploit Third World conflicts to gain political advantage and eventually political preponderance; (e) to underline Carter's commitment to cooperation with allies and new regional influentials, to comprehensive and reciprocal US-Soviet détente and closer relations with Eastern Europe, to maintain sufficient military capability, and to resolve the emerging global issues; (f) brief the Chinese in detail on efforts to enhance the US and NATO defense capabilities; (g) to point out Soviet weaknessess, especially their waning ideological appeal and hostility of East Europe without taking an anti-Soviet posture; (h) to indicate that the US does not object to allies exporting technology to the

PRC; (i) to brief Peking on the strategic and conventional balances and the SALT II negotiations; and (j) to encourage Peking to assist in resolving the regional conflicts in Africa, Southeast Asia, the Middle East, and the Korean peninsula. Regarding normalization, the second purpose of his trip, Brzezinski was instructed to state: (a) the US accepts the three Chinese key points regarding normalization and reaffirms the five points made by Nixon and Ford, and that it "has made up its mind" to engage in active negotiations to remove obstacles to normalization; and (b) the US expects Peking not to contradict the US unilateral statement that the issue of Taiwan would be resolved peacefully and that the US will continue to sell Taiwan military equipment for defensive purposes. Informally, he was: (a) to explore the possibility of developing "an American formula" for a continuing non-diplomatic relationship with Taiwan that would help maintain US credibility since a crisis of confidence in it would be exploited by Moscow; and (b) to indicate that the US is planning to reduce further its military presence in Taiwan this year, to widen opportunities for the export of commercial technology to the PRC, to invite trade and military delegations to visit the US, and to increase direct contacts on a scheduled basis.[95] Carter's instructions transformed a consultative mission into a major initiative.

In Peking Brzezinski repeatedly: (a) stressed the need to cooperate against the common threat. "For one of the central features of our era – a feature which causes us to draw together – is the emergence of the Soviet Union as a global power"; (b) outlined Moscow's strategy as involving an attempt to achieve strategic superiority, to gain political preponderance in Western Europe, to radicalize the Middle East, to destabilize southern Asia, to penetrate the Indian Ocean region, and to encircle the PRC; and (c) reaffirmed the Shanghai communique as the basis of the US-PRC relationship emphasizing the PRC's "central role in the maintenance of the global equilibrium," that "a strong and independent China is a force for peace in our pluralistic world," and that the US-PRC relationship "is an enduring relationship. It has long-term strategic importance. It is not only a tactical anti-Soviet expedient."[96] While declarations a and b reflected his belief that Soviet military power and expansionism made the USSR the greatest threat to peace, c was inconsistent with his belief that the PRC's revolutionary commitment made it a long-range threat to peace and that US-PRC rapprochement was for Peking a transitional and expedient arrangement. Indeed, this belief had led him to attack Nixon's opening to Peking for improving the international position of the PRC without undermining its commitment to revolution. Brzezinski also proposed the exchange of Cabinet-level visits, trade delegations and military missions, and indicated Carter's willingness to modify COCOM procedures to facilitate the transfer of technology to the PRC. He urged the Chinese to support US efforts in the Middle East, to assist those opposing Soviet expansion in Africa through Cuba and in Southeast Asia through the Vietnamese, and to cooperate more closely with the US in aiding Afghanistan and Pakistan.[97] In discussing Carter's commitment to normalization with Deng, Brzezinski noted the domestic difficulties issuing from the Taiwan issue and warned that the US military withdrawal from Taiwan must proceed in a manner that could not be exploited by the USSR during the "historically transitional period" after normalization and before the eventual reunification.[98]

Peking responded to Brzezinski's presentation through Foreign Minister Huang Hua and Vice-Premier Deng Xiaoping. Stressing their concern with Soviet expansionism, they questioned America's will in opposing it, emphasized the risks of SALT, and expressed the view that for fear of offending Moscow Carter would not sell technology to the PRC. Nevertheless, they acknowledged the need for cooperation to stop Soviet expansion. Brzezinski responded that he personally was not concerned with offending Moscow (implying that others might be), that SALT coupled with renewed defense efforts was designed to obtain strategic stability, and that the US had been opposing Moscow's expansion longer than the PRC. He also urged them to stop their anti-American propaganda portraying the US as both hegemonistic and weak, and they did.[99]

Brzezinski's public reiteration, shortly after his return, of the Soviet strategy as he outlined it in Peking and his declaration that Moscow's exploitation of regional conflicts by Cuban military proxy was incompatible with détente and that only through patient negotiations and demonstration of resolve the US can convince Moscow that the benefits of accommodation are greater than the shortsighted attempts to exploit global conflicts, led to a rebuke from Carter and a new clash with Vance. Both feared that Brzezinski's visit to Peking and his declarations were undermining SALT and détente. Carter wondered whether to write Brezhnev to reiterate his commitment to SALT, while Vance argued that a more cooperative Soviet attitude could be encouraged if the US paid conspicuous attention to the sense of equality to which Moscow attached great importance.[100] Vance's conviction in equal treatment was manifest in his recommendation on June 13 that the public announcement of PRC recognition be made mid-December since if SALT could be completed by then both SALT and normalization would be sent to Congress at about the same time, with normalization preceding SALT ratification. Carter and Brzezinski agreed since better relations with Peking would help the ratification of SALT II.[101]

Brzezinski's handling of normalization was inconsistent with his and

Carter's belief in open diplomatic initiatives. Like Kissinger, Brzezinski during his discussions with Deng limited the number of members of the US delegation present and proposed that the negotiations regarding normalization be "highly confidential."[102] His memorandums to Carter urged the "outmost confidentiality," and Carter, sharing his fear that leaks could damage the initiative by arousing opposition from supporters of Taiwan and excessive expectations, kept the meetings on PRC policy limited to Brzezinski, Vance, Brown, and Jordan, and instructed that dispatches and the negotiating information be strictly limited to the President's Daily Brief (PDB). Brzezinski supported Vance's proposal that instructions to Ambassador Leonard Woodcock who conducted the negotiations be sent jointly by them through the White House system of communications.[103] But he opposed Vance's suggestion to consult Congress in secret about the negotiations to avoid a political backlash. In short, while Carter's belief in collegiality led to the participation of other cabinet members in the US-PRC negotiations, their advocacy for open diplomacy did not stop them from excluding the bureaucracy and Congress from the negotiations with Peking.[104]

Brzezinski's handling of US-PRC normalization also demonstrated his beliefs in summitry and in taking bold initiatives. He hinted the possibility of a summit in Washington during his discussions with Deng Xiaoping in Peking and in his personal consultations with Ambassador Chai Zemin he raised the possibility of a summit with the Chinese leader in the US upon normalization. With Carter's encouragement he pursued his initiative.[105] When the negotiations slowed down due to US insistence to sell arms to Taiwan and Vance's initiative to initiate diplomatic relations with Vietnam, Brzezinski as an incentive for Peking offered an invitation to Deng or Hua to visit Washington before Carter's meeting with Brezhnev and Deng accepted. Moreover, having publicly labeled Vietnam a Soviet proxy, Brzezinski opposed Vance's Vietnam initiative as a "pro-Soviet, anti-Chinese move," and Carter who originally considered simultaneous recognition for the PRC and Vietnam instructed Vance to condemn Vietnam for promoting the exodus of refugees.[106]

Deng Xiaoping's revelation during his visit to Washington in January 1979 that Peking will "teach Vietnam a lesson" for its occupation of Cambodia which threatened the long-term stability of Southeast Asia, led to a new Vance/Brzezinski controversy and actions by Brzezinski which reflected his belief in using force to demonstrate one's political will. Carter responded to Deng's request for "moral support" internationally by urging restraint, fearing, as Vance did, the lesson's destabilizing international impact and the damage to domestic support for normalization.[107]

Brzezinski shared their latter fear but, concerned that Peking might be forced to withdraw by a Soviet nuclear threat and be criticized by Carter under pressure from world opinion and the State Department, proposed that criticism of Peking's military action be coupled with a condemnation of the Vietnamese occupation of Cambodia and the demand that both pull out their forces, knowing that this would be unacceptable to Hanoi and Moscow. For him, it was vital to register US disapproval of Peking's action, without joining Moscow's condemnation of it. At an NSC meeting, after the action began, Brzezinski proposed that a demand to Moscow not to exacerbate the situation through military deployments or other forms of military actions be coupled with the statement that the US will exercise similar restraint, implying "a willingness to respond militarily if Moscow acted." The implied message reflected his belief in the need to demonstrate Carter's political will both to Moscow and Peking. Vance aquiesced,[108] but proposed the cancellation of Blumenthal's scheduled trip to Peking as an expression of US disapproval. Brzezinski, supported by Holbrooke, got Carter's approval for the trip by arguing that Peking's action against Vietnam should not affect bilateral relations with either the PRC or the USSR.[109] For Brzezinski, Carter's actions enhanced US credibility by convincing Peking that the US was not a "paper tiger" and that the US-PRC relationship had reciprocal long-range security benefits, while Peking's action, despite its military ineffectiveness, demonstrated the limits of Soviet power, thus encouraging those opposing it.[110]

Brzezinski's efforts to counterbalance Moscow with Peking was also manifest in his suggestion during Deng's visit that Carter in toasts and comments to the press remove assurances that the new US-PRC relationship was not directed against the USSR. When Vance opposed the use of the term "hegemony" in the joint communique, which the Chinese wanted, viewing it as a provocation to Moscow and a concession to Peking, Brzezinski proposed using "hegemony or domination over others" – in his view, a formal reassertion that US-PRC relations were based on their common objective of ending Moscow's geopolitical ambitions. Moreover, he strongly opposed Vance's demand that the statement at the end of Deng's visit stress that while an improvment in US-PRC relations can contribute to the stable structure of peace, there is an equal need to complete SALT and improve the US-Soviet relationship. For Brzezinski, Vance's statement would have reinforced the perception that Carter lacked political will.[111]

The Vance/Brzezinski controversy regarding the granting of MFN status to the PRC also reflected Brzezinski's belief that the USSR's military power and expansionism made it a greater threat to peace than the

PRC. Vance and Blumenthal, who had initiated the trade negotiations with the PRC, proposed in March 1979 the simultaneous granting of MFN status to both the USSR and the PRC. For Vance, the US had to be "evenhanded," meaning, granting trade privileges to both the USSR and the PRC without engaging in military relationships. Brzezinski, however, in view of Moscow's rigidity in SALT, its exploitation of anti-Americanism in Iran, and its support of military activities by Vietnam, opposed Vance's recommendation fearing that the Senate's linkage of MFN status to human rights in the USSR would kill MFN and damage relations with Peking. Convinced that Vance's evenhanded approach favored the USSR, Brzezinski stressed that the US approach to the PRC must be a "balanced" one, taking into account not only Moscow's concerns but the significant disparities of power between the PRC and the USSR.[112] To gain Carter's approval for granting MFN status to the PRC alone Brzezinski sought bureaucratic allies by scheduling trips for Cabinet members to Peking. Assisted by Mondale, whose trip to Peking Brzezinski supported despite Carter's and Vance's reluctance, Brzezinski unlinked the granting of MFN status to the USSR from that to PRC and the decision to grant it only to the PRC was announced by Mondale in Peking.[113]

Brzezinski's belief in linkage became clearly evident in early 1978 in the debate regarding "dual-use" US technology transfer and arms sales by allies to the PRC. Vance, in view of Carter's 1977 reaffirmation of the US prohibition of arms sales to the PRC, sought to limit the relationship to the diplomatic sphere while gradually expanding the economic relationship. Hence, he opposed the transfer of US technology and advised West Europeans, who were seeking Carter's aquiescence, not to sell arms to Peking. But Brown and Brzezinski, who had been pushing for a US-PRC security relationship to increase the pressure on the USSR's eastern flank, supported the transfer of US technology and suggested "benign neutrality" regarding European arms sales to the PRC. The debate intensified after Deng's visit, and in April 1979, concerned with Moscow's expansionism in Iran, Afghanistan, South Yemen, and especially with its increased military presence in Vietnam, Brzezinski and Brown, supported by Carter's informal remarks to allied leaders that he did not oppose European arms sales to the PRC, convinced Vance to inform London that the US did not oppose their sale of arms to the PRC but that it preferred that the sale not be submitted to COCOM for approval where it could generate a dispute. In July, in a compromise, Vance, Brown, and Brzezinski agreed to give the PRC some civil advanced imaging systems and some small jets with sophisticated navigational equipment that the US would not sell the USSR.[114] Moreover, to overcome Vance's strong opposition to a US-PRC security relationship, Brzezinski suggested to Mondale in late July that an announcement during his visit of a trip by Brown would be welcomed in Peking and urged the Chinese to accept Mondale's suggestion. Vance opposed Brown's trip fearing that it would demonstrate a "tilt" toward the PRC thus jeopardizing the development of a more stable and predictable US-Soviet relationship. Mondale who had earlier opposed the development of a US-PRC security relationship got Carter's approval for Brown's visit to enhance the political significance of his own trip. Brown visited Peking in January 1980, and the Soviet invasion of Afghanistan on December 25, 1979, enhanced the importance of his trip.[115]

The invasion of Afghanistan facilitated Brzezinski's efforts to gain Carter's approval for his initiative to liberalize trade regulations to strengthen the security link with Peking. Indeed, in 1980, the State and Commerce Departments liberalized a number of regulations which permitted the export of military support equipment to the PRC. The sale of US military equipment and visits by military officials to Washington and Peking demonstrated Brzezinski's success in developing a US-PRC security relationship – an accomplishment consistent with his belief that the PRC is useful for counterbalancing the USSR but inconsistent with his other belief that the PRC was still a long-term revolutionary threat to peace.[116]

In the 1980s, Brzezinski's suggestions regarding the US-PRC relationship reflected his belief that the USSR is a greater threat to peace than the PRC. He argued that even if Sino-Soviet relations become less hostile, a strong PRC pursuing its own objectives is a major obstacle to Soviet efforts to achieve hegemony in the Far East. To preclude Soviet miscalculations regarding the US interest in the security of the PRC, Brzezinski recommended that US security policy must convey that the US would view its interests as threatened by any hostile actions that sought to undermine the security of the PRC.[117] However, he recognized that since normalization Peking, while basing its long-term modernization on economic relations with the West, no longer seeks an overt and binding military-political alliance. Nevertheless, emphasizing Moscow's desire to derail the PRC's modernization to preclude the emergence of another modern power in the Far East and stressing that a rapidly modernizing PRC could assist in preventing Moscow's domination of Eurasia, Brzezinski recommended that the US and Japan actively support the PRC's economic modernization and quietly expand the scope of informal security consultations with Peking in order to establish an informal geopolitical triangle in the Far East.[118] In short, in the 1980s, while Brzezinski has become even more preoccupied with the Soviet threat to peace, he did not even hint that the PRC was once considered by him a long-term revolutionary threat to peace.

CONCLUSION

The analysis of US policy toward the USSR and the PRC reveals both consistency and inconsistency between Brzezinski's recommendations and/or actions while in office and his beliefs. This is also manifest in his policy proposals after 1981. The declaratory strategy originally outlined by Carter, while reiterating beliefs shared by all the principal policymakers, is most notable for reasserting Brzezinski's beliefs in both the moral and architectural approaches to politics, in the need for reciprocity and comprehensiveness as the bases of the US-Soviet relationship, and in the protracted nature of the East-West conflict. However, as it evolved, the strategy also reaffirmed Brzezinski's beliefs that Soviet military power and its use in regional conflicts is the greatest threat to peace and that Moscow's actions dictated an active US role and a willingness to match Soviet military power and to use force. The fact that the strategy despite its evolution placed great emphasis on SALT as a means for improving US-Soviet relations and indicated a reluctance to using force can be partly explained by Carter's and Vance's belief in arms control and opposition to using force. Carter's belief in collegiality and determination to personally control policy prevented Brzezinski from gaining absolute control of Presidential speeches despite his efforts to do so, consistent with his belief in their importance for setting priorities and launching new initiatives.

By focusing primarily on the US-Soviet relationship and then on the normalization of relations with the PRC, Brzezinski was acting consistently with his beliefs that Soviet military power makes the USSR a greater threat to peace than the PRC and that the PRC is useful to the US for counterbalancing the USSR in the Far East, beliefs also evident in his efforts to achieve normalization rapidly and to develop a US-PRC security relationship. However, his struggle to grant MFN status to the PRC alone and to transfer "dual-use" technology to the PRC was inconsistent with his other belief, namely, that the PRC was still a long-term revolutionary threat to peace. Consistent with his belief that US military superiority is vital for precluding Soviet foreign policy successes that reignite the USSR's revolutionary tendencies, Brzezinski urged Carter to approve PD-18, the new MX missile, and made every effort to establish the RDF and a new war-fighting strategic doctrine. While Brzezinski's attempts to counterbalance the USSR by new strategic weapons programs and a closer relationship with Peking reveal that he, like Kissinger, is a power-realist, his public insistence on linking human rights to other aspects of the US-Soviet relationship reflected his belief in the moral approach to politics. Moreover, his efforts to normalize relations with the PRC gave tangible expression to his belief in the non-ideological approach to politics. In the 1980s, Brzezinski's recommendations have been consistent with those beliefs. Reasserting that the USSR is still pursuing a world-wide communist society, he insists on the need for an integrated strategy and military capability to check the massive buildup of Soviet military power and on a closer informal strategic relationship with the PRC. For him, both are essential to maintain the geopolitical balance of power, the prerequisite to peace.

The rationale of Brzezinski's recommendations and actions in support of new strategic weapons programs and SALT, and of the normalization of US-PRC relations, were also consistent with some of his other beliefs. His efforts to force a decision on the MX and his insistence on Soviet geopolitical restraint while pursuing SALT reflected his beliefs in linkage, in the limited utility of arms control, and in reciprocal and comprehensive détente which he did not equate with SALT. Brzezinski's belief in linkage was also evident in his attempts to link human rights to US-Soviet trade and to grant MFN status to the PRC alone. Consistent with his belief in the need to demonstrate political will, he repeatedly urged Carter not to make concessions in order to speed up the SALT negotiations and to threaten the use of force in the Horn of Africa and southwest Asia. His efforts to slow down the pace of SALT also demonstrated his belief that patience and toughness are vital in negotiations with the East. Brzezinski's struggle to have Carter declare his determination to defend vital US interests by force and to develop the strategic doctrine and the capability for doing so also reflected his belief that the use of force is a necessary means for enhancing US credibility by demonstrating political will, a belief also manifest in his support for Peking's attempt to teach "Vietnam a lesson." His initiative for establishing the RDF was consistent with his belief that the ability to react quickly is vital to global engagement. Consistent with his beliefs in summitry and in taking bold initiatives, Brzezinski personally pursued the idea of a US-PRC summit with the Chinese. However, by opposing Carter's repeated offers to Brezhnev for a summit and proposing a meeting in Alaska, he was acting consistently with his belief that formal summits should not be used since by overselling détente they undermine the West's will to resist Soviet challenges to peace. In the 1980s, Brzezinski has been reasserting his beliefs that only by linking arms control to Soviet geopolitical restraint and by demonstrating US power and political will can the US convince Moscow to end its challenges to peace.

The inconsistency found between Brzezinski's belief that the PRC is a long-term revolutionary threat to peace and his push for developing a US-PRC security relationship is also manifest between his proposals and/or actions and his beliefs in open diplomacy and in prudent leadership. Brzezinski's insistence on utmost confidentiality in the negotiations with Peking, his opposition to consulting Congress about them, and his willingness to hold consultative meetings with Dobrynin and the Chinese were inconsistent with his belief in open diplomacy and attacks on Kissinger's backchannel initiatives. Moreover, inconsistent with his belief that goals are pursued most effectively through prudent leadership which involves cooperation, joint planning, and consultation, Brzezinski, to overcome Vance's opposition and Carter's hesitation, personally hinted at the possibility of a summit to the Chinese, let Carter know that he was willing to engage the Soviets in a broader dialogue to stress that Soviet military intervention is incompatible with détente, forced a decision on the MX, pushed an NSC initiative for the establishement of the RDF, and created a new committee under his control to direct initiatives toward the PRC. However, these actions being consistent with his belief in bold initiatives reflect his implicit acceptance of Kissinger's concept of leadership.

10 Kissinger and the Allies: Seeking a Common Policy

The study of the Atlantic Alliance led Kissinger to criticize US policies toward it and to advocate the creation of an Atlantic community. Hence, it was not suprising that Europeans perceived his appointment as a demonstration of Nixon's determination to fulfill his campaign pledge to resolve the dilemmas undermining NATO unity. Few noted that Kissinger had concluded that no final solution to NATO's strategic dilemmas is possible so long as it remains composed of sovereign states and that European and US interests are not identical everywhere. This chapter examines Kissinger's impact on US alliance, and particularly NATO, policy by analyzing the consistency between his beliefs regarding world politics and strategy and tactics for achieving national goals and his policy preferences and/or actions as it became evident in the rationale of policies in official statements and in his memoranda to Nixon, in his approach to issues and in the agreements with allies. The impact of those beliefs on Kissinger's behavior is also determined by analyzing their consistency with his policy recommendations after he left office.

THE NIXON DOCTRINE: GENUINE PARTNERSHIP

The corollary to Kissinger's triangular balance was partnership with allies. The 1970 Report to Congress declared:

> Genuine *partnership* must increasingly characterize our alliance. For if we cannot maintain and develop further such a relationship with our North Atlantic allies, the prospects for achieving it with our other friends and allies around the world are slim indeed.[1]

The emphasis on partnership reflected Kissinger's belief that the unity of the US alliance system is essential for establishing a stable international system since its resources and manpower help maintain the equilibrium of power and its acceptance of the present system enhances its legitimacy. Subsequent Reports to Congress reiterated it.[2] Genuine partnership, however, would develop in the context of the Nixon Doctrine[3] which as

215

elaborated by Kiṣsinger redefined containment. According to the 1970 Report to Congress:

> Its central thesis is that the United States will participate in the defense and development of allies and friends, but that America cannot, and will not, conceive *all* the plans, design *all* the programs, execute *all* the decisions and undertake *all* the defense of the free nations of the world. We will help where it makes a real difference and is considered in our interest.[4]

Evident here is Kissinger's belief in limited objectives: the US would retreat from the limitless support for anticommunism everywhere and identify priorities, recognizing that some regions are more important than others. For Kissinger, this approach would encourage other nations to do their part thus undermining the growing isolationism and generate the necessary domestic support for the Administration's policies. However, concerned that the Doctrine's emphasis on limited objectives might undermine US credibility which he and Nixon viewed as vital to a succcessful foreign policy the Reports to Congress reiterated their belief that "Peace in the world will continue to require us to maintain our commitments – and we will."[5] Kissinger feared that a sudden withdrawal from the world would lead to shifts in the regional and eventually global equilibrium and it would cause disruption and invite aggression thus making the establishment of a stable international order impossible.[6] The Doctrine did not rule out new commitments but stressed that a more rigorous criteria would be used before assuming them; the 1970 Report declared: "our interests must shape our commitments, rather than the other way around."[7]

Nixon's trip to Europe starting on February 23, 1969, revealed that the Administration set NATO apart from all other commitments. For Nixon and Kissinger, it was essential to reassure West Europeans because, despite their criticism of US dominance and assertions of autonomy, they feared US disengagement – a fear intensified by 1969 due to Congressional pressures for unilateral troop withdrawals. Kissinger was concerned that if not reassured, they would refuse to share the common defense burden thus threatening his efforts to maintain the power equilibrium and, more importantly, they would pursue independent diplomatic initiatives toward the USSR, thus undermining his use of linkage. The reassurance came in the Reports to Congress which reiterated Kissinger's belief that "we can no more disengage from Europe than from Alaska,"[8] because "The peace of Europe is crucial to the peace of the world . . . For the foreseeable future, Europe must be the cornerstone of the structure of a durable peace."[9]

Nixon's trip and repeated declarations convinced West Europeans that Nixon was fulfilling his pledge to attach more importance to NATO than his predecessors. What they did not grasp was that behind the acceptable aspects of his policy he was contemplating some adjustments in US-West European relations. For Nixon and Kissinger, broadly construed, the Doctrine implied a restructuring of the Atlantic relationship around the three elements of the structure of peace: partnership, strength, and willingness to negotiate.[10]

In the near future, however, the Reports to Congress stressed: "the tangible expression of the new partnership is in greater material contributions by other countries."[11] For Nixon and Kissinger, "the balance of burdens and responsibilities must gradually be adjusted, to reflect the economic and political realities of European progress. Our allies will deserve a voice in the Alliance and its decisions commensurate with their growing power and contributions."[12] But unlike his predecesors, Nixon tried to convince them that they would not be pressured to pay for programs conceived in Washington. According to the 1971 Report to Congress:

> The Nixon Doctrine, then, should not be thought of primarily as the sharing of burdens or the lightening of our load. It has a more positive meaning for other nations and for ourselves. In effect we are encouraging countries to participate fully in the creation of plans and the designing of programs. They must define the nature of their own security and determine the path of their own progress. For only in this manner will they think of their fate as truly their own.[13]

This rationale reflected Kissinger's belief in the need for a psychological reorientation, namely, that "when countries feel responsible for the formulation of plans they are more apt to furnish the assets needed to make them work."[14]

Nixon and Kissinger realized that negotiations with adversaries will test the new trans-Atlantic partnership. Reflecting Kissinger's belief that "the Western countries do not have identical national concerns and cannot be expected to agree automatically on priorities or solutions," the 1971 Report to Congress noted differences on some major issues, i.e., Berlin, Mutual and Balanced Force Reductions (MBFR), the Conference on Security and Cooperation in Europe (CSCE), the "German question," and US-Soviet détente. Reiterating his belief that "Each ally is the best judge of its own national interests," it stated: "our principal objective should be to harmonize our policies and insure that our efforts for détente are complementary" because "a differentiated détente, limited to the USSR and certain

Western allies but not others would be illusory."[15] The conviction that this objective could be achieved was manifest in the repetition of Kissinger's belief that "European and American interests in defense and East-West diplomacy are fundamentally parallel and give sufficient incentive for coordinating independent policies."[16] However, the emphasis on greater allied contributions to the formulation of common policies did not imply an abandonment of US leadership. Reflecting Nixon's and Kissinger's belief in leadership the Report stated: "This new sharing requires a new, more subtle form of leadership" because US allies "still look to America for leadership in European diplomacy and defense even while they assert their autonomy."[17] When Nixon sought reassurance about the need for US leadership in light of the progress in European integration, Kissinger's memorandum reminded him that "American weight and leadership were still needed."[18]

In short, the elaboration of the Nixon Doctrine and genuine partnership reflected Kissinger's belief that since political multipolarity makes it impossible to impose a US design the Administration had to evoke the creativity of a pluralistic world. The ideal partnership under the Doctrine was a relationship among "equals," meaning, a retreat from the heavy-handedness and arrogance that had often characterized US relations with Western Europe in the past. "This Administration," the 1971 Report to Congress stated, "does not view our allies as pieces in an American Grand Design."[19] But it also required greater West European unity and the assumption of a more equitable share of the common alliance burden. The Doctrine, however, retained the dominant US role in containing the USSR but at a lower level of effort and with greater material assistance from allies. In other words, it reflected Kissinger's belief that since the US manages the military equilibrium vis-à-vis the USSR it should determine not only the military strategy of NATO but also the diplomatic strategy toward the East. This was essential given Kissinger's dependence on linkage which rested on the ability to control all incentives and penalties necessary to convince Moscow to accept what he considered to be the acceptable goals and methods of foreign policy.

THE DILEMMAS OF COMMON DEFENSE: MAINTAINING THE POWER EQUILIBRIUM

In the 1970s the strategic debate in NATO revolved around five issues: (a) the credibility of the US deterrent; (b) SALT; (c) reductions of US troops in Europe; (d) burden-sharing; and (e) the role of tactical nuclear weapons. Kissinger's approach to them reflected his beliefs that since these cannot be resolved so long as NATO remains composed of sovereign states, allies should not be pressured to accept unilateral US changes in nuclear strategy as official NATO doctrine. His efforts to resolve those issues also demonstrated that while the US-West European relationship was subordinate to US-Soviet détente and US-PRC rapprochement, their resolution was consistent with Kissinger's global strategy and the Nixon Doctrine.

Kissinger's concept of strategic sufficiency, although a unilateral change of US strategy, did not ignite a debate in NATO as the concept of flexible response had done. Its purposefully designed ambiguity permitted the US to deploy strategic weapons to sustain the credibility of its NATO commitments while pursuing SALT. The 1971 Report to Congress stressed: "sufficiency means the maintainance of forces adequate to prevent us and our allies from being coerced,"[20] and declared:

(. . .) *we shall provide a shield if a nuclear power threatens the freedom of a nation allied with us or of a nation whose survival we consider vital to our security.* Nuclear power is the element of security that our friends either cannot provide or could provide only with great and disruptive efforts . . . Their concern would be magnified if we were to leave them defenseless against nuclear blackmail, or conventional aggression backed by nuclear power. (his italics)[21]

Such declarations and the continued deployment of strategic forces appeared to reassure West Europeans who doubted the credibility of the US nuclear guarantee but were not any more prepared than Kissinger to put NATO's strategic dilemmas on the agenda. Indeed, while the 1970 Report to Congress declared: "we can no more disengage from Europe than from Alaska,"[22] West Europeans, in Brandt's words, stressed: "Europe . . . would no more be able to detach itself from America than it could from itself."[23] Both sides conveniently overlooked what Kissinger had emphasized prior to 1969, namely, Alaska not being sovereign could be defended by a strategy which might be unacceptable to West Europeans. Their acceptance of strategic sufficiency confirmed Kissinger's belief that for them the incentives for working within the NATO framework outweigh those to supplant the US military dominance despite differences over economic and monetary matters. Despite the elaboration of strategic sufficiency, Kissinger did not seek to change NATO strategy believing that it would only intensify the strategic debate at a time when its cohesion was vital to the successful implementation of his global strategy.

Kissinger and Brzezinski

In the context of strategic parity in the 1970s, *"strength"* in the Atlantic Alliance meant essentially maintaining the credibility of the US deterrent against Soviet aggression, and strategic sufficiency made this possible.

West European leaders viewed SALT as consonant with their efforts to secure a more general relaxation of East-West tensions so they urged Nixon during his 1969 visit to start the talks and to consult them as they progressed. The Administration's delay to review options and link SALT to other issues led many allied leaders to stress its urgency.[24] In the US, supporters of SALT criticized the delay by arguing that West Europeans desired SALT. However, the enthusiasm of allied leaders waned when the talks started and they were briefed about the implications of ratifying strategic parity. In Kissinger's view, some feared that a SALT agreement ratifying parity would leave the USSR with a substantial conventional superiority in Europe thus weakening the overall deterrent against Soviet attacks, while others (mainly in FRG) feared that the linkage between SALT and political issues would not be maintained[25] (an unlikely possibility given Nixon's and Kissinger's belief in linkage). The greatest fear, however, was that Nixon and Kissinger might become so intoxicated politically by negotiating directly and privately with the Soviet leaders as to diminish the value of political intimacy within NATO.[26] Realizing those concerns, Kissinger sought to maintain NATO unity which he viewed as essential to his Soviet policy by returning from Moscow by way of Paris, Bonn, and London, to brief them on the progress of the negotiations. In addition, US representatives regularly briefed the NATO Council on US positions and on the progress in Helsinki and Vienna.[27] Kissinger's briefings, however, being secretive and bilateral and limited to major allies, although dealing with matters of critical concern to NATO, did not satisfy all NATO members. His reluctance to seek a consensus on SALT reflected his beliefs that since NATO's strategic dilemmas could not be resolved, consultation would only solve peripheral issues while NATO's bureaucracy would limit his flexibility. But Kissinger was not prepared to limit his freedom of action while the Europeans refused to constrain their own.[28] On the whole, however, the regular briefings succeeded in containing West European nervousness both on technical matters and on the important issue of political intent.

Kissinger's belief in maintaining the European balance of power was manifest in his rejection of Soviet demands to include the FBS and British and French ballistic-missiles submarines within the scope of SALT limitations.[29] While the ABM Treaty prolonged the deterrent capability of the British and French nuclear forces by leaving many targets of value for them outside the ABM covered area, the Administration sought to enhance it by asserting that Article IX, which prohibits the transfer of ABM technology to third countries, did not establish a precedent for a parallel prohibition in the case of strategic offensive weapons technology.[30] This was necessary since the British Polaris force was heavily dependent on US cooperation. Kissinger's willingness to explore the possibilities of nuclear cooperation with France and, in fact, permit France to acquire some of the military sensitive information and equipment that the US used to withold removed the French *force de frappe* from being a point of political contention in NATO.[31] Those actions, reversing the previous policy, reflected Kissinger's view that the European nuclear forces should be seen not as an alternative to US strategic forces but as a complement.[32] Indeed, the Reports to Congress stated: "The nuclear forces of the United States, supplemented by the nuclear forces of our allies, remain the backbone of our deterrent."[33] Kissinger's efforts, however, did not remove all anxiety regarding the SALT agreements.[34]

The belief that Western Europe is vital to the global equilibrium of power was manifest in Kissinger's handling of Brezhnev's proposal for the APNW. Convinced that a US-Soviet agreement renouncing the use of nuclear weapons against each other was designed to "dismantle the military strategy of NATO"[35] since it did not preclude the use of nuclear weapons in a war involving NATO and the Warsaw Pact, Kissinger insisted on the inclusion of Article VI which stated: "nothing in this Agreement shall affect or impair: (a) the inherent right of individual or collective self-defense as envisaged by Article 51 of the Charter of the United Nations . . . and (c) the obligations undertaken by either Party towards its allies or other countries in treaties, agreements, and other appropriate documents."[36] He feared that, without Article VI, by protecting the superpowers against nuclear destruction in a European war while guaranteeing the devastation of Europe, the APNW would have destroyed NATO whose defense rested on the US nuclear guarantee.[37] Kissinger had briefed Brandt, Heath, and Pompidou about the APNW but the foreign and defense ministries had not been consulted and this generated concern that the US response in a crisis might depend upon the uncertain outcome of US-Soviet consultations.[38] Indeed, in June 1973, at the NATO Council the agreement was strongly criticized by the British representative even though it was largely a British draft. The FRG's representative supported the criticism.[39] After the October War, French Foreign Minister Michel Jobert challenged Kissinger to reconcile the requirement for NATO consultation in a nuclear crisis with the US commitment (Article IV of the APNW) to consult the USSR in similar circumstances.[40] As in the case of SALT, the unwillingness to consult the US and West European bureaucracies about the APNW reflected Kissinger's beliefs that only a non-bureaucratic approach can increase a statesman's flexibility and that consultation could only resolve the peripheral issue – right to be consulted – but not NATO's strategic dilemma which generated the West European fears. Moreover, his actions reflected his conviction that disagreement on peripheral issues was the price for unity on the issues that really matter, namely, preventing nuclear war and establishing a stable international system. He felt that those goals could be achieved if Moscow observed Article II and refrained from the threat or use of force in its international conduct; the essential requisite of legitimacy/peace.[41]

The belief that the European balance of power was vital to the global equilibrium, especially with the approaching strategic parity, led Kissinger to lead the Administration's efforts to defeat several Senate Resolutions sponsored by Senator Mansfield and others which called for unilateral reductions of US troops in Europe. He repeatedly urged Nixon to stress the US commitment to maintain strong US forces in Europe, but to emphasize that Congressional support required proportionate European contributions.[42] The importance Kissinger attached to this issue was evident in his request for NSSM 84 in November 1969, and the number of NSC meetings during the summer and fall of 1970 to review the study.[43] In summing up the strategic problem for Nixon, Kissinger revealed the rationale of his actions by stating:

> (. . .) we and our Allies must maintain strong enough conventional forces to be able to meet Soviet aggression or the threat of it implicit in their substantial forces. Unless we and our Allies rework our NATO strategy and forces so that they can provide this capability, we will soon experience the gradual "neutralization" of Western Europe. To avoid this situation, we must act vigorously to maintain NATO's conventional capability while developing a strategy for its use that makes sense in this fundamentaly new strategic situation.[44]

Evident here is his belief that maintaining NATO's capability for a conventional war, even for a limited time, enhances deterrence,[45] since it would drive the USSR into a scale of attack which would remove any doubt about its objective, thus making the threat of US retaliation convincing. In the NSC meeting in November 19, it was agreed to strongly reaffirm the US troop commitment to NATO[46] which Rogers did at the NATO Foreign Ministers meeting in December 1970 by announcing Nixon's decision to maintain current levels until at least July 1972 "unless there is reciprocal action [reductions] by our adversaries."[47] (The time period was extended later). Kissinger's belief in the need for a large NATO conventional capability was also evident in his support of the recommendations of the studies produced by NSSM 84 and by the US-supported NATO review AD-70; those called for improving equipment, supplies, and deployments.

Kissinger's opposition to unilateral troop withdrawals were supported by the bureaucracy. State opposed reductions believing that they would undermine NATO cohesion and the Western bargaining position in future talks with the Warsaw Pact on MBFR. The JCS seeking to maintain the European military balance took a similar line. Only Laird, in September 1969, recommended a 10 percent reduction to prevent larger cuts by Congress, and Kissinger responded by establishing the DRPC in the NSC system to enable him and the other agencies to prevent unilateral cuts by administrative fiat.[48] Kissinger's opposition to troop withdrawals was total. In May 1971, he rejected a compromise, proposed by the Administration's supporters in the Senate and favored by Rogers and others, calling for negotiating reductions with both the USSR and West Europeans and semiannual reports to Congress. He feared it would establish the principle of reductions and the reports would revive pressures for unilateral withdrawals. The efforts to defeat the Mansfield Amendment of May 1971, calling for a 50 percent unilateral cut by the end of the year, were added by the bipartisan consensus on the issue,[49] West European public warnings about the negative impact on NATO's credibility, and Brezhnev's declaration of the Soviet readiness to start negotiations on MBFR.[50]

Kissinger's beliefs that improving NATO's conventional forces and maintaining its unity were vital to the global equilibrium of power and thus to US Soviet policy were also evident in his approach to burden-sharing. The 1970 Report to Congress stressed:

> The conception of burden-sharing in previous administrations was that our allies should share our burden; the thrust of the Nixon Doctrine is that their primary task is to shoulder their own. The emphasis is no longer on their sharing the cost of America's military commitment to Europe – although financial arrangements may play a part – but on their providing the national forces needed in conjuction with ours in support of an effective common strategy.[51]

Senator Mansfield argued that his amendments were intended to induce a larger European contribution to NATO since the West European economies were flourishing. Kissinger, however, believing that West Europeans had resisted US pressures to strengthen their conventional forces fearing that this would undermine nuclear deterrence, supported a proposal by the British Minister of Defense Denis Healey in 1969 to establish the Eurogroup which undertook the European Defense Improvement Program (EDIP). He saw EDIP as "sparse and essentially irrelevant" since it could not create the needed conventional capability but accepted it since it achieved its immediate purpose; it neutralized Congressional criticism that Europeans were not doing enough and thus helped to defeat the amendments.[52] By not exerting any "real" pressure on West Europeans for further increases in the EDIP Kissinger avoided a dispute over an unsolvable issue – the role of conventional forces – that could have threatened NATO unity. Instead, the Reports to Congress praised EDIP.[53]

Having criticized US policymakers for not dealing with the "real" issue in NATO requiring urgent attention, namely, the role of tactical nuclear weapons, one would assume that with strategic parity and Soviet superiority in conventional forces, Kissinger would take the lead in trying to resolve it.[54] However, believing that NATO's strategic dilemmas could not be resolved so long as it remains composed of sovereign states, he was not prepared to tackle an issue that since 1968 had produced serious disputes in NATO's Nuclear Planning Group (NPG) and thus undermine Atlantic unity which he viewed as vital to a true relaxation of East-West tensions. Instead, he noted the issue's existence in the Reports to Congress,[55] and accepted a temporary compromise on the issue that emerged from the NPG's discussions initiated by the Europeans in 1968.[56] Opposed to the needed massive buildup of conventional forces both sides of the Alliance concurred in giving tactical nuclear weapons a crucial role in deterrence by flexible response. But while the US views tactical nuclear weapons as devices to implement the nuclear guarantee while postponing and/or avoiding a strategic nuclear war and seeks options to use them without crossing the strategic threshold, the Europeans, for whom any tactical nuclear engagement would be a disaster, regard tactical nuclear weapons as the trigger of the US strategic forces and seek options to preclude their use. A British "solution" of the issue, supported by the FRG, was adopted in 1969 by the NPG. The "demonstrative use" of tactical nuclear weapons meant using such a weapon in some remote location, i.e., in the air over the Mediterranean which did not involve many casualties, as a signal to Moscow that the situation was getting out of control and that the West was willing to escalate to a strategic exchange if the warning failed. For West Europeans, the demonstrative use of tactical nuclear weapons could spare their countries from devastation early in the conflict while it guaranteed a US nuclear response. To avoid a dispute Kissinger acquiesced but stated:

I never had much use for this concept. I believed that the Soviet Union would not attack Western Europe without anticipating a nuclear response. A reaction that was designed to be of no military relevance would show more hesitation than determination; It would thus be more likely to spur the attack than defer it. If nuclear weapons were to be used, we needed a concept by which they could stop an attack on the ground. A hesitant or ineffective response ran the risk of leaving us with no choices other than surrender or holocaust.[57]

For Kissinger, the NPG decision manifested the West's lack of political will, and the nuclear alert during the October War revealed his belief in demonstrating that the West had both the capability and the will to challenge Moscow's geopolitical ambitions.[58] Nonetheless, the 1972 Report to Congress praised the NPG for its review of NATO's nuclear doctrine and while noting the existence of divergent views, it declared: "we will not impose our view."[59] This declaration reflected Kissinger's belief that since NATO's nuclear dilemmas would not be resolved the US must not pressure the West Europeans to accept changes in US strategic doctrine as NATO doctrine.

In the 1980s, looking at the precarious combination of NATO reliance on nuclear defense, trends toward nuclear stalemate, growing nuclear pacifism, and continued deficiencies in conventional forces, Kissinger reiterated his belief that "if we are reluctant to resort to nuclear weapons, and if we continue to evade the necessity for conventional forces, the Western Alliance is left with no defense policy at all, and we are risking the collapse of the military balance in Europe" that has made possible European security, prosperity, and world peace since 1945.[60] He was particularly concerned with the anti-nuclear movements which in his view were pushing the West toward unilateral psychological and eventually physical disarmament. Kissinger's rejection of the 1982 proposal by Robert McNamara, McGeorge Bundy, George Kennan, and Gerard Smith that NATO should renounce the first use of nuclear weapons and rely exclusively on conventional weapons for the defense of Europe reflected his belief in the need for maintaining the European balance of power. He opposed such a declaratory policy for four reasons: (a) without immediate, serious, and sustained efforts to buildup conventional forces, a no-first-use policy will leave NATO psychologically naked until the conventional balance is achieved; (b) it might increase the risk of war by convincing Moscow that, since the West fears nuclear war, a reversal of its strategic doctrine to one that a war in Europe cannot be limited to nuclear weapons will face the West with the choice of surrender or a war the West will be incapable of fighting; (c) the West should not create the impression that a conventional defeat in Europe is preferable to a first use of nuclear weapons since conventional deterrence had failed in the past; and (d) a no-first-use declaration will demoralize allies outside of Europe which depend on the US guarantee. Kissinger reiterated his belief that "the West has no choice but to give greater priority to its conventional defense . . . it *must* be our policy to reduce reliance on nuclear war to the greatest extent possible, by creating other means to resist aggression" (his italics). [61] In his view, since Moscow has effectivelly used MBFR to thwart "the desperately needed Western conventional buildup," only by closing the gap in conventional forces will NATO convince Moscow to negotiate seriously about MBFR. [62] For Kissinger, without an immediate Western conventional buildup or a substantial reduction in Soviet conventional forces, more strategic arms control agreements would further undermine the credibility of deterrence. Hence, he opposed the Reykjavik formula calling for a 50 percent reduction of strategic forces to follow the INF agreement. [63]

Kissinger declared that the increasing NATO disputes over strategy could be resolved only if US and West European leaders participate in a joint effort to redefine the requirements of Western security. This declaration reiterated the Nixon Doctrine which reflected his belief that states are more likely to pay the political costs and make the sacrifices for implementing strategies and programs if they feel responsible for their formulation. Reiterating his belief that this cannot be done by consultation, he stressed the need for "an explicit act of statesmanship . . . to give new meaning to Western unity and a new vitality to NATO," and recommended the following. First, a more significant role for Europe within NATO since by analyzing its security needs it will find, as he believed, that cooperation with the US is essential. He specifically suggested that by 1990 Europe should assume the major responsibility for conventional ground defense, that the Supreme Allied Commander Europe (SACEUR) be a European officer to make defense planning a more explicit European task and to give a new perspective to NATO strategic planning, that Europeans take over arms control negotiations dealing with weapons stationed in Europe, i.e., INF and MBFR, and that with greater emphasis on political coordination the Secretary General should be an American. Evident here is Kissinger's belief that political initiatives must remain under US control. Second, redeployment of NATO forces with Europe concentrating on the conventional defense of the Continent while the US focuses on maintaining the global balance of power by developing highly mobile conventional forces capable of backing up Europe and defending US interests in regions (Middle East, Asia, or the Western hemisphere) where the West Europeans do not see their interests immediately engaged but conflict is much more likely. This is a reiteration of his belief that since the Europeans are unlikely to play a significant global role US-West European cooperation must concentrate on issues within the Atlantic area. Third, Kissinger urged: (a) that the existing US land-based air power on the Continent be strengthened; (b) that the present naval US deployments be continued; and (c) that the US maintain the responsibility for strategic and tactical nuclear defense, assuming there is an agreement on the use of the latter. By these steps the US would demonstrate that Western Europe is a vital US interest, thus precluding European neutralism. In his view, the intermediate-range missiles should remain in Europe so long as West European leaders want them to "couple" the nuclear defenses of Europe and the US. Indeed, while he opposed the INF negotiations Kissinger accepted the INF Treaty as an accomplished fact and urged its ratification to maintain NATO unity. However, convinced that West Europeans will not build a full conventional defense to provide an alternative to nuclear deterrence which public opinion rejects, Kissinger warned that a gradual withdrawal of perhaps up to half the present ground US forces would be a logical result. But he stressed, the redeployed forces must be added to US strategic reserves since their demobilization would weaken the overall defense. Evident in Kissinger's proposals is the desire to undermine both US isolationism and European pacifism and neutralism which could result from a deployment that is losing its rationale and thus intensifying disputes about it. Kissinger warned, however, that redeployment must not be imposed by the US budgetary process or for its own sake since it will shock Europe into neutralism and mislead Moscow thus tempting aggression.[64] For Kissinger, the US "must make clear that no scheme involving the complete withdrawal of American forces from Europe can be considered."[65] Reiterating his belief that "defense requires . . . *some* agreed political purpose in the name of which it is conducted" (his italics), Kissinger declared: "The Atlantic Alliance must urgently develop a grand strategy for East-West problems and Third World relations applicable for the rest of this century."[66]

EUROPEAN UNITY: PAYING THE ECONOMIC PRICE FOR IT

The Soames/de Gaulle controversy in February 1969 gave Kissinger the opportunity to establish the US position on European unity. The controversy started when de Gaulle outlined his vision of the future of Europe to the British Ambassador to Paris, Christopher Soames, in terms that appeared to threaten both NATO and the EEC. Britain considered de

Gaulle's proposals very important and, although its views of NATO, the US, and the EEC differed from his, it was willing to discuss them further only if all NATO members were kept fully informed. By informing other allies about them, Britain unintentionally generated the fear that de Gaulle was trying to break up NATO. French efforts to reassure NATO members that this was not his goal failed.[67] US opponents of de Gaulle inside and outside the Administration urged Nixon to seize the opportunity to reaffirm the US commitment to a federal Europe, and to reject de Gaulle's proposal for a West European concert. The proposal had not been submitted to the US and Kissinger determined to avoid a dispute with de Gaulle, a day before Nixon's European trip began, recommended that Nixon affirm US support for NATO, for European unity, including British entry into the EEC, but to stress that the structure of Europe was fundamentaly the concern of the Europeans.[68] Indeed, Nixon stressed those points in discussions with West European leaders and Kissinger in briefings to the press, and they reappeared in the Reports to Congress thus establishing the US position on the issue.[69]

Kissinger's approach to the Soames/de Gaulle controversy avoided a dispute with France and reflected his beliefs that: (a) France was the pivot of US problems in NATO, hence, the improvement of US-French relations was the key to resolving them;[70] (b) US efforts to isolate de Gaulle were "mistaken and doomed to failure" because on East-West relations his views represented "the dominant trend in Europe"; (c) in NATO the US may prevail against France on technical issues but not in a prolonged political contest over strategic doctrine;[71] (d) Britain shared de Gaulle's rejection of European unity on a supranational model, thus her entry into EEC should not be a direct US objective;[72] and (e) the US federal experience is not applicable to Europe where history stressed national identity. In addition, it reflected his and Nixon's hope that since France had diplomatic relations with Hanoi and Peking it could assist them in ending the war in Vietnam and in establishing rapprochement with the PRC.[73]

The refusal to push for a federal Europe and the efforts to improve relations with France led to charges that the Administration was accepting de Gaulle's view of European political unity and of an independent role for Europe in world affairs – a sharp break from the traditional concept of Western Europe as a component of the Atlantic pole in a bipolar or tripolar balance.[74] De Gaulle's concept of a loosely unified Western Europe appealed to Kissinger and Nixon who believed that it would produce some immediate progress on unity without foreclosing the future while providing more access points and greater opportunity for US influence than could be expected in relations with a single political entity.[75] His position also reflected his belief that since US and European interests are not identical outside of Europe, a single European entity is unlikely to share the burdens and responsibilities of world leadership despite its resources and its degree of unity. Indeed, Kissinger resolved issues that, in whole or in part, fell within the jurisdiction of the EEC on a bilateral basis, arguing in the Report to Congress that:

> We believe that we can render support to the process of European coalescence not only by our role in the North Atlantic Alliance and by our relationship with European institutions, but also by our bilateral relations with the several European countries. For many years to come, these relations will provide essential trans-Atlantic bonds; and we will therefore continue to broaden and deepen them.[76]

For Kissinger, triangular diplomacy dictated the pursuit of Atlantic unity but not necessarily West European unity on a federal model since he believed that such a Europe will be in a better position to insist on a specifically European view of global affairs, thus challenging US hegemony in Atlantic policy.

Those beliefs and the desire to improve relations with de Gaulle, who opposed the political pretensions of the EEC Commission, led to a calculated neglect of it by Kissinger and Nixon. While visiting Europe in 1969 Nixon emphasized the US commitment to NATO by going to its headquarters for discussions with the Council and the Secretary General, but invited the Commission to a meeting at his suite at the Hilton, despite the fact that its headquarters was less than five minutes from the hotel.[77] Kissinger supported the informal regular consultation which began in 1970 between the Commission and the US, and welcomed suggestions for expanding consultation, including the possibility of a higher-level EEC representation in Washington, but it was left to West Europeans to make proposals that could be implemented.[78] They, however, were just as opposed as Kissinger to enhancing the role of the Commission.[79] By excluding the State Department and its European missions, which supported the EEC Commission, from the decision-making process Kissinger perpetuated the neglect of the Commission. This was consistent with his beliefs and his global strategy. He believed that through NATO he could manage the process of European détente since dependence on the US nuclear guarantee made European acquiescence to US policies possible.[80] But the US was not a member of the EEC and, more importantly, from Kissinger's view, there were no penalties for noncooperation. Since the US and the EEC had never agreed on a common trade policy toward the East and the EEC's economic interests often coincided with France's political goal to assert a more independent role for Europe,[81] he feared a stronger Commission could threaten Atlantic unity and challenge his policy toward Moscow, especially regarding trade, the second vital element in his linkage strategy. Moscow already was looking to Western Europe for capital and technology to reduce US leverage. For Kissinger, support for the expansion of the EEC represented a necessary concession to an incipient West European consciousness in order to preserve Atlantic unity which was essential for the implementation of his global strategy.

The expansion of the EEC resulted from Prime Minister Harold Wilson's decision to renew Britain's application to the EEC. By supporting Britain's entry into the EEC to balance his Ostpolitik, Brandt made it more attractive to France which feared a more independent course by the FRG.[82] In 1970, when the EEC Commission began negotiating with Britain, Norway, Denmark, and Ireland for their full membership, and began talks with Sweden, Austria, Switzerland, and other members of the European Free Trade Association (EFTA) looking toward some lesser form of relationship, US businesses and the Departments of Treasury, Commerce, and Agriculture began to pressure Nixon for assurances that US trade interests would be protected. They feared that Nixon and Kissinger, by stressing NATO unity and focusing on strategic and political issues, were sacrificing US economic interests. Their concern intensified when the 1970 Report to Congress reiterated Kissinger's belief that:

> We recognize that our interests will necessarily be affected by Europe's evolution, and we may have to make sacrifices in the common interest. We consider that the possible economic price of a truly unified Europe is outweighed by the gain in the political vitality of the West as a whole.[83]

But the Departments, unlike Kissinger, were not prepared to pay the economic price and at an interagency meeting on May 13, 1970, insisted on an official reinterpretation of the Report and on using Britain's entry into the EEC to attack the EEC's trade restrictions and preferential trading arrangements with other countries. At the same time, a restrictive trade bill, aimed at Europe and Japan, was being pushed in Congress. Fearing a trade war that could undermine Atlantic unity, Kissinger, supported by the State Department, and especially its European Bureau, the most ardent advocate of European unity, opposed the demands of the other Departments.[84]

To undermine opposition to European unity Kissinger proposed negotiations to place the Departmental and Congressional concerns before the

EEC. In addition, he permitted the economic Departments to join the USC. Kissinger admitted that the expansion of the USC was "in reality a device to let the economic agencies 'win' on the reinterpretation of the Presidential report, but at the same time to treat it as a foreign policy rather than economic issue through the State Department chairmanship of the committee dealing with the subject." Moreover, the Departmental demand that disputed issues be referred to Nixon, "guaranteed," according to Kissinger, that "I would have an opportunity to weigh in (if not have the last word) if purely commercial considerations threatened to overwhelm foreign policy imperatives."[85] The reassurance that economic interests would not be sacrificed came in the 1971 Report to Congress which declared:

> European unity will also pose problems for American policy, which it would be idle to ignore . . . . And unity happens to be coming fastest in the economic sphere – the area of policy in which competition seems to have the least immediate penalty and our common interest will take the most effort to insure . . . The common interest requires the prosperity of both Western Europe and the United States. This means freer and expanded trade and restraint in protecting special interests. We must negotiate a reduction in our trade restrictions . . . In short, we must define our self-interest in the widest terms and fix our sights on our fundamental rather than tactical purposes.[86]

The negotiations with the EEC that Kissinger proposed began on October 10, 1970, but dragged on inconclusively until August 15, 1971, when Nixon imposed the New Economic Policy (NEP).[87]

Kissinger's belief that there is a price to be paid for European unity and his willingness to pay it was evident in his efforts to resolve the crisis generated by NEP which reflected the fear of Treasury Secretary John Connally that if Britain, a large importer of US agricultural products, was put behind the EEC's protective wall it would damage US economic interests.[88] The West Europeans (and the Japanese, and the Canadians), who were not consulted in advance,[89] viewed NEP as a declaration of economic war and began to talk about a "European solution." Kissinger, fearing that the economic conflict would create disarray in NATO just before the impending Peking and Moscow summits sought to resolve the crisis. He proposed the formation of a small group which established a negotiating position and recommended a summit of the Western leaders. When the summit was rejected by the Europeans he proposed the bilateral meetings that led to the settlement of the issue.[90] Indeed, it was Kissinger who at the Nixon-Pompidou meeting in the Azores on December 14, over breakfast with Pompidou, settled the amount by which France was willing to revalue the franc in exchange for the devaluation of the dollar.[91] This agreement led to a conference of the Group of Ten a week later at the Smithsonian in Washington. The Smithsonian Agreement ratified the new monetary arrangements which ended the economic crisis. In short, by pushing for the resolution of the crisis, Kissinger appeared to be paying the economic price to maintain Atlantic unity which was essential for the implementation of his global strategy.

In the 1980s Kissinger reiterated his belief that "European unity, strength, and self-confidence are essential for the future of the West," since it is beyond the psychological and physical resources of the US to be the only or even the principal center of initiative and responsibility in the non-Communist world – a reiteration of the Nixon Doctrine. Arguing that US support for European unity is based on self-interest, he indicated a willingness to pay a price for it occasionally provided that Europe and the US agreed on fundamentals.[92] Moreover, for Kissinger, the special relationship characterizing US-British relations should be "replicate it on a wider plane of America's relations with *all* its European allies" (his italics). However, he continued to insist that whether this is done bilaterally or with a politically united EEC, "is for Europe to decide."[93]

"SELECTIVE DÉTENTE": OSTPOLITIK, BERLIN, AND THE CSCE

In 1969, while Kissinger was looking to the PRC to gain leverage on the USSR, Moscow was exploiting Western European interest in MBFR and a European Security Conference, later known as the CSCE, to gain leverage over Washington. But Brandt's election as Chancellor on October 21 alarmed Kissinger[94] because the new coalition of Social Democrats and Free Democrats had pledged new initiatives toward the East. His opposition to Ostpolitik became evident in the NSC staff meetings,[95] and the rationale for it in his memorandums to Nixon which stressed that Ostpolitik, which many viewed as a progressive policy for establishing détente, could turn into an new form of classic German nationalism which in foreign policy meant to maneuver freely between East and West and that such an attempt "would prove disastrous for the peace of the world"[96] – a conviction consistent with his criticism of Johnson for urging Bonn to take independent initiatives toward the East.[97] Aware of Kissinger's and Nixon's alarm, and before being formally installed, Brandt asked them to receive Egon Bahr, his political confidant, to iron out any differences.

But on October 13, 1969, while informing Kissinger of the course Brandt intended to follow and stressing that he wanted to pursue it in cooperation with Washington, Bahr made it clear that Ostpolitik itself was not subject to discussion, and rejected Kissinger's view that it was more likely to lead to a permanent division of Germany than toward unification. This meeting led to a dispute with Rogers and to the establishment of a backchannel so that Kissinger and Bahr could resolve important issues outside formal procedures.[98] For Kissinger, Brandt's Ostpolitik and the interest in MBFR and the CSCE raised the risk of "selective détente," that is, Moscow could play to the West European interests while remaining intrasigent on global issues of concern to Washington (Vietnam, Middle East), thus isolating the US from its allies and undermining the global equilibrium.[99]

On November 11, 1969, Brandt's offers to the USSR and the GDR to renounce the use of force and accept the status quo in Central Europe made this risk real. Kissinger feared that a direct accommodation between Bonn and Moscow by excluding the US from the solution of a major European problem would set a precedent that might lead other allies to look increasingly to Moscow rather than to Washington. Moreover, Brandt's acceptance of the European status quo would compound the isolation of the PRC. Despite his concern that Ostpolitik could undermine NATO unity, Kissinger recognized he could not derail it because: (a) the SPD/FDP coalition had been elected on the program Brandt was implementing, thus, the US could derail Ostopolitik only by intervening heavily in the FRG's internal politics; (b) opposing it would have alienated Pompidou and Wilson who endorsed it publicly, and privately pressed Nixon to follow suit because they feared FRG's "liberation policy." Pompidou feared that only the refashioning of NATO into a US-FRG alliance for the liberation of Eastern Europe might stop Brandt; and (c) domestically, the Administration would have been charged with destroying prospects for improving the harsh conditions of the division of Germany. Having no alternative to offer, Kissinger sought to control Ostpolitik to preclude Brandt's dependence on the goodwill of Moscow for the achievement of his goals.[100]

For Kissinger, Brandt could not conduct Ostpolitik on a purely national basis given NATO's dependence on the US strategic guarantee and the isolation of Berlin.[101] Indeed, for Kissinger "Berlin became the key to the whole puzzle." The treaties negotiated by Brandt had to be ratified by the Bundestag where his coalition had a slim twelve-vote majority. Therefore, he could ill afford to provide more ammunition for the Christian Democratic oposition which was already charging him with a complete sell out of German interests in the East. In Kissinger's view "an agreement improving the security of Berlin was the most tangible and convincing quid pro quo for Brandt's controversial treaties . . . It became clear that only with a Berlin agreement would Brandt's Eastern treaties be ratified."[102] While a Berlin agreement required the concurrence of the four wartime powers, only the US could guarantee its security, thus it had a major voice in the negotiating process, however it was started. In December 1969, the NATO Foreign Ministers meeting in Brussels, at Kissinger's urging made the holding of a European Security Conference conditional on Soviet concessions on Berlin, on the intra-German and Soviet-German negotiations, and on MBFR.[103] For Kissinger, "linkage was inherent." By relating Ostpolitik to issues involving NATO as a whole, he sought both to strengthen Brandt's negotiating position while setting limits beyond which he could not go without an allied consensus and to generate incentives for Moscow to make concessions.[104] However, the linkage between Berlin and US-Soviet détente was never made explicit.

The Four-Power talks on Berlin began at the ambassadorial level, on March 26, 1970, and were seen by Kissinger and West Europeans as a "test case" regarding the seriousness of Soviet interest both in détente and in long-term cooperation in Europe. Kissinger opposed the talks originally[105] – a stand reflecting his belief that Berlin's isolation limits the possible concessions the West can make without undermining its freedom and, more importantly, the credibility of the US guarantee.[106] Indeed, his belief in credibility was evident during the mini-crisis generated by Soviet protests and GDR's harassment of civilian traffic to Berlin prior the election of the FRG's President in Berlin on March 5. Kissinger recommended that Nixon, in his first meeting with Dobrynin on February 17, 1969, warn Moscow that interference with access to Berlin was a matter of direct concern to the US. Kissinger repeated the warning to Dobrynin on February 22, the day before Nixon left for Europe, and shortly before the election. To underline his warning he recommended and Nixon ordered, despite strong opposition from the State Department, increased US military traffic over the access routes to Berlin reaffirming the US commitment to the city.[107] The strong measures recommended by Kissinger also reflected his belief that since Berlin had become the touchstone of the West's European policy, a "defeat" in Berlin would demoralize the FRG, become a warning to all European states of the folly of resisting Soviet pressure, and demonstrate to the rest of the world the irresistible nature of the communist advance.[108]

Nixon reiterated the US commitment to defend Berlin in a speech on February 27, 1969, at the Siemens Factory, and expressed the hope that Berlin could become the object of "negotiation . . . and reconciliation."[109] Nixon's willingness to negotiate on Berlin resulted from the lobbying efforts of Chancellor Kiesinger and Foreign Minister Brandt.[110] Indeed, only they, urged the rapid acceptance of Gromyko's suggestion of July 10, 1969, for Four-Power talks to prevent future crisis. They hoped that the easing of tensions would benefit their parties in the September parliamentary election. The US, Britain, and France were highly suspicious of Moscow's intensions but on August 7, after Nixon's visit to Rumania, suggested exploratory talks to test them.[111] While accepting on September 12, Moscow resisted any discussion of improved access to Berlin, and wanted the talks to focus on limiting the FRG's activities in West Berlin.[112]

Believing that US-Soviet détente could not be pursued globaly without Atlantic unity, Kissinger sought to prevent Moscow from using Berlin to isolate the US from its allies. To test Moscow's flexibility and to satisfy Brandt's need for movement on Berlin Nixon, in a letter to Kosygin on March 26, repeated his offer to discuss Berlin. But when Kosygin replied on May 27 that Moscow would discuss Berlin but Bonn was to blame for the tensions, Kissinger, concerned with West European and specifically Brandt's reaction to bilateral talks, recommended an end to discussing Berlin until consultations with the new government of the FRG.[113] On October 20, when Dobrynin proposed to Nixon a bilateral formal exchange of views, Kissinger, in view of Moscow's evasions about discussing improvements of access and Brandt's charges that the US was pursuing selective détente, told Nixon, "we should not encourage the notion of bilateral U.S.- Soviet talks on Berlin at this stage. The Soviets would use them to stir up suspicions among the Allies and to play us off against each other. I believe we would do best to keep this issue in the quadripartite forum for the moment and not to press too much ourselves."[114]

The Quadripartite Talks gave the State Department the strongest hand in interagency discussions since it staffed the Bonn Group, the Berlin Task Force, and its Assistant Secretary for European Affairs, Martin J. Hillenbrand, chaired the European IG of the NSC. Kissinger controlled the process by assigning NSSM 111 on December 29, 1970, to prepare a US draft of an allied proposal for a Berlin agreement and NSSM 136 on July 30, 1971, to examine concessions that could be made to the USSR, and through the SRG which evaluated those policy studies prepared by the European IG.[115] Kissinger became personally involved in the negotiations in February 1971, and sought to control the process through the backchannels with US Ambassador Kenneth Rush in Bonn, Bahr and Dobrynin. The backchannels permitted him to bypass the State Department which opposed the linkage of Berlin to the security conference which it viewed as a forum that could produce results on either MBFR or on principles of coexistence,[116] and to curb Bahr's propensity for moving too fast unilaterally and for claiming credit for Bonn for all concessions made.[117] Kissinger feared that Brandt by making concessions too fast would undermine his efforts to implement linkage to influence Moscow's international behavior.

Kissinger viewed the Berlin/Ostpolitik linkage as "his ace in the hole," and despite Brandt's calls for speeding up the talks, consistent with his belief in the need to avoid the quest for quick diplomatic victories in the protracted East-West conflict, he recommended a slower pace. For Kissinger the US position on Berlin would improve once the Eastern treaties were completed since Moscow would be eager to ratify them. Brandt, however, sought to use the Berlin talks for leverage, and more dangerous for Kissinger, to shift the responsibility for any failure of Ostpolitik to Washington.[118] This was not a new concern. In criticizing Johnson's support of Bonn's policy of "small steps" toward the East, Kissinger stressed that if Bonn is determined to pursue this course "there is nothing we can do to prevent it. But we should make certain that the West cannot be blamed."[119] Indeed, when Brandt, prior to signing the Bonn-Moscow Treaty in Moscow on August 12, 1970, linked its ratification to a satisfactory Berlin settlement, Kissinger was disturbed although he had insisted on it. He feared that he would be held responsible if the talks collapsed. Moreover, while convinced that the FRG's acceptance of its eastern borders was essential to a unification program he had stressed: "it is an important tactical question at what point the [FRG] should renounce its claims."[120] Now, he felt Brandt had renounced them too soon, thus depriving the West of the opportunity to get substantive Soviet concessions for recognizing the European status quo.[121] Kissinger's efforts to control the process of European détente was clear to Brandt who stated "I gained the impression . . . that he would rather have taken personal charge of the delicate complex of East-West problems in its entirety."[122]

Kissinger's uneasiness with Brandt's tendency to deal too rapidly and bilaterally with Moscow and other East European states was evident in the 1971 Report to Congress which stated:

> Obviously, the Western countries do not have identical national concerns and cannot be expected to agree automatically on priorities or solutions. Each ally is the best judge of its own national interest. But our principal objective should be to harmonize our policies and insure that our efforts for détente are complementary. A differentiated détente, limited to the USSR and certain Western allies but not others, would be illusory. It would cause strains among allies. It would turn the desire for détente into an instrument of political warfare. Far from contributing to reconciliation in Europe, it would postpone it indefinitely.[123]

The Report also indicated that Brandt had given much more than he had received in the Moscow and Warsaw Treaties.

Kissinger's linkage of Berlin to US-Soviet détente was evident in 1971. In May, when Moscow tried to exploit the double backchannel system during the SALT talks through Semenov's offer to Smith of an ABM agreement without simultaneity in offensive limitations (an offer Kissinger had rejected six weeks earlier in talks with Dobrynin), Kissinger exploited Moscow's need for an early Berlin agreement by instructing Rush to postpone the May 19 meeting with the Soviet Ambassador. Realizing that Smith's efforts to get this "compromise" accepted led to public and Congressional pressure that could have undermined the backchannel, he also told Dobrynin on May 11 that he would shift the Berlin talks to official channels thus postponing the ratification of the Eastern treaties. But following the May 20 SALT breakthrough Kissinger permitted the Berlin talks to proceed.[124] However, when Gromyko made final agreement to a Moscow summit (tentatively scheduled for September 1971) conditional on the conclusion of the Berlin talks and Kissinger realized that there would be no summit, he once again instructed Rush to delay the talks until after July 15 despite pressure from the Europeans to conclude them rapidly. By delaying the talks until after the announcement of his visit to Peking, Kissinger sought to prevent Moscow from using it as a pretext to launch a new crisis.[125] Seeing the opening to Peking as an attempt to isolate it, Moscow compromised. Kissinger also compromised to assure Moscow that US-PRC rapprochement would not disrupt US-Soviet détente.[126] To bypass the opposition of the Departments of State and Defense and the CIA, he conceded in the backchannel, with Nixon's approval, a Soviet consulate in West Berlin.[127] In addition, the Western Three and Bonn agreed to reduce FRG's presence in West Berlin. But Moscow for the first time guaranteed unimpeded access from FRG to West Berlin, accepted the right of West Berliners to visit the GDR and East Berlin and their right to travel on FRG passports, and Bonn's right to represent West Berlin in international agreement bodies.[128] Agreement was reached on August 18, and initialed on August 23. But Rogers, not aware that the consulate decision was Nixon's, pointed to a NSDM which ordered the negotiators not to agree to it without Nixon's approval and threatened an "intensive review." But Nixon's intervention and Brandt's endorsement, on Kissinger's suggestion, ended the bureaucratic debate. The Quadripartite Agreement was officially signed on September 3. Even Kissinger's critics later acknowledged that it improved the lives and safety of Berlin's population.[129]

Kissinger's efforts to control the process of European détente by linkage was also evident in his handling of Moscow's formal proposal on March

17, 1969, for an early European Security Conference, better known as
Conference on Security and Cooperation in Europe (CSCE). The Budapest
Appeal put forward as a means to enhance European security was notable
for its omission of anti-German polemics (notable in previous proposals)
and the continued exclusion of the US. For Kissinger this was "the maximum Soviet program for Europe."[130] Hence, his initial reaction (shared by
some Allies) was very cool. He viewed the Budapest Appeal as a Soviet
ploy to achieve the formal ratification of the status quo in Europe without
making any concessions. Indeed, on April 3, when Dobrynin gave him the
proposal in their channel noting that it no longer called for the dissolution
of alliances and told Kissinger that Moscow would not object to US
participation, Kissinger wrote Nixon that those were absurd preconditions
not concessions. However, at the NATO meeting in Washington in April,
Brandt urged its members to examine Moscow's proposal arguing, "it
would be a mistake for the West to pursue détente on a selective basis"
– implying the US should not expect West Europeans to reject Moscow's
conciliatory gestures while it negotiated with it. Moreover, he argued that a
conference would legitimize the US role in Europe. Italian Foreign Minister
Pietro Nenni supported Brandt by proposing the West take the lead in
calling for a security conference. Pompidou supported Brandt in order
to involve Bonn in a multilateral framework and preclude independent
initiatives towards the East, while the British advocated it as a means to
transcend the Cold War.[131]

This reaction convinced Kissinger that rejection would lead to US
isolation in NATO, hence he recommended to Nixon that its acceptance
in principle depend on progress on concrete European issues, especially
Berlin. In a memorandum on April 8, he noted:

> Without such progress, a conference would probably find the East Euro-
> pean countries closely aligned with a rigid Soviet position, while the
> western participants would be competing with each other to find ways
> to "break the deadlock." The new result . . . would tend to set back
> prospects for an eventual resolution of European issues. Consequently,
> our emphasis should be on the need for talks on concrete issues and
> for consultations within NATO designed to develop coherent western
> positions on such issues.[132]

This reflects his belief that NATO unity is vital to pursuing détente.
The communique at the end of the meeting offered to explore "concrete issues" with the Warsaw Pact, but insisted on US and Canadian
participation. Kissinger's influence on the issue was evident to Brandt

who reported that at the meeting Nixon informed them about the prelude to the SALT talks, and declared that in moving toward an "age of negotiation . . . the West must not . . . be drawn into a selective détente which would leave the Soviet Union more or less free to determine where it considered détente appropriate or a continuation of the Cold War expedient." For Brandt, "Kissinger's handwriting was clearly discernible [in Nixon's statement]." [133]

Kissinger's stand on the CSCE also reflected his belief that it should be linked to global issues of concern to the US. Rejecting Dobrynin's proposal that the conference meet in the first half of 1970 to discuss the renunciation of the use of force in Europe and the widening of commercial, economic, technical and scientific relations, he felt that by waiting until the Bundestag's ratification of the German-Soviet treaties he could induce Moscow to restrain its actions, particularly in Vietnam. [134] In addition, by slowing down the expansion of trade he prevented Moscow from getting the needed technology from Western Europe thus depriving him of positive incentives. A multilateral preparatory conference on CSCE opened on Helsinki on November 22, 1972. Consistent with his belief in avoiding the quest for quick diplomatic victories in the protracted conflict with the USSR, Kissinger opposed West European pressure during the October War for a summit to conclude the CSCE. [135]

In the late 1970s and in the 1980s, the threat of selective détente had materialized for Kissinger in the form of a dangerous West European dependency on economic ties in some areas with the East. In his view, this was evident in the inability of the Carter and Reagan Administrations to get West European cooperation in restricting East-West trade, by stopping the sale of certain commodities and interrupting long-term projects, i.e., the gas pipeline, when the USSR invaded Afghanistan and suppressed freedom in Poland. He was concerned with the US perception, magnified by the pipeline dispute, that the West Europeans were sacrificing long-term strategy to short term economic and political gain, and the West European view, generated by the lifting of the grain embargo by Reagan, that the US was unwilling to pay the price and was playing global politics with their assets. He criticized Western governments for increasingly acting on the premise that the immediate employment gains outweigh the polical risks in strengthening a hostile and aggressive political system and for justifying the continuation of trade by arguing that sanctions never work and that sanctions are tantamount to an act of war. Kissinger was distressed by the increasing competition between Western governments which provide concessional credits to aid their national industries thus allowing Moscow to play off the Western countries and industries to obtain benefits unjustified by the economic balance of advantages and by the political conditions and, more importantly, by the fact that the increasing economic ties induce Western restraint in the face of Moscow's assault on the global equilibrium. Criticizing the frivolous use of the West's overwhelming economic power, he reiterated his belief that this was the result of the lack of will or the leadership to organize a coherent response rather than stop-and-go sanctions. In his view, selective détente could be controlled if the West agreed on a political criteria for progress in economic cooperation or at least on letting market conditions determine the level of East-West trade and credit[136] – a reiteration of his beliefs in the primacy of politics and in exacting a political quid pro quo for economic benefits that Moscow could not acquire elsewhere. Moreover, Kissinger feared that Atlantic divisions over the assessment of Soviet conduct, military strategy, arms control and issues outside the NATO area invite Moscow to apply détente selectively in order to split the West and undermine the global equilibrium while avoiding its own structural dilemmas.[137] For Kissinger, it is incompatible with the Alliance that its members agree on no major policy around the world.[138]

THE YEAR OF EUROPE: SEEKING ATLANTIC UNITY

By the end of 1972, having established new relationships with Moscow and Peking and convinced that the Vietnam negotiations were close to completion, Kissinger sought to develop an Atlantic community which he believed to be vital for retaining the West's relevance in the rest of the world and for establishing a stable world order. When consultations with West European leaders (but not the Japanese) revealed a lack of support about the idea Kissinger did not abandon it – an action consistent with his belief that the effective pursuit of goals requires leadership.[139] As with previous major policy initiatives Rogers was not consulted and its implementation was controlled by Kissinger who in September 1973 also became the Secretary of State.[140]

The initiative appeared in the form of the "Year of Europe" address by Kissinger on April 23, at the annual meeting of the Associated Press editors in New York. Expressing his concern about the growing US isolationism and criticisms of the West European disregard of US economic interests and reluctance to share the common defense burden and about the West European fears that the US is trying to divide Europe economically, desert it militarily and bypass it diplomatically, and noting that Europe's appeals for greater independence and its veto of US independent policies are made in the name of Atlantic unity, Kissinger declared that this was "an appeal for a joint effort of creativity" to "articulate a clear set of common objectives." Emphasizing the linkage of political, military, and economic issues, Kissinger stressed the need "to deal with [them] comprehensively . . . at the highest level" since a technical approach will waste the opportunity. He underlined the centrality of the Alliance "in building a new structure of peace," and emphasized the need to gear it less to crisis and more to opportunities by drawing inspiration from its goals rather than its fears. Kissinger promised continued US support for European unity as a component of a larger Atlantic partnership and more US concessions to promote its further growth, but he insisted on reciprocity. He reaffirmed the US commitment to the defense of Western Europe and opposition to unilateral troop withdrawals, and praised allied efforts to improve their forces, but stressed the need for greater allied contributions to the common defense. Acknowledging differences over the pursuit of détente by uncoordinated independent initiatives, he declared that "we can no longer afford to pursue national or regional self-interest without a unifying framework." He urged cooperation on new common problems, especially energy, and invited Japan's cooperation. Consistent with his belief that the Europeans would not assume greater global responsibilities, he stressed: "the United States has global interests and responsibilities. Our European allies have regional interests. These are not necessarily in conflict, but in the new era neither are they automatically identical."[141] In brief, the address reiterated Kissinger's beliefs in linkage, summitry, European unity, Atlantic community, regional balance of power, and leadership. Those beliefs reappeared in the 1973 Report to Congress in May and in Kissinger's address to the Society of Pilgrims in London on December 12 where he reiterated his proposal with minor modifications.[142]

The West Europeans ignored Kissinger's proposal that the new Atlantic Charter be worked out by the end of the year by promising to study it. France objected to confining Europe to a "regional role," and feared that efforts to foster Atlantic unity might undermine the simultaneous European attempts to build political unity under her leadership, pressure her to rejoin NATO or pressure the EEC in the forthcoming trade negotiations. Moreover, France feared that the Atlantic Declaration would permit Nixon to act as a spokesman of all Atlantic states in the forthcoming Nixon-Brezhnev summit in Washington in June thus undermining her independent role. On France's request Kissinger bypassed the EEC in order to give Paris the leading role in shaping the European response to his initiative – an action consistent with his previous efforts to improve relations with France on the belief that on political issues France is not as isolated in Europe as many believed and that this allowed her to kill US initiatives. Britain, Italy, and the FRG, shared the French concerns and were ready to follow her lead. Brandt, in particular, wanted to avoid closer Atlantic bonds to preserve his freedom of action for Ostpolitik. The smaller states followed their lead. Kissinger's insistence on an Atlantic summit to deal with his initiative reflected his beliefs in the need for political will and rejection of policymaking by bureaucratic means. Watergate, however, increased the West European reluctance to accept an initiative that Nixon's domestic critics saw as a diversion. Hence, while pressing Nixon to attend a collective summit to conclude the CSCE, they proposed bilateral consultations among the Big Four as a means to formulate the Atlantic Declaration. But when Kissinger pursued bilateral consultations the Europeans insisted on developing a joint response by EEC consultations and without US participation.[143]

The October War further undermined Kissinger's initiative. Rejecting his view that their oil supplies could be best guaranteed by a united NATO response that would reduce Moscow's role in the Middle East, the West Europeans sought dissociation from the US by arguing that NATO's obligations do not extend to the Middle East. In other words, despite their previous criticisms they now defended the regional role assigned Europe in the initiative. In their view, the supply of oil could be assured only by a pro-Arab tilt, that is, by insisting that the US pressure Israel to return to the 1967 borders. Hence, they did not permit the US to use its European bases for the airlift of arms to Israel and banned US overflight of their territory while the USSR overflew their airspace in its airlift to the Arabs. Moreover, Britain and France rejected Kissinger's proposals for a UN cease-fire resolution that urged a return to the status quo ante, and later objected to a UN Emergency Force which Sadat accepted. In addition, while they criticised détente for not preventing the war they invoked it in order to end it. Indeed, they refused to reduce their economic exchanges with the USSR and pressed for concluding the CSCE. For Kissinger, it appeared that West Europeans were seeking to reduce their dependence on the US by multiplying contacts with the USSR.[144]

The oil embargo and the nuclear alert intensified West European efforts to dissociate themselves from US policy and led them to criticize Kissinger for not consulting over the alert which involved US troops stationed in Europe. His actions, however, reflected his belief that since consultations could not create a consensus but could be used by allies to veto US initiatives, consultations about the alert would have undermined the demonstration of political will and the willingness to run risks – the aim of the alert – which he considered vital for maintaining the global equilibrium. Moreover, by not consulting he assured the rapid application of US capabilities which he viewed as essential for advancing one's interests.[145]

To give concrete expression to Atlantic unity, Kissinger, in his address to the Society of Pilgrims in London on December 12, 1973, invited the industrial democracies to form an Energy Action Group (EAG) which would promote alternative sources of energy and conservation and give producers an incentive to increase the supply of oil. In his view, the energy crisis of 1973 provided an opportunity for such an initiative. To reduce the tensions generated by the Year of Europe address, he affirmed Europe's global responsibilities and promised to consult, but he repeated his conviction that "even the best consultative machinery cannot substitute for common vision and shared goals." To reassure those who felt that his initiative was intended to undermine European unity, he left it to the West Europeans to decide whether to respond as the EEC.[146] The West Europeans, however, while interested in enlisting US technology to develop alternatives sources of energy and in sharing supplies in an emergency, ignored his proposals regarding the EAG and for improving consultation. Under French leadership, the EEC decided to pursue its own initiative in the Middle East by proposing a separate "European-Arab dialogue." The EEC's call for a comprehensive solution, however, was in conflict with Kissinger's step-by-step approach – a reflection of the growing divergence that Kissinger believed would result from greater European unity. France opposed the EAG convinced that it would lead to a cutoff of oil,[147] and to maintain her independence proposed bilateral deals with the oil producers. Those who accepted the principle of consumer cooperation defined it in terms that also permitted the independent policy favored by France.[148] Kissinger's belief that in times of ambiguity the US must lead was evident in his proposal for an energy conference in Washington. On January 9, 1974, Nixon invited the West Europeans, Japan, and the EEC. While the West European leaders accepted the invitation they were reluctant to establish a permanent consumer group for fear of provoking the Arabs. France sought to undermine the initiative by proposing an alternative UN conference on energy problems which in its view might moderate the positions of producers, consumers, and developing states, and later a European energy grouping which would exclude the US.[149]

The EEC's actions seemed to confirm Kissinger's belief that since European and US interests are not identical everywhere a united Europe would be in a better position to insist on differences thus magnifying Atlantic disputes. By leading the opposition to Kissinger's initiatives and succeeding in developing a European response in the Middle East, France demonstrated that Kissinger had been correct in assuming that when the economic interests of the EEC coincide with the political goal of France it leads to a more independent role for Europe in world affairs. The result of Kissinger's initiatives was the declaration on security principles, known as the Declaration on Atlantic Relations, agreed to at the Ottawa NATO Council meeting on June 19, 1974.[150]

Despite the failure of his "Year of Europe" and the EGA initiatives, since 1977 Kissinger has been reasserting his belief that "the unity of the industrial democracies remains crucial to the survival of democratic values and of the global equilibrium,"[151] and has insisted on dealing with the problems of the Alliance immediately since the increasing intensity of disagreements over nuclear strategy, East-West relations, economic policy, arms control, the Middle East, Central America, and Africa, will eventually impair the security relationship which has maintained world peace.[152] He specifically criticized West Europeans for condemning US actions in Grenada and other Third World areas convinced that since they could not influence them it was safe to appease "progressives" at home and radicals abroad. He feared the rush to condemn the US would eventually affect its willingness to run risks even for Europe's defense.[153] For Kissinger, the USSR has successfully exploited opportunities to undermine the global equilibrium despite its profound systemic crisis because of the lack of a united Western response. The absence of a forum for addressing the future in a concrete way and for harmonizing disagreements or implementing common policies concerned Kissinger, who while reiterating his belief that summits are of limited utility since they can only call the leaders' attention to major problems in an informal, unsystematic way, he recommended them as a means for injecting political will into policymaking of the Alliance. Moreover, while repeating his belief in the limited utility of consultation he continued to suggest that it should be improved as a first step for coordinating Western policies.[154] Blaming the failure of Western leadership for Moscow's successes he declared: "the solutions to the West's problems are, to a significant degree, in our own hands" – a reflection of his belief that with political imagination and will man can shape history.[155]

CONCLUSION

The analysis of US policy toward the Atlantic Alliance reveals that Kissinger's policy proposals and/or actions while in office were consistent with his beliefs. This consistency is also found in his policy recommendations after 1977. Believing that the unity of NATO is vital for establishing a stable international order, Kissinger made partnership with the European allies the corollary to his strategy toward the USSR and the PRC. However, his belief in limits led him to use the Nixon Doctrine to redefine partnership to mean that while the US would help where it makes a real difference it would not conceive all plans, design all programs, and undertake all the defense of the free world. Consistent with his belief that political multipolarity makes it impossible to impose an American design, Kissinger stressed that while partnership meant greater material contributions by allies these would be for programs they designed. But believing that only the US can guarantee the security of NATO, he strove to maintain the credibility of the US commitment to it and to enhance its deterrent by military means since uncertainty would lead West Europeans to pursue more independent initiatives toward the East thus undermining his use of linkage to make Moscow more cooperative on global issues vital to the US. Convinced that while West European and US interests are not identical everywhere, in defense and East-West diplomacy are fundamentaly parallel, he insisted that policies in these areas be harmonized. When this did not materialize, consistent with his belief that leadership is inherent in power, he used NATO's dependence on the US nuclear guarantee to control West European diplomatic initiatives toward the East to preclude selective détente.

Kissinger's efforts to maintain NATO's military strength reflected his belief that the European balance of power is vital for maintaining the global equilibrium of power – a prerequisite to peace. However, consistent with his beliefs that NATO's strategic dilemmas could not be resolved as long as it remains composed of sovereign states and that US efforts to impose solutions unilaterally undermine its unity, he: (a) insisted on strategic sufficiency which permitted the US to deploy new strategic weapons programs to sustain the credibility of the nuclear guarantee to Western Europe while pursuing SALT; and (b) acquiesced with the NPG's decision regarding the demonstrative use of tactical nuclear weapons even though he viewed it as a reflection of the West's lack of political will. His acquiescence reflected his belief in the need for NATO unity which would have been undermined by his rejection of the NPG's decision which emerged from a European initiative. However, consistent with his belief in leadership, during the October War he used the nuclear alert to demonstrate that the US had both the capability and the will to meet Soviet threats to peace. To maintain the European balance of power in the context of strategic parity without undermining Atlantic unity, Kissinger: (a) rejected Soviet demands to include the FBS and the British and French nuclear systems in SALT; (b) asserted that Article IX of the ABM treaty does not prohibit the transfer of offensive weapons technology to Britain and France; (c) insisted on the inclusion of Article VI in the APNW which protected US obligations to NATO; (d) led the efforts to defeat several Senate resolutions which called for unilateral reductions of US troops in Europe; and (e) redefined burden-sharing and praised EDIP. By dealing with the role of conventional forces through the EDIP which did not create the needed conventional capability and that of tactical nuclear weapons through the NPG decision which demonstrated the West's lack of political will, Kissinger was acting inconsistently with his belief in the need to establish a relationship between power and will. However, he was acting consistently with his belief that to maintain NATO's unity the US must avoid the tendency to impose solutions on strategic issues by unilateral initiatives. His insistence on limiting consultations on SALT and the APNW, reflected his belief that consultations cannot create a consensus but they can be used by allies to veto US initiatives. Since 1977, Kissinger's recommendations have been consistent with those beliefs. Reasserting the need to maintain the European balance of power by strengthening NATO's conventional forces and by maintaining the US nuclear guarantee, he has opposed both the no-first-use initiative and the Reykjavik formula. Consistent with his belief that West Europeans would not play a global role, he recommended that they concentrate on their own defense in order to permit the redeployment of US forces to develop the capability for defending the most likely attacks to Western interests outside NATO. In addition, reiterating his belief in the need for a Western strategy and for increased West European initiatives in NATO, he stressed that these require not just consultation but an act of statesmanship.

The consistency between proposals and/or actions and beliefs is also evident in Kissinger's reaction to West European initiatives to strengthen European unity. Consistent with his belief that negotiations with the USSR and the PRC dictate Atlantic unity, Kissinger recommended that the US affirm support for European unity, including British entry into the EEC, but not to use the Soames/de Gaulle controversy to promote the federal model. His refusal to push this model reflected his beliefs that the US experience is not applicable to Europe, that both Britain and de Gaulle opposed unity on a supranational model, that political multipolarity makes it impossible to impose US designs, and that since US and West European interests are not identical everywhere a federal Europe will be in a better position to challenge US hegemony in Atlantic policy which he viewed as essential for pursuing his initiatives to the East. His calculated neglect of the EEC Commission also reflected the last belief. NATO's dependence on the US nuclear guarantee permits the US to influence political and diplomatic initiatives, but since the US is not a member of the EEC and penalties for non-cooperation do not exist, in the absence of a common trade policy a stronger Commission would have challenged his trade policy toward the East with which he tried to create incentives for Moscow's cooperation. However, consistent with his belief that there is an economic price to be paid for European unity which is essential to Atlantic unity, he tried to resolve the crisis generated by NEP. Kissinger's Year of Europe initiative reiterated his beliefs in linkage, European and Atlantic unity, a regional role for Europe, summitry, conceptualization and leadership. Consistent with his belief that leadership is the willingness to stand alone, he pursued this initiative despite his knowledge of the lack of West European support for it. Since 1977, Kissinger has been reiterating his beliefs that while West European unity is vital it must result from European initiatives and that the unity of the industrial democracies is crucial to the global equilibrium of power – a prerequisite to peace.

The fact that Kissinger's recommendations and/or actions toward Western Europe were influenced by his strategy toward the USSR and the PRC was evident in his handling of Ostpolitik, the Berlin negotiations, and the CSCE. He insisted that NATO make the holding of the CSCE conditional on Soviet concessions on Berlin, on the intra-German and Soviet-German negotiations, and on MBFR, and linked Berlin and the CSCE to global issues of concern to the US. Consistent with his belief in the need to avoid the quest for quick diplomatic victories in the protracted conflict with the East, Kissinger repeatedly slowed down the Berlin negotiations to induce Moscow to make concessions in SALT and on Berlin but let them proceed after his opening to Peking. By doing this through the backchannels he demonstrated his belief in leadership.

11 Brzezinski and Alliances: Trilateral Cooperation?

INTRODUCTION: THE CHALLENGE OF COLLECTIVE
LEADERSHIP

Carter's reiteration during the campaign of Brzezinski's attacks on the Nixon Shocks, the Nixon Doctrine, and the Year of Europe, and his reaffirmation of Brzezinski's declaration that the active promotion of trilateral cooperation must be the central priority of US policy, led many to believe that Carter would seek to develop a partnership with Western Europe and Japan through consultations, and joint leadership. Brzezinski's appointment was seen as a demonstration of Carter's determination to fulfill his campaign pledge, as was the appointment of Vance and Brown who had also served in the Trilateral Commission. This chapter examines Brzezinski's impact on US alliance policy by analyzing the consistency between his beliefs on world politics and strategy and tactics for achieving national goals and his recommendations and/or actions as it became evident in the rationale of policies in official statements, in his memoranda to Carter, in his approach to issues and in the agreements with allies. The impact of those beliefs on Brzezinski's actions is also ascertained by analyzing their consistency with his policy recommendations since his departure from the NSC. This chapter also highlights the similarities and differences between Brzezinski's proposals and/or actions and those of Kissinger.

THE NEED FOR ARCHITECTURE

President-elect Carter dramatized his commitment to trilateral cooperation by announcing in early January 1977 that Mondale would travel to Europe and the Far East in the first week after the inauguration to discuss his foreign policy plans and to consult on preparations for the upcoming Economic summit.[1] This demonstration of his intention to consult the West Europeans and the Japanese was followed by a more explicit, although indirect, promise not to push unilateral changes of US policy on them. In his UN speech on March 17, 1977, Carter declared that in pursuing the goals of arms control, a more cooperative international economic system, and the advancement of human rights, "I realize that the United States cannot solve the problems of the world. We can sometimes help others resolve their differences, but we cannot do so by imposing our own particular solutions." According to Carter, the US objectives regarding trilateral cooperation were: (a) to "promote the health of the industrial economies"; (b) to support the efforts of allies "to strengthen the democratic institutions in Europe, and particularly in Portugal and Spain"; and (c) to work closely with the West Europeans on the review of CSCE to assure that the Helsinki agreement is fully implemented and that progress is made to further East-West cooperation. He expressed the hope that the leaders of the industrial democracies would discuss these issues at the London summit.[2] While Carter's declarations reflected Brzezinski's beliefs in the need to avoid unilateral initiatives in relations with allies, in pursuing common goals by joint initiatives and collective leadership, in the necessity to resolve the economic problems of the industrial democracies, and in linking détente to the implementation of the Helsinki accords, those beliefs were shared by Vance and Brown as well.

In the Notre Dame address in May 22, 1977, Carter, reasserted Brzezinski's belief that "together, our democracies can help to shape the wider architecture of global cooperation."[3] But while expressing Brzezinski's belief, which he shared, that relations with Western Europe and Japan provide the strategic hard core for both global stability and progress, Carter, exuding optimism, did not admit as Brzezinski did in 1976 that Western Europe and Japan were unwilling to play a major global role – a belief of Kissinger that had influenced the policies of the Nixon and Ford Administrations.

In 1978, the change in strategy toward the USSR and the PRC was also evident in the strategy regarding US relations with allies and friends. To dispel the myth that, as a result of the codification of the nuclear balance by the SALT agreements and Moscow's ominous inclination to use its military power to expand its influence, the US was pulling back from protecting its interests and its friends around the world, Carter declared: "our security depends on strong bonds with our allies . . . "[4] Noting the threat of political blackmail resulting from the massive buildup of Soviet conventional forces, he asserted: "We will match, together with our allies and friends, any threatening power through a combination of military forces, political efforts, and economic programs." In Carter's view, one of the ways to insure that the USSR does not gain military superiority was to work closely with West Europeans to strengthen and modernize the defenses in Europe. To allay fears regarding the US commitment to strengthen extended deterrence, Carter stated: "For 30 years and more we've been committed to the defense of Europe, bound by the knowledge that Western Europe's security is vital to our own . . . "[5] Carter's emphasis on the need to counterbalance the Soviet military buildup to preclude its use for political blackmail was consistent with Brzezinski's belief in military superiority. Indeed, since 1977 he had been urging Carter to approve new strategic programs to strengthen the US nuclear and conventional capabilities. But the strategy also reflects a reluctance, shared by all key policymakers, to admit what Kissinger had maintained since the 1950s and Nixon and Ford had discovered; namely, that (a) US allies will not build up their forces to provide a real alternative to the US nuclear guarantee fearing that this would lead to US withdrawal; and (b) most allies do not share US perceptions regarding the Soviet threat, particularly outside of Europe. However, unlike his efforts to dominate US policy towards the USSR and the PRC, Brzezinski, inconsistently with his belief that the active promotion of trilateral cooperation must be the central priority of US policy, played an "essentially supportive" role in the formulation of strategy regarding US relations with Western Europe and Japan.[6]

THE COMMON DEFENSE: THE EUROPEAN MILITARY BALANCE

During the Carter Administration US-West European security relations were dominated by three issues: (a) increasing NATO's defense spending and burden-sharing by West Europeans; (b) the Enhanced Radiation Weapon (ERW) – the neutron bomb; and (c) SALT II and theater nuclear force (TNF) modernization. Although Vance and Brown took the lead in dealing with those issues, Brzezinski's recommendations reflected his beliefs in the need for consultation, summitry, bold initiatives, collective leadership, linkage, and in the balance of power.

Mondale stressed Carter's commitment to strengthen NATO defenses during his European visit. But while reassuring West Europeans that the proposed $6–$7 billion cut in US defense spending would not affect NATO, he emphasized that increased US spending would be linked to commensurate West European increases. Carter himself called for increased defense spending by NATO in his address to NATO leaders following the London Economic summit in May 1977. Through the winter of 1977 and spring of 1978 the NATO members developed the Long-Term Defense Program (LTDP) calling for increased defense spending to strengthen conventional, TNF and reinforcement capabilities.

The NATO Council meeting in Washington adopted the LTDP on May 30, 1978, which stressed the buildup of antitank weapons and the integration of air defenses.[7] The 1979 US budget included a 3 percent increase for NATO as pledged. The NATO Defense Planning Committee met in Brussels in May 1979, and agreed to a 3 percent increase through 1985.[8] But the West Europeans had agreed to the increase with great reluctance.[9] While Brown led the negotiations to secure European compliance to raise appropriations for NATO, Brzezinski, consistent with his beliefs in the need to improve the European military balance and demonstrate political will, strongly supported Carter's call for increased burden-sharing convinced that it would buttress the resolve of all NATO members to step up defense efforts and demonstrate to Moscow that the West had political will. His stand also indicated his recognition that Congressional pressures for reducing the defense budget made the Western European contribution necessary. However, despite the West European reluctance to strongly support the increased defense efforts, Brzezinski's surprise with Bonn's announcement on November 1, 1980, that it would not be meeting the 3 percent annual increase as promised, manifested his refusal to admit, as Kissinger had, that West Europeans would not provide a real alternative to the US nuclear guarantee, fearing that this would undermine its credibility and lead to US withdrawal.[10]

Brzezinski's belief in the need to maintain the military balance by building up the US strategic and conventional capabilities was also manifest in the policy debates regarding PD-18. With Brown's support, he opposed the State Department's preference for considering the reduction of US forces in Europe and South Korea, and urged Carter to approve PD-18 which reaffirmed NATO's strategy for forward defense. Brzezinski's urging during 1977 and 1978 led the Administration to increase conventional forces in Europe by 35 000 men, to decide to station two more combat brigades there, and to store full sets of arms and equipment for three additional divisions. In the nuclear forces area, the Administration quietly changed the assignment of SLBMs available to SACEUR from five Polaris submarines with 80 warheads to 400 Poseidon warheads. These were in addition to the entire US strategic force which serves a deterrent role for NATO and provides contingent war-fighting capabilities. In addition, in 1977 the number of F-111 long-range fighter-bombers based in Britain was doubled, from 80 to 164.[11] Brzezinski's belief in the need to maintain the military balance in Europe was also manifest in his lack of interest in MBFR; a disinterest which also revealed his belief in the limited utility of arms control as a means for building peace.[12] However, his reluctance to push MBFR was inconsistent with his attacks on the Nixon-Kissinger timid approach to multilateral negotiations as a complement to bilateral US-Soviet relations to allay West European fears about a US-Soviet condominium.

Brzezinski was much more active on the ERW issue which was inherited by Carter from Ford whose 1978 budget provided for the Lance missile version of it. This, however, did not help Carter when the controversy regarding the ERW began on June 7, 1977, when *The Washington Post* described its planned deployment in Europe.[13] The portrayal of the ERW as the bomb that destroys people and not property raised fears in Europe that the US intended to wage a nuclear war in Europe to escape damage to itself. The West European fears were exploited by Moscow to divert attention from its deployment of the SS-20s. Lost in the controversy was the fact that the ERW was designed to counter the Warsaw Pact advantage in tanks by knocking out tank crews with intensified radiation while reducing blast damage to troops and civilians in the area, and the fact that its deployment would not have changed the tactical nuclear doctrine or the strategic nuclear balance. Carter's immediate response was to defend the ERW, to ask Congress to maintain the funds, and to order a Defense Department study of the issue to be submitted by August 15. On August 11, Brzezinski urged Carter to support the existing program until the final study was reviewed, and Brown, after the review, recommended its continuation. Carter approved the recommendation but his commitment to arms control and non-proliferation made him reluctant to order the ERW's production and deployment. Indeed, he was prepared to use the West European disinterest in it as the basis for killing the ERW. But Vance, Brown, and Brzezinski agreed to pressure the West Europeans to show greater interest in deploying the ERW to save the program.[14] Brzezinski's willingness to pressure West Europeans appears inconsistent with his belief in collective leadership and more in line with Kissinger's unilateralism which he had attacked. However, unlike Brzezinski, Kissinger, believing that NATO's nuclear dilemmas would not be resolved as long as it remained composed of sovereign states, had not pressured West Europeans to accept unilateral US decisions on nuclear issues. Brzezinski, not sharing Kissinger's belief in the inherent limitations in NATO's nuclear dilemmas, was prepared to push the issue.

Consultations in NATO's NPG revealed that without a clear US commitment to produce and deploy the ERW West European leaders were reluctant to make their support explicit and some argued that they had never supported it in the NPG, even though the Ford Administration had been consulting with them. Chancellor Schmidt, trying to keep the left wing of the SPD from openly opposing its deployment and concerned with

Moscow's response, maintained that since the US is the leader in NATO defense, production of the ERW was solely a US decision and that the issue of its deployment should be decided later collectively, not as a bilateral US-FRG agreement. Brzezinski's support for consultations regarding the ERW reflected his belief that more extensive consultations could create the necessary consensus to save the US initiative. His realization, however, that consultations would not resolve the issue led him to consider the possibility of linking the ERW to the overall nuclear balance and to offer Moscow not to deploy it in exchange for a withdrawal of Soviet tanks from central Europe – a consideration reflecting his beliefs in linkage and in the need to counterbalance the Soviet conventional superiority. But Schmidt's speech in London on October 28, 1977, on the Eurostrategic balance, by underscoring the threat to Western Europe from the SS-20s and by criticizing SALT II for not addressing this threat, made such an approach unacceptable.[15]

The consistency between Brzezinski's beliefs and his recommendations was manifest at the SCC meeting on November 16, 1977. Brzezinski insisted that Carter: (a) must order the production of the ERW; (b) "should tell the Europeans affirmatively" to associate themselves with its deployment; (c) start high-level discussions with the Europeans on security issues; and (d) in light of these discussions offer Moscow a deferral of the ERW deployment in return for not deploying the SS-20. Suggestion A and B reflect his belief in taking bold initiatives to demonstrate political will, suggestion C is consistent with his belief in summitry, and suggestion D reveals his belief in linkage. Indeed, he reiterated those beliefs on November 24, in his draft for a letter from Carter to Schmidt which called for high-level discussions in which the US would accept Schmidt's suggestion on linking the ERW to arms control, and specifically to SS-20s, and suggested that the offer to Moscow be timed with the announcement that the ERW would be produced and deployed.[16] Schmidt accepted the idea for consultations but insisted on an early US decision to produce the ERW to be used as a bargaining chip to reduce Soviet tanks and that the decision to deploy the ERW must be a collective one; in practical terms, another continental NATO member had to accept the ERW. Consultations between January and March 1978 led to a compromise which in essence was the Brzezinski proposal contained in Carter's letter to Schmidt. It was agreed: (a) that the US would produce the ERW; (b) to offer Moscow not to deploy it in exchange for not deploying the SS-20s; and (c) to announce that NATO would deploy the ERW in two years if arms control negotiations failed. A meeting of the NATO Council was set for March 28, 1978, to consider the final proposal. But despite support for the compromise by

Vance, Brown, and Brzezinski, who submitted their joint memorandum to Carter on March 18, Carter decided that they could not make any statements on the ERW without his specific authorization and instructed Vance to cancel the NATO meeting. This decision reflected both Carter's determination to personally control national security policy and his belief in arms control.[17]

Brzezinski's reaction to Carter's decision reflected his belief in taking bold initiatives to demonstrate political will in order to enhance US credibility, but was inconsistent with his belief in collective leadership. In a number of meetings with Carter he emphasized that not going through with the proposals made to Schmidt would indicate a lack of political will thus undermining US credibility and in turn weaking NATO. Brzezinski told Carter in the morning national security briefing on March 26 that "leadership means making decisions which the Europeans are not prepared to make" – a statement inconsistent with his belief in collective leadership and joint initiatives and more in line with Kissinger's conception of leadership which he had criticized, namely, the willingness to stand alone when the situation requires it. Yet, Brzezinski's insistence for taking bold initiatives reflected his implicit acceptance of Kissinger's conception of leadership. He also emphasized to Carter that a negative decision on the ERW "will affect the credibility of his leadership and will sow dissension within the alliance."[18] However, failing to get explicit statements of support from Schmidt and Callaghan, Carter informed his advisers on March 27 that he had decided against the production and deployment of the ERW.[19]

Carter's decision, however, did not stop Brzezinski from insisting on saving the ERW. In preparing Carter for his meeting with Foreign Minister Genscher, he urged him "to press Genscher for a firm commitment to deploy." Failing that, he insisted that Carter defer the decision and link the ERW to Soviet reductions in both conventional and nuclear forces, but in effect be willing to produce and deploy it within two years. For Brzezinski, a decision not to produce the ERW "would be the worst Presidential decision of the first fourteen months." Brzezinski's insistence led Carter to note: "Zbig, I must say that you never give up." But Bonn's firm commitment was not secured and on April 8, 1978, the White House announced that the US would defer production of the ERW, pending demonstrations of Soviet restraint in the deployment of the SS-20s – a decision reflecting Carter's commitment to reducing nuclear weapons.[20]

Brzezinski's support for the ERW reflected his beliefs in leadership (as Kissinger defined it), in credibility, in linkage, and in the necessity to counterbalance the Soviet conventional superiority in Europe. For Brzezinski, Carter's decision damaged his personal credibility as a strong eader thus undermining his influence on other issues and it sowed dissention in NATO. In retrospect, Brzezinski argued that stronger support from Vance, Brown, and Mondale who did not get involved, would have saved the ERW. Critical of himself for misreading Carter's reluctance to deploy the ERW, he concluded that the US should have "quietly" produced the ERW but "it would [have been] better for the sake of allied unity not to press the issue of deployment."[21] This, Kissinger had argued, should be the US approach in dealing with NATO's nuclear issues since they could not be resolved in the foreseeable future. In short, Brzezinski who had criticized Kissinger's approach, believing that consultations could both create and implement a consensus, now accepted Kissinger's view of the limited utility of consultations.

Brzezinski was also actively involved in the TNF modernization issue which surfaced as the SALT II negotiations were gaining momentum. West Europeans feared that the Soviet deployment of SS-20s and the Backfire bomber would permit Moscow to exert a greater degree of political pressure at a time when Carter's commitment to arms reductions indicated a greater US reluctance to respond to Soviet provocations or attack. This fear was expressed by Schmidt in a speech in London on October 28, 1977. He declared:

> SALT neutralizes [the US and Soviet] strategic nuclear capabilities. In Europe this magnifies the significance of the disparities between East and West in nuclear tactical and conventional weapons . . . . Strategic arms limitations confined to the United States and the Soviet Union will inevitably impair the security of the West European members of the Alliance vis-à-vis Soviet military superiority in Europe if we do not succeed in removing the disparities of military power in Europe parallel to the SALT negotiations.[22]

Schmidt's speech and private consultations on TNFs led to the establishment of a special NATO High Level Group to examine force modernization and to develop a consensus on a program. In February 1978, it endorsed in principle the need for modern weapons. The SCC under Brzezinski's chairmanship reviewed the political and military aspects of TNFs and arms control and although he and Vance originally doubted the necessity for new missiles based in Europe he was convinced by his staff that after the ERW decision it was politically vital to deploy a European-based nuclear counter to the SS-20s and to deal with the TNF issue firmly, with NATO united under US leadership.[23] Vance and Brown shared this view.

Brzezinski's initial reluctance to push for TNF modernization was

inconsistent with his belief in maintaining the European military balance
However, his reluctance probably emanated from his conclusion, after his
discussions with Schmidt, Callaghan, and Giscard d'Estaing in Europe in
October 1978, that despite their concern with the Eurostrategic balance
they were not ready to support a concrete solution. In his view, talks
at the highest-level and the avoidance of a unilateral US decision migh
allay their concern. Indeed, he supported Schmidt's suggestion that the
big four most directly engaged in security issues should meet informally
to discuss them since the larger NATO summit or the economic summit
were not conducive to open and frank discussion of the political and
strategic issues. Brzezinski's only concern was to structure the meeting
so that it would not appear as the "directoire" which when proposed
by de Gaulle had led to a controversy in NATO. The big four met at
Guadeloupe on January 5 and 6, 1979. The meeting dealt with nuclear
issues, US-Soviet and US-PRC relations, the Iranian crisis and other issues
but had the result Brzezinski feared, thus no similar meetings were held.
Although no conclusion was reached on TNF modernization, Brzezinski
felt that the discussions contributed to the shaping of a strategic consensus.
Therefore, after Guadeloupe he urged the transformation of the annual
economic summit into a strategic summit dealing with both political and
economic issues. Evident here are Brzezinski's beliefs in summitry without
fanfare and in collective leadership.[24]

In July 1979, the SCC dealt with the size of the TNF force and only
Brzezinski and the JCS pushed for the upper limit of 572 – 108 Pershing
IIs and 464 GLCMs. Consistent with his belief in linkage, Brzezinski
argued for the 572 TNFs since they would provide an incentive for
Moscow to agree to limits in the eventual arms control negotiations
and be useful in the negotiations with the West Europeans who, given
their reluctance to deploy a new nuclear weapon, would ask for a lower
mumber. On August 1979, Carter approved the Brzezinski/JCS recommendation and on October 4, the NATO High Level Group accepted the
US proposal. On October 6, Brezhnev, warning that TNF modernization
would undermine arms control and threaten the strategic balance, offered
to withraw 20 000 troops and 1000 tanks from the GDR during 1980 if
NATO abadoned TNF modernization and hinted that Soviet modernization
would be limited as well. However, he did not offer to withdraw the
SS-20s which made TNF modernization essential. Brzezinski feared that
Brezhnev's offer would mobilize European public opinion against the
NATO program, but consultations with the West Europeans by David
Aaron in October led Brzezinski to conclude that NATO was closer to
a firm consensus on the US proposal since the governments of Britain,

the FRG, and Italy had internally decided to support it.[25] On December 12, 1979, NATO decided to deploy 108 Pershing IIs to replace the Pershing Is and 464 new GLCMs beginning in 1983, and to pursue negotiations with Moscow to limit TNFs. It also decided to withdraw 1000 warheads to demonstrate that it was not increasing its reliance on nuclear weapons.[26] Recognizing the West European reluctance to deploy the new missiles on December 28, Brzezinski opposed Vance's efforts to separate SALT from other issues and advised Carter to blame the Soviet invasion of Afghanistan for the delay of SALT ratification since it would permit the US to insist that NATO proceed with the deployment; this advice reflected his belief in linkage.[27] Moscow's attack on the two-track decision and the withdrawal of its offer to negotiate on TNF in early January 1980 increased the likelihood that the new missiles would be deployed.

West Europeans were concerned with Carter's acceptance of Brzezinski's recommendations to strengthen the US military capabilities, to include war-fighting as part of the US strategic doctrine, and particularly to link SALT II to Soviet geopolitical restraint. The deferral of the SALT II treaty ratification which Carter had made the central element of US-Soviet détente raised the prospect of an intensified nuclear arms race and this worried West Europeans who considered arms control as a critical part of NATO's strategy for preserving the nuclear balance in Europe. Indeed, while Brzezinski was more interested in part one of NATO's two-track decision, to deploy the 572 TNFs, West Europeans were in favor of part two, the emphasis on negotiating the reduction of TNF. But since TNF limitations were to be discussed in SALT III, they feared that due to the deferral of the ratification of the SALT II treaty they would be forced to deploy the Pershings IIs and the new GLCMs – politically this was a dangerous decision given the opposition to the proposed deployment within most West European states.[28] Carter's repeated pledges that he would not abandon his efforts to ratify the SALT II treaty did not assure West Europeans that he was not seeking to dismantle détente and return to the cold war.[29]

The Soviet invasion of Afghanistan increased the tension in US-Soviet relations and in turn the West European reluctance to deploy the new missiles. Schmidt, in particular, seeking to avoid domestic criticism and to maintain his role as the West's intermediary with Moscow, made ambiguous public statements in the spring of 1980 which were interpreted as a proposal for a freeze on TNF deployment on both sides (but it was not). Brzezinski, concerned that a freeze would legitimize and make permanent the Eurostrategic imbalance, shortly before the

Venice economic summit telephoned Schmidt's national security adviser for clarification and was reassured that Schmidt was misinterpreted. Nevertheless, he, Brown, and Muskie supported an initiative for a formal letter from Carter to Schmidt which noted that although misinterpreted the statements could be harmful to collective defense efforts, hence, it was vital that the NATO decision be supported unambiguously.[30] The letter was leaked and it led to increased tension between Carter and Schmidt whose personal relations were not good. But during the Venice summit, on Brzezinski's recommendation, the two appeared before the press and stated that they were in full agreement on Afghanistan and TNF.[31] Brzezinski's determination to secure West European support for TNF deployment and maintain US leadership in NATO was also evident on July 2, when Genscher visited Washington to report on Schmidt's trip to Moscow on June 30. Rejecting Genscher's characterization of Soviet hints of flexibility on TNF negotiations as a serious offer, Brzezinski offered a suggestion accepted by all, namely, that the Soviet offer would be examined in a constructive spirit. He also supported Carter's decision for preliminary talks with Moscow on limiting TNF since they could be useful given the West European reluctance to fully support the TNF deployment.[32] His rationale for supporting the talks reflected his belief in the limited utility of arms control for resolving the major strategic issues. The TNF talks opened in Geneva on October 17, 1980.

In the 1980s, Brzezinski reasserted his belief that the Soviet conventional advantage in Europe makes the US strategic forces and Europe-based US conventional forces vital to deterring a conventional war in Europe and Moscow's intimidation of Western Europe.[33] Indeed, believing that extended deterrence rests on the fear of nuclear escalation, he, like Kissinger, opposed the "no-first-use" proposal since he was now more certain that it is highly unlikely that NATO would buildup its conventional capabilities to match those of the USSR.[34] However, seeing that US conventional forces are stronger in Europe where allies have the greatest capacity to do more for their own defense and that West Europeans would not help defend Western interests outside of Europe, Brzezinski, like Kissinger, argued that the US must gradually but only partially redeploy European-based troops to enlarge the RDF for defending US interests in Central America and the southwestern strategic front where the US is the most vulnerable and its forces are the weakest.[35] Although his call for partial reductions appears inconsistent with his belief in strengthening the Western conventional capability and his efforts to do so under Carter, it is not, when one examines his suggestions that US reductions could be offset by the introduction of new technologies in conventional defense. He specifically recommends a joint US-West European anti-tactical missile (ATM) project to develop a defense for protecting key West European military assets and the use of SDI technologies to conventional warfare. For Brzezinski, the joint projects would also allay the fear that SDI and the reductions would decouple West European security from that of the US.[36] Moreover, he insisted that while the manpower from the partial reductions must be used for additional light divisions to enlarge the RDF, the budgetary savings must go into the expansion of the US airlift capability. In short, those recommendations are consistent both with his beliefs in maintaining the conventional military balance, if not strengthening it, and in the necessity for flexibility and strategic mobility to rapidly and credibly project US power into regions where no US forces are prepositioned to deter Moscow from exploiting local conflicts.[37] Like Kissinger, then, Brzezinski advocated the redeployment of European-based US forces since their demobilization would weaken the overall Western military capabilities which both viewed as vital to maintaining global stability.

However, in the 1980s, Brzezinski, perhaps as a result of his experience under Carter, showed a greater awareness of the West European reluctance to either increase their defense spending or share the burdens of competing with the USSR outside of Europe.[38] Indeed, he argued that the partial reductions of US forces might induce the Western Europeans to address the issue of their own defense.[39] Convinced that in the foreseeable future a more self-reliant Western Europe would not emerge on the initiative of the Europeans themselves, he urged the US to encourage the development of a politically and militarily integrated Western Europe, less dependent on the US but still tied to it by a strategic alliance. This could be achieved in his view by encouraging greater Franco-German defense cooperation, pressing for a greater European contribution to the common defense, and by gradually but partially reducing US forces in Europe.[40] The last two suggestions while inconsistent with his belief in collective leadership reflect his belief in taking bold initiatives – an implicit acceptance of Kissinger's conception of leadership. This acceptance is also evident in his call for "consensual leadership" which still requires a dynamic and powerful America. Indeed, he insists that "America's partners will continue to want the United States to play [a leading world role]."[41] But can the US play such a role without the willingness to stand alone and take unilateral actions? Brzezinski has not answered this question explicitly.

THE THREAT OF SELECTIVE DÉTENTE: AFGHANISTAN AND POLAND

The Soviet invasion of Afghanistan and the crisis in Poland increased tensions between the US and its European allies over the issue of responding to Moscow's challenges inside and outside of Europe. The West European response to US reactions to Afghanistan and Poland demonstrated what Kissinger believed and had acted upon, namely, that there is a serious divergence of views between the US and Western Europe as to what constitutes a balanced policy toward the USSR, particularly outside of Europe. The West European desire to protect the concrete gains of détente made allied leaders reluctant to react to Moscow's challenges as strongly as Brzezinski believed that the West should do. In their view, it was a US task to deter Soviet challenges both inside and, particularly, outside of Europe. The divergent perceptions became manifest in 1977. Carter's emphasis on nuclear non-proliferation, and especially his public opposition to sales of nuclear technology by the FRG to Brazil, and his criticism of Soviet and Eastern European human rights abuses, evoked fears in Western Europe about US unilateralism. On April 3, 1977, noting Schmidt's resistance to US initiatives, Brzezinski warned Carter that unless he was more responsive to West European concerns the London economic summit scheduled for May would be a failure.[42] Brzezinski's concern reflected his beliefs in the need for consultations and in joint initiatives as the means for creating a Western consensus and maintaining unity when dealing with the East.

US-West European Differences on Policy Toward the East

In the mid-1970s, US-West European differences on policy toward the East centered on the divergent conceptions of détente. West Europeans viewed détente as a continuing, self-perpetuating peace process in Europe, based on the recognition of the status quo, on reciprocal political concessions, economic interdependence, and – ultimately – on military disengagement by both sides. But the US (and the USSR) conceived détente as a policy for managing the protracted East-West conflict under new international conditions and with slightly altered methods.[43] Brzezinski had criticized the Nixon-Kissinger passive approach to détente because it lacked the necessary linkage between the expansion of US-Soviet political and economic ties and the reduction of Soviet restraints on more extensive cultural and social contacts. In his view, a linkage essential to a reciprocal and comprehensive détente.

The divergence between Brzezinski's and West European conceptions of détente became evident during the London economic summit. Despite his advice to Carter prior to the summit to be responsive to West European concerns, Brzezinski responded to Schmidt's statement that Radio Free Europe (RFE) was incompatible with détente and that it should be removed from the FRG, by declaring that RFE was an important tool of US policy toward the East, including policy regarding the security of the FRG, and that its status could not be decided unilaterally or outside the larger security context.[44] Indeed, consistent with his belief that RFE was the best means for influencing the political transformation of communist systems and that more use should be made of it, he pressed for more funds for RFE and used the NSC staff to free it from excessive control from the State Department which restricted its use for encouraging political change in order to avoid negative reactions from East European governments.[45] Convinced that RFE broadcasts should deliberately encourage political change by addressing the internal problems of communist systems and offering genuine alternatives to communist policies, he encouraged its use to maintain pressure on Moscow and East European governments to comply with the Helsinki accords. Dismissing the State Department's and West European objections Brzezinski pushed hard for a more assertive US posture in the CSCE, arguing that the US "take the lead and be perceived as . . . pushing CSCE toward higher standards." Indeed, he even suggested that a study examine the advisability of a confrontationist approach, admitting that his objective was to "stiffen" the back of the State Department.[46] To achieve his objective in the CSCE he blocked the State Department's relatively unknown nominee for head of the US delegation to the CSCE and got Carter to appoint his own choice who was more likely to give the issue the visibility he believed it desired.[47] Brzezinski's position on the CSCE was consistent with his belief that a reciprocal and comprehensive détente requires the reduction of restraints on more extensive cultural and social contacts with the West. In short, Brzezinski's attacks on Kissinger's unilateralism and calls for joint initiatives did not prevent him from taking bold initiatives when allied support was not forthcoming, as was not in the case of publicly criticizing human rights abuses in Eastern Europe and the USSR.

Like Kissinger, Brzezinski viewed Moscow's courting of Bonn as an attempt at selective détente. Moscow's efforts had the effect of underlining the divergence in conceptions of détente and in perceptions of the USSR in the US and Western Europe, and particularly in Bonn and Washington. This was evident in July 1977, when Schmidt during his visit to Washington urged that Carter be more responsive to the "good Brezhnev who is promoting détente and . . . needs our help," and offered to set up private, direct contacts between Carter and Brezhnev with himself as the intermediary. Brzezinski, however, consistent with his belief that in dealing with Moscow the West must demonstrate political will, seeing Schmidt as "soft" since he opposed stronger public criticism of Soviet policies, urged Carter not to accept Schmidt's offer.[48] When Schmidt repeated his offer in a letter to Carter in September, Brzezinski again opposed it. While agreeing that a high-level emmisary could be useful in contacts with Brezhnev, he warned against using Schmidt since his unilateral pursuit of détente was undermining NATO unity and US initiatives toward Moscow. Brzezinski also feared that NATO unity would be further undermined by the negative reaction of other allies who could not be informed of Schmidt's role.[49]

For Brzezinski, Moscow's pursuit of selective détente was further facilitated by Giscard d'Estaing's efforts to assert France's leadership in Europe. In his view, France would not succeed without the support of the FRG, and Schmidt's actions indicated that such support was not forthcoming. Brzezinski was concerned since France's inability to exercise its leadership alone and Schmidt's pursuit of an independent policy was stimulating the Franco-German race to Moscow. But sharing Kissinger's belief that while France was too weak to achieve its objectives alone, it could undermine US initiatives since other European allies shared some of her views, he, like Kissinger, placed Paris at the center of his efforts to shape a common Western policy toward the East. Indeed, he personally consulted with Giscard d'Estaing and his advisers more frequently than with either the British or the Germans and, despite Vance's objections, urged Carter to approve nuclear collaboration with France convinced that the separate nuclear capability gave Paris some genuine foreign policy choices. The degree of nuclear collaboration was greater under Carter than under Nixon and Ford who supported it on Kissinger's recommendation.[50]

West European concern about Moscow's negative reaction to US initiatives toward Eastern Europe did not stop Brzezinski from urging Carter to pursue selective détente in Eastern Europe. He argued that the US could effectively respond to opportunities to promote change in Eastern Europe only by not treating the Soviet bloc either as a monolithic adversary or simply as a group of uniformly friendly neighbors. He reiterated his belief that the long-term goal of Western policy should be to transform the Soviet bloc into a more pluralistic and diversified entity since such a policy offered a better way of dealing with Moscow's challenge in Europe than considering the USSR either as the leader of a totally hostile coalition or as a partner in an undifferentiated détente.[51] Carter's policy toward

Eastern Europe was a critical factor in US-West European relations, and Brzezinski's recommendations reflect that when consultations could not develop joint initiatives, he was ready to act unilaterally to preclude Soviet gains. Rejecting the West European preference, shared by Vance, for expanding contacts with all the East European states, Brzezinski strongly pushed for the expansion of relations with states which were relatively more liberal internally and/or more independent of Moscow; a reiteration of a recommendation he made in 1965,[52] and a reflection of his belief that only by this approach could the US encourage polycentrism and pluralism in the region.[53] Carter accepted Bzrezinski's recommendation and on September 13, 1977, signed PD-21 which stated that preference would be given to states which were more liberal internally and/or more independent of Moscow.

The new approach toward Eastern Europe was evident in US-Polish relations. Convinced that the processes of liberalization were gaining momentum in Poland, Brzezinski urged Carter to visit Poland in order to encourage it and to demonstrate his more forthcoming approach toward Eastern Europe. Carter, having criticized Ford during the campaign for stating that he did not consider Poland under domination, decided to visit Poland on his first world trip in December 1977, despite the State Department's warning that Moscow would view the visit as provocative.[54] During the visit, Carter accepted Brzezinski's recommendation to symbolically demonstrate his support for Polish independence and for greater ties between Poland and the West – a recommendation reflecting his belief in the importance of symbolic actions to make a lasting investment in popular goodwill.[55] Moreover, despite the CIA's assessment that Poland was a poor credit risk, Brzezinski, consistent with his belief that economic assistance to Eastern Europe should be guided primarily by political, not economic, considerations,[56] strongly pushed for increased economic aid to Poland to encourage Warsaw to assert a greater degree of independence from Moscow.[57]

The US and West European responses to repression in Poland manifested the divergence in their perceptions of the Soviet threat in Europe. In the middle of 1979, informed that pro-Soviet elements were deliberately undermining Polish economic programs to keep Poland dependent on Moscow, Brzezinski reasserted his belief that the Polish situation indicated the decrease of Soviet control and advised Carter in early September to increase US-Polish contacts as well as economic assistance. In August 1980, when the Solidarity free trade union was challenging Party control, Brzezinski sought to influence Soviet calculations against intervention by confronting Moscow with a united Western response. The West European preference for opposing Moscow rhetorically and unwillingness to reduce economic relations with it, led him to urge Carter to emphasize the US interest in the Polish situation and his concern over possible Soviet intervention by writing to Margaret Thatcher, Giscard d'Estaing, and Schmidt and by initiating consultations on the issue in order to develop joint initiatives. Carter's letter led to consultations between the State Department and West Europeans on possible contingency measures in case of Soviet intervention.[58] Convinced that after the ERW experience the demonstration of US leadership was vital to the development of a common Western policy, Brzezinski felt that such a demonstration was undermined by Carter's approval of Muskie's initiative to inform the Soviet Ambassador that the Administration was not involved with the AFL-CIO decision to provide financial assistance to Solidarity. Therefore, he prevailed on Muskie to call in the Polish Ambassador as well to preclude the misperception that the US accepted Soviet domination of Poland since that would have undermined efforts to create a common Western policy.[59] By early October 1980, when it appeared that Moscow might intervene, Brzezinski started to convene the SCC to review contingencies for a possible crisis and urged Muskie to make it clear to Gromyko that the US would view a Soviet intervention as a threat to peace. By the third week of October, his influence on policy was evident in the SCC approval of a series of specific steps designed to penalize Moscow severely if it intervened militarily. Those steps became the basis of further allied consultations on the issue.

For Brzezinski, it was vital for the US to avoid the mistake it made in 1968 when it failed to communicate to Moscow prior to its intervention in Czechoslovakia the costs of it to East-West relations and to the USSR specifically. In his view, by publicizing the sanctions that could be adopted, Moscow could be convinced that Carter would react. To publicize the US position, in late November he send a memo to Muskie and Brown, sure that it would be leaked, which stated his judgment that Soviet intervention would: (a) rupture political détente in Europe; (b) disrupt East-West economic cooperation; (c) generate increases in Western defense budgets; (d) produce severe strains between Western European Communist parties and Moscow; (e) further alienate the Non-aligned Movement from the USSR; (f) possibly precipitate turmoil elsewhere in the Soviet bloc; and (g) lead to overt US-PRC military cooperation. He also reiterated those points in background briefings to the press. On December 3, when Soviet intervention appeared imminent Brzezinski convened a meeting with Muskie, Brown, and Turner which led to a joint recommendation to Carter to publicly declare that Soviet intervention would directly and very adversely affect US-Soviet relations and to reassert this message in a letter to Brezhnev, which would also reassure him that the US would not exploit the Polish situation in a way that would threaten Soviet security. Moreover, Brzezinski personally sought the support of the AFL-CIO to organize a worldwide boycott on the shipment of goods to the USSR. Relying on the Defense Department's ability to leak, he indirectly raised the possibility of greater US-PRC cooperation by instructing it to prepare lists of weapons that might be transferred to Peking if Moscow invaded Poland.[60] In addition, through personal channels, Brzezinski alerted the Solidarity leaders to avoid detention and briefed the Pope, thus depriving Moscow of the element of surprise and increasing the cost of intervention.[61] Evident in Brzezinski's recommendations and actions are his beliefs in linkage, as in the hint of greater US-PRC cooperation, in the need for bold initiatives, and in implementing one's conceptions.

The publicity generated by Brzezinski was probably responsible for Schmidt's pledge that Bonn would adopt economic sanctions if Moscow intervened militarily and Giscard d'Estaing's strong warning to Moscow against intervention. Their support of the US position was very important to US efforts to deter Moscow given the large scale of German credits and trade with the USSR and Giscard d'Estaing's friendly meeting with Brezhnev in Poland after the invasion of Afghanistan which was seen as a manifestation of Moscow's success in pursuing selective détente. West European opposition to Soviet intervention in Poland was also evident in the expressions of concern to Moscow by West European Communist Parties.[62] For Brzezinski, the united Western response and the strong US reaction to the invasion of Afghanistan propably tipped the balance in Moscow in favor of those opposing military intervention.[63]

In the 1980s, Brzezinski's recommendations regarding US policy toward Western and Eastern Europe reflected his belief that the USSR is the main threat to peace. Concerned that Moscow was succeeding in exploiting the absence of a united Europe, the mounting US frustration with the unwillingness of West Europeans to do more for their defense and to assist the US in defending Western interests outside of Europe, and the appeal of escapist notions as nuclear freezes to achieve selective détente, Brzezinski reasserted his belief in the need for a common Western policy. The real danger, in his view, is a neutralized Western Europe, autonomous internally but deferential to Soviet foreign policy goals. His main focus again was the FRG – the linchpin state in Western Europe – since Moscow could exploit German nationalism, evident in the desires for greater ties with the GDR and for reviving Germany's traditional special relationship with Russia, to neutralize the FRG. A neutral FRG, according to Brzezinski, would not dismantle NATO or the EEC as such but would deprive them of any political or military substance thus removing a major politico-military barrier to

Soviet attempts to dominate the first strategic front.[64] Brzezinski's concern about the future of the FRG and its desire for a grand deal with Moscow was shared in Paris and London. Noting that such a deal would parallel in its geopolitical consequences the US-PRC rapprochment, he seemed relieved that the systemic crisis in Eastern Europe reduced Moscow's ability to permit German unification since it would deprive itself of its key – the GDR – to exercising effective control over Poland, Czechoslovakia, and Hungary. For Brzezinski, Moscow was deterred from making such a deal by the fact that a neutralized FRG would be disruptive both for NATO and the Warsaw Pact.[65]

Brzezinski feared that Moscow's strategy of political attrition could weaken US-West European relations without precipitating massive fears in Western Europe or strong US reactions to the progressive and piecemeal neutralization of Western Europe – a fear similar to Kissinger's regarding what he called Moscow's strategy of ambiguity. Brzezinski reaffirmed his view that the massive buildup of Soviet conventional forces facilitates Moscow's policy of political intimidation which leads West Europeans to pressure the US to make concessions for the sake of a relaxation of tensions rather than increase their defense spending and/or oppose Moscow's increasing military aggression outside of Europe. He also maintained that the inadequate West European response to the Soviet military buildup feeds the neutralist and anti-American sentiments.[66] For Brzezinski, the evolution in the foreign policy positions of the SPD demonstrated the danger of selective détente and de facto neutralism. He criticized the 1985 action of the SPD, which joined the Communist Party of the GDR, in advocating the long-standing Soviet propaganda proposals for an unverifiable ban on chemical warfare and a joint consideration of a nuclear-free zone in central Europe, and ex-chancellor Schmidt for publicly endorsing the crushing of Solidarity when other West European Socialists condemned it,[67] a criticism reflecting his belief that the West must develop a common policy for encouraging political change in Eastern Europe. This change he believed would eventually influence change in the USSR.

Consistent with his belief that the broad thrust of West European development is toward increasing cooperation, Brzezinski insists that in order to defeat Moscow's strategy of political attrition the US must encourage the development of a politically and militarily integrated Western Europe. However, believing that a positive regionalism has yet to mature, he urged the gradual and partial reduction of US troops in Europe to induce West Europeans to move in that direction by doing more for their own defense.[68] Unlike Kissinger, Brzezinski does not fear that a politically and militarily integrated Western Europe, less dependent on the US for its defense, is likely to challenge US hegemony in Atlantic policy by insisting on a specifically European view of world affairs, thus further undermining efforts to develop a common Western strategy toward the East. If he did, unlike Kissinger, Brzezinski did not state his willingness to pay the price. His lack of concern was probably a reflection of his belief that the common Western values would eventually lead to trilateral cooperation. Moreover, he reiterated his view that, in the long-term, the US should welcome closer multilateral ties between a more integrated Western Europe and Eastern Europe since they could eventually lead to the US and Soviet disengagement from Europe.[69] Indeed, he urged the US to encourage the EEC to provide Eastern Europe with economic aid since increased all-European economic cooperation would inevitably lead to closer political ties.[70]

In the 1980s, Brzezinski's attention in Eastern Europe was again focused on Poland – the linchpin state – since he viewed Soviet domination over it as being central to Moscow's control over Eastern Europe[71] and to the long-term policy of seducing or subordinating the FRG.[72] He argued that Moscow's insistence on continued ideological political subordination of Poland would further intensify resentments, thereby making Poland even more susceptible to external attraction from the West.[73] Brzezinski reiterated his recommendation that the US should promote the creation of an independent-minded and increasingly assertive East European public opinion through radio broadcasts and other new communication techniques, such as videocassettes, miniaturized printers, and word processors.[74] Looking at the economic failure and political unrest, Brzezinski concluded that Eastern Europe is in a classic prerevolutionary situation. He predicted that while the failure of *perestroika* in the USSR could make the systemic crisis of Eastern Europe a more general crisis of Communism itself, a major explosion in Eastern Europe would "almost certainly" precipitate Soviet intervention, the end of *perestroika*, and it would damage East-West relations. Reasserting his belief that the US and its European allies should focus actively on an effort to forge a more stable relationship with Eastern Europe, he reiterated the need for a more coordinated Western policy of political and economic engagement to facilitate the evolutionary change in Eastern Europe.[75]

West European Reaction to US Initiative to Contain Soviet Third World Expansionism

The Administration's inability to develop a united Western response to Soviet expansionism in the Horn of Africa and to the Soviet invasion of

Afghanistan demonstrated what Kissinger believed and acted upon and Brzezinski acknowledged in 1976, that is, that Western Europe and Japan would not play a global role despite their wealth and/or degree of unity. West European rhetorical condemnation of Soviet expansionism was not followed by punative actions that could have suspended détente in Europe. Indeed, Brzezinski, who had attributed the damage to US relations with its allies to Kissinger's personal and secretive diplomacy, now admitted that "the differences that emerged were deep-seated and not merely a reflection of personalities."[76] In short, he accepted Kissinger's belief that due to structural changes Western Europe would not share with the US the burdens and responsibilities of world leadership, meaning it would pursue neither parallel nor identical policies, especially outside Europe.

The West European reluctance to follow the US lead in linking Soviet expansionism to East-West détente became manifest in 1978 when they did not support Brzezinski's efforts to organize a tougher Western reaction to the Soviet-Cuban military intervention in the Horn of Africa. West European leaders opposed his recommendations to link SALT II to Soviet restraint, to reduce economic relations and high-level visits with the USSR, and to cooperate in a demonstation of Western military power by deploying forces in the region. At the NATO meeting in Washington in May 1978, PM Callaghan, rejecting Brzezinski's belief that Soviet military intervention presented long-term dangers to peace, ridiculed those "Columbuses who have lately discovered Africa."[77] Giscard d'Estaing, however, shared Brzezinski's concern about the long-term dangers of Soviet expansionism in the Horn and warned Carter several times regarding the threats to Saudi Arabia's security emanating from the Soviet military buildup in the region.[78] Therefore, he was the only West European leader to be informed of Sadat's offer to deploy Egyptian forces in Somalia, and to get a letter from Carter asking him to warn Moscow that its military intervention in the Horn was endangering East-West détente.[79] Giscard d'Estaing's expressions of concern led Brzezinski to suggest that France join the US in deploying aircraft carriers in the area. But since Carter rejected Brzezinski's suggestion France did not have to act.[80] Giscard d'Estaing was more willing than other West Europeans to support US policy because: (a) he shared Brzezinski's view regarding the threat of Soviet expansionism; (b) Carter, at Brzezinski's urging, supported closer US-French nuclear collaboration; and (c) France was treated as the leader in Europe.[81]

However, while rejecting Brzezinski's recommendations to link Soviet expansionism to East-West détente and to cooperate in a demonstration of force, West Europeans supported Vance's efforts to deal with the crisis

in the Horn of Africa as a local issue with diplomatic means. Sharing
Vance's view that providing military aid to Somalia would not resolve
the issue and would probably lead to an even larger Soviet and Cuban
presence, Britain, France, and the FRG joined the US in agreeing not
to supply defense arms to Somalia until it withdrew from the Ogaden.
In late January 1978, the US, Britain, France, Italy, and the FRG met to
coordinate policy for the Horn and decided to press more vigorously for a
negotiated settlement of the Ogaden crisis. In February, they also agreed to
seek a cease-fire that would protect Somali forces and Somali inhabitants
of the Ogaden as they withdrew. For Brzezinski, the sole dependence on
diplomacy demonstrated the West's lack of political will and undermined
the policy of deterrence.[82]

While Carter accepted Brzezinski's advice for a tougher and wider
response to Soviet expansionism after the invasion of Afghanistan, the
reaction of West Europeans to the US sanctions highlighted the difficulty
in developing a united Western response to the Soviet challenges outside
of Europe. Seeing the invasion as the beginning of a regional crisis of
strategic significance since it brought Soviet forces closer to the Persian
Gulf from where they could threaten the West's oil supply, Brzezinski
pressured West Europeans to assist in strengthening the security of the oil
fields and access to the Gulf by increasing their own defense capabilities in
Europe to compensate for US forces redirected to the Persian Gulf–Middle
East region.[83] Most West Europeans, however, rejected Brzezinski's view
that Afghanistan set a dangerous precedent for a wider Soviet strategic
challenge that must be met with increasing defense capabilities. This
became evident in November 1980 when Bonn announced that it would not
be meeting the 3 percent annual increase in defense spending. Nevertheless,
they did take some limited measures to help strengthen the security of the
Gulf. Britain assisted in the expansion of the naval and air facilities on
the island of Diego Garcia in the Indian ocean, and Girscard d'Estaing
responded to Carter's proposal, after the start of the Iraqi-Iran war in
September 1980, for a joint US-French naval presence in the Arabian Gulf
to keep the Strait of Hormuz open.[84] In addition, Britain, France, the FRG,
and Italy collaborated with the US in an international financial consortium
to assist Pakistan. The divergent perceptions regarding the Soviet threat
were also manifest in the argument by several allies that the US could
do more for Western interests in the region by seeking a solution to the
Palestinian problem.[85]

The West Europeans and the Japanese demonstrated their agreement
that the West must deter further Soviet expansionism primarily through
diplomatic means. After the Venice economic summit the seven leaders

supported Brzezinski's suggestion to issue a strong statement condemning the Soviet invasion of Afghanistan. It declared: "the Soviet military occupation of Afghanistan is unacceptable now and [we] are determined not to accept it in the future . . . [it] undermines the foundations of peace both in the region and in the world."[86] They also supported a strong condemnation of the USSR in the UN and they instructed their ambassadors not to attend the Soviet National Day (November 7) parade in Moscow.[87] The FRG, reluctantly, and Japan also joined the US boycott of the Moscow Olympics.[88] However, no US ally followed the US lead in reducing its trade and credits to the USSR as Brzezinski recommended. Indeed, within a few months, France, Italy, Japan, and the FRG held high-level bilateral talks with Moscow on the expansion of their trade with the USSR. While US-Soviet trade was reduced by 60 percent in 1980, after Moscow turned to Western Europe and Japan, in the same year, French-Soviet trade increased by 100 percent, German-Soviet trade by 65 percent, and Soviet-Japanese and Soviet-Italian trade by 35 percent each.[89] The speed with which US allies picked up the slack in US-Soviet trade contributed to intra-alliance tension over policy toward the USSR. In short, while they strongly disapproved of Soviet expansionism, the West Europeans and the Japanese were unwilling to link the expansion of their political and economic relations to Soviet geopolitical restraint fearing that their support of US sanctions would increase tensions in Europe and result in the loss of the concrete benefits of détente.

The speed with which Carter imposed the punitive sanctions raised the issue of consultation. Convinced that Carter's acceptance of Brzezinski's recommendations would lead to a renewed cold war, West Europeans criticized the inadequate consultations on a common Western policy before announcing the sanctions. They felt that the US had adopted a confrontational strategy without considering European interests and then unfairly criticized them for inadequate cooperation.[90] A British parliamentary committee noted the "inadequate consultation among alliance members before it was decided to impose sanctions."[91] Some resented pressure from Brzezinski to accept US actions as the "common" Western policy. Indeed, Schmidt, whose offers to act as an intermediary with Brezhnev had been opposed by Brzezinski, as was his June 30, 1980, visit to Moscow, urged Carter to dismiss Brzezinski because he had a negative influence on East-West relations.[92] Even Giscard d'Estaing, who shared Brzezinski's belief in the need to stop Soviet expansionism and to protect the security of the Persian Gulf without consultation or even advance notification, met Brezhnev in Warsaw in May 1980.[93] The fact that Brzezinski who had advocated trilateral cooperation and consultations, urged Carter to take rapid decisive actions rather than consult in advance in order to develop a common Western policy, manifests that when his beliefs in consultation and cooperation were in conflict with those in bold initiatives, in the need to demonstrate political will, and in the need for rapid responses to prevent a fait accompli, the latter had a greater impact on his actions. In addition, his efforts to maintain allied unity reflected his belief in linkage. Unlike the West Europeans and the Japanese who sought to protect the concrete gains of détente while leaving to the US the task of deterring Soviet aggression outside Europe, Brzezinski stressed the danger of the misperception in allied capitals that West European-Soviet and Japanese-Soviet détente can be isolated from US-Soviet détente and events elsewhere. The West European rejection of linkage was expressed by Giscard d'Estaing who, while sharing Brzezinski's belief in the need to stop Soviet expansionism, spoke of keeping Europe out of US-Soviet bloc politics, declaring: "the balance of power in Europe is a separate problem."[94]

The West European and Japanese reluctance to fully support all US sanctions after Afghanistan reinforced Brzezinski's 1976 recognition that they would not play a global role. Indeed, in the 1980s, their refusal to join the US in patrolling the Persian Gulf led Brzezinski to reiterate Kissinger's belief that "our allies are simply regional powers."[95] This conviction led him to urge that the US must act unilaterally, if necessary, to defend Western interests outside of Europe – advice consistent with his belief in the need to stop Soviet expansionism and in bold initiatives but inconsistent with his beliefs in consultation, and collective leadership. To facilitate this task and avoid disputes with the West Europeans and the Japanese over unilateral US actions he advocated the gradual and partial redeployment of US forces from Europe to strengthen the RDF and expand US airlift capability. For Brzezinski, only a larger RDF and airlift capability would permit the rapid and credible projection of US military power into regions where the US is most vulnerable thus preventing Moscow from exploiting local conflicts to undermine the global balance of power.[96]

CONCLUSION

This examination of US policy toward Western Europe (and Japan) reveals both consistency and inconsistency between Brzezinski's beliefs and his recommendations and/or actions. This is also evident in his recommendations since 1981. Despite his belief that the active promotion of trilateral cooperation must be the central priority of US policy, Brzezinski did not pursue it. However, by allowing Vance and Brown to take the initiative in shaping US policy toward the major allies while he played an essentially supportive role, he demonstrated his belief in collective leadership. But more importantly, his recommendations and/or actions regarding US policy toward Western Europe (and Japan) reflected his belief that the massive Soviet military buildup makes the USSR the main threat to peace. Consistent with this belief, as well as his belief in the need to demonstrate power and political will, Brzezinski strongly supported Carter's call for increased burden-sharing, opposed the State Department's efforts to put under consideration the reduction of US forces in Europe, urged Carter to produce the ERW despite Carter's reluctance to do so, supported TNF modernization, and led efforts to increase US forces in Europe. Since 1981, Brzezinski has been reasserting his belief in the need to maintain the European balance of power. However, his greater awareness of the West European reluctance to increase their defense spending or to share the burdens of competing with the USSR outside of Europe has led him to call for the partial and gradual redeployment of European-based US troops in order to induce West Europeans to address the issue of their own defense. For Brzezinski, the European balance can be maintained by the introduction of new technologies in conventional defense.

Brzezinski's efforts to maintain the European balance of power also reflected a number of his other beliefs. Consistent with his belief in the limited utility of arms control as a means for building peace, he did not support MBFR despite Carter's determination to pursue the issue, he insisted that the ERW be deployed if arms control negotiations failed, and was more interested in deploying the 572 TNFs than negotiating their reductions. His belief in linkage was evident in his insistence on linking the ERW and the TNF modernization to Soviet reductions in both conventional and nuclear forces. Believing that informal summits and consultations are useful for achieving national goals, Brzezinski supported Schmidt's suggestion that led to the Guadeloupe meeting and later urged that the annual economic summit be transformed into a strategic summit. However, his willingness to pressure the West Europeans to support the ERW and TNF modernization was inconsistent with his belief in collective leadership and joint initiatives and more in line with Kissinger's conception of leadership which he implicitly accepted when he stressed the need for bold initiatives to demonstrate political will as he did in the case of the ERW.

Brzezinski's recommendations and/or actions regarding US policy toward Western and Eastern Europe demonstrated his belief that Atlantic unity is vital to dealing with the Soviet challenges to peace. Consistent with his belief in reciprocal and comprehensive détente, he insisted that West Europeans link the expansion of their political and economic relations with Eastern Europe and the USSR to the reduction of restraints on human rights. When the West Europeans refused to pressure the East to comply with the Helsinki accords, inconsistently with his belief in joint initiatives but consistently with his belief in bold initiatives he acted alone. The latter belief led him to try to shape a united Western response to developments in Poland and to the Soviet military intervention in the Horn of Africa and Afghanistan. Brzezinski's advice to Carter to take rapid decisive actions following the Soviet invasion of Afghanistan rather than consult allies in advance in order to develop a common Western policy reflects that, when his beliefs in consultation and trilateral cooperation were in conflict with those in bold initiatives, in the need to demonstrate political will, and in the need for rapid responses to prevent a fait accompli, the latter had a greater impact on his actions. In the 1980s, having accepted Kissinger's beliefs that the intra-alliance disputes are not caused by personalities (i.e., Kissinger) and that the allies are simply regional powers, Brzezinski has been urging that the US take unilateral initiatives to defend Western interests outside of Europe. Moreover, while reasserting his belief that the USSR is the greatest threat to peace, he no longer advocates trilateral cooperation as the central priority of US policy. He now insists that the US must provide the leadership that its allies seek.

12 Conclusions

This study found that, despite Brzezinski's attacks on Kissinger's conceptions and approach to policymaking, they shared many views on world politics and strategy and tactics for achieving national goals. Both believed that international conflicts emanate from the divergent national interests. Conflict characterized Kissinger's conception of peace/stability as well as his models of stable and revolutionary international systems. He conceived peace not as the avoidance of war but as stability based on an equilibrium of power and legitimacy; legitimacy being an international agreement about the nature of workable arrangements and about the permissible aims and methods of foreign policy. In a stable system conflict is limited since states accept its framework and seek to adjust differences within it, while in a revolutionary system conflict is total since a major power is trying to change the system. Brzezinski did not explicitly define peace and did not develop models of international systems, but he shared Kissinger's conception of peace and his belief that the revolutionary power is distinguished by its rejection of the existing international system and its search for absolute security/peace. Both agreed that the USSR and the PRC are revolutionary powers whose commitment to world-wide communist expansion has intensified traditional international conflicts. They also agreed that Soviet military power makes the USSR a greater threat to international stability than the PRC. Their belief that the USSR and the PRC are revolutionary powers did not change despite the Soviet renunciation of the inevitability of war between Capitalism and Socialism and the Sino-Soviet split. However, they believed that the Soviets, unlike the Chinese, having accepted the risk of nuclear war, might be willing to cooperate in the nuclear field in order to reduce it. They also agreed that the bureaucratization of the Soviet political system and/or the convergence in contemporary styles and values did not imply a Soviet acceptance of the present international system. Indeed, both viewed peaceful coexistence as an offensive Soviet tactic to transform the present international system by means short of an all-out nuclear war. However, Kissinger and Brzezinski disagreed about the international impact of the conflict between the PRC and the USSR. Kissinger believed that while the PRC is still a revolutionary power, its concern with the USSR and its less bureaucratic structure may permit Peking to take new international policy initiatives. But Brzezinski believed that despite US-PRC rapprochement, the PRC's efforts to promote revolution by inducing a conflict between the US and the USSR make the PRC the greater long-range threat to peace. Nevertheless, both agreed that, despite ideological differences, the US should respond to any PRC interest in broadening contacts in order not to appear as a tacit partner of the USSR.

For Kissinger and Brzezinski, divergent national interests were the primary cause of conflicts even within the US and Soviet alliance systems. However, the conflicts were limited since allies within each system accepted the framework of that system as well as the permissible aims and methods of foreign policy within it. Unlike Kissinger, however, Brzezinski, believed that while the impact of nationalism in Eastern Europe was increasing, its vitality in Western Europe was declining. They also disagreed about the pace of West European unity and about its impact on US-West European relations. For Kissinger, greater West European unity is likely to increase conflicts within NATO emanating from the incompatibility of national sovereignty with nuclear weapons since Western Europe would be in a better position to challenge US initiatives in Atlantic policy. But until 1976, Brzezinski believed that the common Western values would lead to more joint Western initiatives which would create the basis of a new international system. Nevertheless, both agreed that Western unity is vital to peace. While Kissinger advocated an Atlantic Community, Brzezinski urged trilateral cooperation, which stressed the need for greater Japanese participation. Moreover, both believed that the traditional international conflicts have been further exacerbated by: (a) the increase in the number of states in the international system which inject into their foreign policy the revolutionary fervor that gained them independence; (b) the impact of the scientific and technological revolutions in the fields of weaponry and communications; and (c) the ideological conflict which reduces the distinction between domestic and foreign policy. For Kissinger and Brzezinski, the new states weigh little in the physical balance of power, but they are important to stability since they affect the psychological balance of power. By accepting the present international system these states could prevent the revolutionary powers, and especially the USSR, from exploiting Third World conflicts to subvert the international system. Moreover, both believed that the greatest threat to peace is a Third World conflict in which the superpowers are forced to intervene.

Kissinger and Brzezinski were both pessimistic and optimistic about the eventual realization of their political goals. However, Kissinger's belief that nuclear weapons have eroded the relationship between power and policy, and his belief that the US is at a critical juncture and that only creativity can preclude its decline, made him more pessimistic than Brzezinski about the establishment of a stable international order in the foreseeable future. Yet, he was optimistic given the US potential relative to other states and his belief in man's freedom to act to overcome the limitations imposed by his environment. Brzezinski, believing in America's positive impact in the world and in the emergence of a global consciousness for the first time due to the impact of the technetronic revolution, was more optimistic than Kissinger about trilateral cooperation and the development of a new world order. But like Kissinger, he was also pessimistic since the emerging global consciousness lacks identity, cohesion, and focus, and the increase of pessimism in the world paralyzes effective responses. Kissinger and Brzezinski believed that, despite the unpredictability of specific events, trends in the foreseeable future are predictable, thus man can take action to achieve his goals. They also believed that while man's control of historical development is limited, statesmen can shape history by providing and implementing a vision, and by educating their nations to bridge the gap between history and their vision. Moreover, they agreed that while chance can never be completely eliminated from historical development the task of statesmen is to reduce it to a minimum. Yet, consistently with his greater pessimism, Kissinger, unlike Brzezinski, believed that this is more likely when statesmen recognize and accept limits and act with self-restraint.

While Kissinger and Brzezinski shared many beliefs regarding strategy and tactics for achieving national goals, their conception of some of them differed. For both, national goals must be selected on the basis of the power-realist approach, especially since the USSR and the PRC are still committed to world-wide communist expansion through the use of force. However, while sharing Kissinger's conception of power, Brzezinski emphasized military capabilities more than Kissinger did. Believing that Nixon and Kissinger had applied the power-realist approach successfully in relations with the USSR and the PRC, where its use is necessary, he stressed that it must be employed less in relations with allies and the Third World. Brzezinski advocated the planetary humanist approach for the selection of goals regarding the Third World and, viewing the power-realist and the planetary humanist approaches as compatible, he advocated that the two be combined when dealing with advanced states. Nevertheless, his preoccupation with the Soviet military threat indicated a preference for the power-realist approach. Kissinger believed that the reluctance to use force due to the fear that it would lead to nuclear war dictates the use of the strategic approach which permits the development of a strategic doctrine which defines the goals worth fighting for and determines the degree of force appropriate for achieving them. Brzezinski stressed the need for the architectural approach which was to some degree similar to the strategic approach of Kissinger. Kissinger and Brzezinski agreed that the strategic and architectural approaches rest on the related conceptual approach which permits a conscious intellectual effort to understand and define the present international reality to avoid policy by reaction. However, while Kissinger viewed the development of a conception and its implementation as the lonely tasks of a statesman, Brzezinski viewed conceptualization as a collegial task and separated it from the responsibility of execution. This was evident in his claim that the architectural approach requires cooperation, joint planning, and consultation. Kissinger insisted on a non-ideological/non-moralistic approach to politics believing that an ideological/moral foreign policy – a characteristic of revolutionary states – by seeking absolute objectives undermines stability. Brzezinski, however, distinguished the ideological from the moral approach. He rejected the former, convinced that its use is not necessary since the bureaucratized Soviet doctrine had lost its appeal thus reducing the ideological threat to stability, but advocated the latter believing that being complementary to the planetary humanist approach, the two could tap the moral resources of the American people and world opinion.

Moreover, while Kissinger and Brzezinski agreed on a number of the requirements essential for pursuing national goals effectively, they conceived them differently. Both agreed on the need for leadership. But while Kissinger conceived it as the willingness to stand alone when the situation requires it, Brzezinski conceived it as an open collegial task involving joint planning and consultation. However, Brzezinski also believed in the need for bold initiatives and in this sense he implicitly accepted Kissinger's conception of leadership. For Kissinger, since political multipolarity makes it impossible to impose US designs it is essential to create coalitions of shared purposes. Sharing this belief, Brzezinski advocated trilateral cooperation as the central priority of US policy. For both, the possession of military power is an essential requirement, but while Kissinger rejected numerical superiority, Brzezinski insisted on it. They also agreed that it is essential to use the inherent linkage of issues and to establish a relationship between power and the will to use it by demonstrating political will. Moreover, while Kissinger believed that the control of all factors essential to survival and the clear definition of the strategic transformations one is prepared to resist were essential requirements, Brzezinski insisted on reciprocity in relations with adversaries and the dramatization of political initiatives. In addition, while Kissinger's conception of leadership dictated policymaking by non-bureaucratic means, Brzezinski's conception of leadership led him to insist only on the institutional and political reorganization of the policymaking process.

The difference in Kissinger's and Brzezinski's conceptions of leadership was also evident in their beliefs regarding the calculation, control, and acceptance of risks. Unlike Kissinger who viewed the willingness to take risks as inherent in leadership, Brzezinski's advocacy of prudent leadership and joint initiatives indicated that he was less prepared than Kissinger to take risks. However, both believed that since the major risks arise from miscalculation, they can be controlled by maintaining the necessary strategic force to enhance US credibility. They differed, however, on the requirements of such a force. They also agreed that the control of risks requires a demonstration of the political will to use force to defend Western interests. But while Kissinger maintained that this can be achieved by increasing tactical flexibility through the reduction of bureaucratic control and the development of a strategy for limited war, Brzezinski insisted on prudent leadership and joint initiatives. However, despite their differences, both agreed that since the USSR and the PRC are better suited to revolution and conflict than to protracted global stability, the control of risks requires the total elimination of opportunities that could be exploited by them to subvert the international system.

Kissinger's and Brzezinski's beliefs regarding the best timing of action for advancing one's interests are related to their short-term pessimism and long-term optimism and to their belief that the East-West conflict will be protracted. For Kissinger, the protracted nature of the conflict dictates the willingness to fight indefinitely and to avoid the quest for quick military and diplomatic victories since the side willing to wait can tip the psychological balance whatever the outcome of the physical battle. Sharing Kissinger's belief that by the time risks become self-evident it is usually too late, Brzezinski stressed the need to distinguish the immediate from the long-range threats and to focus on the immediate, but given the protracted nature of the conflict the responses must be taken in the context of long-term goals. However, both agreed that the ability to react quickly to numerous diverse situations is vital since in the nuclear age by the time a threat becomes unambiguous it may be too late. While Kissinger stressed that the Soviet strategy of ambiguity can only be defeated by a policy of precaution, Brzezinski advocated institutional changes that would permit the US to apply elements of its superiority more rapidly than its adversaries.

For Kissinger and Brzezinski, the utility of different means depends on their usefulness for maintaining the equilibrium of power and legitimacy – the prerequisites to stability. Both believed that while all-out nuclear war has lost its utility as a means of policy, except as a last resort, the use of limited force to defend concrete US interests is still vital. To facilitate the use of force in the nuclear era, Kissinger even advanced the view that the US must develop the capability for limited nuclear war. For Kissinger, traditional diplomacy is possible only in a stable international system where agreement about the nature of workable arrangements and about the permissible aims and methods of foreign policy exists. Nevertheless, he believed that although diplomacy cannot resolve the fundamental political conflicts with the USSR and the PRC since they reject the present international system, it is useful for conveying one's intentions thus preventing conflicts due to miscalculation and for identifying the US with the aspirations of humanity. Brzezinski agreed with Kissinger that the USSR's and the PRC's commitment to world-wide communist expansion has reduced the utility of traditional diplomacy, but believed that diplomacy conducted openly with flexibility, patience, toughness, and on the principle of reciprocity, can be useful for preventing conflicts due to miscalculation. Both agreed that summits can be useful. But while Kissinger insisted that summits must be held on the bases of a concrete program for breaking a deadlock, charting a new course, and ratifying agreements, Brzezinski insisted only that they be informal and held regularly without fanfare. The utility of arms control, according to both, is limited to reducing the instability caused by the escalating arms race; hence, it should not be approached with the view that without it all is lost. Both viewed consultations as useful. For Kissinger, however, consultations are better for implementing a consensus than for creating it, while for Brzezinski collective consultations could both create and implement a consensus. Finally, both believed that education is a useful means for developing the domestic and international consensus which is essential for achieving national goals. But unlike Kissinger, Brzezinski did not perceive the limitations inherent in the task of educating public opinion about the realities of the revolutionary threat and about the nature of power in the nuclear age.

This study found that Nixon, (Ford), and Carter, shared many of their respective National Security Advisers' views on world politics and strategy and tactics for achieving national goals. However, the congruence between the President's and the Adviser's views was greater in the case of Nixon, (Ford) and Kissinger than in the case of Carter and Brzezinski. Unlike Brzezinski, Carter, was less concerned with the Soviet military threat, regarded arms control as the core of détente, and did not recognize, as Brzezinski did in 1976, that Western Europe and Japan were not prepared to play a larger global role. This study revealed that the roles of the

National Security Adviser and of the Secretaries of State and Defense were greatly influenced by the President's definition of his own role which was in turn influenced by his conception of leadership. This study also revealed that the organization of the NSC system and the more informal policymaking structures were particularly influenced by the President's and the Adviser's conception of leadership. Nixon's (and Ford's) NSC system and the backchannels which gave Kissinger total control of policymaking reflected Nixon's and Kissinger's belief that leadership is the willingness to act alone when the situation requires it and the related belief that inherent in leadership is the provision and implementation of a vision. Carter's NSC system, the Friday Presidential breakfast, and the V-B-B (and later the M-B-B) luncheon which permitted other principal policymakers to influence policy were consistent with Carter's and Brzezinski's beliefs in collective leadership and in consultation. The fact that Brzezinski, despite his attacks on the Nixon-Kissinger preoccupation with the USSR and the PRC, tried to control through the SCC the issues related to SALT, crisis management, and intelligence also reflected his beliefs that the increasing Soviet military capabilities and Moscow's exploitation of Third World conflicts make the USSR the greatest immediate threat to peace. However, inconsistently with their belief in collective leadership, Carter and Brzezinski agreed on the organization of the NSC system without prior consultation with Vance and Brown. But their action reflected Carter's belief in controlling policy personally and Brzezinski's implicit acceptance of Kissinger's conception of leadership, an acceptance also manifest in Brzezinski's use of procedural means to control national security policymaking and his willingness to hold consultative meetings with the Soviets and the Chinese despite his and Carter's attacks on Kissinger's secretive and personal diplomacy and backchannel initiatives. The efforts of Kissinger and Brzezinski to control policymaking, however, reflected their shared belief that men with a will by taking calculated actions can, within limits, move history in the direction they desire.

Consistently with their belief that Soviet military power makes the USSR the greatest immediate threat to peace, Kissinger and Brzezinski focused their energies on the US-Soviet relationship and sought to counterbalance the USSR by supporting new strategic weapons programs and by promoting a closer US-PRC relationship. Their promotion of the US-PRC relationship reflected their belief that while the US should not promote the Sino-Soviet conflict it can exploit it by using the PRC to counterbalance the USSR. However, Brzezinski's push for the rapid normalization of US-PRC relations and his efforts to establish a security relationship with Peking was inconsistent with his belief that the US should move more slowly since the PRC is still a long-term threat to peace and his attacks on Kissinger for the opening to Peking. The timing of their initiatives toward Peking and their efforts to declare officially that the basis of the US-PRC relationship is the common opposition to Moscow's geopolitical ambitions, revealed that their promotion of the US-PRC relationship was, indeed, influenced by their views of the USSR. Their belief in linkage was clearly evident in their pursuit of the triangular relationship among the US, the USSR, and the PRC. By focusing on relations with Moscow and Peking, Kissinger and Brzezinski were acting consistently with their belief in the power-realist approach to politics. Kissinger's declaration that the objective of détente was to adjust Moscow's external goals, not to transform its political system, and his pursuit of the opening to Peking gave tangible expression to his belief in the non-ideological/non-moralistic approach to politics. Brzezinski's push to normalize relations with the PRC reflected his belief in the non-ideological approach to politics, while his efforts to link human rights to the other aspects of the US-Soviet relationship revealed his belief in the moral approach. Consistent with his belief that legitimacy is the second requirement of stability, Kissinger used the Soviet proposals for the Basic Principles and the APNW to establish an international agreement on what he considered to be the permissible aims and methods of foreign policy. Moreover, by negotiating all agreements with the USSR and the PRC personally, Kissinger demonstrated his belief that statesmanship requires both the provision and implementation of a vision. However, while Brzezinski's personal initiatives toward the PRC were inconsistent with his belief in collective leadership, they were consistent with his belief in the need for bold initiatives. After leaving office, consistent with their belief in the power-realist approach to politics, both have been reasserting that Soviet military power and Moscow's increasing willingness to use it make the USSR the greatest immediate threat to peace and that strategic considerations must govern US relations with the USSR and the PRC. However, while Kissinger insists that US credibility dictates that the US must fulfill its commitment to assist the rearmament of the PRC, Brzezinski, who pushed for it, has been urging that the US assist the economic modernization of the PRC in order to maintain an informal strategic relationship with Peking.

Kissinger's and Brzezinski's recommendations and/or actions regarding the new strategic weapons programs and SALT reflected some of their other beliefs. While their support for new strategic weapons programs was consistent with their belief that the US-Soviet strategic balance is the key to peace, their specific recommendations reflected their different conceptions of that balance. Kissinger's concept of sufficiency, his acceptance of inequality in launchers in SALT I, and his opposition to the Defense Department's "equal aggregates" demands in SALT II, reflected his belief that an adequate retaliatory force, not numerical superiority, is the key to peace. Brzezinski's belief in strategic superiority was manifest in his efforts to force a decision on the MX and his support for an ICBM freeze at the existing US levels which, while it would have stopped the MX, it would have prevented Moscow from achieving qualitative superiority as well by stopping the deployment of new Soviet ICBMs. Their belief in the limited utility of arms control was evident in their strong support for new strategic weapons programs and their insistence on Soviet geopolitical restraint while pursuing SALT. Consistent with their belief in linkage, Kissinger and Brzezinski linked SALT to other issues in the US-Soviet relationship, but the specific linkages in each case reflected their particular conception of détente. Kissinger's belief in the non-ideological/non-moralistic approach to détente led him to link SALT to US-Soviet trade and to Moscow's geopolitical restraint but to oppose the explicit linkage of human rights to US-Soviet trade. For him, the linkage of human rights with trade was implicit, as was the linkage of the US relationships with the USSR and the PRC. Unlike Kissinger, Brzezinski believing in the moral approach to politics linked SALT to Soviet geopolitical restraint, to trade, and to Moscow's willingness to reduce human rights restrictions. For him, the explicit linkage of human rights to other aspects of the US-Soviet relationship was at the core of his conception of reciprocal and comprehensive détente. Moreover, their shared belief that the East-West conflict will be protracted, led both to insist on slowing down the pace of SALT. In Kissinger's case, this also reflected his belief that the quest for quick diplomatic and military victories must be avoided, while in Brzezinski's case, it revealed his belief that patience and toughness are vital in the negotiations with the East. Since leaving office both have been reasserting their beliefs that arms control must be linked to new strategic weapons programs to balance the military power of the USSR and to Soviet geopolitical restraint to prevent Moscow from subverting the international system by exploiting Third World conflicts.

Consistent with their belief that for Moscow peaceful coexistence is an offensive tactic by which to subvert the international system by means short of an all-out nuclear war, Kissinger and Brzezinski while pursuing US-Soviet trade and SALT urged the use of force to defeat Soviet efforts to change the global equilibrium of power by small degrees. Their readiness in every Third World crisis in which the USSR was involved to both negotiate and, more importantly, to use force reflected their beliefs in the need to establish a relationship between power and diplomacy and to strengthen US credibility by demonstrating power and political will. Those beliefs led them to pressure the Pentagon to develop the strategic doctrine and the military capabilities that would facilitate the use of force in contingencies short of an all-out nuclear war. Their pressure on the Pentagon was also consistent with their belief that global engagement requires the ability to react rapidly and credibly to prevent a *fait accompli*. Moreover, Kissinger's requests to the Pentagon to develop flexible strategic options and Brzezinski's efforts to create a war-fighting doctrine and capability reflected their shared belief that although all-out nuclear war has ceased to be an instrument of policy, the capability and the will to fight nuclear war as a last resort are essential for preventing it from occurring by miscalculation. Since leaving office Kissinger and Brzezinski have been stressing that since Moscow is still using peaceful coexistence as a tactic to subvert the international system by small degrees the US must develop a doctrine and the capabilities that permit the use of force in contingencies short of an all-out nuclear war. Indeed, they insist that the US take risks to defend its vital interests in the Third World in order to convince Moscow to end its challenges to peace.

Kissinger's and Brzezinski's recommendations and/or actions regarding US allied policy were also consistent with their beliefs. Believing that the European military balance and Atlantic unity were essential for maintaining the global equilibrium of power both supported the strengthening of NATO's military capabilities and sought to develop a united response toward the PRC and the USSR. However, convinced that NATO's strategic dilemmas cannot be resolved as long as it remains composed of sovereign states, Kissinger tried to strengthen extended deterrence by unilateral means and by accepting West European initiatives in the security field even though he was convinced that they did not create the needed military capability and demonstrated the lack of West European political will. But by avoiding disputes over strategic issues he maintained the political unity which he believed to be essential in dealing with the East. Bzrezinski, believing that NATO's strategic dilemmas can be resolved by consultation, despite the limits imposed by the fusion of sovereignty with nuclear weapons, and inconsistently with his belief in collective leadership, pressured the West Europeans to support new weapons programs convinced they were needed to demonstrate NATO's power and political will. The fact that neither Kissinger nor Brzezinski pushed MBFR and were more supportive of new weapons programs reflected their shared belief that arms control has limited utility for creating stability. Kissinger's beliefs that US and West European interests are not identical everywhere and that a united Western Europe will be in a better position to challenge

US hegemony in Atlantic policy, led him to oppose US intervention in the West European debate regarding the preferred structure of the enlarged EEC and to intentionally neglect the EEC Commission, since by strengthening it, in the absence of a common trade policy it could have challenged his trade policy toward the East. Those actions also reflected his belief that due to political multipolarity the US could no longer impose its own initiatives. However, consistently with his belief that Atlantic unity is vital to dealing with the East, he paid the economic price for the enlarged EEC and pushed the Year of Europe initiative which also revealed his conception of leadership. Moreover, believing that leadership is inherent in power, Kissinger used NATO's dependence on the US nuclear guarantee to control all Western initiatives toward the East. His beliefs in linkage and in avoiding the quest of quick diplomatic victories led him to tie Ostpolitik and the CSCE to global issues of concern to the US and to slow down the pace of the Berlin negotiations until Moscow made concessions. Convinced that consultations are better suited to implementing a consensus than in creating it, Kissinger limited consultations to major allies and only on issues they agreed and pursued his objectives through backchannel initiatives. Since 1977, Kissinger has been reasserting the same beliefs. Brzezinski, however, after leaving office, acknowledged that it would have been better to deal with NATO's security issues the way Kissinger did.

Brzezinski, however, inconsistently with his belief that the active promotion of trilateral cooperation must be the central priority of US policy, did not pursue it. But by allowing Vance and Brown to take the initiative in shaping US policy toward NATO and Japan, he was acting consistently with his belief in collective leadership. Moreover, despite his belief that the common values of the US, Western Europe, and Japan permit trilateral cooperation through deliberate, closer and more institutionalized political consultations, Brzezinski, like Kissinger, limited his consultations to the major allies and especially the French who shared his belief about Moscow's objectives in the Persian Gulf and the Middle East. When consultations failed to produce a common Western policy toward the USSR, Brzezinski urged unilateral US action and then pressured West Europeans to get his desired response to Moscow's actions in Eastern Europe, in the Horn of Africa and in Afghanistan. His willingness to take unilateral actions reflected his belief in bold initiatives – an implicit acceptance of Kissinger's conception of leadership. Indeed, since 1981, reasserting Kissinger's belief that the West European allies are just regional powers, Brzezinski has deemphasized consultations as a means for developing trilateral cooperation and has been advocating unilateral US initiatives to defend Western interests outside of Europe. Moreover, reiterating the need for both West European and Atlantic unity, he has been declaring that since neither will emerge from European initiatives the US should exercise the leadership that its allies seek.

This study found enough similarities between Kissinger and Brezinski to raise the question: Can a consensus on national security policy be created if those struggling to control that policy admit, as Brezizinski did, that most of the attacks on each other that undermine the needed consensus are the result of campaign politics? I believe that it can be created, but to stop the attacks and to start a dialogue requires the demonstration of political will, and that in itself is an act of leadership.

Notes

Chapter 1: Introduction

1. Their official title was Assistant to the President for National Security Affairs. This study, however, uses the more popularly known National Security Adviser.
2. John G. Stoessinger, *Henry Kissinger: The Anguish of Power* (New York: W. W. Norton & Company, Inc., 1976), pp. 137–38; George W. Ball, *Diplomacy for a Crowded World* (Boston: Little, Brown and Company, 1976), pp. 155–56; Peter W. Dickson, *Kissinger and the Meaning of History* (New York: Cambridge University Press, 1978), pp. 113–14; Richard A. Falk, *What's Wrong with Henry Kissinger's Foreign Policy* (Princeton University, 1974), pp. 5–6; David Landau, *Kissinger: The Uses of Power* (Boston: Houghton Mifflin Company, 1972), pp. 114–15; Zbigniew Brzezinski, "Half Past Nixon," *Foreign Policy* 3 (Summer 1971):3–20, "U.S. Foreign Policy: The Search for Focus," *Foreign Affairs* 51 (July 1973):708–27, "The Deceptive Structure of Peace," *Foreign Policy* 14 (Spring 1974):35–55, "Shifting Mood and System," *The Atlantic Community Quarterly* 12 (Fall 1974):319–26, "America in a Hostile World," *Foreign Policy* 23 (Summer 1976):65–96; Stanley Hoffmann, "Choices," *Foreign Policy* 12 (Fall 1973):3–42; J. Robert Schaetzel, "Some European Questions for Dr. Kissinger," *Foreign Policy* 12 (Fall 1973):66–74. Vincent Davis, *Henry Kissinger and Bureaucratic Politics* Essay Series, No. 9 (Institute of International Studies, University of South Carolina, 1979).
3. Suetonious, "Born to Skim," *The New Republic* 176 (January 1977):8; Robert Scheer, "Carter's Man Zbig: Profound or Banal?" *Los Angeles Times* (January 23, 1977), pp. 24–25; Russell Watson and others, "Life at Brzezinski U," *Newsweek* LXXXIX:63 (May 9, 1977); Victor Zorza, "A Man to Out-Kissinger Kissinger," *Washington Post* (January 19, 1977), p. 23; A. Stang, "Zbig Brother," *American Opinion* 21 (February 1978):99; E. Bettiga, "Jimmy Who? and Zbigniew Who?" *Survey* 22 (Summer/Autumn 1976):20; Herman Nickel, "Why Zbig is Not Quite on Top of the World," *Fortune* 99 (April 23, 1979):71; Ernest Conine, "Foreign Policy Under President Carter," *Los Angeles Times* (August 20, 1976), p. 7; David Butler and others, "An Exodus from Zbig," *Newsweek* 93 (June 9, 1979):71; "A Hard-liner on Russia, Who Will Fill Key White House Post?" *U.S. News and World Report* 81 (December 27, 1976):29; Cummings Bruce, "Chinatown: Foreign Policy and Elite Realignment," in *The Hidden Election*, ed. Thomas Ferguson and Joel

Rogers (New York: Pantheon Books, 1981), pp. 196–231.

4. Many of their conceptions were also a product of general life experience and upbringing, not necessarily their academic experience. Bruce Mazlish, *Kissinger: The European Mind in American Policy* (New York: Basic Books, Inc., 1976); Dana Ward, "Kissinger: A Psychohistory," in *Henry Kissinger: His Personality and Policies*, ed. Dan Caldwell (Durham, N.C.: Duke Press Policy Studies, 1983), pp. 24–63.

5. Alexander L. George, "The 'Operational Code': A Neglected Approach to the Study of Political Leaders and Decision-Making," *International Studies Quarterly* 13 (June 1969):190–222. See pp. 201–5 for philosophical questions and pp. 205–16 for instrumental questions.

6. George, "The 'Operational Code'," pp. 201–2, 221.

7. Ibid., pp. 216–21; and "The Causal Nexus between Cognitive Beliefs and Decision-making Behavior: The 'Operational Code' Belief System," in *Psychological Models in International Politics*, ed. Lawrence S. Falkowski (Boulder, CO: Westview Press, 1979), p. 99; Also see Loch K. Johnson, "Operational Codes and the Prediction of Leadership Behavior: Senator Frank Church at Midcareer," in *A Psychological Examination of Political Leaders*, eds. Margaret G. Hermann with Thomas W. Milburn (New York: The Free Press, 1977), pp. 109–13

8. Ole R. Holsti, "The 'Operational Code' Approach to the Study of Political Leaders: John Foster Dulles' Philosophical and Instrumental Beliefs," p. 153, *Canadian Journal of Political Science* 3:1 (March 1970). George, "The 'Operational Code'," p. 200; Harvey Starr, *Henry Kissinger: Perceptions of International Politics* (Lexington, KY: The University of Kentucky Press, 1984), p. 47.

9. George, "The Causal Nexus between Cognitive Beliefs and Decision-making Behavior," p. 101.

10. Ibid., p. 102.

11. Ole R. Holsti, "Foreign Policy Formation Viewed Cognitively." In *Structure of Decision*, ed. Robert Axelrod (Princeton, NJ: Princeton University Press, 1976), pp. 18–54.

12. George, "The Causal Nexus between Cognitive Beliefs and Decision-making Behavior," pp. 102, 112–13.

13. Ibid., p. 103.

14. Ibid., pp. 103, 113.

15. Ibid. George states that "Viewed from a slightly different standpoint, a person's operational code beliefs structure and channel the way in which he copes and deals with the cognitive limits of rationality; they serve to define his particular type of 'bounded rationality'."

16. George, "The 'Operational Code'," pp. 196–97.

17. George, "The Causal Nexus between Cognitive Beliefs and Decision-making Behavior," p. 114. He states: The two leaders would be approximately the same age and (except for their beliefs) have similar personalities; they would have lived in the same sociohistorical

epoch and undergone similar political socialization experiences; they would embrace the same ideology and occupy similar political roles – that is, they would be members of the same political elite occupying comparable positions at a given decision-making level. Further, they would receive the same informational inputs about emergent situations and have similar responsibilities for decision-making or, at least, for formulating responsible judgments and advice regarding the preferred option or strategy to pursue.

18. Mazlish, *Kissinger: The European Mind in American Policy*, p. 21; Elizabeth Drew, "A Reporter At Large: Brzezinski," *The New Yorker* (May 1, 1978), p. 90.
19. Davis, *Henry Kissinger and Bureaucratic Politics*, pp. 19–20.
20. Ibid., pp. 17–18. Kissinger received three degrees from Harvard, a B.A. in 1950, an M.A. in 1952, and a Ph.D. in 1953. Brzezinski received his B.A. and M.A. from McGill University, and his Ph.D. from Harvard in 1953.
21. Ibid., pp. 20–21. In the 1968 presidential campaign Kissinger advised Nelson Rockefeller and Brzezinski advised Hubert H. Humphrey. In the 1972 presidential campaign Brzezinski advised George McGovern and in 1976 Carter.
22. Starr, *Henry Kissinger*, pp. 48–49. Starr maintains that Kissinger is "an ideal subject for an operational code study." But I think that his comment also applies to Brzezinski who meets the reasons Starr uses to justify his comment.
23. Stephen R. Graubard, *Kissinger: Portrait of a Mind* (New York: W. W. Norton & Company, Inc., 1973), p. 6. In his discussion of Kissinger's undergraduate thesis, "The Meaning of History: Reflections on Spengler, Toynbee and Kant," Graubard observes, "Much of what he learned at Harvard was incorporated into a thesis that pretended to deal with selected philosophies of history since the eighteenth century; it was, in fact, a kind of personal testament."
24. Harvey Starr, "The Kissinger Years: Studying Individuals and Foreign Policy," *International Studies Quarterly* 24:4 (December 1980), p. 474, and in *Henry Kissinger*, p. 49.

Chapter 2: The Philosophical Beliefs of Henry Kissinger

1. Henry A. Kissinger, *White House Years* (Boston: Little, Brown and Company, 1979), p. 54.
2. Kissinger, "The Meaning of History" (Unpublished Undergraduate Thesis, Harvard University, 1950), pp. 347–48.
3. Kissinger, *A World Restored: Europe After Napoleon* (Glouster, Mass: Peter Smith, 1973). Kissinger used the terms "stable order" and "legitimate order" interchangeably.
4. Ibid,. p. 1; Kissinger, "The White Revolutionary: Reflections on Bis-

marck," *Daedalus* 97 (Summer 1968):899–900; Dickson, *Kissinger and the Meaning of History*, p. 20.

5. Kissinger, *A World Restored*, pp. 1–2; Henry A. Kissinger, *Nuclear Weapons and Foreign Policy* (New York: Harper & Brothers, 1957), pp. 141–42, 317; abridged edn (New York: W. W. Norton & Company, Inc., 1969), pp. 44, 122.

6. Stoessinger, *Henry Kissinger*, p. 12; Falk, *What's Wrong with Henry Kissinger's Foreign Policy*, pp. 17, 25, 29. Falk stated that "any kind of ideological or moralistic posturing by a government or its leaders is abhorrent to Kissinger."

7. Kissinger, *Nuclear Weapons and Foreign Policy*, p. 316; abridged edn, p. 43; He argued that Napoleonic France, Nazi Germany, and Communist Russia were equally threatening to international stability since they based their foreign policy on ideologies committed to transform the international system. Falk, *What's Wrong with Henry Kissinger's Foreign Policy*, p. 17. Falk maintained that "To Kissinger it makes almost no difference whether a revolutionary is red or white. Both are equally dangerous to international stability, and stability is the overriding, virtually the exclusive, objective of statesman."

8. Kissinger, *A World Restored*, p. 3.

9. Ibid., p. 2. *Nuclear Weapons and Foreign Policy*, abridged edn, p. 77; 1957 edn, pp. 358–59.

10. Kissinger, *A World Restored*, p. 145.

11. Ibid., p. 181.

12. Ibid., p. 145.

13. Ibid., p. 1. *Nuclear Weapons and Foreign Policy*, p. 428; abridged edn p. 244.

14. Kissinger, *Nuclear Weapons and Foreign Policy*, p. 328; abridged edn, p. 53.

15. Ibid., p. 4; abridged edn, p. 2.

16. Kissinger, *Nuclear Weapons and Foreign Policy*, pp. 5–6; abridged edn, pp. 2–3; Falk, *What's Wrong with Henry Kissinger's Foreign Policy*, pp. 8–11. Stoessinger, *Henry Kissinger*, p. 12. He stated: "The impact of these discoveries on Kissinger was profound and permanent."

17. Kissinger, *American Foreign Policy* (New York: W. W. Norton & Company, Inc., 1969), pp. 53–55; *Nuclear Weapons and Foreign Policy*, pp. 5–6; abridged edn, pp. 2–3; *The Necessity for Choice* (New York: Harper and Brothers, 1961), pp. 2, 6. Falk, *What's Wrong with Henry Kissinger's Foreign Policy*, p. 14. Falk recognized the shift in emphasis in Kissinger's writings but stated that it became evident in *The Necessity for Choice*.

18. Kissinger, *Nuclear Weapons and Foreign Policy*, p. 5; abridged edn, p. 3.

19. Ibid., pp. 6–7; abridged edn, pp. 3–4.

20. Ibid., p. 7; abridged edn, pp. 3, 49.

21. Ibid., p. 323.
22. Kissinger, *A World Restored*, p. 2.
23. Kissinger, *Nuclear Weapons and Foreign Policy*, pp. 358–59, see also pp. 357–58, 318–19; abridged edn, pp. 77, 76, 45; Falk, *What's Wrong with Henry Kissinger's Foreign Policy*, p. 12.
24. Kissinger, *Nuclear Weapons and Foreign Policy*, p. 358; abridged edn p. 76.
25. Ibid., p. 16; abridged edn, pp. 11–12; *American Foreign Policy*, p. 87.
26. Kissinger, *American Foreign Policy*, pp. 55–56.
27. Kissinger, *Nuclear Weapons and Foreign Policy*, abridged edn, pp. 50–51; 1957 edn, p. 325.
28. Ibid., abridged edn, pp. 3, 51, 86; 1957 edn, pp. 6, 325, 367.
29. Ibid., abridged edn, p. 11; 1957 edn, pp. 15–16; *American Foreign Policy*, p. 87; Stoessinger, *Henry Kissinger*, pp.43–44. Stoessinger saw a radical change in Kissinger's view of the opponent. He argued that Kissinger anchored his grand design for a stable world order to "his belief that the Soviet Union and China had *ceased to be 'revolutionary' states*." Stoessinger's argument rests on his understanding of the term "revolutionary" which in his view "was reserved for nations that were irrevocably committed to the destruction of their adversaries." He argued that "in Kissinger's opinion . . . the leaders of China and the Soviet Union were no longer comparable to Napoleon or Hitler," for the following reasons: (a) a greater degree of rationality seemed to govern their behavior; (b) the approaching strategic balance between the US and the USSR served as a deterrent against irresponsible behavior; and (c) the Sino-Soviet split. Stoessinger's argument derives from his analysis of Rockefeller's campaign speeches in 1968 which were written by Kissinger. However, this change is not evident in Kissinger's academic writings.
30. Kissinger, *American Foreign Policy*, p. 85; *Nuclear Weapons and Foreign Policy*, abridged edn, p.11; 1957 edn, pp. 15–16. *The Necessity for Choice*, p. 97. Stoessinger, *Henry Kissinger*, pp. 80–81. Stoessinger states: "Before the Cuban Missile crisis Kissinger viewed the Soviet Union as the World's leading 'revolutionary' power, insatiably bent on global conquest. By the time he joined the government in 1969, Kissinger had changed his mind." I disagree. Kissinger modified his views but he did not change his mind.
31. Kissinger, *American Foreign Policy*, p. 87.
32. Kissinger, *Nuclear Weapons and Foreign Policy*, abridged edn, pp. 126–27. Kissinger pointed out that "while it is difficult to predict the precise circumstances of a possible split within the Soviet orbit . . . relations between China and the Soviet Union may become cooler if the alliance forces either partner to shoulder risks for objectives which are of no benefit to it."
33. Kissinger, *The Necessity for Choice*, p. 202. *The Troubled Partnership*, pp. 59–60.

34. Kissinger, *American Foreign Policy*, p. 129.
35. Kissinger, *Nuclear Weapons and Foreign Policy*, abridged edn, p. 111; 1957 edn, p. 126.
36. Ibid., abridged edn, pp. 70–71, 74–76; 1957 edn, pp. 142–43, 350–51; *The Necessity for Choice*, p. 97.
37. Kissinger, *The Necessity for Choice*, p. 97.
38. Kissinger, *Nuclear Weapons and Foreign Policy*, abridged edn, p. 70; 1957 edn, p. 350;
39. Ibid., abridged edn, pp. 99, 91, 50; 1957 edn, pp. 386–87, 325. He believed: "the consistency of Soviet behavior would indicate that on questions of doctrine the Kremlin generally does mean what it says"(p. 91). "Since the Soviet leadership derives its claim to superiority from its theoretical insight, a doctrinal dispute in the USSR has not only a philosophical, but an eminently practical significance. Throughout the history of Soviet communism, almost every dispute over doctrine has reflected a disagreement on policy, and almost every change of doctrine has sooner or later been translated into action" (p. 99).
40. Ibid., abridged edn, p. 74; 1957 edn, p. 354.
41. Ibid., abridged edn, pp. 3, 48–49; 1957 edn, pp. 323, 7.
42. Ibid., abridged edn, p. 75; 1957 edn, p. 356. *The Necessity for Choice*, p. 172.
43. Kissinger, *Nuclear Weapons and Foreign Policy*, p. 142.
44. Kissinger, *American Foreign Policy*, p. 89.
45. Ibid., p. 87.
46. Kissinger, *A World Restored*, p. 2.
47. Kissinger, *Nuclear Weapons and Foreign Policy*, pp. 353, 359; abridged edn, pp. 72, 78.
48. Kissinger, *The Necessity for Choice*, pp. 197–202. *American Foreign Policy*, p. 38.
49. Kissinger, *Nuclear Weapons and Foreign Policy*, p. 357; abridged edn, pp. 76–77. He argued that in Russia this "would almost inevitably imply a much larger role for the military."
50. Kissinger, *American Foreign Policy*, p. 38.
51. Ibid., p. 57.
52. Kissinger, *Nuclear Weapons and Foreign Policy*, abridged edn, p. 201.
53. Kissinger, *American Foreign Policy*, p. 75. *The Troubled Partnership*, pp. 166, 169.
54. Kissinger, *The Troubled Partnership*, p. 177.
55. Ibid., pp. 106, 169.
56. Ibid., pp. 22, 15.
57. Ibid., pp. 169, 17.
58. Kissinger, *American Foreign Policy*, pp. 89–90; *The Troubled Partnership*, pp. 248–51.
59. Kissinger, *The Troubled Partnership*, p. 169.

60. Ibid., pp. 27–28, 241, 232. *American Foreign Policy*, p. 68.
61. Kissinger, *The Troubled Partnership*, pp. 232, 27–28.
62. Kissinger, *American Foreign Policy*, pp. 70–72. He pointed out that prior to World War II America had the resources but was unwilling to conduct a global policy. *The Troubled Partnership*, p. 9.
63. Kissinger, *The Troubled Partnership*, pp. 232, 40, 21.
64. Ibid., p. 11; *Nuclear Weapons and Foreign Policy*, pp. 237–38; abridged edn, pp. 197–98.
65. Kissinger, *The Troubled Partnership*, p. 11.
66. Ibid., pp. 11–12; *American Foreign Policy*, p. 67.
67. Kissinger, *American Foreign Policy*, pp. 65–66; *Nuclear Weapons and Foreign Policy*, p. 238; abridged edn, p. 198.
68. The North Atlantic Treaty, *State Bulletin* (20 March 1949), p. 340.
69. Kissinger *The Troubled Partnership*, p. 169.
70. Ibid., pp. 15, 162, 117–18, 170.
71. Ibid., p. 12.
72. Kissinger, *Nuclear Weapons and Foreign Policy*, p. 245.
73. Kissinger, *The Troubled Partnership*, pp. 5, 10.
74. Kissinger, *American Foreign Policy*, pp. 66–67.
75. Ibid., pp. 56, 66–67; also see *Nuclear Weapons and Foreign Policy*, pp. 246–54; abridged edn, pp. 206–11.
76. Kissinger, *Nuclear Weapons and Foreign Policy*, p. 254; *The Troubled Partnership*, pp. 10, 15, 21.
77. Kissinger, *The Troubled Partnership*, pp. 248–50, 28.
78. Kissinger, *American Foreign Policy*, p. 81.
79. Kissinger, *Nuclear Weapons and Foreign Policy*, p. 255; abridged edn, p. 212.
80. Kissinger, *American Foreign Policy*, pp. 80–81; also see *Nuclear Weapons and Foreign Policy*, pp. 261–62; abridged edn, pp. 217–18.
81. Kissinger, *American Foreign Policy*, p. 56.
82. Kissinger, *Nuclear Weapons and Foreign Policy*, p. 5; abridged edn, p. 3.
83. Ibid., p. 256; abridged edn, p. 213.
84. Ibid., pp. 258–59; abridged edn, pp. 215–16.
85. Ibid., pp. 259–60; abridged edn, p. 216.
86. Ibid., p. 266; abridged edn, p. 222.
87. Ibid., pp. 261–62; abridged edn, pp. 217–18.
88. Ibid., p. 262; abridged edn, pp. 218–19.
89. Ibid., abridged edn, p. 220; 1957 edn, p. 263.
90. Oriana Fallaci, "Kissinger," *The New Republic* (December 16, 1972), p. 22. Kissinger stated: "In a sense, however, I am a fatalist. I believe in fate." Dickson, *Kissinger and the Meaning of History*, pp. 28, 72, 79, 85, 86. He stated: Kissinger's outlook on life was "fundamentally pessimistic, even fatalistic . . . Some of Kissinger's policies in fact seemed to flow presisely from such an attitude." Stoessinger, *Henry Kissinger*, p. 19.

91. Dickson, *Kissinger and the Meaning of History*, pp. 79, 86. Seeing Kissinger's conditional optimism, Dickson argued: "Yet, it would be difficult to find an individual who has exhibited more desire and determination to influence events, to advance national interests, and to fullfill his own personal goals than Henry Kissinger. His faith in the power of man's freedom to act was most apparent . . . " Brandon, *The Retreat of American Power*, p. 36.
92. Kissinger, *Nuclear Weapons and Foreign Policy*, p. 247; abridged edn, p. 207; Dickson, *Kissinger and the Meaning of History*, pp. 76, 80.
93. Kissinger, *American Foreign Policy*, p. 54.
94. Ibid., p. 56.
95. Kissinger, *Nuclear Weapons and Foreign Policy*, pp. 264, 428; abridged edn, pp. 220, 244; *The Necessity for Choice*, p. 9.
96. Dickson, *Kissinger and the Meaning of History*, pp. 83–116. He argued the notion of limits is vital to understanding Kissinger, and devoted a chapter to it; Mazlish, *Kissinger*, pp. 177–86. He stated: "Kissinger was, and is, obsessed with the notion of 'limits'. It is a major theme, both in his life and in his writings."
97. Kissinger, *A World Restored*, pp. 2–3.
98. Ibid., p. 316. He also viewed Alexander I as revolutionary.
99. Kissinger, "The Meaning of History," pp. 345–46; Dickson, *Kissinger and the Meaning of History*, pp. 95–98.
100. Mazlish, *Kissinger*, pp. 177, 180; Dickson, *Kissinger and the Meaning of History*, pp. 100, 97–98. Dickson stated that "for Kissinger a realistic appraisal of the human situation not the validity of moral principles demonstrates the need for moderation and self-restraint."
101. Kissinger, *American Foreign Policy*, pp. 59–60.
102. Kissinger, *The Troubled Partnership*, p. 162.
103. Ibid., p. 170.
104. Kissinger, *The Necessity for Choice*, p. 357.
105. Kissinger, *Nuclear Weapons and Foreign Policy*, pp. 423–31; abridged edn, pp. 239–46; Nutter, *Kissinger's Grand Strategy*, p. 7. Nutter notes Kissinger's "unmistakable vision of the West in decline."
106. Ibid., pp. 435–36, 429; abridged edn, pp. 251, 245.
107. Ibid., p. 431; abridged edn, p. 246.
108. Dickson, *Kissinger and the Meaning of History*, p. 86; Mazlish, *Kissinger*, pp. 182–83. Like Dickson, Mazlish maintained that "we have all the opposing concepts made familiar to us in Kissinger's undergraduate thesis: limits, recognition of them (resignation), and yet transcendence of them, and thus choice." Nutter, *Kissinger's Grand Design*, p. 8. He notes that Kissinger did not believe in historical determinism and "conceive[d] a critical role for human will and imagination in shaping the course of events within the constraints forged by facts and circumstances."
109. Kissinger, *The Troubled Partnership*, p. 250.
110. Ibid., pp. 248–50, 28.

111. Ibid., p. 65; *Nuclear Weapons and Foreign Policy*, p. 170; abridged edn, pp. 141–42.
112. Kissinger, *The Necessity for Choice*, p. 357. Dickson, *Kissinger and the Meaning of History*, p. 46.
113. Kissinger, *The Troubled Partnership*, pp. 23–24; Stoessinger, *Henry Kissinger*, p. 18.
114. Kissinger, *The Troubled Partnership*, pp. 170, 15, 21, 117–18, 162.
115. Ibid., p. 248.
116. Ibid., p. 19.
117. Ibid., pp. 232–33, 241, 27.
118. Ibid., p. 40.
119. Ibid., p. 25.
120. Kissinger, *American Foreign Policy, p. 55.*
121. Ibid., p. 75; *The Troubled Partnership*, p. 169.
122. Kissinger, *A World Restored*, p. 326; Stoessinger, *Henry Kissinger*, p. 18.
123. Kissinger, *American Foreign Policy*, p. 14.
124. Kissinger, *A World Restored*, pp. 328–29.
125. Kissinger, *The Necessity for Choice*, p. 358; Stoessinger, *Henry Kissinger*, pp. 18–19. Stoessinger wrote: "In this recognition of the limits of the statesman, but also in the simultaneous affirmation of his possibilites, we find the core of Kissinger's belief."
126. Kissinger. *The Necessity for Choice*, p. 357. Nutter, *Kissinger's Grand Design*, p. 8.
127. Dickson, *Kissinger and the Meaning of History*, p. 82.
128. Kissinger, *A World Restored*, p. 331.
129. Kissinger, "The Meaning of History," pp. 347–48; Dickson, *Kissinger and the Meaning of History*, p. 70.
130. Kissinger, *The Troubled Partnership*, p. 251; Dickson, *Kissinger and the Meaning of History*, p. 74.
131. Kissinger, *A World Restored*, p. 324.
132. Kissinger, *The Necessity for Choice*, p. 2.
133. Kissinger, *A World Restored*, pp. 324–25; Dickson, *Kissinger and the Meaning of History*, p. 50. He discussed Kissinger's belief, rarely made explicit, "that the human spirit is historical in character . . . For Kissinger, man is a spiritual being endowed with freedom but he is also lost in an historical process that has no ultimate end or transendent meaning."
134. Kissinger, *A World Restored*, p. 325.
135. Ibid., pp. 213, 326, 329.
136. Ibid., pp. 329–30, 326.
137. Ibid., p. 327.
138. Ibid., pp. 326, 329; Dickson, *Kissinger and the Meaning of History*, p. 70.
139. Kissinger, *A World Restored*, p. 322; Mazlish, *Kissinger*, pp. 181–82. He argued: many misinterpreted Kissinger when they "see Metternich

as Kissinger's inspiration. However, such a view (while partially true) overlooks the fact that Metternich offered Kissinger only the stress on limits. Missing was the emphasis on creative activism."
140. Kissinger, *A World Restored*, p. 213; Mazlish, *Kissinger*, p. 182.
141. Kissinger, "The Meaning of History," pp. 22–23; Dickson, *Kissinger and the Meaning of History*, p. 39.
142. Dickson, *Kissinger and the Meaning of History*, p. 46.
143. Kissinger, "The White Revolutionary," pp. 888–89.
144. Kissinger, *American Foreign Policy*, pp. 24–25.
145. Kissinger, "The White Revolutionary," p. 893. Stoessinger, *Henry Kissinger*, pp. 18–19. He stated: "Kissinger knew and emphasized the role of accident in history."
146. Kissinger, *Nuclear Weapons and Foreign Policy*, pp. 435–36; abridged edn, pp. 251. *A World Restored*, pp. 326, 329.
147. Kissinger, *Nuclear Weapons and Foreign Policy*, p. 424; abridged edn, p. 240;
148. Kissinger, *The Necessity for Choice*, p. 355.
149. Kissinger, *American Foreign Policy*, p. 18.
150. Kissinger, *Nuclear Weapons and Foreign Policy*, pp. 435–36; abridged edn, p. 251.
151. Ibid., p. 429; abridged edn, p. 245.

Chapter 3: The Philosophical Beliefs of Zbigniew Brzezinski

1. Brzezinski, "U.S. Foreign Policy," pp. 714–15. According to Brzezinski this assessment is based on Nixon's *Foreign Affairs* article of October 1967, which foreshadows the changed China policy, his acceptance speech of 1968 which pointed to the need for reshaping alliance relationships, and his Guam interview of early 1969, which spelled out the broad framework for the policies of subsequent years.
2.. Ibid., p. 721. "Toward Cooperative Activism," *Current* 175 (September 1975):43.
3. Brzezinski, *Between Two Ages: America's Role in the Technetronic Era*. (New York: The Viking Press, 1970), pp. 54, 275.
4. Ibid., pp. 283, 275.
5. Brzezinski, *Ideology and Power in Soviet Politics*, (New York: Frederick A. Praeger, 1962) pp. 112–13; Revised edn, pp. 146–47. *The Soviet Bloc: Unity and Conflict*, revised edn (New York: Praeger, 1961) p. 391; Revised and enlarged edn (Cambridge, MA: Harvard University Press, 1967), p. 493.
6. Zbigniew K. Brzezinski, *Ideology and Power in Soviet Politics*, pp. 98–101, 103. Brzezinski viewed Soviet ideology as a "combination of Marxist doctrine, Russian revolutionary experience, social economic backwardness, and the vested interest of the ruling Bolshevic Party." In the revised edn, 1967, pp. 132–35, 37; *Between Two Ages*, p. 145; *The*

Soviet Bloc, pp. 385, 387–89; *The Soviet Bloc*, revised and enlarged edn, pp. 487, 490–91. Here Brzezinski states that both Communism and Fascism or Nazism are revolutionary ideologies.

7. Brzezinski, *Idelology and Power in Soviet Politics*, p. 98; revised edn, p. 132. *The Soviet Bloc*, Revised edn., p. 383; revised and enlarged edn, p. 485.

8. Zbigniew Brzezinski and Samuel P. Huntington, *Political Power: USA/USSR* (New York: The Viking Press, 1964), p. 409.

9. Brzezinski, *Ideology and Power in Soviet Politics*, pp. 103–6; revised edn, pp. 137–40.

10. Ibid., p. 224.

11. Ibid., pp. 222–23, 227.

12. Brzezinski, *Between Two Ages*, pp. 4–5, 9, 52–53, 293, 307–08.

13. Ibid., pp. 9–10. He explained: "The post-industrial society is becoming a technetronic society: a society that is shaped culturally, psychologically, socially, and economically by the impact of technology and electronics – particularly in the area of computers and communications."

14. Ibid., pp. 25, 31. "America in a Hostile World," p. 91. He points to both US scientific and technological influence and to the less tangible but no less pervasive US impact on mass culture, youth mores, and lifestyles.

15. Brzezinski, *Between Two Ages*, p. 24.

16. Ibid., p. 34; "America in a Hostile World," pp. 65–96.

17. Brzezinski, "America in a Hostile World," p. 91.

18. Brzezinski, *Between Two Ages*, pp. 5–6, 3. He explained that the principal thrust of contemporary change is the simultaneous increase in the unification and fragmentation of humanity at a time when the differences in the condition of the separate societies are widening. In his view, "under these circumstances proximity, instead of promoting unity, gives rise to tensions prompted by a new sense of global congestion."

19. Ibid., pp. 19, 5–6, 284, 287.

20. Ibid., p. 17.

21. Ibid., pp. 23, 115–21. "Not War But Anarchy," p. 47.

22. Brzezinski, *Between Two Ages*, pp. 117–20, 305. In his view the "rapid scientific change, the massive educational explosion, and the intense communications implosion" generate "highly volatile beliefs and reactions and create a situation in which subjective feelings are more important than collective commitment to a blueprint for social action and organization."

23. Ibid., pp. 111–12, 112–15. He claimed that "the search for forms in which the idea of equality can be expressed is currently the strongest motivating impulse behind the activities" of the youthful critics of both the Eastern and Western elites and institutions respectively, and also guides the relations between the races in the US and Africa, and between the developing and the developed worlds."

24. Brzezinski, "Recognizing The Crisis," *Foreign Policy* 17 (Winter 1974–75):65–66.
25. Brzezinski, *Between Two Ages*, p. 24. "The Degeneration of Peace," *Newsweek* (January 24, 1972), p. 36.
26. Brzezinski, "Half Past Nixon," *Foreign Policy* 3 (Summer 1971):12, 24. "The Degeneration of Peace," p. 36.
27. Brzezinski, *Ideology and Power in Soviet Politics*, pp. 115, 123; revised edn, pp. 217, 223, 227, 232, 235; *Between Two Ages*, pp. 125, 126, 138; *The Soviet Bloc*, revised edn, pp. 384–86; revised and enlarged edn, pp. 486–88, 508.
28. Brzezinski, *Ideology and Power in Soviet Politics*, pp. 119, 126, 134; revised edn, pp. 153, 160, 168, 213; *Political Power: USA/USSR*, p. 428; *Alternative to Partition: For a Broader Conception of America's Role in Europe* (New York: McGraw-Hill Book Company, 1965), pp. 40–41. *Between Two Ages*, pp. 124, 150; *The Soviet Bloc*, Revised edn, pp. 494, 507, 511; revised and enlarged edn, p. 396.
29. Brzezinski, *The Soviet Bloc*, revised and enlarged edn, pp. 398–406. In Sino-Soviet relations Brzezinski saw "a dynamic escalation of the Moscow-Peking dialogue into a dispute, then a conflict, and finally a rift." In these pages he summarized the issues dividing Moscow and Peking under three general headings: party-ideological, foreign policy, and state issues.
30. Brzezinski, *Ideology and Power in Soviet Politics*, p. 113; revised edn, p. 147.
31. Kissinger, *A World Restored*, p. 3.
32. Brzezinski, *The Soviet Bloc*, revised edn, pp. 384–85, 387–89; revised and enlarged edn, pp. 486–87, 490–91.
33. Kissinger, *Nuclear Weapons and Foreign Policy*, p. 316; abridged edn, p. 43. Kissinger makes the same point regarding Napoleonic France, Nazi Germany, and Communist Russia.
34. James Wooten, "Here Comes ZBIG!" *Esquire* (November 1979), p. 122.
35. Kissinger, *A World Restored*, p. 2.
36. Brzezinski, *Ideology and Power in Soviet Politics*, pp. 107–8; revised edn, pp. 141–42.
37. Ibid., p. 111; revised edn, p. 145.
38. Kissinger, *A World Restored*, p. 181.
39. Brzezinski and Huntington, *Political Power: USA/USSR*, p. 409.
40. Brzezinski, *Ideology and Power in Soviet Politics*, revised edn, pp. 224–25. He used the Cuban missile crisis to demostrate this. *Between Two Ages*, pp. 136–37. Brzezinski argued that "internationalism, often violated in practice – it did restraint Great Russian nationalism." "Sufficiency For War or Peace?" *Newsweek* (April 26, 1971), p. 45.
41. Brzezinski, *Ideology and Power in Soviet Politics*, pp. 3–4; revised edn, pp. 4–5.

42. Ibid., pp. 138–39; revised edn, pp. 172–73. In his view, "this ersatz method of revitalizing the ideology is not entirely a matter of conscious design."
43. Ibid., pp. 115–16; revised edn, pp. 149–50. He saw Leninism, Stalinism and Khrushchevism, and the relatively violent transitions from one to the other, as part of this dialectical relationship.
44. Ibid., p. 152.
45. Brzezinski. *The Soviet Bloc*, revised and enlarged edn, pp. x, 430–31. He makes a number of predictions regarding the possibility of war between the USSR and the PRC in the 1970s.
46. Brzezinski, *Ideology and Power in Soviet Politics*, pp. 131–33, 92–93, 113, 146; revised edn, pp. 165–67, 92–93, 147. *The Soviet Bloc*, revised and enlarged edn, pp. 399–400, 407. *Between Two Ages*, pp. 145–46. The Soviet conception that wars were inevitable as long as capitalism, and in particular imperialism, created the economic basis for them, and that the only outcome of a war in which the USSR was drawn into would be the end of capitalism, changed at the 20th Party Congress.
47. Brzezinski, *Between Two Ages*, pp. 146–47.
48. Brzezinski, *Ideology and Power in Soviet Politics*, pp. 133–34; revised edn, pp. 167–68.
49. Brzezinski, *Between Two Ages*, pp. 145–46. Kissinger, *The Necessity for Choice*, p. 97.
50. Brzezinski, *Ideology and Power in Soviet Politics*, p. 98; revised edn, p. 132.
51. Ibid., p. 92; revised edn, p. 92.
52. Ibid., p. 126; revised edn, p. 160. Brzezinski suggested that "one should increasingly speak not of Communist ideology but of Soviet Communist ideology, Chinese Communist ideology, Yugoslav Communist ideology, ..."
53. Ibid., pp. 140, 135–40; revised edn, pp. 174, 169–74.
54. Ibid., pp. 133–34, 135–40; revised edn, pp. 167–68, 169–74.
55. Brzezinski, *Between Two Ages*, p. 175.
56. Ibid., pp. 145–46. Brzezinski states: "This theme runs like a thread through all major speeches, foreign policy analysis, or scholarly commentaries on world affairs." *The Soviet Bloc*, revised and enlarged edn, pp. 399–400.
57. Brzezinski, *Between Two Ages*, p. 146.
58. Brzezinski, *Ideology and Power in Soviet Politics*, pp. 92–93; revised edn, pp. 92–93. *Between Two Ages*, pp. 145–46.
59. Brzezinski and Huntington, *Political Power: USA/USSR*, pp. 424, 434–35. He argued: "the bureaucrats know the main source of the danger to the stability of the political system: any decline in the ideological and political monopoly of the ruling party."
60. Brzezinski, *Between Two Ages*, p. 148.
61. Brzezinski, *Ideology and Power in Soviet Politics*, pp. 93, 138–40; revised edn, pp. 93, 172–74.

62. Brzezinski, *Between Two Ages*, pp. 123, 138–39.
63. Brzezinski, *Ideology and Power in Soviet Politics*, pp. 144–45; *The Soviet Bloc*, revised and enlarged edn, pp. 397–400.
64. Brzezinski, *Alternatives to Partition*, p. 135.
65. Brzezinski, *The Soviet Bloc*, revised and enlarged edn, pp. 402, 398. This accusation was most fully spelled out by Peking, for the first time, in 1965.
66. Brzezinski, *Ideology and Power in Soviet Politics*, p. 145. *The Soviet Bloc*, revised and enlarged edn, pp. 401–2.
67. Brzezinski, *Ideology and Power in Soviet Politics*, revised edition, p. 232; 1962 edn, pp. 158–59. In 1962, he argued that "A China capable of unilateral action could be very dangerous." If the PRC left the bloc on its own initiative and carried with it a significant number of the Communist parties, it could develop a more active militant line to which the USSR would respond with a more radical attitude in an effort to regain leadership of the Communist camp.
68. Ibid., revised edn, pp. 226–27, 221–23. Brzezinski pointed to PRC statements which in his view make it clear that its strategy rests on "slighting imperialism strategically" and on "respecting it tactically," but he stressed, that "as the revolutionary Communism gains in strength, the Chinese may eventually expect to be able to 'slight' imperialism tactically as well, thereby precipitating a major threat to peace."
69. Brzezinski, *Between Two Ages*, pp. 124–5, 187.
70. Ibid., pp. 124–25.
71. Brzezinski, *Ideology and Power in Soviet Politics*, revised edn, p. 217. *Alternative to Partition*, p. 41; *The Soviet Bloc*, revised and enlarged edn, pp. 397–406.
72. Brzezinski, *Ideology and Power in Soviet Politics*, revised edn, pp. 213–14.
73. Ibid., revised edn, pp. 221–23. *The Soviet Bloc*, revised and enlarged edn, p. 398.
74. Brzezinski, "Meeting Moscow's 'Limited Coexistence'," *The New Leader* (November 16, 1968), p. 13.
75. Brzezinski, *Ideology and Power in Soviet Politics*, p. 88; revised edn, p. 88; *Political Power: USA/USSR*, pp. 434–35.
76. Brzezinski, *Ideology and Power in Soviet Politics*, p. 82; revised edn, p. 82; he argued that this would be the case even if indoctrination is already highly ritualized and may no longer involve the general individual commitment. *Political Power: USA/USSR*, pp. 424, 434–35.
77. Brzezinski, *Between Two Ages*, pp. 141–42. He viewed efforts to reassert and expand ideological training as partially compensating for the decline of coercion as a key means of integrating Soviet society with the political system. *Political Power: USA/USSR*, pp. 424, 434–35.
78. Brzezinski and Huntington, *Political Power: USA/USSR*, p. 435.
79. Ibid., p. 430. They argued that reforms must go beyond the introduction of more formal and regular procedures which in themselves would

not undermine one-Party rule or challenge the Soviet socio-economic system, but acknowledged that any formalization in the long run would result in some democratization.

80. Brzezinski, *Ideology and Power in Soviet Politics*, p. 94; revised edn, p. 94.

81. Ibid., pp. 91–92; revised edn, pp. 91–92. He saw Kennan's thesis that political containment would lead to a domestic mellowing or breakdown of the Soviet system as premature since it assumed a relationship between external and domestic politics that did not exist in Stalin's time. But it exists today in a much different way.

82. Brzezinski, *Ideology and Power in Soviet Politics*, p. 94; revised edn, p. 94.

83. Ibid., pp. 92–93; revised edn, pp. 92–93. *Between Two Ages*, pp. 145–46.

84. Brzezinski and Huntington, *Political Power: USA/USSR*, p. 419.

85. Ibid., p. 436; *Ideology and Power in Soviet Politics*, revised edn, pp. 213–14.

86. Brzezinski and Huntington, *Political Power: USA/USSR*, pp. 429–30; Brzezinski, *Alternative to Partition*, pp. 145, 172.

87. Brzezinski and Huntington, *Political Power: USA/USSR*, pp. 436, 430. Specifically, he argued that the structure of power, the access to leadership, the role of ideology, and the relationship of the political system to the individual are not likely to undergo a radical change in either system. Brzezinski (ed.), *Dilemmas of Change in Soviet Politics* (New York: Columbia University Press, 1969), p. 1.

88. Brzezinski and Huntington, *Political Power: USA/USSR*, pp. 419–21. Brzezinski, *Between Two Ages*, p. 154. "Shifting Mood and System," *The Atlantic Community Quarterly* 12 (Fall 1974), p. 325.

89. Brzezinski and Huntington, *Political Power: USA/USSR*, pp. 424, 434–35; Brzezinski, *Alternative to Partition*, p. 53. *Between Two Ages*, pp. 144, 148.

90. Brzezinski, *Between Two Ages*, p. 144, see his footnote. *Alternative to Partition*, pp. 145, 172. E. Modrzhinskaya, "Anti-Communism Disguised as Evolutionism," *International Affairs* 1 (Moscow, 1969), p. 16. The Soviets also viewed Walt Rostow's theory of stages in economic growth and Raymond Aron's doctrine of the single industrial society as efforts to subvert the ideological foundations of Soviet power.

91. Brzezinski and Huntington, *Political Power: USA/USSR*, p. 429; Brzezinski, *Alternative to Partition*, pp. 43–44, 136, 172.

92. Brzezinski, *Alternative to Partition*, p. 44. For him "the immodest stress on national achievements and on Soviet primacy as a great power [has become] the main link between the people and the rulers, and the dominant motif in the Soviet outlook."

93. Brzezinski, *Between Two Ages*, p. 283.

94. Brzezinski, "The Deceptive Structure of Peace," p. 43. "What Kind of Détente?", p. 289.

95. Brzezinski, "What Kind of Détente?" *The Atlantic Community Quarterly* 13 (Fall 1975):289–90. "The Deceptive Structure of Peace," pp. 41–45. In 1974 he stressed the Soviets' justification of severe restrictions of human rights by proclaiming domestically that the ideological conflict must go on unabated.

96. Brzezinski, "How the Cold War was Played," pp. 207–9; "U.S. Foreign Policy," pp. 716, 720.

97. Brzezinski, "The Deceptive Structure of Peace," pp. 41–45; "Half Past Nixon," p. 15.

98. Brzezinski, "The Deceptive Structure of Peace," pp. 41–45; "Half Past Nixon," p. 15. Before the SALT agreements were signed Brzezinski credited the Nixon Administration for recognizing the possibility that some Soviet leaders may be tempted to exploit SALT to establish such superiority. "Memorandum For The President," p. 50. "Sufficiency For War of Peace," p. 45.

99. Brzezinski, *Alternative to Partition*, pp. 152–54, he insisted on this linkage.

100. Brzezinski, "China's New Diplomacy," *Problems of Communism* 20 (November–December 1971), pp. 25–26.

101. Brzezinski, *Alternative to Partition*, p. 1. Kissinger, *The Troubled Partnership*, p. 3.

102. Brzezinski. *Alternatives to Partition*, pp. 2–3, x. Also see chapters 1 and 2. Kissinger, *The Troubled Partnership*, pp. 5, 10. Here Kissinger makes the same point, stating: "no one man could have disrupted the Alliance by himself." Both studies were sponsored by the Council on Foreign Relations.

103. Brzezinski. *Alternatives to Partition*, pp. 4–5.

104. Ibid., pp. 2–5; Kissinger, *The Troubled Partnership*, pp. 27–28, 232–33, 241. Kissinger stressed that the differences in US and West European interests are greater outside of Europe.

105. Brzezinski, *Between Two Ages*, pp. 54, 275, 283.

106. Brzezinski, *Alternative to Partition*, pp. 5–6, 22. He points out that "Gheorghiu-Dej criticisms of tight integration might have been borrowed directly from De Gaulle." Even their policy of pinpricks against the former hegemones was similar. *Ideology and Power in Soviet Politics*, p. 142

107. Brzezinski, *Alternative to Partition*, pp. 10–11, 20–22. The Soviet claim was made during the Congress of the CPSU, the last one attended by Stalin. For Brzezinski, the Rumanian veto of Soviet prescriptions for CEMA in 1964 demonstrated that national sovereignty can frustrate common communist policies.

108. Ibid., pp. 12–13. For Brzezinski, "the Soviets always had a dual interest in controlling East Europe: First, it provided a defensive buffer and a strategically advanced jump-off point toward West Europe; second, it satisfied the ideological desire to create stable, and in the end, popularly accepted communist regimes in East Europe."

109. Kissinger, *The Troubled Partnership*, p. 21. Criticizing US policies toward the Allies for underestimating the importance of nationalism he stated: "Our penchant for treating the Atlantic area as if it were a single unit runs counter to the fact that the Alliance is still composed of sovereign states."

110. Brzezinski, *Alternative to Partition*, pp. 74–75. *The Soviet Bloc*, revised and enlarged edn, pp. 496–507.

111. Brzezinski, *Ideology and Power in Soviet Politics*, pp. 142, 141–43. Brzezinski saw the Moscow Conference on December 6, 1960, as the turning point in the transformation of the Soviet bloc into a Communist one. *Alternatives to Partition*, pp. 74–75.

112. Brzezinski, *Alternative to Partition*, pp. 136–37, 22, 28.

113. Ibid., pp. 24–25, 13–14, 22.

114. Ibid., pp. 35–36.

115. Ibid., p. 53.

116. Brzezinski, *The Soviet Bloc*, revised and enlarged edn, pp. 494–95; revised edn, pp. 395–96.

117. Brzezinski, *Alternative to Partition*, pp. 49–58.

118. Ibid., pp. 22, 28.

119. Ibid., pp. 28, 45, 112.

120. Ibid., p. 37. For Brzezinski, today Eastern Europe is going through a period of technocratic-nationalist-communist dictatorships.

121. Ibid., pp. 89–91, 103.

122. Ibid., p. 86.

123. Ibid., pp. 37, 136. He stated that this inclination was shared even by the Yugoslavs.

124. Ibid., p. 75.

125. Ibid., pp. 46–47.

126. Ibid., p. 59–60, 112; *The Soviet Bloc*, revised and enlarged edn, pp. 482–84.

127. Brzezinski, *Alternative to Partition*, pp. 70–71, 72.

128. Ibid., pp. 74–75. He concluded that European politics reflect the renewed vitality of nation-states while European economics undeline the ideological neutraltity of the technological revolution.

129. Ibid., pp. 6–7.

130. Brzezinski, *Between Two Ages*, p. 294; *Alternative to Partition*, pp. 6–7.

131. Brzezinski, *Between Two Ages*, pp. 294–95.

132. Brzezinski, *Alternative to Partition*, pp. 6–7, 8. He argued that the US approach, being less ideological, was less offensive, and much more cooperative. Therefore, even French-inspired anti-American pressures did not preclude efforts to built closer ties among the West European nations.

133. Ibid., pp. 13–14, 20–22; *The Soviet Bloc*, revised and enlarged edn, pp. 482–84.

134. Brzezinski, *Alternative to Partition*, p. 10.

135. Brzezinski, *Between Two Ages*, pp. 293–94.
136. Ibid., pp. 295–97, 304–5. He suggested in phase one the community of advanced states could also include Australia, Israel, and Mexico. In phase two, links with the more advanced communist states (including the USSR) could begin. In "Needed: An Alternative," p. 53, he changed advanced communist states to the "more cooperative" communist states.
137. Brzezinski. "America in a Hostile World," pp. 92–93; Kissinger, *American Foreign Policy*, pp. 68, 70–72; *The Troubled Partnership*, pp. 27–28.
138. Brzezinski, *Between Two Ages*, p. 296. In his words, such a community "will not preclude more homogeneous relations within the larger entity . . . " and states "will continue for a long time to enjoy more intimate relationship within their own areas."
139. Brzezinski, *Alternative to Partition*, p. 132.
140. Ibid., *Between Two Ages*, p. 302.
141. Brzezinski, *Between Two Ages*, p. 35.
142. Ibid., pp. 39–40.
143. Ibid., p. 36.
144. Ibid., pp. 53–54. "Half Past Nixon," p. 12.
145. Brzezinski, *Between Two Ages*, pp. 56, 55.
146. Ibid., p. 85.
147. Ibid., pp. 52–53.
148. Ibid., p. 186.
149. Ibid., p. 192.
150. Brzezinski, "America in a Hostile World," pp. 65–66.
151. Brzezinski, *Between Two Ages*, pp. 112–13; "America in a Hostile World," pp. 72, 95.
152. Brzezinski, *Between Two Ages*, p. 113. For Brzezinski, while Third World socialism shares the Marxist analysis of capitalism and the Leninist description of imperialism, the leaders stress that their economic approach avoids the errors of both capitalism and communism. *Ideology and Power in Soviet Politics*, p. 157.
153. Brzezinski, "U.S. Foreign Policy," pp. 717–26; "The Deceptive Structure of Peace," pp. 39–40.
154. Brzezinski, "America in a Hostile World," pp. 65–67, 72–73.
155. Brzezinski, *Between Two Ages*, pp. 48–50. Brzezinski argued that the North-South conflict was fed by the concept of "neo-colonialism" which provided the rationale for stimulating suspicion in the Third World masses about the political motives of economic aid given by advanced countries, and the charges of graft, corruption, and inefficiency made by the donor states against the recipients of that aid.
156. Ibid., p. 281.
157. Brzezinski, "America in a Hostile World," pp. 91, 95. *Between Two Ages*, p. 24.
158. Brzezinski, *Between Two Ages*, p. xvii. For Brzezinski "the positive potential of the third American revolution lies in its promise to link

liberty with equality."

159. Ibid., pp. 58–60, 303. Such institutions are the World Health Organization, the World Bank, etc., while the new yardsticks are GNP figures, per-capita income, consumption data, educational opportunities etc.
160. Brzezinski, "U.S. Foreign Policy," p. 724; *Between Two Ages*, p. 296.
161. Brzezinski, *Between Two Ages*, p. 296. "Facing Democracy's Crisis," p. 58.
162. Brzezinski, "Shifting Mood and System," pp. 319, 322. He also saw a decline in revolutionary optimism in the communist states. "Toward Cooperative Actvism," p. 44. "Facing Democracy's Crisis," pp. 57, 59. He believed that a call on the nation to sacrifice would contribute a great deal to the restoration of optimism. "Recognizing the Crisis," p. 68. "Not War But Anarchy," p. 47.
163. Brzezinski, *Between Two Ages*, p. xvii.
164. Ibid., pp. 61–62. "Peace and Power," *Encounter* 5 (November 1968), p. 13.
165. Brzezinski, *Between Two Ages*, pp. 3, 5.
166. Brzezinski, "Purpose and Planning in Foreign Policy," *Public Interest* 14 (Winter 1969):59. Discussing "the importance of forecasting" in foreign policy he stated: "Policy-planning has to involve, to an important extent, the anticipation of future events. It thus has to rely on a reasonably accurate estimate of likely developments . . . "
167. Brzezinski, *Between Two Ages*, p. 35.
168. Ibid., p. 167. In this case he specified that the short run meant "during the 1970s."
169. Ibid., pp. 175–76.
170. Ibid., p. 281.
171. Ibid., p. 283. He was referring to the 1970s.
172. Ibid., p. 277.
173. Ibid., p. 275. *Ideology and Power in Soviet Politics*, p. 140.
174. Brzezinski, *Between Two Ages*, p. 54.
175. Ibid., p. 281.
176. Ibid., p. 50.
177. Ibid., pp. 190–91.
178. Ibid., pp. 279–81; "Recognizing the Crisis," pp. 65–66.
179. Brzezinski, "Purpose and Planning in Foreign Policy," p. 57.
180. Brzezinski, *Ideology and Power in Soviet Politics*, p. 134. revised edn, pp. 214–15.
181. Ibid., revised edn, pp. 214–15.
182. Ibid., p. 161.
183. Brzezinski, *Between Two Ages*, pp. 69–71, 35.
184. Ibid., pp. 72, 74.
185. Ibid., p. 73. Pierre Teilhard de Chardin, *The Phenomenon of Man* (New York: 1961), p. 211.
186. Brzezinski, *Between Two Ages*, pp. 75, 77, 123. For Brzezinski, then, Marxism "provided a unique intellectual tool for understanding and

harnessing the fundamental forces of our time," but given its neglect of the spiritual element, "it does not suffice as the sole basis for meaningful comprehension of our reality."

187. Brzezinski, "The Deceptive Structure of Peace," p. 48; "America in a Hostile World," p. 96.
188. Brzezinski, *Between Two Ages*, p. 306.
189. Brzezinski, "Half Past Nixon," p. 18.
190. Brzezinski, "The Deceptive Structure of Peace," p. 49.
191. Brzezinski, "Half Past Nixon," pp. 11–13, 18; "The Deceptive Structure of Peace," pp. 49, 53. "Purpose and Planning in Foreign Policy," p. 58.
192. Brzezinski, "The Deceptive Structure of Peace," pp. 51–52.
193. Kissinger, *A World Restored*, pp. 326, 329–30.
194. Brzezinski, "Purpose and Planning in Foreign Policy," p. 59.
195. Brzezinski, *Between Two Ages*, pp. 256–57.
196. Ibid., p. 35.
197. Ibid., p. 155. Brzezinski and Huntington, *Political Power*, p. 418. Discussing future developments in the USSR Brzezinski pointed out that events would depend essentially on unpredictable factors, such as accident, personality, coincidence.
198. Brzezinski, *Between Two Ages*, pp. 188–89.
199. Brzezinski, "Purpose and Planning in Foreign Policy," pp. 56–57.

Chapter 4: The Instrumental Beliefs of Henry Kissinger

1. Brzezinski, "The Deceptive Structure of Peace," pp. 49–55.
2. Kissinger, *Nuclear Weapons and Foreign Policy*, p. 7; abridged edn, p. 4. *American Foreign Policy*, pp. 59–64. *A World Restored*, p. 5. John Lewis Gaddis, *Strategies of Containment* (New York: Oxford University Press, 1982), p. 277.
3. Kissinger, *Nuclear Weapons and Foreign Policy*, abridged edn, pp. 103, 69–70; 1957 edn, p. 349.
4. Kissinger. *American Foreign Policy*, pp. 60–61.
5. Kissinger, *Nuclear Weapons and Foreign Policy*, abridged edn, p. 82; 1957 edn, p. 363. Referring to Soviet doctrine, he noted: "the result was a tour de force, masterful in its comprehension of psychological factors, brutal in its consistency, and ruthless in its sense of direction."
6. Ibid., abridged edn, pp. 79, 128; 1957 edn, p. 360.
7. Ibid., abridged edn, p. 45; 1957 edn, p. 318.
8. Ibid., abridged edn, p. 243; 1957 edn, p. 427. *American Foreign Policy*, pp. 92, 95–96.
9. Kissinger, *Nuclear Weapons and Foreign Policy*, abridged edn, p. 45; 1957 edn, p. 318.
10. Ibid., abridged edn, p. 243; 1957 edn, pp. 427–28.
11. Ibid., abridged edn, pp. 220, 223; 1957 edn, pp. 264, 267–68.

12. Kissinger, *American Foreign Policy*, pp. 57–58.
13. Kissinger, *Nuclear Weapons and Foreign Policy*, pp. 6–7, 60; abridged edn, pp. 3–4, 42.
14. Kissinger, *American Foreign Policy*, pp. 30–31.
15. Ibid., pp. 32–33. *The Necessity for Choice*, pp. 346–47.
16. Kissinger, *American Foreign Policy*, pp. 29–31. *The Necessity for Choice*, pp. 333–34.
17. Kissinger, *American Foreign Policy*, pp. 30–31.
18. Kissinger, *Nuclear Weapons and Foreign Policy*, abridged edn, p. 240; 1957 edn, p. 424.
19. Ibid., abridged edn, p. 224; 1957 edn, pp. 403–4.
20. Ibid., abridged edn, pp. 225–26; 1957 edn, p. 405.
21. Ibid., pp. 7–8; abridged edn, p. 4.
22. Ibid., abridged edn, p. 224; 1957 edn, p. 403.
23. Falk, *What's Wrong with Henry Kissinger's Foreign Policy*, pp. 17–18. Falk noted Kissinger's abhorrence of ideological or moralistic posturing by leaders and to "[his] tendency to remove the moral question from the sphere of international diplomacy [which] is a tremendous asset in the search for domestic political support in the United States." Landau, *Kissinger*, pp. 7, 10. Brandon, *The Retreat of American Power*, p. 35.
24. Kissinger, *Nuclear Weapons and Foreign Policy*, abridged edn, pp. 243–44; 1957 edn, pp. 427–28.
25. Ibid., abridged edn, p. 7; 1957 edn, p. 11.
26. Ibid., abridged edn, p. 16; 1957 edn, p. 21.
27. Kissinger, *American Foreign Policy*, p. 79.
28. Kissinger, *Nuclear Weapons and Foreign Policy*, abridged edn, p. 245; 1957 edn, p. 429.
29. Ibid., abridged edn, pp. 2–3, 61; 1957 edn, pp. 5–6, 337. *American Foreign Policy*, p. 96.
30. Kissinger, *A World Restored*, pp. 330, 326, 213.
31. Kissinger, *Nuclear Weapons and Foreign Policy*, abridged edn, pp. 249–50; 1957 edn, pp. 433–34. *American Foreign Policy*, pp. 29–34. He maintained that training in industry and law has a negative impact on foreign policy.
32. Kissinger, *Nuclear Weapons and Foreign Policy*, abridged edn, p. 248; 1957 edn, p. 432. *American Foreign Policy*, p. 19.
33. Kissinger, *Nuclear Weapons and Foreign Policy*, abridged edn, p. 247; 1957 edn, pp. 431–32.
34. Kissinger, *A World Restored*, pp. 326–27, 210. *Nuclear Weapons and Foreign Policy*, abridged edn, pp. 246–51; 1957 edn, pp. 431–36. *American Foreign Policy*, p. 18. Graubard, *Kissinger*, pp. 50–51, 101–2, 228–32. Gaddis, *Strategies of Containment*, p. 302.
35. *Kissinger, American Foreign Policy*, pp. 97, 79, 57. Gaddis, *Strategies of Containment*, p. 277.
36. Kissinger, *American Foreign Policy*, pp. 17–20.
37. Kissinger, *Nuclear Weapons and Foreign Policy*, abridged edn,

pp. 246–8; 1957 edn, pp. 431–2. *American Foreign Policy*, pp. 17–22.

38. Kissinger, *Nuclear Weapons and Foreign Policy*, abridged edn, p. 240; 1957 edn, p. 424. *The Necessity for Choice*, pp. 340–48.
39. Kissinger, *Nuclear Weapons and Foreign Policy*, abridged edn, p. 227; 1957 edn, pp. 406–7. *The Necessity for Choice*, pp. 343–44.
40. Kissinger, *Nuclear Weapons and Foreign Policy*, abridged edn, pp. 223, 209; 1957 edn, pp. 267–68, 251.
41. Ibid., abridged edn, p. 247; 1957 edn, p. 431. *A World Restored*, p. 329.
42. Kissinger, *The Necessity for Choice*, pp. 3–4.
43. Kissinger, *Nuclear Weapons and Foreign Policy*, abridged edn, p. 245; 1957 edn, p. 429.
44. Ibid., abridged edn, pp. 244, 196; 1957 edn, pp. 428–29. *A World Restored*, p. 1. *The Necessity for Choice*, p. 176.
45. Kissinger, *Nuclear Weapons and Foreign Policy*, abridged edn, p. 76; 1957 edn, p. 357.
46. Kissinger, *Nuclear Weapons and Foreign Policy*, abridged edn, pp. 42, 14, 112, 157, 166 ; 1957 edn, pp. 60, 18, 189, 199, 128. *The Necessity for Choice*, pp. 179–80.
47. Kissinger, *Nuclear Weapons and Foreign Policy*, abridged edn, p. 14; 1957 edn, p. 18.
48. Ibid., abridged edn, p. 41; 1957 edn, p. 60.
49. Kissinger, *The Troubled Partnership*, p. 109.
50. Kissinger, *Nuclear Weapons and Foreign Policy*, abridged edn, pp. 95, 79; 1957 edn, pp. 379, 360.
51. Ibid., abridged edn, p. 244; 1957 edn, p. 429.
52. Ibid., abridged edn, pp. 14, 4; 1957 edn, pp. 18, 7.
53. Ibid., abridged edition, pp. 103, 20; 1957 edn, p. 26.
54. Ibid., abridged edition, pp. 14–15, 12; 1957 edn, pp. 19–20.
55. Ibid., abridged edition, pp. 9, 26, 34; 1957 edn, pp. 13, 35.
56. Ibid., abridged edition, p. 79; 1957 edn, p. 360.
57. Ibid., abridged edition, pp. 8–9; 1957 edn, pp. 12–13. *The Necessity for Choice* p. 176.
58. Kissinger, *Nuclear Weapons and Foreign Policy*, abridged edition, p. 9; 1957 edn, p. 13.
59. Ibid., abridged edition, p. 12; 1957 edn, p. 16.
60. Ibid., abridged edition, p. 11, 115; 1957 edn, pp. 15–16, 133. *The Necessity for Choice*, p. 56.
61. Kissinger, *Nuclear Weapons and Foreign Policy*, abridged edition, p. 36; 1957 edn, p. 51. *The Necessity for Choice*, pp. 176–80.
62. Kissinger, *Nuclear Weapons and Foreign Policy*, abridged edition, p. 33; 1957 edn, p. 47.
63. Ibid., abridged edition, p. 28.
64. Kissinger, *The Necessity for Choice*, p. 345.
65. Kissinger, *American Foreign Policy*, pp. 29, 33. Gaddis, *Strategies of*

Containment, pp. 294–95.
66. Kissinger, *Nuclear Weapons and Foreign Policy*, p. 10; abridged edn, p. 6.
67. Ibid., pp. 8–9, 10; abridged edn, pp. 4–6.
68. Kissinger, *American Foreign Policy*, pp. 58–60.
69. Ibid., p. 97.
70. Ibid., pp. 68, 72.
71. Kissinger, *The Troubled Partnership*, pp. 248–49, 28.
72. Kissinger, *A World Restored*, p. 327.
73. Kissinger, *Nuclear Weapons and Foreign Policy*, abridged edn, p. 240; 1957 edn, p. 424.
74. Ibid., abridged edn, p. 247; 1957 edn, pp. 431–2.
75. Ibid., abridged edn, pp. 166–67, 144; 1957 edn, pp. 201, 173, 199. He argued that an all-out war between the superpowers "has to be planned on the assumption that it is likely to be a nuclear war." *The Necessity for Choice*, p. 59.
76. Kissinger, *Nuclear Weapons and Foreign Policy*, abridged edn, p. 78; 1957 edn, p. 359.
77. Ibid., abridged edn, pp. 115–16; 1957 edn, p. 134.
78. Ibid.
79. Ibid., abridged edn, pp. 140, 33, 157, 99; 1957 edn, pp. 168, 47, 189, 387. *The Necessity for Choice*, p. 48.
80. Kissinger, *Nuclear Weapons and Foreign Policy*, abridged edn, pp. 112, 166; 1957 edn, pp. 131, 199–200.
81. Ibid., abridged edn, p. 59; 1957 edn, p. 335. *The Necessity for Choice*, pp. 48, 88.
82. Kissinger, *Nuclear Weapons and Foreign Policy*, abridged edn, p. 33; 1957 edn, pp. 387, 47–48.
83. Ibid., abridged edn, pp. 167, 112; 1957 edn, pp. 199–200, 131.
84. Ibid., abridged edn, pp. 77–78; 1957 edn, p. 359.
85. Ibid., abridged edn, pp. 22–24, 12; 1957 edn, pp. 28, 30.
86. Kissinger, *The Necessity for Choice*, p. 29.
87. Kissinger, *Nuclear Weapons and Foreign Policy*, abridged edn, pp. 43–80; 1957 edn, pp. 316–61.
88. Kissinger, *The Necessity for Choice*, p. 42.
89. Kissinger, *Nuclear Weapons and Foreign Policy*, abridged edn, pp. 22–24, 12; 1957 edn, pp. 28, 30.
90. Ibid., abridged edn, p. 105; 1957 edn, p. 87. In his view it also comes "when there exists so deep a schism between the contenders that the total destruction of the enemy appears as the only goal worth contending for."
91. Ibid., abridged edn, pp. 143–44, 166; 1957 edn, pp. 172, 175–76, 199. His view of the utility of limited nuclear war changed over the years but not his belief that such a war represents the most effective strategy against nuclear powers or against a major power which can substitute manpower for technology. *The Necessity for Choice*. p. 81.

92. Ibid., abridged edn, p. 117; 1957 edn, p. 136.
93. Kissinger, *The Necessity for Choice*, p. 48.
94. Ibid., p. 15.
95. Ibid., p. 81.
96. Ibid., pp. 46–47.
97. Ibid., pp. 57, 56.
98. Kissinger, *Nuclear Weapons and Foreign Policy*, abridged edn, p. 247; 1957 edn, pp. 431–32.
99. Kissinger, *American Foreign Policy*, pp. 17–18.
100. Ibid., p. 23.
101. Kissinger, *Nuclear Weapons and Foreign Policy*, abridged edn, pp. 78–9; 1957 edn, p. 360. *The Necessity for Choice*, p. 175.
102. Kissinger, *Nuclear Weapons and Foreign Policy*, abridged edn, p. 77; 1957 edn, pp. 358–59.
103. Ibid., abridged edn, p. 79; 1957 edn, p. 360.
104. Ibid., abridged edn, pp. 68–69, 66; 1957 edn, pp. 348–49, 344. Kissinger found Mao's essays on Protracted War, "remarkable for their sense of proportion."
105. Ibid., abridged edn, pp. 69–70; 1957 edn, p. 349.
106. Ibid., abridged edn, p. 70; 1957 edn, p. 350. *The Necessity for Choice* p. 175. He noted that "many of the erratic tendencies in American policy are traceable to our impatience . . . and discomfort when faced with protracted deadlock."
107. Kissinger, *Nuclear Weapons and Foreign Policy*, abridged edn, p. 17; 1957 edn, p. 22.
108. Ibid., abridged edn, p. 5; 1957 edn, p. 9.
109. Ibid., abridged edn, p. 240. *American Foreign Policy*, p. 20.
110. Kissinger, *American Foreign Policy*, pp. 29–30.
111. Kissinger, *Nuclear Weapons and Foreign Policy*, abridged edn, pp. 58–59, 46–47; 1957 edn, pp. 334–35, 320.
112. Ibid., abridged edn, pp. 111, 124, 167; 1957 edn, p. 128.
113. Ibid., abridged edn, p. 78; 1957 edn, p. 359.
114. Ibid., abridged edn, p. 111; 1957 edn, p. 128.
115. Ibid., abridged edn, pp. 111, 124, 167; 1957 edn, p. 128.
116. Ibid., abridged edn, p. 157; 1957 edn, pp. 189.
117. Ibid., abridged edn, pp. 42, 16, 166; 1957 edn, pp. 60, 189, 199.
118. Ibid., abridged edn, p. 166; 1957 edn, p. 199.
119. Ibid., abridged edn, pp. 148, 194–95; 1957 edn, pp. 178–79, 231–2.
120. Ibid., abridged edn, p. 3; 1957 edn, p. 6.
121. Ibid., abridged edn, p. 185; 1957 edn, p. 192.
122. Ibid., abridged edn, pp. 120–21, 124; 1957 edn, p. 141.
123. Ibid., abridged edn, pp. 122–23; 1957 edn, pp. 143–44.
124. Ibid., abridged edn, p. 125; 1957 edn, p. 147.
125. Kissinger, *The Necessity for Choice*, p. 65.
126. Kissinger, *Nuclear Weapons and Foreign Policy*, abridged edn, p. 127; 1957 edn, p. 148.

127. Ibid., abridged edn, pp. 123–24; 1957 edn, p. 145.
128. Ibid., abridged edn, p. 4; 1957 edn, pp. 7–8.
129. Ibid., abridged edn, pp. 129–30; 1957 edn, pp. 155–56.
130. Ibid., abridged edn, pp. 130–31; 1957 edn, pp. 156–57.
131. Ibid., abridged edn, p. 131; 1957 edn, p. 157.
132. Ibid., abridged edn, pp. 131–9; 1957 edn, pp. 157–67. Although beyond the scope of the present study, it should be pointed out that Kissinger discussed in greater detail specific changes that must be made in the capability and doctrine of each one of the armed services in order to develop the necessary forces for limited war. Moreover, believing that "a revolution in technology carries with it a revolution in tactics," he made specific proposals regarding new military tactics – abridged edn, pp. 149–50; 1957 edn, pp. 179–80. He specifically stressed the need for "small, highly mobile, self-contained units, relying on air transport even within the combat zone." For specifics on tactics see pp. 150–68 in the abridged edn and pp. 179–202 in the 1957 edn. Nutter, *Kissinger's Grand Design*, p. 4.
133. Kissinger, *The Necessity for Choice*, pp. 64–65.
134. Kissinger, *A World Restored*, p. 2. Kissinger also viewed diplomacy as "the art of restraining the exersice of power."
135. Kissinger, *Nuclear Weapons and Foreign Policy*, abridged edn, p. 171; 1957 edn, p. 205.
136. Ibid., abridged edn, pp. 168, 171; 1957 edn, pp. 201–2, 205.
137. Ibid., abridged edn, p. 61; 1957 edn, p. 337.
138. Ibid., abridged edn, pp. 3, 243; 1957 edn, pp. 6, 427–28.
139. Ibid., abridged edn, pp. 61–63; 1957 edn, pp. 337–40. Nutter, *Kissinger's Grand Design*, p. 13.
140. Kissinger, *Nuclear Weapons and Foreign Policy*, abridged edn, p. 63; 1957 edn, p. 339. *The Necessity for Choice*, pp. 169–91. *American Foreign Policy*, pp. 35–36, 47–48.
141. Kissinger, *Nuclear Weapons and Foreign Policy*, abridged edn, pp. 44–64; 1957 edn, pp. 316–40. *The Necessity for Choice*, pp. 184, 196. *American Foreign Policy*, pp. 87–90. Nutter, *Kissinger's Grand Design*, pp. 6–7.
142. Kissinger, *The Necessity for Choice*, pp. 187–88, 180–88.
143. Ibid., pp. 190–91. Nutter, *Kissinger's Grand Design*, pp. 7, 78–83.
144. Kissinger, *Nuclear Weapons and Foreign Policy*, abridged edn, p. 170; 1957 edn, p. 204.
145. Kissinger, *The Necessity for Choice*, p. 213. *American Foreign Policy*, pp. 88–89.
146. Kissinger, *The Necessity for Choice*, pp. 210–13.
147. Ibid., pp. 284–6.
148. Ibid., p. 213. Nutter, *Kissinger's Grand Design*, pp. 6, 61–67.
149. Kissinger, *The Necessity for Choice*, p. 280.
150. Ibid., p. 254. Nutter, *Kissinger's Grand Design*, pp. 6, 61–67.
151. Kissinger, *The Necessity for Choice*, p. 281.

152. Ibid., p. 281.
153. Kissinger, *The Troubled Parnership*, p. 227.
154. Ibid., pp. 227–29; *American Foreign Policy* pp. 72–74.
155. Kissinger, *American Foreign Policy* p. 85.
156. Ibid., p. 55. *Nuclear Weapons and Foreign Policy*, abridged edn, pp. 3, 143; 1957 edn, pp. 171–72.
157. Kissinger, *A World Restored, pp. 328–30.*

Chapter 5: The Instrumental Beliefs of Zbigniew Brzezinski

1. Brzezinski, "Half Past Nixon," p. 18.
2. Brzezinski, "America in a Hostile World," pp. 73–74.
3. Brzezinski, "U.S. Foreign Policy," pp. 716–17.
4. Brzezinski, "The Deceptive Structure Of Peace," pp. 36, 49. "U.S. Foreign Policy," p. 715.
5. Brzezinski, "America in a Hostile World," p. 85; "U.S. Foreign Policy," p. 726.
6. Karen De Witt, "Brzezinski, the Power and the Glory," *The Washington Post* (February 4, 1977), p. B1. Brzezinski, "The Deceptive Structure of Peace," pp. 49–55.
7. Brzezinski, *Between Two Ages*, pp. 275, 282–83, 286. "Facing Democracy's Crisis," p. 61. "Crisis and Parity," *Newsweek* (January 3, 1972), p. 26. "Peace and Power," p. 10.
8. Brzezinski, *Ideology and Power in Soviet Politics*, revised edn, pp. 227–28, 167–68; 1962 edn, pp. 133–34; "Peace and Power," p. 12. *Between Two Ages*, pp. 286–87. "U.S. Foreign Policy," p. 727.
9. Brzezinski, "Sufficiency For War or Peace?" p. 45. He used superiority in quotation marks to indicate that in a setting of mutual non-survivability it has less and less meaning. "U.S. Foreign Policy," pp. 720–21. "What Kind of Détente?", p. 290.
10. Brzezinski, "The Deceptive Structure of Peace," pp. 41–42. *Between Two Ages*, pp. 286–87. He argued that US technological superiority would provide the necessary degree of ambiguity to the qualititive and quantitive power relationship between the superpowers.
11. Brzezinski, "The Deceptive Structure of Peace," pp. 39, 50. "Half Past Nixon," pp. 17–19. In 1971 he gave the Administration a (C) for its defense policy.
12. Brzezinski, "Toward Cooperative Activism," p. 43.
13. Brzezinski, "U.S. Foreign Policy," pp. 719–20. "The Deceptive Structure of Peace," pp. 53–54.
14. Brzezinski, "U.S. Foreign Policy," pp. 721, 716. In his words, Nixon's foreign policy "involved an admirably intelligent application of the power-realist approach, skillfully adapted to prevailing domestic circumstances." "Facing Democracy's Crisis," p. 61.

15. Brzezinski, "U.S. Foreign Policy," pp. 712–14, 721, 727.
16. Brzezinski, "Needed: An Alternative," p. 53. He stated that "in a foreign policy alternatives are not so much a matter of contrast as of emphasis." "The Balance of Power Delusion," p. 58.
17. Brzezinski, "U.S. Foreign Policy," pp. 721, 727, 712–14. "Toward Cooperative Activism," p. 43.
18. Brzezinski, "U.S. Foreign Policy," pp. 720–21. "Toward Cooperative Activism," p. 43.
19. Brzezinski, "U.S. Foreign Policy," p. 720.
20. Brzezinski, "Peace and Power," pp. 8–9. Criticizing the tendency to focus more on the allegedly peaceful character of Soviet intentions and to downgrade the importance of increased Soviet capabilities, he declared that the scope of capabilities does make a difference irrespective of motives.
21. Brzezinski, "Purpose and Planning in Foreign Policy," p. 73.
22. Ibid., pp. 52, 55–56.
23. Brzezinski, "U.S. Foreign Policy," p. 720.
24. Brzezinski, "Purpose and Planning in Foreign Policy," pp. 53–54, 56. "The Deceptive Structure Of Peace," pp. 36–37. Kissinger, *Nuclear Weapons and Foreign Policy*, abridged edn, pp. 249–50; 1957 edn, pp. 433–34. *American Foreign Policy*, pp. 29–34.
25. Kissinger, *American Foreign Policy*, pp. 17–20.
26. Brzezinski, "Purpose and Planning in Foreign Policy," pp. 57–58, 64–68. He proposed that the Council must be reduced in size, upgraded in status, and closely related to the Secretary of State. Its chairman should be someone enjoying the Secretary's personal confidence. The new body, the Council of International Affairs Advisers, must include both career officials and outside experts. *Between Two Ages*, pp. 291–93. Here he stressed the urgent needs to reform the US policymaking process and to free it from its dependence on the bureaucratic process.
27. Kissinger, *A World Restored*, pp. 326, 330.
28. Brzezinski, "Purpose and Planning in Foreign Policy," pp. 56, 59, 60–61. He did not see the generation of new ideas as the planner's most important function, although he recognized the desirability of new initiatives.
29. Brzezinski, "U.S. Foreign Policy," pp. 726, 715. "The Deceptive Structure of Peace," p. 52.
30. Brzezinski, "The Deceptive Structure of Peace," pp. 51–53.
31. Kissinger, *A World Restored*, pp. 325–26, 329–30. *American Foreign Policy*, p. 19.
32. Brzezinski, "Recognizing the Crisis," p. 66. "Shifting Mood and System," p. 324.
33. Brzezinski, "Shifting Mood and System," p. 324.
34. Kissinger, *A World Restored*, pp. 1–2, 328–29. *American Foreign Policy*, p. 58.

35. Brzezinski, "The Deceptive Structure Of Peace," pp. 53, 49–55. "Recognizing the Crisis," p. 73.
36. Brzezinski, *Between Two Ages*, p. 285.
37. Ibid., p. 305.
38. Ibid., pp. 308, 61. Such as famine, overpopulation, radiation, disease, drugs, pollution, etc.
39. Brzezinski, "America in a Hostile World," pp. 76, 95.
40. Brzezinski, *Between Two Ages*, pp. 286, 285. *Alternative to Partition*, p. 8.
41. Brzezinski, "Japan's Global Engagement," p. 281.
42. Brzezinski, *Between Two Ages*, p. 255.
43. Brzezinski, "U.S. Foreign Policy," p. 719. "The Deceptive Structure of Peace," pp. 39, 45. "What Kind of Détente," p. 21. "Facing Democracy's Crisis," p. 61.
44. Brzezinski, "Crisis and Parity," p. 26. This argument was made with reference to the Nixon-Kissinger stand in the Indo-Pakistani war.
45. Brzezinski, "U.S. Foreign Policy," p. 719. "Facing Democracy's Crisis," p. 61. He felt that the deceptive and unpredictable Nixon-Kissinger policy came at a time when US moral authority and clarity were very much needed.
46. Brzezinski, "Recognizing the Crisis," p. 66. "The Deceptive Structure of Peace," p. 45. He approved of Nixon's call for less overt and assertive US leadership in relations with allies. "Shifting Mood and System," p. 322. He called for more patient and prudent leadership.
47. Brzezinski, "Purpose and Planning in Foreign Policy," p. 64. "Shifting Mood and System," p. 324.
48. Brzezinski, "The Deceptive Structure of Peace," pp. 48–49, 51. "Shifting Mood and System," p. 322. He claimed that US unilateralism created fissures in the alliance which "could have been avoided by more patient and more prudent leadership."
49. Brzezinski, "America in a Hostile World," pp. 89–90.
50. Brzezinski, "Half Past Nixon," p. 13. For him the doctrine was "a negative concept reacting to the excesses of the past." "Facing Democracy's Crisis," p. 57. He claimed that the weakness of US leadership, a weak Congress confronting a weak president, undermined optimism.
51. Brzezinski, "A Moment for Restraint," *Newsweek* (July 19, 1971), p. 37. He stressed the need for a US initiative in Vietnam. Kissinger, *Nuclear Weapons and Foreign Policy*, abridged edn, pp. 223, 209; 1957 edn, pp. 267–68. 251.
52. Brzezinski, *Alternative to Partition*, pp. 132–33. Here he suggests a US initiative to end peacefully the partition of Europe.
53. Brzezinski, "Peace and Power," p. 12. *Between Two Ages*, pp. 277, 283–4, 304–5, 307–8. "Facing Democracy's Crisis," p. 61. "Recognizing the Crisis," p. 69.
54. Brzezinski, *Between Two Ages*, pp. 307–8. "Facing Democracy's Crisis," p. 61.

55. Brzezinski, *Between Two Ages*, p. 305. "Peace and Power," p. 12.
56. Brzezinski, *Alternatives to Partition*, pp. ix, 132–33.
57. Brzezinski, "Recognizing the Crisis," pp. 69–70. "Shifting Mood and System," p. 324. "America and Europe," pp. 22–23.
58. Brzezinski, "U.S. Foreign Policy," p. 723.
59. Brzezinski, "The Deceptive Structure of Peace," p. 51. "Shifting Mood and System," p. 324.
60. Brzezinski, "The Balance of Power Delusion," pp. 55–56. For him Western Europe and Japan were not true powers because they lacked effective military power and clear political purposes. They were uncertain quantities.
61. Brzezinski, *Alternative to Partition*, pp. 117–18. "Meeting Moscow's 'Limited Coexistence'," *The New Leader* (December 16, 1968), p. 13.
62. Brzezinski, "Sufficiency For War or Peace?" p. 45. "Half Past Nixon," pp. 17–18. "Crisis and Parity," p. 26.
63. Brzezinski, "New Nuclear Ideas," p. 55. "Crisis And Parity," p. 26. Here he argued that the Indo-Pakistani war demonstrated that the Nixon Administration was unable to achieve its objectives in a situation of parity because of the lack of will and power.
64. Brzezinski, "Recognizing the Crisis," pp. 64, 70, 72.
65. Brzezinski, "America in a Hostile World," pp. 80–82, 90. "Not War but Anarchy," p. 47. He felt that in struggles between powerful and weak nations, the latter are capable of undertaking an all-out effort that the former cannot match spiritually.
66. Brzezinski, "Shifting Mood and System," p. 325. "Half Past Nixon," p. 11.
67. Brzezinski, "U.S. Foreign Policy," pp. 719–21. "What Kind of Détente?" , pp. 289–90. "Memorandum for the President," p. 50.
68. Brzezinski, "The Deceptive Structure of Peace," pp. 40, 45.
69. Brzezinski, "Memorandum for the President," p. 50.
70. Brzezinski, "Shifting Mood and System," pp. 325–26.
71. Brzezinski, *Alternative to Partition*, p. 152. "Memorandum for the President," p. 50. "The Deceptive Structure of Peace," pp. 40–45.
72. Brzezinski, "Recognizing the Crisis," pp. 72–73, 66. "The Deceptive Structure Of Peace," pp. 49–52, 55.
73. Brzezinski, "Recognizing the Crisis," pp. 73–74. "Purpose and Planning in Foreign Policy," pp. 64–65, 68–70. Here he had urged the creation of a new body to integrate institutionally all foreign policy planning. "Facing Democracy's Crisis," p. 61.
74. Brzezinski, "Purpose and Planning in Foreign Policy," pp. 64–65.
75. Brzezinski, *Between Two Ages*, pp. 304–5. "U.S. Foreign Policy," pp. 722–23.
76. Brzezinski, "U.S. Foreign Policy," p. 723. "Half Past Nixon," p. 13. "Peace and Power," p. 11. *Between Two Ages*, pp. 293–97, 308. "Needed: An Alternative," p. 53.
77. Brzezinski, "The Balance of Power Delusion," p. 59.

78. Brzezinski, *Between Two Ages*, pp. 304–5.
79. Brzezinski, "U.S. Foreign Policy," p. 723. "Peace and Power," p. 13. *Between Two Ages*, p. 305. "Shifting Mood and System," pp. 322, 324.
80. Brzezinski, "U.S. Foreign Policy," pp. 722–24. "The Balance of Power Delusion," p. 59. "Memorandum for the President," p. 50. "The Degeneration of Peace," p. 36. "America and Europe," p. 29.
81. Brzezinski, "Peace and Power," p. 12.
82. Brzezinski, "America in a Hostile World," pp. 92–93. "Recognizing the Crisis," pp. 64, 67. He points to the increasing unilateralism on the part of the allies on economic issues that inhibit collective responses. "Shifting Mood and System," p. 321.
83. Kissinger, *The Troubled Partneship*, pp. 27–28, 248–49. Prior to 1973 he advocated an Atlantic Commonwealth, but in the Year of Europe Japan was included. Brzezinski, *Between Two Ages*, pp. 296–97.
84. Brzezinski, "Peace and Power," pp. 12–13.
85. Brzezinski, "What Kind of Détente?" pp. 291–92, 290.
86. Brzezinski, "Recognizing the Crisis," pp. 72–73. He urged the dramatization of the energy, inflation, and global social equity problems. "Facing Democracy's Crisis," p. 59. *Alternative to Partition*, pp. 168–69.
87. Brzezinski, *Between Two Ages*, pp. 300, 307–8. He urged intensive efforts to shape a new world monetary structure despite his recognition that there will be some consequent risk to the present relatively favorable US position. "America in a Hostile World," p. 91. He rejected isolationism and accepted the risks inherent in global involvement in order to prevent a vacuum that would be filled by escalating anarchy which could eventually threaten the US domestically.
88. Brzezinski, *Ideology and Power in Soviet Politics*, revised edn, pp. 227–28. *Alternative to Partition*, pp. 134–35, 139. "Peace and Power," pp. 10, 12. He maintained that parity cannot be defined given the differences in perceived needs, in commitments, in industrial-population distributions and in historical perspectives.
89. Brzezinski, "Sufficiency for War or Peace," p. 45. "U.S. Foreign Policy," pp. 720–21.
90. Brzezinski, "U.S. Foreign Policy," pp. 720–21. "What Kind of Détente?" p. 290.
91. Brzezinski, *Alternative to Partition*, pp. 134–35. *Ideology and Power in Soviet Politics*, revised edn, p. 227.
92. Brzezinski, *Alternative to Partition*, p. 135.
93. Brzezinski, "Peace and Power," p. 10. "Crisis and Parity," p. 26.
94. Brzezinski and Huntington, *Political Power: USA/USSR*, p. 429.
95. Brzezinski, "Crisis and Parity," p. 26. "How the Cold War was Played," pp. 206–7.
96. Brzezinski, "New Guidelines for the West," pp. 13–14.
97. Brzezinski, "Crisis and Parity," p. 26. He stated that the USSR has

always been prudent, with only the exception of the Cuban missile crisis, because it had to operate in the context of relative weakness in relation to the US. "Peace and Power," pp. 6, 10.

98. Brzezinski, *Between Two Ages*, pp. 304–5.
99. Brzezinski, "Purpose and Planning in Foreign Policy," p. 52.
100. Brzezinski, *Alternative to Partition*, p. 155. Here he referred specifically to dependence on Congress to exercise negative economic sanctions in relations with Communist states.
101. Brzezinski, "America in a Hostile World," p. 85.
102. Brzezinski, "Recognizing the Crisis," pp. 66–69.
103. Brzezinski, "Sufficiency For War or Peace?" p. 45.
104. Brzezinski, *Ideology and Power in Soviet Politics*, revised edn, pp. 232, 227.
105. Brzezinski, "Recognizing the Crisis," p. 69.
106. Brzezinski, "U.S. Foreign Policy," p. 724.
107. Brzezinski, "Shifting Mood and System," pp. 322, 325–26.
108. Brzezinski, "New Guideliness for the West," pp. 13–14.
109. Brzezinski, *Between Two Ages*, pp. 285–86.
110. Brzezinski, "Not War but Anarchy," p. 47. "U.S. Foreign Policy," p. 720. "Toward Cooperative Activism," p. 43. "Recognizing the Crisis," p. 69. Here he argued that military action in response to economic policies is neither morally warranted nor politically feasible.
111. Brzezinski, "U.S. Foreign Policy," pp. 723–24, 726. "Not War But Anarchy," p. 47. "America and Europe," pp. 29–30. "Japan's Global Engagement," pp. 280–81. *Between Two Ages*, p. 297.
112. Brzezinski, "Shifting Mood and System," p. 323.
113. Brzezinski, "The Deceptive Structure of Peace," pp. 55, 52. Here he called for collective consultations. "America and Europe," pp. 29–30.
114. Brzezinski, "Recognizing the Crisis," pp. 66, 72–73.
115. Brzezinski, "The Deceptive Structure of Peace," p. 39. "Half Past Nixon," p. 14. "America and Europe," p. 17.
116. Brzezinski, "The Deceptive Structure of Peace," p. 47. "Japan's Global Involvement," p. 272. "Substance and Style," p. 41.
117. Brzezinski, "The Deceptive Structure of Peace," pp. 51–52.
118. Brzezinski, "Peace and Power," pp. 10, 12.
119. Brzezinski, "U.S. Foreign Policy," p. 720. *Between Two Ages*, p. 286.
120. Brzezinski, "The Deceptive Structure of Peace," pp. 41–42, 44. "Half Past Nixon," p. 15. "What Kind of Détente?" p. 290.
121. Brzezinski, *Ideology and Power in Soviet Politics*, revised edn, p. 228. Here he was talking about disarmament but the thrust of his argument also applied to arms control.
122. Brzezinski, "The Deceptive Structure of Peace," pp. 41–42. "Half Past Nixon," p. 15.
123. Brzezinski, "The Deceptive Structure of Peace," pp. 51, 47. "America in a Hostile World," p. 73.

124. Brzezinski, "The Deceptive Structure of Peace," p. 41. He was referring specifically to SALT I. "Shifting Mood and System," p. 322. "America and Europe," pp. 24–25.
125. Brzezinski, "America and Europe," pp. 22–24.
126. Brzezinski, "Crisis and Summit," p. 57.
127. Brzezinski, "The Degeneration of Peace," p. 36. "Fortune-Cookie Diplomacy," p. 46. "Memorandum for the President," p. 50.
128. Brzezinski, "Peace and Power," p. 13. He recommended that such meetings be held one year in Alaska and the next in the Soviet Far East.
129. Brzezinski, "What Kind of Détente?" p. 290.
130. Brzezinski, *Alternative to Partition*, pp. 152, 159–61.
131. Brzezinski, "The Deceptive Structure of Peace," pp. 37–39, 52.
132. Kissinger, *A World Restored*, p. 329.
133. Brzezinski, "The Deceptive Structure of Peace," pp. 52, 55. "What Kind of Détente?" p. 291. "Peace and Power," pp. 12–13. Here he discussed reciprocity of treatment as an educational exercise.

Chapter 6: Kissinger Organizing Power for Decision-Making

1. Richard Nixon, *The Memoirs of Richard Nixon* (New York: Grosset & Dunlap, 1978), p. 340.
2. Oriana Fallaci, "Kissinger: An Interview," *The New Republic* 1967 (December 16, 1972), pp. 20–21. Danielle Hunebelle, *Dear Henry* (New York: 1972), p. 43.
3. Kissinger, *White House Years*, p. 7. Marvin Kalb and Bernard Kalb, *Kissinger* (Boston: Little Brown and Company, 1974), pp. 15–16, 19, 21. Hunebelle, *Dear Henry*, p. 60.
4. Nixon, *The Memoirs of Richard Nixon*, pp. 340–41. Dickson, *Kissinger and the Meaning of History*, p. 146.
5. Nixon, *The Memoirs of Richard Nixon*, p. 340.
6. Ibid., p. 344.
7. Nixon, "Asia After Viet Nam," *Foreign Affairs* (October 1967):122. "Nixon Speaks," in *Nixon: a Political Portrait*. By Earl Mazo and Stephen Hess (New York: Harper & Row, 1968), pp. 32–33.
8. Nixon, *The Memoirs of Richard Nixon*, pp. 212–13.
9. *The New York Times* (August 7 and 9, 1968). He saw the PRC as "the next superpower."
10. Nixon, *The Memoirs of Richard Nixon*, pp. 281–82. "Nixon Speaks," pp. 312–13. "Asia After Viet Nam," pp. 121–13.
11. Nixon, "Asia After Viet Nam," pp. 122–23. "Nixon Speaks," p. 313.
12. Nixon, "Asia After Viet Nam," p. 122. "Nixon Speaks," p. 312.
13. Nixon, *Six Crises* (New York: Pyramid Books, 1968), p. 41.
14. *The New York Times* (7 August 1968). "Nixon Speaks," p 313. "The Time to Save NATO," *Atlantic Community Quarterly* (Winter 1968–69):481–82.

15. Nixon, "Asia After Viet Nam," pp. 115, 122–23. "Nixon Speaks," pp. 309–10. *The New York Times* (October 9, 1968).
16. *The New York Times* (August 9, 1968).
17. *The New York Times* (August 9, 1968).
18. Nixon, "Asia After Viet Nam," p. 111.
19. *The New York Times* (August 2 and 7, 1968).
20. *The New York Times* (August 9, 1968).
21. Nixon, "Asia After Viet Nam," pp. 122–23. "Nixon Speaks," p. 313.
22. *The New York Times* (August 9, 1968).
23. Nixon, "Asia After Viet Nam," pp. 117–18.
24. Nixon, *Six Crises*, pp. x, xxviii.
25. Nixon, "The Nature of the Presidency," in Hedley Donovan, *Roosevelt to Reagan* (New York: Harper & Row, 1985), p. 112. "Nixon Speaks," p. 314.
26. *The New York Times* (August 9, 1968).
27. Nixon, "Asia After Viet Nam," p. 114.
28. *The New York Times* (October 25, 1969).
29. *The New York Times* (August 7 and 9, 1968). Nixon, *The Memoirs of Richard Nixon*, pp. 340–41.
30. *The New York Times* (August 2, 1968).
31. Nixon, *The Memoirs of Richard Nixon*, p. 343.
32. *The New York Times* (August 2, 1968).
33. Gerald R. Ford, *A Time to Heal* (New York: Berkley Books, 1980), pp. 28–29, 126. Ford states that after meeting with Nixon who recommended that he keep Kissinger but not give him a totally free hand, he called Kissinger and told him, "'Henry . . . I need you. The country needs you. I want you to stay. I'll do everything to work with you.'"
34. Nixon, *Six Crises* p. 319.
35. *The New York Times* (December 3, 1968).
36. Ibid.
37. Nixon, *The Memoirs of Richard Nixon*, p. 339. Kissinger, *White House Years*, pp. 26–29. Morris, *Uncertain Greatness*, pp. 85–86.
38. Nixon, *The Memoirs of Richard Nixon*, p. 339. Kissinger, *White House Years*, pp. 32–33. Morris, *Uncertain Greatness*, pp. 87–88.
39. Ford, *A Time to Heal*, pp. 117, 315–16.
40. *The New York Times* (October 25, 1968).
41. Kissinger, *White House Years*, p. 77.
42. Nixon, *US Foreign Policy for the 1970's: A New Strategy for Peace*, (Washington, D.C.: GPO, 1970) pp. 17–23. *US Foreign Policy for the 1970s: Building for Peace*, (Washington, D.C.: GPO, 1971), pp. 226–29. *US Foreign Policy for the 1970s: The Emerging Structure of Peace*, (Washington, D.C.: GPO, 1972), pp. 208–11. Kalb and Kalb, *Kissinger*, pp. 85–86. Morris, *Uncertain Greatness*, pp. 80–81. I. M. Destler, *Presidents, Bureaucrats and Foreign Policy*, (Princeton, NJ: Princeton University Press, 1974), pp. 118–23. John P.

Leacacos, "Kissinger's Apparat." *Foreign Policy* 5 (Winter 1971–72), pp. 3–14.

43. 000"Morris,*UncertainGreatness*,pp.80–81.Destler,*Presidents,Bureaucrats and Foreign Policy*, pp. 132–37.

44. Kissinger, *White House Years*, p. 45. Morris, *Uncertain Greatness*, pp. 89–90.

45. Kissinger, *White House Years*, pp. 42–46, 36. Morris, *Uncertain Greatness*, pp. 81, 88–90.

46. Nixon, *US Foreign Policy for the 1970's: A New Strategy for Peace*, pp. 17–23; *US Foreign Policy for the 1970s: Building for Peace*, pp. 226–29; *US Foreign Policy for the 1970s: The Emerging Structure of Peace*, pp. 208–12.

47. Kissinger, *White House Years*, pp. 158–59. He suggested it during the transition period. Nixon decided his report would appear a month before the State Department's, p. 1127; the State Department had never published such reports before and never did again. *Years of Upheaval*, p. 159.

48. Destler, *Presidents, Bureaucrats and Foreign Policy*, pp. 123–24, 133. In two and a half years Nixon held 63 NSC meetings. Leacacos, "Kissinger's Apparat," pp. 5–6, 13, 25–27.

49. Nixon, *US Foreign Policy for the 1970's: A New Strategy for Peace*, pp. 20–23. *US Foreign Policy for the 1970s: Building for Peace*, pp. 228–29. *US Foreign Policy for the 1970s: The Emerging Structure of Peace*, pp. 210–11. Kalb and Kalb, *Kissinger*, pp. 86–87. Leacacos, "Kissinger's Apparat," pp. 5–9. Destler, *Presidents, Bureaucrats and Foreign Policy*, pp. 127–28.

50. Kissinger, *White House Years*, p. 47, 805–6, 369. *Years of Upheaval*, p. 263.

51. I. M. Destler, "National Security Advice to US Presidents: Some Lessons from Thirty Years," *World Politics* 2 (January 1977):150, 155, 158–9. Ford, *A Time to Heal*, pp. 315–16.

52. Kissinger, *White House Years*, pp. 28–29. He writes that Nixon initiated the backchannels. Nixon, *The Memoirs of Richard Nixon*, p. 369. Nixon writes that Kissinger suggested the development of a private channel between Dobrynin and him.

53. Kissinger, *White House Years*, pp. 47–48. Destler, *Presidents, Bureaucrats and Foreign Policy*, pp. 125–26.

54. Kissinger, *White House Years*, p. 805. *Years of Upheaval*, pp. 415–16. on changes on Nixon's style after Watergate.

55. Kissinger, *White House Years*, p. 48; Morris, *Uncertain Greatness*, p. 145. Morris reports that by early spring of 1969, and even after, Kissinger had acquired, through mutual interest, a near monopoly on the time, attention, and respect of the President on all matters of foreign policy. His was literally the first and final word on policy decisions.

56. Kissinger, *White House Years*, pp. 28–29, 48, 805. Nixon met with

Soviet Ambassador Anatoly Dobrynin on February 17, 1969. The practice of excluding Rogers – established before Kissinger's position was settled – continued throughout Nixon's term of office. When a state visitor was received in the Oval Office by Nixon for a lengthy discussion Kissinger was the only other American present. U. Alexis Johnson, *The Right Hand of Power* (Englewood, Cliffs, N.J.: Prentice-Hall, Inc., 1984), pp. 552–53. Ambassador Johnson agrees that this was indeed the practice.

57. *The New York Times* (December 3, 1968). Kissinger, *White House Years*, p. 315. He notes this inconsistency.
58. Kissinger, *American Foreign Policy*, p. 23.
59. Kissinger, *White House Years*, pp. 1084, 1140.

Chapter 7: Brzezinski Organizing Power for Decision-Making

1. Jimmy Carter, *Keeping Faith: Memoirs of a President* (New York: Bantam Books, 1982), pp. 51–52. Brzezinski, *Power and Principle: Memoirs of the National Security Adviser 1977–1981* (New York: Farrar, Straus, Giroux, 1983), pp. 5, 7–9. Leslie H. Gelb. "Brzezinski Viewed as Key Advisor to Carter," *The New York Times* (October 6, 1976). Gelb wrote that Brzezinski was the only person to whom Carter publicly promised a top job if elected. Hamilton Jordan, *Crisis* (New York: G. P. Putnam's Sons, 1982), pp. 45–47. He states Brzezinski became Carter's friend, Vance his acquaintance.
2. *The New York Times* (December 17, 1976). Carter, *Keeping Faith*, p. 51.
3. Committee on House Administration, U.S. House of Representatives. *The Presidential Campaign 1976*. Vol. 1, Part 1, Jimmy Carter (Washington, D.C.: Government Printing Office, 1978), Speech, American Chamber of Commerce, Tokyo, Japan, May 28, 1975, pp. 66, 68.
4. Ibid., Position Papers VI, p. 682.
5. Ibid., Speech, Foreign Policy Association, New York, June 23, 1976, pp. 267, 271. Speech, Chicago Council on Foreign Relations, March 15, 1976, p. 110.
6. Ibid., Speech, Chicago Council on Foreign Relations, p. 113. Position Papers VI, p. 682. Vol. 3. The Debates (Washington, D.C.: Government Printing Office, 1979), Second debate on October 6, 1976, p. 105. Brzezinski, "U.S. Foreign Policy," pp. 715–16, 720–21.
7. *The Presidential Campaign 1976*. Vol. 1, Part 1, Speech, Chicago Council on Foreign Relations, pp. 116, 110. Speech, American Chamber of Commerce, Tokyo, p. 69.
8. Ibid., Vol. 3, Second Debate, p. 93.
9. Ibid., Vol. 1, Part 1, Speech, Chicago Council on Foreign Relations, p. 116.

10. Ibid., Vol. 1, Part 1, Speech, Foreign Policy Association, p. 273.

11. Ibid., Speech, Chicago Council on Foreign Relations, p. 116.

12. Ibid., Speech, Foreign Policy Association, p. 271. Vol. 3, Second Debate, p. 104.

13. Ibid., Vol. 3, Second Debate, pp. 104–5.

14. Ibid., Vol. 1, Part 1, Speech, Foreign Policy Association, p. 268. Brzezinski, *Between Two Ages*, p. 296.

15. *The Presidential Campaign 1976.* Vol. 1, Part 1, Speech, Foreign Policy Association, p. 267. Brzezinski, *Between Two Ages*, p. 294.

16. *The Presidential Campaign 1976.* Vol. 1, Part 1, Speech, Foreign Policy Association, p. 273. Speech, Chicago Council on Foreign Relations, pp. 114–15.

17. Ibid., Vol. 3, Second Debate, p. 93. See Brzezinski, "The Deceptive Structure of Peace."

18. *The Presidential Campaign 1976.* Vol. 3, Second Debate, p. 105. Vol. 1, Part 1, Speech accepting the Democratic nomination for President, July 15, 1976, p. 352.

19. Ibid., Vol. 1, Part 1, Position Papers VI, p. 683. Speech at the United Nations, May 13, 1976, p. 194. See Brzezinski, "U.S. Foreign Policy," pp. 721, 727.

20. *The Presidential Campaign 1976.* Vol. 1, Part 1, Speech, Foreign Policy Association, p. 274. Acceptance Speech, p. 351. See Brzezinski, "The Deceptive Structure of Peace."

21. *The Presidential Campaign 1976.* Vol. 1, Part 1, Speech, Foreign Policy Association, p. 270. See Brzezinski, "America in a Hostile World," p. 76

22. *The Presidential Campaign 1976.* Vol. 1, Part 1, Speech, Foreign Policy Association, pp. 267, 270. Address to UN, p. 193.

23. Ibid., Vol. 1, Part 1, Acceptance Speech, pp. 349, 350–52. Vol. 3, Second Debate, p. 97. Brzezinski, *Between Two Ages*, p. 255.

24. *The Presidential Campaign 1976.* Vol. 1, Part 1, Speech, Foreign Policy Association, p. 270. Vol. 3, Second Debate, p. 100. Brzezinski, "What Kind of Détente?" p. 291.

25. *The Presidential Campaign 1976.* Vol. 3, Second Debate, pp. 112, 94. For Carter: "Mr. Ford and Kissinger have continued with the policies and failures of Richard Nixon." See Brzezinski, "The Deceptive Structure of Peace," and "U.S. Foreign Policy."

26. *The Presidential Campaign 1976.* Vol. 1, Part 1, Acceptance Speech, p. 349. Vol. 3, Second Debate, p. 108.

27. *The New York Times,* (December 4, 1976). *The Presidential Campaign 1976.* Vol 1, Part 2, Campaign rally in Alexandria, Virginia, October 23, 1976, p. 1082.

28. *The Presidential Campaign 1976.* Vol. 1, Part 1, Speech, Foreign Policy Association, pp. 267–68.

29. Vol 3, Second Debate, pp. 93, 109. See Brzezinski, "America in a Hostile World," and "Toward Cooperative Activism," p. 43.

30. *The Presidential Campaign 1976*, Vol. 1, Part 1, Acceptance Speech, p. 352.
31. Ibid., Vol. 3, Second Debate, pp. 97, 105. Vol. 1, Part 1, Acceptance Speech, p. 349; Speech, Chicago Council on Foreign Relations, pp. 110–11. Brzezinski, *Power and Principle*, p. 8. He states that he urged Carter to omit the anti-Kissinger stuff he got from Ball, but they compromised on the "Lone Ranger" reference to it.
32. *The Presidential Campaign 1976*, Vol. 3, Second Debate, p. 98.
33. Ibid., Vol. 1, Part 1, Speech, Foreign Policy Association, pp. 268–69. See Brzezinski, "Peace and Power," p. 13; and "Recognizing the Crisis," p. 72.
34. *The Presidential Campaign 1976*. Vol. 3, Second Debate, p. 98.
35. Ibid., Vol. 1, Part 1, Address to UN, p. 188; Vol. 1, Part 2, Speech on Nuclear Proliferation in San Diego, CA, September 25, 1976, p. 817. See Brzezinski, "The Deceptive Structure of Peace," pp. 41–42, 44.
36. *The Presidential Campaign 1976*. Vol. 1, Part 1, Speech, Chicago Council on Foreign Relations, p. 116.
37. Ibid., Vol. 1, Part 1, Speech, Foreign Policy Association, p. 272. Vol. 1, Part 2, pp. 818, 856. Vol. 3, Second Debate, p. 108.
38. Ibid., Vol. 1, Part 1, Address at UN, pp. 193, 187; Vol. 1, Part 2, p. 815.
39. Ibid., Vol. 3, Second Debate, p. 112. Vol. 1, Part 2, p. 816.
40. Ibid., Vol. 1, Part 1, Address at UN, p. 191.
41. Ibid., Vol. 3, Second Debate, p. 93.
42. Ibid., Vol. 1, Part 1, Speech, Foreign Policy Association, p. 274.
43. *The Washington Post* (December 27, 1976). Carter, *Keeping Faith*, p. 52. Burton M. Sapin, "What Every New Administration Should Know About Foreign Policy," Unpublished manuscript. The George Washington University, 1984, pp. 49–51.
44. *The New York Times* (December 4, 1976).
45. Carter, *Keeping Faith*, p. 52. Carter states that Brzezinski recommended Vance for the post.
46. *The New York Times* (December 4, 1976).
47. *The New York Times* (December 17, 1976). Carter, *Keeping Faith*, p. 52. Carter states that some cautioned him that Brzezinski might not be deferential to Vance and that he might speak out too forcefully on controversial issues. But Vance recommended him for the job.
48. *The Washington Post* (December 27, 1976). Carter, *Keeping Faith*, p. 55.
49. Brzezinski, *Power and Principle*, pp. 58–59. He proposed that the NSC consist of seven committees, three of which would be chaired by him while the rest would be chaired by the Secretaries of State, Defense and Treasury, and occasionally the Director of the CIA.
50. Ibid., p. 62. Brzezinski admitted that he worried whether Carter would approve the assignment of SALT and crisis management to the SCC and whether this would be accepted by the Secretaries.

51.   Robert E. Hunter, *Presidential Control of Foreign Policy: Management or Mishap?* (New York: Praeger, 1982), pp. 105–8. Brzezinski, *Power and Principle*, pp. 58–62.
52.   Brzezinski, *Power and Principle*, p. 61. Hunter, *Presidential Control of Foreign Policy*, pp. 103–4.
53.   Brzezinski, *Power and Principle*, pp. 62–63. Cyrus Vance, *Hard Choices: Critical Years in America's Foreign Policy* (New York: Simon and Schuster, 1983), pp. 36–37.
54.   Brzezinski, *Power and Principle*, pp. 60–61, 64, 72–73. Carter, *Keeping Faith*, p. 116.
55.   Brzezinski, *Power and Principle*, pp. 501–2. At a special meeting at Camp David to deal formally with Muskie's objections Carter supported the existing structure as he did again when Muskie sought to bypass Brzezinski by going directly to him.
56.   Ibid., pp. 63–67. Hunter, *Presidential Control of Foreign Policy*, pp. 8–28. Carter, *Keeping Faith*, pp. 51–57. Vance, *Hard Choices*, pp. 36–39.
57.   Brzezinski, "Purpose and Planning in Foreign Policy," pp. 60, 65.
58.   Brzezinski, *Power and Principle*, pp. 67–68. Vance, *Hard Choices*, pp. 38–39. Carter, *Keeping Faith*, pp. 55–56.
59.   Brzezinski, *Power and Principle*, pp. 70–71. Vance, *Hard Choices*, p. 39.
60.   Brzezinski, *Power and Principle*, pp. 153, 167, 173, 179–80, 338–39, for meetings with Dobrynin. pp. 203, 226–27, 419, for meetings with the Chinese.
61.   Ibid., pp. 226–28, initiatives toward the PRC, pp. 338–39, deals with Dobrynin. Tad Szulc, "Springtime For Carter," *Foreign Policy* 27 (Summer 1977):180.

Chapter 8: Kissinger and the Adversaries: The USSR and the PRC

1.   Landau, *Kissinger*, pp. 103–4. Brown, *The Crisis of Power*, pp. 16–17.
2.   Nixon, *US Foreign Policy for the 1970s: A New Strategy for Peace*, p. 2.
3.   Ibid., pp. 1–13; *US Foreign Policy for the 1970s: Building for Peace*, pp. 3–7; *US Foreign Policy for the 1970s: The Emerging Structure of Peace*, pp. 2–4; *US Foreign Policy for the 1970s: Shaping a Durable Peace*, pp. 2–10.
4.   Nixon, *US Foreign Policy for the 1970s: A New Strategy for Peace*, p. 4; *US Foreign Policy for the 1970s: Building for Peace*, p. 6.
5.   Nixon, *US Foreign Policy for the 1970s: A New Strategy For Peace*, pp. 4–5, 156; *US Foreign Policy for the 1970s: Building for Peace*, p. 7.
6.   Nixon, *US Foreign Policy for the 1970s: Building for Peace*, p. 105;

US Foreign Policy for the 1970s: A New Strategy for Peace, p. 142; *US Foreign Policy for the 1970s: Shaping a Durable Peace*, p. 16.

7.   Nixon, *US Foreign Policy for the 1970s: A New Strategy for Peace*, pp. 1–13; *US Foreign Policy for the 1970s: The Emerging Structure of Peace*, pp. 3–4.

8.   Nixon, *US Foreign Policy for the 1970s: A New Strategy for Peace*, pp. 12, 134–5, 140; *US Foreign Policy for the 1970s: Building for Peace*, p. 105. *US Foreign Policy for the 1970s: Shaping a Durable Peace*, p. 16.

9.   Nixon, *US Foreign Policy for the 1970s: A New Strategy for Peace*, pp. 134–35.

10. See Kissinger, *White House Years*, pp. 135–36, for the text of the letter which was really intended for Rogers.

11. Ibid., pp. 133–36, Kissinger's discussion of opposition to linkage; pp. 137–38, for Smith's and Rogers' efforts to undermine it by pushing Nixon into SALT talks.

12. Nixon, *US Foreign Policy for the 1970s: A New Strategy for Peace*, pp. 135–36.

13. Kissinger, *White House Years*, pp. 129–30, 135–36.

14. *Time*, January 3, 1972, pp. 14–15. *Presidential Documents*, vol. 7, no. 28 (July 1971), p. 1036. Nixon talked of "five great economic superpowers." Kissinger, *White House Years*, pp. 749, 1049. He reports Chou En-Lai rejected the appellation of superpower. It was also rejected in the Shanghai Communique. Szulc, *The Illusion of Peace*, pp. 412–13. He states Kissinger agreed with Nixon's pentagonal vision.

15. Kissinger, *American Foreign Policy*, p. 57. These elements were: stable technology, limited domestic claims, the multiplicity of major powers.

16. Graubard, *Kissinger*, pp. 252, 250. Stoessinger, *Henry Kissinger*, pp. 43–44. Both state Rockefeller's foreign policy speeches were written by Kissinger.

17. Nixon, *US Foreign Policy for the 1970s: A New Strategy for Peace*, pp. 125–26. *US Foreign Policy for the 1970s: Building for Peace*, pp. 169, 176. Kissinger, *White House Years*, p. 172. Both Nixon and Kissinger viewed the PRC as the aggressor in the Sino-Soviet border clashes that began on March 2 on the Damansky/Chenpao island in the Ussuri River.

18. Kissinger, *White House Years*, Kissinger discusses a number of developments that led him to push for the opening to Peking: p. 177, discussion of the May 20 and June 10 clashes on the Shinkiang border that convinced him the USSR was the aggressor; pp. 172–73, Dobrynin suggested to Kissinger common action on March 11 and April 3 to remove the Chinese threat; p. 178, SRG met on May 15 to discuss NSC study on PRC; p. 178, Brezhnev proposed Asian collective security system on June 8 to isolate the PRC; p. 183, Soviet asked about US reaction to a nuclear strike on August 18; p. 185, Soviets hint about "fraternal help," referring to a

doctrine that Socialist states have the right to intervene in each others affairs to protect socialism, on September 16; p. 182, Nixon declared at the NSC meeting on August 14, that the USSR was the aggressor in the border clashes and that it was in the US interest to prevent the defeat of the PRC in a Sino-Soviet war. He also points to Moscow's readiness to open the SALT talks and its increased support for Hanoi. Hersh, *The Price of Power*, p. 355. On June 13 Moscow recognized the Provisional Revolutionary Government of South Vietnam and endorsed the Vietcong's National Liberation Front's ten-point peace program. Michael Ledeen and William Lewis, *Debacle: The American Failure in Iran* (New York: Vintage Books, 1982), p. 47.

19. Kissinger, *White House Years*, p. 179. Steps for easing restrictions emerged from NSSM-35, "Trade with Communist China," ordered by Kissinger on March 28, 1969. The USC, under Richardson's chairmanship prepared the specific steps. See pp. 180–81, for Nixon's signals to the PRC; pp. 181–82, Rogers' signals in a speech on August 8, 1969, in Canberra, Austalia; p. 184, Helms' signals in a backgrounder on August 27, on the possibility of a Soviet attack on Chinese nuclear installations, and Richardson's signals in a speech to the APSA in New York on September 5. See Nixon, *US Foreign Policy for the 1970s: The Emerging Structure for Peace*, pp. 28–33, for specific steps easing trade from 1969 to 1971.

20. Nixon, *US Foreign Policy for the 1970s: A New Strategy for Peace*, p. 140.

21. Ibid., p. 142; *US Foreign Policy for the 1970s: Building for Peace*, p. 105–6; *US Foreign Policy for the 1970s: Shaping a Durable Peace*, p. 16. Kissinger, *White House Years*, pp. 688–89. He states that this was a message to Peking.

22. Kissinger, *White House Years*, pp. 220–22. He launched a reexamination of the "2 1/2 war" strategy and recommended the "1 1/2 war" to Nixon on October 2, 1969.

23. Nixon, *US Foreign Policy for the 1970s: A New Strategy for Peace*, p. 129. *US Foreign Policy for the 1970s: Building for Peace*, p. 178. Kissinger, *White House Years*, pp. 688–89, 221–22.

24. Kissinger, *White House Years*, For his report to Nixon in June p. 179; on September 29, p. 186; on October 20, p. 187; for report after trip to Peking pp. 754–55; in October 1970, pp. 764–65. Also see pp. 1053, 1063, 1076.

25. Nixon, *US Foreign Policy for the 1970s: Shaping a Durable Peace*, p. 16.

26. Kissinger, *White House Years*, pp. 712, 764, 836, 1062, 1066, 1073, 1078, 1080, 1089–90. *Years of Upheaval*, pp. 685, 689–90, 693.

27. Kissinger, *White House Years*, p. 178, for SRG meeting on May 15 to discuss study on PRC ordered by NSSM-14 on February 5, 1969; p. 183, WSAG meets in San Clemente on August 25 to discuss Soviet inquiry about US reaction to Soviet attack on the PRC's nuclear installations.

Szulc, *The Illusion of Peace*, pp. 22–23, on July 3, NSSM-63 ordered a study on "Sino-Soviet Relations."

28. Kissinger, *White House Years*, p. 167, on November 29, 1968, before Kissinger's appointment, Johnson with Nixon's approval accepted Peking's offer to resume the Warsaw talks; p. 188, on September 9, 1969, Kissinger urged US Ambassador to Poland, Walter Stoessel, to tell the Chinese Ambassador that the Administration was prepared for serious talks. On December 11, Stoessel was invited to the PRC's embassy.

29. Ibid., p. 690.

30. Ibid., pp. 182, 188–90, State Department opposition to linkage came from Llewellyn Thompson, former Ambassador to the USSR and Charles Bohlen, who upon hearing of plans for easing trade restrictions against the PRC warned Nixon against the use of the PRC against the USSR.

31. Ibid., p. 765; see also p. 179, for his report to Nixon in June 1969.

32. Ibid., pp. 688, 724–25, His views on impact on Japan and other Asian allies. pp. 762–63. His views on initiative's impact on allies. He admits that Peking was suspicious of the secrecy and saw it as a device to permit a quick reversal of policy.

33. Ibid., pp. 686–93. He describes the struggle with State to include discussion of special emissary's visit in the instructions for the May 20, 1970, Warsaw talks. Rogers' report to Nixon on March 10 stated the Department's position. On March 17, Marshall Green, Assistant Secretary for East Asian and Pacific Affairs, pressed Kissinger for resolution of the bilateral issues.

34. Nixon, *US Foreign Policy for the 1970s: The Emerging Structure for Peace*, pp. 33–34.

35. Kissinger, *White House Years*, pp. 746–47, 773–74. Rogers' push of the dual representation formula prior to Nixon's trip did not jeopardize it; p. 1062, Kissinger's reports Mao's concern with the USSR, not Taiwan; pp. 1073–74, he reports Chou treated Vietnam in the context of long-term Soviet expansion in South East Asia.

36. Ibid., pp. 781–83. It was negotiated during Kissinger's second trip to Peking in October 1971, but Nixon had seen and approved Kissinger's draft, pp. 1082–84, Rogers was shown the Communique the last minute because Nixon fearing leaks vetoed Kissinger's suggestion to include Green on the negotiating team.

37. *Presidential Documents*, vol. 8, no. 9 (February 28, 1972), p. 475.

38. Kissinger, *White House Years*, pp. 781–83.

39. Ibid., pp. 1085–7. *Years of Upheaval*, pp. 60–63. Discussion of Chou proposal for Liaison Offices.

40. Kissinger, *For The Record: Selected Statements 1977–1980*, (Boston: Little, Brown, 1981), p. 270. *Observations: Selected Speeches and Essays 1982–1984* (Boston: Little, Brown, 1985), p. 144.

41. Kissinger, *Observations*, pp. 145–46.
42. Ibid., p. 149. On technology transfer he gave the PRC the same status as India and Yugoslavia.
43. Ibid., p. 146. *For The Record*, p. 270. "The Rearming of Japan – and the Rest of Asia," *The Washington Post* (January 29, 1987), p. A25. He states that the Soviet threat to Asia equals that to Europe and notes common US-PRC interests.
44. Kissinger, *Observations*, pp. 146–48.
45. Landau, *Kissinger*, pp. 104–5. He states that the Nixon-Kissinger policy was geared primarily to the behavior of the USSR. Mazlish, *Kissinger*, p. 234. Stoessinger, *Henry Kissinger*, p. 214.
46. Nixon, *US Foreign Policy for the 1970s: Building for Peace*, p. 157. Nutter, *Kissinger's Grand Design*, p. 15. He states: Kissinger never altered his view that the transformation of Soviet society will be a slow evolutionary process essentially beyond the influence of outside pressure.
47. *State Bulletin*, vol. 70, no. 1814 (April 1, 1974), p. 323. Stoessinger, *Henry Kissinger*, p. 81. Morris, *Uncertain Greatness*, p. 210. He claims, Kissinger's vision of détente was clear and premeditated as were Nixon's political instincts on the subject.
48. Kissinger, *White House Years*, p. 1254. *Years of Upheaval*, pp. 245, 982.
49. *State Department Bulletin*, no. 1547 (February 17, 1969), p. 143. Nixon's news conference on January 27, 1969, explaining why he supported sufficiency. Mazlish, *Kissinger*, p. 236. Brown, *The Faces of Power*, p. 337.
50. Nixon, *US Foreign Policy for the 1970s: Building for Peace*, pp. 170–71.
51. Ibid.
52. Kissinger, *White House Years*, pp. 216–17.
53. Nixon, *US Foreign Policy for the 1970s: The Emerging Structure of Peace*, p. 158.
54. Kissinger, *White House Years*, p. 217.
55. Kissinger, *White House Years*, pp. 198, 204; pp. 535, 539–40, for NSC meeting on March 25, 1970, where Rogers and Smith opposed both the ABM and MIRV programs; Laird, Packard, and General Wheeler supported MIRVs but were lukewarm on ABM. *Years of Upheaval*, pp. 237, 273–74; p. 1002–4 for his support for Trident, B-1, and the cruise missile.
56. Nixon, *US Foreign Policy for the 1970s: Building for Peace*, p. 174. Kissinger, *White House Years*, p. 202.
57. Kissinger, *White House Years*, pp. 211–12, 535.
58. Ibid., 1143.
59. Nixon, *US Foreign Policy for the 1970s: The Emerging Structure of Peace*, p. 158.
60. Kissinger, *Years of Upheaval*, pp. 259, 262, 1009–10, 1015.

61. Stoessinger, *Henry Kissinger*, p. 82; Mazlish, *Kissinger*, p. 235. He states: on the issue of SALT it seems to have been Kissinger who moved Nixon around to favoring it.

62. Graubard, *Kissinger*, p. 274. He states that "Kissinger's object was to secure a stable international order. That purpose transcended all others; in his mind, it was the necessary precondition of peace." Stoessinger, *Henry Kissinger*, pp. 36–37, 45.

63. Kissinger, *White House Years*, p. 127, Kissinger expressed this view to Boris Sedov on December 18, 1968 at the Pierre Hotel; p. 135, at the NSC meeting on January 25; pp. 132–33, in a backgrounder on February 6; and p. 141, in his memo to Nixon before the Nixon/Dobrynin meeting on February 17; pp. 802–4, Kissinger proposal to Nixon to link Berlin to SALT and telling Dobrynin about it on January 2 and 23, 1971.

64. Ibid., pp. 133–35 for pressures on Nixon; pp. 136–38, for efforts by Rogers and Smith to push Nixon into talks by public statements and leaks.

65. Ibid., pp. 138, 145, 147.

66. Ibid., p. 541, for options presented to NSC on April 8, 1970; pp. 546, 1486, the initiative for negotiating a freeze on offensive weapons originated in the Pentagon in a memorandum from Deputy Secretary David Packard in October 1970. See also, *Years of Upheaval*, pp. 259–60. Nixon, *US Foreign Policy for the 1970s: Building for Peace*, p. 176.

67. Kissinger, *White House Years*, p. 128; p. 143, Kissinger's memo to Nixon on February 18, 1969, reflects views on simultaniety.

68. Ibid., pp. 535, 813.

69. Ibid., pp. 552–54, 556, Kissinger admits that Nixon's summit idea led to major disagreement between them but he discussed the idea with Dobrynin.

70. Ibid., p. 536.

71. Ibid., pp. 548–49, 815.

72. Kissinger, *Years of Upheaval*, p. 1010.

73. Kissinger, *White House Years*, pp. 817–18, Soviet efforts to exploit the two channels; pp. 819–21, for moves leading to the breakthrough and its announcement on May 20.

74. Ibid., pp. 1216, 1219.

75. *State Bulletin*, vol. 66 (June 26, 1972), pp. 918–20.

76. *State Bulletin*, vol. 71 (July 29, 1974), pp. 216–17.

77. Kissinger, *Years of Upheaval*, pp. 1165–66.

78. *State Bulletin*, vol. 66 (June 26, 1972), pp. 920–21.

79. Kissinger, *White House Years*, pp. 1244–45; pp. 1232–33, for impact of Johnson's decisions on SALT. *Years of Upheaval*, pp. 268, 1007, 1012–13.

80. Kissinger, *Years of Upheaval*, pp. 1007–9, 1026.

81. Morris, *Uncertain Greatness*, p. 212.

82. Nixon, *US Foreign Policy for the 1970s: The Emerging Structure of Peace*, p. 175. These agreements had been worked out in parallel with the main arms negotiations. Dickson, *Kissinger and the Meaning of History*, pp. 130–32. He argues US policy toward the PRC as a version of power politics, not the so called "linkage" policy, was the prime factor accounting for Kissinger's success with the Soviets at the negotiating table.

83. Kissinger, *Years of Upheaval*, pp. 264–65; see his note on the strategic significance of equal aggregates.

84. Ibid., pp. 265, 270, 1012.

85. Ibid., p. 265; p. 267; for Departmental positions at the Verification Panel (VP) meetings in February and March 1973; p. 270, for their positions in the VP meetings on April 25, 27, and 30.

86. Ibid., pp. 1013, 1015, 1026–27.

87. Ibid., pp. 1011–12, 1016.

88. Ibid., pp. 273, 1002–5.

89. Ibid., p. 271.

90. Ibid., pp. 1018–20, 1016. Nixon approved it at the end of the meeting and Kissinger proposed it to Moscow through Dobrynin in an oral note prior to his visit on March 24.

91. Ibid., pp. 1022–25, 1153. Brezhnev proposed 1100 MIRVed launchers for the US and 1000 for the USSR which Kissinger found unacceptable.

92. Ibid., pp. 1017–18, for the agencies' preferred options; pp. 1027–28, 1154–59, for Schlesinger's views on equal aggregates and Kissinger's admission that differences with Schlesinger "were more personal than intellectual."

93. Kissinger, *For the Record*, pp. 193, 209.

94. Ibid., pp. 193–94; see also pp. 279, 295.

95. Ibid., p. 202.

96. Ibid., p. 198.

97. Ibid., pp. 281–82; pp. 290–91, 218–19, he criticized the Vienna summit for not focusing on the key issue of Soviet political restraint.

98. Ibid., pp. 205, 211, 226. *Years of Upheaval*, pp. 261. He argued that Carter's actions did not speed up SALT negotiations or improve the treaty's terms.

99. Kissinger, *For the Record* pp. 201, 280.

100. Ibid., pp. 224, 226; he stated that the new defense program must accelerate the development of a counterforce capability, i.e., MX, Trident II, TNF, and forces for regional defense, especially the modernization and expansion of the Navy.

101. Kissinger, *Observations*, pp. 38–40, 66.

102. Kissinger, "Kissinger: How to Deal With Gorbachev," *Newsweek* (March 2, 1987), pp. 47, 42.

103. *The Washington Post* (19 January 1988). Kissinger, "The Dangers Ahead," *Newsweek* (December 21, 1987), pp. 34–36, and "Kissinger:

How to Deal With Gorbachev," pp. 42, 47. He urged ratification of INF to maintain the unity of NATO.

104. Kissinger, *Years of Upheaval*, p. 1010. *For the Record*, pp. 217, 272.
105. Kissinger, *White House Years*, p. 1132. He states that one reason for pursuing the Soviet proposal was that similar principles were included in the Shanghai Communique.
106. Ibid., pp. 1131–32. He stalled by asking Dobrynin for a draft on February 7 and March 9, when Dobrynin reiterated his proposal. He responded on March 17 (after the Peking summit) to preclude the impression of a US-Soviet condominium that could have undermined the opening to Peking.
107. Ibid., pp. 1150–51, This was a counterdraft to a Soviet counterdraft, to Kissinger's original draft; pp. 1205, 1209, the Agreement surfaced by Gromyko at the summit, on Kissinger's suggestion to Brezhnev to avoid a controversy with Rogers. Nixon repeated the suggestion to Brezhnev.
108. *State Bulletin*, vol. 66 (June 26, 1972), pp. 898–99.
109. Ibid.
110. Kissinger, *Years of Upheaval*, pp. 274–75, 286. *White House Years*, p. 1251. Brezhnev reiterated his proposal to Nixon at the Moscow summit.
111. Kissinger, *Years of Upheaval*, pp. 275–78. Dobryning gave Kissinger the first draft on May 12, and the second on July 21, 1972.
112. *State Bulletin*, vol. 69, no. 1778 (July 23, 1973), pp. 160–61.
113. Kissinger, *Years of Upheaval*, pp. 284–85. He had made the same point in a Nixon letter to Brezhnev on June 7.
114. Ibid., pp. 277–79, 282–83. Those were stated in his paper to Dobrynin on September 7, 1972; repeated to Brezhnev by Kissinger during his September 1972 visit to Moscow; reiterated in the draft given to Gromyko in Washington on October 2, and appeared on the US draft, completed by Sir Thomas Brimelow, a British Soviet expert of the Foreign Office, given by Kissinger to Brezhnev at Zavidovo in May 1973.
115. Ibid., p. 285.
116. Kissinger, *White House Years*, pp. 152–53. He states that Nixon offered Dobrynin increased trade for help in Vietnam. pp 1151–52. Kissinger repeated this to Brezhnev during his secret trip to Moscow on April 1972.
117. Ibid., p. 1133. Gromyko raised the issue with Nixon in their meeting in September 1971. Dobrynin proposed an exchange of visits by Cabinet officers responsible for trade.
118. Ibid., pp. 153–54. The other requests were for materials for a foundry at a new truck plant and for the sale of 15 million tons of corn.
119. Ibid., pp. 154–55. In July 1969 he stopped Commerce from announcing decontrol of 30 items for export to the USSR and Eastern Europe. In October he rejected a joint State/Commerce request for a sale

of computers to the USSR and the request of Commerce Secretary Maurice Stans to decontrol 135 items. Their success would have ended Kissinger's use of trade to restrain Soviet intransigence.

120. Ibid., pp. 1133–34, 1269–70. *Years of Upheaval*, p. 248. For the Kissinger/Butz controvercy over control of trade. Hersh *The Price of Power*, pp. 335, 343. He discusses the linkage between SALT and grain.
121. Kissinger, *White House Years*, pp. 840, 153–54.
122. Ibid., p. 1151–52.
123. Ibid., pp. 1269–71; pp. 1213–14, at summit Nixon links trade and credit to SALT.
124. *State Bulletin*, vol. 66 (June 26, 1972), pp. 898–99. Article 8 dealt with cooperation in science and technology.
125. Kissinger, *White House Years*, pp. 1271–72. Nixon, *US Foreign Policy for the 1970s: Shaping A Durable Peace*, pp. 34–35 for specifics of those and other agreements. Garthoff, *Détente and Confrontation*, p. 307.
126. Morris, *Uncertain Greatness*, pp. 283–84. He states that détente was not the cause of the disarray of the American domestic food market and skyrocketing grocery prices.
127. Stoessinger, *Henry Kissinger*, p. 100.
128. Kissinger, *Years of Upheaval*, pp. 250, 986–87. The Kissinger/Jackson controversy over the trade/emigration issue, originating on October 4, 1972 in response to a Soviet education "exit tax" on emigration, brought the critics of détente together and by 1974 led to the introduction of other amendments in various trade bills explicitly linking trade to emigration. Garthoff, *Détente and Confrontation*, pp. 453–63. For discussion of the evolution of the Kissinger/Jackson controversy.
129. Kissinger, "The Trade Reform Act," *State Bulletin*, vol. 70, no. 1814 (April 1, 1974), pp. 323–24.
130. Kissinger, "Détente with the Soviet Union: The Reality of Competition and the Imperative of Cooperation," *State Bulletin*, vol. 71, no. 1842 (October 14, 1974), pp. 511–12. *Years of Upheaval*, pp. 254, 986–89. Garthoff, *Détente and Confrontation*, pp. 453–63.
131. Kissinger, *Years of Upheaval*, pp. 252, 994–96. For the Kissinger talks with Gromyko and Dobrynin that led to the 45 000 target.
132. Kissinger, *For the Record*, p. 152.
133. Kissinger, *Observations*, pp. 223, 45–46, 121, 85.
134. Ibid., p. 120. *For the Record*, pp. 40–41.
135. Kissinger, *For the Record*, pp. 40–41. *Observations*, p. 45.
136. Kissinger, *Observations*, pp. 43, 45, 120–21, 85–86.
137. Kissinger, *For the Record*, pp. 41–42. *Observations*, pp. 46–47.
138. Kissinger, *White House Years*, p. 594, He referred specifically to Jordan, Cienfuegos and Chile. pp. 640–41. He discusses the Soviet strategy of ambiguity in the context of Cienfuegos.

139. Ibid., p. 789. *Years of Upheaval*, pp. 118–19, 123, 168, 242, 980–81, discusses USSR's ambiguous challenge.
140. Kissinger, *White House Years*, pp. 594, 599–600, 605–6, 608–9, 611–12, 615–19, 623, 625, 627, 630–31. Here he discussed moves for deterring Moscow.
141. Ibid., pp. 626, 629–30. For debates in the NSC meetings on September 21 and 23, see pp. 598–99, 602, 607–8, 625–26.
142. Ibid., pp. 596–97, 604, 617. For his and Nixon's views on credibility.
143. Nixon, *US Foreign Policy for the 1970s: Building for Peace*, p. 19.
144. Kissinger, *White House Years*, p. 641. Garthoff, *Détente and Confrontation*, pp. 76–83.
145. Kissinger, *White House Years*, pp. 640–41. Rogers proposed to discuss the issue with Gromyko in late October at the UN; p. 642, he maintained Nixon feared confrontation believing that Cuba had cost him the 1960 election. Nixon, *The Memoirs of Richard Nixon*, p. 487. He discusses Rogers' recommendation.
146. Kissinger, *White House Years*, pp. 645–52. For his negotiations with Dobrynin. Nixon, *The Memoirs of Richard Nixon*, pp. 487–89.
147. Kissinger, *Years of Upheaval*, p. 470, he told Haig "we had better be tough as nails." p. 536, Nixon agreed stating: "we can't allow a Soviet-supported operation to succeed against an American-supported operation. If it does, our credibility everywhere is severely shaken." See also, pp. 508, 521, 468.
148. Ibid., p. 493.
149. Ibid., pp. 455, 470, 584. Quandt, *Decade of Decisions*, p. 197.
150. Kissinger, *Years of Upheaval*, pp. 455, 475, On October 6, he asked General Scowcroft before the WSAG meeting for plans about the movement of the 6th Fleet and its reinforcement.
151. Ibid., pp. 478–81, 493–95, for debate in WSAG regarding military aid to Israel on October 6 and 9; p. 512, Kissinger decides on all-out airlift; p. 529, October 14, WSAG settled problems with an all-out US airlift of arms to Israel; pp. 501, 514, for demand of resignations. Nixon, *The Memoirs of Richard Nixon*, pp. 924, 927.
152. Quandt, *Decade of Decisions*, p. 197. Nixon, *The Memoirs of Richard Nixon*, pp. 938–39.
153. Kissinger, *Years of Upheaval*, p. 583, Text of Brezhnev's note; pp. 579–80, Discussion of Sadat's request; pp. 587–9, for specific moves regarding US forces.
154. Ibid., pp. 580, 587, 592.
155. *State Bulletin*, vol. 69, no. 1788 (October 29, 1973), p. 529.
156. Garthoff, *Détente and Confrontation*, pp. 509–10.
157. Ibid., p. 520. *State Bulletin*, vol. 73 (December 1, 1975), p. 768, and vol. 74 (February 23, 1976), pp. 219, 213.
158. *State Bulletin*, vol. 74 (January 19, 1976), p. 69, and (February 2, 1976), p. 125. Garthoff, *Détente and Confrontation*, pp. 521–22.
159. *State Bulletin*, vol. 74 (March 8, 1976), pp. 288, 289, and (March

1, 1976), p. 260. See also vol. 74 (February 23, 1976), p. 209, and (February 2, 1976), p. 128.
160. *State Bulletin*, vol. 74 (February 16, 1976), pp. 175, 179.
161. *State Bulletin*, vol. 74 (February 23, 1976), p. 209. Kissinger, *For the Record*, pp. 141, 284. Garthoff, *Détente and Confrontation*, pp. 519–26.
162. Kissinger, *For the Record*, p. 75.
163. Ibid., p. 136.
164. Ibid., pp. 284, 265, 217; *Observations*, pp. 115, 185.
165. Kissinger, *For the Record*, pp. 218–19, 290–91. He criticized the Vienna summit for not dealing with the key issue of political restraint.
166. Kissinger, *Observations*, p. 147.
167. Ibid., pp. 185, 115. *For the Record, pp. 194, 218–19, 223.*
168. Kissinger, *For the Record*, pp. 223–24, 228–29. He outlined a criteria of acceptable political conduct and urged that the President be required to submit an annual report to the Senate indicating the degree to which Moscow meets it and that the Senate vote every two years its judgment whether Moscow observes the criteria. If it does not the Senate must vote on whether SALT should continue.

Chapter 9: Brzezinski and the Adversaries: The USSR and the PRC

1. Brzezinski, *Power and Principle*, pp. 146–47.
2. Ibid., pp. 81, 151.
3. Carter, "A Foreign Policy Based on America's Essential Character," Notre Dame University address, *State Bulletin*, vol. 76 (June 13, 1977), pp. 621–25. Also in *State Bulletin* by Carter, "Peace, Arms Control, World Economic Progress, Human Rights: Basic Priorities of US Foreign Policy," Address to UN on March 17, vol. 76 (April 11, 1977), pp. 329–33. Pan American Day Address on April 14, vol. 76 (May 9, 1977), pp. 453–57. Speech at Charleston, S.C. on July 21, vol. 77 (August 15, 1977), pp. 193–97.
4. Carter, "Peace, Arms Control, World Economic Progress, Human Rights," p. 329. Noting the US military strength, Carter declared: "we hope never to use again," p. 330, Carter offered US help to resolve conflicts among nations but stressed: "we cannot do so by imposing our own particular solutions." Address at the Commencement Exercises on the US Naval Academy, *Presidential Documents*, vol. 14 (June 7, 1978), pp. 1052–53, 1054. Brzezinski, *Power and Principle*, p. 147, he notes his disputes with Vance over the insertion of the terms reciprocal and comprehensive in Carter's speeches to describe détente. Vance, *Hard Choices*, pp. 441–42, Appendix I, for Vance's memo to Carter on October 1976 on the foreign policy issues and positions.
5. Address at Wake Forest University, *Presidential Documents*, vol. 14

(March 24, 1978), pp. 531–35. Garthoff, *Détente and Confrontation*, pp. 593–94. Vance commented on a draft but did not see the final version until it was delivered. Brzezinski, *Power and Principle*, pp. 188–89. He notes the speech was "a good one and set us on the right course," but did not make up for the lack of determination to oppose Moscow in the Horn.

6. Address at the Commencement Exercises on the US Naval Academy, *Presidential Documents*, vol. 14 (June 7, 1978), pp. 1052–53, 1057.

7. Brzezinski, *Power and Principle*, pp. 320–21.

8. Sapin, "What Every New Administration Should Know About Foreign Policy," p. 66. He notes the absence of a strategy toward the USSR and that Brzezinski's views of the USSR never won Carter's full acceptance.

9. Hoffmann, "Muscle and Brains," *Foreign Policy*, 37 (Winter 1979–80), pp. 3–4. Jordan, *Crisis*, p. 48. He states when Vance and Brzezinski differed on Soviet policy Carter sided with Cy three out of four times. Sapin, "What Every New Administration Should Know About Foreign Policy," pp. 71–73. He notes changes in Carter's original initiatives and failure to communicate a coherent and consistent foreign policy.

10. Brzezinski, *Power and Principle*, pp. 151–53, describes Vance's draft as "a little too eager and too gushy." He made the suggestions directly to Carter and to Vance. Carter, *Keeping Faith*, pp. 216–18, on the first letter to Brezhnev and decision to limit knowledge of private letters to himself, Mondale, Vance and Brzezinski despite attacks on secret diplomacy. Sapin, "What Every New Administration Should Know About Foreign Policy," pp. 51, 66. He notes: Carter's original approach toward Moscow was personalist and naïvely optimistic.

11. Carter, "US Interests and Ideals," *State Bulletin*, vol. 80 (June 1980), p. 7.

12. Carter, State of the Union Message, *State Bulletin*, vol. 80 (February 1980), p. H. See also State of the Union Address, where Carter declared: "I am determined that the United States will remain the strongest of all nations . . . ," p. A. Carter, "US Interests and Ideals," *State Bulletin*, vol. 80 (June , 1980) p. 5. Carter, "National Security Goals," *State Bulletin*, vol. 80 (March 1980), p. A.

13. Carter, State of the Union Message, *State Bulletin*, vol. 80 (February 1980), pp. G–H.

14. Carter, State of the Union Address, *State Bulletin*, vol. 80 (February 1980), p. B.

15. Carter, "US Interests and Ideals," p. 7.

16. Brown, *The Faces of Power*, p. 552.

17. Brzezinski, *Power and Principle*, pp. 177–78, 335. Robert G. Kaiser, "Disputed Memo Assesses US Soviet Strength." *The Washington Post* (July 6, 1977). Charles Mohr, "Carter Orders Steps to Increase Ability to Meet War Threats: Secret Directive on Strategy." *The New York Times* (August 26, 1977).

18. Brzezinski, *Power and Principle*, p. 333. For him the Air Force's hardened tunnels proposal raised problems of verifiability. In 1978 the DOD's multiple aim point basing mode was opposed by the SALT negotiating team and rejected by Moscow; pp. 333–34, Brzezinski, favoring a ground mobile system, rejected Brown's proposal for an air mobile system and urged Carter to ask for a good analysis of the ground-based mobile system.

19. Ibid., p. 334, Carter told Brzezinski he was jamming the decision down his throat; pp. 334–35, Brown assures Carter the US needs the triad but does not strongly support the new missile; p. 335, Vance questioned at the June 4, 1979 NSC meeting, dealing with strategic arms policy and US-Soviet relations, Brzezinski's claim that the US would face a "strategic dip" in the 1980s; p. 336, Carter critical of Brzezinski for stressing Soviet superiority. Smith, *Morality, Reason and Power*, pp. 83–84.

20. Brzezinski, *Power and Principle*, p. 336, he opposed the development of a smaller common missile suited to both ground and sea based deployment; p. 337, Vance's and Christopher's support for the MX facilitated Carter's decision; pp. 337–38, he urged the appointment of General George Seignious to replace Warnke as ACDA Director in 1979 and he supported the MX. Vance, *Hard Choices*, pp. 137–38, on Carter's approval of the MX and his own decision to support it in order to reassure the JCS and Congressional opponents and redress the theoretical vulnerability of US ICBMs. Carter, *Keeping Faith*, p. 241, on difficulties with MX deployment.

21. Brzezinski, *Power and Principle*, pp. 455–56.

22. Ibid., pp. 455, 459, on Soviet war-fighting capabilities; pp. 456–57, for specifics of PDs in 1978, 1979, and 1980; p. 459, for PD-59 issued in July 1980. It expanded strategic flexibility beyond the existing options by placing greater targeting emphasis on military targets, on C3I, and on Soviet war-supporting industries. C3I was treated as a broader requirement, for control of both strategic and conventional forces in a protracted conflict, and it called for a "look-shoot-look" capability for identifying new and moving targets. The Secure Reserve Force was to be increased for influencing military campaigns, not only for psychological coercion, and acquisition policy was tied to employment policy for the first time. Garthoff, *Détente and Confrontation*, pp. 789–90, notes the Brzezinski/Brown collaboration on PD-59, but argues that while Brown emphasized concepts and capabilities for countervailing deterrence, Brzezinski stressed war-fighting concepts and capabilities in support of deterrence.

23. Brzezinski, *Game Plan: How to Conduct the US-Soviet Contest* (Boston: The Atlantic Monthly Press, 1986), pp. 246–47, 102, 256–57, 100; pp. 244, 190, on maintaining the military balance. See also, "America's New Geostrategy," *Foreign Affairs* (Spring 1988), pp. 682, 694.

24. Brzezinski, *Game Plan*, pp. 100, 256, on protracted competition;

p. 100, on centrality of military power; p. 259, for him the US must maintain a military capability sufficient to: (a) preclude Soviet blackmail of strategic US friends and allies; (b) block direct and indirect Soviet expansionism; (c) eliminate Soviet certainty of quick conventional victory on Eurasia's three strategic fronts and increase the uncertainty about US nuclear escalation; (d) counter the Soviet war-fighting capability at all levels of nuclear escalation; and (e) maintain a secure second-strike capability; pp. 191–93, on the integrated strategic framework. See also, "America's New Geostrategy," p. 684, where he argues that "space control is likely to become tantamount to earth control"; pp. 683–86, on the need for a flexible mix of nuclear and conventional forces.

25. Brzezinski, *Game Plan*, p. 261, specific proposals for mutual strategic security; pp. 261–62, specifics for global conventional flexibility; pp. 185, 262, on SDI; p. 263, on objectives of an integrated strategy; p. 164, on imperative for limited strategic defense; pp. 167–68, on the ABM treaty; pp. 161–62, on the prudent mix of strategic forces.

26. Brzezinski, "America's New Geostrategy," pp. 694, 699. *Game Plan*, pp. 141, 259.

27. Brzezinski, *Power and Principle*, pp. 146–47; pp. 171, 173, for other issues he linked to SALT; pp. 185–86, March 2 SCC meeting and dispute with Vance over linkage, and March 3 memo insisting on comprehensive and reciprocal détente. Vance, *Hard Choices*, p. 45; pp. 445–46, Appendix I; pp, 99–100, 102, on differences on SALT and his rejection of linkage. Carter, *Keeping Faith*, pp. 212–13, his hopes for SALT; pp. 214, 220, his rejection of linkage.

28. Brzezinski, News Conference, *State Bulletin*, vol. 76 (April 25, 1977), pp. 415, the SALT proposal was linked to limiting the superpower military presence in the Indian Ocean and conventional arms transfers to third parties, talks about a CTB, controls on antisatellite capabilities, etc. Brzezinski, *Power and Principle*, pp. 171, 173. His July 1977 report to Carter on US initiatives to make détente comprehensive.

29. Brzezinski, *Power and Principle*, p. 158.

30. Ibid., p. 160, on his insistence on standing firm; p. 159, for specifics of SALT options considered by NSC. He disputes the thesis that he and Brown foisted the deep-cuts option on Carter. Vance, *Hard Choices*, pp. 48–49, he preferred the option based on Vladivostok since it would have led to an early agreement.

31. Brzezinski, *Power and Principle*, p. 162.

32. Ibid., p. 167 Jordan's role; pp. 168–70 for Vance's and Warnke's views; p. 172, Vance's memo on steps to "stabilize" US-Soviet relations; p. 173, Brzezinski cover memo rejecting Vance's suggestions.

33. Brzezinski, News Conference, *State Bulletin*, vol. 76 (April 25, 1977), pp. 415–16, on the impact of the ICBM freeze on the Soviet and US strategic programs. See also Carter's UN speech, vol. 76 (April 11 1977), p. 331, and Charleston speech, vol. 77 (August 15, 1977),

p. 195. Brzezinski, *Power and Principle*, pp. 158–59. On the March 10, 1977 SCC meeting for ICBM freeze, he was supported by Brown. He preferred strategic delivery systems to be reduced approximately to 2000.

34. Brzezinski, *Power and Principle*, pp. 164–65. Prime Minister Callaghan and Chancellor Schmidt, in late spring and early summer, were urging Carter to be more conciliatory; p. 176, for Schmidt's letter to Carter in September 1977 urging conciliation.

35. Ibid., pp. 149–50, his February 1976 memo to Carter (co-authored by Richard Gardner) criticizing Nixon and Kissinger; pp. 152–53, Carter's first letter to Brezhnev expressing hope for a early summit; pp. 165–66 his suggestion for an Alaska meeting as it appeared in Carter's letter to Brezhnev on June 9. Vance, *Hard Choices*, pp. 109, 138, on Carter's desire for an early summit.

36. Brzezinski, *Power and Principle*, pp. 175–76. The Harriman initiative and Vance's November 1977 draft letter to Moscow expressing hope for a summit. Vance *Hard Choices*, pp. 445–46, his October 1976 memo to Carter suggesting that a summit be delayed for six months and that its purpose be to conclude SALT II. Carter, *Keeping Faith*, pp. 232–33, desire for a summit led him to approve Vance's trip to Moscow in September 1978 which he previously opposed.

37. Brzezinski, *Power and Principle*, pp. 340–41, for his advise to Carter and Vance's memo on June 8; p. 341, Carter's push for maximum objectives; pp. 342–43, Carter's tough statement on Soviet activities in Africa, Vietnam and Middle East; p. 344, his assessment of the summit's success. Vance, *Hard Choices*, pp. 138–39, on the "sharp exchange" regarding Moscow's intervention in the Third World. Carter, *Keeping Faith*, pp. 240–41, on desire for maximum goals and the reluctance of advisers to go along; p. 254, Carter's statement regarding Soviet military intervention in the Third World.

38. Brzezinski, Address to the Chicago Council on Foreign Relations. *State Bulletin*, vol. 79 (May 1979), pp. 49–50.

39. Ibid., p. 50.

40. Brzezinski, *Power and Principle*, p. 520, pp. 431–32, on being informed by Carter that ratification will be postponed; pp. 432, 444–45, 448, 459–60, on the importance of emulating Truman.

41. Brzezinski, *Game Plan*, pp. 148, 155, 260. He warns of "Strategic Impotence: The Threat of Arms Control"; p. 246, his criticism of arms control as the central platform of détente; pp. 153–54, on linkage of arms control to geopolitical restraint; pp. 157–58, damage to US-Soviet stability due to Soviet strategic secrecy; pp. 192–93, arms control as an integral part of an effort to deny Moscow a politically decisive military edge.

42. Brzezinski, "After Reykjavik: What Reagan should do," *US News & World Report* (November 3, 1986), pp. 31–32.

43. For Carter's speeches at UN, *State Bulletin*, vol. 76 (April 11, 1977),

pp. 330, 332–33; at OAS, vol. 76 (May 9, 1977), pp. 454, 456; at Notre Dame, vol. 76 (June 13, 1977), pp. 622–23; at Charleston, vol. 77 (August 1977), p. 196.

44. Brzezinski, *Power and Principle*, pp. 149, 188, 162. Vance, *Hard Choices*, p. 46, implicitly confirms Brzezinski's desire to use human rights mainly as an instrument in the political offensive against Moscow. Carter, *Keeping Faith*, pp. 149–50, on using human rights as "a good weapon" in the peaceful struggle for influence.

45. Carter's Charleston speech, *State Bulletin*, vol. 77 (August 15, 1977), p. 196, he stressed human rights was not "aimed specifically at them or is an attack on their vital interests. There are no hidden meanings in our commitment to human rights." Brzezinski, *Power and Principle*, pp. 153–54. Response to Brezhnev's letter of February 4, 1977. Carter, *Keeping Faith*, p. 146, on reassuring Brezhnev and Dobrynin.

46. Brzezinski, *Power and Principle*, pp. 153–54. Vance, *Hard Choices*, p. 46.

47. Brzezinski, *Power and Principle*, p. 156. Vance and Brzezinski drafted response to Sakharov. Carter, *Keeping Faith*, p. 146, on letter to Sakharov.

48. *Presidential Documents*, vol. 14 (June 6, 1978), p. 1054. Brzezinski, *Power and Principle*, pp. 320–21.

49. Brzezinski, *Power and Principle*, p. 188.

50. Ibid., pp. 338–39. For specifics of this initiative. Carter, *Keeping Faith*, pp. 147–49, on prisoner exchange.

51. Brzezinski, *Power and Principle*, pp. 322–23, he states that domestic advisers convinced Carter; p. 323, specific steps of trade restraint.

52. Ibid., p. 323, Carter at foreign policy breakfast tells Vance to drop new trade initiatives; pp. 324–25, August 10, Commerce approved Dresser applications but Carter fearing that Kreps would resign did not want Brzezinski to push the issue.

53. Ibid., pp. 416–18. Carter, *Keeping Faith*, p. 201–2.

54. Brzezinski, "After Reykjavik," p. 31.

55. Brzezinski, *Power and Principle*, pp. 178–79, 181, 186–87. Vance, *Hard Choices*, p. 84, on Brzezinski's view of the issue and their dispute; pp. 73–75, his view of the issue and preferred solution.

56. Brzezinski, *Power and Principle*, pp. 179–78, on warning Dobrynin; p. 180, on briefing the press. In Carter's letter to Brezhnev in late December Brzezinski stressed the need to resolve regional conflicts and avoid direct or indirect involvement in order to improve the US-Soviet relationship; pp. 180–81, on Gromyko's suggestion. Vance, *Hard Choices*, pp. 84–85, on Brzezinski's effort to counter Moscow to maintain credibility; p. 87, he warns Dobrynin.

57. Brzezinski, *Power and Principle*, p. 181, memos to Carter on January 11 and 18. Vance, *Hard Choices*, p. 75, on Brzezinski's desire to increase the cost of Soviet intervention.

58. Brzezinski, *Power and Principle*, pp. 182–83, Vance's and Brown's

Notes to pp. 195–198 339
opposition to the task force proposal. Vance, *Hard Choices*, p. 87, on Brzezinski's proposal and Brown's opposition to it.

59. Brzezinski, *Power and Principle*, p. 184, for January 18 memo and February SCC discusion of technology transfer to PRC.
60. Ibid., pp. 187–88, 560–61, for weekly reports.
61. Ibid., p. 185, Carters statement at the National Press Club. pp. 185–86, Vance rejected the linkage in the SCC meeting on March 2. Vance, *Hard Choices*, pp. 87–88, on Carter's and Brzezinski's linkage of SALT to the Horn. pp. 91–92, his and Brzezinski's views on linking SALT to the Horn.
62. *Presidential Documents*, Wake Forest speech, vol. 14 (March 24, 1978), pp. 531–32. Naval Academy speech, vol. 14 (June 7, 1978), pp. 1054, 1056.
63. Brzezinski, *Power and Principle*, pp. 346–47, on July 4 and August 14 warns Carter about impact on SALT; p. 347, issue not vital so he, Carter and Brown take their vacations; pp. 346–51, Vance's views; p. 349, Vance supported by Mondale and Cutler; pp. 346, 348–52, Brzezinski's links brigade to Soviet and Cuban adventurism; p. 348, he argues for a tougher position but quiet resolution and suggests a way out; p. 350, his September memo urging specific steps; pp. 347–48, Senator Frank Church publicized issue on August 30 after briefing from State; pp. 347–48, discussions on V-B-B meeting and PRC meetings on September 4 and 5; pp. 350–51, he and Brown accused of seeking to revive the cold war. Vance, *Hard Choices*, pp. 358–9, privately in July Senator Richard Stone demands firm action; p. 361, Senators link SALT to brigade and stop hearings on SALT; pp. 362–3, Soviets reject Vance's proposal for unilateral moves; p. 364, on Cuba as an isolated incident; p. 362, claims his demand for withdrawal misperceived; p. 390, military ties with Peking an ineffective counter to the brigade. Carter, *Keeping Faith*, pp. 262–64, his fear of losing SALT.
64. Brzezinski, *Power and Principle*, p. 349, his analogy to the Berlin Wall crisis; pp. 350, 352, seeking to make Carter a Truman-type leader. Vance, *Hard Choices*, pp. 363–64, Vance suggests senior statesmen meeting.
65. Carter, "Soviet Troops in Cuba and SALT," *State Bulletin*, vol. 79 (November 1979), pp. 7–9.
66. Brzezinski, *Power and Principle*, p. 351, on October 4 he tells Carter the address damaged US credibility and Carter implied he was advocating war over Cuba.
67. Ibid., p. 426, at the end of March 1979, with Brown's support, he prevailed on Vance and Christopher to formally register US concern; p. 427, in April, despite opposition from State, with Mondale's support Brzezinski pushed through the SCC a decision to aid the resistance in Afghanistan. On July 23, Carter approved Brzezinski's proposal to publicize an analysis indicating that Moscow would remove PM Hafizullah Amin; Vance opposed it; pp. 426–27, on warning Carter in March, April and May.

68. Ibid., p. 428, for weekly report and State opposition to an NSC proposed press back-grounder on Soviet intervention in Afganistan. On December 17, at an SCC meeting State opposed but Brown and Turner supported Brzezinski's approach.
69. Ibid., p. 429. for SCC and NSC meetings; p. 230, he feared Vance might prevail on Carter to treat Afghanistan as an isolated issue. Carter, *Keeping Faith*, p. 472, message to Brezhnev by the hot line. Vance, *Hard Choices*, p. 388, on his and Brzezinski's views on the situation; Carter's decision to make it costly for Moscow but not link SALT to it. He implies closer US-Soviet relations might have prevented it.
70. Brzezinski, *Power and Principle*, pp. 430–31, for NSC meetings, proposals and objections; p. 433, he supported grain embargo to undermine opposition to stronger controls on technology transfer to the USSR. Also on Mondale's proposal. Carter, *Keeping Faith*, p. 476, on Mondale's opposition to the grain embargo, and State's advocacy for stronger action than Brzezinski; p. 482–83, Mondale and Stu Eizenstat opposed Vance's proposal for draft registration. Vance, *Hard Choices*, p. 391, his views on the draft; p. 393, on lessons of Afghanistan and his commitment to SALT.
71. Carter, Address on the Soviet invasion of Afghanistan, *State Bulletin*, vol. 80 (January 1980), pp. A–B.
72. Carter, State of the Union Address, *State Bulletin*, vol. 80 (February 1980), p. B. Here he announced the boycott of the Olympics.
73. Ibid.
74. *Brzezinski, Power and Principle*, pp. 443–45, on how he generated support for those declarations; p. 445, Vance and Cutler opposed the idea of "a regional security framework" but Jody Powell allowed Brzezinski to pencil it in the final version of the speech; p. 446, February 28, 1979, memo urging Carter to abandon the objective of demilitarizing the Indian Ocean; State was still supporting it. Brzezinski, interview on "Issues and Answers," *State Bulletin*, vol. 80 (June 1980), p. 49. His views of the three central strategic zones.
75. Brzezinski, *Power and Principle*, p. 434, on confidencial meetings and international force proposal; pp. 435–36, Vance proposed a formal Vance-Gromyko meeting, a message to Brezhnev by sending Shulman to Moscow, and a letter to Gromyko discussing neutrality for Pakistan and Iran. Mondale at Brzezinski's urging opposed Vance's proposals. Vance, *Hard Choices*, pp. 394–95, on efforts to reestablish dialogue by meeting Gromyko and sending Shulman to Moscow.
76. Brzezinski, *Game Plan*, pp. 247–50, 267.
77. Ibid., pp. 264–65, 266, 36, 41, 50–51. p. 254, He sees Iran or the combination of Afghanistan and Pakistan as linchpin states on the southwestern front, and argues that the prospects of a Soviet breakthrough are far greater in this region. See also, "America's New Geostrategy," pp. 688–90.
78. Brzezinski, *Game Plan*, pp. 78–79, 90, 255–56, 267; pp. 240–41, 143,

98, he argues that if Central America becomes a contested zone in the US-Soviet contest, it would represent a defeat for the US irrespective of the outcome since it would open-up a fourth central strategic front.

79. Ibid., p. 242. See also, "America's New Geostrategy," pp. 690–92.

80. Brzezinski, *Game Plan*, p. 266.

81. Ibid., p. 264. He sees the Philippines as a linchpin state on the far eastern front. Here he urged cooperation with Japan to resolve the economic causes of the unrest.

82. Brzezinski, *Power and Principle*, p. 199, Vance wanted to visit Peking in August; p. 197, in April PRM-24 was also issued in an effort to define US policy toward the PRC.

83. Vance, *Hard Choices*, pp. 76–77, memo and PRM-24; p. 76 on December 1976 study on normalization and Defense Department push for security links.

84. Brzezinski, *Power and Principle*, pp. 196–98.

85. Vance, *Hard Choices*, pp. 78, 114, on Brzezinski's and Brown's support for "security enhancements" , i.e. exchange of military attaches and access to "dual-use" technology.

86. Carter, Notre Dame Address, *State Bulletin*, vol. 76 (June 13, 1977), p. 625. Brzezinski, *Power and Principle*, p.199.

87. Brzezinski, *Power and Principle*, p. 199, dinner with the head of its Mission in Washington.

88. Ibid., p. 198–99. p. 198, Nixon's five points.

89. Ibid., pp. 199–200, Carter's marginal notes to Brzezinski's memo. pp. 200–201, in PRC meeting considering RPM-24 Brzezinski urged commitment to normalization during Vance's visit and deemphasis on relations with Taiwan. He reiterated those views in a national security briefing in early July before Carter met the US Liaison Mission head in Peking Leonard Woodcock; p. 201, on July 30, in a meeting preparing for Vance's trip Carter decided to go for normalization. Carter, *Keeping Faith*, p. 191, on decision to go slow; pp. 199–200, he credits Nixon for the opening to Peking; Vance, *Hard Choices*, pp. 78–79, on PRC's global role and impact on Moscow.

90. Brzezinski, *Power and Principle*, pp. 202–3. He encouraged the invitation through NSC staffer for Chinese affairs, Michel Oksenberg. Szulc, "Springtime for Carter," p. 180. He argued that Kissinger's backchannel system was functioning again. Carter, *Keeping Faith*, p. 193, on other pressing issues and Vance's demands to control policy toward Peking. Vance, *Hard Choices*, pp. 79, 82, on draft communique to be issued in Peking; p. 77, he states Brzezinski was ready to compromise the security of Taiwan.

91. Brzezinski, *Power and Principle*, pp. 203–4, Vance's position; pp. 205, 207, Carter's concern for Vance's views and Vance's effort to send Mondale to Peking. Vance, *Hard Choices*, pp. 114–15, on opposing Brzezinski's trip and Mondale's desire to go to PRC.

92. Brzezinski, *Power and Principle*, pp. 203–4; pp. 204–6, role of

Mondale and Brown which he argues influenced Carter's decision.
93. Ibid., p. 206.
94. Ibid., pp. 208–9. Vance, *Hard Choices*, pp. 70–71, his opposition to dealing with the issue as "an East-West 'test of strength'"; pp. 90–91, his debate with Brzezinski over Zaire.
95. Brzezinski, *Power and Principle*, Annex I, for instructions in full. pp. 206–7. At the end of April, he, Carter, Vance, and Brown agreed to move toward normalization and on May 12 Carter told him to move in that direction; p. 207, for specific areas where Peking could assist; p. 208, PRC's points were: termination of US relations with Taiwan, removal of all US military personnel and installations from Taiwan, and the abrogation of the US-Taiwan Security Treaty. Carter, *Keeping Faith*, pp. 190–91, 197, for his conditions for normalization.
96. Brzezinski, *Power and Principle*, pp. 211, 216–17, 220, his views regarding the Soviet threat and the PRC's vital world role; pp. 213–14, 217, for views of Shanghai communique.
97. Ibid., pp. 211–12, he hinted that Carter would approve the sale of an infrared scanning system; pp. 406–7, his note to Carter during talks with Deng urging reiteration of the areas in which to cooperate.
98. Ibid., pp. 213–14, 218. He repeatedly stated that the "US has made up its mind on this issue."
99. Ibid., pp. 212, 216, Hua's views; pp. 214–15, Deng's views; pp. 212, 215, urges an end to anti-American propaganda; p. 214, irritated with Peking's doubts about US will.
100. Ibid., p. 220, declaration on Soviet threat on *Meet the Press*. pp. 220–22, on disputes with Carter and Vance.
101. Ibid., pp. 223–24. pp. 207, 223, on preferred timing for normalization. Vance, *Hard Choices*, p. 116, on timing of normalization. Carter, *Keeping Faith*, p, 194, on combining SALT and normalization.
102. Brzezinski, *Power and Principle*, pp. 213–14; only NSC Chinese expert Oksenberg and Ambassador Woodcock were present. Richard Holbrooke from State protested his exclusion.
103. Ibid., pp. 223–25. PDB was available only to Carter, Mondale, Vance, Brown, and Brzezinski. Vance, *Hard Choices*, p. 117, he and Holbrooke suggested the use of White House system.
104. Carter, *Keeping Faith*, pp. 197, 199, on the need for secrecy. Vance, *Hard Choices*, pp. 118–19, suggestion to consult Congress.
105. Brzezinski, *Power and Principle*, p. 215, he offered Deng a reciprocal dinner in his home in Washington. pp. 227–28, consultation with Zemin. Carter, *Keeping Faith*, p. 198, invitation to Deng Xiaoping.
106. Brzezinski, *Power and Principle*, pp. 228–29, Vietnam and arms to Taiwan; pp. 230–31, invitation to Deng; pp. 416–17, State's efforts to normalize relations with Vietnam. Vance, *Hard Choices*, pp. 122–23, on benefits of relations with Vietnam.
107. Brzezinski, *Power and Principle*, pp. 408–10, Deng informs Carter about his plans. Carter, *Keeping Faith*, pp. 206, 208–9, his response

to Deng's revelation.

108. Brzezinski, *Power and Principle*, p. 412, pp. 409–10, Brzezinski's concerns with Peking's military action; pp. 411–12, his proposed response; p. 412, NSC meeting; p. 414, Carter's advisers agreed to warn Moscow that a military presence in Cam Ranh Bay would lead to a reevaluation of the US security position in the Far East; an implicit step toward a wider US-PRC relationship. Vance, *Hard Choices*, pp. 121–22.

109. Brzezinski, *Power and Principle*, pp. 413–14, State opposed Blumenthal's trip at SCC meeting. When Blumenthal in Peking condemned PRC's actions, Brzezinski, instructed him to concentrate entirely on trade.

110. Ibid., p. 414.

111. Ibid., pp. 407–8, dispute over communique and final statement. Vance, *Hard Choices*, pp. 110–12, he argues that Soviet inflexibility in the winter of 1978–79 was due primarily to the manner and timing of the announcement of US-PRC normalization, and especially the use of the term "hegemony" in the communique.

112. Brzezinski, *Power and Principle*, pp. 415–16, MFN debate.

113. Ibid., pp. 417–18. p. 418, Mondale's personal appeal to Vance to propose MFN status for the PRC. Carter, *Keeping Faith*, p. 202, he preferred to grant MFN status to both states simultaneously.

114. Brzezinski, *Power and Principle*, p. 420, in January 1979, Carter informally at Guadeloupe hinted to the leaders of France, Britain and FRG that he was not unhappy with a more relaxed Western attitude regarding Chinese arms purchases; p. 421, sale of technology to PRC; pp. 431, 433, Vance opposed technology transfer; Vance, *Hard Choices*, pp. 113–14, his views on allied arms sales to Peking; p. 114, on Carter's go ahead to President Giscard d'Estaing in January 1978; p. 390, on his opposition to "dual-use" technology transfer.

115. Brzezinski, *Power and Principle*, pp. 421–23, debate over Brown's visit. Vance, *Hard Choices*, pp. 390–91, on opposition to Brown's trip.

116. Brzezinski, *Power and Principle*, p. 424, specific steps taken by State and Commerce. The head of the PRC's Military Commission Vice-Premier Geng Biao visited Washington in May 1980 and in September high-level Pentagon officials visited Peking; p. 431, his proposal to expand the US-PRC security relashionship. Vance, *Hard Choices*, pp. 390–91, Carter's decision to give military technology to PRC.

117. Brzezinski, *Game Plan*, pp. 211–12.

118. Ibid., pp. 264, 196, 216.

Chapter 10: Kissinger and the Allies: Seeking a Common Policy

1. Nixon, *US Foreign Policy for the 1970s: A New Strategy for Peace*, p. 28.
2. Nixon, *US Foreign Policy for the 1970s: Building for Peace*, pp. 25, 7, 12.
3. *Presidential Documents*. pp. 544–56. Nixon's statements in Guam on July 25, 1969. Kissinger, *White House Years*, pp. 223–4. For his account of how the Doctrine emerged in his talks with Nixon when preparing for the Asian trip in the summer of 1969. Nixon, *The Memoirs of Richard Nixon*, pp. 340–41.
4. Nixon, *US Foreign Policy for the 1970s: A New Strategy for Peace*, p. 6. *US Foreign Policy for the 1970s: Building for Peace*, p. 14.
5. Nixon, *US Foreign Policy for the 1970s: A New Strategy for Peace*, p. 7. Hahn, "The Nixon Doctrine: Design and Dilemmas," *ORBIS* 2 (Summer 1972), p. 370.
6. Nixon, *US Foreign Policy for the 1970s: Building For Peace*, pp. 12–13.
7. Nixon, *US Foreign Policy for the 1970s: A New Strategy for Peace*, p. 7. *US Foreign Policy for the 1970s: Building for Peace*, p. 13.
8. Nixon, *US Foreign Policy for the 1970s: A New Strategy for Peace*, p. 31; and *US Foreign Policy for the 1970s: Building for Peace*, pp. 24–8.
9. Nixon, *US Foreign Policy for the 1970s: A New Strategy For Peace*, p. 27; and *US Foreign Policy for the 1970s: Building for Peace*, p. 24.
10. Nixon, *US Foreign Policy for the 1970s: A New Strategy for Peace*, p. 8; *US Foreign Policy for the 1970s: Building for Peace*, p. 24. Hahn, "The Nixon Doctrine: Design and Dilemmas," pp. 369–70; and Werner Kaltefleiter, "Europe and the Nixon Doctrine: A German Point of View," *ORBIS* 1 (Spring 1973), pp. 75–77.
11. Nixon, *US Foreign Policy for the 1970s: Building for Peace*, p. 11.
12. Nixon, *US Foreign Policy for the 1970s: A New Strategy for Peace*, p. 31; and *US Foreign Policy for the 1970s: Building for Peace*, pp. 11–12.
13. Nixon, *US Foreign Policy for the 1970s: Building for Peace*, p. 12, 11.
14. Ibid., p. 11.
15. Ibid., p. 39.
16. Ibid., pp. 30, 29. *US Foreign Policy for the 1970s: The Emerging Structure of Peace*, p. 40.
17. Nixon, *US Foreign Policy for the 1970s: Building for Peace*. pp. 12, 26, 28. George Liska, *Beyond Kissinger* (Baltimore: The John Hopkins University Press, 1975), pp. 64–65. Stanley Hoffman, *Primacy and World Order* (New York: McGraw-Hill, 1978), pp. 46–48.

18. Kissinger, *White House Years*, pp. 381–82. It was written in March 1970.
19. Nixon, *US Foreign Policy for the 1970s: Building for Peace*, p. 25.
20. Ibid., p. 170.
21. Ibid., pp. 13–14.
22. Nixon, *US Foreign Policy for the 1970s: A New Strategy for Peace*, p. 31.
23. Willy Brandt, *People and Politics: The Years 1960–1975*, trans. J. Maxwell Brownjohn (Boston: Little, Brown and Company, 1978), p. 285. Statement in Washington in April 1970.
24. Kissinger, *White House Years*, pp. 403–4. De Gaulle and British Foreign Secretary Michael Stewart strongly urged Nixon to start SALT. Walter Scheel, leader of the Free Democratic Party (FDP) and later foreign minister, visiting Washington argued: West Europeans no longer feared a US-Soviet condominium. Smart, "Perspectives from Europe," p. 189.
25. Kissinger, *White House Years*, pp. 404–5. He wrote: Josef Luns, Dutch Foreign Minister said to Nixon that the notion of parity was one of the most shocking propositions that he had ever heard. Chancellor Kiesinger commented that it had come to something of a "thought-provoking" surprise to realize how close the two sides were to equality. The UK representative at the NATO Council questioned whether this was the moment for talks; p. 404, his memo on July 10, 1969, about allied fears regarding SALT.
26. Smart, "Perspectives from Europe," pp. 185, 188.
27. Roger Morgan, *The United States and West Germany 1945–1973* (London: Oxford University Press, 1974), pp. 209–10. J. Robert Schaetzel, *The Unhinged Alliance* (New York: Harper & Row Publishers, 1975), pp. 52–53.
28. Kissinger, *White House Years*, p. 387.
29. The conventional role of the FBS was (and is) a concern of the US that may not have been (or is) equally shared by the Allies who emphasize the nuclear role of the FBS.
30. *State Bulletin*, vol. 66 (June 26, 1972), pp. 918–20; vol. 67 (July 3, 1972), pp. 11–14. The unilateral US interpretation stated: "In regard to this Article [IX] . . . The U.S. side wishes to make clear that the provisions of this Article do not set a precedent for whatever provision may be considered for a treaty on Limiting Strategic Offensive Arms. The question of transfer of strategic offensive arms is a far more complex issue, which may require a different solution."
31. Kissinger, *White House Years*, p. 389. He stated: "not even the possibility of limited cooperation in the nuclear field was excluded." Osgood *et al.*, *Retreat From Empire?* p. 182. Richard H. Ullman, "The Covert French Connection," *Foreign Policy* 75 (Summer 1989):91–92, on Kissinger's offer to Jobert in June 1973 to assist the French nuclear program.

32. Kissinger, *The Troubled Partnership*, p. 166.
33. Nixon, *US Foreign Policy for the 1970s: The Emerging Structure of Peace*, p. 43; and *US Foreign Policy for the 1970s: A New Strategy for Peace*, p. 34.
34. Kissinger, *White House Years*, pp. 1273–74. He wrote: all heads of government sent congratulatory letters "(which may or may not have accorded with their private views)." But influential middle-level officials (the defense ministries and the disarmament sections of the foreign ministries) and publicists expressed a lingering uneasiness, "which reflected in part Europe's inability to articulate its own objectives."
35. Kissinger, *Years of Upheaval*, p. 275. He also feared that it would isolate the PRC.
36. Ibid., pp. 276, 284, 1235. *State Bulletin*, vol. 69 (July 23, 1973), pp. 160–61.
37. Kissinger, *Years of Upheaval*, pp. 275–77; p. 278, he wrote: in the summer of 1972 the major European allies and the PRC were briefed on the Soviet proposal.
38. Ibid., p. 286. He reported that Heath, Brandt (and Bahr) supported the agreement but for reasons of their own did not inform their bureaucracies and that Pompidou had been wary. Also, Cromwell, "Europe and the 'Structure of Peace'," p. 21.
39. Kissinger, *Years of Upheaval*, pp. 278–86. He discussed the British role in drafting the agreement.
40. Ibid., p. 723. *The New York Times*, (December 11, 1973).
41. Kissinger, *Years of Upheaval*, pp. 285–86. *State Bulletin*, vol. 69 (July 23, 1973), pp. 160–61.
42. Kissinger, *White House Years*, p. 386. Memo on April 9, 1969, preparing Nixon for NATO's 20th anniversary celebration in Washington; pp. 391–92, June 17 and August 19, 1969, memos stressing need for improving conventional forces.
43. Wilfrid L. Kohl, "The Nixon-Kissinger Foreign Policy System and U.S.-European Relations: Patterns of Policy Making," *World Politics*, vol. XXVIII, no. 1 (October 1975), pp. 27–28. Leacacos, "Kissinger's Apparat," pp. 25–27.
44. Kissinger, *White House Years*, p. 402. *Years of Upheaval*, p. 134.
45. Nutter, *Kissinger's Grand Design*, p. 13. He stated: despite all the other changes in his thinking, Kissinger has not wavered in his insistence on strong conventional forces to defend Europe. He has steadfastly opposed any reduction in US forces and pressed for a buildup in European military strength.
46. Kissinger, *White House Years*, p. 402. For options discussed see John Yochelson, "The American Military Presence in Europe: Current Debate in the United States," *ORBIS*, XV (Fall 1971), p. 793.
47. *The New York Times* (December 4, 1970), p. 1.
48. Kissinger, *White House Years*, pp. 394–96. He discusses Laird's pro-

posed cuts. p. 396, On September 19 he recommended the creation of the DRPC. Yochelson, "The American Military Presence in Europe," pp. 794–95; *The New York Times*, (December 25, 1970), p. 6; Kohl, "The Nixon-Kissinger Foreign Policy System and U.S.-European Relation," pp. 28–29.

49. Kissinger, *White House Years*, pp. 938–46; he discusses efforts to defeat the May 11, 1971 Amendment to the Draft Extension Act, and the support given by nearly all living former Secretaries of State and Defense, their deputies, former NATO commanders, and Truman and Johnson; pp. 941–42, his rejection of the compromise; Kohl, "The Nixon-Kissinger Foreign Policy System and U.S.-European Relations," p. 29; Kaplan, "NATO and the Nixon Doctrine Ten Years Later," p. 153; for President Johnson's statement see *The New York Times*, (May 13 and 16, 1971).

50. Kissinger, *White House Years*, p. 945, for statements by Brandt and NATO Secretary General Manlio Brosio; pp. 946–47, for impact of Brezhnev's speech. Kohl, "The Nixon-Kissinger Foreign Policy System and U.S.-European Relations," pp. 29–30; Yochelson, "The American Military Presence in Europe," p. 785.

51. Nixon, *US Foreign Policy for the 1970s: Building for Peace*, pp. 35–36.

52. Kissinger, *White House Years*, p. 386. His recommendation on Eurogroup; pp. 400, 402, for view of EDIP. *Years of Upheaval*, pp. 134–35. For specifics of EDIP see Nixon, *US Foreign Policy for the 1970s: The Emerging Structure of Peace*, p. 45; *US Foreign Policy for the 1970s: Shaping A Durable Peace*, p. 83.

53. Nixon, *US Foreign Policy for the 1970s: Building for Peace*, p. 36. EDIP called: "a landmark in the history of NATO – an effort undertaken, organized, and financed entirely by our European allies." *US Foreign Policy for the 1970s: Shaping A Durable Peace*, p. 83.

54. Kissinger, *The Troubled Partnership*, pp. 177–86.

55. Nixon, *US Foreign Policy for the 1970s: A New Strategy For Peace*, pp. 33–34; *US Foreign Policy for the 1970s: Building For Peace*, p. 32; *US Foreign Policy for the 1970s: The Emerging Structure of Peace*, pp. 42–4; *US Foreign Policy for the 1970s: Shaping a Durable Peace*, p. 85.

56. Kissinger, *White House Years*, pp. 218–20. The NPG, created by McNamara to give Europe a voice in nuclear decisions, was composed of four permanent members, US, Britain, FRG, and Italy, and three members rotated at eighteen-month intervals. To maintain independence in nuclear matters France did not participate. Osgood *et al.*, *Retreat From Empire?*, p. 167. Paul Buteux, *The Politics of Nuclear Consultation in NATO 1965–1980* (London: Cambridge University Press, 1983), pp. 110–45.

57. Kissinger, *White House Years*, p. 219. Healey explained the British proposal to Nixon during his visit to London in February 1969. Buteux,

The Politics of Nuclear Consultation in NATO 1965–1980, pp. 223–27. He reports that the US was far more sceptical as to the value of a demonstration option than were the authors of the Anglo-German working paper from which the political guidelines on initial use of tactical nuclear weapons were developed; they, it was reported, favored an earlier and more limited use of nuclear weapons than did the US. *The Times*, London (May 31, 1969).

58. Kissinger, *White House Years*, pp. 587–89. Morris, *Uncertain Greatness*, pp. 247–49.
59. Nixon, *US Foreign Policy for the 1970s: The Emerging Structure of Peace*, pp. 43–44.
60. Kissinger, *Observations*, pp. 34, 172.
61. Ibid., pp. 34–36, 84, 169–72 he hoped that NATO can repel any level of conventional attack by conventional means. "Dealing with Moscow: A New Balance," *The Washington Post* (February 7, 1989); "Arms Control Fever" (January 19, 1988); "The Dangers Ahead," *Newsweek* (December 21, 1987), pp. 34, 36, 41.
62. Kissinger, *Observations*, pp. 203–4, 41.
63. Ibid., pp. 41, 163, 170. "Arms Control Fever," *The Washington Post* (January 19, 1988); "The Dangers Ahead," *Newsweek* (December 21, 1987), pp. 34–35, he called the 50 percent reduction "a fateful step."
64. Kissinger, *Observations*, pp. 207–15, 183, "The Dangers Ahead," pp. 41, 34. He stated that the failure to ratify the INF Treaty "would wreck" NATO. "Dealing with Moscow," *The Washington Post* (February 7, 1989).
65. Kissinger, "Dealing with Moscow," *The Washington Post* (February 7, 1989).
66. Kissinger, *Observations*, p. 215.
67. Kissinger, *White House Years*, p. 87. De Gaulle's terms: (a) a truly independent Western Europe that could play an effective international role requires freedom from NATO which perpetuates US domination. An effective political organization dictates a concert composed of France, Britain, the FRG, and Italy, but its core would be Anglo-French cooperation; (b) this required the replacement of the EEC with a broad, free-trade area especially for agricultural products; (c) to facilitate Anglo-French cooperation de Gaulle was ready to hoid "private" bilateral discussions with Britain on political, economic, monetary, and financial problems; pp. 87–88, for Britain's briefing of other allies. Edward A. Kolodziej, *French International Policy Under de Gaulle and Pompidou* (Ithaca, NY: Cornell University Press, 1974), pp. 401–3.
68. Kissinger, *White House Years*, pp. 88–89. Memo to Nixon on February 22, and his comments to the press on February 21, 1969.
69. Nixon, *US Foreign Policy for the 1970s: A New Strategy for Peace*, p. 32. "The structure of Western Europe itself – the organization of its unity – is fundamentally the concern of the Europeans. We cannot

unify Europe and we do not believe that there is only one road to that goal. When the United States in previous Administrations turned into an ardent advocate, it harmed rather than helped progress." *US Foreign Policy for the 1970s: Building for Peace*, p. 29. Kissinger, *Year of Upheaval*, p. 139.

70. Kissinger, *The Troubled Partnership*, p. 32. He believed that France has the power to prevent the US from realizing its objectives in Europe.
71. United States Senate, Committee on Foreign Relations, *United States Policy Toward Europe* (Washington: GPO, 1966), p. 137.
72. Kissinger, *The Troubled Partnership*, pp. 76, 239–40, 242–43. *American Foreign Policy*, p. 74.
73. Nixon, *The Memoirs of Richard Nixon*, p. 370.
74. Cromwell, "Europe and the 'Structure of Peace'," p. 12.
75. Kissinger, *The Troubled Partnership*, p. 244, wrote favorably about the Fouchet plan. Kissinger's statement in *United States Policy Toward Europe*, p. 175.
76. Nixon, *US Foreign Policy for the 1970s: A New Strategy for Peace*, p. 32. Schaetzel, *The Unhinged Alliance*, p. 49. He stated: the Administration resolved serious issues bilaterally with France, Britain, and Germany, and in that order.
77. Schaetzel, *The Unhinged Alliance* p. 49. p. 51, He stated: Kissinger's beliefs were "a critical factor" in neglecting the Commission. Cromwell, "Europe and the 'Structure of Peace'," p. 18.
78. Nixon, *US Foreign Policy for the 1970s: Building for Peace*, p. 30.
79. Schaetzel, *The Unhinged Alliance*, p. 145. They refused to assign an ambassador as head of the Commission's Washington mission.
80. Kissinger, *White House Years*, p. 385.
81. Kissinger, *The Troubled Partnership*, p. 8.
82. Brandt, *People and Politics*, p. 254. He stated: "In reality Ostpolitik was one of our reasons for wanting progress in the West", pp. 245–46; France proposed the EEC summit on December 2, 1969, where it was announced that the EEC was prepared to negotiate with Britain about political cooperation within "the context of enlargement." Kissinger, *White House Years*, p. 389.
83. Nixon, *US Foreign Policy for the 1970s: A New Strategy for Peace*, p. 32. *US Foreign Policy for the 1970s: Building for Peace*, p. 29.
84. Kissinger, *White House Years*, pp. 426–27. The Bureau feared, since France welcomed British entry into the EEC, if negotiations broke down, the US opposition would provide the scapegoat.
85. Ibid., p. 428.
86. Nixon, *US Foreign Policy for the 1970s: Building for Peace*, pp. 29–30.
87. Kissinger, *White House Years*, p. 429. NEP would levy a 10 percent surcharge on all imports, end the convertability of the dollar into gold, and establish wage and price controls.

88. Brandon, *The Retreat of American Power*, p. 229. Kohl, "The Nixon-Kissinger Foreign Policy System and US-European Relations," p. 19. Absent from the Camp David meeting on August 13 and 14, where NEP was decided were Kissinger, Rogers, and representatives of other foreign economic policy agencies, i.e., Commerce Department and Office of the Special Trade Representative. Kissinger, *White House Years*, p. 950.

89. Brandon, *The Retreat of American Power*, p. 224. On August 14, Paul A. Volcker, Treasury Under-Secretary for Monetary Affairs, who shared Connally's views, went to Paris to explain the thinking behind the policy to West European finance ministers.

90. Kissinger, *White House Years*, pp. 957–58. The group included Kissinger, Connally, Paul W. McCracken (Chairman of the Council of Economic Advisers), and George P. Shultz (the Director of the Budget). Arthur Burns was kept advised, p. 958; Pompidou, the key to resolving the crisis, rejected the summit knowing Europe could not develop a common policy. Prime Minister Edward Heath, was not interested because he wanted to avoid choosing sides between the US and France, and Brandt was not interested because in case of a stalemate would have been under pressure to side with the US thus alienating France; p. 959, meetings were scheduled with Heath in Bermuda for December 20–21 and with Brandt in Key Biscayne for 28–29. Brandon, *The Retreat of American Power*, pp. 233, 235–36. Also Kohl, "The Nixon-Kissinger Foreign Policy System and US-European Relations," p. 38.

91. Brandon, *The Retreat of American Power*, pp. 240–41; for specific proposals see Kohl, "The Nixon-Kissinger Foreign Policy System and US-European Relations," p. 38; Kissinger. *White House Years*, pp. 959–62.

92. Kissinger, *Observations*, p. 14.

93. Ibid., p. 11. p. 208, he encourages European unity in the defense field.

94. Kissinger, *White House Years*, p. 408. After the election of September 28, Nixon, assured the CDU/CSU plurality meant that Kiesinger would continue as Chancellor, telephoned to congratulate him. The Bundestag elected Brandt by 251 votes to 235. Brandt, *People and Politics*, pp. 223–24.

95. Hersh, *The Price of Power*, p. 416. For comments by NSC staff members Roger Morris and Robert E. Osgood on Kissinger's negative view of Ostpolitik.

96. Kissinger, *The Necessity of Choice*, p. 132; *The Troubled Partnership*, pp. 215–16. *White House Years*, pp. 408–9, His October 1969 memo stressing the risks of Ostpolitik; pp. 529–30, February 16, 1970, memo stressed the long-term dangers of Ostpolitik. He feared that once Brandt achieved normalization and the hoped-for benefits failed to develop the Germans, having already invested heavily in their Eastern policy, would face agonizing choices. Noting that in the 1950s, many Germans in

the SPD under Schumacher and in conservative quarters traditionally fascinated with the East or enthralled by the vision of Germany as a bridge between East and West were against Bonn's incorporation in Western institutions convinced that it would forever seal Germany's division, and preclude the restoration of an active German role in the East, he argued that this kind of debate about Germany's position might recur in more divisive form thus inflaming German domestic affairs and generating suspicions in NATO about its reliability as a partner. *Years of Upheaval*, pp. 144–46; on dangers of Ostpolitik; pp. 146–18, on Bahr's nationalism and his view of Ostpolitik as an alternative to security policy. Hersh, *The Price of Power*, p. 416. He noted Kissinger's opposition to Ostpolitik but not the rationale for it.

97. Kissinger, *The Necessity for Choice*, p. 132; *The Troubled Partnership*, pp. 211–16.

98. Kissinger, *White House Years*, pp. 411–12. He thought by receiving Bahr he could reduce the distrust produced by Nixon's call to Kiesinger. *Years of Upheaval*, pp. 145–17, on Bahr's views about Ostpolitik. Hersh, *The Price of Power*, p. 417. Bahr states "I made clear we'd inform them in advance of what we would do but we would do it anyway"; p. 416, Hersh noted, Brandt like Nixon kept his foreign office out of the negotiations with Moscow, Warsaw, and the GDR.

99. Kissinger, *White House Years*, pp. 132, 410, 528. He used the terms "selective détente" and "differential détente" interchangeably. *Years of Upheaval*, pp. 136, 143.

100. Kissinger, *White House Years*, pp. 529–30. He admitted: "the sole option available to us was to give [Ostpolitik] a constructive direction." p. 410. He credits Brandt for his historic initiative and admits that this was not his immediate view. p. 411; He stated: Paris opposed Ostpolitik but was unwilling to make its opposition explicit. *Years of Upheaval*, p. 146. Brandt, *People and Politics*, p. 284. Brandt reported that his talks with Kissinger at Camp David in April 1970 revealed "Kissinger's interest in our Ostpolitik was lively but not untinged with skepticism. I gained the impression – one which occasionally recurred in later years – that he would rather have taken personal charge of the delicate complex of East-West problems in its entirety."

101. Kissinger, *White House Years*, pp. 410, 530. He stated: "we were not without recourse." Also see *Years of Upheaval*, p. 136.

102. Kissinger, *White House Years*, pp. 530–31, 824. *Years of Upheaval*, p. 145.

103. Kissinger, *White House Years*, pp. 412, 415, 531; Catudal, Jr., *The Diplomacy of the Quadripartite Agreement on Berlin*, pp. 65–66; *The Washington Post*, (February 11, 1970).

104. Kissinger, *White House Years*, pp. 410, 412. Catudal, Jr., *The Diplomacy of the Quadripartite Agreement on Berlin*, p. 69.

105. Catudal, Jr., *The Diplomacy of the Quadripartite Agreement on Berlin*, pp. 95–96.

106. Kissinger, *The Necessity for Choice*, pp. 139–41; *The Troubled Partnership*, p. 71.
107. Kissinger, *White House Years*, pp. 145, 406–7, Moscow's protests came in December 1968 but Johnson left the response to Nixon. On January 22, a State Department draft rejecting the Soviet protest was held up by Kissinger who although agreeing with it sought to avoid an acrimonious exchange with Moscow.
108. Kissinger, *The Necessity For Choice*, p. 139.
109. Kissinger, *White House Years*, pp. 146, 407.
110. Brandt, *People and Politics*, p. 194. Catudal, Jr., *The Diplomacy of the Quadripartite Agreement on Berlin*, p. 55.
111. Kissinger, *White House Years*, pp. 146, 407–8. Catudal, Jr., *The Diplomacy of the Quadripartite Agreement on Berlin*, p. 59, Gromyko's speech to the Supreme Soviet; pp. 60–61, for the response of the allies.
112. Kissinger, *White House Years*, pp. 146, 408.
113. Ibid., p. 407. Dobrynin's first hint to Kissinger before the FRG election about "positive possibilities" to talk on access procedures to Berlin.
114. Ibid., p. 408, 146.
115. Kohl, "The Nixon-Kissinger Foreign Policy System and US-European Relations," p. 26; Catudal, Jr., *The Diplomacy of the Quadripartite Agreement on Berlin*, pp. 88–90.
116. Kissinger, *White House Years*, p. 415.
117. Ibid., p. 825; Hersh, *The Price of Power*, pp. 417–18.
118. Kissinger, *White House Years*, pp. 531–32. Brandt's letter to Nixon on February 25, 1970 urged the early opening of the talks. After stalling for 6 months, Moscow on February 10, 1970, formally invited the Western Three to begin talks on February 18. He recommended acceptance of the invitation, but phasing the talks to prevent Moscow from using the short deadline to divide the Allies by using two simultaneous sets of talks.
119. Kissinger, *The Troubled Partnership*, pp. 215, 212–13.
120. Ibid., pp. 219–20.
121. Kissinger, *White House Years*, pp. 533–34. He stated: "Bonn forswore its national claims in return for an improvement of the atmosphere and easing of inter-German contacts, which should never have been interrupted to begin with." Catudal, Jr., *The Diplomacy of the Quadripartite Agreement on Berlin*, pp. 118–19; London and Paris also reacted negatively to Brandt's linkage. *Newsweek* (August 10, 1970).
122. Brandt, *People and Politics*, pp. 284, 288. He did not perceive Kissinger's doubts about Ostpolitik.
123. Nixon, *US Foreign Policy For the 1970s: Building for Peace*, pp. 39–40.
124. Kissinger, *White House Years*, pp. 817–18, 821, 829.
125. Ibid., pp. 829–30.
126. Ibid., pp. 731, 828–33.; Catudal, Jr., *The Diplomacy of the*

Quadripartite Agreement on Berlin, pp. 189, 178. Dickson, *Kissinger and the Measuring of History*, pp. 130–31.

127. Kissinger, *White House Years*, p. 830. He saw this as a face-saving device because "it was of no help to the Soviet theory of separating West Berlin from the Federal Republic, since Soviet consulates exist in West German cities." Hersh, *The Price of Power*, pp. 419–20. For Departmental and NSC staff opposition to the consulate, see Catudal, Jr., *The Diplomacy of the Quadripartite Agreement on Berlin*, p. 178; p. 164 Bahr urged the US to accept Soviet consulate.

128. Press and Information Office of the Federal Government, *The Quadripartite Agreement on Berlin* (Bonn, 1971), pp. 12–13.

129. Kissinger, *White House Years*, pp. 831–32, for Rogers' opposition. Hersh, *The Price of Power*, pp. 420–21, for conflict with Rogers; p. 422. for later views of critics.

130. Kissinger, *White House Years*, p. 414, put forth in Budapest at a meeting of the Political Consultative Committee of the Warsaw Pact, it called for inviolability of existing European borders; recognition of the GDR and FRG; renunciation by Bonn of possession of nuclear weapons in any form and its claim to represent the entire German people; strengthening of political, economic, and cultural contacts; and recognition of West Berlin's separation from the FRG. Catudal, Jr., *The Diplomacy of the Quadripartite Agreement on Berlin*, pp. 57–59.

131. Kissinger, *White House Years*, p. 414. Italian PM Mariano Rumor urged Nixon to accept it. p. 424, on Brandt's misperception of his views on CSCE. Brandt, *People and Politics*, p. 156; p. 289, for Brandt's fears of US-Soviet bilateralism. Catudal, Jr., *The Diplomacy of the Quadripartite Agreement on Berlin*, pp. 58–59, for Brandt's lobbying.

132. Kissinger, *White House Years*, pp. 414–15.

133. Brandt, *People and Politics*, p. 156.

134. Kissinger, *White House Years*, pp. 415, 1128, 1149–50.

135. Kissinger, *Years of Upheaval*, pp. 710–71. Garthoff, *Détente and Confrontation*, p. 402.

136. Kissinger, *Observations*, pp. 42–47, 85–86, 121. *For the Record*, p. 291.

137. Kissinger, *Observations*, p. 123.

138. Ibid., p. 86.

139. Kissinger, *Years of Upheaval*, p. 130, on December 8, 1972, Kissinger raised the idea with Pompidou in Paris and suggested a summit for defining the common purposes and Pompidou encouraged it as he also did in an interview with New York Times columnist James Reston. p. 139, In January he consulted Jean Monnet who urged that Nixon visit the EC Council of Ministers and join Europe in a declaration of common goals, and to treat Europe as a political unity. Nixon receptive but balked at treating Europe as a unit immediately; pp. 140–43, in February Nixon tells Heath about Year of Europe and suggested a US-UK study group to coordinate goals and strategies and proposed a summit of leaders of

industrial democracies. Heath agreed on the need for a new initiative but after Europe's institutions had developed; p. 151, on April 19, London got an advanced copy of speech; p. 147, in January and April Kissinger told Bahr about the initiative, but Bahr opposed its objective; pp. 148–19, on March 29, Kissinger told French Ambassador Nixon welcomes Pompidou's summit idea and proposed a meeting between Nixon and Pompidou. In April, Paris agreed. On April 13, outline of speech given to the French Ambassador; pp. 149–50, on April 17, Nixon tells PM Andreotti about the initiative; pp. 150–51, on Japan. *The New York Times*, (December 14, 1972), for Reston interview.

140.   Kissinger, *Years of Upheaval*, p. 175. A meeting on foreign policy by foreign ministers was used to exclude Rogers from the Nixon-Pompidou meetings at the Reykjavik summit on May 31 and June 1, 1973. Kohl, "The Nixon-Kissinger Foreign Policy System and US-European Relations," pp. 16–17.

141.   Kissinger, "The Year of Europe", *State Bulletin*, vol. 68 (May 14, 1973), pp. 593–98.

142.   Nixon, *US Foreign Policy for the 1970s: Shaping a Durable Peace*, pp. 92–93. Kissinger, "The United States and a Unifying Europe: the Necessity for Partnership," *State Bulletin*, vol. 69 (December 31, 1973), pp. 777–82. He affirmed Europe's global responsibilities.

143.   Kissinger, *Years of Upheaval*, French criticims in pp. 154, 164, 173–74, 177–78, 181, 183, 187, 189, 700–1, 704, 728; British objections in pp. 154, 162–63, 165, 172, 189, 192; FRG objections in pp. 154–55, 156–57, 185–87, 731–32; Italy's views in p. 155; p. 179, Pompidou proposes bilateral consultations; p. 181, Jobert insists on them; p. 185. Brandt agrees to bilateral talks; pp. 187, 702, Allied pressure for collective summit; pp. 186–88, 701, Allied efforts to avoid meeting Nixon; pp. 188, 701, Allies insist on joint EEC response; pp. 186, 188, 701, 702–3, 705, he argues that by refusing to meet Nixon and dealing with the initiative throught the EEC the Europeans undermined its purpose.

144.   Ibid., pp. 708–9, for negative responses of allies to US airlift; pp. 708, 713, Britain and France reject Kissinger's UN proposals; pp. 709–11, Jobert attacks on US and USSR; pp. 711, 716, 723, Allies insist on NATO's regional role.

145.   Ibid., pp. 712, 714, 718, 720–21, 723, alert and dispute over consultation; pp. 712–13, Kissinger on considerations of timing; p. 718, France seeks a common European policy; pp. 718–19, 723, attacks on superpower condominium by Jobert and Brandt; p. 728, by Pompidou; p. 723, Kissinger suggests regular meetings of deputy foreign ministers for improving consultations on matters outside NATO. Nixon, *The Memoirs of Richard Nixon*, pp. 921, 926, on Allied response to the October War.

146.   Kissinger, "The United States and a Unifying Europe," *State Bulletin*, vol. 69 (December 31, 1973), pp. 780–81.

147.   Kissinger, *Years of Upheaval*, pp.726–27, EEC response to the Pilgrims

speech; pp. 727, 898–99, France seeks a "European-Arab dialogue"; pp. 728, 897, Pompidou rejects EAG.
148. Ibid., pp. 898–900, Jobert's alternative proposals to the EAG.
149. Ibid., For French proposal regarding a UN conference on energy p. 903; regarding a European energy grouping, p. 917.
150. *State Bulletin*, vol. 71 (July 8, 1974), pp. 42–44. Kissinger, *Years of Upheaval*, pp. 933–34.
151. Kissinger, *Observations*, pp. 22, 29, 123, 217.
152. Ibid., pp. 23, 29, 123.
153. Ibid., pp. 205–6.
154. Ibid., pp. 25, 46–47, 138, he was discussing economic summits; pp. 25, 204–5 on consultation.
155. Ibid., pp. 25, 85. "Something is Deeply Wrong in the Atlantic Alliance," *The Washington Post* (December 21, 1981), p. A21. He stated: "We have the power to shape our own future."

Chapter 11: Brzezinski and Alliances: Trilateral Cooperation?

1. Brzezinski, *Power and Principle*, p. 292.
2. Carter, UN Address, *State Bulletin*, p. 330.
3. Carter, Notre Dame Address, *State Bulletin*, p. 623. They agreed to widen economic cooperation, to promote free trade, to promote nuclear non-proliferation, on proposals for meeting Third World development and on efforts to reinforce and modernize NATO's defense.
4. Carter, Wake Forest Address, *Presidential Documents*, p. 531. See also Carter's Naval Academy Address, *Presidential Documents*, p. 1055.
5. Carter, Wake Forest Address, *Presidential Documents*, pp. 532–33, See also Carter's Naval Academy Address, *Presidential Documents*, p. 1056.
6. Brzezinski, *Power and Principle*, p. 290, on his role in the handling of most inter-allied issues.
7. Carter, Wake Forest Address, *Presidential Documents*, pp. 533–34.
8. Brzezinski, *Power and Principle*, pp. 292–93.
9. Vance, *Hard Choices*, p. 65. He notes the most controversial decision at the London summit was the agreement to increase defense spending by 3 percent.
10. Brzezinski, *Power and Principle*, p. 311.
11. Carthoff, *Détente and Confrontation*, p. 850. The F-111 is capable of all-weather delivery of nuclear weapons into the USSR.
12. Brzezinski, *Power and Principle*, pp. 177–78, on PD-18; p. 172, on MBFR.
13. *The Washington Post*, June 6, 7, 9, and July 1, 6, 8, 1977. Articles by Walter Pincus.
14. Brzezinski, *Power and Principle*, pp. 301–2. They agreed on this on the V-B-B lunch on August 17. Vance, *Hard Choices*, pp. 67–69.

15. Brzezinski. *Power and Principle*, pp. 302–3. Vance, *Hard Choices*, pp. 68–69. on Schmidt's position on ERW.

16. Brzezinski, *Power and Principle*, p. 303. Vance, *Hard Choices*, p. 69, on the letter to Schmidt.

17. Brzezinski, *Power and Principle*, pp. 303–4. Vance, *Hard Choices*, pp. 92–93, on consultations with allies and the position of the FRG, UK, France and others; NATO support was cast in terms of confidence in Carter's leadership; p. 94, on Carter's orders.

18. Brzezinski, *Power and Principle*, p. 304, March 20, 1978 statement to Carter on meeting Brown and Vance attended; pp. 304–5, on leadership; p. 306, on credibility. Vance, *Hard Choices*, p. 94, on Carter not appreciating the damage to his prestige and US leadship from opposing a NATO consensus worked out in his name.

19. Carter, *Keeping Faith*, pp. 225–26, on FRG and UK positions on ERW deployment; pp. 226–27, on Vance's, Brown's and Brzezinski's advice for production and deployment and his aggravation for ignoring his views; p. 227, on Callaghan's opposition to deloyment.

20. Brzezinski, *Power and Principle*, pp. 305–6, on pressuring Carter and on Carter's note. Vance, *Hard Choices*, pp. 94–95, on meeting with Genscher and Carter's decision. Carter, *Keeping Faith*, pp. 227–28, on Bonn's position; p. 228, on linking the ERW to MBFR, CTB, and SALT; p. 229, on compatibility of ERW decision with his commitment to arms control and the desires of West Europeans.

21. Brzezinski, *Power and Principle*, p. 306.

22. Schmidt, "The 1977 Alastair Buchan Memorial Lecture," (October 28, 1977), *Survival* vol. 20 (January-February 1978), pp. 3–4. Brzezinski, *Power and Principle*, pp. 290, 307.

23. Brzezinski, *Power and Principle*, pp. 307–8. Vance, *Hard Choices*, pp. 64–65, on need for TNF modernization; p. 65, on High Level Group.

24. Brzezinski, *Power and Principle*, p. 294, on his meetings with European leaders; pp. 294–95, on Schmidt's idea for informal meeting; pp. 295–96, in a speech in Paris in the summer of 1980 he urged the transformation of the economic summit. Carter, *Keeping Faith*, pp. 234–36, on Guadeloupe summit; p. 235, on European unwillingness to deploy the Pershing II and the GLCM, and comments by Giscard, Schmidt and Callaghan.

25. Brzezinski, *Power and Principle*, pp. 307–8, for July 1979 SCC meeting; p. 308, on Aaron's consultations and his conclusions in his weekly report on October 26.

26. Ibid., p. 309. Vance, *Hard Choices*, pp. 96–97. State of the Union Message, *State Bulletin*, vol. 80 (February 1980), p. J.

27. Brzezinski, *Power and Principle*, p. 566.

28. Vance, *Hard Choices*, pp. 392, 98.

29. Ibid., p. 393. State of the Union Message, *State Bulletin*, vol. 80 (February 1980), p. G.

30. Brzezinski, *Power and Principle*, pp. 462–63, on Schmidt's statements and the letter initiated by Aaron, Walter Slocombe from the Defense Department and Reginald Bartholomew from the State Department; p. 309, V-B-M on June 11 agreed on letter to Schmidt. Carter, *Keeping Faith*, pp. 535–36, on Schmidt's statements and his letter to Schmidt.
31. Brzezinski, *Power and Principle*, pp. 309–10 on his suggestion in Venice. Carter, *Keeping Faith*, pp. 536–37, on Schmidt's criticism of the letter in Venice and Brzezinski's response. Smith, *Morality, Reason and Power*, p. 223.
32. Brzezinski, *Power and Principle*, p. 310.
33. Brzezinski, *Game Plan*, pp. 178–79, 257.
34. Ibid., pp. 150–51.
35. Ibid., pp. 261–62, 205–6, 175, p. 181, he suggests a reduction by 100 000 troops. "America's New Geostrategy," p. 686. "We Need More Muscle in the Gulf, Less in NATO," *The Washington Post*, p. B2 (June 7, 1987).
36. Brzezinski, *Game Plan*, pp. 262, 180.
37. Ibid., pp. 262, 181–83. "America's New Geostrategy," p. 685.
38. Brzezinski, *Game Plan*, pp. 172, 179.
39. Ibid., pp. 263, 205–7. "We Need More Muscle in the Gulf, Less in NATO," pp. B1–B2. "The Future of Yalta," *Foreign Affairs* 63:2 (Winter 1984/85, pp. 299–300).
40. Brzezinski, *Game Plan*, pp. 205–7, 263, 196–97. "The Future of Yalta," pp. 299–300.
41. Brzezinski, "America's New Geostrategy," pp. 695–96, 699. "The Future of Yalta," p. 300, he suggests that the US can act unilaterally; p. 298, he states the US "should take the lead" in Eastern Europe.
42. Brzezinski, *Power and Principle*, p. 292, he notes that Schmidt's problems in the FRG were in part caused by US actions. Vance, *Hard Choices*, pp. 391, 393, he notes the divergence between US and West European views.
43. Sodaro, "US-Soviet Relations: Détente or Cold War," p. 4.
44. Brzezinski, *Power and Principle*, p. 293.
45. Ibid., p. 300.
46. Ibid., p. 297.
47. Ibid., p. 300.
48. Ibid., p. 307, Schmidt made the offer at a State Department luncheon on July 13.
49. Ibid., p. 176, for his note to Carter on September 14. He notes that Schmidt was put up to it by Egon Bahr who had made a similar proposal to him.
50. Ibid., pp. 313–14. Ullman, "The Covert French Connection," pp. 18–20; p. 18, for degree of nuclear collaboration from Nixon to Carter; p. 20, Vance's objections.
51. Brzezinski, *Power and Principle*, pp. 300–1.
52. Brzezinski, *Alternative to Partition*, p. 154.

53. Brzezinski, *Power and Principle*, pp. 296–97, his views at PRC meeting on April 14, 1977 to consider PRM-9, a study on US-East European relations.
54. Ibid., p. 297, his comments at PRC meeting on August 23 which dealt with the study on Eastern Europe. The warning came from Shulman the principal Soviet affairs adviser.
55. Brzezinski, *Alternative to Partition*, pp. 157–58.
56. Ibid., pp. 154, 156.
57. Brzezinski, *Power and Principle*, pp. 298–99. He suggested a visit with Cardinal Wyszynski and the laying of a wreath at the monument to the Home Army; p. 299, for specifics on the economic aid. Turner, *Secrecy and Democracy*, p. 119, on Brzezinski's reaction to the CIA report.
58. Brzezinski, *Power and Principle*, pp. 463–64. His suggestions discussed in the PRC and SCC in late 1979 and early 1980. Carter also wrote to the Pope. Carter, *Keeping Faith*, p. 584. He notes that West Europeans were not at all emphatic or persistent in opposing Soviet actions.
59. Brzezinski, *Power and Principle*, p. 464.
60. Ibid., p. 465, on memo to Muskie and Brown; pp. 465–6, on December 3 suggestions; p. 467, on AFL-CIO and memo to DoD. Also, PM Gandhi was prevailed upon to register strongly to Brezhnev on his forthcoming trip to India concerns over the possible invasion. Carter, *Keeping Faith*, pp. 584–85.
61. Brzezinski, *Power and Principle*, pp. 466–68. Carter, *Keeping Faith*, pp. 584–85. He claims credit for warning the Polish opposition.
62. Brzezinski, *Power and Principle*, pp. 466, 468, on Schmidt's pledge to oppose Soviet intervention. Carter, *Keeping Faith*, pp. 538, on the Giscard-Brezhnev meeting in Poland.
63. Brzezinski, *Power and Principle*, p. 465.
64. Brzezinski, *Game Plan*, pp. 44, 68, 144, 254, 52. He defines a linchpin state as one that is strategically important and in some sense "up for grabs"; pp. 203–4, on the real danger.
65. Brzezinski, "America's New Geostrategy," pp. 687–88.
66. Brzezinski, *Game Plan*, pp. 68–69.
67. Ibid., pp. 199, 144. "The Future of Yalta," p. 298.
68. Brzezinski, *Game Plan*, pp. 263, 203–6; pp. 208, 210, on the desirability of a more self-reliant Europe.
69. Ibid., pp. 263, 203. *Alternative to Partition*, p. 161.
70. Brzezinski, *Game Plan*, pp. 265, 207–8.
71. Ibid., pp. 52–53, 254.
72. Ibid., p. 55.
73. Ibid., p. 255.
74. Ibid., pp. 265–66, 93–94.
75. Brzezinski, "America's New Geostrategy," pp. 686–87.
76. Brzezinski, *Power and Principle*, p. 307.

77. Ibid., p. 321; p. 317, on his weekly report on early April 1978 urging international condemnation of Soviet activities.
78. Ibid., pp. 178–79.
79. Ibid., p. 181.
80. Ibid., p. 183.
81. Ullman, "The Covert French Connection," p. 19. Brzezinski, *Power and Principle*, p. 313. He hints about the nuclear collaboration.
82. Vance, *Hard Choices*, pp. 85–86; p. 74, for West European views in October 1977.
83. Brzezinski, *Power and Principle*, p. 450. Vance, *Hard Choices*, pp. 391-92
84. Brzezinski, *Power and Principle*, p. 453. Vance, *Hard Choices*, p. 392.
85. Vance, *Hard Choices*, p. 392.
86. Brzezinski, *Power and Principle*, p. 461.
87. The ambassadors of all NATO members did not attend in 1980 and 1981.
88. Brzezinski, *Power and Principle*, p. 462, on Carter's concern with Schmidt's refusal to commit publicly to the boycott.
89. Garthoff, *Détente and Confrontation*, p. 977.
90. Vance, *Hard Choices*, p. 393.
91. Garthoff, *Détente and Confrontation*, p. 977.
92. Brzezinski, *Power and Principle*, p. 463. He notes that Carter received Schmidt's message from two Cabinet members who on Schmidt's request spoke privately with him after his Moscow trip, and that Carter told him about it personally.
93. Carter, *Keeping Faith*, p. 538.
94. James O. Goldsborough, "Europe Cashes in on Carter's Cold War," *The New York Times Magazine* (April 27, 1980), p. 42. Garthoff, *Détente and Confrontation*, p. 978.
95. Brzezinski, "We Need More Muscle in the Gulf, Less in NATO," p. B2.
96. Brzezinski, *Game Plan*, pp. 180–83, 261–62.

Select Bibliography

PRIMARY SOURCES

Books

Brzezinski , Zbigniew. *Game Plan: How to Conduct the US-Soviet Contest*. Boston: The Atlantic Monthly Press, 1986.
——. *Power and Principle: Memoirs of the National Security Adviser 1977–1981*. New York: Farrar, Straus, Giroux, 1983.
——. *The Fragile Blossom: Crisis and Change in Japan*. New York: Harper and Row, 1972.
——. *Between Two Ages: America's Role in the Technetronic Era*. New York: Viking Press, 1970.
——, ed. *Dilemmas of Change in Soviet Politics*. New York: Columbia University Press, 1969.
——. *Ideology and Power in Soviet Politics*. Revised edn, New York: Praeger, 1967.
——. *The Soviet Bloc: Unity and Conflict*. Revised and Enlarged edn, Cambridge, MA: Harvard University Press, 1967.
——. *Alternative to Partition: For a Broader Conception of America's Role in Europe*. Atlantic Policy Studies. New York: McGraw Hill, 1965.
——, ed. *Africa and the Communist World*. Hoover Institution Publication, No. 5. Stanford, CA: Stanford University Press, 1963.
—— and Huntington Samuel, P. *Political Power: USA/USSR*. New York: Viking Press, 1963.
——. *Ideology and Power in Soviet Politics*. New York: Praeger, 1962.
——. *The Soviet Bloc: Unity and Conflict*. Revised edn, New York: Praeger, 1961.
——. *The Permanent Purge: Politics in Soviet Totalitarianism*. Cambridge, MA: Harvard University Press, 1956.
—— and Friedrich, Carl. *Totalitarian Dictatorship and Autocracy*. New York: Praeger, 1956.
Carter, Jimmy. *Keeping Faith: Memoirs of a President*. New York: Bantam Books, 1982.
Ford, Gerald R. *A Time to Heal*. New York: Berkley Books, 1980.
Jordan, Hamilton. *Crisis: The Last Year of the Carter Presidency*. New York: G. P. Putnam's Sons, 1982.
Kissinger, Henry A. *Observations: Selected Speeches and Essays 1982–1984*. Boston: Little, Brown and Company, 1985.
——. *Years of Upheaval*. Boston: Little, Brown and Company, 1982.
——. *White House Years*. Boston: Little, Brown and Company, 1979.

——. *For the Record. Boston: Little, Brown and Company, 1977.*

——. *A World Restored: Europe After Napoleon.* Gloucester, MA: Peter Smith, 1973.

——. *American Foreign Policy.* New York: W. W. Norton & Company, Inc., p. 1969.

——. *Nuclear Weapons and Foreign Policy.* Abridged Edition. New York: W. W. Norton & Company, 1969.

——. *The Troubled Partnership.* New York: McGraw-Hill Book Company, 1965.

——, ed. *Problems of National Strategy.* New York: Frederick A. Praeger, 1965.

——. *The Necessity for Choice.* New York: Harper & Brothers, Company, 1960.

——. *Nuclear Weapons and Foreign Policy.* Foreword by Gordon Dean. New York: Harper & Brothers, 1957.

——. "The Meaning of History: Reflections on Spengler, Toynbee and Kant." Undergraduate Honors Thesis, Harvard University, 1950.

Nixon, Richard M. *The Memoirs of Richard Nixon.* New York: Grosset & Dunlap, 1978.

——. *Six Crises.* New York: Pyramid Books, 1968.

Powell, Jody. *The Other Side of the Story.* New York: William Morrow and Company, Inc., 1984.

Vance, Cyrus. *Hard Choices: Critical Years in American Foreign Policy.* New York: Simon and Schuster, 1983.

Turner, Stansfield. *Secrecy and Democracy: The CIA in Transition.* Boston: Houghton Mifflin Company, 1985.

Articles

Brzezinski, Zbigniew. "Entering the Age of Defense." *The Washington Post* (October 2, 1988):C2.

——. "Help Pakistan Stay on Course." *The Washington Post* (August 26, 1988):A21.

——. "America's New Geostrategy." *Foreign Affairs* 55:4 (Spring 1988):680–99.

——. "NSC's Midlife Crisis." *Foreign Policy* 69 (Winter 1987–88):80–99.

——. "Reagan's INF Treaty Moves US Toward a New Europe." *The Washington Post* (September 27, 1987):D1–D2.

——. "What the US Should Have Told Iran." *The Washington Post* (August 6, 1987):A21.

——. "We Need More Muscle in the Gulf, Less in NATO." *The Washington Post* (June 7, 1987):B1–B2.

——. "After Reykjavik: What Reagan should do." *US News & World Report* (November 3, 1986):31–32.

——. "The Future of Yalta." *Foreign Affairs* 63:2 (Winter 1984/85):279–302.

——. "Brzezinski Details Administration's Position." *Aviation Week and*

Space Technology 106 (April 18, 1977):34–39.

——. "America in a Hostile World. *"Foreign Policy* 23 (Summer 1976):65–97.

——. "An Exchange on Middle East." *Foreign Policy* 21 (Winter 1975–76):212–23.

——. "Toward Cooperative Activism." *Current* 175 (September 1975): 42–44.

——. "What Kind of Détente?" *The Atlantic Community Quarterly* 13 (Fall 1975):289–92.

—— *et al.* "Peace in an International Framework." *Foreign Policy* 19 (Summer 1975):3–17.

——. "Facing Democracy's Crisis." *Current* 172 (April 1975):56–61.

——. "Recognizing the Crisis." *Foreign Policy* 17 (Winter 1974–75):63–74.

——. "Shifting Mood and System: Subjective and Objective Changes Affect US-EC Relations." *The Atlantic Community Quarterly* 12:3 (Fall 1974):319–26.

——. "The Economics of Détente: A US Portfolio in the USSR?" *The New Leader* 57:16 (August 5, 1974):5–7.

——. "The Deceptive Structure of Peace." *Foreign Policy* 14 (Spring 1974): 35–55.

——. "Separating Security from Territory; A Plan for Peace in the Middle East." *The New Leader* 57:1 (January 7, 1974):7–9.

——. "US Foreign policy: The Search for Focus." *Foreign Affairs* 51:4 (July 1973):708–27.

——. "Negotiating from Weakness: The Second Nixon-Brezhnev Summit." *The New Leader* 56:12 (June 11, 1973):4–5.

——. "Debating Détente." *The New Leader* 55:19 (October 2, 1972):5–6.

——. "How the Cold War was Played." *Foreign Affairs* 51:1 (October 1972): 181–209.

——. "The International and the Planetary." *Encounter* 39:2 (August 1972): 49–55.

——. "The Balance of Power Delusion." *Foreign Policy* 7 (Summer 1972):54–59.

——. "Crisis and Summit." *Newsweek* (May 29, 1972):57.

——. "Memorandum For The President." *Newsweek* (May 8, 1972):50.

——. "The Politics of Zero Growth." *Newsweek* (March 27, 1972):54.

——. "Needed: An Alternative." *Newsweek* (March 6, 1972):53.

——. "Fortune-Cookie Diplomacy." *Newsweek* (February 14, 1972):46.

——. "U.S.-Soviet Policies in Crisis." *Current* 137 (February 1972):61–63.

——. "The Degeneration Of Peace." *Newsweek* (January 24, 1972):36.

——. "Crisis and Parity." *Newsweek* (January 3, 1972):26.

——. "China's New Diplomacy." *Problems of Communism* 20:6 (November–December 1971):25–26.

——. "Half Past Nixon." *Foreign Policy* 3 (Summer 1971):3–21.

——. "New Nuclear Ideas." *Newsweek* (June 7, 1971):55.

——. "The New Triangle." *Newsweek* (June 28, 1971):51.

——. "A Moment for Restraint." *Newsweek* (July 19, 1971):37.

——. "Substance and Style." *Newsweek* (August 9, 1971):41.

——. "Sufficiency For War or Peace?" *Newsweek* (April 26, 1971):45

——. "Not War But Anarchy." *Newsweek* (April 5, 1971):47.

——. "America and Europe." *Foreign Affairs* 49:1 (October 1970):11–30.

——. "The Soviet Past and Future." *Encounter* 34:3 (March 1970):3–16.

——. "Détente in the 70s." *New Republic* 162:1 (January 3, 1970):17–18.

——. "Purpose and Planning in Foreign Policy." *Public Interest* 14 (Winter 1969):52–73.

——. "Meeting Moscow's Limited Coexistence." *The New Leader* 51:24 (December 16, 1968):11–13.

——. "Peace and Power." *Encounter* 31:5 (November 1968):3–13.

——. "Revolution and Counterrevolution." *New Republic* 158:22 (June 1, 1968): 23–25.

——. "Reflections on the Soviet System." *Problems of Communism* 17:2 (May-June):44–48.

——. "U.S. will be Involved for the Rest of the Century." *Current* 94 (April 1968):10–12.

——. "America in the Technetronic Age." *Atlantic Community Quarterly* 6:2 (Summer 1968):175–82.

——. "The Framework of East-West Reconciliation." *Foreign Affairs* 46:2 (January 1968):256–75.

——. "American Transition." *New Republic* 157:26 (December 23, 1967):18–21.

——. "Communism is Dead." *The New Leader* 50:16 (July 17, 1967):10–13.

——. "New Guidelines for the West." *The New Leader* (March 28, 1966):12–6.

——. "Toward a Community of the Developed Nations." *Department of State Bulletin* 56:1446 (March 13, 1967):414–20.

——. "Shifts in the Satellites." *New Republic* 134:24 (June 11, 1956):37–41.

Kissinger, Henry A. "Seeking a New Balance in Asia." *Newsweek* (May 22, 1989):51–56.

——. "Dealing with Moscow: A New Balance." *The Washington Post* (February 7, 1989):A25.

——. "First, a Breakthrough with Mexico." *The Washington Post* (January 11, 1989):A21.

——. "Gorbachev and the West's Wishful Thinkers." *The Washington Post* (December 20, 1988):A25.

——. "The Challenge of a 'European Home'." *The Washington Post* (December 4, 1988):L7.

——. "Arms-Control Fever." *The Washington Post* (January 19, 1988):A15.

——. "The Dangers Ahead." *Newsweek* (December 21, 1987):34–41.

——. "Kissinger: A New Era for NATO." *Newsweek* (October 12, 1987):57–60.

——. "Wandering in the Gulf." *The Washington Post* (June 21, 1987):B7.

——. "Kissinger: How to Deal with Gorbachev." *Newsweek* (March 2,

1987):39–47.

——. "The Rearming of Japan and the Rest of Asia." *The Washington Post* (January 29, 1987):A25.

——. "Something is Deeply Wrong in the Atlantic Alliance." *The Washington Post* (December 21, 1981):A21.

——. "The White Revolutionary: Reflections on Bismarck." *Daedalus* 97 (Summer 1968):888–924.

——. "NATO: Evolution or Decline?" *The Texas Quarterly* 9 (Autumn 1966):110–18.

——. "For a New Atlantic Alliance." *The Reporter* 35 (July 14, 1966):18–27.

——. "Illusionist: Why We Misread de Gaulle." *Harper's Magazine* 230 (March 1965):69–70.

——. "The Price of German Unity." *The Reporter* 32 (April 22, 1965):12–17.

——. "The Essentials of Solidarity in the Western Alliance." *The Conservative Papers* (Chicago: Quadrangle Books,1964):18–38.

——. "Coalition Diplomacy in the Nuclear Age." *Foreign Affairs* 42 (July 1964):525–45.

——. "Strains on the Alliance." *Foreign Affairs* 41 (January 1963):261–85.

——. "The Skybolt Affair." *The Reporter* 28 (January 17, 1963):15–6.

——. "NATO's Nuclear Dilemma." *The Reporter* 28 (March 28, 1963):22–33f.

——. "The Unresolved Problems of European Defense." *Foreign Affairs* 40 (July 1962):515–41.

——. "For an Atlantic Confederacy." *The Reporter* 24 (February 2, 1961):16–20.

——. "Limited War: Nuclear or Conventional? A Reappraisal." *Daedalus* 89 (Fall 1960):800–17.

——. "The New Cult of Neutralism." *The Reporter* 23 (November 24, 1960):26–29.

——. "As Urgent as the Moscow Threat." *The New York Times Magazine* (March 8, 1959):19ff.

——. "The Search for Stability." *Foreign Affairs* 37 (July 1959):537–560.

——. "Missiles and the Western Alliance." *Foreign Affairs* 36 (April 1958):383–400.

——. "Nuclear Testing and the Problem of Peace." *Foreign Affairs* 37 (October 1958):1–18.

——. "Military Policy and the Defense of the 'Gray' Areas." *Foreign Affairs* 33 (April 1955):416–28.

——. "The Limitations of Diplomacy." *The New Republic* (9 May 1955):7–8.

——. "American Policy and Preventive War." *Yale Review* 44:3 (Spring 1955):321–39.

Nixon, Richard M. "Asia after Vietnam." *Foreign Affairs* 46 (October 1967): 112–25.

——. "The Time to Save NATO." *Atlantic Community Quarterly* (Winter 1968–9):481–82.

Schmidt, Helmut. "The 1977 Alastair Buchan Memorial Lecture." *Survival* 20 (January–February 1987):3–4.

Official Documents

The Eurogroup. Brussels: NATO Information Service, Aspects of NATO Series, 1972.

Nixon, Richard M. *U.S. Foreign Policy for the 1970s: A New Strategy for Peace*. Washington, D.C.: Government Printing Office, 1970.

——. *U.S. Foreign Policy for the 1970s: Building for Peace*. Washington, D.C.: Government Printing Office, 1971.

——. *U.S. Foreign Policy for the 1970s: The Emerging Structure of Peace*. Washington, D.C.: Government Printing Office, 1972.

——. *U.S. Foreign Policy for the 1970s: Shaping a Durable Peace*. Washington, D.C.: Government Printing Office, 1973.

Press and Information Office of the Government of the Federal Republic of Germany. *Documentation Relating to the Federal Government's Policy of Détente*. Bonn, 1974.

——. *The Development of the Relations between the Federal Republic of Germany and the German Democratic Republic*. Bonn, 1973.

——. *The European Group in the North Atlantic Alliance*. Bonn: The Federal Ministry of Defense, 1972.

Weekly Compilation of Presidential Documents. Washington, D.C.: Government Printing Office, 1969–1980.

United States Congress. *Report on the Fifth Meeting of Members of Congress and of the European Parliament*. 93rd Congress, 2nd Session. Washington, D.C.: Government Printing Office, 1974.

United States Department of Defense. *Defense Report: Fiscal Year 1971 Defense Report and Budget*. Washington, D.C.: Government Printing Office, 1970.

——. *Defense Report: Fiscal Year 1972–76 Defense Program and the 1972 Defense Budget*. Washington, D.C.: Government Printing Office, 1971.

——. *Defense Report: Fiscal Year 1973 Defense Budget and Fiscal Year 1973–1977 Program*. Washington, D.C.: Government Printing Office, 1972.

United States Department of State. *United States Foreign Policy, 1969–1970: A Report of the Secretary of State*. Washington, D.C.: Department of State Publication 8575, GPO, 1971.

——. *United States Foreign Policy, 1971: A Report of the Secretary of State*. Washington, D.C.: Department of State Publication 8634, GPO, 1972.

——. *United States Foreign Policy, 1972: A Report of the Secretary of State*. Washington, D.C.: Department of State Publication 8699, GPO, 1973.

——. *Department of State Bulletin,* "North Atlantic Treaty." Vol. XX, No. 507, March 20, 1949, pp. 339–342.

——. *Department of State Bulletin,* "The Year of Europe." Vol. LXVIII, No. 1768, May 14, 1973, pp. 593–98.

United States House of Representatives, Committee on Armed Services. *U.S. Military Commitments to Europe.* 93rd Congress, 2nd Session. Washington, D.C.: Government Printing Office, 1974.

——, Committee on House Administration. *The Presidential Campaign 1976.* Vol. 1. Jimmy Carter. Washington, D.C: Government Printing Office, 1978.

——. *The Presidential Campaign 1976.* Vol. 3. The Debates. Washington, D.C: Government Printing Office, 1979.

United States Senate, Committee on Foreign Relations. *United States Policy Toward Europe and Related Matters.* 89th Congress, 2nd Session. Washington, D.C.: Government Printing Office, 1966.

——. *Nuclear War Strategy: Hearing on Presidential Directive* 59. 96th Congress, 2nd Session. Washington, D.C.: Government Printing Office, 1981.

——. *U.S. Security Issues in Europe: Burden Sharing and Offset, MBFR and Nuclear Weapons.* 93rd Congress, 1st Session. Washington, D.C.: Government Printing Office, 1973.

SECONDARY SOURCES

Books

Aron, Raymond. *The Imperial Republic: The United States and the World 1945–1973.* Translated by Frank Jellinek. Cambridge, MA: Winthrop Publishers, Inc., 1974.

Ball, George W. *Diplomacy for a Crowded World.* Boston: Little, Brown and Company, 1976.

Barnet, Richard J. *The Alliance: America-Europe-Japan Makers of the Postwar World.* New York: Simon and Schuster, 1983.

——. *The Giants: Russia and America.* New York: A Touchstone Book, 1977.

Bell, Coral. *The Diplomacy of Détente: The Kissinger Era.* New York: St. Martin's Press, 1977.

Binder, David. *The Other German: Willy Brandt's Life & Times.* Washington, D.C.: The New Republic Book Company, Inc., 1975.

Brandon, Henry. *The Retreat of American Power.* Garden City, NY: Doubleday & Company, Inc., 1973.

Brandt, Willy. *People and Politics: The Years 1960–1975.* Translated by Maxwell Brownjohn. Boston: Little, Brown and Company, 1976.

——. *A Peace Policy For Europe.* Translated by Joel Carmichael. New York: Holt, Rinehart and Winston, 1969.

Brezhnev, Leonid. *Peace, Détente, and Soviet-American Relations.* New York: Harcourt Brace Jovonovich, 1979.

——. *On the Policy of the Soviet Union and the International Situation.* Garden City, NY: Doubleday Company, Inc., 1973.

Broadhurst, Arlene Idol, ed. *The Future of European Alliance Systems: NATO and the Warsaw Pact.* Boulder, CO: Westview Press, 1982.

Brown, Seyom. *The Crises of Power: An Interpretation of United States Foreign Policy During the Kissinger Years.* New York: Columbia University Press, 1979.

——. *The Faces of Power: Constancy and Change in United States Foreign Policy from Truman to Reagan.* New York: Columbia University Press, 1983.

Burrows, Bernard and Edwards, Geoffrey. *The Defense of Western Europe.* London: Butterworth Scientific, 1982.

Buteux, Paul. *The Politics of Nuclear Consultation in NATO 1965–1980.* London: Cambridge University Press, 1983.

Caldwell, Dan, ed. *Henry Kissinger: His Personality and Policies.* Durham, NC: Duke Press Policy Studies, 1983.

——. *American-Soviet Relations: From 1947 to the Nixon-Kissinger Grand Design.* Contributions in Political Science, No. 61. Westport, Conn: Greenwood Press, 1981.

Caldwell, Lawrence T. and Diebold, William, Jr. *Soviet-American Relations in the 1980s: Superpower Politics and East-West Trade.* New York: McGraw-Hill Book Company, 1981.

Catlin, George, Sir. *Kissinger's Atlantic Charter.* Gerrards Cross, Buckinghamshire: Colin Smythe, 1974.

Catudal, Honore M., Jr. *The Diplomacy of the Quadripartite Agreement on Berlin.* Foreword by Ambassador Kenneth Rush. Berlin: Berlin-Verlag, 1978.

——. *A Balance Sheet of the Quadripartite Agreement on Berlin* Foreword by Ambassador Kenneth Rush. Berlin: Berlin-Verlag, 1978.

Chomsky, Noam. *Towards a New Cold War.* New York: Pantheon Books, 1982.

Close, Robert. *Europe Without Defense?* New York: Pentagon Press, 1979.

Cromwell, William C. *The Eurogroup and NATO.* Research Monograph Series, No. 18. Philadelphia, Penn: Foreign Policy Research Institute, 1974.

Davis, Vincent. *Henry Kissinger and Bureaucratic Politics.* Essay Series, No. 9, Institute of International Studies the University of South Carolina, 1979.

DePorte, A. W. *Europe Between the Super-Powers: The Enduring Balance.* New Haven: Yale University Press, 1979.

Destler, I. M. *Presidents, Bureaucrats and Foreign Policy.* Princeton, NJ: Princeton University Press, 1974.

Destler, I. M.; Gelb, Leslie H.; and Lake, Anthony. *Our Own Worst Enemy.* New York: Simon and Schuster, 1984.

Dickson, Peter W. *Kissinger and the Meaning of History.* New York: Cambridge University Press, 1978.

Dougherty, James E. and Pfaltzgraff, Robert B., Jr., eds. *Contending Theories of International Relations.* 2nd Revised Edition. New York: Harper & Row, Publishers, 1981.

Ehrlichman, John. *Witness to Power: The Nixon Years.* New York: Simon and Schuster, 1982.

Evans, Rowland and Novak, Robert D. *Nixon in the White House.* New York: Vintage Books, 1972.

Foster, Richard B.; Beaufre, Andre; and Joshua, Wynfred, eds. *Strategy for the West: American-Allied Relations in Transition.* New York: Crane, Russak & Company, Inc., 1974.

Frankel, Joseph. *British Foreign Policy 1945–1973.* New York: Oxford University Press, 1975

Gaddis, John L. *Strategies of Containment.* New York: Oxford University Press, 1982.

——. *Russia, the Soviet Union and the United States.* New York: John Wiley and Sons, Inc., 1978.

Garnett, John C., ed. *The Defense of Western Europe.* New York: St. Martin's Press.

Garthoff, Raymond L. *Détente and Confrontation.* Washington, D.C.: The Brookings Institution, 1985.

Gatzke, Hans W. *Germany and the United States: A "Special Relationship"?* Cambridge, Mass: Harvard University Press, 1980.

George, Alexander L. *Presidential Decisionmaking in Foreign Policy.* Boulder, CO: Westview Press, 1980.

Golan, Matti. *The Secret Conversations of Henry Kissinger.* Translated by Ruth Geyra Stern and Sol Stern. New York: Bantam Books, 1976.

Goldman, Marshall I. *Détente and Dollars.* New York: Basic Books, Inc., 1975.

Goodman, Elliot R. *The Fate of the Atlantic Community.* New York: Praeger Publishers, 1975.

Graubard, Stephen R. *Kissinger: Portrait of a Mind.* New York: W. W. Norton & Company, Inc., 1973.

Hanrieder, Wolfram F., ed. *Helmut Schmidt: Perspectives on Politics.* Boulder, CO: Westview Press, 1982.

——, ed. *The United States and Western Europe.* Cambridge, Mass: Winthrop Publishers, Inc., 1974.

Hartley, A. *American Foreign Policy in the Nixon Era.* Adelphi Papers, No. 110. London: The International Institute for Strategic Studies, 1974.

Hermann, Margaret G. and Milburn, Thomas W., eds. *A Psychological Examination of Political Leaders.* New York: The Free Press, 1977.

Hill, Christopher, ed. *National Foreign Policies and European Political Cooperation.* London: George Allen and Unwin Ltd., 1983.

Hoffmann, Stanley. *Primacy or World Order.* New York: McGraw-Hill Book Company, 1978.

Hunebelle, Danielle. *Dear Henry.* New York: Berkley Medallion Books, 1972.

Hunter, Robert E. *Presidential Control of Foreign Policy: Management or Mishap?* Foreword by Brent Scowcroft. New York: Praeger, 1982.

Hyland, William G. *Mortal Rivals: Superpower Relations From Nixon To Reagan.* New York: Random House, 1987.

Johnson, U. Alexis and McAllister, Jef Olivarius. *The Right Hand of Power.* Englewood, Cliffs, NJ: Prentice-Hall, Inc., 1984.

Joiner, Harry M. *American Foreign Policy in the Kissinger Era.* Huntsville, Alabama: The Strode Publishers, Inc., 1977.

Kahan, Jerome H. *Security in the Nuclear Age: Developing U.S. Strategic Arms Policy.* Washington, D.C.: The Brookings Institution, 1975.

Kaiser, Karl and Schwarz, Hans-Peter, eds. *America and Western Europe.* Lexington, MA: Lexington Books, 1977.

Kalb, Marvin and Kalb, Bernard. *Kissinger.* Boston: Little, Brown and Company, 1974.

Kaplan, Lawrence S. and Clawson, Robert W., eds. *NATO After Thirty Years.* Wilmington, Delaware: Scholarly Resources Inc., 1981.

Kaplan, Morton. *The Rational for NATO: European Collective Security Past and Future.* Washington, D.C.: American Enterprise Institute for Public Policy Research, 1973.

——, ed. *SALT: Problems & Prospects.* Morristown, NJ: General Learning Press, 1973.

Kegley, Charles W. Jr., and McGowan, Pat., eds. *Foreign Policy USA/USSR.* Beverly Hills: Sage Publications, 1982.

Kegley, Charles W. Jr. and Wittkopf, Eugene R. *World Politics: Trend and Transformation.* New York: St. Martin's Press, 1981.

Kintner, William R. and Pfaltzgraff, Robert L. Jr., eds. *SALT: Implications For Arms Control in the 1970s.* University of Pittsburgh Press, 1973.

Kleiman, Robert. *Atlantic Crisis: American Diplomacy Confronts a Resurgent Europe.* New York: W. W. Norton and Company, Inc., 1964.

Kolodziej, Edward A. *French International Policy Under De Gaulle and Pompidou.* Ithaca, NY: Cornell University Press, 1974.

Korbel, Josef. *Détente in Europe: Real or Imaginary?* Princeton, NJ: Princeton University Press, 1972.

Labrie, Roger P., ed. *SALT Hand Book: Key Documents and Issues 1972–1979.* Washington, D.C.: American Enterprise Institute for Public Policy Research, 1979.

LaFeber, Walter. *America, Russia, and the Cold War 1945–1975*, 3rd edn. New York: John Wiley and Sons, Inc., 1976.

Landau, David. *Kissinger: The Uses of Power.* Boston: Houghton Mifflin Company, 1972.

Ledeen, Michael and Lewis, William. *Debacle: The American Failure in Iran.* New York: Vintage Books, 1981.

Liska, George. *Beyond Kissinger: Ways of Conservative Statecraft.* Baltimore: The John Hopkins University Press, 1975.

Litwak, Robert S. *Détente and the Pursuit of Stability 1969–1976*. London: Cambridge University Press, 1984.

Malraux, Andre. *Felled Oaks: Conversation with de Gaulle*. New York: Holt, Rinehart and Winston, 1971.

Mayall, James and Navari, Cornelia, eds. *The End of the Post-War Era: Documents on Great-Power Relations 1968–1975*. London: Cambridge University Press, 1980.

Mazlish, Bruce. *Kissinger: The European Mind in American Policy*. New York: Basic Books, 1976.

Mazo, Earl and Hess, Stephen. *Nixon: A Political Portrait*. New York: Harper and Row, 1968.

McNamara, Robert S. *The Essence of Security*. New York: Harper and Row, 1968.

Melanson, Richard A., ed. *Neither Cold War nor Détente*. Charlottesville: University Press of Virginia, 1982.

Morgan, Roger. *The United States and West Germany 1945–73: A Study in Alliance Politics*. London: Oxford University Press, 1974.

———. *West Germany's Foreign Policy Agenda*. The Washington Papers, Vol. VI, No. 54. Beverly Hills: Sage Publications, 1978.

Moreton, Edwina and Segal, Gerald, eds. *Soviet Strategy Toward Western Europe*. London: George Allen & Unwin, 1984.

Morris, Roger. *Uncertain Greatness: Henry Kissinger and American Foreign Policy*. New York: Harper & Row, 1977.

Myers, Kenneth A., ed. *NATO: The Next Thirty Years*. Boulder, CO: Westview Press, 1980.

———. *Ostpolitik and American Security Interests in Europe*. Washington, D.C.: The Center for Strategic and International Studies, 1972.

Nathan, James A. and Oliver, James K. *United States Foreign Policy and World Order*, 2nd edn. Boston: Little, Brown and Company, 1981.

Neal, Fred Warner and Harvey, Mary Kersey, eds. *The Nixon-Kissinger Foreign Policy: Opportunities and Contradictions*. Pacem in Terris III, Vol. I. Santa Barbara, CA: Center for the Study of Democratic Institutions, 1973.

Newhouse, John. *Cold Dawn the Story of SALT*. New York: Holt, Rinehart and Winston, 1973.

Newhouse, John et al. *U.S. Troups in Europe: Issues, Costs and Choices*. Washington, D.C.: The Brookings Institution, 1971.

Newsom, David D. *The Soviet Brigade in Cuba*. Foreward by Admiral Stansfield Turner. Indianapolis: Indiana University Press, 1987.

Nutter, Warren G. *Kissinger's Grand Design*. Washington, D.C.: American Enterprise Institute for Public Policy Research, 1975.

Osgood, Robert E., *Containment, Soviet Behavior, and Grand Strategy*. Berkeley, CA: Institute of International Studies, University of California, 1981.

Osgood, Robert E. et al. *Retreat from Empire?: The First Nixon Administration*. Baltimore, MD: The John Hopkins University Press, 1973.

Pranger, Robert J., ed. *Détente and Defense*. Washington, D.C.: American Enterprise Institute for Public Policy Research, 1976.

Quandt, William B. *Decade of Decisions: American Policy Toward the Arab-Israeli Conflict, 1967–1976*. Berkeley: 1977.

Reich, Bernard. *Quest for Peace*. New Brunswick, NJ: Transaction Books, 1977.

Reichley, A. James. *Conservatives in an Age of Change:The Nixon and Ford Administrations*. Washington, D.C.: The Brookings Institution, 1981.

Rush, Kenneth; Scowcroft, Brent; and Wolf, Joseph. *Strengthening Deterrence*. Cambridge, Mass: Ballinger Publishing Company, 1981.

Saeter, Martin. *The Federal Republic, Europe and the World*. Translated by Susan Hoivik Norwegian Foreign Policy Studies, No. 31. Oslo: Universitetsforlaget, 1980.

Sapin, Burton M. "What Every New Administration Should Know About Foreign Policy." Unpublished Manuscript. The George Washington University, 1984.

Schaetzel, Robert J. .*The Unhinged Alliance: America and the European Community*. New York: Harper & Row, 1975.

Schwartz, David N. *NATO's Nuclear Dilemmas*. Washington, D.C.: The Brookings Institution, 1983.

Serfaty, Simon. *Fading Partnership: American and Europe after 30 Years*. New York: Praeger, 1979.

Smith, Gaddis. *Morality, Reason and Power*. New York: Hill and Wang, 1986.

Smith, Gerard. *Doubletalk: The Story of the First Strategic Arms Limitation Talks*. Garden City, NY: Doubleday & Company, Inc., 1980.

Snyder, Richard; Bruck, H. W.; and Sapin, M. Burton. *Foreign Policy Decision-Making*. New York: Free Press, 1962.

Sobel, Lester A., ed. *Kissinger & Détente*. New York: Facts on File, Inc., 1975.

Spanier, John. *American Foreign Policy since World War II*. 7th edn. New York: Praeger, 1977.

Spengler, Oswald. *The Decline of the West*. Abridged Edition by Helmut Werner. English Abridged Edition by Arthur Helps from the Translation by Charles Francis Atkison. New York: Alfred A. Knopf, 1962.

Stanley, Timothy W. and Whitt, Darnell M. *Détente Diplomacy: United States and European Security in the 1970s*. New York: The Dunellen Company, Inc., 1970.

Starr, Harvey. *Henry Kissinger:Perceptions of International Politics*. Lexington, KY: The University of Kentucky Press, 1984.

Steele, Jonathan. *World Power: Soviet Foreign Policy under Brezhnev and Andropov*. London: Michael Joseph, 1983.

Steibel, Gerald L. *Détente: Promises and Pitfalls*. New York: Crane, Russak & Company, Inc., 1975.

Stoessinger, John G. *Henry Kissinger: The Anguish of Power*. New York: W.

W. Norton & Company, Inc., 1976.

Szulc, Tad. *The Illusion of Peace: Foreign Policy in the Nixon Years.* New York: The Viking Press, 1978.

Trezise, Philip H. *The Atlantic Connection.* Washington, D.C.: The Brookings Institution, 1975.

Ulam, Adam B. *Dangerous Relations: The Soviet Union in World Politics 1970–1982.* New York: Oxford University Press, 1983.

Willrich, Mason and Rhinelander, John B. *SALT The Moscow Agreements and Beyond.* New York: The Free Press, 1974.

Woodward Bob and Bernstein Carl. *The Final Days.* New York: Simon & Schuster, 1976.

Yost, David S., ed. *NATO's Strategic Options: Arms Control and Defense.* New York: Pergamon Press, 1981.

——. *European Security and the SALT Process.* The Washington Papers, Vol. IX, No. 85. Beverly Hills: Sage Publications, 1981.

Articles

Aron, Raymond. "Richard Nixon and the Future of American Foreign Policy." *Daedalus* 101 (Fall 1972):1–24.

Bare, Cordon C. "Burden-sharing in NATO: The Economics of Alliance." *ORBIS* 2 (Summer 1976):417–36.

Bergsten, Fred C. "Mr. Kissinger: No Economic Superstar." *New York Times*, 12 December 1973.

Bettiga, E. "Jimmy Who? and Zbigniew Who?" *Survey* 22 (Summer/Autumn 1976):19–21.

Brady, Linda P. "Negotiating European Security: Mutual and Balanced Force Reductions." *International Security Review* 2 (Summer 1981):189–208.

Brenner, Michael J. "The Problem of Innovation and the Nixon-Kissinger Foreign Policy." *International Studies Quarterly* 3 (September 1973):255–94.

——. "The Theorist as Actor, the Actor as Theorist: Strategy in the Nixon Administration." *Stanford Journal of International Studies* 7 (Spring 1972):109–31.

Brody, Richard A. "Cognition and Behavior: A Model of International Relations." In *Experience Structure and Adaptability.* Edited by O. G. Harvey. New York: Springer, 1966.

Butler, David et al. "An Exodus from Zbig." *Newsweek* 93 (June 11, 1979):71.

Conine, Ernest. "Foreign Policy Under President Carter." *Los Angeles Times* 20 August 1976, p. 7.

Cromwell, William C. "Europe and the 'Structure of Peace'." *ORBIS* 1 (Spring 1978):11–36.

Cummings, Bruce. "Chinatown: Foreign Policy and Elite Realignment." In *The Hidden Election.* pp. 196–231. Edited by Thomas Ferguson and Joel Rogers. New York: Pantheon Books, 1981.

De Witt, Karen. "Brzezinski, the Power and the Glory." *The Washington Post,* (4 February 1977):B1

Fallaci, Oriana. "Kissinger: An Interview." *The New Republic* 167 (December 16, 1972):17–22.

Flynn, Gregory A. "The Content of European Détente." *ORBIS* 2 (Summer 1976):401–16.

Garret, Stephen A. "Nixonian Foreign Policy: A New Balance of Power or a Revived Concert?" *Polity* 8 (Spring 1976):389–421.

Gelb, Leslie H. "Brzezinski Says He'll Give Advise to Carter Only When He Asks For It." *The New York Times, 17 December 1976, p.5.*

———. *"Brzezinski Viewed as Key Advisor to Carter." The New York Times,* 6 October 1976, p. 24.

George, Alexander L. "The Causal Nexus between Cognitive Beliefs and Decision-Making Behavior: The 'Operational Code' Belief System." In *Psychological Models in International Politics,* pp. 95–124. Edited by Lawrence S. Falkowski. Boulder, CO: Westview Press, 1979.

———. "The 'Operational Code': A Neglected Approach to the Study of Political Leaders and Decision-Making." *International Studies Quarterly* 13 (June 1969):190–222.

Goldsborough, James O. "Europe Cashes in on Carter's Cold War." *The New York Times Magazine* (April 27, 1980): 42.

Hahn, Walter F. "West Germany's Ostpolitic: The Grand Design of Egon Barh." *ORBIS* 4 (Winter 1973):859–80.

———. "The Nixon Doctrine: Design and Dilemmas." *ORBIS* 2 (Summer 1972):361–76.

Hoffmann, Stanley. "The Case of Dr. Kissinger." *The New York Review of Books.* (December 6, 1979):14–29.

———. "Muscle and Brains." *Foreign Policy* 37 (Winter 79–80):3–27.

Holsti, Ole R. "The Operational Code Approach: Problems and Some Solutions." In *Cognitive Dynamics and International Politics,* pp. 75–90. Edited by Christer Jonsson. New York: St Martin's Press, 1982.

———. "Foreign Policy Decision-Makers Viewed Psychologically." In *In Search for Global Patterns,* Edited by James N. Rosenau. New York: Free Press, 1976.

———. "Foreign Policy Formation Viewed Cognitively." In *Structure of Decision,* pp. 18–53. Edited by Robert Axelrod. Princeton, NJ: Princeton University Press, 1976.

———. "The 'Operational Code' Approach to the Study of Political Leaders: John Foster Dulles' Philosophical and Instrumental Beliefs." *Canadian Journal of Political Science* 3:1 (March 1970):123–57.

———. "The Belief System and National Images: A Case Study." *Journal of Conflict Resolution* 6 (1962):244–52.

Johnson, Loch K. "Operational Codes and the Prediction of Leadership Behavior: Senator Frank Church at Midcareer." In *A Psychological Examination of Political Leaders,* pp. 80–119. Edited by Margaret G. Hermann. New York: The Free Press, 1977.

Leacacos, John P. "Kissinger's Apparat." *Foreign Policy* 5 (Winter 1971–72):3–27.

Legvold, Robert. "European Security Conference." *Survey* (Summer, 1970):41–52.

Kaltefleiter, Werner. "Europe and the Nixon Doctrine: A German Point of View." *ORBIS* 1 (Spring 1973):75–94.

Kaplan, Lawrence S. "NATO and the Nixon Doctrine Ten Years Later." *ORBIS* 1 (Spring 1980):149–64.

Klein, Jean. "European and French Points of View on Mutual and Balanced Force Reductions in Europe: Historic and Current Perspectives." *Stanford Journal of International Studies* (Spring 1979):53–70.

Kohl, Wilfrid L. "The Nixon-Kissinger Foreign Policy System and U.S.-West European Relations: Patterns of Policy Making." *World Politics* 1 (October 1975):1–43.

Kohl, Wilfrid L. and Taubman, William. "American Policy Toward Europe: The Next Phase." *ORBIS* 1 (Spring 1973):51–74.

Kostko, Y. "Mutual Force Reductions in Europe." *Survival* (September–October 1972):236–38.

Kristol, Irving. "The Meaning of Kissinger." *Wall Street Journal* (April 11, 1974):12.

Lewis, Anthony. "Kissinger Now." *The New York Review of Books* (October 27, 1977):8–10.

Lindblom, Charles E. "The Science of 'Muddling' Through." *Public Administration Quarterly* 29 (Spring 1959):79–88.

Martin, Laurence. "The Nixon Doctrine and Europe." In *The Defense of Western Europe*. Edited by John C. Garnett. New York: St. Martin's Press, 1974.

Montgomery, John D. "The Education of Henry Kissinger." *Journal of International Affairs* 1 (1975):49–62.

Nickel, Herman. "Why Zbig is Not Quite on Top of the World." *Fortune* 99 (April 23, 1979):71.

Pierre, Andrew J. "The Future of America's Commitments and Alliances." *ORBIS* 3 (Fall 1972):696–719.

Pipes, Richard. "America, Russia, and Europe in the Light of the Nixon Doctrine." In *Strategy for the West*. Edited by Richard B. Foster *et al.* New York: Crane, Russak & Company, Inc., 1974.

Plaltzgraff, Robert L. "The United States and Europe: Partners in a Multipolar World?" *ORBIS* 1 (Spring 1973):31–50.

Scheer, Robert. "Carter's Man Zbig: Profound or Banal?" *Los Angeles Times* 23 January 1977, pp. 24–25.

Serfaty, Simon. "America and Europe in the 1970's: Integration or Disintegration?" *ORBIS* 1 (Spring 1973):95–109.

———. "Brzezinski; Play it Again Zbig." *Foreign Policy* 32 (Fall 1978):3–21.

Sjoblom, Gunnar. "Some Problems of the Operational Code Approach." In *Cognitive Dynamics and International Politics*, pp. 37–74. Edited by Christer Jonsson. New York: St. Martin's Press, 1982.

Smart, Ian. "MBFR Assailed: A Critical View of the Proposed Negotiation of Mutual and Balanced Force Reduction." *Occasional Paper* No. 3, Ithaca, New York: Cornell University Peace Studies Program, 1972.

Stang, A. "Zbig Brother." *American Opinion* 21 (February 1978):99.

Starr, Harvey. "Kissinger's Operational Code." *Korea and World Affairs* 4:4 (Winter 1980):582–606.

———. "Henry Kissinger's Belief System and World Order: Perception and Policy." In *World in Transition: Challenges to Human Rights, Development and World Order*, pp. 239–55. Edited by Henry H. Hann. Washington, D.C.: University Press of America, 1979.

Suetonious. "Born to Skim." *The New Republic* 176 (January 1977):8.

Szulc, Tad. "Springtime for Carter." *Foreign Policy* 27 (Summer 1977):178–91.

Ward, Dana. "Kissinger: A Psychohistory." In *Henry Kissinger: His Personality and Policies*, pp. 24–63. Edited by Dan Caldwell. Durham, NC: Duke Press Policy Studies, 1983.

Watson, Russell *et al.* "Life at Brzezinski U." *Newsweek* LXXXIX:63 (May 9, 1977).

West, Diana. "The World According to Brzezinski." *Insight* (September 8, 1986):56–57.

Wolin, Seldon. "Consistent Kissinger." *The New York Review of Books* (December 9, 1976):20–31.

Yochelson, John. "MFR: West European and American Perspectives." In *The United States and Western Europe*. Edited by Wolfram Hanrieder. Cambridge, Mass: Winthrop Publishers, Inc., 1974.

———. "MBFR: The Search for an American Approach." *ORBIS* 1 (Spring 1973):155–75.

———. "The American Military Presence in Europe: Current Debate in the United States." *ORBIS* 15 (Fall 1971):784–807.

Zorza, Victor. "A Man to Out-Kissinger Kissinger." *Washington Post* (January 19, 1977), p, 23.

Other Sources

International Herald Tribune.
Newsweek.
The Los Angeles Times.
The New York Times.
The Times.
The Washington Post.
Time.
US News and World Report.
Wall Street Journal.

Index

Aaron, David, 140, 256
ABM, 157, 159, 186, 220–1, 237
  and Treaty terms, 160
Afghanistan, 154, 169, 173, 194,
  198–9, 200–1, 207, 211, 257,
  260, 269
AFL-CIO, 264–5
Alaska, 189, 213, 216, 219
Alliance, *see* NATO
allies, *see* NATO
Angola, 136, 154, 169–70, 172–3
APNW (Agreement on the Prevention
  of Nuclear War), 163–6, 221–2
  see also Kissinger
arms control, *see* Brzezinski, Carter,
  Kissinger, Nixon, SALT
  and Vance
Atlantic Alliance, *see* NATO
Atlantic Commonwealth, *see* Kissinger

B-1 bomber, 157, 161–2
backchannels, *see* Kissinger *and*
  Brzezinski
Bahr, Egon, 232–3, 235–6
balance of power, *see* Brzezinski,
  Carter, Kissinger *and* Nixon
Berlin, 158, 166–7, 175, 217, 233–5
Bismarck, Otto von, 34
Blumenthal, Michael, 141, 190, 193,
  202, 210
Bonn, 220–1, 224, 230, 235,
  see also FRG, Brandt, Ostpolitik
  and Schmidt
Brandt, Willy, 219, 221, 235
  and Ostpolitik, 230, 232–3,
  236–9, 242
Brezhnev, Leonid, 150, 159–3, 165,
  167–8, 172, 182, 189–90, 192
  doctrine of, 19
  see also Kissinger
Britain, 220–1, 224, 227–8, 238,
  269–70
  and EEC, 227–8, 230

  and nuclear forces of, 220–1

Brown, Harold, 139, 141, 145,
  157, 248–9
  and Brzezinski, 184–5, 188, 193
  and ERW, 252, 253–4
  and NATO, 251
  and PRC, 202, 203–4, 208, 210–11
  and Soviet-Cuban intervention, 195
  and TNF, 255, 258
  and V-B-B, 143
  and Western Europe, 250
burden-sharing, 124, 217
  see also Brzezinski *and* Kissinger
Butz, Earl, 167–8
Brzezinski, Zbigniew, 1, 2, 3, 8, 10,
  76, 133, 138, 154, 178, 180, 183
  and Afghanistan, 198–9,
  200–1, 207, 257, 260, 265,
  269–70, 273
  and AFL-CIO, 265
  and anti-Americanism in new
  states, 61, 67
  and architectural approach, 101,
  104–5, 106, 116, 120, 135,
  180, 212, 249, 277
  and arms control, 115–17, 121, 136,
  145, 191, 213, 251, 258, 272,
  279, 282–3
  and arms sales to PRC, 210–11
  and backchannels, 144–6
  and balance of power (Western
  Europe), 251, 256, 272
  and bold initiatives, 107, 253–4,
  259, 261, 265, 271–3, 277,
  281, 284
  and Brown, 141, 143; 188, 193, 195,
  203–4, 210–11, 264, 272, 284
  and burden-sharing, 250–1, 259, 272
  and Carter, 133, 145
  and Carter doctrine, 199–200
  and Carter's speeches, 179,
  180–2, 249

and CEMA, 59, 60
and chance, role of, 71–2, 75, 276
and communism in new states,
  62–3, 67–8, 74
and conception of détente, 109, 111,
  134, 144, 179, 181–2, 187,
  273, 282
and conceptual approach, 70, 101,
  103–4, 120, 277
and conflict in international system,
  39–42, 46, 55, 72, 274–5
and control of history, 69–71, 75,
  276, 280
and consultations, 70, 104, 115–16,
  121, 136–7, 145, 253, 255, 260,
  270, 271–3, 279, 280, 284
and conventional forces (NATO),
  184–5, 187, 251, 258–9,
  266–7, 271–2
and convergence theory, 51–2,
  73, 274
and CPSU, 46, 48, 51, 73
and credibility, 112, 121, 191, 195,
  197–8, 200, 203, 205–6, 209,
  254, 278, 283
and CSCE, 249, 261
and Cuban missile crisis, 48, 112–13
and de Gaulle, 55–6, 58, 73, 107
and diplomacy, 117–18, 121,
  214, 279
and Dobrynin, 144–6, 189–90, 193,
  195, 214
and Eastern Europe, 55–60, 74,
  118–19, 261–7, 273, 275
and education of public opinion,
  70–1, 75, 115, 118–19
and EEC, 59, 116, 276
and emerging global consciousness,
  41–2, 64–6, 72, 74–5, 118, 276
and equality, 42, 63, 74
and ERW, 250, 252–5, 264, 272
and Estaing, Giscard' d', 256,
  262, 264–5
and force, *see* use of force
and Friday Presidential Breakfast,
  143, 145
and global city, concept of, 41–2
and global village, concept of, 41
and Helsinki Accords, 261, 273

and Horn of Africa, 194–6,
  268–9, 273
and human rights, 192–4, 196,
  212–13, 261, 273, 281
and ideology, 42, 47
and international system, 39, 42, 46,
  65–6, 133
and Iran, 198–200, 210
and Japan, 54, 59, 60, 65, 73,
  108, 110–11, 116, 211, 249,
  268, 280
and Kissinger on, 4, 38, 43, 54,
  55–6, 63, 70, 100–1, 104–6,
  108–10, 113–14, 117–19, 134,
  136, 188–9, 192–3, 202–3,
  204, 268
and leadership, conception of, 103,
  106–8, 112–13, 120, 136, 145,
  214, 249, 252, 254, 256, 259,
  271–2, 277–8, 280–1, 284
and leadership of new states,
  63–4, 74
and Lenin, 39, 70
and liberalization/democratization
  of USSR, 50–1, 73
and linkage, 54, 106, 109, 120, 187,
  190–4, 196, 202, 213, 253,
  256–7, 260, 264–5, 268, 271–2,
  277, 281–2
and London economic summit,
  260–1
and Mao Tse-tung, on, 48, 70
and MBFR, 251, 272, 283
and MFN status (to PRC), 193–4,
  209–10, 212–13
and military superiority, 101–2, 108,
  112, 117, 121, 183–4, 186–7,
  194, 212–3, 250, 277, 282
and Mondale, 188, 199, 203–4,
  210–11
and moral approach, 101, 105–6,
  120, 135, 144, 180, 192, 212,
  277, 281–2
and Muskie, 264
and nationalism, 39, 42, 53, 55–60,
  62, 69–70, 73–4, 274–5
and nationalism in Eastern Europe,
  56–8, 60, 74
and nationalism in FRG, 265–6

and nationalism in new states,
62–3, 67–8
and NATO, 55–6, 251–2, 258–9,
262, 265–6, 272, 275, 283
and neutralism of Western Europe,
265–6
and new states (Third World), 61–4,
67–8, 74–5, 190, 275
and Nixon on, 38, 54, 56, 63, 70,
100, 104–7, 109–10, 116–19,
134, 136, 188–9, 202–3
and Nixon doctrine, 42, 70, 107, 110
and no-first-use, 258
and non-ideological approach,
101, 105, 120, 135, 144, 213,
277, 281
and NSC, 140–2, 145–6, 184–5,
187–8, 193, 199, 201, 209, 261
and nuclear war, 115–16, 121,
279, 283
and nuclear weapons, 45, 184
and optimism, 65–6, 71, 75, 275–6
and PD-18, 184–5, 212, 251
and peaceful coexistence, 45–8,
51, 53, 58, 72, 101, 181,
274, 282–3
and perestroika, 267
and Pershing IIs, 256–7
and pessimism, 66, 75, 275–6
and planetary humanism, 38, 101–2,
106, 109, 119, 133, 144, 276
and Poland, 263–5, 267, 273
and policy-planning/making, 68,
104, 109–10, 120
and political will, 106, 108–9,
111, 115, 120, 187–8, 191,
193–8, 200–1, 205, 208–9,
213, 251, 253–4, 269, 271–3,
277–8, 283
and power, concept of, 101,
119, 276
and power-realism, 38, 101–3, 109,
119, 144, 212, 276, 281
and PRC, 39–46, 48–50, 54, 60, 72,
114, 144–6, 202, 211–12, 250,
274–6, 278, 280–1
and predictability of political future, 66–9, 75,
276

and racism in new states, 62–3, 68,
74
and Radio Free Europe, 119, 261
and RDF, 184–5, 187, 212–14,
258–9, 271
and reciprocity, 106, 111, 120, 134,
180, 198, 212, 277
and revolutionary powers, 43–6, 48,
50, 52–4, 72, 274
and Reykjavik, 191, 194
and risks, 112–13, 120–1, 278, 283
and role of, 138–40, 145
and SALT I, 54, 101–3, 116–17,
141, 145
and SALT II, 116, 184–8, 189–91,
196–8, 207, 210, 213, 257, 282
and SCC, 140–2, 145–6
and Schmidt, 258, 261–2, 264–6
and SDI, 186, 191, 259
and selective détente, 192,
261–2, 265–6
and Shanghai Communique, 206
and Sino-Soviet split, 43, 45, 48, 50,
54, 57–8, 60, 68, 73
and sovereignty, 56, 60, 73–4
and Soviet brigade, 196–7
and Soviet communist ideology,
39–40, 42–7, 50–1, 72–3
and Soviet-Cuban intervention,
194–6
and Soviet-East European relations,
57–9, 262–3
and speeches (presidential), 104,
111, 142, 145, 180–2, 212
and Spengler on, 70, 119
and SS-20s, 253–5
and statesman's role on, 70–1, 75
and sufficiency (strategic), 101, 108
and summitry, 115, 117–18, 121,
145, 189–92, 208, 213, 253,
256, 272, 279
and technetronic revolution, 40, 42,
59, 61, 65, 72, 74, 276
and Teilhard de Chardin on, 69
and timing, 113–15, 121, 278
and TNF, 250, 255–8, 272
and trilateral cooperation, 60,
65–6, 75, 105–6, 108, 110–13,
115–16, 120, 134, 144–5,

248–50, 267, 270–1, 273, 275–7, 284–5
and Turner, 141–2, 264
and use of force, 108, 113, 115–16, 121, 180, 187, 195, 200–1, 212–3, 268, 272, 278–9, 283
and US global impact, 40–2, 61, 65–7, 71–2, 74–5
and US leadership, 107–8, 136, 187, 208, 254, 259, 264, 273, 285
and US leaders on, 103
and US-PRC normalization, 195–9, 201–12, 264–5, 280–1
and US-PRC rapprochement, 54, 73, 144, 206
and US-Soviet détente, 53–4, 73, 109, 111, 179, 183–4, 189–90, 192–4, 196, 213, 260–1, 271, 282
and US-Soviet rivalry, 40, 52–3, 61, 65, 67, 73, 75, 114–15, 121, 180–1, 186, 188, 191, 200–1, 205
and US-Soviet trade, 190, 193–4, 199, 209–13, 270, 282
and USSR, 39–46, 48–54, 57–8, 60, 65, 67, 72, 101–3, 111, 113–14, 116–17, 141, 144–6, 182–7, 195–6, 200, 202, 206, 209, 211–12, 250, 258, 261, 262–4, 265–6, 270–6, 278, 280–1
and Vance, 141, 143–4, 181–2, 187–90, 194, 197–8, 203–4, 207–10, 272, 284
and V-B-B luncheon, 143, 145
and Vienna summit, 189–90
and Western European unity, 59, 74, 108, 266–7, 275
and Western Europe, 59–60, 65, 73–4, 249, 251–2, 265–70, 272–3, 275, 280
and Year of Europe, 108, 110, 113, 116

Carter, Jimmy, 1, 4, 133, 154, 169, 173, 175, 178–9
and Afghanistan, 183, 198–200
and architectural approach, 135
and arms control, 137–8, 145, 179–82, 212, 249, 252, 254–5, 260, 279
and arms sales to PRC, 210
and balance of power, 135
and Brown's role, 139, 143, 145
and Brzezinski, 133, 138–9, 183–5, 187, 189–90, 193, 195–200, 205–7, 252, 254, 261–4, 269, 272, 279–80
and Brzezinski's role, 138–9, 145
and consultations, 136–7, 145, 280
and control of policy, 138–9, 141–3, 145, 180, 204, 212, 254, 280
and CSCE, 249
and détente, conception of, 134, 137, 144–5
and diplomacy (Lone-Ranger), conception of, 136–7, 139, 145
and doctrine of, 183, 199–200
and ERW, 252–5
and Ford, 134–7, 252
and Friday Presidential Breakfast, 143, 145
and Helsinki Accords, 136, 192, 249
and human rights, 135–6, 144, 179, 192–4, 249, 260
and Japan, 134, 145, 248, 279–80
and Kissinger, 4, 134, 136–7, 178, 204
and leadership, conception of, 136, 145
and linkage, 187, 190, 196
and London economic summit, 250
and MBFR, 179, 182
and Middle East, 179–80, 182
and moral approach, 135–6, 144, 179–80
and NATO, 179–81, 184, 249–51
and Nixon, on, 134
and non-ideological approach, 135–6, 144
and non-proliferation, 137–8
and NSC, 140–3, 199, 280
and optimism of, 179
and planetary humanism, 133, 135, 144
and Poland, 263–4
and power, conception of, 136

and power-realism, 135, 144,
    180–1, 183
and PRC 134–5, 144, 178, 180
and SALT I, 137, 145, 162–3,
    178, 182
and SALT II, 183–5, 187–9, 196–7,
    199, 207, 257
and SALT II ratification, 183,
    197, 199
and Schmidt, 258
and Soviet-Cuban intervention,
    194–7
and speeches of, 179–81, 249
and summitry, 137, 145, 182,
    189–90
and Third World, 134, 180
and TNF, 256, 258
and trilateral cooperation, 134–5,
    144–5, 179, 248–9
and use of force, 180–1, 183
and US leadership, 136, 145, 280
and US-PRC normalization, 134,
    144, 180, 202, 208
and US-Soviet détente, 134, 179,
    181, 183, 268
and US-Soviet trade, 193, 199,
    210, 239
and USSR, 134–6, 144, 178–81,
    183, 189–90, 197, 249–50,
    264, 279
and Vance's role, 138, 143, 145,
    188, 204
and Vienna summit, 189–90
and Vietnam, 208–9
and Vladivostok agreement, 137
and Western Europe, 134, 145,
    248–50, 264, 269–70, 279–80
Callaghan, James, 256, 268
Ceausescu, Nicolae, 150–1
Central America, 173, 201
Cienfuegos, 170–1, 173, 176, 196,
    see also Kissinger
CEMA (Council of Economic Mutual
    Assistance), 59–60
CENTO (Central Treaty Organization),
    24–5
chance, role of, *see* Brzezinski *and*
    Kissinger
China, *see* PRC

Chou En-lai, 153
Christopher, Warren, 198–9
CIA (Central Intelligence Agency),
    127–8, 142, 263
COCOM (Coordinating Committee
    on Export Controls), 167, 169,
    207, 210
    see also Kissinger
conceptual approach, *see* Brzezinski,
    Carter, Kissinger *and* Nixon
conflict, in international system, *see*
    Brzezinski *and* Kissinger
community of the developed states, *see*
    Trilateral cooperation
Connally, John, 231
consultations, *see* Brzezinski, Carter,
    Kissinger, Nixon *and* Vance
control of history, *see* Brzezinski *and*
    Kissinger
convergence theory, *see under*
    Brzezinski *and* Kissinger
credibility, *see* Brzezinski, Kissinger
    and Nixon
CPSU (Communist Party of the Soviet
    Union), 20, 36, 46, 48
    see also Brzezinski *and* Kissinger
CSCE, 217, 232–4, 238, 242, 249, 261
Cuban missile crisis, 18, 36, 48,
    112–13
    see also Brzezinski, Kissinger
    and Nixon
Czechoslovakia, 108

Defense Department, 161–2,
    171–2, 175
and equal aggregates, 161–2
de Gaulle, Charles, 24, 55–6, 58, 73,
    107, 123, 246, 256
and controversy with Soames,
    227–8
    see also Brzezinski *and* Kissinger
Deng Xiaoping, 207–9
Détente, 53–4, 73, 109, 111, 155, 157,
    172, 174–6, 179, 181–4, 189–90,
    192–4, 196, 213, 217–18, 234–5,
    260–1, 271
    see also Brzezinski, Carter,
    Kissinger, Nixon *and*
    selective détente

differentiated détente, *see* selective détente
diplomacy, *see* Brzezinski, Carter, Kissinger, Nixon *and* Vance
Dobrynin, Anatoly, 144, 164, 183, 189–90, 193, 195, 234–5
DPRC (Defense Program Review Committee), 129, 223

EAG (Energy Action Group), 243–4
EDIP (European Defense Improvement Program), 224
EEC, 116, 227–32, 242–4, 246, 265, 267
and Commission of, 229–30, 247
see also Brzezinski, France *and* Kissinger
EFTA (European Free Trade Association), 230
Egypt, 194, 199
equal aggregates, *see under* Defense Department *and* Kissinger
ERW (Enhanced Radiation Weapon), 250, 252
Estaing, Valery Giscard' d', 256, 262, 264–5, 268–71
Ethiopia, 154, 169, 173, 194–6
Eurogroup, 224
Europe (East), 56–9, 74, 118–19, 261–7, 273, 275
and nationalism in, 56–8, 60, 74
see also Brzezinski
Europe (West)
unity of, 22, 30, 36, 55–6, 59, 73–4, 227–8
see also Brzezinski *and* Kissinger

flexibility, *see* Kissinger
force, use of, *see under* Brzezinski *and* Kissinger
Ford, Gerald R., 125, 129–30, 134–7, 162, 192, 252, 263, 279–80
and Kissinger, 125, 129–30
and Vladivostok, 162
France, 55, 220, 262, 268–70
and EAG, 243
and EEC, 227–8, 230
and nuclear forces (*force de frappe*), 220–1

and Year of Europe, 241–4
Friday Presidential Breakfast, 143, 145, 280
see also Brzezinski, Carter *and* Vance
FRG (Federal Republic of Germany), 55, 58, 220–1, 224, 230, 235, 265–7, 269–70
and nationalism of, 232, 265–6
and Olympics (Moscow), 270
see also Bahr, Berlin, Brandt *and* Schmidt

GDR (German Democratic Republic), 108, 233–4
Genscher, Hans-Dietrich, 254, 258
George, Alexander L., *see* Operational Code
German nationalism, *see under* Brzezinski, FRG *and* Kissinger
Germany (West) *see* FRG
global city, *see* Brzezinski
global village, *see* Brzezinski
Gromyko, Andrei, 164, 195, 205, 235, 237, 264

Harriman, W. Averell, 189
Healey, Denis, 224
Heath, Edward, 221
Helms, Richard, 151
Helsinki Accords, 135–6, 192, 249
see also Brzezinski *and* Carter
High Level Group (NATO), 255–6
Horn of Africa, 194–6, 204, 268–9, 273
see also Somali-Ethiopian War, Brzezinski *and* Vance
Hua Huang, 207–8
human rights, *see* Brzezinski, Carter *and* Kissinger

ideology, 14, 16, 42
see also Brzezinski *and* Kissinger
IGs (Interdepartmental Groups), 127–8, 140, 235
Indo-Pakistani War, 113
INF, (intermediate nuclear forces), 226–7
see also Kissinger

Interim Agreement, 160–2
international systems, *see* Brzezinski
    and Kissinger
  and terms of 160
Iran, 154, 173, 198–200, 210
Israel, 134

Jackson, Henry M., 162, 168–9
Jackson-Vanik amendment, 169
Japan, 21–2, 54, 59–60, 65, 73, 108,
    110–11, 116, 152, 211, 249,
    268–271
  and Olympics (Moscow), 270
JCS (Joint Chiefs of Staff), 127, 161,
    223, 256
Jobert, Michel, 221
Johnson, Lyndon B., 124–5, 127, 157,
    160, 232, 236
Jordan, 170–2, 173, 176
Jordan, Hamilton, 143, 188, 208

Kennedy, John. F., 125, 127
Khan, Yahya, 150–1
Khrushchev, Nikita, 19–20, 45
Kissinger, Henry, 1–4, 8, 10,
    147–8, 180
  and ABM, 157, 159–60, 175–6,
    220–1, 237, 246
  and Angola, 154, 169–70, 172–3,
    176
  and anti-Americanism in new
    states, 26–7
  and APNW, 163, 165–6, 171, 176,
    221–2, 246, 281
  and arms control, 91, 95–6, 99, 148,
    158–9, 163, 175, 279, 282–3
  and Atlantic Commonwealth, 25,
    29–30, 36, 85, 215, 240–1,
    244, 275
  and backchannels, 130–2, 171–2,
    233, 235, 237, 247, 280, 284
  and Bahr, 232–3, 235–6
  and balance of power, 77–8, 85,
    148–50, 169, 215–16, 283
  and balance of power in Europe, 225
  and Basic Principles, 163–4, 166,
    168, 171–2, 176, 281
  and Berlin, 158, 166–7, 217, 233–8,
    247, 284

  and bipolarity, 25, 28, 151, 155
  and Bismarck, 32, 34
  and Brezhnev, 159–62, 165, 167–8
  and burden-sharing, 22, 217–18,
    223, 246
  and bureaucracy and policy, on, 78,
    80, 88–90, 98, 110, 152
  and bureaucratization of USSR,
    20, 274
  and Carter, on, 154, 162–3, 169,
    173, 175
  and CENTO, 24–5
  and chance, role of, 34–5, 37, 276
  and CIA, 128
  and Cienfuegos, 170–1
  and COCOM, 167, 169
  and conceptual approach, 80–1,
    97–8, 104, 148, 174, 277
  and conflict in international system,
    13–14, 21, 35, 274–5
  and consultations, 91, 96, 99, 152,
    220–2, 243–4, 246, 255,
    279, 284
  and control of history, 32–5, 37,
    244, 276, 280
  and conventional forces (NATO),
    93, 96, 157, 222–7, 241,
    246, 258
  and convergence, theory of, 20,
    36, 274
  and CPSU, 20, 36
  and credibility, 85, 87–8, 98, 124–5,
    131, 149–50, 156, 163, 165,
    167, 169–71, 173–4, 176, 203,
    216, 220, 234, 245, 278, 283
  and CSCE, 217, 232–4, 238–9,
    247, 284
  and Cuban missile crisis, 18, 36
  and decolonization, 16, 22
  and de Gaulle, on, 24, 55, 73
  and diplomacy, 91, 94–5, 99,
    148, 279
  and Dobrynin, 234, 237–9
  and EAG, 243–4
  and education of public opinion, 33,
    37, 71, 91, 96–7, 99, 119, 129
  and EEC, 227–32, 242–4, 246, 284
  and EEC Commission, 229–30,
    247, 284

and equal aggregates, 161, 175
and Europe on unity, 22, 30, 36, 85, 227–32, 241, 246–7, 275
and first-use policy, 91–2, 225–6
and flexibility, 88–9, 98–9, 131–2, 220, 278
and foreign policy, conception of, 31, 34–5, 80
and history, conception of, 13, 32–3
and ideology, 14, 16, 21
and INF, 226–7
and Japan, 152, 241
and Khrushchev, on, 19–20
and Laird, 171
and leaders of new states, 25–7
and leadership, conception of, 80–2, 85–6, 98, 106, 120, 124, 131, 245, 247, 254, 277, 280, 284
and legitimacy, conception of, 14, 21, 148, 274, 281
and Lenin, 18, 34
and limits, 28–30, 32, 37, 216, 245
and limited war, 15, 19, 30, 87, 91–4, 98–9, 278–9
and linkage, 81, 84, 98, 124–5, 132, 149, 153–4, 159, 162–3, 165, 173–6, 216, 218, 220, 234–9, 241, 245, 277, 281–2
and Mao Tse-tung, on, 17–18
and MBFR, 217, 226, 232–4, 283
and Metternich, 32–33
and MFN status (to USSR), 167–8
and MIRVs, 157, 160–2
and morality, 35, 82
and Moscow summits, 159–60, 167
and multipolarity, 25, 78, 85, 98, 151, 218, 245–6, 277, 284
and nationalism, 21, 24, 26, 274–5
and nationalism in FRG, 232
and NATO, 21–3, 25, 29, 85, 96, 148, 152–3, 157, 165, 215–16, 220, 224, 227, 229–32, 238–9, 241, 245–7, 275, 283–4
and NATO strategy, 22, 24, 30, 215, 218–22, 225–6, 245, 252
and NEP, 231–2, 247
and neutralism in Western Europe, 22, 24, 227
and neutralism in new states, 26–7

and new states, 16, 21, 25–7, 36–7, 275
and Nixon doctrine, 215–18, 223, 226, 232, 245
and Nixon, 122, 130, 156–9, 161, 176–7, 222, 234–5, 238
and no-first-use, 225–6, 246, 258
and non-ideological/non-moralistic approach, 79–80, 97, 124, 149–51, 153, 155, 164, 168–9, 174–5, 277, 281–2
and NPG (NATO), 224–5, 227, 245–6
and NSC, 127–30, 159, 162, 166–7, 170, 222, 232
and nuclear war (all-out), 18–19, 21, 24, 83–7, 91–2, 94, 98–9, 156–7, 176, 226, 279, 283
and nuclear weapons, 23–4, 29, 36–7, 78, 97, 275–6
and optimism, 28–30, 37, 99, 275–6
and Ostpolitik, 232–3, 236, 284
and peace, conception of, 14–15, 82, 148, 174, 274
and peaceful coexistence, 19–20, 36, 95, 123, 131, 164, 170, 175–6, 274, 282–3
and pessimism, 28–30, 37, 99, 275–6
and policy, conception of, 31, 34–5, 80
and policy of precaution, 89, 90, 99
and political will, 81, 83, 98
and power, conception of, 77, 97, 124
and power-realism, 77–8, 80, 97, 131, 174–5, 276, 281
and PRC, 16–18, 21, 35–6, 77–8, 92, 94, 123, 131, 148, 151–2, 166, 174–5, 274–6, 278, 280–1
and predictability of political future, 30–31, 37, 276
and Reagan, 154, 162–3, 169, 175
and Reports to Congress (on US Foreign Policy), 129, 147
and Reykjavik, 163, 226, 246
and risks, 30–31, 34–5, 37, 82, 85–9, 98, 124, 131, 151, 155, 170–1, 174, 243, 278, 283

and revolutionary international
  systems, 14, 16, 28, 35, 274
and revolutionary powers, 14–18,
  20, 79, 97, 123, 131, 148, 174
and Rogers, 152–3, 158, 170, 233
and SACEUR, 226
and Safeguard ABM program,
  157, 159
and SALT I, 156–62, 175–6, 188,
  246, 282
and SALT II, 161–2, 175
and SALT II ratification, 163,
  173, 176
and SDI, 163
and SEATO, 24–5
and selective détente, 217–18, 233,
  235–41, 245
and Shanghai Communique,
  153–4, 175
and simultaneity, 159, 175–6
and Sino-Soviet split, 19, 148, 151
and Soames-de Gaulle controversy,
  227–8, 246
and sovereignty, 24, 29, 31
and Soviet doctrine of protracted
  conflict, 17–20, 89, 148–9,
  159, 176
and Soviet strategy of ambiguity,
  83, 87–90, 99, 155, 170–1,
  173–4, 278
and SRG, 127–8
and stability, 14–15, 97
and stable international systems, 14,
  17, 21, 28, 35–37, 77–8, 99,
  148, 150, 155, 158, 163, 174,
  215–16, 240, 274, 276
and statesmanship, 33, 37, 80, 82,
  96, 104, 129–30, 132, 166,
  177, 226, 246, 281
and State Department, 152–3, 161,
  167, 171–2
and strategic approach, 78, 80, 84,
  97, 276–7
and strategic balance, 21, 77, 81, 97,
  148–9, 151–5, 157–8, 162–3,
  169, 173, 176, 186, 226,
  245, 277
and strategic doctrine, 78–9, 82–5,
  97, 151, 152

and sufficiency, (strategic), 155–6,
  174–5, 219–20, 245, 277, 282
and summitry, 91, 95–6, 99, 161,
  176, 189, 241, 244, 279
and survival, 28, 37, 82
and third-force dangers, 21–2
and timing, 89–90, 99, 174, 176,
  236, 239, 278
and TNF, 93, 224–5, 227, 245–6
and Trident, 157, 161–2
and US leadership, 27, 85, 148, 150,
  152, 174, 218, 240, 243–6
and US leaders, 78, 80
and use of force, 78, 83, 87, 91–2,
  95, 98–9, 124, 132, 170–1, 176,
  225, 278–9, 283
and US-PRC rapprochement,
  150, 152–4, 161, 163, 165,
  173–5, 202–3, 228, 232,
  237, 280–1
and US-Soviet détente, 155,
  157, 168, 175, 217–18,
  234–5, 281–2
and US-Soviet trade, 166–70,
  229–30, 239–40, 282
and USSR, 16–18, 27, 35–6,
  77–8, 86, 92, 94, 123,
  131, 148, 150–5, 157–61,
  163, 166, 169, 171–2,
  174–5, 274–6, 278,
  280–1
and Vietnam, 149, 151, 158–9, 165,
  175–6, 228, 239
and Year of Europe, 240–4,
  247, 284
Kosygin, Alexei, 235
Kreps, Juanita, 190, 193

Laird, Melvin, 128, 155, 171,
  223
and role of, 126, 132
leadership, *see* Brzezinski, Carter,
  Kissinger *and* Nixon
Lenin, Vladimir Ilych Ulyanov, *see*
  Brzezinski *and* Kissinger
limited war, *see* Kissinger
linkage, *see* Brzezinski, Carter,
  Kissinger, Nixon *and* Vance
London, *see* Britain

LTDP (Long-Term Defense Program), 250–1

Mansfield Amendments, 222–3
Mao Tse-tung, 17–18, 48, 70, 153
MBFR (Mutual and Balanced Force Reductions), 179, 182, 217, 223, 226, 232–4, 251, 272, 283
see also Brzezinski, Carter *and* Kissinger
Metternich, Prince Klemens von, *see* Kissinger
MFN (Most Favored Nation) status, 167–8, 193–4, 209–10, 212–13
see also Brzezinski, Kissinger *and* Vance
Middle East, 158, 166, 170–2, 175, 179
MIRV, 157, 160–2
Mondale, Walter F., 143, 188, 199, 203–4, 210–11, 248, 250, 255
Morgenthau, Hans, 55
Moscow, *see* USSR
Moscow summits, *see under* Kissinger *and* Nixon
Muskie, Edmund S., 142, 258, 264
MX, 157, 162, 184–5, 188, 190, 212–14, 282

Napoleon, Bonaparte, 28, 32
National Security Adviser, 1, 2, 122, 133, 138–9
and role of, 1, 3, 125–6, 127
nationalism, *see* Brzezinski, FRG *and* Kissinger
NATO, 21–3, 55, 123–4, 227–8, 242, 265–6
and consultation, 220–1
and conventional forces, 222–3, 225–7
and INF, 226
and neutralism of, 22, 24, 227, 265–6
and no-first-use, 225–6
and nuclear war, 22
and Pershing IIs, 256–7
and SALT, 220
and sovereignty, 24, 29, 30, 37
and strategy, 24, 29–30,
37, 55, 215, 218–19, 221
and TNF, 224–5, 227, 255–7
and unity of, 22–5, 36, 55–6, 96, 148, 152–3, 157, 165, 215–16, 220, 230
see also Brzezinski, Carter, Kissinger *and* Nixon
Nenni, Pietro, 238
NEP (New Economic Policy), 231–2, 247
see also Kissinger
neutralism, *see* Brzezinski, Kissinger, NATO *and* new states
new states, 16, 21, 25–6, 36–7
and anti-Americanism of, 26–7, 37, 61, 67
and communism, 62–3, 68, 74
and equality in, 42, 63, 74
and leaders of, 25–7, 36, 63–4, 74
and nationalism in, 26, 62–3, 67–8, 74
and neutralism, 26–7, 37
and racism in, 62–3, 68, 74
and Soviet bloc, 26–7, 68, 74
and technetronic revolution, impact on, 42, 61, 63
see also, Brzezinski *and* Kissinger
Nicaragua, 201
Nixon doctrine, 42, 70, 107, 110, 215–18, 223, 226, 232
see also Brzezinski *and* Kissinger
Nixon, Richard M., 1, 38, 54, 56, 63, 70, 122, 125, 134, 147–9, 163, 171–2, 239
and administration of, 100, 102, 104–5, 115–18, 147, 149
and Berlin, 234–5
and burden-sharing, 124
and control of foreign policy, 122, 125–6, 128, 132
and credibility, 124–5, 131, 170, 216
and Cuban missile crisis, 123
and European unity, 123, 228–30
and Kissinger, 122, 126, 156–9, 161, 176, 279–80
and leadership, 124–5, 131–2, 218, 280

and linkage, 124–5, 132, 149, 158, 220
and military intervention, 123–4, 131–2
and Moscow summit (1972), 159–60, 167
and national security adviser, 122, 125–6, 128, 132
and NATO, 123–4, 131, 215–17, 229–30
and NEP, 231
and non-ideological approach, 124, 131
and NSC, 125–30, 132
and peaceful coexistence, 123, 131
and political will, 131–2
and power, 124–5, 131
and PRC, 123, 131, 150–1, 161
and risks, 124, 131
and Rogers, 126, 128, 153, 159, 171
and Safeguard ABM program, 150
and SALT I, 158–9, 188
and sufficiency, 155
and Third World, 123–4, 131
and USSR, 123, 131, 151, 167
and Vietnam, 123–5, 158–9
and Washington summit (1973), 163
and Watergate, 162
see also Brzezinski *and* Kissinger
no-first-use, *see* Brzezinski *and* Kissinger
NPG (NATO), 224–5, 245
see also Kissinger
NSC (National Security Council), 1, 81, 125–30, 139–42, 280
see also Brzezinski, Carter, Kissinger *and* Nixon
NSDM (National Security Decision Memorandum), 128, 141, 237
NSSM (National Security Study Memorandum), 127–9, 141, 222–3, 235
nuclear war, *see* Brzezinski *and* Kissinger

October War, 170–3, 176, 242
Olympics (Moscow), 199, 270
Operational Code, 5–8, 10
and instrumental beliefs of, 5, 7, 9

and opponents in, 6, 7
and philosophical beliefs of, 5, 7, 9
optimism, *see* Brzezinski *and* Kissinger
Ostpolitik, 230, 232–3, 236–9, 242, 284
see also Brandt *and* Kissinger
Owen, Henry, 141

Pakistan, 136, 150–1, 198–200, 207
Paris, *see* France
Partial Test-Ban Treaty, 19
PD (Presidential Directive), 140–2, 184–6, 212, 251, 263
peaceful coexistence, *see* Brzezinski, Kissinger *and* Nixon
Peking, *see* PRC
Pentagon, 156, 185
perestroika, *see under* Brzezinski
Pershing IIs, 256–7
pessimism, *see* Brzezinski *and* Kissinger
Peterson, Peter, 168
Pilgrims (Society of), 241, 243
planetary humanism, *see* Brzezinski *and* Carter
Poland, 57, 169, 260, 263–4
see also Brzezinski *and* Carter
Policy Review Committee, 140–2, 197–8
political will, *see* Brzezinski, Kissinger *and* Nixon
Pompidou, Georges, 221, 232–3, 238
Powell, Jody, 143
power-realism, *see* Brzezinski, Carter, Kissinger *and* Nixon
PRC (People's Republic of China), 16–18, 21, 26, 39–46, 48–50, 54, 60, 72, 77–8, 92, 94, 114, 123, 131, 144, 145–6, 148, 151–2, 166, 174–5, 202, 207, 211–12, 250, 274–6, 278, 280–1
and MFN status, 209–10
and new states, 21
see also Brown, Brzezinski, Carter, Kissinger, Nixon, *and* Vance

predictability, *see* Brzezinski *and* Kissinger
PRM (Policy Review Memorandum), 140–3, 183–4

Radio Free Europe, 119, 261
RDF (Rapid Deployment Force), 184–5, 187, 212–14, 258–9, 271
Reagan, Ronald, 154, 162–3, 169, 175, 194, 239
revolutionary powers, *see* Brzezinski *and* Kissinger
Reykjavik Framework, 163, 191, 194, 226
   see also Brzezinski *and* Kissinger
Richardson, Elliot, 151
risks, *see* Brzezinski, Kissinger, *and* Nixon
Rockefeller, Nelson, 122, 150
Rogers, William P., 128–9, 132, 152–3, 159, 204, 222, 237, 240
   and role of, 126, 132
   and US-PRC rapprochement, 152–3, 203
   and US-Soviet détente, 152–3, 158–9, 167, 170–1
Rumania, 56, 58, 151
Rush, Kenneth, 235, 237

SACEUR (Supreme Allied Commander Europe), 226, 251
   see also Kissinger
Sadat, Anwar, 195, 268
Safeguard (ABM), 150, 157, 159
Sakharov, Andrei, 192
SALT, 101–3, 116–17, 156–61, 163, 173, 175–6, 179, 181, 183–91, 196–8, 204, 207, 209–10, 213, 220–1, 255, 257
   and ratification of SALT II, 163, 173, 199
   and terms of SALT I, 160
   and terms of SALT II, 190
   see also Brzezinski, Carter, Kissinger, Nixon *and* Vance
Sato, Eisaku, 152
Saudi Arabia, 199
SCC (Special Coordination Committee), 140–3, 145–6, 187–8,

195, 197, 198, 253, 255–6, 264, 280
   see also Brzezinski
Schlesinger, James R., 157, 162
Schmidt, Helmut, 252–8, 260–2, 264–5, 270
   and ERW, 252–3
   see also Brzezinski *and* Carter
Schultze, Charles, 141
Scowcroft, Brent, 129–30
SDI (Strategic Defense Initiative), 163, 186, 191
SEATO (Southeast Asia Treaty Organization), 24–5
selective détente, 192, 217–18, 233, 235–41, 261–2, 265–6
   see also Brzezinski *and* Kissinger
Shanghai Communique, 153–4, 163, 175, 206
   see also Brzezinski *and* Kissinger
Shcharansky, Anatoly, 193
Shultz, George, 154
simultaneity, *see under* Kissinger
Sino-Soviet bloc, 19, 26–7
Sino-Soviet split, *see* Brzezinski *and* Kissinger
SLBM (submarine-launched ballistic missiles), 160, 251
Smith, Gerard, 158–9, 237
Smithsonian Agreement, 232
Soames, Christopher, 227–8
   see also Kissinger
Solidarity, 196, 263–6
Solzhenitsyn, Alexander, 192
Somali-Ethiopian War, 194–5, 269
   see also Horn of Africa
sovereignty, *see* Brzezinski *and* Kissinger
Soviet brigade, *see under* Brzezinski *and* Vance
Soviet-Cuban intervention, 169, 194–6
   see also Brzezinski, Carter *and* Vance
Soviet Union, *see* USSR
Spengler, Oswald, *see under* Brzezinski
Sputnik, 48
SRG (Senior Review Group), 127–8, 150, 152, 235

SS-20s, 252–6
see also Brzezinski
START (Strategic Arms Reduction
    Talks), 191
State Department, 128, 132
    and PRC, 152–3
    and SALT, 161
    and US-Soviet trade, 167
strategic approach, see Brzezinski,
    Kissinger and Nixon
sufficiency, (strategic), 101,
    108, 155–7
    see also Brzezinski and Kissinger
summitry, see under Brzezinski,
    Carter, Kissinger and Nixon

Taiwan, 54, 153–4, 206–8
technetronic revolution, see under
    Brzezinski and new states
Teilhard de Chardin, Pierre, see under
    Brzezinski
Thatcher, Margaret, 264
Third World, 21, 61–4, 67–8, 74–5,
    114, 123–4, 131, 190, 275
    see also new states, Brzezinski and
    Kissinger
timing, see Brzezinski and Kissinger
TNF (theater nuclear forces),
    224–5, 225–8
    see also Brzezinski, Carter,
    Kissinger and Vance
Trident, 157, 161–3
Trilateral Commission, 133, 139
trilateral cooperation, see Brzezinski
    and Carter
trilateral energy proposal, 108
Turner, Stansfield, 141–2, 264

US (United States of America), 18,
    21, 40–1
    and global impact, 40–2, 61, 65, 67,
    71–2, 74, 78
    and leaders of, 78, 80, 103
    and leadership, 107–8, 136, 145,
    187, 208, 254, 259, 264, 273,
    280, 285
    and NATO, 21–22, 123–4
    and new states, 26–7
    and nuclear guarantee, 22, 36

    and US-PRC normalization, 195–9,
    201–12, 264–5, 280–1
    and US-PRC rapprochement, 54,
    73, 144, 150, 152–4, 161, 163,
    165, 173–5, 202–3, 206, 228,
    232, 237, 280–1
    and US-Soviet détente, 53–4, 73,
    109, 111, 155, 157, 179,
    183–4, 189–90, 192–4, 196,
    213, 217–8, 234–5, 260–1,
    271, 281–2
    and US-Soviet rivalry, 40, 52–3,
    61, 65, 67, 73, 75, 114–15,
    121, 180–1, 186, 188, 191,
    200–1, 205
    and US-Soviet trade, 166–70, 190,
    193–4, 199, 209–13, 229–30,
    239–40, 270, 282
    see also Brzezinski, Carter,
    Kissinger, Nixon and Vance
USC (Under Secretaries Committee),
    127, 231
USSR, 16–18, 26, 39–46, 48–54,
    57–8, 60, 65, 67, 72, 101–2,
    103, 111, 113–14, 116–17, 141,
    144–6, 182–3, 184–7, 195–6,
    200, 202, 206, 209, 211–2, 230,
    250, 258, 261, 262–6, 270–6,
    278, 280–1
    and Afghanistan, 191, 198–9, 257
    and Berlin, 234–7
    and bureaucratization of, 20, 274
    and CSCE, 232, 238–9
    and Cuban missile crisis, 18, 36
    and doctrine of, 17–19
    and ERW, 252–4
    and liberalization/democratization
    of, 20, 50–1, 73
    and MFN status, 210
    and new states, 21, 26–7
    and peaceful coexistence, 19–20, 36
    and SS-20s, 252–4, 256
    and US-Soviet détente, 53–4, 73,
    109, 111, 179, 183–4, 189–90,
    192–4, 196, 213, 260–1,
    271, 282
    and US-Soviet rivalry, 40,
    52–3, 61, 65, 67, 73, 75,
    114–15, 121, 180–1,

186, 188, 191, 200–1,
205
and US-Soviet trade, 190, 193–4,
199, 209–13, 270, 282
see also Brzezinski, Carter,
Kissinger, Nixon *and* Vance

Vance, Cyrus, 154, 248–9, 262–3
and Afghanistan, 198–200
and arms control, 180, 182
and arms sales to PRC, 210–11
and Brzezinski, 141, 143–4, 181–2,
187, 190, 194, 197–8, 203–4,
207, 209
and ERW, 252–4
and Friday Presidential Breakfast,
143
and Horn of Africa, 268–9
and linkage, 187, 190, 196, 198, 202
and MFN status, 193–4, 209–10
and NSC, 140
and Olympics (Moscow), 199
and PRC normalization, 201–4,
207–9
and role of, 138, 145
and SALT, 141, 182, 185, 187–9,
190, 196–7, 204, 209, 257
and Soviet brigade, 197
and Soviet-Cuban intervention,
194–6
and TNF, 255
and use of force, 180
and USSR, 180, 182, 190, 193, 197,
204–5, 207, 209, 211
and V-B-B luncheon, 143, 280
and Vienna summit, 189–90
and Vietnam, 208–9
and Western Europe, 250, 252
V-B-B, *see under* Brown, Brzezinski
and Vance
Verification Panel (VP), 129, 141
Vienna summit, 189–90
Vietnam, 123–5, 136, 148–9, 151, 153,
158, 166, 175, 179, 208–10, 228
see also Brzezinski, Carter,
Kissinger, Nixon *and* Vance
Vladivostok Agreement, 137,
162, 188
see also Ford

VSSG (Vietnam Special Studies
Group), 129

Warnke, Paul, 188
Warsaw Pact Treaty Organization
(WTO), 60
Warsaw talks, 152
Washington, *see* US
Washington summit (1973), 163
Watergate, 162, 242
Western Europe(ans),
and Afghanistan, 269–71
and APNW, 221–2
and Berlin talks, 234
and CSCE, 232, 234, 238–9,
242, 261
and defense (NATO), 216–17,
219–21, 223–4, 226–7, 250–3,
258–9, 272
and EAG, 243
and EEC, 230–1, 242
and ERW, 252–3
and MBFR, 226
and NEP, 231–2
and neutralism of, 22, 24, 227
and October War, 221, 242
and Pershing IIs, 256–7
and SALT, 220–1, 255, 257
and TNF, 224, 255–8
and US-Soviet détente, 260, 268–71
and USSR, 263–6, 268–70
and Year of Europe, 241–2, 247
see also NATO
will, *see* political will
Wilson, Harold, 230, 233
Woodcock, Leonard, 208
WSAG (Washington Special
Actions Group), 129, 141, 150,
152, 170–2

Year of Europe, 108, 110, 113, 116,
240–2, 247, 284
see also Brzezinski, France *and*
Kissinger
Yom Kippur War, 116
see also October War
Young, Andrew, 195
Yugoslavia, 56–7

DATE DUE